D0212088

American Ethnic Writers

MAGILL'S CHOICE

American Ethnic Writers

Volume 2

Henry Louis Gates, Jr.—Grace Paley

Editors, Revised Edition
The Editors of Salem Press

Editor, First Edition
David Peck
California State University, Long Beach

SALEM PRESS, INC.
Pasadena, California   Hackensack, New Jersey

Cover image: © Ejla/Dreamstime.com

These essays originally appeared in *Issues and Identities in Literature* (1997), edited by David Peck; *Critical Survey of Drama, Second Revised Edition* (2003); *Critical Survey of Long Fiction, Second Revised Edition* (2000); *Critical Survey of Poetry, Second Revised Edition* (2002); *Cyclopedia of World Authors, Fourth Revised Edition* (2003); *Magill Book Reviews* (online); *Magill's Survey of American Literature* (2006); *Masterplots II, African American Literature Series* (1994); *Masterplots II, Women's Literature Series* (1995); *Notable African American Writers* (2006); and *Notable Latino Writers* (2005). New material has been added.

∞ The paper used in these volumes conforms to the American National Standard for Permanence of Paper for Printed Library Materials, Z39.48-1992 (R1997).

Library of Congress Cataloging-in-Publication Data

American ethnic writers / editors, the editors of Salem Press. — Rev. ed.

p. cm. — (Magill's choice)

Includes bibliographical references and index.

ISBN 978-1-58765-462-6 (set : alk. paper) — ISBN 978-1-58765-463-3 (vol. 1 : alk. paper) — ISBN 978-1-58765-464-0 (vol. 2 : alk. paper) — ISBN 978-1-58765-465-7 (vol. 3 : alk. paper) 1. American literature—Minority authors—Bio-bibliography—Dictionaries. 2. Minority authors—United States—Biography—Dictionaries. 3. Ethnic groups in literature—Dictionaries. 4. Minorities in literature—Dictionaries. I. Salem Press.

PS153.M56A414 2008

810.9′920693—dc22

2008018357

First Printing

PRINTED IN CANADA

Contents

Pronunciation Guide

Many of the names of personages covered in *American Ethnic Writers* may be unfamiliar to students and general readers. For these unfamiliar names, guides to pronunciation have been provided upon first mention of the names in the text. These guidelines do not purport to achieve the subtleties of the languages in question but will offer readers a rough equivalent of how English speakers may approximate the proper pronunciation.

Vowel Sounds

Symbol	*Spelled (Pronounced)*
a	answer (AN-suhr), laugh (laf), sample (SAM-puhl), that (that)
ah	father (FAH-thur), hospital (HAHS-pih-tuhl)
aw	awful (AW-fuhl), caught (kawt)
ay	blaze (blayz), fade (fayd), waiter (WAYT-ur), weigh (way)
eh	bed (behd), head (hehd), said (sehd)
ee	believe (bee-LEEV), cedar (SEE-dur), leader (LEED-ur), liter (LEE-tur)
ew	boot (bewt), lose (lewz)
i	buy (bi), height (hit), lie (li), surprise (sur-PRIZ)
ih	bitter (BIH-tur), pill (pihl)
o	cotton (KO-tuhn), hot (hot)
oh	below (bee-LOH), coat (koht), note (noht), wholesome (HOHL-suhm)
oo	good (good), look (look)
ow	couch (kowch), how (how)
oy	boy (boy), coin (koyn)
uh	about (uh-BOWT), butter (BUH-tuhr), enough (ee-NUHF), other (UH-thur)

Consonant Sounds

Symbol	*Spelled (Pronounced)*
ch	beach (beech), chimp (chihmp)
g	beg (behg), disguise (dihs-GIZ), get (geht)
j	digit (DIH-juht), edge (ehj), jet (jeht)
k	cat (kat), kitten (KIH-tuhn), hex (hehks)
s	cellar (SEHL-ur), save (sayv), scent (sehnt)
sh	champagne (sham-PAYN), issue (IH-shew), shop (shop)
ur	birth (burth), disturb (dihs-TURB), earth (urth), letter (LEH-tur)
y	useful (YEWS-fuhl), young (yuhng)
z	business (BIHZ-nehs), zest (zehst)
zh	vision (VIH-zhuhn)

Complete List of Contents

Volume 1

Volume 2

Volume 3

American Ethnic Writers

Henry Louis Gates, Jr.

Born: Keyser, West Virginia; September 16, 1950

African American

The dean of African American literary studies, Gates is considered one of the most prominent black American intellectuals of the late twentieth and early twenty-first centuries.

Principal works

NONFICTION: *Figures in Black: Words, Signs, and the "Racial Self,"* 1987; *The Signifying Monkey: A Theory of Afro-American Literary Criticism*, 1988; *Loose Canons: Notes on the Cultural Wars*, 1992; *The Amistad Chronology of African-American History, 1445-1990*, 1993; *Colored People: A Memoir*, 1994; *Speaking of Race, Speaking of Sex: Hate Speech, Civil Rights, and Civil Liberties*, 1994; *The Future of the Race*, 1996 (with Cornel West); *Thirteen Ways to Look at a Black Man*, 1997; *Wonders of the African World*, 1999; *The African-American Century: How Black Americans Have Shaped Our Country*, 2000 (with West); *The Trials of Phillis Wheatley: America's First Black Poet and Her Encounters with the Founding Fathers*, 2003; *America Behind the Color Line: Dialogues with African Americans*, 2004; *Finding Oprah's Roots: Finding Yours*, 2007

EDITED TEXTS: *Black Is the Color of the Cosmos: Essays on Afro-American Literature and Culture, 1942-1981*, 1982 (Charles T. Davis's essays); *Our Nig: Or, Sketches from the Life of a Free Black, in a Two-Story White House, North, Showing That Slavery's Shadows Fall Even There*, 1983 (by Harriet E. Wilson); *Black Literature and Literary Theory*, 1984, 1990; *The Slave's Narrative*, 1985 (with Charles T. Davis); *"Race," Writing, and Difference*, 1986; *Wole Soyinka: A Bibliography of Primary and Secondary Sources*, 1986 (with James Gibbs and Ketutto Katrak); *The Classic Slave Narratives*, 1987; *The Schomburg Library of Nineteenth-Century Black Women Writers*, 1987 (30 volumes); *Reading Black, Reading Feminist: A Critical Anthology*, 1990; *Bearing Witness: Selections from African-American Autobiography in the Twentieth Century*, 1991; *Black Biography, 1790-1950: A Cumulative Index*, 1991 (3 volumes; with Randall K. Burkett and Nancy Hall Burkett); *Alice Walker: Critical Perspectives Past and Present*, 1993; *Gloria Naylor: Critical Perspectives Past and Present*, 1993; *Langston Hughes: Critical Perspectives Past and Present*, 1993; *Richard Wright: Critical Perspectives Past and Present*, 1993; *Toni Morrison: Critical Perspectives Past and Present*, 1993; *Zora Neale Hurston: Critical Perspectives*

Past and Present, 1993; *Identities*, 1995 (with Kwame Anthony Appiah); *The Dictionary of Global Culture*, 1996 (with Appiah); *The Norton Anthology of African American Literature*, 1996 (with Nellie Y. McKay); *Pioneers of the Black Atlantic: Five Slave Narratives from the Enlightenment, 1772-1815*, 1998 (with William L. Andrews); *Black Imagination and the Middle Passage*, 1999 (with Maria Diedrich and Carl Pedersen); *The Civitas Anthology of African-American Slave Narrative*, 1999 (with Andrews); *The Souls of Black Folk*, 1999 (with Terri Hume Oliver); *The Bondwoman's Narrative*, 2002 (by Hannah Crafts); *Unchained Memories: Readings from the Slave Narratives*, 2002; *African American Lives*, 2004 (with Evelyn Brooks Higginbotham); *In Search of Hannah Crafts: Critical Essays on "The Bondswoman's Narrative,"* 2004 (with Hollis Robbins)

West Virginia was racially segregated when Henry Louis Gates, Jr., was born in Keyser on September 16, 1950. Keyser's schools were not integrated until Gates was in secondary school, and integration came to Keyser with less protest than it had elsewhere in the South. In 1968, Gates, named valedictorian of his high school graduating class, gave a militant speech heavily influenced by his study of African history.

Gates's father, Henry Louis Gates, Sr., was a loader in Keyser's paper mill, the major employer in town. He also moonlighted as a janitor for the telephone company. Given his family's financial situation, it had not occurred to Gates to attend college outside West Virginia. In September, 1968, he enrolled in Potomac State College of West Virginia University, planning on taking courses that would prepare him for medical school.

One of Gates's Potomac State professors, Duke Anthony Whitmore, recognized Gates's promise and urged him to transfer to an Ivy League institution. Gates applied for admission to Yale University and was admitted. In 1970-1971, still interested in medicine, Gates worked as general anesthetist at the Anglican Mission Hospital in Kilimatinde, Tanzania, but he returned to Yale to complete his bachelor's degree summa cum laude in 1973.

Following his graduation from Yale University, Gates continued his studies at Clare College, Cambridge University, and received a master's degree in 1974 and a Ph.D. in 1979. He then became a staff correspondent for *Time* magazine's London bureau. From 1976 until 1979, he was a lecturer at Yale University, after which he became director of Cornell University's undergraduate Black Studies Program.

Gates advanced from assistant to associate professor and, in 1985, was named W. E. B. Du Bois Professor of Literature at Cornell. In 1988, he assumed the John Spencer Bassett Professorship in English and Literature at Duke University. He left that position in 1990 to become W. E. B. Du Bois Professor of Humanities, professor of English, and director of the African American studies program at Harvard University, which had struggled to attract students interested in African American history and culture.

Gates immediately enlivened Harvard's African American studies program by bringing in a variety of exciting lecturers, including Jamaica Kincaid, Wole Soyinka, and Spike Lee. Within a short time, Gates's dynamic efforts resulted in a threefold increase in the number of African American studies majors.

Henry Louis Gates, Jr. (Library of Congress)

Gates made a major contribution to black studies with the publication in 1988 of *The Signifying Monkey: A Theory of Afro-American Literary Criticism*. This book offered a new theoretical approach to viewing writing by blacks. A landmark work, it was informed by the critical theories of major theorists such as Jacques Derrida, Jacques Lacan, and Claude Levi-Strauss but reconsidered such theories in the light of the uniqueness of literature produced by blacks both in the United States and abroad. Besides his academic achievements, Gates is one of the three most prominent black public intellectuals in the United States, sharing that distinction with Cornel West and Kwame Anthony Appiah.

The Signifying Monkey

Type of work: Literary theory
First published: 1988

Gates dealt with some of the questions raised in this book in his first major work, *Figures in Black: Words, Signs, and the "Racial" Self*, published in 1987, one year before *The Signifying Monkey*. Gates's use of the term "signifying," sometimes rendered "signifyin(g)" to suggest the dialect of many blacks, posits the notion that many writers of all races have to deal with the oppressive weight of their literary predecessors and often do so initially by trying to copy them. They then reach a second stage in which they seek to transfigure them, to move beyond them, and to create their own literary worlds.

Gates attempts to determine the boundaries of an African American literary tradition by showing how it intentionally misquotes itself. For Gates, past and future are deconstructed into a riverlike strand, a continuous present. "Signifying" generally refers simply to denoting or representing, but Gates suggests a difference that is present in denoting or representing black literature by rendering the term with a capital *S* and a parenthesized *g*: Signifyin(g). The final *g* in words that end with *-ing* words is often dropped in the black vernacular.

Gates analyzes some dialogue—actually passages of a rap monologue—by H. Rapp Brown, carefully interpreting all its rhymes, rhythms, and repetitions. The Brown lyrics have a remarkable originality that imparts a calculated exhilaration to those who hear them. These are the lyrics of black street talk, and even though one can legitimately compare them to some of Walt Whitman's most excessive writing, they are the unique lyrics of the black culture that produced H. Rapp Brown.

Although Gates is quite aware that many black writers were directly influenced by their white colleagues, in *The Signifying Monkey* he limits his literary-historical definition of signifying to the influence of black texts on other black texts, an important limitation that gives his argument the focus it demands.

Loose Canons

Type of work: Essays and speeches
First published: 1992

Loose Canons is a collection of essays and speeches Gates made between 1986 to 1973. Gates concerns himself with examining the implications of nationalistic upheavals and the politics of identity for various aspects of American culture and education. His book is divided into three sections, "Literature," "The Profession," and "Society."

Gates compiled this book with a broad readership in mind. He avoids the professional jargon of his earlier writing, which made it too specialized for many readers. As a result, *Loose Canons* is great fun to read. Gates takes outrageous jabs at many academics involved in critical theory. With tongue in cheek, he accuses Harvard's Helen Vendler of doing the dirty work of the literature and cultural mafia. He cites the spurious contention that Harold Bloom, who is credited with doing a great deal of canon formation, killed off a whole list of venerated writers—from Matthew Arnold to Robert Lowell—consigning them to obscurity.

In reading Gates's book, one must remember that he is trying to justify an expansion, long overdue, of the literary canon to include black literature. Many works by African Americans not only were ignored until relatively recently but also had not even been discovered. Gates's herculean efforts to correct this omission are commendable; his struggle to reexamine, redefine, and renew the canon is both understandable and admirable.

Colored People

Type of work: Memoir
First published: 1994

Having grown up in the segregated South, Gates might well have viewed his past as a period of repression and unhappiness. Such is certainly not the case in *Colored*

People, which is an intimate, mellow account of Gates's youth and of his relationship to the community where he lived. Many people write memoirs to sort out their experience and come to a better understanding of themselves, and this appears to be the case in this elegantly written and beautifully recollected glimpse into Gates's past.

Keyser, in Piedmont, West Virginia, was a one-industry town. Its paper mill, which cast a malodorous pall over Keyser most of the time, employed blacks only as loaders of its trucks and machines. Gates's father was employed in this capacity, but he earned so little that he took a second part-time job as a janitor.

Gates's mother was bipolar, and her illness began to surface when Henry (nicknamed Skip) was about twelve. Bewildered by the changes in his mother's personality and disposition, he turned to religion, joining a Baptist church that he describes as restrictively fundamentalistic. For many years, Gates did not know that his mother had been active in the Civil Rights movement before his birth and that she had led one of the early civil rights protest marches in the United States.

A yearly event in Keyser was a picnic hosted by the paper mill for all of its black employees. Gates always looked forward to and greatly enjoyed this event. The fact that it was segregated did not seem important to him. He writes with great nostalgia and warmth about this picnic and also about the sense of community that blacks had in this small town. Members of the black community were protective and were truly kind and generous toward one another. Keyser's blacks did not want whites at their picnic because their celebration would have been restrained by white attendees.

Gates was unaware of the color line in Keyser until he was twelve or thirteen. Until then, he, like many young people brought up under segregation, considered the separation of the races normal. Also, he was probably influenced by his father's disdain for blacks. Like many black people, the elder Gates had harsh opinions of blacks who brought dishonor upon their race.

Gates writes frankly about his religious fanaticism during the mid-1960's and about his repressed romance with a white girl. He comments on the transition from "colored" society in the 1950's—note the title of his book—to the "Negro" society of the early 1960's and then to the "black" society of the later 1960's. In the choice of terms to describe themselves, African Americans more or less chronicled a significant change in outlook and attitude.

Changes came with the civil rights advances of the 1960's, and most blacks in Keyser learned about them through television and newspaper reports. As a result of new legislation, blacks could eat in restaurants once open only to whites. They could sit where they wished in movie theaters, and schools were now integrated. Gates believes, however, that the introduction of these freedoms also ushered in the disappearance of the sheltering institutions that protected blacks within their own communities.

Among the most touching accounts in the book is that of how Gates's mother, Pauline, who looked down upon whites, dreamed of one day owning a house of her own. When the Gates family tried to buy the house of a white family for whom she had worked, she hesitated. Finally she broke down in tears, saying that this house reminded her of the cruelty and humiliation she had received from the owners as their domestic servant.

The Future of the Race

Type of work: Essays and memoirs
First published: 1996

Gates collaborated with Cornel West on this book, which is often read by young adults. The authors take their lead from W. E. B. Du Bois's brief essay, "The Talented Tenth," published in 1903 in *The Souls of Black Folk*. In it, Du Bois issued a clarion call to gifted young blacks, "the talented tenth," who were well educated, to dedicate themselves to working for the betterment of their race. Du Bois's call to educated blacks fell short of its mark, largely because he overestimated the altruistic motives of educated blacks and underestimated the power of an individual's desire to gain an education and elevate his or her socioeconomic status.

Gates and West question the wisdom of establishing a black elite, as Du Bois initially suggested in his essay (he shrank somewhat from this position in a 1948 revision). Gates describes his experiences as a student at Yale, and he writes about two of his talented black classmates there who did not survive and to whom the book is dedicated. Interestingly, he notes that contemporary blacks may find more antiblack racism within their own black communities than in the white community. At least in the white community, one might anticipate such a sentiment and proceed with caution, but many blacks make the mistake of thinking that they can depend upon the support of their black brothers, which is sometimes unrealistic. Gates knew that his own father harbored a deep antiblack prejudice.

Suggested Readings

Adell, Sandra. "A Function at the Junction." *Diacritics: A Review of Contemporary Criticism* 20 (Winter, 1990).

Branam, Harold. "Henry Louis Gates, Jr." In *Encyclopedia of Literary Critics and Criticism*, edited by Chris Murray. Chicago: Fitzroy Dearborn, 1999.

Bucknell, Brad. "Henry Louis Gates, Jr., and the Theory of 'Signifyin(g).'" *Ariel: A Review of International English Literature* 21 (January, 1990).

Gates, Henry Louis, Jr. "An Interview with Henry Louis Gates, Jr." Interview by Charles H. Rowell. *Callaloo: A Journal of African American and African Arts and Letters* 14, no. 2 (Spring, 1991).

_______. "Interview with Henry Louis Gates, Jr." Interview by Jerry W. Ward, Jr. *New Literary History: A Journal of Theory and Interpretation* 22 (Autumn, 1991).

Olney, James. "Henry Louis Gates, Jr." In *Modern American Critics Since 1955*, edited by Gregory S. Jay. Vol. 67 in *Dictionary of Literary Biography*. Detroit: Gale Group, 1988.

Contributor: R. Baird Shuman

Allen Ginsberg

Born: Newark, New Jersey; June 3, 1926
Died: New York, New York; April 5, 1997

Jewish

Ginsberg helped inaugurate major literary, social, and cultural changes in the post-World War II United States through his role as one of the members of the Beat generation.

Principal works

POETRY: *Howl, and Other Poems*, 1956, 1996; *Empty Mirror: Early Poems*, 1961; *Kaddish, and Other Poems, 1958-1960*, 1961; *The Change*, 1963; *Reality Sandwiches*, 1963; *Kral Majales*, 1965; *Wichita Vortex Sutra*, 1966; *T.V. Baby Poems*, 1967; *Airplane Dreams: Compositions from Journals*, 1968; *Ankor Wat*, 1968; *Planet News, 1961-1967*, 1968; *The Moments Return*, 1970; *Ginsberg's Improvised Poetics*, 1971; *Bixby Canyon Ocean Path Word Breeze*, 1972; *The Fall of America: Poems of These States, 1965-1971*, 1972; *The Gates of Wrath: Rhymed Poems, 1948-1952*, 1972; *Iron Horse*, 1972; *Open Head*, 1972; *First Blues: Rags, Ballads, and Harmonium Songs, 1971-1974*, 1975; *Sad Dust Glories: Poems During Work Summer in Woods*, 1975; *Mind Breaths: Poems, 1972-1977*, 1977; *Mostly Sitting Haiku*, 1978; *Poems All over the Place: Mostly Seventies*, 1978; *Plutonian Ode: Poems, 1977-1980*, 1982; *Collected Poems, 1947-1980*, 1984; *White Shroud: Poems, 1980-1985*, 1986; *Hydrogen Jukebox*, 1990 (music by Philip Glass); *Collected Poems*, 1992; *Cosmopolitan Greetings: Poems, 1986-1992*, 1994; *Making It Up: Poetry Composed at St. Marks Church on May 9, 1979*, 1994 (with Kenneth Koch); *Selected Poems, 1947-1995*, 1996; *Death and Fame: Poems, 1993-1997*, 1999; *Collected Poems, 1947-1997*, 2006

NONFICTION: *Indian Journals*, 1963; *The Yage Letters*, 1963 (with William Burroughs); *Indian Journals, March 1962-May 1963: Notebooks, Diary, Blank Pages, Writings*, 1970; *Allen Verbatim: Lectures on Poetry, Politics, Consciousness*, 1974; *Gay Sunshine Interview*, 1974; *Visions of the Great Rememberer*, 1974; *To Eberhart from Ginsberg*, 1976; *As Ever: The Collected Correspondence of Allen Ginsberg and Neal Cassady*, 1977; *Journals: Early Fifties, Early Sixties*, 1977, 1992; *Composed on the Tongue: Literary Conversations, 1967-1977*, 1980; *Allen Ginsberg Photographs*, 1990; *Snapshot Poetics: A Photographic Memoir of the Beat Era*, 1993; *Journals Mid-Fifties, 1954-1958*, 1995; *Deliberate Prose: Selected Essays, 1952-1995*, 2000; *Family Business: Selected Letters Between a Father and Son*, 2001 (with Louis Ginsberg); *Spontaneous Mind: Selected Interviews, 1958-1996*, 2001

EDITED TEXT: *Poems for the Nation: A Collection of Contemporary Political Poems*, 2000

MISCELLANEOUS: *Beat Legacy, Connections, Influences: Poems and Letters by Allen Ginsberg*, 1994; *The Book of Matyrdom and Artifice: First Journals and Poems, 1937-1952*, 2006

Allen Ginsberg (GIHNZ-burg) is usually associated with the Beat generation, a literary movement popular with the counterculture of the late 1950's and early 1960's. He was born into a fairly typical middle-class Jewish family. His father, a schoolteacher, was a poet, but the stability of his home life was shattered by his mother's periods of mental illness. She was finally institutionalized until her death in 1956. Ginsberg himself spent eight months in Columbia Presbyterian Psychiatric Institute in 1949, and madness, along with visionary hallucinations, became a central image in his poetry. Ginsberg drew on memories of his mother's illness, as well as his own experience inside the mental institution, for the raw material in "Kaddish" (1959), an elegy for his mother that many critics consider his best work.

While attending Columbia University, Ginsberg met two of the most influential figures of his early years: Jack Kerouac and William S. Burroughs. Kerouac later wrote *On the Road* (1957), a central document of the Beat movement. Burroughs, a New York City literary impresario and a homosexual drug addict, later wrote the innovative novel *Naked Lunch* (1959). Burroughs was then just beginning to experiment with fictional techniques, and his approach of combining spontaneous composition, random associations, and raw confessional autobiographical material appealed to Ginsberg's need to transform the ecstatic chaos of his life into the controlled substance of art. Their homosexuality was another shared characteristic, and under the influence of Burroughs and the bisexual Kerouac (Ginsberg was temporarily expelled from Columbia when the two were found in bed together), Ginsberg came to regard his homosexuality as an asset rather than a liability, an early example of gay pride.

The relationship between the inchoate madness of experience and the organizing principles of poetry is a central theme in Ginsberg's work. Much of his fascination with the shaping aspect of art is derived from two other notable influences on his style: the eighteenth century English mystic and poet William Blake and the nineteenth century American poet Walt Whitman. From Blake, Ginsberg discovered the power of incongruous apocalyptic images, of disjunctive narrative, and of the juxtaposition of mundane events with extraordinary perception. From Whitman, Ginsberg appropriated the effective use of the long line, the catalog technique of accumulating details, and the craft of weaving scraps of autobiography into the whole cloth of historical myth. Ginsberg acknowledged Blake's influence in the poem "Sunflower Sutra" (1956). Echoing themes from Blake, "Sunflower" contrasts the natural beauty of the world with human beings' capacity to corrupt it. The poet's point of view is distinctly dystopian, lamenting the fall from a prelapsarian Eden into the sewer of contemporary America. In his frequently anthologized poem "A Supermarket in California" (1956), Ginsberg addresses Whitman directly, complaining of the American lack of imagination that converts a vital land of hope and plentitude into a crass commercial wasteland.

After being expelled from Columbia University for scrawling pornographic images in the scum of his dormitory window, Ginsberg set off to see the world, traveling on merchant tankers, picking up menial jobs, and living with friends. He eventually did return to graduate from Columbia, and afterward he accepted a job as a market researcher in San Francisco, but the allure of the other side of San Francisco life, the jazzy bohemian arts scene, was too tempting, and Ginsberg soon joined those who congregated around Lawrence Ferlinghetti's City Lights Bookstore, the mecca for the West Coast Beat poets.

When Ferlinghetti published the 1956 poem "Howl," Ginsberg's career was launched. Along with Kerouac's *On the Road*, "Howl" became the most important publication of the Beat movement, a status only underlined when Ferlinghetti was charged with distributing obscene material in publishing it. An extended trial, during which the artistic merits of the poem were thoroughly debated, ended with Ferlinghetti's acquittal and Ginsberg's reputation made. In "Howl," just as Kerouac in his novels attempted to immortalize his circle of friends, Ginsberg portrayed Kerouac and the others as visionary troubadours, "angelheaded hipsters burning for the ancient heavenly connection." The poem is at once a history, an account of the exploits of Ginsberg and his friends, and a portrait of a generation Ginsberg idolized as rebels persecuted by a callous society bent on punishing those who refused to conform to rigid standards of behavior. "Howl," at once vicious and playful, comical and apocalyptic, manages to summarize the philosophic and poetic sensibility of an entire literary movement while simultaneously extending its audience and creating a new subculture in response to it.

During the 1960's and 1970's Ginsberg became a celebrity of sorts. His earlier involvement with pacifism and Eastern mysticism, and his experiments with drugs, prefigured, defined, and sustained cultural movements as diverse as that of the "hippies," the radical political Left, and the antiwar movement during the Vietnam conflict. Ginsberg was outspoken in his support for liberal causes, actively working for social and political reforms. In 1994 Stanford University acquired his memorabilia and papers as part of their permanent collection. He died on April 5, 1997, in New York, from complications of liver cancer and hepatitis.

Howl

Type of work: Poetry
First published: 1956

The protagonists of *Howl*, Ginsberg's best-known book, are marginalized because of their rejection of, or failure to measure up to, the social, religious, and sexual values of American capitalism. The poem "Howl," central to the book, is divided into three sections. Part 1 eulogizes "the best minds of my generation," whose individual battles with social, religious, and sexual uniformity leave them "de-

Allen Ginsberg (George Holmes)

stroyed by madness, starving hysterical naked." Ginsberg said that his use of the long line in *Howl*, inspired by Walt Whitman, is an attempt to "free speech for emotional expression." The poem is structured to give voice to those otherwise silenced by the dominant culture, to produce from their silence a "cry that shivers the cities down to the last radio."

Part 2 focuses on Moloch, the god for whom parents burned their children in sacrifice. Moloch symbolizes the physical and psychological effects of American capitalism. From America's "mind" of "pure machinery" emerges Moloch's military-industrial complex, whose bomb threatens to destroy the world.

Part 3 is structured as a call-and-response litany, specifically directed to Carl Solomon, whom Ginsberg met in 1949 when both were committed to the Columbia Presbyterian Psychiatric Institute. Solomon, to whom the poem is dedicated, represents the postwar counterculture, all of those whose "madness basically is rebellion against Moloch." The addendum to the poem, "Footnote to Howl," celebrates the holy cleansing that follows the apocalyptic confrontation dramatized in the poem.

Ginsberg termed crucial those elements of the poem that specifically describe the gay and bisexual practices of his protagonists as "saintly" and "ecstatic." Drawing from Ginsberg's experiences as a gay man in the sexually conformist 1940's and 1950's, the poem affirms gay eroticism as a natural form of sexual expression, replacing, as he said, "vulgar stereotype with a statement of act." The sexual explicitness of the poem prompted the San Francisco police to seize *Howl* and to charge Ginsberg's publisher, Lawrence Ferlinghetti, with obscenity. The judge in the case found the book to be "not obscene" because of its "redeeming social importance." The *Howl* case remains a landmark victory for freedom of expression in the twentieth century.

Kaddish

Type of work: Poetry
First published: 1961

Kaddish is Ginsberg's elegy for his mother, Naomi. In *Kaddish* Ginsberg portrays the course of Naomi's mental illness and its effect on the extended Ginsberg family. The perceptions of Ginsberg, the narrator, are crucial to understanding how sexual and religious themes of identity work in the poem. Naomi's worsening condition coincides with Ginsberg's realization as a young boy that he is gay and with his emerging discomfort with traditional American religious institutions.

Invoking both "prophesy as in the Hebrew Anthem" and "the Buddhist Book of Answers," section 1 remembers Naomi's childhood. Naomi passes through major American cultural institutions—school, work, marriage—all of which contribute to her illness. Section 2 details her descent into madness and its harrowing effects on the family. Throughout the poem, Ginsberg seeks rescue from Naomi's madness yet recognizes that her condition also inspires his own critique of the United States. "Naomi's mad idealism" frightens him; it also helps him understand the sinister qualities of middle-class American institutions. As he admits that Naomi's condition caused him sexual confusion, he also confers imaginative inspiration to her. She is the "glorious muse that bore me from the womb, gave suck/ first mystic life"; and it was from her "pained/ head I first took vision." Unlike Naomi, the truly mad in *Kaddish* are those incapable of compassion, such as the psychiatric authorities who brutalize Naomi with electroshock treatments, leaving her "tortured and beaten in the skull."

By the end of *Kaddish*, Ginsberg seeks to redeem Naomi's life according to the Eastern and Western religious traditions that inform the poem. The final sections of *Kaddish* seek to transform the trauma of Naomi's illness into sacred poetry. The key to this transformation is Ginsberg's revision of the Kaddish, the Jewish prayer for the dead. The Kaddish was not said at Naomi's grave because the required minimum of ten Jewish adults—a *minyan*, in traditional Judaism—was not present, as required by Jewish law. Therefore, the poem accomplishes what Naomi's original mourners could not: Ginsberg eulogizes Naomi with his Kaddish, and by doing so he offers his own revision of traditional Judaic law.

Suggested Readings

Aronson, Jerry. *The Life and Times of Allen Ginsberg*. Video. New York: First Run Icarus Films, 1993.

Caveney, Graham. *Screaming with Joy: The Life of Allen Ginsberg*. New York: Broadway Books, 1999.

Ginsberg, Allen. *Spontaneous Mind: Selected Interviews, 1958-1996*. Preface by Václav Havel. Introduction by Edmund White. Edited by David Carter. New York: HarperCollins, 2001.

Hyde, Lewis, ed. *On the Poetry of Allen Ginsberg*. Ann Arbor: University of Michigan Press, 1984.

Kramer, Jane. *Allen Ginsberg in America*. New York: Random House, 1969.

Landas, John. *The Bop Apocalypse*. Champaign: University of Illinois Press, 2001.

Merrill, Thomas F. *Allen Ginsberg*. New York: Twayne, 1969.

Miles, Barry. *The Beat Hotel: Ginsberg, Burroughs, and Corso in Paris, 1958-1963*. New York: Grove Press, 2000.

_______. *Ginsberg: A Biography*. New York: Simon & Schuster, 1989.

Molesworth, Charles. *The Fierce Embrace*. Columbia: University of Missouri Press, 1979.

Morgan, Bill. *I Celebrate Myself: The Somewhat Private Life of Allen Ginsberg*. New York: Viking Press, 2006.

Portugés, Paul. *The Visionary Poetics of Allen Ginsberg*. Santa Barbara, Calif.: Ross-Erikson, 1978.

Schumacher, Michael. *Dharma Lion: A Biography of Allen Ginsberg*. New York: St. Martin's Press, 1992.

Tonkinson, Carol, ed. *Big Sky Mind: Buddhism and the Beat Generation*. New York: Riverhead Books, 1995.

Contributors: Jeff Johnson and Tony Trigilio

Nikki Giovanni

Born: Knoxville, Tennessee; June 7, 1943

African American

Giovanni's works have earned critical acclaim and have remained in print in an era when poetry typically does not sell.

Principal works

POETRY: *Black Feeling, Black Talk*, 1968; *Black Judgement*, 1968; *Black Feeling, Black Talk, Black Judgement*, 1970; *Poem of Angela Yvonne Davis*, 1970; *Re: Creation*, 1970; *Spin a Soft Black Song: Poems for Children*, 1971 (revised 1987; juvenile); *My House*, 1972; *Ego-Tripping, and Other Poems for Young Readers*, 1973 (juvenile); *The Women and the Men*, 1975; *Cotton Candy on a Rainy Day*, 1978; *Vacation Time*, 1980 (juvenile); *Those Who Ride the Night Winds*, 1983 (juvenile); *Knoxville, Tennessee*, 1994 (juvenile); *Life: Through Black Eyes*, 1995; *The Genie in the Jar*, 1996 (juvenile); *The Selected Poems of Nikki Giovanni*, 1996; *The Sun Is So Quiet*, 1996 (juvenile); *Love Poems*, 1997; *Blues: For All the Changes*, 1999; *Quilting the Black-Eyed Pea: Poems and Not Quite Poems*, 2002; *The Collected Poetry of Nikki Giovanni, 1968-1998*, 2003; *Just for You! The Girls in the Circle*, 2004 (juvenile); *Acolytes*, 2007

NONFICTION: *Gemini: An Extended Autobiographical Statement on My First Twenty-five Years of Being a Black Poet*, 1971; *A Dialogue: James Baldwin and Nikki Giovanni*, 1973; *A Poetic Equation: Conversations Between Nikki Giovanni and Margaret Walker*, 1974; *Sacred Cows . . . and Other Edibles*, 1988; *Conversations with Nikki Giovanni*, 1992 (Virginia C. Fowler, editor); *Racism 101*, 1994; *The Prosaic Soul of Nikki Giovanni*, 2003 (includes *Gemini*, *Sacred Cows*, and *Racism 101*)

EDITED TEXTS: *Night Comes Softly: Anthology of Black Female Voices*, 1970; *Appalachian Elders: A Warm Hearth Sampler*, 1991 (with Cathee Dennison); *Grand Mothers: Poems, Reminiscences, and Short Stories About the Keepers of Our Traditions*, 1994; *Shimmy Shimmy Shimmy Like My Sister Kate: Looking at the Harlem Renaissance Through Poems*, 1996; *Grand Fathers: Reminiscences, Poems, Recipes, and Photos of the Keepers of Our Traditions*, 1999

When Nikki Giovanni (jee-oh-VAH-nee) began to appear on the literary scene in the late 1960's, critics praised her work for its themes of militancy, black pride, and revolution. The majority of poems in her volumes, however, address themes such as love, family, and friendship. Her militant poems received more attention, however, and they reflected Giovanni's own activism. It was not accurate,

Nikki Giovanni (© Jill Krementz)

therefore, when critics argued that Giovanni abandoned the cause of black militancy in the 1970's, when her poems became more personal. The change was not as marked as some believed.

Giovanni's work took on a different perspective in 1970, when she became a mother. That year she published *Re: Creation*, whose themes are black female identity and motherhood. In *My House*, Giovanni more clearly addresses issues of family, love, and a twofold perspective on life, which is revealed in the two divisions of the book. With poems about the "inside" and "outside," Giovanni acknowledges the importance of not only the personal but also the world at large. Another dimension of this two-part unity is seen in *The Women and the Men*. Giovanni's poetry, over time, also seems to have undergone another change—an increased awareness of the outside world. After 1978, her poetry reflected her interest in the human condition. The poems became more meditative, more introspective, and eventually more hopeful, focusing on life's realities.

Examined as a whole, Giovanni's work reveals concerns for identity, self-exploration, and self-realization. These concerns also appear in her works of other genres: recorded poetry, read to music; children's poetry, which she wrote to present positive images to black children; and essays. Giovanni's most consistent theme is the continual, evolving exploration of personal identity and individualism amid familial, social, and political realities.

Black Feeling, Black Talk

Type of work: Poetry
First published: 1968

Although Giovanni's reputation as a revolutionary poet is based on this work, fewer than half its poems address the theme of revolution. Critics point to often-quoted incendiary poems in this collection to indicate Giovanni's revolutionary stance. They also note the poems about political figures and poems addressing black identity to illustrate Giovanni's militancy. These poems are important in this volume, but they are not Giovanni's sole concern.

What has been overlooked are the highly personal poems. In tallying the themes that appear in this work, it becomes apparent that love, loss, and loneliness are important to Giovanni. She also writes personal tributes and reminiscences to those who helped shape her life and ideology. Then there are Giovanni's personal responses to political events. She mourns the deaths of John F. Kennedy, Martin Luther King, Jr., and Robert Kennedy. She states that the 1960's were one long funeral day. She also notes atrocities in Germany, Vietnam, and Israel and compares them to 1960's America.

Black Feeling, Black Talk, then, is a compilation of political and personal poetry. Amid calls for revolution and affirmations of blackness is an insistence on maintaining one's individuality in the face of the political. There is also the importance of acknowledging the contributions of others in one's development. Thus, what is central to Giovanni's revolution is helping people to think about new ways of viewing and understanding their lives, personally and politically. *Black Feeling, Black Talk* is not a call for revolution that will destroy the world. The book is about how people, in the words of its final poem, may "build what we can become when we dream."

Gemini

Type of work: Essays
First published: 1971

Nominated for a National Book Award in 1973, *Gemini: An Extended Autobiographical Statement on My First Twenty-five Years of Being a Black Poet* offers scenes from Giovanni's life as a child and mother. However, *Gemini* is in a sense neither an autobiography nor an extended statement; rather, it is a collection of thirteen essays, about half of which discuss aspects of Giovanni's life. Readers learn something of Giovanni's life, but *Gemini* reveals more of her ideas. All of the essays involve personal observations mingled with political concerns, as the final lines of the essay "400 Mulvaney Street" illustrate: "They had come to say Welcome Home. And I thought Tommy, my son, must know about this. He must know we come from somewhere. That we belong." These lines are a capsule of Giovanni's major themes: family and belonging, identity, and one's relationship to the world. As the people of Knoxville come to hear her, Giovanni realizes her connection to a place and people. Sharing this with her son underscores the importance of family and passing on legacies, a lesson for not only him but also all blacks. To know that they come from somewhere and therefore belong is part of the message in this work.

The central message in *Gemini* is love. Giovanni claims, "If you don't love your mama and papa then you don't love yourself." This includes racial love; Giovanni provides tributes to black writer Charles Waddell Chesnutt and to black musicians

Lena Horne and Aretha Franklin. Giovanni states that black people "must become the critics and protectors" of black music and literature. Love of oneself leads to a sense of identity: This is Giovanni's second message.

Giovanni cautions blacks against carelessly adopting "white philosophies." Her advice is to "know who's playing the music before you dance." Giovanni discusses respect as an outgrowth of love and identity, particularly for blacks of other nationalities and for the elderly. In Giovanni's discussion of the black revolution, she emphasizes the need to change the world. She addresses what one should be willing to live for: hope to change the world or some aspect of it. The essays of *Gemini* combine to give readers a sense of Giovanni, her world, and their world.

My House

Type of work: Poetry
First published: 1972

In the 1960's, poetry was to be a witness of the times—"it's so important to record" ("Records"), but Giovanni's poetry proved to be her house: *My House* shows her assimilation and transformation of the world into her castle. In "Poem (For Nina)" from that volume, she begins by asserting that "we are all imprisoned *in the castle of our skins*"; though her imagination will color her world "Black Gold": "my castle shall become/ my rendezvous/ my courtyard will bloom with hyacinths and jack-in-the-pulpits/ my moat will not restrict me but will be filled/ with dolphins. . . ." In "A Very Simple Wish" she wants through her poetry to make a patchwork quilt of the world, including all that seems to be left behind by world history: "i've a mind to build/ a new world/ want to play."

In *My House* Giovanni began to exhibit increased sophistication and maturity. Her viewpoint had broadened beyond a rigid black revolutionary consciousness to balance a wide range of social concerns. Her rhymes had also become more pronounced, more lyrical, more gentle. The themes of family love, loneliness, and frustration, which Giovanni had defiantly explored in her earlier works, find much deeper expression in *My House*. Her change from an incendiary radical to a nurturing poet is traced in the poem "Revolutionary Dreams": from dreaming "militant dreams/ of taking over america," she

> . . . awoke and dug
> that if i dreamed natural
> dreams of being a natural
> woman doing what a woman
> does when she's natural
> i would have a revolution

This changed perspective accords with the conclusion of "When I Die": "And if ever i touched a life i hope that life knows/ that i know that touching was and still is and will/ always be the true/ revolution." Love and sex form the subject matter of many of her poems. She will "scream and stamp and shout/ for more beautiful beautiful beautiful/ black men with outasight afros" in "Beautiful Black Men" and propose "counterrevolutionary" sex in "Seduction" and "That Day": "if you've got the dough/ then i've got the heat/ we can use my oven/ til it's warm and sweet."

This bold and playful manner, however, is usually modulated by the complications of any long-term relationship between men and women. While she explains in *Gemini*: "to me sex is an essence. . . . It's a basic of human relationships. And sex is conflict; it could be considered a miniwar between two people," marriage is "'give and take—you give and he takes.'" In "Woman" her acknowledgment of the difficulty of a black man maintaining his self-respect in America has led to her acceptance of his failings: "she decided to become/ a woman/ and though he still refused/ to be a man/ she decided it was all/ right."

Cotton Candy on a Rainy Day

Type of work: Poetry
First published: 1978

The title poem of this collection hints at the tempering of Giovanni's vision. When Giovanni published *Cotton Candy on a Rainy Day*, critics viewed it as one of her most somber works. They noted the focus on emotional ups and downs, fear and insecurity, and the weight of everyday responsibilities. The title poem tells of "the gray of my mornings/ Or the blues of every night" in a decade known for "loneliness." Life is likened to nebulous cotton candy: "The sweet soft essence/ of possibility/ Never quite maturing." Her attitude tired, her potential stillborn, she is unable to categorize life as easily as before, "To put a three-dimensional picture/ On a one-dimensional surface."

One reason for her growth in vision seems to be her realization of the complexity of a woman's life. The black woman's negative self-image depicted in "Adulthood" was not solved by adopting the role of Revolutionary Black Poet. In "Woman Poem," "Untitled," "Once a Lady Told Me," "Each Sunday," and "The Winter Storm," the women with compromised lives are other women. In "A Poem Off Center," however, she includes herself in this condition: "maybe i shouldn't feel sorry/ for myself/ but the more i understand women/ the more i do." A comparison of "All I Gotta Do" ("is sit and wait") to "Choice," two poems alike in their subject matter and their syncopated beat, shows that a woman's only choice is to cry.

Sacred Cows . . . and Other Edibles

Type of work: Essays
First published: 1988

A reader of this difficult-to-classify assortment might at first think that the principal topic of the book is humor. In a column in which Giovanni mulls over a race for the Cincinnati City Council, she proposes annexing Northern Kentucky and the Jack Nicklaus Sports Complex. A mock-serious piece warns that handicapped parking spaces may engender a new wave of segregation: Are "white" and "colored" wheelchair zones in the offing? These essays, however, aim at much more than inducing a few chuckles. The author has endured much hardship in her life, and several of her columns portray both her sorrow and her ability to take life as it comes. She describes with moving economy of tone the death of her father from cancer; in the midst of her despair she marvels at the maturity with which her twelve-year-old son responds to his grandfather's passing.

Giovanni's comments are by no means limited to personal events. She participated actively in the Civil Rights movement, and feminist issues concern her greatly. One can vividly sense the anger she feels over the exploitation of women in pornography. Even on social issues, however, her touch of whimsical humor is rarely absent.

Giovanni's view of the ways in which life and literature relate to each other is yet another of her themes. She strongly opposes a formalist position that regards poetry as a world apart. To her, writing is a way of dealing with life. Although she acknowledges that many of her poems have been occasioned by rage at injustice, her overall outlook is one of accepting life, rather than bemoaning fate. Giovanni is a genuine original; whether she is discussing seat belts or Bob Dylan, she always has some fresh angle to explore.

Racism 101

Type of work: Essays
First published: 1994

Many of these essays are autobiographical, and most contain biographical elements. Nikki Giovanni identifies her intellectual origins as like those of Alex Haley, listening to her grandparents talk evenings on their porch in Knoxville, Tennessee. She tells about her family, about growing up in Ohio and Tennessee, raising her son, returning to her family home after her father's stroke, accepting and then fighting to keep a professorship at Virginia Polytechnic.

Only two of the essays speak directly about her practice and aims as a writer: "Meatloaf: A View of Poetry" and "Appalachian Elders: The Warm Hearth Writers' Workshop." Ideas about her art appear in many pieces, however, including especially her reviews of Spike Lee's *Malcolm* and of the works of Toni Morrison.

The title, *Racism 101*, suggests that the book will be a primer on American racism, but this is not quite the case. Giovanni's observations of American culture often focus on problems of racial justice. In "Remembering Fisk . . . Thinking About Du Bois," she excoriates black conservatives for adopting a form of individualism that denigrates their cultural roots: "No one chooses misery, and our efforts to make this a choice will be the damnation of our souls." Her title piece offers practical advice to black students on Virginia Polytechnic's predominantly white campus. Two other topics that recur in these pieces are the positions of black women and the praise of black achievers.

From her "Author's Note" to the "Postscript," Giovanni's collection is unified by her voice, which is intimate, down-home, friendly, eloquent, tough, and—especially when it is a matter of justice—uncompromising. Readers who know her poetry will recognize her voice here.

Blues: For All the Changes

Type of work: Poetry
First published: 1999

As the twentieth century came to a close, readers found a bit of the younger, more political Giovanni in several of the poems of her collection *Blues: For All the Changes*. While sociopolitical commentary in poetry often fails because it loses touch with humanity, Giovanni continues to keep focus on people: Here she spars with ills that confront Americans, but every struggle has a human face. There is a real estate developer who is destroying the woodland adjacent to Giovanni's home in preparation for a new housing development ("Road Rage"). There is a young basketball star ("Iverson"), who, when harassed for his youth and style, finds a compassionate but stern sister in Giovanni. And there is President Bill Clinton, who is subject to Giovanni's opinions ("The President's Penis"). Giovanni writes in this collection with an authority informed by experience and shared with heart-stealing candor.

Pop culture and pleasure find a place in the collection as well. She writes about tennis player Pete Sampras and her own tennis playing, and she pays tribute to Jackie Robinson, soul singer Regina Belle, the late blues singer Alberta Hunter, and Betty Shabazz, the late widow of Malcolm X. She also writes fondly of her memories of going to the ballpark with her father to see the Cincinnati Reds.

Her battle with illness is captured in "Me and Mrs. Robin," which deals with Giovanni's convalescence from cancer surgery and the family of robins she observed with delight and sympathy from her window. Yet this gentle poem also revisits the real estate developer, who, the poem notes, has destroyed trees and "confused the birds and murdered the possum and groundhog." As she identifies with an injured robin, Giovanni's language invokes a gnostic cosmogony: God takes care of individuals; Mother Nature wreaks havoc left and right. "No one ever says 'Mother Nature have mercy.' Mother nature don't give a damn," Giovanni says; "that's why God is so important."

Suggested Readings

Baldwin, James, and Nikki Giovanni. *A Dialogue: James Baldwin and Nikki Giovanni*. Philadelphia: Lippincott, 1973.

Bigsby, C. W. E. *The Second Black Renaissance: Essays in Black Literature*. Westport, Conn.: Greenwood Press, 1980.

Fowler, Virginia C. *Nikki Giovanni*. New York: Twayne, 1992.

Giovanni, Nikki. *Conversations with Nikki Giovanni*. Edited by Virginia C. Fowler. Jackson: University Press of Mississippi, 1992.

Gould, Jean. "Nikki Giovanni." In *Modern American Women Poets*. New York: Dodd, Mead, 1984.

McDowell, Margaret B. "Groundwork for a More Comprehensive Criticism of Nikki Giovanni." In *Belief vs. Theory in Black American Literary Criticism*, edited by Joseph Weixlmann and Chester J. Fontenot. Greenwood, Fla.: Penkevill, 1986.

Walters, Jennifer. "Nikki Giovanni and Rita Dove: Poets Redefining." *The Journal of Negro History* 85, no. 3 (Summer, 2000): 210-217.

White, Evelyn C. "The Poet and the Rapper." *Essence* 30, no. 1 (May, 1999): 122-124.

Contributors: Paula C. Barnes, Sarah Hilbert, and Honora Rankine-Galloway

Joanne Greenberg
(Hannah Green)

Born: Brooklyn, New York; September 24, 1932

Jewish

Drawing on her Jewish heritage in many of her novels, Greenberg will be best remembered for her sensitive and illuminating portrayal of mental illness in I Never Promised You a Rose Garden.

Principal works

LONG FICTION: *The King's Persons*, 1963; *I Never Promised You a Rose Garden*, 1964 (as Hannah Green); *The Monday Voices*, 1965; *In This Sign*, 1968; *Founder's Praise*, 1976; *A Season of Delight*, 1981; *The Far Side of Victory*, 1983; *Simple Gifts*, 1986; *Age of Consent*, 1987; *Of Such Small Differences*, 1988; *No Reck'ning Made*, 1993; *Where the Road Goes*, 1998; *Appearances*, 2006

SHORT FICTION: *Summering*, 1966; *Rites of Passage*, 1972; *High Crimes and Misdemeanors*, 1979; *With the Snow Queen*, 1991

Joanne Greenberg's novels and short stories made her an important voice for those members of American society who have become alienated because of an illness, weakness, or obsession that makes it difficult for them to communicate with the mainstream culture. She was born Joanne Goldenberg to Julius Lester Goldenberg and Rosalie (Bernstein) Goldenberg. Although she came from a Jewish background and has drawn on that background and heritage in some of her writing, she received almost no formal religious training. She earned a bachelor's degree in anthropology from American University, and in 1955 she married Albert Greenberg, whom she had met at the university.

During her teenage years, she had been treated for schizophrenia and eventually institutionalized. Her therapist was Frieda Fromm-Reichmann, an active proponent of the use of psychoanalysis for schizophrenia patients (in contradiction of Sigmund Freud, who, though he had originated the psychoanalytic method, did not believe that it could be used for such patients). In the course of the therapy, the two women formed a close relationship and planned to collaborate on a book about schizophrenia. When Fromm-Reichmann died in 1957, Greenberg decided to undertake the project herself by writing a fictionalized account of her illness in *I Never Promised You a Rose Garden*.

Her career as a social worker and psychoanalyst brought Greenberg into contact with the subcultures of the handicapped and disadvantaged, whom she represented in several of her works. In her third novel, *The Monday Voices*, she deals with the frustrations of a social worker as he tries to find help for his clients. In the 1960's, when Albert Greenberg was working with the deaf community around Denver, they both began to learn sign language. Greenberg's fourth novel, *In This Sign*, follows Janice and Abel Ryder, a deaf couple, through nearly fifty years of marriage. Greenberg accurately depicts the communication between the couple: All the words and expressions they use can be said in the limited vocabulary of signing. Greenberg returned to writing about the deaf community in *Of Such Small Differences*, where she describes the particular difficulties of those who are both deaf and blind.

Another cluster of Greenberg's works focuses on religious themes. Her first novel, *The King's Persons*, is a historical account of anti-Semitism in twelfth century England. *Founder's Praise* describes the founding of a new religious sect in a small American town, the depth of feeling of the new adherents, and their sense of betrayal as the sect begins to die. *A Season of Delight* shows a middle-class Jewish housewife trying to understand her children's rejection of their religious heritage. (This novel also includes vivid descriptions of the workings of a small-town fire department and rescue team.) Through the protagonists of these novels Greenberg shows that feelings about religion can be just as uncontrollable and alienating as the handicapping conditions described in others of Greenberg's works. Yet whatever struggles she believes adherence to religion may create, Greenberg treats religion seriously and with respect.

Greenberg's later novels usually have contemporary settings and revolve around a central character. These characters face ethical and deep emotional issues in their efforts to survive. Eric Gordon, in *The Far Side of Victory*, drives drunk, killing several people in another car, and then falls in love with one of the survivors. Reconstructive surgeon Daniel Sanborn of *Age of Consent* is examined as he tries to repair lives after his displacement from Israel. Greenberg takes a broader look at family dynamics, social issues, and American life in *Where the Road Goes*, a well-crafted succession of letters between a traveling grandmother and her family in Colorado.

Greenberg's short stories deal with many of the same themes as do her novels, and they present the same range of characters and settings. The stories in *Summering*, *Rites of Passage*, and *High Crimes and Misdemeanors* deal with good and evil, faith and doubt, and the need for communication. The characters include the deaf, the isolated, the insane, the aged, the self-destructive, and the questioning—in short, the kind of people who are usually ignored. As in the novels, not all the characters find happy endings. In her fourth collection, *With the Snow Queen*, Greenberg focuses on connections in her usual cast of characters—connections between people and others, and connections between people and themselves.

Although Greenberg's characters often face frightening illness or handicapping conditions, she avoids the trap of excessive sentimentality or predictability. Her protagonists demonstrate the same capacity for selfishness and pride as everyone else, but they do have special needs that are not always being met by society, and Greenberg intends her work to be a plea in their behalf.

None of Greenberg's later works was as popular as *I Never Promised You a Rose Garden*, but all have been greeted with respect and praise from the critics, and they have drawn a modest audience of faithful readers. This is partly a response to the fact that Greenberg has, throughout her writing career, involved herself in her Colorado community. She has been a teacher's aide in a rural school teaching the history of the English language, a certified medical technician with the rescue team of her local fire department, and an adjunct professor of anthropology at the Colorado School of Mines. She has also served as an interpreter and guide at conventions for the deaf and blind and has delivered lectures on mental health care for the deaf.

I Never Promised You a Rose Garden

Type of work: Novel
First published: 1964

In this novel, her most popular and the one that eventually made her famous, Greenberg chronicles her treatment for schizophrenia. The protagonist, Deborah Blau, who suffers from schizophrenia, creates a mythical kingdom called Yr to which she retreats when reality becomes too overwhelming. She attempts suicide, is hospitalized, and undergoes treatment with a Dr. Fried, who is patterned on Fromm-Reichmann. The book was widely praised by critics and psychoanalysts alike for its sensitive and illuminating portrayal of mental illness, but it did not sell well until it was published in paperback, when it attracted a large audience, especially among teenage girls. Millions of copies were sold in more than a dozen languages, and the novel was made into a film in 1977. The title was also used in a popular song, and the expression "I never promised you a rose garden" became a commonplace in American English.

Although she had published one novel, *The King's Persons*, under her own name, Greenberg chose to publish *I Never Promised You a Rose Garden* under the pseudonym Hannah Green. Because it was commonly believed in the 1960's that schizophrenia was incurable, Greenberg wanted to keep her own mental illness a secret to protect her two young sons. It was not until the 1970's that she acknowledged her authorship.

Of Such Small Differences

Type of work: Novel
First published: 1988

Greenberg here creates a hauntingly perceptive and poetic tour de force that proves her one of America's best storytellers. Entering John Moon's life is to enter a world of synesthesia, unexpectedly abrupt accidents, inexplicable abandonments, and ceaseless quests into unknown areas that may be mapped only by stepping carefully through endlessly dark silence.

Blind at birth and permanently deafened at age nine by his drunken father, John is twenty-six, lives alone in a Denver apartment, and works at "the workshop" when the story begins. He is also a poet, earning money for his poems that are printed on Handicards and sold to hearing-sighted people. Trapped more by the expectations of those around him than by his own physical limitations, John finds his life "continually being defined and interpreted to him because direct experience was too perilous to dare." Likewise, his publisher wants only poems which deemphasize human differences and speak of life from the perspective of a hearing-sighted person; thus John derives poems from stories he has read in Braille by such writers as Herman Melville and Charles Dickens.

Falling in love with Leda, a hearing-sighted actress, changes John's life and poetry profoundly. Yet there are complications: John's deaf-blind friends warn him against the relationship, his family thinks Leda is using him, and Leda's friends think John is using her. John's triumphs in overcoming obstacles in the material world are extended here into triumphs of the heart over mental constructs that often darken rather than illuminate human potential.

Suggested Readings

Diamond, R. "The Archetype of Death and Renewal in *I Never Promised You a Rose Garden.*" *Perspectives in Psychiatric Care* 8 (January-March, 1975): 21-24.

Fromm-Reichmann, Frieda. "Frieda Fromm-Reichmann Discusses the 'Rose Garden' Case." *Psychiatry* 45, no. 2 (1982): 128-136.

Greenberg, Joanne. "Go Where You're Sent: An Interview with Joanne Greenberg." Interview by K. L. Gibble. *Christian Century* 102 (November 20, 1985): 1063-1067.

_______. Interview by Susan Koppelman. *Belles Lettres* 8, no. 4 (Summer, 1993): 32.

_______. "Joanne Greenberg." Interview by Sybil S. Steinberg. *Publishers Weekly* 234 (September 23, 1988): 50-51.

Wisse, Ruth. "Rediscovering Judaism." Review of *A Season of Delight*, by Joanne Greenberg. *Commentary* 73 (May, 1982): 84-87.

Wolfe, K. K., and G. K. Wolfe. "Metaphors of Madness: Popular Psychological Narratives." *Journal of Popular Culture* 10 (Spring, 1976): 895-907.

Contributor: Cynthia A. Bily

Jessica Hagedorn

Born: Manila, Philippines; 1949

Filipino American

Hagedorn expresses the "tough and noble" lives of Asian immigrants who feel only partially assimilated.

Principal works

DRAMA: *Chiquita Banana*, pb. 1972; *Where the Mississippi Meets the Amazon*, pr. 1977 (with Thulani Davis and Ntozake Shange); *Mango Tango*, pr. 1978; *Tenement Lover: no palm trees/in new york city*, pr. 1981, pb. 1990; *Holy Food*, pr. 1988 (staged; pr. 1989, radio play); *Teenytown*, pr. 1990 (with Laurie Carlos and Robbie McCauley); *Black: Her Story*, pr., pb. 1993; *Airport Music*, pr. 1994 (with Han Ong); *Silent Movie*, pr. 1997 (as part of *The Square*); *Dogeaters*, pr. 1998, pb. 2003 (adaptation of her novel)

LONG FICTION: *Dogeaters*, 1990; *The Gangster of Love*, 1997; *Dream Jungle*, 2003

POETRY: *The Woman Who Thought She Was More than a Samba*, 1978; *Visions of a Daughter, Foretold*, 1994

SCREENPLAY: *Fresh Kill*, 1994

EDITED TEXTS: *Charlie Chan Is Dead: An Anthology of Contemporary Asian American Fiction*, 1993; *Charlie Chan Is Dead II: At Home in the World, an Anthology of Contemporary Asian American Fiction*, 2004

MISCELLANEOUS: *Dangerous Music*, 1975; *Pet Food and Tropical Apparitions*, 1981; *Danger and Beauty*, 1993

Born and raised in the Philippines, Jessica Hagedorn (HA-geh-dohrn) experienced the United States through the eyes of her mother and through images provided by American textbooks and movies. "The colonization of our imagination was relentless," she has said. Only when she started living in California in 1963 did she begin to appreciate what was precious in the Filipino extended family, a cultural feature partially left behind. In California, she began to feel allied with persons of various national origins who challenged American myths. Kenneth Rexroth, who had been patron of the Beat generation in San Francisco during the 1950's, introduced her to the poets who gathered at the City Lights Bookstore. In 1973, Rexroth helped her publish her first poems, later collectively titled "The Death of Anna May Wong." Her principal concern was the exploitation of Filipino workers.

Her poetry became more and more influenced by the rhythms of popular street music. In 1975, she gathered together a volume of prose and poetry called *Dangerous Music*. That same year Hagedorn formed her band, The West Coast Gangster

Choir, and sang lyrics of her own invention with them. In 1978, she left San Francisco without her band and established herself in New York City. There, along with Ntozake Shange and Thulani Davis, she performed her poetry at Joseph Papp's Public Theater. In 1981, Hagedorn published her second collection of mixed prose and poetry. During the 1980's she worked on her first novel, *Dogeaters*, which exposes corruption in her homeland as a result of Ferdinand Marcos's years of "constitutional authoritarianism." *Dogeaters* is also a novel that she has described as a love letter to her motherland. The characters in her novel for the most part are trapped by consumerism; this plight is caused by the Filipinos' long history as a colony and by their dreams of success, which too often come from American soap operas. Hagedorn's work is devoted to substituting for such stereotypes the complexities visible among people in Metro Manila and the urban reaches of the American coasts. Her anthology, *Charlie Chan Is Dead*, signifies a new image for Asians.

Dangerous Music

Type of work: Poetry
First published: 1975

The poems in *Dangerous Music* were composed after Hagedorn began "discovering myself as a Filipino-American writer" in California. Orientalist Kenneth Rexroth had placed five of her early poems in his 1973 anthology, *Four Young Women Poets*. "The Death of Anna May Wong," included in that edition, signified the poet's rejection of Hollywood stereotypes of Asian women as demure or exotically sinister. *Dangerous Music* continues the author's search for authentic images of non-Europeans that describe her own situation as well as those of other minorities. The intensity of many of these lyrics, written while she was performing with her West Coast Gangster Choir, became a way of expressing whole dimensions of society largely ignored or misunderstood by generations of European Americans. Although on the page such poems resemble songs without music, their occasional arrangement in ballad quatrains sometimes imitates blues music. The influence of Latino or African music is visible in the more jagged, syncopated lines of such poems as "Latin Music in New York" or "Canto Negro."

The cultural environment that is so much a part of the voices she assumes in *Dangerous Music* can readily be imagined. "Something About You," for example, affectionately connects Hagedorn with fellow artists Ntozake Shange and Thulani Davis, with whom she performed poems set to music for New York's Public Theater. Other poems identify her with Puerto Rican or Cuban musicians. More typical poems, however, describe a love-hate relationship with the American Dream. In "Natural Death," a Cuban refugee seems satisfied with fantasies of cosmetic splendor, though warned about bodies buried in saran wrap on a California beach. Loneliness and anger are conveyed by the mocking refrain: "o the grandeur of it." Yet the Philippines, which is remembered in "Sometimes" ("life is very cheap"), is equally far from being ideal. "Justifiable Homicide" warns of urban dangers anywhere in the world, when differences among people become cause for mutual indifference.

The only defense against the insanity that comes from cultural and economic stress is found in singing, according to "Sorcery" and "Easter Sunday," even if the songs themselves are passionate outcries of pain, not lullabies. The unacceptable alternative to release through song is to surrender one's memories of better dreams or, as in the case of "The Blossoming of Bongbong," the one prose fantasy included with these poems, total forgetfulness of one's personal identity.

Jessica Hagedorn (Nancy Wong)

Danger and Beauty

Type of work: Poetry
First published: 1993

Before her novel *Dogeaters*, Hagedorn had published poetry in anthologies such as *Four Young Women Poets*, and two books of her short fiction were issued by an underground press. *Danger and Beauty* reprints some of this material; it also includes some of her more recent works. New or old, the writing is strangely haunting literary experimentation. Music consumed Hagedorn during the 1970's when she formed her band, the West Coast Gangster Choir, and music pulses here in her language. The unconventional melodies may not suit everyone, but words rise boldly off the pages none the less, demanding to be heard.

Music also seems ever-present in the lives of most of Hagedorn's characters; the persona in "Seeing You Again Makes Me Wanna Wash the Dishes" muses against the background of "martha & the vandellas/ crooning/ come/ and/ get/ these/ memories." However, music is not always such innocent stuff. In her poem "Sorcery," Hagedorn looks at the power of words to create illusion. She says, "They most likely/ be saying them,/ breathing poems/ so rhythmic/ you can't help/ but dance./ and once/ you start dancing/ to words/ you might never stop."

Hagedorn's second book, *Pet Food and Tropical Apparitions*, is reprinted in its entirety. Here, her voice becomes fierce and hard. In the novella *Pet Food*, the teenage Filipino narrator, George Sand, is writing a musical about her life on the streets of San Francisco and tells of sex, drugs, and murder as part of daily existence. This work is representative of *Danger and Beauty*, an amalgam of Filipino roots and urban American experiences that never fully blends. In "Carnal," one of the more recent pieces, Hagedorn returns to San Francisco and says, "I'm home, in spite of myself." It has been a long journey, and some readers may have a similar experience with this collection. Others, though, may find that the underlying beat of such personal and artistic exploration resonates with them in powerful ways.

The Gangster of Love

Type of work: Novel
First published: 1997

The protagonist of this novel, Rocky, is a strong, literary-minded, ambitious girl with no idea of what she wants to do with her life. Her older brother, Voltaire, is no better off. They live with their stubborn, beauty-queen mother and help her with her catering business. Voltaire often brings home street artists, and one time brings home Elvis Chang. Rocky and Elvis immediately move in together. Soon after Rocky meets Elvis, she meets Keiko. Keiko is an artist of obscure ethnic origin who swallows fire on the streets for cash. Rocky, Elvis, and Keiko all decide to move to New York and soon after Rocky starts her band, The Gangsters of Love, with Elvis as the guitarist.

In New York, Rocky lives a decade of her life with no direction. Her life is a constant rotation of trying to earn enough money to keep the band going, working with the band, and partying with drugs and alcohol. Keiko becomes a famous artist, and eventually Elvis and Rocky break up. Once she reaches her thirties, Rocky begins to realize that this pointless lifestyle is not what she wants, so when she becomes pregnant she decides to keep the baby and make some changes.

Throughout the dead-end courses that Rocky always seems to choose, there is threaded the rich heritage of her Filipino upbringing. The decisions she makes are based on the unusual circumstances of her life; the navigation between the clashing cultures of the Philippines and the United States. After she gives birth to her daughter, Venus, and her mother dies, Rocky realizes that she has been running away from her life and her past. The band and partying were only a means of escape. Yet it is not until she is called to her father's sickbed in the Philippines that she realizes how far she has run trying to escape who she is. It is then that she finds a sense of closure to her extended youth, when she finally grows up.

Suggested Readings

Ancheta, Shirley. Review of *Danger and Beauty*, by Jessica Hagedorn. *Amerasia Journal* 20, no. 1 (1994).

Bloom, Harold. "Jessica Hagedorn." In *Asian American Writers*, edited by Harold Bloom. Philadelphia: Chelsea House, 1997.

Casper, Leonard. "*Bangugot* and the Philippine Dream in Hagedorn." *Pilipinas* 15 (1990).

Doyle, Jacqueline. "'A Love Letter to My Motherland': Maternal Discourses in Jessica Hagedorn's *Dogeaters*." *Hitting Critical Mass: A Journal of Asian American Cultural Criticism* 4, no. 2 (Summer, 1997): 1-25.

Evangelista, Susan. "Jessica Hagedorn and Manila Magic." *MELUS* 18, no. 4 (1993/1994).

Hau, Caroline. "*Dogeaters*, Postmodernism, and the 'Worlding' of the Philippines." In *Philippine Post-Colonial Studies: Essay on Language and Literature*. Quezon City: University of the Philippines Press, 1993.

Jenkins, Joyce. "Jessica Hagedorn: An Interview with a Filipina Novelist." In *The Asian Pacific American Heritage: A Companion to Literature and Arts*, edited by George J. Leonard. New York: Garland, 1999.

Lee, Rachel C. *The Americas of Asian American Literature: Gendered Fictions of Nation and Transnation*. Princeton, N.J.: Princeton University Press, 1999.

Mendible, Myra. "Desiring Images: Spectacle and Representation in *Dogeaters*." *Critique* 43, no. 3 (2002).

Quintana, Alvina E. "Borders Be Damned: Creolizing Literary Traditions." *Cultural Studies* 13, no. 2 (1999).

Contributor: Leonard Casper

Janet Campbell Hale

Born: Riverside, California; January 11, 1946

Native American

Hale's books present the trials and tribulations of life as a Native American both on the reservation and in urban America.

Principal works

LONG FICTION: *The Owl's Song*, 1974; *The Jailing of Cecelia Capture*, 1985; *Women on the Run*, 1999

POETRY: *Custer Lives in Humboldt County, and Other Poems*, 1978

NONFICTION: *Bloodlines: Odyssey of a Native Daughter*, 1993

Janet Campbell Hale, a member of the Coeur d'Alene tribe of Northern Idaho, was born in Riverside, California, on January 11, 1946, the youngest of four daughters of Nicholas Patrick Campbell, a full-blooded Coeur d'Alene tribal member, and Margaret O'Sullivan Campbell, who was part Kootenay Indian and part Irish. A brother died in infancy a year before Hale's birth. She lived with her parents on the reservation until the age of ten. All of her sisters were married by that time, and she and her mother and father lived in a rural, isolated area near Tacoma, Washington. Their home was twenty miles removed from their nearest neighbor. It had no electricity or running water, and temperatures in that region sometimes dropped to 40 degrees below zero.

As an American Indian who lived both on tribal reservations and in urban American society, Hale experienced life in different cultures and endured the prejudice that exists against people of her heritage. Her books present the trials and tribulations of life under these circumstances and the battles waged to overcome them. Hale suffered verbal and psychological abuse from her mother and, when they lived at home, her siblings. Hale's father was an alcoholic who abused her mother. After leaving to escape her alcoholic husband, Margaret Campbell and her daughter lived in three states; Janet attended twenty-one schools. Her mother was an intelligent but uneducated woman who denied her Indian roots. Because she was uneducated, she was limited to working at menial jobs. At the age of twelve, Hale lived with her mother in the Yakima tribal reservation town of Wapato, Washington. She remained in poverty throughout her childhood and dropped out of school in the ninth grade. She always knew, though, that she was destined to write.

Hale left home and moved to Santa Fe, New Mexico. There she met and married Arthur Dudley III and attended the Institute of American Indian Arts. During this short-lived marriage she had a son, Aaron Nicholas. Hale was abused by her white husband, and, after one year of marriage, she and Dudley divorced in 1965. She moved to San Francisco. Single, uneducated, and with a child, she struggled to provide for herself and her son.

A turning point in her life arrived when, at the age of twenty-one, she learned of an open admissions, tuition-free program at the City College of San Francisco (CCSF) that permitted her to attend without having completed high school. She was able to place her son in a government-funded day care program while she attended college. Enrolling in CCSF enabled her to gain confidence and self-esteem. She completed her studies at CCSF in 1968. While attending school, she received a grade of D in one of her writing courses. This discouraged her from writing, and she decided to study law. She enrolled in Boalt Hall School of Law at the University of California at Berkeley. There she met her second husband, Stephen Dinsmore Hale. In 1970 they married and had a daughter, Jennifer Elizabeth. Hale earned a bachelor's degree in rhetoric from Berkeley in 1974. She later attended the University of California, Davis, where she earned a master of arts degree in English in 1984.

Hale's writing career began in her childhood. At the age of nine she wrote poetry, which she continued throughout her teenage years. In 1978 she published a book of poems titled *Custer Lives in Humboldt County, and Other Poems*. Her first novel, *The Owl's Song*, was published in 1974. In this novel, Hale draws upon her experiences as a young American Indian seeking a better life away from the reservation. The book parallels Hale's life, and it speaks of the prejudices she has encountered.

In 1985 Hale's second novel, *The Jailing of Cecelia Capture*, was published. This book received literary acclaim and was nominated for a Pulitzer Prize. Imprisoned and trapped between two worlds, Cecelia seeks her identity amid difficult odds. She is an American Indian caught between ties to her past and her culture and a world in which she is not truly accepted. After she is jailed for drunk driving, it is discovered that, in the past, she committed welfare fraud. Cecelia Capture's life in many ways parallels the life of Janet Campbell Hale in that both had alcoholic fathers and abusive mothers. Hale's fourth book, *Bloodlines: Odyssey of a Native Daughter*, published in 1993, consists of autobiographical essays. *Women on the Run* was published in 1999.

In addition to being nominated for a Pulitzer Prize for *The Jailing of Cecelia Capture*, Hale received literary distinction in being awarded the New York Poetry Day Award in 1964 and the American Book Award for *Bloodlines* in 1994. She has worked as an educator, holding numerous teaching positions at colleges and universities, including the University of Oregon, Western Washington University, and the University of California, Davis. Also an artist, she painted what would become the cover of *Women on the Run*, as well as a mural at the Coeur d'Alene tribal school.

The Jailing of Cecelia Capture

Type of work: Novel
First published: 1985

The Jailing of Cecelia Capture was Hale's first adult novel, and in it she skillfully constructed a poignant tale that provides a keen look into the life of a modern Native American woman. In this absorbing character study, the protagonist, Cecelia Capture Welles, is a thirty-year-old law student, wife, and mother. She is jailed on a drunk-driving charge the night of her birthday and reflects back on her life in an effort to understand how she arrived at this point. Cecelia's childhood on a reservation in Idaho and in various western slum communities was marked by a father who drank, a nagging mother, and indifferent older sisters. A runaway at sixteen, Cecelia secures a job as a waitress, then meets a young soldier about to depart for Vietnam. She becomes pregnant, the man is killed, and Cecelia becomes an unwed mother on welfare. While struggling to eke out a living for her child as she attends college, she meets and marries one of her former instructors. Cecelia remains dissatisfied and unhappy and decides to enroll in a law school in another state, against her husband's wishes. After being arrested, Cecelia realizes that she has known many kinds of prison, some worse than the reality of jail. For years, she has tried to live her life by other people's standards and rules. She realizes that most of her actions have been reactions to those around her, instead of an acting out of her own desires. This realization signifies the beginning of her freedom.

Suggested Readings

Bataille, Gretchen M., and Laurie Lisa, eds. *Native American Women: A Biographical Dictionary*. 2d ed. New York: Routledge, 2001.

Charles, Jim. "Contemporary American Indian Life in *The Owl's Song* and 'Smoke Signals.'" *English Journal* 90, no. 3 (January, 2001): 54-59.

Hale, Frederick. *Janet Campbell Hale*. Boise, Idaho: Boise State University Press, 1996.

Steinberg, Sybil. Review of *Women on the Run*, by Janet Campbell Hale. *Publishers Weekly* 246, no. 39 (September 27, 1999): 71.

Contributor: Vivian R. Alexander

Alex Haley

Born: Ithaca, New York; August 11, 1921
Died: Seattle, Washington; February 10, 1992

African American

Haley's Roots, *a monumental chronicle of seven generations of Haley's African American ancestors launched a genealogy craze among Americans of all ethnicities, not just African Americans.*

Principal works

LONG FICTION: *Roots: The Saga of an American Family*, 1976; *A Different Kind of Christmas*, 1988; *Alex Haley's Queen: The Story of an American Family*, 1993 (with David Stevens); *Mama Flora's Family*, 1998 (with Stevens)
TELEPLAY: *Palmerstown, U.S.A.*, 1980
NONFICTION: *The Playboy Interviews*, 1993 (Murray Fisher, editor)
EDITED TEXT: *The Autobiography of Malcolm X*, 1965

Alex Haley (HAY-lee) was born in Ithaca, New York, in 1921 to Bertha George Palmer and Simon Alexander Haley, graduate students at Cornell University. As a young boy, Haley moved with his family back to his parents' hometown of Henning, Tennessee. Growing up in Henning surrounded by a large extended family, Haley and his younger brothers enjoyed listening to their grandmother and aunts tell stories about their family's history. One story that particularly fascinated Haley was the tale of a slave ancestor named Kunta Kinte, also referred to as "the African," who had arrived on a ship that landed in a place called "Naplis"—which Haley much later learned was Annapolis, Maryland—and worked on a plantation in Spotsylvania County, Virginia.

After attending teacher's college in North Carolina for two years, Haley joined the U.S. Coast Guard in 1939. In 1941, he married Nannie Branch, with whom he had two children, Lydia and William. Haley served as a mess boy and later as a cook at the beginning of his Coast Guard career, but he took up writing as a hobby when he found that his writing skills were in demand among coworkers who needed help composing love letters. This experience led Haley to try his hand as a romance writer, and he submitted numerous romance stories to popular magazines, but without success. Undaunted, Haley next tried his hand at history, writing mainly about the history of the Coast Guard, and he published several of these articles in magazines. In 1949, Haley was promoted to the position of Coast Guard journalist, a position that he held until his retirement from service in 1958.

After retiring from the Coast Guard, Haley authored a successful series of articles in *Playboy* magazine about prominent African Americans, including jazz musician Miles Davis, boxer Cassius Clay (later known as Muhammad Ali), and Nation of Islam leader Malcolm X, among others. His *Playboy* interview with Malcolm X led Haley to take on a larger project, which became his first book, *The Autobiography of Malcolm X*, published in 1965. Haley met with Malcolm X frequently over a two-year period to conduct the interviews for the book, which sold six million copies and was translated into eight languages. Its critical and popular acclaim helped Haley obtain a contract with the publisher Doubleday to write his next book, *Roots*.

Haley's first marriage ended in 1964, and he married Juliette Collins, with whom he had one child, Cynthia, before their divorce in 1972. Between the publication of *The Autobiography of Malcolm X* in 1965 and *Roots* in 1976, Haley spent most of his time conducting the painstaking historical and genealogical research for *Roots*. His research ultimately led him to Gambia, West Africa, where he met a *griot*, or ancestral storyteller, who told Haley the African side of his family's stories about Kunta Kinte. Haley describes this encounter as the "peak experience" of his life.

In 1976, *Roots* was published and immediately became a best seller. Almost overnight, the book sparked a genealogy fad among Americans of all ethnicities but particularly among African Americans. Read by millions, the story of *Roots* became even more well known in 1977 when it was adapted for television as a miniseries that was viewed by 130 million people.

Not long after the publication of *Roots* and the airing of the miniseries, several

Alex Haley (AP/Wide World Photos)

writers brought plagiarism lawsuits against Haley. Although judges dismissed two of the suits, Haley paid $650,000 in an out-of-court settlement to Harold Courlander, author of a 1967 novel called *The African*. Some people believe that Haley's settlement payment was an admission of guilt; others believe that Haley agreed to the payment simply to avoid a lengthy trial. A few years later, several historians questioned whether *Roots* was historically accurate and whether Haley's genealogical research was reliable. However, despite questions about its authenticity, *Roots* continues to be important for its influence on popular culture and for its realistic portrayal of slavery and the lives of African Americans.

Haley died of cardiac arrest in 1992 in Seattle, Washington. He was seventy years old.

The Autobiography of Malcolm X

Type of work: Autobiography
First published: 1965

Although the author of this autobiography is the legendary black activist Malcolm X, Haley in many ways is the book's creator. To conduct the interviews that would become *The Autobiography of Malcolm X*, Haley met with Malcolm X almost daily throughout 1963 and 1964. According to Haley, Malcolm insisted that the story be told in his own words, with no "biographical interpretation" on Haley's part. This limited Haley's role as a biographer: Because he followed Malcolm's ban on interpretation, the reader learns only what Malcolm chooses to reveal. However, despite this rather significant limitation, Haley's work is a success. He managed to take the raw data of hundreds of hours of interviews and weave together a life story that is not only coherent but also powerfully lucid, revealing to a great extent the logical development of Malcolm X's theories about race and religion. However misguided some of Malcolm X's racial beliefs seem, Haley's articulate writing serves to create understanding—understanding of how these beliefs make a great deal of sense in the world inhabited by Malcolm X and millions of other young men like him. *The Autobiography of Malcolm X* was named by *Time* magazine as one of the ten most important nonfiction books of the twentieth century.

Roots: The Saga of an American Family

Type of work: Novel
First published: 1976

Some critics have found it difficult to evaluate *Roots* because it is unclear whether the book is essentially fact or essentially fiction. Although based on genealogical and historical research, it is not a book of history, because most of its details and dialogue are (by necessity) invented. However, unlike most historical fiction, *Roots* is much more than a fictional story placed against a real historical background, with a few famous historical figures making cameo appearances. Haley himself called the book “faction,” a mix of fact and fiction.

Roots opens with the birth of Kunta Kinte in 1750 and tells the story of his childhood in a Muslim family, part of a Mandinka tribe in the small Gambian village of Juffure in West Africa. One day when Kunta is about seventeen, he is captured and endures the horrors of the Middle Passage—the voyage across the Atlantic Ocean on a crowded, stinking, disease-ridden slave ship, an experience shared by perhaps 20 million Africans over the four hundred years of the slave trade.

Landing at Annapolis and arriving at a plantation in Virginia, Kunta is shocked to find that the other black people there are not Africans—they speak English, practice Christianity, and, worst of all, seem to accept the fact that they are slaves. Kunta vows never to assimilate, and for this he endures unspeakably brutal treatment. His African ways and stubborn individuality become the tales and legends of his descendants: his daughter Kizzy, who is sold away from her parents as a teenager; Kizzy’s son, the colorful character Chicken George, born of rape by Kizzy’s plantation owner; and all the generations down to Alex Haley’s own grandparents, aunts, and parents, who share stories about Kunta, “the African,” with Haley and his brothers.

Critics who consider *Roots* to be a work of history have sometimes faulted it for containing historical inaccuracies. For instance, it is unlikely that Kunta’s village, Juffure, was as peaceful and democratic in the eighteenth century as Haley portrays it, and it is also doubtful whether Kunta’s northern Virginia plantation would have produced cotton in the late 1700’s. These kinds of factual errors bother some critics, but others overlook them and judge the book on its literary merits rather than its historical correctness.

The literary merits of *Roots* are many. Most important is the skill with which Haley portrays the reality of slavery and the slave trade. Haley’s writing shatters the myth of the happy-go-lucky slave who loves his master and has no desire to be freed. Haley was not the first writer to portray slavery realistically, but he was the first to reach a mass audience of Americans of all colors and ethnicities. This feat was partly the result of perfect timing. The Civil Rights movement of the 1960’s had made some progress in changing mainstream attitudes toward African Americans, so *Roots* was able to find a wide audience that might not have been ready to hear the book’s message twenty years earlier. However, the book’s success also is a result of its compelling story line and characters. Haley’s skillful writing easily draws readers in, helping them identify with and care about the characters’ triumphs and sorrows. *Roots* received a 1977 National Book Award, and Haley was awarded a Pulitzer Prize and the Spingarn Medal of the National Association for the Advancement of Colored People (NAACP) for outstanding achievement by a black American.

Roots also succeeds in its resonance with African Americans whose family histories were lost or obscured by the institution of slavery. The book elicited a very personal response among many African Americans, who felt that *Roots* had returned their identity to them. Beyond the personal scale, however, the novel changed American culture by demonstrating that it was possible to do serious historical research into African American history and genealogy. Indeed, the study of African American history in schools and colleges became commonplace only after the publication of *Roots*.

Roots has a universal appeal that accounts for its commercial success. Although it tells the unique story of African Americans, it also tells a story with which all Americans can identify. Most Americans' ancestors originally were settlers from other continents. Just like Haley's family, many American families tell stories about their forebears and raise their children to know their roots. Finally, all Americans can sympathize with what many believe to be the worst horror of slavery—not the beatings or the lack of freedom but the forced separation of families. For these reasons, *Roots* found a receptive audience not only among African Americans but also among Americans of all ethnicities and backgrounds.

Suggested Readings

Blayney, Michael Steward. "*Roots* and the Noble Savage." *North Dakota Quarterly* 54 (Winter, 1986): 1-17.

Courlander, Harold. "Kunta Kinte's Struggle to Be African." *Phylon* 47 (December, 1986): 294-302.

Demarest, David P., Jr. "*The Autobiography of Malcolm X:* Beyond Didacticism." *College Language Association Journal* 16 (1972).

Gerber, David. "Haley's *Roots* and Our Own: An Inquiry into the Nature of Popular Phenomenon." *Journal of Ethnic Studies* 5 (Fall, 1977): 87-111.

Haley, Alex. Interview by Jeffrey Elliot. *Negro History Bulletin* 41, no. 1 (January/February, 1978): 782-785.

Miller, R. Baxter. "Kneeling at the Fireplace: Black Vulcan—*Roots* and the Double Artificer." *MELUS* 9 (Spring, 1982): 73-84.

Othow, Helen Chavis. "*Roots* and the Heroic Search for Identity." *College Language Association Journal* 26 (March, 1983): 311-324.

Pinsker, Sanford. "Magic Realism, Historical Truth, and the Quest for a Liberating Identity: Reflections on Alex Haley's *Roots* and Toni Morrison's *Song of Solomon*." In *Black American Prose Theory*, edited by Joe Weixlmann and Chester J. Fontenot. Vol. 1 in *Studies in Black American Literature*. Greenwood, Fla.: Penkevill, 1984.

Staples, Robert. "A Symposium on *Roots*." *The Black Scholar* 8, no. 7 (May, 1977): 36-42.

Tucker, Lauren R., and Hemant Shah. "Race and the Transformation of Culture: The Making of the Television Miniseries *Roots*." *Critical Studies in Mass Communication* 9 (December, 1992).

Contributor: Karen Antell

Virginia Hamilton

Born: Yellow Springs, Ohio; March 12, 1936
Died: Dayton, Ohio; February 19, 2002

African American

The prolific Hamilton, one of the best writers of children's fiction in the twentieth century, also wrote biographies of African Americans who set positive examples and fostered black pride.

Principal works

CHILDREN'S LITERATURE: *Zeely*, 1967; *The House of Dies Drear*, 1968; *The Planet of Junior Brown*, 1971; *M. C. Higgins the Great*, 1974; *Justice and Her Brothers*, 1978; *Dustland*, 1980; *Jahdu*, 1980; *The Gathering*, 1981; *Sweet Whispers, Brother Rush*, 1982; *Willie Bea and the Time the Martians Landed*, 1983; *The People Could Fly: American Black Folktales*, 1985; *The Mystery of Drear House*, 1987; *A White Romance*, 1987; *Anthony Burns: The Defeat and Triumph of a Fugitive Slave*, 1988; *In the Beginning: Creation Stories from Around the World*, 1988; *Bells of Christmas*, 1989; *Cousins*, 1990; *The Dark Way: Stories from the Spirit World*, 1990; *Many Thousand Gone: African Americans from Slavery to Freedom*, 1992; *Plain City*, 1993; *Her Stories: African American Folktales, Fairy Tales, and True Tales*, 1995; *When Birds Could Talk and Bats Could Sing*, 1996; *A Ring of Tricksters: Animal Tales from America, the West Indies, and Africa*, 1997; *The Magical Adventures of Pretty Pearl*, 1998; *Second Cousins*, 1998; *Bluish*, 1999; *The Girl Who Spun Gold*, 2000; *Wee Winnie Witch's Skinny: An Original Scare Tale for Halloween*, 2001; *Time Pieces: The Book of Times*, 2002

NONFICTION: *W. E. B. Du Bois: A Biography*, 1972; *Paul Robeson: The Life and Times of a Free Black Man*, 1974

Virginia Esther Hamilton, the youngest of five children, was born and raised in Yellow Springs, Ohio, a descendant of an African American man who escaped to Ohio from slavery. Her parents were Kenneth James Hamilton, a musician, and Etta Belle Perry Hamilton. She attended school in Yellow Springs, graduating with honors, and went on to Yellow Springs' Antioch College on a full scholarship. Her writing courses there reinforced her long-standing conviction that becoming an author was her destiny. She completed further study at Ohio State University and The New School for Social Research in New York.

In New York, she supported herself through various activities, including work as a singer in obscure nightclubs. She mingled with other writers, musicians, and artists and ultimately met her future husband, poet Arnold Adoff, whom she married in March, 1960. The two traveled to Spain and North Africa, destinations she had long wanted to visit. It was after this lengthy trip (lasting several months) that she wrote her first book, *Zeely*. She had tried to write, even at a very early age, and had concentrated her efforts on short stories. However, an editor at Macmillan Publishing Company (with whom she had attended Antioch College) suggested that she try book-length fiction for young adults. *Zeely* was the result of Hamilton's efforts to transform a short story she had written in college into a short novel.

The success of her award-winning first book was balanced with a few critics' comments on flaws in the novel's character development. Still, she was encouraged to continue, knowing that she had begun to establish a reputation for an impressive style and imaginative narratives. Her second book came out in 1968, and she had produced seven more by 1974, interspersing her fiction with biographies of the notable African Americans W. E. B. Du Bois and Paul Robeson. She chose these biographical subjects because they fit in with her strong belief in the ability of African Americans to survive against unfair odds and in the importance of nurturing African American racial pride. These concepts are prominent themes in many of her fictional works.

Though her husband had been a teacher in New York and she had lived there while attending school and working in different capacities (one of her jobs was as a cost accountant for an engineering firm), after fifteen years of off-and-on residence, Hamilton felt the city was so mentally stimulating that it was difficult for her to find the meditative quiet she needed as a writer. Consequently, she moved with her husband and their two children back to Ohio and settled on land that had been owned by her family since the late nineteenth century. Hamilton and Adoff built a large redwood-and-glass home, where they both worked at their craft. She produced scores of books, most of them award winners, before dying of breast cancer in 2002. She was sixty-five years old.

Zeely

Type of work: Children's literature
First published: 1967

Virginia Hamilton is known internationally for the major contributions her young adult fiction makes to the fields of children's literature and African American literature. Her dozens of fiction and nonfiction works portray the African American experience in a unique and honest way that had rarely been attempted by another American writer. Her main characters are solemn children who are faced with situations or conditions that are at least peculiar, and often bizarre or even perilous. These children face their circumstances with purpose and dignity and eventually come to understand what it means to be African American in America and to be worthy human beings.

Such a figure is Zeely Tayber, the protagonist of *Zeely*. She is an older girl who lives on a farm and raises hogs. More than six feet tall, she is regal and mysterious, and to the young girl Geeder, visiting a neighboring farm with her brother, Zeely seems as marvelous as a Watutsi queen, like one pictured in a magazine Geeder reads in her uncle's house. Geeder sees Zeely as a proud and dignified role model and wants to be like her and to become her friend. When the two finally meet, first at a disastrous hog market and later when Zeely summons her to a catalpa forest, Geeder at last learns about Zeely's mysterious background.

Zeely was Hamilton's first book. It was named one of the American Library Association's Notable Books and also received a Nancy Block Award. Some critics, however, took exception with her character development and to certain episodes that they felt were anticlimactic. For example, in one scene the hogs are brought to market and Geeder is slightly injured; this scene was critiqued as insufficiently realized. The author was praised, however, for her use of language and her ability to create a story and style that appeals to young female readers.

The House of Dies Drear

Type of work: Children's literature
First published: 1968

Written in 1968, *The House of Dies Drear* tells the story of a family that relocates from North Carolina to a house in an Ohio town that was an Underground Railroad station. The father, a history professor, is fascinated by the house and the legends surrounding it. However, his thirteen-year-old son Thomas and the rest of the family are uneasy living in a house where, as legend has it, the former owner, a Dutch immigrant abolitionist named Drear, and two runaway slaves were murdered. The ghosts of the slaves and Drear are supposed to be haunting the house. Thomas explores the tunnels and secret passageways in and around the house and encounters the old caretaker, Mr. Pluto, who seems evil to Thomas. The youth is convinced the house is dangerous, and the family is warned that they must leave before disaster strikes. However, Thomas and his father join forces, and together they try to unlock the mystery of the house.

This book received the Ohioana Book Award and the Edgar Allan Poe Award for best juvenile mystery. A sequel, *The Mystery of Drear House*, was written eighteen years later and revealed the house's mysteries. A movie based on *The House of Dies Drear* was made in 1984; Hamilton wrote the screenplay.

The Planet of Junior Brown

Type of work: Children's literature
First published: 1971

Junior Brown is a neurotic, three-hundred-pound eighth-grader with musical talent. His family circumstances are miserable: a sickly, overprotective mother and an often-absent father. Music is the one bright spot in his life, but, despite his talent, his music teacher won't allow him to practice his lessons on the grand piano in her apartment. The excuses she offers only increase the fantasies that gradually consume the boy. His friends are few: There is only Mr. Pool, the school janitor, and Buddy Clark. Buddy is an orphan who has lived most of his young life on the streets. He and Junior so rarely go to school that on the infrequent occasions when they do show up, some teachers don't recognize them. Life becomes so complicated for them that Junior begins to lose his grip on reality, and Buddy and Mr. Pool are the only people with the loyalty and affection to support him in his decision to run away from home and in his encounter with his piano teacher's mysterious "relative."

Some critics consider the characters Junior and Buddy to be as memorable and original as any in modern fiction written for young readers. The story is one of courage in the face of despair and of heroism and survival, and it promotes the notion that human beings must be interdependent. *The Planet of Junior Brown*, with its themes of the brotherhood of man and the indomitability of the human spirit, won Hamilton's first Newbery Honor Book award.

M. C. Higgins the Great

Type of work: Children's literature
First published: 1974

Mayo Cornelius Higgins, nicknamed M. C., is a youngster living with his family on land that has been in the family since his great-grandmother came there as a runaway slave. When strip-mining on the nearby mountain threatens to ruin their land, M. C. envisions escaping with his family to a better place. However, strangers come to the area, bringing with them the possibility that M. C. can do something to try to save the mountain that is part of their home instead of merely trying to escape the impending ugliness.

Called by some reviewers a brilliantly conceived novel, *M. C. Higgins the Great* has the elements of a rite-of-passage story, showing a youngster coping with conflicts with a difficult father and dealing with the need to grow up and show maturity and the capacity to take responsibility. Though it won a Newbery Medal, a National Book Award, and the Boston Globe Award, it also received some criticism. Its opening passages were said to be "almost impenetrable" because of the "heavy prose." Still, others commend it as a fine piece of writing, "moving, poetic, and unsentimental," "warm, humane, and hopeful."

Suggested Readings

Farrell, Kirby. "Virginia Hamilton's *Sweet Whispers, Brother Rush* and the Case for a Radical Existential Criticism." *Contemporary Literature* 31, no. 2 (Summer, 1990): 161-176.

Giovanni, Nikki. Review of *M. C. Higgins, the Great*, by Virginia Hamilton. *The New York Times Book Review*, September 22, 1974, 8.

Hamilton, Virginia. "The Mind of a Novel: The Heart of the Book." *Children's Literature Association Quarterly* 8 (Winter, 1983): 10-14.

_______. "Talking with Virginia Hamilton." Interview by Yolanda Robinson Coles. *American Visions* 10 (December/January, 1995): 31-32.

_______. "Writing the Source: In Other Words." *The Horn Book Magazine* 14 (December, 1978): 609-619.

Mikkelsen, Nina. *Virginia Hamilton*. New York: Twayne, 1994.

Paterson, Katherine. "Family Visions." *The New York Times Book Review*, November 14, 1982, 41, 56.

Scholl, Kathleen. "Black Traditions in *M. C. Higgins, the Great*." *Language Arts* 17 (April, 1980): 420-424.

Townsend, John Rowe. "Virginia Hamilton." In *A Sounding of Storytellers*. Philadelphia: J. B. Lippincott, 1979.

Contributor: Jane L. Ball

Lorraine Hansberry

Born: Chicago, Illinois; May 19, 1930
Died: New York, New York; January 12, 1965

African American

Hansberry is credited with being the first African American woman playwright to have a play produced on Broadway.

Principal works

DRAMA: *A Raisin in the Sun*, pr., pb. 1959; *The Sign in Sidney Brustein's Window*, pr. 1964, pb. 1965; *To Be Young, Gifted, and Black*, pr. 1969, pb. 1971; *Les Blancs*, pr. 1970, pb. 1972; *Les Blancs: The Collected Last Plays of Lorraine Hansberry*, pb. 1972 (Robert Nemiroff, editor; includes *Les Blancs*, *The Drinking Gourd*, and *What Use Are Flowers?*); *The Drinking Gourd*, pb. 1972; *What Use Are Flowers?*, pb. 1972

NONFICTION: *The Movement: Documentary of a Struggle for Equality*, 1964 (includes photographs); *To Be Young, Gifted, and Black: Lorraine Hansberry in Her Own Words*, 1969 (Robert Nemiroff, editor)

With the successful Broadway opening in 1959 of *A Raisin in the Sun*, Lorraine Hansberry (HAHNZ-bur-ree) became a major voice in behalf of racial, sexual, economic, and class justice. During Hansberry's childhood, her father, a successful real estate broker, and her mother, a schoolteacher, were involved in politics and were active supporters of the National Association for the Advancement of Colored People and its causes. Hansberry grew up in a Chicago household where racial issues, oppression, African American identity, and the struggle against discrimination were major concerns. Her early intellectual development was influenced by her uncle, William Leo Hansberry, a professor and scholar at Howard University and writer of African history. He put Hansberry in contact with her African roots and introduced her to a world of articulate black artists and thinkers who personified the struggle to overcome discrimination in American society.

Hansberry was a student in the segregated Chicago public school system. She proceeded to the University of Wisconsin, where she became the first African American woman to live in her dormitory. At the university she was active in politics and developed an interest in the theater and its power.

Dropping out of school, Hansberry moved to New York and became a writer and associate editor for the progressive newspaper *Freedom*. She championed civil rights causes, writing not only on behalf of blacks but also on behalf of other socially repressed groups, including women and gays. With encouragement and inspiration from such luminaries as W. E. B. Du Bois, Langston Hughes, and Paul Robeson, her active professional and intellectual life in Harlem soon blossomed into stories, poems, and plays.

After marrying Robert Nemiroff in 1953, Hansberry left *Freedom* to devote all her attention to writing. Drawing upon her Chicago experiences, she completed *A Raisin in the Sun*, a play that explores the tensions that arise as a black family in Chicago tries to escape the ghetto. The family faces white hostility as it plans to move into a white neighborhood. The play was a phenomenal success.

Hansberry's second Broadway production, *The Sign in Sidney Brustein's Window*, explores such topics as prostitution, marriage, homosexuality, and anti-Semitism. The play's depictions of the plight of those oppressed and discriminated against and of the nature of society's reaction to injustice and prejudice are vivid and thoughtful. Hansberry died from cancer at the age of only thirty-four. Her call for justice and human sympathy continues to reverberate in the work she left behind.

A Raisin in the Sun

Type of work: Drama
First produced: 1959, pb. 1959

A Raisin in the Sun, Hansberry's most celebrated play, is a realistic portrait of a working-class black family struggling to achieve the American Dream of careers and home ownership while gripped by the reality of their lives as African Americans who must survive in a racist society.

Hansberry based her play on her knowledge of life in Chicago's black ghetto and the families to whom her father, a successful real estate broker, rented low-income housing. The action takes place in the cramped, roach-infested apartment of the Youngers, where three generations of the family have resided for years. With the death of her husband, Lena (Mama) becomes the head of the family. She has the right to decide how to use the $10,000 in life insurance money that has come with her husband's death.

Tensions develop quickly. Mama dreams of using the money to move out of the apartment into a new, large home where her family can breathe the free, clean air outside the ghetto. Her son Walter, seeing himself as the new head of the family, envisions the money as a way to free himself and his family from poverty by investing in a liquor store. Walter's intellectual sister hopes the windfall may be a way for her to break racist and sexist barriers by getting a college education and becoming a doctor.

As the play unfolds, Hansberry explores issues of African American identity, pride, male-female relationships within the black family, and the problems of segregation. Mama makes a down payment on a house in a white neighborhood. Fearing that her exercise of authority will diminish her son's sense of masculine self-worth, and in spite of her opposition to buying a liquor store, she re-

Lorraine Hansberry (Library of Congress)

minds Walter of his sister's right to some of the money for a college education and entrusts him with what is left of the money after the down payment. When he returns despairingly after losing all of it, he considers that the only way to recoup the loss is to humiliate himself and his family by making a deal with the Clybourne Park Association, a group of white homeowners who want to buy back the new home in order to keep their neighborhood white.

In a dramatic conclusion, the disillusioned Walter enacts the dilemma of the modern African American male. Trapped at the bottom of the economic ladder, he must again submit to matriarchal authority. Mama despairs at having to take control and wield the authority she knows is destroying her son's masculine identity. Walter finally realizes that he cannot accept the degradation he would bring upon himself, his family, and his father's memory by accepting the association's offer. Discovering his manhood and his responsibility to his family and his race, he refuses to sell back the house. When the association's representative appeals to Mama to reverse her son's decision, she poignantly and pridefully says, "I am afraid you don't understand. My son said we was going to move and there ain't nothing left for me to say." The play closes with the family leaving their cramped apartment for their new home and the challenges that surely await them there.

The Sign in Sidney Brustein's Window

Type of work: Drama
First produced: 1964, pb. 1965

Hansberry's second play, *The Sign in Sidney Brustein's Window*, never matched the success of her first, but it, too, uses a realistic format and was drawn from her own life. Instead of South Side Chicago, it is set in Greenwich Village, Hansberry's home during the early years of her marriage with Robert Nemiroff, and the central character is one who must have resembled many of Hansberry's friends. He is Sidney Brustein, a lapsed liberal, an intellectual, a former insurgent who has lost faith in his ability to bring about constructive change. As the play opens, Sidney moves from one project, a nightclub that failed, to another, the publication of a local newspaper, which Sidney insists will be apolitical. His motto at the opening of the play is

"Presume no commitment, disavow all engagement, mock all great expectations. And above all else, avoid the impulse to correct." Sidney's past efforts have failed, and his lost faith is much the same as Beneatha's in *A Raisin in the Sun*.

The surrounding environment goes a long way toward explaining Sidney's cynicism. His wife, Iris, has been in psychoanalysis for two years, and her troubled soul threatens their marriage. Iris's older sister, Mavis, is anti-Semitic, and her other sister, Gloria, is a high-class call girl who masquerades as a model. Sidney's upstairs neighbor, David Ragin, is a homosexual playwright whose plays invariably assert "the isolation of the soul of man, the alienation of the human spirit, the desolation of all love, all possible communication." Organized crime controls politics in the neighborhood, and drug addiction is rampant; one of Sidney's employees at the defunct nightclub, Sal Peretti, died of addiction at the age of seventeen, despite Sidney's efforts to help him. Faced with these grim realities, Sidney longs to live in a high, wooded land, far from civilization, in a simpler, easier world.

The resultant atmosphere is one of disillusionment as characters lash out in anger while trying to protect themselves from pain. One of the targets of the intellectual barbs of the group is Mavis, an average, settled housewife who fusses over Iris and pretends to no intellectual stature. When the wit gets too pointed, though, Mavis cuts through the verbiage with a telling remark: "I was taught to believe that creativity and great intelligence ought to make one expansive and understanding. That if ordinary people . . . could not expect understanding from artists . . . then where indeed might we look for it at all." Only Sidney is moved by this remark; he is unable to maintain the pretense of cynicism, admitting, "I *care*. I care about it all. It takes too much energy *not* to care." Thus, Sidney lets himself be drawn into another cause, the election of Wally O'Hara to public office as an independent, someone who will oppose the drug culture and gangster rule of the neighborhood.

As Sidney throws himself into this new cause, he uses his newspaper to further the campaign, and even puts a sign, "Vote for Wally O'Hara," in his window. Idealism seems to have won out, and indeed Wally wins the election, but Sidney is put to a severe test as Iris seems about to leave him, and it is discovered that Wally is on the payroll of the gangsters. Added to all this is Gloria's suicide in Sidney's bathroom. Her death brings Sidney to a moment of crisis, and when Wally O'Hara comes into the room to offer condolences and to warn against any hasty actions, Sidney achieves a clarity of vision that reveals his heroism. Sidney says,

> *This world*—this swirling, seething madness—which you ask us to accept, to maintain—has done this . . . maimed my friends . . . emptied these rooms and my very bed. And now it has taken my sister. *This* world. Therefore, to live, to breathe—I shall *have* to fight it.

When Wally accuses Sidney of being a fool, he agrees:

> A fool who believes that death is waste and love is sweet and that the earth turns and that men change every day . . . and that people wanna be better than they are . . . and that I hurt terribly today, and that hurt is desperation and desperation is energy and energy can *move* things.

In this moment, Sidney learns true commitment and his responsibility to make the world what it ought to be. The play closes with Iris and Sidney holding each other on the couch, Iris crying in pain, with Sidney enjoining her: "Yes . . . weep now, darling, weep. Let us both weep. That is the first thing: to let ourselves feel again . . . then, tomorrow, we shall make something strong of this sorrow."

As the curtain closes, the audience can scarcely fail to apply these closing words to themselves. Only if they permit themselves to feel the pain, Hansberry claims, will it be possible to do anything to ease that pain in the future. James Baldwin, referring to the play, said, "it is about nothing less than our responsibility to ourselves and to others," a consistent theme in Hansberry's drama. Again and again, she reminds the audience of their responsibility to act in behalf of a better future, and the basis for this message is her affirmative vision. Robert Nemiroff says that she found reason to hope "in the most unlikely place of all: the lives most of us lead today. Precisely, in short, where *we* cannot find it. It was the mark of her respect for us all."

To Be Young, Gifted, and Black

Type of work: Drama
First produced: 1969, pb. 1971

After Hansberry's untimely death, Robert Nemiroff, her former husband and literary executor, edited versions of her writings and adapted them for the stage under the title *To Be Young, Gifted, and Black*. He also expanded that work into an informal autobiography of the same title. In Nemiroff's words, the work is "biography and autobiography, part fact, part fiction, an act of re-creation utilizing first person materials as well as, inferentially, autobiographical projections of herself in her characters."

"Never before, in the entire history of the American theater, had so much truth of black people's lives been seen on the stage," James Baldwin said of *To Be Young, Gifted, and Black*. Characters from Hansberry's plays, including the character of Lorraine Hansberry herself, portray and relate various strands of African American life in modern America. Walter Lee, for example, embodies the frustrations of black men trying to cope in an economic system that promises advancement but holds them back because of their race. His sister, Beneatha, is an example of the gifted, intelligent black woman (not unlike Hansberry herself) who aspires to participate fully in the American culture. She also, as does Asagai, the Africanist intellectual, strives to remember her African roots.

Then there is Sidney Brustein of *The Sign in Sidney Brustein's Window* (1964), the play most represented in *To Be Young, Gifted, and Black*. Sidney, after leading a life of sleepy noncommitment, grows to care about himself and his society; he takes action, political and otherwise, to improve things. This sort of character growth, in one way or another apparent in all of Hansberry's work, defines her own belief in the possibility for human goodness to prevail. It is this conviction that allows her to anticipate a healing of familial and social ills that comes when people are moved to dedicate themselves to change.

To Be Young, Gifted, and Black also addresses the deep connections between black Americans and emerging African nations, black empowerment, sexual relationships, the generation gap, and black art. Woven throughout *To Be Young, Gifted, and Black* is the character of Lorraine Hansberry herself, who, at the beginning of the work, states perhaps somewhat despairingly: "I was born on the South Side of Chicago. I was born black and female," but by the end is proclaiming proudly, "My name is Lorraine Hansberry. I am a writer." She has ceased allowing the ghetto, with its economic, social, and cultural deprivation, to define her. She has overthrown her enslavement by oppressive sexual stereotypes. In this, the character of Lorraine Hansberry and the playwright are one in the embodiment of a hope for the black race and the female sex. Just as they have, through commitment and perseverance, discovered and defined themselves in name and vocation, so, too, must their people insist on partaking of that vital experience and self-definition that lead to a discovery of self-worth, purpose, and genuine human sympathy.

Les Blancs

Type of work: Drama
First produced: 1970, pb. 1972

Hansberry's last play of significance, *Les Blancs*, was not in finished form when she died and did not open onstage until November 15, 1970, at the Longacre Theatre, years after her death. Nemiroff completed and edited the text, though it is to a very large degree Hansberry's play. It was her least successful play, running for only forty-seven performances, but it did spark considerable controversy, garnering both extravagant praise and passionate denunciation. Some attacked the play as advocating racial warfare, while others claimed it was the best play of the year, incisive and compassionate. The play is set not in a locale drawn from Hansberry's own experience but in a place that long held her interest: Africa.

Les Blancs is Hansberry's most complex and difficult play. It takes as its subject white colonialism and various possible responses to it. At the center of the play are the members of the Matoseh family: Abioseh Senior, the father, who is not actually part of the play, having died before it opens, but who is important in that his whole life defined the various responses possible (acceptance, attempts at lawful change, rebellion); in addition, there are his sons, Abioseh, Eric, and, most important, Tshembe. Hansberry attempts to shed some light on the movement for African independence by showing the relationships of the Matosehs to the whites living in Africa. The whites of importance are Major Rice, the military commander of the colony; Charlie Morris, a reporter; Madame Neilsen; and her husband, Dr. Neilsen, a character never appearing onstage but one responsible for the presence of all the others.

Dr. Neilsen has for many years run a makeshift hospital in the jungle; he is cut in the mold of Albert Schweitzer, for he has dedicated his life to tending the medical ills of the natives. It is because of him that all the other doctors are there and because of him, too, that Charlie Morris is in Africa, for Charlie has come to write a story about the famous doctor.

Whereas Charlie comes to Africa for the first time, Tshembe and Abioseh are called back to Africa by the death of their father. Abioseh comes back a Catholic priest, having renounced his African heritage and embraced the culture and beliefs of the colonialists. Tshembe, too, has taken much from the colonial culture, including his education and a European bride. He has not, however, rejected his heritage, and he is sensitive to the injustice of the colonial system. Though he sees colonialism as evil, he does not want to commit himself to opposing it. He wants to return to his wife and child and lead a comfortable, secure life.

For both Charlie and Tshembe, the visit to Africa brings the unexpected, for they return in the midst of an uprising, called "terror" by the whites and "resistance" by the blacks. Charlie gradually learns the true nature of colonialism, and Tshembe, after great struggle, learns that he cannot avoid his obligation to oppose colonialism actively.

While Charlie waits for Dr. Neilsen to return from another village, he learns from Madame Neilsen that the doctor's efforts seem to be less and less appreciated. When Tshembe comes on the scene, Charlie is immediately interested in him and repeatedly tries to engage the former student of Madame Neilsen and the doctor in conversation, but they fail to understand each other. Tshembe will accept none of the assumptions that Charlie has brought with him to Africa: He rejects the efforts of Dr. Neilsen, however well-intentioned, as representing the guilty conscience of colonialism while perpetrating the system. He also rejects Charlie's confident assumption that the facilities are so backward because of the superstitions of the natives. Charlie, on the other hand, cannot understand how Tshembe can speak so bitterly against colonialism yet not do anything to oppose it. Tshembe explains that he is one of those "who see too much to take sides," but his position becomes increasingly untenable. He is approached by members of the resistance and is asked to lead them, at which point he learns that it was his father who conceived the movement when it became clear that the colonialists, including Dr. Neilsen, saw themselves in the position of father rather than brother to the natives and would never give them freedom.

Still, Tshembe resists the commitment, but Charlie, as he leaves the scene, convinced now that the resistance is necessary, asks Tshembe, "Where are you running, man? Back to Europe? To watch the action on your telly?" Charlie reminds Tshembe that "we do what we can." Madame Neilsen herself makes Tshembe face the needs of his people. Tshembe by this time knows what his choice must be, but he is unable to make it. In his despair, he turns to Madame Neilsen, imploring her help. She tells him, "You have forgotten your geometry if you are despairing, Tshembe. I once taught you that a line goes into infinity unless it is bisected. Our country needs *warriors*, Tshembe Matoseh."

In the final scene of the play, Tshembe takes up arms against the colonialists, and Hansberry makes his decision all the more dramatic by having him kill his brother Abioseh, who has taken the colonial side. Yet, lest anyone misunderstand the agony of his choice, Hansberry ends the play with Tshembe on his knees before the bodies of those he has loved, committed but in agony, deeply engulfed by grief that such commitment is necessary.

Les Blancs is less an answer to the problem of colonialism than it is another expression of Hansberry's deep and abiding belief in the need for individual commitment and in the ability of the individual, once committed, to bring about positive change for the future, even if that requires suffering in the present. Surely her commitment to her writing will guarantee her work an audience far into the future.

Suggested Readings

Carter, Steven R. *Hansberry's Drama: Commitment Amid Complexity*. Urbana: University of Illinois Press, 1991.

Cheney, Anne. *Lorraine Hansberry*. New York: Twayne, 1994.

Domina, Lynn. *Understanding "A Raisin in the Sun": A Student Casebook to Issues, Sources, and Historical Documents*. Westport, Conn.: Greenwood Press, 1998.

Effiong, Philip U. *In Search of a Model for African American Drama: A Study of Selected Plays by Lorraine Hansberry, Amiri Baraka, and Ntozake Shange*. Lanham, Md.: University Press of America, 2000.

Kappel, Lawrence, ed. *Readings on "A Raisin in the Sun."* San Diego, Calif.: Greenhaven Press, 2001.

Keppel, Ben. *The Work of Democracy: Ralph Bunche, Kenneth B. Clark, Lorraine Hansberry, and the Cultural Politics of Race*. Cambridge, Mass.: Harvard University Press, 1995.

Leeson, Richard M. *Lorraine Hansberry: A Research and Production Sourcebook*. Westport, Conn.: Greenwood Press, 1997.

Scheader, Catherine. *Lorraine Hansberry: A Playwright and Voice of Justice*. Springfield, N.J.: Enslow, 1998.

Contributors: Richard M. Leeson, Katherine Lederer, and Hugh Short

Joy Harjo

Born: Tulsa, Oklahoma; May 9, 1951

Native American

Harjo's poetry has won acclaim for its substance, style, and themes, combining many elements of Native American and mainstream American experience.

Principal works

CHILDREN'S LITERATURE: *The Good Luck Cat*, 2000

POETRY: *The Last Song*, 1975; *What Moon Drove Me to This?*, 1980; *She Had Some Horses*, 1983; *Secrets from the Center of the World*, 1989; *In Mad Love and War*, 1990; *The Woman Who Fell from the Sky*, 1996; *How We Became Human: New and Selected Poems, 1975-2001*, 2002

SCREENPLAY: *Origin of Apache Crown Dance*, 1985

SHORT FICTION: "Boston," 1991; "Northern Lights," 1991; "The Flood," 1991; "The Woman Who Fell from the Sky," 1996; "Warrior Road," 1997

NONFICTION: *The Spiral of Memories: Interviews*, 1996 (Laura Coltelli, editor)

EDITED TEXT: *Reinventing the Enemy's Language: Contemporary Native Women's Writing of North America*, 1997 (with Gloria Bird)

MISCELLANEOUS: *A Map to the Next World: Poetry and Tales*, 2000

In her poetry, Joy Harjo (HAHR-joh) expresses a close relationship to the environment and the particularities of the Native American and white cultures from which she is descended. She is an enrolled member of the Creek tribe, the mother of two children (a son, Phil, and a daughter, Rainy Dawn) and a grandmother. Various forms of art were always a part of her life, even in childhood. Her grandmother and aunt were painters. In high school, she trained as a dancer and toured as a dancer and actress with one of the first Indian dance troupes in the country. When her tour ended, she returned to Oklahoma, where her son was born when she was seventeen years old. She left her son's father to move to New Mexico, enrolling at the university as a pre-med student. After one semester, she decided that her interest in art was compelling enough to engage in its formal study.

Educated at the Institute of American Indian Arts in Santa Fe, New Mexico, where she later worked as an instructor, she received a bachelor's degree from the University of New Mexico and a master's degree in fine arts from the University of Iowa. She was a professor of English at both the University of Arizona and the University of New Mexico.

Harjo has received numerous awards for her writing, including the William

Carlos Williams award from the Poetry Society of America, the Delmore Schwartz Award, the American Indian Distinguished Achievement in the Arts Award, and two creative writing fellowships from the National Endowment for the Arts. Harjo's poetry has been increasingly influenced by her interest in music, especially jazz. She plays the saxophone in a band, Poetic Justice, that combines the musical influences of jazz and reggae with her poetry. Many of her poems are tributes to the various musicians who have influenced her work, including saxophonists John Coltrane and Jim Pepper.

The history and mythology of her people and the current state of their oppression also are prominent themes in her work. As she states in the explanation of her poem "Witness": "The Indian wars never ended in this country . . . we were hated for our difference by our enemies."

In Mad Love and War

Type of work: Poetry
First published: 1990

In Mad Love and War is composed of two sections of poems expressing the conflicts and joys of Harjo's experiences as a Native American woman living in contemporary American culture. The poems draw on a wealth of experiences, including those relating to tribal tradition and sacredness of the land. Such positive experiences are compared with the sometimes grim realities inherent in the modern society in which Harjo lives.

Joy Harjo

The first section, titled "The Wars," offers poetry that imagistically develops themes relating to oppression and to survival in the face of daunting problems of poverty, alcoholism, and deferred dreams. In her notable poem "Deer Dancer," Harjo retells a traditional myth in the contemporary setting of "a bar of broken survivors, the club of shotgun, knife wound, of poison by culture." Through the dance, the deer dancer becomes "the myth slipped down through dreamtime. The promise of feast we all knew was coming." Like many of Harjo's poems, "The Deer Dancer" ends with beauty being experienced amid lost hope and despair.

Many of the other poems in "The Wars" are political in nature, containing stark images of violence and deprivation, most notably her poem dedicated to Anna Mae Pictou Aquash, a member of the American Indian Movement whose murdered body was found on the Pine Ridge Reservation, and the poems "We Must Call a Meeting," "Autobiography," "The Real Revolution Is Love," and "Resurrection."

The poems of the second section, "Mad Love," are more personal in their treatment of subject, more lyrical in their voice, and quieter in their tone. In a poem titled with the name of Harjo's daughter, "Rainy Dawn," Harjo concludes by expressing the joy of Rainy Dawn's birth.

> And when you were born I held you wet and unfolding, like a butterfly newly born from the chrysalis of my body. And breathed with you as you breathed your first breath. Then was your promise to take it on like the rest of us, the immense journey, for love, for rain.

In Mad Love and War encompasses a variety of styles, from narrative poems written in expansive lines to tightly chiseled lyrics. Many of the poems in the "Mad Love" section are prose poems, whose unlined stanzas create a notable incongruity with respect to the increasingly personal, softer mood of the pieces. The book offers a journey from the ruins of dislocation to the joys of membership and love. In the final masterful poem of the collection, "The Eagle," Harjo writes, "That we must take the utmost care/ And kindness in all things. . . . We pray that it will be done/ In beauty/ In beauty."

The Woman Who Fell from the Sky

Type of work: Poetry
First published: 1996

The Woman Who Fell from the Sky, Harjo's seventh collection of poetry, consists primarily of prose poems. The collection is divided into two sections, "Tribal Memory" and "The World Ends Here," which express the lore of Harjo's Native American ancestry and her observations of contemporary life. These poems show a concern for content over style. The poetry is presented without conventions of patterned rhyme or meter; the imagery is stark and unadorned.

Each poem is followed by an explanation that contextualizes the piece by offering a brief history of the genesis of the poem or commenting on themes elucidated by the writing. The majority of the book's poems are narrative, developing stories that explain the destinies of Native American characters who retain identity despite the onslaught of European culture, which strips away their language, lore, and religion. The poems create a universe of oppositions: darkness and light, violence and peace.

Other poems relate stories of ancestry on a more personal level, illuminating a view of many worlds existing at once, interconnected and affecting one another. In "The Naming," a grandmother "who never had any peace in this life" is "blessed with animals and songs"; after the birth of a "daughter-born-of-my-son . . . the earth is wet with happiness." As Harjo notes in the explanation of this piece, "When my granddaughter Haleigh was born I felt the spirit of this grandmother in the hospital room. Her presence was a blessing." In the world that Harjo creates, the living and the dead are united and the physical universe is animate, pulsing with feeling of its own.

"The World Ends Here" offers shorter and more concrete poems than those in "Tribal Memory." In addition, the poems are concerned with wounds suffered through a history of genocide inflicted upon Native Americans. "When a people institute a bureaucratic department to serve justice then be suspicious," Harjo warns in "Wolf Warrior." "The Indian wars never ended in this country," she writes in the postscript to "Witness." The poems do not, however, fall into despair. The beauty of nature, the rich rewards of friendship, the joys of music, and the hope of love are continually evident, emerging with their healing power. As Harjo writes in "Perhaps the World Ends Here:" "The gifts of earth are brought and prepared, set on the table. So it has been since creation, and so it will go on."

Suggested Readings

Andrews, Jennifer. "In the Belly of a Laughing God: Reading Humor and Irony in the Poetry of Joy Harjo." *American Indian Quarterly* 24, no. 2 (2000): 200-218.

Clark, C. B. "Joy Harjo (Creek)." In *The Heath Anthology of American Literature*, edited by Paul Lauter et al. Vol. 2. Boston: Houghton Mifflin, 1998.

Coltelli, Laura, ed. *The Spiral of Memory: Interviews, Joy Harjo*. Ann Arbor: University of Michigan Press, 1996.

Donovan, Kathleen. *Feminist Readings of Native American Literature*. Tucson: University of Arizona Press, 1998.

Lang, Nancy. "'Twin Gods Bending Over': Joy Harjo and Poetic Memory." *MELUS* 18, no. 3 (Fall, 1993): 41-49.

Pettit, Rhonda. *Joy Harjo*. Boise, Idaho: Boise State University Western Writer Series, 1998.

Scarry, John. "Joy Harjo." In *Smoke Rising: The Native North American Literary Companion*, edited by Janet Witalec. Detroit, Mich.: Gale Research, 1995.

Wilson, Norma C. "The Ground Speaks: The Poetry of Joy Harjo." In *The Nature of Native American Poetry*. Albuquerque: University of New Mexico Press, 2001.

Witalec, Janet, ed. *Native North American Literature: Biographical and Critical Information on Native Writers and Orators from the United States and Canada from Historical Times to the Present*. New York: Gale Research, 1994.

Womack, Craig S. "Joy Harjo: Creek Writer from the End of the Twentieth Century." In *Red on Red: Native American Literary Separatism*. Minneapolis: University of Minnesota Press, 1999.

Contributor: Robert Haight

Michael S. Harper

Born: Brooklyn, New York; March 18, 1938

African American

Harper's poetry synthesizes diverse ethnic, racial, and historic components to create an inclusive perspective on American culture.

Principal works

POETRY: *Dear John, Dear Coltrane*, 1970; *History Is Your Own Heartbeat*, 1971; *Photographs, Negatives: History as Apple Tree*, 1972; *Song: I Want a Witness*, 1972; *Debridement*, 1973; *Nightmare Begins Responsibility*, 1974; *Images of Kin: New and Selected Poems*, 1977; *Rhode Island: Eight Poems*, 1981; *Healing Song for the Inner Ear*, 1985; *Honorable Amendments*, 1995; *Songlines in Michaeltree: New and Collected Poems*, 2000

EDITED TEXTS: *Every Shut Eye Ain't Asleep: An Anthology of Poetry by African Americans Since 1945*, 1994 (with Anthony Walton); *Chant of Saints: A Gathering of Afro-American Literature, Art, and Scholarship*, 1979 (with Robert B. Stepto); *The Carleton Miscellany: A Ralph Ellison Festival*, 1980 (with John Wright); *The Collected Poems of Sterling A. Brown*, 1980; *The Vintage Book of African American Poetry*, 2000 (with Walton); *Selected Poems*, 2002 (edited and introduced by Ronald A. Sharp)

The first son in his middle-class African American family, Michael Steven Harper was encouraged to follow the career path of his grandfather and great-grandfather: medicine. An intense interest in the rhythms of language and in exploring the apparent schisms in American society, however, led Harper to his dual vocations of writer and scholar.

In the Harper home, music and poetry were important parts of family life. Poems by Langston Hughes were a familiar presence in Harper's childhood home. Harper's parents also owned an extensive collection of contemporary jazz recordings. The poet recalled spending many happy hours listening to, among others, Bessie Smith, Billie Holiday, Charlie Parker, and John Coltrane.

As an adolescent, Harper was forced into an awareness of racism in America. The family moved from New York to West Los Angeles, where African Americans were the targets of racial violence. During high school, Harper began experimenting with creative writing. In college, he continued writing in addition to working full-time for the post office. He later attended the famous Iowa Writers Workshop at the University of Iowa in Iowa City.

Michael S. Harper (© John Foraste)

As the only African American student in the poetry and fiction workshop classes, Harper endured misunderstanding and prejudice. These experiences motivated him to confront the dualism inherent in being an African American writer. Harper refused exclusive containment in either the African American or in the American category. Rather, he affirmed his identity in both groups.

Harper interrupted his studies at Iowa to enter the student teacher program at Pasadena City College in 1962. He became the first African American to complete the program, and after finishing his courses at Iowa, he accepted an instructorship at Contra Costa College in San Pablo, California. This was the beginning of an extensive and distinguished teaching career, including professorships at Colgate University, Brown University, and Harvard University. In addition to eight volumes of poetry, Harper has contributed to numerous journals and anthologies and has edited several anthologies of poetry.

Dear John, Dear Coltrane

Type of work: Poetry
First published: 1970

In an interview with Abraham Chapman, Michael Harper identifies the poetic technique of much of his work as "modality," an abstract musical concept that he uses as a metaphor for his ethical vision as well as for his subjective principle of composition. Many of Harper's poems lend themselves to performance; they are meant to be read aloud. In hearing them, one hears, through a range of idiom, dialect, and individual voices, the past fused with the contemporary, the individual speaking forth from communal experience and the black American's kinship, simultaneously tragic and heroic, to the whole of American cultural values. Rooted in classic jazz patterns from such musicians as Duke Ellington, Charlie Parker, and John Coltrane, modality is "about relationships" and "about energy, energy irreducible and true only unto itself." As a philosophical, ethical perspective, modality is a "particular frequency" for expressing and articulating "the special nature of the Black man and his condition and his contributions" to the American synthesis of cultural values. As such, modality refutes "the Western orientation of division between denotative/connotative, body/mind, life/spirit, soul/body, mind/heart" and affirms a unity of being and experience: "modality is always about unity." Consequently, Harper's poetry gathers fragments from private and public experience, past and present, and seeks to rejuvenate spiritual forces historically suppressed by bringing them to the surface in a poetry of "tensions resolved through a morality worked out between people."

In the early poems of *Dear John, Dear Coltrane*, Harper's modal experiments succeed in a variety of forms that nevertheless remain unified in the power of his particular voice. In "Brother John," Harper eulogizes Charlie Parker, the "Bird/ baddest nightdreamer/ on sax in the ornithology-world," Miles Davis, "bug-eyed, unspeakable,/ Miles, sweet Mute,/ sweat Miles, black Miles," and John Coltrane, who serves as a mythic center for the poem and the volume as well as several later poems. Typical of Harper's multiple allusions in naming, however, both the poem and the volume also eulogize John O. Stewart, a friend and fiction writer; nor is Coltrane merely a mythic figure, for Harper maintained a personal friendship with him until his death in 1967; in addition, the name "John" also conjures echoes from Harper's great-grandfather, who spent several years in South Africa, and, further, evokes John Brown, who figures prominently in later poems by Harper. Thus, from early in his work, Harper uses modality to reconcile past and present, myth and history, and private and public; personal mourning becomes part of a universal experience and a communal celebration. Drawing inspiration from both the suffering and the achievement of jazz artists in this poem and in subsequent poems in his career, Harper establishes the modal wordplay that affirms his philosophical stance as an activist of the conscience: "I'm a black man; I am; / black; I am; I'm a black/ man; I am; I am," and his own cry of being, refusing any limiting universality of humanness that is blind to ethnic heritage and experience: "I am; I'm a black man; / I am."

In other poems from this first volume, Harper links past and present as well as private and public by exploring larger patterns of history. In "American History," Harper asserts the invisibility of black suffering to mainstream America by juxtaposing "Those four black girls blown up/ in that Alabama church" with "five hundred/ middle passage blacks,/ in a net, under water . . . so *redcoats* wouldn't find them." Concluding in an ironic but colloquial idiom, he asks: "Can't find what you can't see/ can you?" In "Reuben, Reuben," Harper uses the death of his own son to overcome his pain in the transcendence of creative energy, just as blues singers have always done when faced with the horror of loss: "I reach from pain/ to music great enough/ to bring me back . . . we've lost a son/ the music, *jazz*, comes in."

History Is Your Own Heartbeat

Type of work: Poetry
First published: 1971

Harper's early poems test the possibilities of modality, and, in such techniques as concrete imaging, literary allusions, sprung syntax, enjambment, blues refrains, idioms, variable line lengths, and innovative cadences, he discovers in modality a formalism strong enough to bear diverse experiments in free-verse forms and yet a visionary field large enough to draw from virtually any relationship, however intimate or distant, however painful or joyful, for individual affirmation. In his second collection, *History Is Your Own Heartbeat*, Harper uses modality to reconstruct personal history, integrating it with a mythic sense of spiritual unity. Divided into three sections, the book begins with a twenty-poem sequence, "Ruth's Blues," which employs his white mother-in-law's physical deterioration as an extended metaphor for the denial of black and white kinship. In tribute to Ruth's endurance in her quest for physical and psychological health, Harper shows the potential for a unified American sensibility, one that respects cultural differences yet realizes from the pain of division that American experience "is all a well-knit family;/ *a love supreme*," if one chooses to affirm multiple origins. The following two sections, "History as Personality" and "High Modes," pay homage, respectively, to influential personalities such as Martin Luther King, Jr., and Gwendolyn Brooks and, in the latter, to the painter Oliver Lee Jackson. Throughout these sections, Harper emphasizes the unity of a historical and cultural continuum that reaches back to Africa and comes forward to his own family, claiming his own past and an American history that is freed of its delusions, confronting its origins in the slavery of Africans and the genocide of Native Americans, to whom Harper also unearths literal kinship. In several ways, then, this volume, as the title suggests, builds from literal links of kinship with a diversity of races and cultures to a holistic view of American values, in contrast to the exclusive emphasis on European origins characteristic of traditional American history. By healing himself of narrow stereotypes, Harper offers "a love supreme" to his fellow citizens, asserting kinship even where citizenship has been denied and is diminished by racism.

Song: I Want a Witness

Type of work: Poetry
First published: 1972

Subsequent books extend Harper's sense of kinship and develop the aesthetic of modality. In *Song: I Want a Witness*, he explores the black American religious heritage, using the metaphor of testifying, and conceptualizes the literary process as essentially one of an ethical affirmation of heroic character. Tracing American culture back both to Native America (by a link with a great-great-grandmother who was Chippewa) and to the Puritan legacies of Roger Williams and John Winthrop (by a link to the spirit of place where he lives), Harper, in "History as Appletree," develops an organic metaphor that embodies history and family while also bringing the negative, through an extended photographic metaphor of those ignored by history, to present light and image. In this vision, the fruit of the tree, American culture itself, blossoms with the fertility of long-forgotten bones whose dust nurtures the root system.

Debridement

Type of work: Poetry
First published: 1973

"Debridement" is a medical term for cutting away the dead flesh of a wound so that it will not infect the healthy body and a metaphor for revising stereotyped versions of American history. The title of this collection, therefore, honors the heroic actions of John Brown, Richard Wright, and the fictional John Henry Louis. Together, the three sections, each revolving around its respective persona, correct the myth that Americans who have fought against racism were insane, zealous, hysterical. Instead, Harper argues through the modality of these poems, they were, and are, themselves the victims of racism, surviving because they have pursued a truth that has for the most part been hidden from them.

Nightmare Begins Responsibility

Type of work: Poetry
First published: 1974

In *Nightmare Begins Responsibility*, the poet extends a logic that runs through the previous two books. Once one realizes that the pejorative American myth is false, then one must act to overcome the cultural insensitivity of racism and the apathy toward the land, both as physical and cultural environment. Alienation and isolation yield only to courageous, often unpopular action, and the American Dream and manifest destiny are concepts of death riddled with literal exploitation and genocide unless one replaces them with the values of kinship and acts to establish historical knowledge and contemporary intimacy as the basis for defining oneself as an American.

Healing Song for the Inner Ear

Type of work: Poetry
First published: 1985

Healing Song for the Inner Ear expands the modality of celebrating friends, family, musicians, and poets by bringing them into Harper's constantly expanding vision of history. Functioning much like his first book, this collection moves both backward and forward, but it also moves toward a more international perspective than that found in any of his earlier collections. From the American perspective of "Goin' to the Territory," which salutes the influence of Ralph Ellison and witnesses his aesthetic endurance, and "The Pen," which gives voice to an oral tradition become literary artifact, embodying values inherent in both black American and Native American lives, a modality in which "patterns of the word fling out into destiny/ as a prairie used to when the Indians/ were called Kiowa, Crow, Dakota, Cheyenne," to a series of poems set in South Africa, Harper explores the complexity of image and story embedded in history and the enduring truth of experience excavated in modal expression.

In the poem "The Militance of a Photograph in the Passbook of a Bantu Under Detention," Harper meditates on the history behind the photograph that identifies a black South African from Soweto, and he asserts: "This is no simple mug shot/ of a runaway boy in a training/ film. . . ." Harper senses his own history here; the runaway might have been a nineteenth century slave, the training film could well serve as a powerful tool for the suppression of historical facts, and the mug shot suggests that color itself (since only blacks must carry passbooks) is the crime. Personally, Harper must also unite his great-grandfather's experience in South Africa with the strategies of apartheid, and, in uniting the past personal association with the contemporary public policies of racism, Harper affirms the courage of the oppressed: "The Zulu lullaby/ I cannot sing in Bantu/ is this song in the body/ of a passbook/ and the book passes/ into a shirt/ and the back that wears it." Perhaps the modality of such a link between Americans and South Africans, between forgotten language and forgotten people, serves as the celebration of Harper's enduring theme, as in the epigraph to the poem: "Peace is the active presence of Justice."

Songlines in Michaeltree

Type of work: Poetry
First published: 2000

In this retrospective collection, which culls poetry from eight previous volumes, Harper returns to his characteristic progressive, improvisatory power that respects a variety of traditions in the arts. He celebrates the accomplishments of outstanding figures of the African American community while also tenderly exploring the "Michaeltree," an emblem of his own life, with deeply felt poems about members of his family. Serving as figurative bookends to the volume is a poem of six stanzas, each line repeated three times, beginning with the triad, "when there is no history," followed by an image of "a blind nation in a storm," that is "belted in these ruins." Here Harper asserts a reclamation from silent and suppression of the many-centuried struggle of African Americans in the United States and sets the tone for the collection.

Poems from past collections are balanced by Harper with additional material to assist the reader in understanding his life of teaching and writing. "Notes to the Poem" functions as a teaching text and provides background to Harper's familiar themes, elucidating his use of historical data that might be obscure to those who don't share his expertise. "To the Reader" invites the reader on a journey that explores the evolution of his creative consciousness. Here he acknowledges his debt to the "pioneering writers: Robert Hayden, Sterling A. Brown, and Ralph Ellison."

He also notes the influences of family members and, through anecdotal notes, that of his experiences with publicly reading his poetry. Finally, "Notes on Form and Fictions" examines his poetic technique and the derivations of his innovations. He notes, "I began to write poems because I could not see those elements of my life that I considered sacred reflected in my courses of study: scientific, literary, and linguistic." The reader thus better understands his overriding attraction to African American music as a source for shape, language, rhythms, and the near-mythic hero-figures of his poetry.

Suggested Readings

Antonucci, Michael. "The Map and the Territory: An Interview with Michael S. Harper." *African American Review* 34, no. 3 (Fall, 2000): 501-508.

Breslin, Paul. "Some Early Returns." *Poetry* 134 (May, 1979): 107-114.

Brown, Joseph A. "Their Long Scars Touch Ours: A Reflection on the Poetry of Michael Harper." *Callaloo* 9, no. 1 (1986): 209-220.

Forbes, Calvin. Review of *Honorable Amendments*, by Michael S. Harper. *African American Review* 32, no. 3 (Fall, 1998): 508-510.

Harper, Michael S. "My Poetic Technique and the Humanization of the American Audience." In *Black American Literature and Humanism*, edited by Miller R. Baxter. Lexington: University Press of Kentucky, 1981.

Jackson, Richard. *Acts of Mind: Conversations with Contemporary Poets*. University: University of Alabama Press, 1983.

Lehman, David. "Politics." *Poetry* 123 (December, 1973): 173-180.

Lieberman, Laurence. *Unassigned Frequencies: American Poetry in Review, 1964-77*. Chicago: University of Illinois Press, 1977.

Stepto, Robert B. "Let's Call Your Mama and Other Lies About Michael S. Harper." *Callaloo* 13, no. 4 (Fall, 1990): 801-804.

Turner, Alberta T., ed. *Fifty Contemporary Poets: The Creative Process*. New York: David McKay, 1977.

Young, Al, Larry Kart, and Michael S. Harper. "Jazz and Letters: A Colloquy." *TriQuarterly* 68 (Winter, 1987): 118-158.

Contributors: Anne B. Mangum, Michael Loudon, Philip K. Jason, and Sarah Hilbert

Wilson Harris

Born: New Amsterdam, British Guiana (now Guyana); March 24, 1921

African American, Native American, Caribbean

As philosopher, novelist, and critic, Harris imagines recent world history and colonialism in order to present a vision of a possible human community that celebrates multiple, mixed, and interrelating identities.

Principal works

LONG FICTION: *Palace of the Peacock*, 1960; *The Far Journey of Oudin*, 1961; *The Whole Armour*, 1962; *The Secret Ladder*, 1963; *Heartland*, 1964; *The Eye of the Scarecrow*, 1965; *The Waiting Room*, 1967; *Tumatumari*, 1968; *Ascent to Omai*, 1970; *Black Marsden*, 1972; *Companions of the Day and Night*, 1975; *Da Silva da Silva's Cultivated Wilderness and Genesis of the Clowns*, 1977; *The Tree of the Sun*, 1978; *The Angel at the Gate*, 1982; *Carnival*, 1985; *The Guyana Quartet*, 1985 (includes *Palace of the Peacock*, *The Far Journey of Oudin*, *The Whole Armour*, and *The Secret Ladder*); *The Infinite Rehearsal*, 1987; *The Four Banks of the River of Space*, 1990; *The Carnival Trilogy*, 1993 (includes *Carnival*, *The Infinite Rehearsal*, and *The Four Banks of the River of Space*); *Resurrection at Sorrow Hill*, 1993; *Jonestown*, 1996; *The Dark Jester*, 2001; *The Mask of the Beggar*, 2003; *The Ghost of Memory*, 2006

POETRY: *Fetish*, 1951 (as Kona Waruk); *Eternity to Season*, 1954

SHORT FICTION: *The Sleepers of Roraima*, 1970; *The Age of the Rainmakers*, 1971

NONFICTION: *Tradition, the Writer, and Society*, 1967; *History, Fable, and Myth in the Caribbean and Guianas*, 1970; *Fossil and Psyche*, 1974; *Explorations: A Selection of Talks and Articles*, 1981; *The Womb of Space: The Cross-Cultural Imagination*, 1983; *The Radical Imagination: Lectures and Talks*, 1992; *Selected Essays of Wilson Harris: The Unfinished Genesis of the Imagination*, 1999

Born in British Guiana, Wilson Harris studied at Queen's College in Georgetown and became a government surveyor before becoming a writer. In 1959 he settled in England and married a Scottish writer, Margaret Burns, his second marriage. He published his first novel, *Palace of the Peacock,* in 1960; it was followed by three more novels—*The Far Journey of Oudin* in 1961, *The Whole Armour* in 1962, and *The Secret Ladder* in 1963—which together with his first form *The Guyana Quartet.* These would be followed by many more novels, including those that form *The Carnival Trilogy*, as well as nonfiction and criticism. Although he and his wife made London their home, Harris has traveled widely as a result of fellowships and visiting professorships in Europe, Australia, India, the Caribbean, Canada, and the United States. These travels have influenced his writing: His trip to Mexico in 1972, for example, led to his use of the Quetzalcoatl legend in *The Carnival Trilogy*. Harris has won honorary doctorates from the University of the West Indies (1984) and the University of Liège (2001), among other institutions of higher learning. He received the English Arts Council Award twice (1968 and 1970) and a Guggenheim Fellowship (1972). In 1992 he won Italy's Mondello Prize for fiction. He was the recipient of the Guyana Prize for Literature in both 1987 and 2002.

Harris is an extremely eclectic and expansive writer. In *The Womb of Space*, he writes that "literature is still constrained by regional and other conventional suffocating categories." Harris has spent his career attempting to transcend notions of genre, tradition, and discipline, constructing texts founded on philosophical speculation. Harris attempts, in his writing, to promote new models for civilization and for creative art.

Influenced by Carl Gustav Jung, Martin Buber, Elizabethan poetry, William Blake, Native American folklore, and nineteenth century expedition literature, Harris investigates the ambiguities of life and death, of history and innovation, of self and other, and of reality and illusion. Harris questions received concepts of origin, history, and reality. It is Harris's hope that such inquisitions of the self may prove crucial in the development of a radical revision of history, origin, and identity.

Opening with a series of nightmare vignettes that awaken into each other, the narrator of Harris's *Palace of the Peacock* declares: "I dreamt I awoke with one dead eye seeing and one living eye closed." The novel hovers between reality and illusion, death and life, insight and blindness. It chronicles an expeditionary party's journey into the interior of Guyana. In this expedition into the territory of the self, each member of the party embodies a part of Guyanese identity. A European, an African, and a Native American set out together in a quest to retrieve renegade farmworkers but find along the way that they are, perhaps, the ghostly repetitions of a party that perished on the same river in the early days of European conquest. The allegorical and existential significances of the quest give Harris the opportunity to delve into the nature of narration, of time, of space, and of being. He asserts that humanity can alter fate through recognition of connections and by articulating and celebrating commonly held identities.

The themes *Palace of the Peacock* raises are also found in the novels that succeed it. In subsequent novels, Harris returns to elaborate and examine the psychological and existential structures by way of which identity ossifies and resists participation in change. By carefully constructing contradictory narrative puzzles, Harris leads his readers into ambiguous regions of understanding where opposites (life and death, reality and illusion, self and other) meet. It is his hope that such expeditions of the imagination will result in greater understanding of identity and community.

Fossil and Psyche

Type of work: Essay
First published: 1974

Fossil and Psyche articulates Wilson Harris's belief that "the potentiality for dialogue, for change, for the miracle of roots, for new community is real." Using the metaphor of archery (psychic arrows and fossil targets), he situates his novels and the work of other writers within a realm of attempts to reach architectonic (mythic) realities. He argues against the opposition of the material to the spiritual and critiques the borders by means of which the real is held separate from the imaginary. Harris asserts the potential of the imaginary to illuminate the transcendent possibilities of history and identity. Such possibilities, if realized, would result in a culturally heterogeneous world community and in an alteration of world power hierarchies.

The "idolatry of absolutes" holds readers and writers hostage to the temporal, spatial, and cultural limitations of literature when in fact those limitations are illusory. Arrows of language and imagination can reach the fossil targets of architectonic, mythic, eternal, atemporal, renewing experience. Novels by authors such as Patrick White and Malcolm Lowry, Harris claims, are dream-expeditions signaling humanity toward "a third perhaps nameless revolutionary dimension of sensibility" that evades commonly held notions of material and spiritual reality. Such an evasion is the key to enriching and understanding the value of the multiplicity of identities. Accessing these wells of timeless connection will "deepen and heighten the role of imaginative literature to wrestle with categories and to visualize the birth of community as other than the animism of fate."

Traditional oppositions lead to inadequate readings of imaginative literature and to misreadings of the processes that underlie imaginative composition. Literature, like every aspect of human experience, is lodged within a matrix of time and space. The literature Harris addresses in *Fossil and Psyche* attempts to transcend this matrix, to confound time and space, to mine the architectonic fossils of human community with present psychic projections of imagination.

Novels of expedition, then, revise history and reveal the hopeful, transformative energies of life locked away in even the most deadly and deadening acts of history. Writers who embrace such a process of revision renew the creative, psychic act of imagination. Such psychic projections of imagination join past to present and future and European to African and Native American.

The Womb of Space

Type of work: Essays
First published: 1983

Harris's *The Womb of Space: The Cross-Cultural Imagination* is a collection of critical essays that attempt to describe how multiculturalism can inform the reading of texts. "Imaginative sensibility," Harris asserts, "is uniquely equipped by forces of dream and paradox to mirror the inimitable activity of subordinated psyche." Harris's cross-cultural rereadings of specific texts in *The Womb of Space* reveal bridges of myth, imagination, and dream that link culture to culture, despite the appearance of disparity.

Harris interprets works by William Faulkner, Edgar Allan Poe, Ralph Ellison, Jean Toomer, Juan Rulfo, Raja Rao, Jean Rhys, Derek Walcott, Edward Brathwaite, and others in order to demonstrate the applicability of a cross-cultural analysis to world literature.

For example, Harris rereads Poe's *The Narrative of Arthur Gordon Pym* (1838) as a psychic text in which the unconscious subtext critiques the cultural hierarchy that the surface of the tale intends to uphold. Instead of emphasizing the tale's narrative focus on the consolidation of Western values, Harris underscores the unconscious "twinships" (pairings) of characters and events that point to an unconsciously scripted psychic, mythic dimension. Such a subversion of the text leads Harris to "perceive the decay of order conditioned by conquest; that order begins to review its daylight deeds . . . in the night-time rebellious dream life of the half-conscious and unconscious psyche." Despite the conscious intentions of Poe, the text is for Harris a revision of pre-Columbian mythic antecedents that illuminate the psychic, mythic, and communal dimensions of the literary imagination.

Harris generalizes that cross-cultural readings reveal, in literature, correlations and unity that spring from the dialectic of explicit statement and implicit subversion of that statement. Stressing the undermining of Western texts by consulting mythic, psychic (often non-Western) roots, Harris hopes to open a cultural dialogue among cultures and identities. Harris suggests that such a dialogue will encourage the growth of broader, multicultural, inclusive communities. The "womb of space" is the generative region where such a community may begin to develop.

"The paradox of cultural heterogeneity, or cross-cultural capacity, lies in the evolutionary thrust it restores to orders of the imagination, the ceaseless dialogue it inserts between hardened conventions and eclipsed or half-eclipsed otherness." By bringing the cross-cultural imagination to bear on a variety of texts in *The Womb of Space*, Wilson Harris affirms his particular vision of literature and of the role texts play in reconstructing identity, culture, and community.

Suggested Readings

Cribb, Tim. "T. W. Harris, Sworn Surveyor." *Journal of Commonwealth Literature* 28, no. 1 (1993): 33-46.

Drake, Sandra. *Wilson Harris and the Modern Tradition: A New Architecture of the World*. Westport, Conn.: Greenwood Press, 1986.

Gilkes, Michael, ed. *The Literate Imagination: Essays on the Novels of Wilson Harris*. London: Macmillan, 1989.

Howard, W. J. "Wilson Harris's *Guyana Quartet:* From Personal Myth to National Identity." *Ariel* 1 (1970): 46-60.

Maes-Jelinek, Hena. *Wilson Harris*. Boston: Twayne, 1982.

Review of Contemporary Fiction 17, no. 2 (Summer, 1997).

Riach, Alan, and Mark Williams. "Reading Wilson Harris." In *Wilson Harris: The Uncompromising Imagination*, edited by Hena Maes-Jelinek. Sydney: Dangaroo Press, 1991.

Sharrad, Paul. "The Art of Memory and the Liberation of History: Wilson Harris's Witnessing of Time." *The Journal of Commonwealth Literature* 27, no. 1 (1992): 110-127.

Slemon, Stephen. "*Carnival* and the Canon." *Ariel* 19, no. 3 (1988): 47-56.

Contributor: Daniel M. Scott III

Robert Hayden

Born: Detroit, Michigan; August 4, 1913
Died: Ann Arbor, Michigan; February 25, 1980

African American

Hayden's poetry provides a learned, kind observer's view of major events and figures in American and African American history.

Principal works

POETRY: *Heart-Shape in the Dust*, 1940; *The Lion and the Archer*, 1948 (with Myron O'Higgins); *Figure of Time: Poems*, 1955; *A Ballad of Remembrance*, 1962; *Selected Poems*, 1966; *Words in the Mourning Time*, 1970; *The Night-Blooming Cereus*, 1972; *Angle of Ascent: New and Selected Poems*, 1975; *American Journal*, 1978; *The Legend of John Brown*, 1978; *Collected Poems*, 1985 (revised 1996)

NONFICTION: *Collected Prose*, 1984

EDITED TEXTS: *Kaleidoscope: Poems by American Negro Poets*, 1967; *Afro-American Literature: An Introduction*, 1971 (with David J. Burrows and Frederick R. Lapides)

Robert Hayden's childhood independence was instrumental to his becoming a scholar and poet. He was reared in a poor Detroit neighborhood, where such distinctions were rare. Soon after he was born Asa Bundy Sheffey, Hayden was adopted by the Haydens, neighbors of his birth parents. A sufferer of extreme myopia as a child, Hayden was separated from his peers into a "sight conservation" class; although his handicap kept him from participating in most sports, the resulting time alone allowed him to read (especially poetry, which demanded less of his vision), write, and play the violin, thereby developing rhythmical and tonal sensitivities that would well serve his eventual vocation.

Several fortuitous events and encounters in Robert Hayden's life supported his choosing texts in African American history, especially the narratives of rebellious slaves, as fruitful subjects for his verse. After attending Detroit City College (which later became Wayne State University), Hayden, in 1936, began working for the Federal Writers' Project of the Works Progress Administration; he was assigned to research "Negro folklore." Two major figures encouraged his ensuing interest in African American history. The first, Erma Inez Morris, a pianist and a teacher in Detroit's public schools, became Hayden's wife and, for a time, his financial support. She also introduced her new husband to Countée Cullen, the Harlem Renaissance poet who admired Hayden's first book, *Heart-Shape in the Dust*, and who motivated Hayden to keep writing. Hayden also found inspiration from the British poet W. H. Auden, also a folklorist, who instructed Hayden at the University of Michigan when the younger poet began graduate work there.

In 1946, Hayden began a twenty-three-year tenure as a professor at Fisk College in segregated Nashville. During this time Hayden wrote steadily, despite being hampered by a heavy teaching load. The quality of Hayden's work was recognized internationally—it was broadcast by the British Broadcasting Company, and his 1962 book *A Ballad of Remembrance* won the Grand Prize for Poetry at the First World Festival of Negro Arts in Dakar, Senegal—before he was discovered in the United States. Eventual recognition included invitations to teach at several universities and to edit anthologies of work by his poetic heroes and contemporaries. In 1975, the year that *Angle of Ascent* was published, Hayden was elected fellow of the Academy of American Poets and Appointed Consultant in Poetry to the Library of Congress.

Hayden's greatest personal successes, however, occurred in the last few months of his life. The poet was publicly celebrated both by President Jimmy Carter, at "A White House Salute to American Poetry," and by his peers at the University of Michigan with "A Tribute to Robert Hayden," the latter occurring the day before Hayden died of a respiratory embolism at age sixty-six. Popular appreciation of Hayden's sensitive lyrics, dramatic monologues, and poignant remembrances has grown since his death.

Poetry

Much of Robert Hayden's poetry reflects one man's wrestling with the sway of poetic influence. His early verse echoes the themes and styles of many of his immediate forebears: Harlem Renaissance poets such as Langston Hughes and Countée Cullen, and American modernists such as Edna St. Vincent Millay and Hart Crane. The subjects of Hayden's later poetry reflect his belief that African American poets need not focus exclusively on sociological study or on protest. Early mentors such as Hughes and Cullen guided Hayden through his years of apprenticeship and obscurity and defended Hayden during his later successful years, when he was often upbraided by some black poets for being insufficiently political. Hayden's persevering confidence in his poetic voice and learning inured him against such criticism.

Throughout most of his career as a poet, from the publication of *Heart-Shape in the Dust* to that of his breakthrough book, *Angle of Ascent*, Hayden was sustained by academic work—heavy teaching loads and an occasional funded research project—more than he was by popular acclaim. Working in the 1930's and 1940's as a researcher for the Federal Writers' Project, and in various university libraries, Hayden found the historical material for some of his most celebrated poems. Interested especially in the motivations of rebellious slaves, Hayden in "The Ballad of Nat Turner" imagines Turner's almost sympathetic understanding of his captors, as the educated slave "Beheld the conqueror faces and, lo,/ they were like mine." In "Runagate Runagate" Hayden celebrates Harriet Tubman as "woman of earth, whipscarred," who has "a shining/ Mean to be free." The culmination of Hayden's study of his political heroes can be found in the perfectly crafted sonnet titled "Frederick Douglass," a poignant paean to "this man, this Douglass, this former slave, this Negro/ beaten to his knees, exiled, visioning a world/ where none is lonely, none hunted, alien."

Robert Hayden (Library of Congress)

Throughout his middle years Hayden himself might have felt like an alien, teaching at Fisk University in segregated Nashville. He was composing often formal, often disinterested poetry in a time when confessional poetry was fashionable. As was the case with Frederick Douglass a century earlier, Robert Hayden did not let his dissimilarity from those around him keep him from speaking his mind. An inherently peaceful person, Hayden was most upset by the violence of the 1960's; the title poem of his 1970 book *Words in the Mourning Time* mourns "for King for Kennedy . . ./ And for America, self-destructive, self-betrayed." Himself feeling betrayed by America's policies in Vietnam, Hayden asks: "Killing people to save, to free them?/ With napalm lighting routes to the future?" Despite this expressed skepticism toward American nationalism, in the 1960's and 1970's Hayden was welcomed by the poetic and political establishment. Named poetry consultant at the Library of Congress and invited to read at the Carter White House, Hayden felt particularly gratified regarding his late ascendancy. His successes corroborated Hayden's belief that literature composed by African Americans should be judged objectively and should meet the same high standards as the best literature written in English.

Suggested Readings

Conniff, Brian. "Robert Hayden and the Rise of the African American Poetic Sequence." *African American Review* 33, no. 3 (Fall, 1999): 487-506.

Davis, Arthur P. "Robert Hayden." In *From the Dark Tower: Afro-American Writers, 1900 to 1960*. Washington, D.C.: Howard University Press, 1982.

Davis, Charles T. "Robert Hayden's Use of History." In *Modern Black Poets: A Collection of Critical Essays*, edited by Donald B. Gibson. Englewood Cliffs, N.J.: Prentice-Hall, 1973.

Fetrow, Fred M. "Portraits and Personae: Characterization in the Poetry of Robert Hayden." In *Black American Poets Between Worlds, 1940-1960*, edited by R. Baxter Miller. Knoxville: University of Tennessee Press, 1986.

_______. *Robert Hayden*. Boston: Twayne, 1984.

Gikandi, Simon. "Race and the Idea of the Aesthetic." *Michigan Quarterly Review* 40, no. 2 (Spring, 2001): 318-350.

Glaysher, Frederick, ed. *Collected Prose: Robert Hayden*. Foreword by William Meredith. Ann Arbor: University of Michigan Press, 1984.

Nicholas, Xavier. "Robert Hayden: Some Introductory Notes." *Michigan Quarterly Review* 31, no. 3 (Summer, 1992): 8.

Su, Adrienne. "The Poetry of Robert Hayden." *Library Cavalcade* 52, no. 2 (October, 1999): 8-11.

Williams, Pontheolla T. *Robert Hayden: A Critical Analysis of His Poetry*. Foreword by Blyden Jackson. Urbana: University of Illinois Press, 1987.

Contributor: Andrew O. Jones

Le Ly Hayslip
(Phung Thi Le Ly)

Born: Ly La, Vietnam; December 19, 1949

Vietnamese American

Hayslip's memoirs chronicle a largely successful merger of her Vietnamese ancestry with her acquired American identity.

Principal works

NONFICTION: *When Heaven and Earth Changed Places: A Vietnamese Woman's Journey from War to Peace*, 1989 (with Jay Wurts); *Child of War, Woman of Peace*, 1993

Born Phung Thi Le Ly in 1949 to Buddhist peasants living under Vietnam's French colonial rule, Le Ly Hayslip (lee li HAY-slihp) ardently supported her nation's struggle for independence. Years later, when Viet Cong soldiers of the North wrongly accused her of treason, she fled her village in central Vietnam to live in Danang and, later, Saigon. After giving birth to her wealthy employer's son and witnessing the cruelty of communist rebels against the peasants they purported to defend, she shifted her allegiance to the republican-backed American forces. She supported herself and her child through black marketeering and other illegal activity and entered into a series of unhappy love affairs with United States servicemen before marrying Ed Munro, an American contractor more than forty years her senior. In 1970, without notifying her family, she left Vietnam for the United States as Munro's bride and the mother of his infant son.

The pattern of being caught in the middle—between the North and the South or between allies and enemies—continued in her new home in suburban San Diego, where Hayslip experienced culture shock, homesickness, and racial antagonism. Soon after Munro's death in 1973, she married Dennis Hayslip, a mentally unstable man by whom she had her third son before he committed suicide. The resilient Hayslip supported herself in the United States as a maid, nurse's aide, and factory worker; with money from her late husband's insurance settlement and trust fund, she purchased stock options, real estate, and a share in a successful restaurant. Combining investment revenues with the proceeds from her memoir about her life in Vietnam (*When Heaven and Earth Changed Places*), Hayslip founded the nonprofit East Meets West Foundation, a humanitarian relief organization that delivers medical and relief supplies to the Vietnamese.

Child of War, Woman of Peace, the sequel to her first memoir and the account of her American acculturation and subsequent return trips to Vietnam, attests Hayslip's ability to endure and heal, which she attributes to her potential to forgive. That second memoir, cowritten with her eldest son, James Hayslip, reveals her ability to embrace America while reconnecting to her Vietnamese past. She explains that her philanthropy, financing her mission in Vietnam through resources acquired in the United States, is the means to bind her old country to her new one, "to sponsor a healing handshake across time and space." The two autobiographies form the basis for Oliver Stone's 1993 film, *Heaven and Earth*, about Hayslip's life in Vietnam and America.

When Heaven and Earth Changed Places

Type of work: Memoir
First published: 1989

When Heaven and Earth Changed Places: A Vietnamese Woman's Journey from War to Peace, cowritten with Jay Wurts, recounts Hayslip's life in war-ravaged Vietnam, her immigration to the United States in 1970, and her dangerous return visit to her homeland in 1986. As a young girl, Phung Thi Le Ly (her name before marriage) promises her father, a devote Buddhist farmer, that she will become a woman warrior. She interprets that charge to mean that she must stay alive in order to nurture other life and preserve her ancestral heritage. The memoir is her means of fulfilling that responsibility. She nevertheless offends her family by her presumed betrayal by marriage to an American civilian contractor and flight from Vietnam to join him in California. The autobiography is her tribute to her ancestral traditions and her testimony that she has not forsaken them.

Le Ly's loyalties shift throughout her autobiography. Like most peasants in her village on the border between North and South Vietnam, she supports the Viet Cong against the republican government and its American backers. She performs many daring acts to advance the communist cause, but the Viet Cong wrongly suspect her of collaborating with the South. She evades their deadly reprisals by fleeing to Danang and, later, Saigon. There she pins her hope for a better life onto the American servicemen she comes to know as she struggles to support her illegitimate son and other family members by working as a nurse's assistant, a black marketeer, and, briefly, a prostitute.

Although Le Ly leaves Vietnam during the war and enters the United States as the wife of one American and marries another when she is widowed, her expatriate status distresses her. She proudly regards her three sons—two born in Vietnam and one in the United States—as Americans but regrets that she is "something else: not quite Vietnamese anymore, but not so American as they." By returning to Vietnam with a fresh perspective to write the account of her family's suffering, she aids in their survival and recovery, thus reconciling with them and healing her divided sense of self. The memoir's dual time frames, which alternate chapters of Le Ly moving toward emigration with ones of her preparing to return, converge near the end of the book when her departure and homecoming are complete. The narrative strategy suggests that the difference between leaving home and remaining there is not significant. Rather than forsaking her homeland by emigrating, Le Ly has protected and prepared herself for the mission of telling its story and preserving its culture.

Suggested Readings

Abramowitz, Rachel. "The Road to 'Heaven.'" *Premiere* 7 (January, 1994): 46-50.

Hayslip, Le Ly. "A Vietnam Memoir." *People Weekly* 32 (December 18, 1989): 147-150.

Hayslip, Le Ly, and James Hayslip. *Child of Peace, Woman of War*. New York: Doubleday, 1993.

Hayslip, Le Ly, and Jay Wurtz. *When Heaven and Earth Changed Places*. New York: Doubleday, 1989.

Klapwald, Thea. "Two Survivors Turn Hell into 'Heaven and Earth.'" *The New York Times* 143 (December 19, 1993): H22.

Mydans, Seth. "Vietnam: A Different Kind of Veteran and Her Healing Mission." *The New York Times* 139 (November 28, 1989): A10.

Contributor: Theresa M. Kanoza

Oscar Hijuelos

Born: New York, New York; August 24, 1951

Cuban American

Hijuelos, a Latino writer, was awarded the 1990 Pulitzer Prize in fiction for The Mambo Kings Play Songs of Love.

Principal works

LONG FICTION: *Our House in the Last World*, 1983; *The Mambo Kings Play Songs of Love*, 1989; *The Fourteen Sisters of Emilio Montez O'Brien*, 1993; *Mr. Ives' Christmas*, 1995; *Empress of the Splendid Season*, 1999; *A Simple Habana Melody: From When the World Was Good*, 2002

Oscar Hijuelos (hih-WAY-lohs), whose family came from Oriente Province in Cuba, was reared amid two divergent worlds: that of Columbia University, teeming with scholars, and that of Morningside Park, overflowing with drug addicts and muggers. At age four, Hijuelos and his mother visited Cuba, and upon his return he succumbed to nephritis. Bedridden, Hijuelos lingered in a hospital for two years. The theme of separation and isolation, especially from family, saturates Hijuelos's novels. After receiving his master's degree in 1976 from the City University of New York, Hijuelos moved to within a few blocks of his childhood home to begin his author's life, supported by a menial job in an advertising agency.

Our House in the Last World is a portrait of his family's exodus from Cuba. The work recalls Hijuelos's family relationships; he both hated and loved his alcoholic father, and he misunderstood and miscommunicated with his mother. *The Mambo Kings Play Songs of Love* also recalls Hijuelos's family life. One of his uncles had been a musician with Xavier Cugat. The elevator operator in Hijuelos's building played music. Hijuelos jumbled these two characters into Cesar Castillo. Cesar and his brother Nestor reach the highest point in their lives when the Mambo Kings appear on the *I Love Lucy* television show. Later, the brothers are separated.

In *The Fourteen Sisters of Emilio Montez O'Brien*, Hijuelos addresses issues of cross-cultural identity with the connection of Cuban and Irish families in a marriage. In *Mr. Ives' Christmas*, Hijuelos examines father-son relationships from the father's perspective. Mr. Ives seeks penance and peace after the disaster of his son's murder.

The Mambo Kings Play Songs of Love

Type of work: Novel
First published: 1989

Hijuelos's life in an advertising agency had little to do with his passion for writing. When he first began thinking of the story that would become *The Mambo Kings Play Songs of Love*, he knew that an uncle and an elevator operator would be his models. The uncle, a musician with Xavier Cugat in the 1930's, and a building superintendent patterned after an elevator-operator-musician merged to become Cesar Castillo, the Mambo King. Cesar's brother, Nestor, laconic, retrospective, lamenting the loss of a lover he left behind in Cuba, writes the song in her memory that draws the attention of Ricky Ricardo. He hears "Beautiful María of My Soul" as he catches the Mambo Kings in a seedy nightclub where gigs are cheap but long. Ricky's interest changes their lives. The book altered Hijuelos's literary career by winning for him the Pulitzer Prize in fiction in 1990.

As the book opens, Cesar rots with his half-empty whiskey glass tipped at the television beaming reruns. He seeks the *I Love Lucy* spot featuring Nestor and him as the Mambo Kings. Nestor has died. Cesar pathetically broods on the aging process, cirrhosis, and the loss of flamboyant times. Cesar's old, scratchy records—brittle and warped—resurrect his music stardom. He laments his brother's death by leafing through fading pictures.

In *The Mambo Kings Play Songs of Love*, Hijuelos presents pre-Castro Cubans, who, after World War II, streamed to New York. All communities may strive for the American Dream, but in Latino quarters, music, the mainstream of a culture, sought to free the oppressed. Hijuelos pursues thematic progression: The Castillo brothers become, for a moment, cultural icons by their appearance on *I Love Lucy*. Their fame does not last, however; Cesar comforts his ego with debauchery, and Nestor dies suddenly. The ironically named Hotel Splendour is where Cesar commits suicide.

The Fourteen Sisters of Emilio Montez O'Brien

Type of work: Novel
First published: 1993

The Fourteen Sisters of Emilio Montez O'Brien is presented in the form of an album of continuous memories, verbal photographs, and nostalgic images clustered around the major events in the lives of the family members. It is recounted in associative rather than chronological order, and it deliberately creates the effect of sorting through a century of family photographs, while a variety of voices comment on the images and recall their different versions of how events fitted together. Both Nelson O'Brien and his only son, Emilio Montez O'Brien, are photographers, and emphasis is placed on visual images and the importance of these pictures through time. The novel reflects on how these images, like the images of memory, represent and reconfigure past events.

The Fourteen Sisters of Emilio Montez O'Brien is a third-person narrative, told primarily from the perspective of Margarita, the book's central and most fully explored character. Margarita is the first of the fourteen daughters of Nelson O'Brien and Mariela Montez, and it is her life span and her perceptions that define the story. Rather than emphasizing exceptional individuals, the novel recounts the stories of ordinary people who live out their lives as best they can, helping one another through the difficult moments and enjoying their times of earthly happiness. It is a novel that celebrates love, sensual pleasures, and human relationships.

Mr. Ives' Christmas

Type of work: Novel
First published: 1995

Hijuelos, born in New York City, grew up in a humble, immigrant Cuban family. At age four, he was exiled from the family by nephritis, a kidney inflammation that crippled his youth with a two-year quarantine from home and loved ones. Perhaps that near-orphan status inspired Hijuelos to develop the Edward Ives of this novel.

The title character of the novel sanely goes through his life with no malice toward fellow man or woman. He seeks the rewards of work and patience that he has become accustomed to earning, but one date, Christmas Eve, consistently seems to interfere with his life. A widowed printmaker visits the orphan Edward Ives on

Oscar Hijuelos (Roberto Koch)

Christmas Eve and, a few Christmases later, adopts him. His adoptive father idyllically rears the dark-skinned child, inspires him to pursue his love for drawing, and eventually guides him to the Art Students League, where he meets, on Christmas Eve, his future wife.

The picture-postcard family image is shattered when, on yet another Christmas Eve, the Iveses' seventeen-year-old son is gunned down as he leaves church choir practice. A fourteen-year-old Puerto Rican kills the boy for ten dollars. Ives devotes his life to obsessive, unerring attempts to rehabilitate the murderer. Symbolically, Ives's favorite book is a signed copy of British novelist Charles Dickens's *A Christmas Carol* (1843). Hijuelos strongly relies on this book to link the two tales. The author emulates Dickens's populous canvases and uses his love of coincidence and contrivance as a metaphor for God's mysterious workings. The temperance of Ives allows him a longing for grace, a gift for contemplation, and a steady curiosity.

Hijuelos draws heavily on images from his New York neighborhood, his coterie of friends, and the milieu of gangs, muggers, and dope addicts at the end of his street. Differing from his other novels, *Mr. Ives' Christmas* leaves no doubt that Hijuelos speaks of faith—a faith that mysteriously probes emotions, tested by death and opportunities for forgiveness.

Suggested Readings

Barbato, Joseph. "Latino Writers in the American Market." *Publishers Weekly* 238, no. 6 (February, 1991): 17-21.

Chávez, Lydia. "Cuban Riffs: Songs of Love." *Los Angeles Times Magazine* 112 (April, 1993): 22-28.

Patteson, Richard F. "Oscar Hijuelos: 'Eternal Homesickness' and the Music of Memory." *Critique* 44, no. 1 (2002): 38-48.

Pérez-Firmat, Gustavo. *Life on the Hyphen: The Cuban-American Way*. Austin: University of Texas Press, 1994.

Shirley, Paula W. "Reading Desi Arnaz in *The Mambo Kings Play Songs of Love*." *MELUS* 20 (September, 1995): 69-78.

Socolovsky, Maya. "The Homelessness of Immigrant American Ghosts: Hauntings and Photographic Narrative in Oscar Hijuelos's *The Fourteen Sisters of Emilio Montez O'Brien*." *Proceedings of the Modern Language Association* 117, no. 2 (2002): 252-264.

Contributor: Craig Gilbert

Chester Himes

Born: Jefferson City, Missouri; July 29, 1909
Died: Moraira, Spain; November 12, 1984

African American

Himes's work evokes the social and psychological burden of being a black man in a white society.

Principal works

LONG FICTION: *If He Hollers Let Him Go*, 1945; *Lonely Crusade*, 1947; *Cast the First Stone*, 1952 (unexpurgated edition pb. as *Yesterday Will Make You Cry*, 1998); *The Third Generation*, 1954; *The Primitive*, 1955 (unexpurgated edition pb. as *The End of a Primitive*, 1997); *For Love of Imabelle*, 1957 (revised as *A Rage in Harlem*, 1965); *Il pluet des coups durs*, 1958 (*The Real Cool Killers*, 1959); *Couché dans le pain*, 1959 (*The Crazy Kill*, 1959); *Dare-dare*, 1959 (*Run Man Run*, 1966); *Tout pour plaire*, 1959 (*The Big Gold Dream*, 1960); *Imbroglio negro*, 1960 (*All Shot Up*, 1960); *Ne nous énervons pas!*, 1961 (*The Heat's On*, 1966; also pb. as *Come Back Charleston Blue*, 1974); *Pinktoes*, 1961; *Une affaire de viol*, 1963 (*A Case of Rape*, 1980); *Retour en Afrique*, 1964 (*Cotton Comes to Harlem*, 1965); *Blind Man with a Pistol*, 1969 (also pb. as *Hot Day, Hot Night*, 1970); *Plan B*, 1983

SHORT FICTION: *The Collected Stories of Chester Himes*, 1990

NONFICTION: *The Quality of Hurt: The Autobiography of Chester Himes, Volume I*, 1972; *My Life of Absurdity: The Autobiography of Chester Himes, Volume II*, 1976

MISCELLANEOUS: *Black on Black: "Baby Sister" and Selected Writings*, 1973

Chester Bomar Himes (himz) was born on July 29, 1909, in Jefferson City, Missouri, the youngest of three sons born to Estelle Charlotte Bomar and Joseph Sandy Himes, a professor of blacksmithing and wheelwrighting and head of the Mechanical Arts Department at Lincoln University. In 1921 Himes's father obtained a position at Normal College in Pine Bluff, Arkansas, and Chester and his brother Joe were enrolled in first-year studies there (with classmates ten years their senior). In the same year, Joe was permanently blinded while conducting a chemistry demonstration he and Chester had prepared. The local hospital's refusal to admit and treat his brother's injury (presumably because of racial prejudice)—one of several such incidents experienced in his youth—made a lasting impression upon Chester and contributed to his often-cited "quality of hurt" (the title of the first volume of his autobiography). In the next two years Himes attended high schools in St. Louis, Missouri, and Cleveland, Ohio, experiencing the loneliness, isolation, and violence frequently accorded the outsider in adolescence (in schoolyard battles he received chipped teeth, lacerations to the head, and a broken shoulder that never healed properly). Himes was graduated, nevertheless, from Cleveland's Glenville High School in January, 1926. Preparing to attend Ohio State University in the fall, he took a job as a busboy in a local hotel. Injured by a fall down an elevator shaft, Himes was awarded a monthly disability pension that allowed him to enter the university directly.

Early enthusiasm for collegiate life turned quickly to personal depression and alienation, undermining Himes's academic fervor and success. This discontent led to his flirtation with illicit lifestyles and his subsequent expulsion from the university. Returning to Cleveland, Himes was swept into the dangers and excitement of underworld activities which, as he noted in his autobiography, exposed him to many of the strange characters who populate his detective series.

After two suspended sentences for burglary and fraud (because of the personal appeals of his parents for leniency), Himes was arrested in September, 1928, charged with armed robbery, and sentenced to twenty to twenty-five years of hard labor at Ohio State Penitentiary. His serious writing began in prison. By the time he was paroled to his mother in 1936, Himes's stories about the frustrations and contradictions of prison life had appeared in *Esquire* and numerous African American newspapers and magazines. In 1937, Himes married Jean Johnson, his sweetheart before imprisonment. Finding employment first as a laborer, then as a research assistant in the Cleveland Public Library, Himes was finally employed by the Ohio State Writers' Project to work on a history of Cleveland. With the start of World War II, Himes moved to Los Angeles, California. His first two novels, *If He Hollers Let Him Go* and *Lonely Crusade*, were based on these experiences. Following trips to New York, back to Los Angeles, and then to New York, where his third novel, *Cast the First Stone*, was published, Himes divorced Jean and left for Europe in 1953, sensing the possibility of a new beginning.

The French admired his life, particularly appreciating the satire of *Pinktoes*, a ribald novel proposing the solution to racial tensions through indiscriminate sexual relationships. It was his French editor who encouraged Himes to write the detective novels set in Harlem, featuring Grave Digger Jones and Coffin Ed Johnson. Himes wrote these in a hurry, desperate for the money, but they turned out to be the perfect match of form and content. Increasingly pessimistic about the violence of his native country, Himes wrote more and more about the radical solution to the racial problem—violence. The Harlem of his detectives, the detectives themselves, and the people among whom they move are all caught up, trapped in a cycle of violent behavior from which they cannot escape.

With so much pain, personal and cultural, experienced from the beginning of his life, Himes did what talented artists do: He confronted it, fashioned it into a personal vision, and, living fully, even found the love and humor in it. Between 1953 and 1957, Himes lived in Paris, London, and Majorca while finishing work on *The Third Generation* and *The Primitive*. Following the international success of his Harlem Domestic series, Himes moved permanently to Spain in 1969 and, with the exception of brief trips to the United States and other parts of Europe, lived there with his second wife, Lesley Packard, until his death on November 12, 1984.

Short Stories

Himes's short stories, he believed, served as his apprenticeship as a writer. They were the first of his writings to be published, and he continued in the genre intermittently for more than forty years. When an anthology of his short fiction was proposed in 1954, he revealed in his autobiography that he could not feel proud of it. The anthology, finally published in 1973, *Black on Black: Baby Sister and Selected Writings*, was highly selective, concentrating on the stories of the first two decades of his career. A 1990 edition, *The Collected Stories of Chester Himes*, contains sixty-one pieces, ranging from 1933 to 1978, with nine updated. Many are prison stories, and not all are of even quality, but as a whole they demonstrate Himes's remarkably versatile range of techniques and the ongoing themes and preoccupations of his longer pieces.

Prison life, horrible as it was, gave Himes the subject of several short stories. "His Last Day," about a condemned man's last few hours before the electric chair, already shows some of Himes's trademarks. Spats, a hardened, ruthless criminal who is condemned to death for killing a police officer, reflects wryly that he would not have been identified if the one person left alive during his robbery of a club had not recognized his fawn-colored spats. Even when he manages to hide out for a few days, he is finally trapped—by his past and by a woman. An old sweetheart whom he had abandoned in her pregnancy shoots the man who had provided Spats with refuge, thus attracting the police. Rivetingly grim, this early effort is marred by the dated slang, but even so, Himes's characteristic grisly humor comes through.

James Baldwin wrote of Himes that he was the only black writer to describe male-female relationships in terms other than violence. One of Himes's earliest love stories, "Her Whole Existence: A Story of True Love," verges on parody in its clichéd language but also shows Himes's imaginative skill. Written from the point of view of Mabel Miles, the beautiful daughter of a successful African American politician, the story leaps suddenly from the romanticism of Mabel's attraction for Richard Riley, an ambitious, successful, and handsome criminal, to an analysis of class conflict. Trapped between the respect for law instilled by her family and her own passion, Mabel first betrays Richard and then helps him to escape. It is the first of Himes's portrayals of unpredictable but strong women.

"A Nigger" suggests, with its shockingly simple denouement, Himes's bitter observations about the sexual relationship between blacks and whites. Mr. Shelton, a rich old white man, drops in unexpectedly on Fay, a black prostitute who lives with a light-skinned common-law husband and who is currently involved with another black man, Joe Wolf. Taken by surprise, Fay shoves Joe into the closet to receive her white lover. Joe hears her cajole and flatter Mr. Shelton out of two hundred dollars and, crouched in the dark, recalls other tired, unattractive white men he has known who have turned to black women not in appreciation but in exhaustion. Such men have convinced themselves, he thinks, that it is only black flesh they touch, animal flesh that has no mind or power to judge. When he is ready to leave, Mr. Shelton opens the door of the closet by mistake, looks in, turns away, and leaves. While Fay is jubilant that Joe was not detected, Joe is so furious that he tries to strangle her. He knows that the white man saw him and simply refused to recognize his existence. Back in his own tiny room, he reflects bitterly that he must count himself a "nigger" for allowing his poverty and dependence on a prostitute to rob him of his manhood.

Chester Himes (Library of Congress)

Though many of Himes's stories—and novels—ram home the pain of being black in the United States, there are other works that portray individuals who can carve a dignified niche in the limited ways available to them. "Headwaiter" presents Dick Small, an African American man in charge of an old-fashioned dining room patronized by a regular white clientele. Imperturbable in this familiar atmosphere, Dick watches over everyone in his care, remembering the personal details of individual customers, waiters, and busboys. In his small way, he does what he can for the less fortunate. When the diners are horrified to learn that one of the best waiters is a former convict, Dick stands firmly by his decision to give the man a second chance, and his polite firmness quells the furor. He is unable, however, to save another waiter who acts drunk; when he has to dismiss him, he does so with sympathy and compassion.

The complementary story "Lunching at the Ritzmore" differs in tone. A satiric view of the laws that required separate public establishments for blacks and whites, this story suggests, lightheartedly, what Himes was seriously to advocate later: the power that lies in a large crowd to hurl down racist barriers. In "the mecca of the motley" in Pershing Square, Los Angeles, a young college student from Vermont argues that there is no discrimination against Negroes. A drifter in the crowd bets him the price of dinner that a young brown-skinned Negro, an unemployed mechanic, will be refused service if the three eat at a restaurant. As the three set off in search of a suitably challenging place to eat, the crowd around them grows and grows because people think that a free giveaway must be the goal of such a gathering. A policeman follows them, wanting to arrest them but not being able to think of a good reason to do so. Finally, an enormous crowd halts outside the very fancy Ritzmore Hotel; there, the debate shifts slightly from race to class, as none of the three is dressed well enough. The diners, the waiters, and the cooks, however, are so stunned by the crowd that the three men are immediately served the only item that they can read on the French menu—ironically enough, it is apple pie. The student wins his bet but has to pay because the drifter is broke.

Few other stories exhibit such lighthearted irony in the face of racial discrimination. "All He Needs Is Feet" is ironic, in the horrifying, brutal way that shocks the reader into realizing why Himes later saw violence as the only solution for African Americans, because they are mistreated so violently by a violent society. Ward, a black man, walking down the sidewalk in Rome, Georgia, steps off to let a white woman and two white men pass. One white man bumps into Ward anyway and provokes him to fight. A crowd that gathers, thinking a lynching is too severe, pours gasoline on Ward's feet and sets him on fire. In jail for assault with a deadly weapon, Ward has his feet amputated. He goes to Chicago with money sent by his family and learns to use crutches and knee pads to work at shining shoes, saving enough money to buy war bonds. In a theater, his crutches tucked out of everyone's way under the seats, Ward cannot stand up for the national anthem at the end of the film. A big, burly man from Arkansas hits him for disrespect to the flag. The ultimate cruelty of the story comes as a punch line, when a policeman arrests the white man: The man from Arkansas blubbers that he could not stand a "nigger" sitting through the national anthem, even if he did not have feet.

The issue of patriotism became very complex for African Americans during World War II, especially for those who fought for democracy against Adolf Hitler and his blatantly racist and fascist goals of a super race and then had to reflect on the racism in their own democracy. Several of Himes's war stories, such as "Two Soldiers," reveal a man struggling to remain patriotic and optimistic. The most effective of these, "So Softly Smiling," springs from the war atmosphere but is really a beautiful love story. Roy Jonny Squires, a lieutenant in the U.S. Army, returns to Harlem for thirty days. Exhausted by the warfare in North Africa, he heads for a bar late at night and meets Mona Morrison, a successful poet. Her "tawny skin like an African veld at sunset" exactly fulfills the ache for love that fiery raids at dawn have brought upon him. This delicate love story is punctuated throughout with dramatic reminders that the lovers' time together is very short, and their courtship and married life proceed at breakneck speed. It is in this story that Himes touches on the race issue during war, lightly, positively; Roy says that he finally enlisted because he heard someone say that the United States belonged to the Negro as much as it did to anyone.

More than two decades later, Himes seemed to have lost such patriotic optimism. In "Tang," a tired, hungry couple sit watching television in their cold-water slum flat in Harlem, when a long cardboard box with a florist's label is delivered to them. They discover inside it an M-14 army gun and a typewritten sheet warning them to learn how to use their weapon and wait for instructions, for freedom is near. The man, T-bone Smith, who had used such a weapon in the Korean War, is absolutely terrified and wants to report the gun to the police. The woman, Tang, once a beautiful, softly rounded woman who has become hard and angular from her life as a poor prostitute, is ecstatic. She hugs the gun as if it were a lover and cherishes the thought that the gun could chop up a white policeman. She is ready to fight for freedom, even pointing the gun at T-bone to stop him from calling the police. Her defiance enrages him; he whips out a spring-blade knife and slashes her to death, crying that he might not be free of whitey, but he is now free of her.

Writing twenty years before Himes's death, the critic Edward Margolies noted that Himes's characters tend to be reflective, interested in ideas and in intellectualizing the predicaments in which they find themselves. As such, they are quite different from such characters as Bigger Thomas, with whom Richard Wright shocked the United States in his *Native Son* (1940). Wright's success trapped other African American writers whom the literary establishment then automatically described as, or expected to be, "protest" writers. Certainly, the range of Himes's short fiction is so vast that it includes stories of strong protest. He wrote, however, stories of individuals caught up in a web of many circumstances. Race is clearly an issue in his fiction, but so are love, sex, poverty, class, war, prison, violence, success, failure, and humor. His short fiction is not only a prelude to his better known novels but also a rewarding world in itself.

Early Novels

Himes wrote nearly twenty novels, the dominant theme of which (like that of his other writing) was often racism: the pain it causes and the hateful legacy it creates. In *If He Hollers, Let Him Go*, Himes uses a wartime West Coast shipyard to set the central confrontation between an educated Northern black man and his poor Southern white coworkers. The results are violent. In spare, functional prose that highlights the psychological paths the novel charts, Himes describes what has been called the American dilemma, or the contrast between a black man believing in democracy and the realities that bruise his dreams. Critics, while not always enamored with the novel, praised Himes for his relentless honesty.

Lonely Crusade, Himes's second novel, treats the betrayal, dislocation, and terror at the nexus of race and sex in United States society. The book makes a laudable effort to understand the relationship between the oppressed and the oppressor.

The Third Generation, thought by many critics to be a thinly veiled autobiography, dramatizes three generations in a family, from slavery to the middle of the twentieth century. It tellingly captures the fear and hatred that can fester in a troubled family, making it perhaps Himes's most ambitious and moving novel.

Detective Novels

Himes left the United States in 1954 for Europe, where he received greater literary recognition than he had ever achieved at home. In France, Himes published sophisticated, fast-paced crime novels. The protagonists, a pair of cynical street-smart black detectives, were hailed by French critics. When, years later, the novels were finally printed in the United States, the series achieved wide success. Among them are *The Crazy Kill*, *The Heat's On*, and *Cotton Comes to Harlem*. Himes also wrote stories that are sometimes painfully funny and often bitterly desolate. In them, cops, robbers, and all-around losers—the people Himes knew well in his youth—trade in the debased currency of lies and secrets.

The connection between the image of Harlem and the violence that derives from fear is particularly apparent in *The Crazy Kill*. The Harlem of this novel is a place, in the words of Coffin Ed, "where anything can happen," and from the narrative's bizarre opening incident to the very last, that sense of the incredibly plausible pervades. When the theft of a bag of money from a grocery store attracts the attention of the Reverend Short, Mamie Pullen's minister and a participant at the wake held across the street for Mamie's husband, the notorious gambler Big Joe Pullen, the storefront preacher leans too far out of a bedroom window under the influence of his favorite concoction, opium and brandy, and falls out. He lands, miraculously, in a basket of bread outside the bakery beneath. He picks himself up and returns to the wake, where he experiences one of his habitual "visions." When Mamie later accompanies the Reverend Short to the window as he explains the circumstances of his fall, she looks down and sees the body of Valentine "Val" Haines, a young hood who has been living with Sister Dulcy and her husband Johnny "Fishtail" Perry, Big Joe's godson. The earlier vision has become reality: a dead man with a hunting knife in his heart.

Grave Digger and Coffin Ed are summoned to discover who murdered Val and, with Detective Sergeant Brody, an Irishman, begin questioning all possible suspects. Perhaps it was Johnny, whose temper is as infamous as his gambling prowess. Perhaps it was Charlie Chink, whose girlfriend, Doll Baby, appeared to be the recent target of Val's affections. Still, why the exotic hunting knife? Why the basket of bread? What conspiracy of silence connects the Reverend Short, Johnny's girl Sister Dulcy, and Mamie Pullen, forcing Johnny to travel to Chicago before returning to Harlem and murdering Charlie Chink?

After the initial several hours of questioning, Sergeant Brody, despite his years of experience, is too dumbfounded to explain the web of illogical complications in this case. Grave Digger tells him, in a statement that recurs throughout the novel and the entire series, epitomizing Himes's vision of the city: "This is Harlem. . . . [A]in't no other place like it in the world. You've got to start from scratch here, because these folks in Harlem do things for reasons nobody else in the world would think of."

The plot unravels through a series of mysterious events, including scenes of rage and violence that are the physical consequences of emotional brutalization. Johnny wakes up to find Charlie Chink wandering around nude in his apartment and shoots him six times, stomps his bloody body until Chink's teeth are "stuck in his calloused heel," and then leans over and clubs Chink's head "into a bloody pulp with his pistol butt." These explosions, Himes's work suggests, derive from the most sublimated forms of frustration and hatred; the same forces can be seen in the degree of murderous intent that accompanies Coffin Ed's frequent loss of equilibrium. The repeated examples of "murderous rage" and the number of characters in the series whose faces are cut or whose bodies are maimed are related to this vision of Harlem as a dehumanizing, prisonlike world. Even the apparently comic purposes of character description tend to underscore this perspective (the Reverend Short, for example, is introduced as having a "mouth shaped like that of a catfish" and eyes that "protrude behind his gold-rimmed spectacles like a bug's under a microscope").

Himes's evocation of a sense of place, however, is not limited to bizarre scenes of physical violence and rage. Beyond the scores of defiant men who are reminders of the repressed nature of manhood in the inner cities, the author gives abundant images of Harlem's social life (rent parties, fish fries, and wakes), its cultural past (Duke Ellington, Billy Eckstein, the Apollo Theatre), its economic and political hierarchies (civil servants, politicians, underworld celebrities), and its peculiar lifestyles and institutions (street gangs, professional gamblers, numbers runners, the homosexual subculture, the heroin trade, evangelists' churches, and soapbox orators). All of this is done with the aplomb of a tour guide whose knowledge of the terrain is complete and whose understanding of the cultural codes of behavior permits explanation to the uninitiated.

A bittersweet, tragicomic tone alternating with an almost Rabelaisian exuberance characterizes Himes's descriptions of the sights, rhythms, and sounds of life in Harlem. Even the diverse enticements and rich peculiarities of African American cooking are a part of Harlem's atmosphere, and the smells and tastes are frequently explored as Himes moves his two detectives through the many greasy spoons that line their beat (at one point in *The Crazy Kill* the author duplicates an entire restaurant menu, from entrées to beverages, from "alligator tail and rice" to "sassafras-root tea").

Humor (if not parody) is reflected in the many unusual names of Himes's characters: Sassafras, Susie Q., Charlie Chink Dawson, H. Exodus Clay, Pigmeat, and Fishtail Perry; it is also reflected in the many instances of gullibility motivated by greed which account for the numerous scams, stings, and swindles that occur.

Himes accomplishes all of this with a remarkable economy of dialogue and language, an astute manipulation of temporal sequence, and a pattern of plots distinguished by a marvelous blend of fantasy and realism: a sense of the magically real that lurks beneath the surface of the commonplace. "Is he crazy or just acting?" asks Sergeant Brody about the Reverend Short's vision. "Maybe both," Grave Digger answers.

The next three novels in the series—*Cotton Comes to Harlem*, *The Heat's On*, and *Blind Man with a Pistol*—continue the character types, stylistic devices, and thematic concerns of the earlier novels. Each one represents a deepening of Himes's artistic control over his material; each one further enhanced his reputation in the genre and increased his notoriety and popularity among the American public. The first two of these, *Cotton Comes to Harlem* and *Come Back Charleston Blue*, were adapted for the screen; the third, reissued in the United States as *Hot Day, Hot Night*, was received as the "apotheosis" of Himes's detective novels. Its author was described (on the jacket cover) as "the best black American novelist writing today."

Autobiographies

Himes's two-volume autobiography, *The Quality of Hurt* and *My Life of Absurdity*, was written in Spain. "I grew to manhood in the Ohio State Penitentiary," writes Himes in *The Quality of Hurt*, a book that is less an organized autobiography than a series of poignant sketches, in which he writes about the many hurts that poisoned his life in the United States. Himes is one of the least known, most prolific African American writers of the twentieth century. Over a fifty-year career, Himes wrote scores of novels, short stories, articles, and poems, all marked by a naked sincerity and raging anger at racism.

Himes began writing, drawing on his experiences as a young man in prison. He gained critical attention first with a short story, "To What Red Hell," a fictionalized account of the 1930 fire that killed more than three hundred inmates at the Ohio State Penitentiary. Released during the Depression, Himes became involved with the Federal Writers' Project, the labor movement, and the Communist Party. He also worked as a journalist in Cleveland. In 1941, Himes moved to California, where he began writing novels of rage and frustration, including *If He Hollers, Let Him Go* (1945), *Lonely Crusade* (1947), and *Cast the First Stone* (1952). By 1953, disgusted with the racism he encountered and the lukewarm, when not hostile, reception his work received, Himes left for Europe.

My Life of Absurdity is not a deep examination of his life so much as a commentary on the meaning of being a black expatriate writer. "No American," he writes, "has lived a life more absurd than mine."

Suggested Readings

Cochran, David. "So Much Nonsense Must Make Sense: The Black Vision of Chester Himes." *The Midwest Quarterly* 38 (Autumn, 1996): 1-30.

Crooks, Robert. "From the Far Side of the Urban Frontier: The Detective Fiction of Chester Himes and Walter Mosley." *College Literature* 22 (October, 1995): 68-90.

Himes, Chester. *Conversations with Chester Himes*. Edited by Michel Fabre and Robert Skinner. Jackson: University Press of Mississippi, 1995.

Margolies, Edward, and Michel Fabre. *The Several Lives of Chester Himes*. Jackson: University Press of Mississippi, 1997.

Muller, Gilbert. *Chester Himes*. Boston: Twayne, 1989.

Rosen, Steven J. "African American Anti-Semitism and Himes's Lonely Crusade." *MELUS* 20 (Summer, 1995): 47-68.

Sallis, James. *Chester Himes: A Life*. New York: Walker, 2001.

Silet, Charles L. P., ed. *The Critical Response to Chester Himes*. Westport, Conn.: Greenwood Press, 1999.

Skinner, Robert E. *Two Guns from Harlem: The Detective Fiction of Chester Himes*. Bowling Green, Ohio: Bowling Green State University Popular Press, 1989.

Contributors: Roland E. Bush, Shakuntala Jayaswal, and Barbara Day

Rolando Hinojosa

Born: Mercedes, Texas; January 21, 1929

Mexican American

Hinojosa's fiction gives a view of Mexican American life in the Rio Grande Valley of Texas in the twentieth century.

Principal works

LONG FICTION: *Estampas del valle, y otras obras/Sketches of the Valley, and Other Works*, 1973 (English revision, *The Valley*, 1983); *Klail City y sus alrededores*, 1976 (*Klail City: A Novel*, 1987); *Mi querido Rafa*, 1981 (*Dear Rafe*, 1985); *Rites and Witnesses*, 1982; *Partners in Crime: A Rafe Buenrostro Mystery*, 1985; *Claros varones de Belken*, 1986 (*Fair Gentlemen of Belken County*, 1986); *Becky and Her Friends*, 1990; *The Useless Servants*, 1993; *Ask a Policeman*, 1998

POETRY: *Korean Love Songs from Klail City Death Trip*, 1978 (printed 1980; includes some prose)

EDITED TEXT: *Tomás Rivera, 1935-1984: The Man and His Work*, 1988 (with Gary D. Keller and Vernon E. Lattin)

MISCELLANEOUS: *Generaciones, Notas, y Brechas/Generations, Notes, and Trails*, 1978; *Agricultural Workers of the Rio Grande and Rio Bravo Valleys*, 1984

Rolando Hinojosa (roh-LAHN-doh hee-noh-HOH-sah) began writing book-length works of fiction in the 1970's when he was in his forties and after he had established a successful academic career. He attended the University of Texas at Austin, but he left to serve in Korea before returning to complete his degree in Spanish in 1953.

In the 1950's, he taught at Brownsville High School. He next took a master's degree in Spanish from New Mexico Highlands University (1962) and a Ph.D. in Spanish from the University of Illinois (1969). He has taught and held administrative posts at various universities in Texas.

Korean Love Songs from Klail City Death Trip, which is poetry, and his novels form the Klail City Death Trip series, which deals with ethnic identity, the perils and rewards of cultural assimilation, and the importance of education. Hinojosa's major characters undergo epic struggles with the issues of identity, moving from a discrete, self-contained Mexican American community of the 1930's into a world in which young Mexican American men fight and die for the institutions that have relegated them to second-class citizenry.

Rolando Hinojosa (Courtesy, University of Texas at Austin)

Hinojosa shows that life in the Rio Grande Valley must change. The Klail City Death Trip series in particular shows the subtle mid-century changes in the social and economic landscape of the small towns of the valley and the ways in which Mexican Americans began to demand equality.

Because many of Hinojosa's characters believe in the American Dream, they become more Americanized and less Chicano as the twentieth century moves forward. By the time of *Partners in Crime* and *Becky and Her Friends*, the main characters have achieved status within the Anglo community and appear to thrive within it.

Klail City

Type of work: Novel
First published: *Klail City y sus alrededores*, 1976 (English translation, 1987)

Klail City is part of the Klail City Death Trip, a chronicle of the Texas Rio Grande Valley. This novel moves between past and present so that the past and the present often appear to be the same. Like most of Hinojosa's novels, *Klail City* lacks linear plot development. A series of vignettes create a sense of place and ultimately present a picture of a changing world. Several narrators, including the main characters of the series, Rafe Buenrostro ("Buenrostro" means "good face") and Jehú Malacara ("Malacara" means "bad face") tell the stories.

P. Galindo, Esteban Echevarría (a kind of wise man throughout the series), Rafe, and Jehú recount a variety of tales ranging from the story of a hastily arranged marriage between the pregnant Jovita de Anda and Joaquín Tamez to tales of the Texas Rangers' abuse of Mexican Americans to the story of how Alejandro Leguizamón planned the murder of Rafe's father, Jesús, and the revenge exacted by Jesús's brother, don Julián. There is also a kind of interior monologue by Jehú as he and Rafe attend their twenty-second high school class reunion.

The past is interwoven with the present, particularly in the scenes that occur in the bars, where the old men, the *viejitos*, sit drinking and talking until don Manuel Guzmán, Klail City's only Mexican American police officer, comes to take them home.

The section entitled "The Searchers" tells the stories of migrant workers as they leave their homes in the valley to travel north to pick produce. The narrator P. Galindo is introduced, and he reveals himself to be a kind of surrogate author for Hinojosa as he explains his interest in preserving a history of these people.

In addition, Rafe gives a personal account of what it was like in the 1940's for Mexican American students in the American high school, and Jehú recounts some of his experiences as an orphan, an acolyte, and a traveling evangelist with Brother Imás. Brother Imás's life story is told, as is Viola Barragán's (Hinojosa's prototype of the liberated woman), along with an account of how the whites used "bought" Mexicans to get their hand-picked candidates elected. This eclectic collection of vignettes makes up a book that, in 1976, won Latin America's most prestigious literary award, the Casa de las Américas prize.

Suggested Readings

Calderón, Héctor. "Texas Border Literature: Cultural Transformation and Historical Reflection in the Works of Américo Paredes, Rolando Hinojosa, and Gloria Anzaldua." *Disposito* 16, no. 41 (1991): 13-27.

Hernandez, Guillermo E. *Chicano Satire: A Study in Literary Culture*. Austin: University of Texas Press, 1991.

Lee, Joyce Glover. *Rolando Hinojosa and the American Dream*. Denton: University of North Texas Press, 1997.

Penzenstadler, Joan. "La frontera, Aztlán, el barrio: Frontiers in Chicano Literature." In *The Frontier Experience and the American Dream*, edited by David Mogen, Mark Busby, and Paul Bryant. College Station: Texas A&M Press, 1989.

Saldivar, José David, ed. *The Rolando Hinojosa Reader: Essays Historical and Critical*. Houston: Arte Público, 1985.

Saldívar, Ramón. *Chicano Narrative: The Dialectics of Difference*. Madison: University of Wisconsin Press, 1990.

Zilles, Klaus. *Rolando Hinojosa: A Reader's Guide*. Albuquerque: University of New Mexico Press, 2001.

Contributor: Joyce J. Glover

Garrett Kaoru Hongo

Born: Volcano, Hawaii; May 30, 1951

Japanese American

Hongo writes lyrically and evocatively about personal history, place of origin, and ethnicity.

Principal works

DRAMA: *Nisei Bar and Grill*, pr. 1976, revised pr. 1992

POETRY: *The Buddha Bandits Down Highway 99*, 1978 (with Alan Chong Lau and Lawson Fusao Inada); *Yellow Light*, 1982; *The River of Heaven*, 1988

NONFICTION: *Volcano: A Memoir of Hawai'i*, 1995 (memoir)

EDITED TEXTS: *The Open Boat: Poems from Asian America*, 1993; *Songs My Mother Taught Me: Stories, Plays, and Memoir*, 1994 (by Wakako Yamauchi); *Under Western Eyes: Personal Essays from Asian America*, 1995

Garrett Kaoru Hongo (GAR-reht kay-OH-roo HON-goh) was born in the shadow of the Kilauea volcano but reared near Los Angeles. When he comes to terms with his origins during his first sojourn to Hawaii at middle age, he liberates his spirit with a moving insight that solidifies his sense of self. His poetry and prose are reverent, precise, and evocative, celebrating male ancestors, early Japanese poets, family, birthplace, and home.

Estranged from his past, Hongo was sheltered from the bitter truths of the World War II internment by his family. Gardena, California, the town where he grew up, boasted the largest community of Japanese Americans on the mainland United States at the time and was bordered on the north by the predominantly black towns of Watts and Compton and on the southwest by Torrance and Redondo Beach, white towns. Thus, Hongo was sensitized to issues of uneasy race relations and urban street life at an early age.

Hongo studied in Japan for a year following graduation from Pomona College, then earned a master's degree in fine arts from the University of California at Irvine. As a poet-in-residence in Seattle, he founded and directed a local theater group called The Asian Exclusion Act. Hongo identifies largely with the West Coast, a mecca for many Asian American writers, and early became a friend and collaborator with Lawson Fusao Inada, a pioneer Japanese American poet. His marriage to white violinist Cynthia Thiessen and their rearing of two sons, Alexander and Hudson, have given Hongo particular sensitivity to the cultural terrain he calls "the borderlands."

As the only Asian member of the faculty at the University of Oregon, Eugene,

Hongo began directing the creative writing program there in 1989 and received several extended leaves that allowed time in Hawaii to work on his prose memoirs, published in 1995 as *Volcano*. Among his most important influences is Wakako Yamauchi, a widely anthologized Japanese American short-story writer and playwright, whose works Hongo collected and edited under the title *Songs My Mother Taught Me*, which was published in 1994.

Volcano

Type of work: Memoir
First published: 1995

Volcano: A Memoir of Hawai'i evocatively describes flora, fauna, and geographical features of an exuberantly lush and exotic landscape. The book contains biographical portraits of a handful of Hongo's flamboyant, melancholy, or mercenary ancestors, intriguing in themselves. In the artful way in which it combines place with personal history, and in which it seeks to reconcile Hongo's Japanese heritage with his American circumstances, the book explores a larger truth: To achieve true peace of mind, it is necessary to seek, acknowledge, and celebrate one's own ethnic, geographical, and biological origins.

Hongo's last name means "homeland," and he conducts a pilgrimage, crossing the Pacific Ocean to immerse himself in the birthplace he left when he was only a few weeks old, Volcano. Growing up near Los Angeles and living as an adult in Missouri and Oregon, Hongo first returns to Volcano when he is thirty years old, his Caucasian violinist wife and their infant son, Alexander, in tow. Having felt a profound sense of estrangement from his past, knowing little about his father or grandfather, Hongo soon makes acquaintances in Volcano with locals and distant relatives, who reveal painful truths about the ravages of the Japanese American internment on his family. His cabin in the rainforest is in the shadow of the Kilauea volcano, which takes on symbolism as his narrative continues. He shops in the general store that his grandfather once owned. He witnesses a volcano erupting in the early morning

Garrett Kaoru Hongo (Ellen Foscue Johnson)

and hikes around lava flows. He eats food such as poi and miso soup, which for him become a wayside of culture and memory.

The first visit makes Hongo eager to return, having given him particulars of ancestral memory and having shown him a way to belong in and to make sense of his world. In the poignancy and drama of coming face-to-face with ugly racial and personal secrets and also with the beauties of place that lift him above the pain, Hongo becomes inspired to compose the poetry that had been locked deep inside. The book ends with the wish that the reader achieve similar healing self-knowledge.

Suggested Readings

Chock, Eric, and Darrell H. Y. Lum, eds. *The Best of Bamboo Ridge: The Hawaii Writer's Quarterly*. Honolulu: Bamboo Ridge Press, 1986.

Evans, Alice. "A Vicious Kind of Tenderness: An Interview with Garrett Hongo." *Poets & Writers Magazine* 20, no. 5 (September/October, 1992): 37-46.

Filipelli, Laurie. *Garrett Hongo*. Boise, Idaho: Boise State University, 1997.

Jarman, Mark. "The Volcano Inside." *The Southern Review* 32, no. 2 (Spring, 1996): 337-343.

Slowik, Mary. "Beyond Lot's Wife: The Immigration Poems of Marilynn Chin, Garrett Hongo, Li-Young Lee, and David Mura." *MELUS* 25, no. 3 (2000): 221-242.

Contributor: Jill B. Gidmark

Bell Hooks
(Gloria Watkins)

BORN: Hopkinsville, Kentucky; September 25, 1952

AFRICAN AMERICAN

Beginning with her acclaimed Ain't I a Woman, *Hooks helped black women find their voices within mainstream feminism.*

PRINCIPAL WORKS

CHILDREN'S LITERATURE: *Happy to Be Nappy*, 1999; *Homemade Love*, 2001; *Be Boy Buzz*, 2002; *Skin Again*, 2004

POETRY: *A Woman's Mourning Song*, 1993; *When Angels Speak of Love*, 2007

NONFICTION: *Ain't I a Woman: Black Women and Feminism*, 1981; *Feminist Theory: From Margin to Center*, 1984, 2000; *Talking Back: Thinking Feminist, Thinking Black*, 1989; *Yearning: Race, Gender, and Cultural Politics*, 1990; *Breaking Bread: Insurgent Black Intellectual Life*, 1991 (with Cornel West); *Black Looks: Race and Representation*, 1992; *Sisters of the Yam: Black Women and Self-Recovery*, 1993; *Outlaw Culture: Resisting Representations*, 1994; *Teaching to Transgress: Education as the Practice of Freedom*, 1994; *Art on My Mind: Visual Politics*, 1995; *Killing Rage: Ending Racism*, 1995; *Reel to Real: Race, Sex, and Class at the Movies*, 1996; *Bone Black: Memories of Girlhood*, 1997; *Wounds of Passion: A Writing Life*, 1997; *Remembered Rapture: The Writer at Work*, 1999; *All About Love: New Visions*, 2000; *Feminism Is for Everybody: Passionate Politics*, 2000; *Where We Stand: Class Matters*, 2000; *Salvation: Black People and Love*, 2001; *Communion: The Female Search for Love*, 2002; *Rock My Soul: Black People and Self-Esteem*, 2003; *Teaching Community: A Pedagogy of Hope*, 2003; *We Real Cool: Black Men and Masculinity*, 2004; *The Will to Change: Men, Masculinity, and Love*, 2004; *Homegrown: Engaged Cultural Criticism*, 2006 (with Amalia Mesa-Bains)

Bell Hooks (whose name is often styled in all-lowercase letters as "bell hooks"), a prolific feminist writer, is one of America's leading intellectual figures. The author of more than a dozen books and numerous essays, Hooks has had a distinguished career as she has sought to locate, describe, and define the shared experiences of black women. Hooks has earned her reputation as an impassioned yet analytical theorist by approaching such subjects as racism, classicism, and sexism with an acute sensitivity.

Hooks was born Gloria Jean Watkins on September 25, 1952, in Hopkinsville,

Kentucky. She is the daughter of Veodis Watkins, a custodian employed by the postal service, and Rosa Bell Watkins, a homemaker. There were seven children, including Gloria, in the Watkins family: one boy and six girls. All the members of the Watkins family shared a love for language, especially poetic language. Hooks remembers that during storms that caused power outages, she would sit with her family in their candlelit living room and stage impromptu talent shows; poetry recitations always figured prominently in these spontaneous family performances. This love for poetry, initiated and sustained by her family, has inspired Hooks throughout her career, and though she chooses to write under the name "Bell Hooks," she does not do so to distinguish or separate herself from her family. Her choice of her pseudonym is a tribute to the wisdom of her great-grandmother, Bell Hooks.

Hooks attended Crispus Attucks High School in Hopkinsville. After graduation she enrolled at Stanford University in Stanford, California; she obtained her B.A. degree in English in 1973. In 1976 she earned her master's degree, also in English, from the University of Wisconsin in Madison. She then began teaching English at the University of Southern California in Los Angeles; she remained there until 1979. In the early 1980's she taught courses in creative writing, African American literature, and composition at several institutions, including the University of California at Santa Cruz. While teaching, Hooks also pursued her Ph.D. She received her doctoral degree from the University of California at Santa Cruz in 1983. Teaching and earning her Ph.D., however, were not the only activities absorbing Hooks's energy during this period. In 1981 she published her first book, *Ain't I a Woman: Black Women and Feminism.*

The publication of *Ain't I a Woman*, a work Hooks began writing when she was nineteen years old, earned her much critical praise. The book was also the harbinger of Hooks's future work. The focus of *Ain't I a Woman*—black women finding their voices within mainstream feminism—is also the central concern of several of Hooks's later works, including *Feminist Theory: From Margin to Center* and *Talking Back: Thinking Feminist, Thinking Black.*

A different concern surfaced in the works Hooks published in the first half of the 1990's. In such works as *Yearning: Race, Gender, and Cultural Politics* and *Black Looks: Race and Representation*, Hooks analyzes, from a black and feminist perspective, such popular cultural phenomenon as films, rap songs, and advertisements. Her specific targets include the videos of the pop-music diva Madonna and the advertisements of the clothing manufacturer Benetton. The purpose of her examination of society and its media representations, Hooks suggests in each of these books, is to illustrate the way African Americans are depicted in film, television, advertisements, and literature. Hooks hopes that by pointing out these images she will help others "see" how prevalent racist images still are in America.

Although Hooks has delved into American popular culture in her books, she has not abandoned all academic pursuits. Besides writing, Hooks has remained active in the classroom. In 1985 she taught African and Afro-American studies and English at Yale University. She has also served as an associate professor of women's studies and American literature at Oberlin College. In 1994 she became the distinguished professor of English at the City College of New York.

Hooks articulated and examined some of her teaching theories in her 1994 work *Teaching to Transgress: Education as the Practice of Freedom.* This volume, according to Hooks, is her attempt to apply the philosophy of the progressive Brazilian educator Paula Freire to American society. She argues in this book that students should do more than merely receive an education; they should participate throughout the process. Hooks has certainly been an active participant in her own education. Through her meticulous observation of and theorizing about such topics as feminism, racism, popular culture, and pedagogical methods, she has cultivated a broad base of knowledge. Her books and essays are her means of synthesizing and disseminating the material that has enriched her own life.

In 1996, Hooks published the first volume of a three-part autobiography, *Bone Black.* She continued with *Wounds of Passion* and *Remembered Rapture.* In 1999, she also began writing children's books, aimed to encourage self-esteem among African American children. In *All About Love*, *Salvation*, and *Communion*, Hooks ventured into territory that verged on self-help, albeit with her typically engaged political consciousness. In these books, Hooks considers the role of love in human lives and how the contentious relations between the sexes in modern American culture came to be and how they can be redressed.

Ain't I a Woman

Type of work: Social criticism
First published: 1981

Ain't I a Woman analyzes how racist and sexist oppression have prevented a positive valuation of black womanhood. As it does so, it critically engages a variety of authors and assumptions, indicating their racist and sexist blind spots. A major theme of the book is how a preoccupation with black male masculinity has hidden and distorted the experiences of black women, leading to mistaken assumptions regarding "strong black women" whose dignity rests on their capacity to cope with and endure oppression and degradation. These assumptions, Hooks argues, have led to the erasure of black women's identity. The term "women" tends to refer primarily to white women; the term "black" or "Negro" tends to refer primarily to black men.

Hooks develops her argument by confronting the widely held view that the predominant damage caused by slavery was the demasculinization of the black male. She shows how, in fact, white patriarchy enabled African males to maintain a semblance of their societally given masculine role; they performed only "masculine" tasks and were encouraged to adopt traditional sex roles in the slave subculture. In contrast, many African women were assigned heavy labor. They were usually bred like cattle. Furthermore, those who worked as "house slaves" were often raped by their owners and brutalized by the owners' wives. To this extent, they came to be seen as the "other," the opposite of the real lady as idealized by the "cult of true womanhood." This patriarchal value system held that women were delicate, chaste, and feminine. Since black women were hardworking, sexually available, and "nonfeminine," they did not count as women at all. Thus, Hooks points out that far from demasculinizing black men, the experience of slavery masculinized black women.

Hooks also shows the continuation of the devaluation of black womanhood after slavery, taking white feminists to task for ignoring the sexist oppression of black women after manumission. For example, she criticizes Susan Brownmiller's *Against Our Will: Men, Women, and Rape* (1975), arguing that Brownmiller fails to acknowledge that the rape of black women has never received the same sort of attention as the rape of white women. Hooks explains that because of the slave system, which led to the designation of black women as sexually depraved, immoral, and loose, black women have been seen by the white public as sexually permissive and eager for sexual assault. Black women have been viewed as incapable of being "raped."

To demonstrate the racist ideology that has made the term "women" synonymous with "white women," Hooks raises arguments against white feminists who have been unwilling to distinguish among varying types and degrees of oppression and discrimination. She points out that white women in the women's movement wanted to project an image of themselves as victims in order to gain entry to the job market. This image clashed, however, with black women's experiences as employees, as the maids and housekeepers of white women's children. Moreover, it ignored the fact that many lower-class women and women of color had to work, that not working was the privilege of middle-class white women. In this respect, Hooks offers a strong critique of Betty Friedan's *The Feminine Mystique* (1963), showing how it made the white middle-class "housewife" into a victim while ignoring the exploitation of poor black and nonblack women in the American economy.

Although much of Hooks's argument exposing the impact of the slave system on understandings of black womanhood focuses on the racism of white feminists, she does not ignore the way in which many black women have themselves internalized racism and sexism. She explains that when confronted with racism in the women's movement, a number of black women responded by forming separate black feminist groups. While she perhaps underestimates the positive role of these groups in facilitating exchanges among black women and giving them a sense of community and purpose, she convincingly details many of the negative repercussions of separatism. First, segregated groups perpetuated the very racism that they were designed to attack, leading to the even greater polarization of the women's movement. Second, they failed to provide a critical assessment of the movement and a notion of feminism untainted by racism. Third, they forfeited the opportunity for coalition-building, enabling white women to continue to think of race and sex as unconnected. Thus, Hooks concludes that separatism serves primarily the interests of white men, pitting women against women and allowing white men to establish the meaning of liberation and freedom, success and opportunity.

Hooks teaches that as long as liberation means having the same power that white men have, white and black women will remain at odds with each other. This power is inherently divisive, denying the connections among people and creating a world of oppression and opposition. Yet once women cease to accept the idea of divisiveness and break through the myths, stereotypes, and assumptions that deny their commonality, they can grasp the connections between race and sex and begin forging a new sisterhood. This sisterhood will be one of accountability, whereby women take responsibility for ending division and oppression and recognizing the dignity and diversity of all people.

Yearning

Type of work: Social criticism
First published: 1990

The analysis of sexism in the black community is one of Hooks's strongest themes. She observes that black male sexism is analyzed differently from white male sexism; popular assumptions in the "liberal" establishment that racism is more oppressive to black men than to black women are based on the acceptance of patriarchal notions of masculinity. These, she notes again and again, are life-threatening to black men. The continuing argument over sexism versus racism misses the point of the interlocking nature of oppressions: They cannot be ranked.

Her stance between various points of view—between black and white, between positions in the black community, between positions in the feminist community—is a foundation of her political belief. This view has characterized her work at least from the time of *Feminist Theory: From Margin to Center*. In *Yearning*, however, she is clearer about the choice to stay on the boundary: "Understanding marginality as position and place of resistance is crucial for oppressed, exploited, colonized people."

The critique of *Writing Culture: The Poetics and Politics of Ethnography* (1986), edited by James Clifford and George Marcus, provides a practical example of the kind of analysis done by cultural critics. Hooks's assessment, which focuses on the omission of articles by non-Western or feminist theorists, spotlights the cover as an ironic visual metaphor for the position of the book. The cover reproduces a photograph of a white male fieldworker taking notes on darker-skinned people who watch him from a distance. Although the brown man seems to be watching with admiration, the brown woman's face is blocked by the graphics of the cover. Although the book itself critiques the traditional exploitative stance of the anthropologist, the cover seems to undercut that critique by reinscribing or reinforcing the colonialist power position.

The cover of *Yearning* also lends itself to analysis, especially considering Hooks's critique of the cover of *Writing Culture*. The image on *Yearning*'s cover appears to be a portion of a nineteenth century etching, in which a barefoot darker-skinned woman, seated on an oriental carpet, tells the fortune of a white woman, lying on a couch above her. The darker-skinned woman is wearing a loose jacket, open to show her cleavage; loose pants with her legs crossed above her bare feet;

scarf; and earrings. She is holding out a card to the lighter-skinned woman. More cards are spread around her. The lighter-skinned woman, dressed in white, reclines on pillows. In this image, the darker-skinned woman is made to seem a sexual object (on the floor, breasts showing, begging), while the lighter-skinned woman's position is literally higher (arms and chest covered, eyes downcast, passive). However, to whom is the darker woman a sexual object? To the white woman? Or to the audience of the etching, playing out a stereotyped notion of the exotic Other? The lighter woman is no less stereotyped: The passive lady, on a couch instead of a pedestal, constricted by corsets and clothing, is taking no active role in public life. Although the cover almost certainly shows a colonial scene from Turkey or Egypt, it could just as likely stand for the situation of the Southern United States during slavery—house slave entertaining plantation mistress.

Read in a different way, the cover could also be saying that the darker woman is prophesying a different future to the white woman, a more egalitarian one in which the colonial world of which the white woman is a part will be overturned by the "underside of history." Perhaps both women are "yearning" for a radical change to their very different oppressive situations.

In all this discussion of cover images undermining ideas of the book, Hooks has not recognized the market forces that usually preclude the author's choice or even approval of the cover. Thus, seeing significance in the cover should perhaps be prefaced by a recognition of the prevailing system. In this particular case, according to South End Press's editorial department, Hooks herself helped to choose the cover.

Suggested Readings

Bauer, Michelle. "Implementing a Liberatory Feminist Pedagogy: Bell Hooks' Strategies for Transforming the Classroom." *MELUS* 25, no. 3 (2000): 265-274.

Cheng, Cliff. "A Review Essay on the Books of Bell Hooks: Organizational Diversity Lessons from a Thoughtful Race and Gender Heretic." *The Academy of Management Review* 22, no. 2 (1997): 553-564.

Florence, Namulundah. *Bell Hooks' Engaged Pedagogy: A Transgressive Education for Critical Consciousness*. Westport, Conn.: Bergin & Garvey, 1998.

Grunnell, Marianne, and Sawitri Saharso. "Bell Hooks and Nira Yuval-Davis on Race, Ethnicity, Class, and Gender." *European Journal of Women's Studies* 6, no. 2 (1999): 203-219.

Martin, Joan M. "The Notion of Difference for Emerging Womanist Ethics." *Journal of Feminist Studies in Religion* 9, no. 1/2 (1993): 39-51.

Valdivia, Angharad N. "Bell Hooks: Ethics from the Margins." *Qualitative Inquiry* 8, no. 4 (2002): 429-447.

Contributors: Traci S. Smrcka, Jodi Dean, and Margaret McFadden

Langston Hughes

Born: Joplin, Missouri; February 1, 1902
Died: New York, New York; May 22, 1967

African American

Hughes's writings reflect on the struggles and triumphs of African American people, in the idiom of black America.

Principal works

children's literature: *Popo and Fijina: Children of Haiti*, 1932 (story; with Arna Bontemps); *The First Book of Negroes*, 1952; *The First Book of Rhythms*, 1954; *The First Book of Jazz*, 1955; *The First Book of the West Indies*, 1955; *The First Book of Africa*, 1960

drama: *Little Ham*, pr. 1935; *Mulatto*, pb. 1935; *Troubled Island*, pr. 1935 (opera libretto); *Don't You Want to Be Free?*, pb. 1938; *Freedom's Plow*, pb. 1943; *Street Scene*, pr., pb. 1947 (lyrics; music by Kurt Weill and Elmer Rice); *Simply Heavenly*, pr. 1957 (opera libretto); *Black Nativity*, pr. 1961; *Five Plays*, pb. 1963 (Walter Smalley, editor); *Tambourines to Glory*, pr., pb. 1963; *Jerico-Jim Crow*, pr. 1964; *The Prodigal Son*, pr. 1965

long fiction: *Not Without Laughter*, 1930; *Tambourines to Glory*, 1958

poetry: *The Weary Blues*, 1926; *Fine Clothes to the Jew*, 1927; *Dear Lovely Death*, 1931; *The Negro Mother, and Other Dramatic Recitations*, 1931; *The Dream Keeper, and Other Poems*, 1932; *Scottsboro Limited: Four Poems and a Play in Verse*, 1932; *A New Song*, 1938; *Shakespeare in Harlem*, 1942; *Jim Crow's Last Stand*, 1943; *Lament for Dark Peoples*, 1944; *Fields of Wonder*, 1947; *One Way Ticket*, 1949; *Montage of a Dream Deferred*, 1951; *Selected Poems of Langston Hughes*, 1959; *Ask Your Mama: Or, Twelve Moods for Jazz*, 1961; *The Panther and the Lash: Or, Poems of Our Times*, 1967; *The Poems, 1921-1940*, 2001 (volume 1 of *The Collected Works of Langston Hughes*; Dolan Hubbard, editor); *The Poems, 1941-1950*, 2001 (volume 2 of *The Collected Works of Langston Hughes*; Hubbard, editor); *The Poems, 1951-1967*, 2001 (volume 3 of *The Collected Works of Langston Hughes*; Hubbard, editor)

screenplay: *Way Down South*, 1939 (with Clarence Muse)

short fiction: *The Ways of White Folks*, 1934; *Simple Speaks His Mind*, 1950; *Laughing to Keep from Crying*, 1952; *Simple Takes a Wife*, 1953; *Simple Stakes a Claim*, 1957; *The Best of Simple*, 1961; *Something in Common, and Other Stories*, 1963; *Simple's Uncle Sam*, 1965; *The Return of Simple*, 1994; *Short Stories*, 1996

translations: *Masters of the Dew*, 1947 (of Jacques Roumain; with Mercer Cook);

Cuba Libre, 1948 (of Nicolás Guillén; with Ben Carruthers); *Gypsy Ballads*, 1951 (of Federico García Lorca); *Selected Poems of Gabriela Mistral*, 1957

NONFICTION: *The Big Sea: An Autobiography*, 1940; *Famous American Negroes*, 1954; *Famous Negro Music Makers*, 1955; *The Sweet Flypaper of Life*, 1955 (photographs by Roy De Carava); *I Wonder as I Wander: An Autobiographical Journey*, 1956; *A Pictorial History of the Negro in America*, 1956 (with Milton Meltzer); *Famous Negro Heroes of America*, 1958; *Fight for Freedom: The Story of the NAACP*, 1962; *Black Magic: A Pictorial History of the Negro in American Entertainment*, 1967 (with Meltzer); *Black Misery*, 1969 (illustrations by Arouni); *Arna Bontemps—Langston Hughes Letters: 1925-1967*, 1980; *Remember Me to Harlem: The Letters of Langston Hughes and Carl Van Vechten, 1925-1964*, 2001 (Emily Bernard, editor)

EDITED TEXTS: *The Poetry of the Negro, 1746-1949*, 1949 (with Arna Bontemps); *The Book of Negro Folklore*, 1959 (with Bontemps); *New Negro Poets: U.S.A.*, 1964; *The Book of Negro Humor*, 1966; *The Best Short Stories by Negro Writers: An Anthology from 1899 to the Present*, 1967

MISCELLANEOUS: *The Langston Hughes Reader*, 1958; *The Collected Works of Langston Hughes*, 2001-2004 (16 volumes)

James Mercer Langston Hughes led an active literary life. His writings extend from the Harlem Renaissance of the 1920's to the Black Arts movement of the 1960's. Hughes's father abandoned his wife and infant son in 1903 to seek wealth in Mexico. His mother, unable to find even menial labor in their hometown of Joplin, Missouri, moved frequently to look for work. In his youth, Hughes lived predominantly with his maternal grandmother in Lawrence, Kansas. Hughes understood poverty, dejection, and loneliness, but from his grandmother he learned the valuable lessons of perseverance and laughter. Her resilience and ingenuity made a lasting impression upon Hughes's imagination, and she seems the prototype of his self-assured female characters.

After his grandmother's death, Hughes reunited with his mother in Lincoln, Illinois, but for a time was placed with his Auntie Reed and her husband, religious people who pressured Hughes into joining their church. Hughes marked this unsuccessful attempt at conversion as the beginning of his religious disbelief, as illustrated in the story "Salvation."

Hughes later moved to Cleveland, where his intellectual growth began in earnest. His earliest poems were influenced by Paul Laurence Dunbar and Carl Sandburg. He read the German philosophers Arthur Schopenhauer and Friedrich Nietzsche and was introduced to socialist ideas. When Hughes's father, having become prosperous, asked Hughes to join him in Mexico in 1920, Hughes rode a train across the Mississippi River at St. Louis and penned the famous "The Negro Speaks of Rivers" on the back of an envelope.

In Mexico, Hughes became dissatisfied with his father's materialism and his plans to send him to a European university. Hughes escaped and attended bullfights and studied Mexican culture. He wrote little of these experiences, although a few pieces were published in *The Brownies' Book*, founded by W. E. B. Du Bois's staff at *Crisis*, the official journal of the National Association for the Advancement of Colored People (NAACP).

Langston Hughes (Library of Congress)

In 1921, Hughes enrolled at Columbia University. He was quickly disillusioned with Columbia's coldness and spent more time in Harlem and at Broadway productions. Consequently, Hughes failed most of his classes and dropped out. He worked odd jobs while devoting his free time to the shaping forces of the Harlem Renaissance. Hughes led a nomadic life for two years as a cabin boy on freighters that took him to Europe and Africa. On his initial voyage, he threw away his books because they reminded him of past hardships. He discovered how cities such as Venice had poor people too. These voyages and observations became the genesis of his first autobiography, *The Big Sea*. Hughes made many influential friends, among them Countée Cullen, James Weldon Johnson, Carl Van Vechten, and Arna Bontemps. Van Vechten helped Hughes find a publisher for his work. Bontemps and Hughes later collaborated on numerous children's books and anthologies.

Hughes matriculated at Lincoln University in Pennsylvania in 1926, the year that his first book, *The Weary Blues*, was published. This book was soon followed by many others. During the 1930's, Hughes made trips to Haiti and to the Soviet Union. In 1937, he was a correspondent in Spain during that country's civil war. He wrote about these excursions in his second autobiography, *I Wonder as I Wander*. During the 1940's, he wrote columns for the *Chicago Defender*, formulating the humorous persona Jesse B. Semple, or "Simple," who would later become the basis of the "Simple" stories. In the 1950's, his politically edged writings made Hughes a brief target of Senator Joseph McCarthy's hunt for communists. In the last years of his life, Hughes continued to produce volumes of edited and creative work. Hughes died following prostate surgery at Polyclinic Hospital in New York City in 1967.

Although perhaps best known for his poetry, Langston Hughes explored almost every literary genre. His prose fiction includes novels, humorous books, translations, lyrics, librettos, plays, and scripts. He wrote the libretti for several operas, a screenplay—*Way Down South*, with Clarence Muse—radio scripts, and song lyrics. His most famous contribution to musical theater was the lyrics he wrote for Kurt Weill and Elmer Rice's musical adaptation of Rice's *Street Scene*. Over the years, Hughes also wrote several nonfiction articles, mainly focused on his role as a poet and his love of black American music—jazz, gospel, and the blues. Perhaps his most important article was his first: "The Negro Artist and the Racial Mountain," published in *The Nation* on June 23, 1926, in defense of the idea of a black American literary style, voice, and subject matter.

The Big Sea

Type of work: Autobiography
First published: 1940

In the opening of Hughes's first autobiography, *The Big Sea*, the author recalls how he heaved his books overboard at the start of his first journey to Africa in 1923. The gesture may be seen as adolescent and anti-intellectual, but it suggests the commencement of Hughes's role as a Renaissance man in Black American letters. The book chronicles the first twenty-seven years of Hughes's life, from the 1920's, when he explored the idiom and jazz rhythms of African Americans in his poetry to the shift to his bitter prose of the 1930's.

The autobiography is written typically as a confession, but it remains comparatively impersonal. Only three guarded personal accounts appear in the text of *The Big Sea*. The first concerns a religious revival Hughes attended at age thirteen at which he waited in vain for Jesus. The second describes the morning in Mexico when he realized that he hated his father. The third, at the book's end, details the break with his patron and mentor, Charlotte Mason. He ties the latter experience to the other two: "The light went out with a sudden crash in the dark, and everything became like that night in Kansas when I had failed to see Jesus and had lied about it afterwards. Or that morning in Mexico when I suddenly hated my father."

Other than these specific episodes, controversy rarely enters the book. Instead, Hughes presents himself as a man who loves his race and is optimistic about his people. He nevertheless carries doubts and fears within himself. The book, furthermore, is peopled by Hughes's many friends, including Jean Toomer, Zora Neale Hurston, and others involved with the Harlem Renaissance. Hughes's publisher, Blanche Knopf, thought that the references were excessive, but Hughes convinced her to retain them. Consequently, *The Big Sea* is perhaps the best chronicle of the Harlem Renaissance.

I Wonder as I Wander

Type of work: Autobiography
First published: 1956

The second autobiography, *I Wonder as I Wander*, received less favor than its predecessor, although Hughes thought that his second autobiography was more important to his future as a writer. Knopf rejected the book, claiming it was "pretty weighted . . . and not a book." Covering his life from 1929 to 1950, it includes his travels to Haiti, Spain, and Russia. More than half of the collection explores his 1932 trip to the Soviet Union, and a second long section covers his excursion to Spain during its civil war. The book seems less a literary life than a political commentary on his travels.

One of the criticisms directed at *I Wonder as I Wander* was its detachment from the personal and reflective. *The Big Sea* contains few enough personal reflections, but those that it contains are balanced between pain and joy. *I Wonder as I Wander* shows a Hughes who is more secure in his world and who is suffering less, despite his poverty (which fame did little to diminish). *I Wonder as I Wander* is a mature recollection, written without radicalism or prejudice.

The Ways of White Folks

Type of work: Short fiction
First published: 1934

During Hughes's travels to Russia in 1931, he became intensely interested in D. H. Lawrence's short fiction. As he later described in *I Wonder as I Wander*, he had never read Lawrence before and remarked that both "The Rocking Horse Winner" and "The Lovely Lady" had made his "hair stand on end." "I could not put the book down," he wrote. Furthermore, he wrote: "If D. H. Lawrence can write such psychologically powerful accounts of folks in England . . . maybe I could write stories like his about folks in America."

This fascination led to *The Ways of White Folks*, a collection of fourteen stories. The title is derived from the story "Berry," an account of a young black man who works as a handyman in a home for handicapped children. Berry is exploited and does more than his share of work for a pittance. He cannot understand why this happens and remarks, "The ways of white folks, I mean some white folks, is too much for me. I rekon they must be a few good ones, but most of 'em ain't good—least wise they don't treat me good. And Lawd knows, I ain't never done nothin' to them, nothin' a-tall."

Overall, the stories comment on the suffering the black community endures at the hands of white society. "Slave on the Block," for example, details how a white couple strives to make a young black artist fit into their aesthetic mold. Humorously, the young man, rebelling, runs off with the cook. In "Father and Son," Bert, a college student, returns home to the South but does not relinquish his independence. Despite warnings to respect white society, Bert ignores them and finds himself and his father hunted by a lynch mob. To save themselves from the disgrace of public hanging, Bert kills his father and himself before the mob overtakes them.

In "Home," Hughes writes of an elderly musician who has returned home; while his career had been successful elsewhere, he is murdered by locals offended by his talking to a white woman. "The Blues I'm Playing" describes how a white patron, a spinster who collects artists, tries to mold a talented black woman into a respectable classical pianist. While the young woman plays exceptional music, she often reverts to her first loves: gospel and blues. Oceola tells her patron, "This is mine. . . . Listen! . . . How sad and gay it is. Blue and happy—laughing and crying. . . . How white like you and black like me." Her music is rooted in "bass notes [that] throb like tomtoms deep in the earth." Her patron, who cannot understand this music's value, prefers looking at the stars, which are unattainable, futile, and distant.

Underlying most of this collection is the difficulty of black-white relationships. Hughes illustrates how blacks are never regarded as individuals but rather as members of a group, how they are always treated with mistrust and hate. Hughes makes it clear in *The Ways of White Folks* that white people do not comprehend their own actions.

Selected Poems of Langston Hughes

TYPE OF WORK: Poetry
FIRST PUBLISHED: 1959

The poems of *Selected Poems of Langston Hughes* were gathered by the poet from several of his earlier collections, including *The Weary Blues*, *Fine Clothes to the Jew*, *Dear Lovely Death*, *Shakespeare in Harlem*, *Fields of Wonder*, *One Way Ticket*, and *Montage of a Dream Deferred*. Representative of the body of Hughes's poetry, the collection includes his best poems: "The Negro Speaks of Rivers," "The Weary Blues," "Song for a Dark Girl," "Sylvester's Dying Bed," "I, Too," "Montage of a Dream Deferred," and "Refugee in America."

Hughes's poetry is an exploration of black identity, not only the sorrows and tribulations faced by black Americans but also the warm joy and humor of Hughes's people. He writes in "Negro": "I am a Negro:/ Black as the night is black,/ Black like the depths of my Africa." This is a resolute proclamation confronting racial adversity: "The Belgians cut off my hands in the Congo./ They lynch me still in Mississippi." Hughes refuses, however, to allow his poetry to become a podium for anger; rather, he offers readers portraits of the black experience and, consequently, draws his readers into a nearer understanding of black identity.

One of the strongest of Hughes's poems is "The Negro Speaks of Rivers." The poem muses upon what rivers mean to black culture and how the rivers symbolize the strength and longevity of a proud race:

> I bathed in the Euphrates when dawns were young.
> I built my hut near the Congo and it lulled me to sleep.
> I looked upon the Nile and raised the pyramids above it.
> I heard the singing of the Mississippi when Abe Lincoln
> went down to New Orleans, and I've seen its muddy
> bosom turn all golden in the sunset.

The beauty of the poem, which reads like a hymn or spiritual, is unmistakable and permanent.

Elsewhere, Hughes experiments with blues rhythms and jazz improvisations, as in "The Weary Blues":

In a deep song voice with a melancholy tone
I heard that Negro sing, that old piano moan—
    "Ain't got nobody in all this world
    Ain't got nobody but ma self.
    I's gwine to quit ma frownin'
    And put ma troubles on the shelf."
Thump, thump, thump, went his foot on the floor.
He played a few chords then he sang some more—
    "I got the Weary Blues
    And I can't be satisfied."

The blues touch upon black sorrow, but the music of the blues makes its listeners feel better. Some of Hughes's characters, as found in the "Madam to You" sequence, are not blue, or troubled, or even angry. Rather, they are secure and pleased with themselves. In "Madam's Calling Cards," Alberta K. Johnson tells the printer: "There's nothing foreign/ To my pedigree:/ Alberta K. Johnson—/ *American* that's me."

Ultimately, Hughes's objective seems to be to provide blacks with identities as Americans, living in a democracy that ensures life without prejudice. Thus, in "I, Too," a poem echoing Walt Whitman's *Leaves of Grass*, the poet looks to a future when a black man can "be at the table/ When company comes" and that "they'll see/ How beautiful I am/ And be ashamed."

Ask Your Mama

Type of work: Poetry
First published: 1961

Ask Your Mama: Or, Twelve Moods for Jazz is dedicated to "Louis Armstrong—the greatest horn blower of them all." In an introductory note, Hughes explains that "the traditional folk melody of the 'Hesitation Blues' is the leitmotif for this poem." The collection was designed to be read or sung with jazz accompaniment, "with room for spontaneous jazz improvisation, particularly between verses, when the voice pauses." Hughes includes suggestions for music to accompany the poetry. Sometimes the instructions are open ("delicate lieder on piano"), and sometimes they are more direct ("suddenly the drums roll like thunder as the music ends sonorously"). There are also suggestions for specific songs to be used, including "Dixie" ("impishly"), "When the Saints Go Marchin' In," and "The Battle Hymn of the Republic." As a final aid, Hughes includes at the end of his collection "Liner Notes" for, as he says, "the Poetically Unhep."

Throughout, the poems in *Ask Your Mama* run the current of protest against "the shadow" of racism that falls over the lives of the earth's darker peoples. Shadows frequently occur as images and symbols, suggesting the fear and the sense of vague existence created by living in oppression. "Show Fare, Please" summarizes the essence of the poet's feeling of being left out because he does not have "show fare," but it also suggests that "the show" may be all illusion anyway. Not all the poems are so stark; the humor of Hughes's earlier work is still very much in evidence. In "Is It True," for example, Hughes notes that "everybody thinks that Negroes have the *most* fun, but, of course, secretly hopes they do not—although curious to find out if they do."

The Panther and the Lash

Type of work: Poetry
First published: 1967

The Panther and the Lash, Hughes's final collection of poems, published the year he died, contains some of his most direct protest poetry, although he never gives vent to the anger that permeated the work of his younger contemporaries. The collection is dedicated "To Rosa Parks of Montgomery who started it all. . . ." in 1955 by refusing to move to the back of a bus. The panther of the title refers to a "Black Panther" who "in his boldness/ Wears no disguise,/ Motivated by the truest/ Of the oldest/ Lies"; the lash refers to the white backlash of the times (in "The Backlash Blues").

The book has seven sections, each dealing with a particular part of the subject. "Words on Fire" has poems on the coming of the Third World revolution, while "American Heartbreak" deals with the consequences of "the great mistake/ That Jamestown made/ Long ago"; that is, slavery. The final section, "Daybreak in Alabama," does, however, offer hope. In spite of past and existing conditions, the poet hopes for a time when he can compose a song about "daybreak in Alabama" that will touch everybody "with kind fingers."

The Return of Simple

Type of work: Short fiction
First published: 1994

Between 1943 and 1965, Hughes delighted readers of the Chicago *Defender* and the *New York Post* with the ideas and opinions voiced by his fictional folk character Jesse B. Semple. Though numerous Simple "stories" (they are actually conversations between Simple and a more educated acquaintance, set in Harlem saloons) were collected in five previous volumes, more than half of the pieces in this collection had not been published in book form. Arranged by the editor under four subject groupings—Women; Race, Riots, Police, Prices, and Politics; Africa and Black

Pride; and Parting Lines (Miscellaneous)—Simple's conversations cover a wide range of topics, running the gamut from bedbugs to race riots. His views on the various social and political issues he addresses represent the unique perspective of the lower-class African American male. Yet, as Simple expresses his ideas on life around him, his remarks often transcend the categories of race, class, and gender and enter the realm of the universal.

The Simple stories are justly famous for their humor, but Hughes was not aiming to be merely amusing in them. Simple's conversations with his more educated and refined companion reflect the tensions and conflicts that Hughes struggled to resolve in himself. The mood of one of Simple's conversations may shift suddenly from the lighthearted to the somber. As Arnold Rampersad (Hughes's biographer) observes in his introduction, an undercurrent of sadness runs beneath Simple's narratives, and Simple's sense of humor is at times all that prevents him from sliding into deep despair.

Suggested Readings

Berry, Faith. *Langston Hughes: Before and Beyond Harlem*. New York: Wings Books, 1995.

Bloom, Harold, ed. *Langston Hughes*. New York: Chelsea House, 1989.

Cooper, Floyd. *Coming Home: From the Life of Langston Hughes*. New York: Philomel Books, 1994.

Harper, Donna Sullivan. *Not So Simple: The "Simple" Stories by Langston Hughes*. Columbia: University of Missouri Press, 1995.

Haskins, James. *Always Movin' On: The Life of Langston Hughes*. Trenton, N.J.: Africa World Press, 1993.

Hokanson, Robert O'Brien. "Jazzing It Up: The Be-bop Modernism of Langston Hughes." *Mosaic* 31 (December, 1998): 61-82.

Leach, Laurie F. *Langston Hughes: A Biography*. Westport, Conn.: Greenwood Press, 2004.

Ostrom, Hans. *Langston Hughes: A Study of the Short Fiction*. New York: Twayne, 1993.

Rampersad, Arnold. *The Life of Langston Hughes*. 2 vols. New York: Oxford University Press, 1986-1988.

Schwarz, A. B. Christa. *Gay Voices of the Harlem Renaissance*. Bloomington: Indiana University Press, 2003.

Tracy, Steven C. *Langston Hughes and the Blues*. Urbana: University of Illinois Press, 1988.

Trotman, C. James, ed. *Langston Hughes: The Man, His Art, and His Continuing Influence*. New York: Garland, 1995.

Contributors: Mark Sanders, Emma Coburn Norris, Mary Rohrberger, and Edward E. Waldron

Zora Neale Hurston

Born: Eatonville, Florida; January 7, 1891
Died: Fort Pierce, Florida; January 28, 1960

African American

Hurston depicts the plight and records the language of her people.

Principal works

DRAMA: *Color Struck*, pb. 1926; *The First One*, pb. 1927; *Mule Bone*, pb. 1931 (with Langston Hughes); *Polk County*, pb. 1944, pr. 2002

LONG FICTION: *Jonah's Gourd Vine*, 1934; *Their Eyes Were Watching God*, 1937; *Moses, Man of the Mountain*, 1939; *Seraph on the Suwanee*, 1948

SHORT FICTION: *Spunk: The Selected Short Stories of Zora Neale Hurston*, 1985; *The Complete Stories*, 1995

NONFICTION: *Mules and Men*, 1935; *Tell My Horse*, 1938; *Dust Tracks on a Road*, 1942; *The Sanctified Church*, 1981; *Folklore, Memoirs, and Other Writings*, 1995; *Go Gator and Muddy the Water: Writings*, 1999 (Pamela Bordelon, editor); *Every Tongue Got to Confess: Negro Folk-Tales from the Gulf States*, 2001; *Zora Neale Hurston: A Life in Letters*, 2002 (Carla Kaplan, editor)

MISCELLANEOUS: *I Love Myself When I Am Laughing . . . and Then Again When I Am Looking Mean and Impressive: A Zora Neale Hurston Reader*, 1979

Zora Neale Hurston (HUR-stuhn) was born in the first incorporated all-black town in America; her father was one of its influential citizens. Her identity was formed in Eatonville; her works clearly show her attachments to that community. When Hurston was nine, her mother died. Hurston was moved among relatives, deprived of a stable home.

She worked to support herself from an early age; at only fourteen she worked as a maid with a touring Gilbert and Sullivan troupe. She later went to night school in Baltimore to catch up on her schooling, to Howard University, and to Barnard College as a scholarship student. She loved learning. Settled in New York in the early 1920's, Hurston filled her life with people who encouraged her work and gave her advice. Some of the most important of these were white: novelist Fanny Hurst and anthropologist Franz Boas, for example. Yet her identity comes from her own people: African American folklore was the focus of her research, and black women's experience informs her best work.

Hurston was influenced by the Harlem Renaissance of the 1920's and is considered one of its stars, but she was not readily accepted in the movement at the time.

Protest writers such as Richard Wright and Ralph Ellison found her writing "quaint" and "romantic." She speaks in a clear feminine voice that, if not full of protest, affirms the black woman's identity. Hurston was equally at home with upper-class whites and poor blacks, but she never forgot her heritage.

Hurston's most important works were published during the 1930's: her collection of folklore, *Mules and Men*, in 1935; her novels *Jonah's Gourd Vine* and her masterpiece *Their Eyes Were Watching God* in 1934 and 1937, respectively. An autobiography, *Dust Tracks on a Road*, was published in 1942. She was married and divorced twice.

Throughout her life Hurston was compelled to discover and translate the Southern black, often female, existence. In her collections of folklore, her fiction, her articles, and her life, she presented her people honestly and sympathetically, faithfully recording their language and their beliefs. Not until after her death was the significance of her work fully appreciated. She died in a welfare home in 1960 and was buried in an unmarked grave. In 1973, acclaimed black writer Alice Walker found Hurston's grave and led a revival of interest in her work.

"John Redding Goes to Sea"

Type of work: Short fiction
First published: 1921, in *Stylus*

In many ways, Hurston's short stories are apprentice works to her novels. In these stories, she introduced most of the themes, character types, settings, techniques, and concerns upon which she later elaborated during her most productive and artistic period, the 1930's. This observation, however, does not suggest that her short stories are inferior works. On the contrary, much of the best of Hurston can be found in these early stories.

Hurston's first published short story is entitled "John Redding Goes to Sea." It was published in the May, 1921, issue of the *Stylus*, the literary magazine of Howard University, and was reprinted in the January, 1926, issue of *Opportunity*. While the story is obviously the work of a novice writer, with its highly contrived plot, excessive sentimentality, and shallow characterizations, its strengths are many, strengths upon which Hurston would continue to draw and develop throughout her career.

The plot is a simple one: Young John Redding, the titular character, wants to leave his hometown to see and explore parts and things unknown. Several circumstances conspire, however, to keep him from realizing his dream. First, John's mother, the pitifully possessive, obsessive, and superstitious Matty Redding, is determined not to let John pursue his ambitions; in fact, she pleads illness and threatens to disown him if he leaves. Second, John's marriage to Stella Kanty seems to tie him permanently to his surroundings, as his new wife joins forces with his mother to discourage John's desire to travel. Further, his mother's tantrums keep John from even joining the Navy when that opportunity comes his way. Later, when John is

Zora Neale Hurston (Library of Congress)

killed in a tempest while working with a crew to build a bridge on the St. John's River, his father forbids his body to be retrieved from the river as it floats toward the ocean. At last, John will get his wish to travel and see the world, although in death.

If the plot seems overdone and the sentimentality overwhelming, "John Redding Goes to Sea" does provide the reader with the first of many glimpses of life among black Floridians—their habits, superstitions, strengths, and shortcomings. For example, one of the more telling aspects of the story is that Matty believes that her son was cursed with "travel dust" at his birth; thus, John's desire to travel is Matty's punishment for having married his father away from a rival suitor. Hurston suspends judgment on Matty's beliefs; rather, she shows that these and other beliefs are integral parts of the life of the folk.

Another strength that is easily discernible in Hurston's first short story is her detailed rendering of setting. Hurston has a keen eye for detail, and nowhere is this more evident than in her descriptions of the lushness of Florida. This adeptness is especially present in "John Redding Goes to Sea" and in most of Hurston's other work as well.

By far the most important aspect of "John Redding Goes to Sea" is its theme that people must be free to develop and pursue their own dreams, a recurring theme in the Hurston canon. John Redding is deprived of self-expression and self-determination because the wishes and interpretations of others are imposed upon him. Hurston clearly has no sympathy with those who would deprive another of freedom and independence; indeed, she would adamantly oppose all such restrictive efforts throughout her career as a writer and folklorist.

"Spunk"

Type of work: Short fiction
First published: 1925, in *Opportunity*

Another early short story that treats a variation of this theme is "Spunk," published in the June, 1925, issue of *Opportunity*. The central character, Spunk Banks, has the spunk to live his life as he chooses, which includes taking another man's wife and parading openly around town with her. While Hurston passes no moral judgment on Banks, she makes it clear that she appreciates and admires his brassiness and his will to live his life according to his own terms.

When the story opens, Spunk Banks and Lena Kanty are openly flaunting their affair in front of the Eatonville townspeople, including Lena's husband, Joe Kanty. The other town residents make fun of Joe's weakness, his refusal to confront Spunk Banks. Later, when Joe desperately attacks Spunk with a razor, Spunk shoots and kills him. Spunk is tried and acquitted but is killed in a work-related accident, cut to death by a circular saw.

Again, superstition plays an important role here, for Spunk claims that he has been haunted by Joe Kanty's ghost. In fact, Spunk is convinced that Joe's ghost pushed him into the circular saw, and at least one other townsman agrees. As is customary in Hurston's stories, however, she makes no judgment of the rightness or wrongness of such beliefs but points out that these beliefs are very much a part of the cultural milieu of Eatonville.

"Sweat"

Type of work: Short fiction
First published: 1926, in *Fire!*

Another early Eatonville story is "Sweat," published in 1926 in the only issue of the ill-fated literary magazine *Fire!*, founded by Hurston, Hughes, and Wallace Thurman. "Sweat" shows Hurston's power as a fiction writer and as a master of the short-story form. Again, the story line is a simple one. Delia Jones is a hardworking, temperate Christian woman being tormented by her arrogant, mean-spirited, and cruel husband of fifteen years, Sykes Jones, who has become tired of her and desires a new wife. Rather than simply leaving her, though, he wants to drive her away by making her life miserable. At stake is the house for which Delia's "sweat" has paid: Sykes wants it for his new mistress, but Delia refuses to leave the fruit of her labor.

Sykes uses both physical and mental cruelty to antagonize Delia, the most far-reaching of which exploits Delia's intense fear of snakes. When Delia's fear of the caged rattlesnake that Sykes places outside her back door subsides, Sykes places the rattlesnake in the dirty clothes hamper, hoping that it will bite and kill Delia. In an ironic twist, however, Delia escapes, and the rattlesnake bites Sykes as he fumbles for a match in the dark house. Delia listens and watches as Sykes dies a painful, agonizing death.

While "Sweat" makes use of the same superstitious beliefs as Hurston's other stories, a more complex characterization and an elaborate system of symbols are central to the story's development. In Delia, for example, readers are presented with an essentially good Christian woman who is capable of great compassion and long suffering and who discovers the capacity to hate as intensely as she loves; in

Sykes, readers are shown unadulterated evil reduced to one at once pitiful and horrible in his suffering. In addition, the Christian symbolism, including the snake and the beast of burden, adds considerable interest and texture to the story. It is this texture that makes "Sweat" Hurston's most rewarding work of short fiction, for it shows her at her best as literary artist and cultural articulator.

Jonah's Gourd Vine

Type of work: Novel
First published: 1934

Jonah's Gourd Vine, Hurston's first novel, portrays the tragic experience of a black preacher caught between black cultural values and the values imposed by his white-influenced church. The novel charts the life of John Pearson—laborer, foreman, and carpenter—who discovers that he has an extraordinary talent for preaching. With his linguistic skills and his wife Lucy's wise counsel, he becomes pastor of the large church Zion Hope and ultimately moderator of a Florida Baptist convention. His sexual promiscuity, however, eventually destroys his marriage and his career.

Though his verbal skills make him a success while his promiscuity ruins him, the novel shows that both his linguistic gifts and his sexual vitality are part of the same cultural heritage. His sexual conduct is pagan and so is his preaching. In praying, according to the narrator, it was as if he "rolled his African drum up to the altar, and called his Congo Gods by Christian names." Both aspects of his cultural heritage speak through him. Indeed, they speak through all members of the African American community, if most intensely through John. A key moment early in the novel, when John crosses over Big Creek, marks the symbolic beginning of his life and shows the double cultural heritage he brings to it. John heads down to the Creek, "singing a new song and stomping the beats." He makes up "some words to go with the drums of the Creek," with the animal noises in the woods, and with the hound dog's cry. He begins to think about the girls living on the other side of Big Creek: "John almost trumpeted exultantly at the new sun. He breathed lustily. He stripped and carried his clothes across, then recrossed and plunged into the swift water and breasted strongly over."

To understand why two expressions of the same heritage have such different effects on John's life, one has to turn to the community to which he belongs. Members of his congregation subscribe to differing views of the spiritual life. The view most often endorsed by the novel emerges from the folk culture. As Larry Neal, one of Hurston's best critics, explains in his introduction to the 1971 reprint of the novel, that view belongs to "a formerly enslaved communal society, non-Christian in background," which does not strictly dichotomize body and soul. The other view comes out of a white culture. It is "more rigid, being a blend of Puritan concepts and the fire-and-brimstone imagery of the white evangelical tradition." That view insists that John, as a preacher, exercise self-restraint. The cultural conflict over spirituality pervades his congregation. While the deacons, whom Hurston often portrays satirically, pressure him to stop preaching, he still has some loyal supporters among his parishioners.

White America's cultural styles and perceptions invade Pearson's community in other ways as well. By means of a kind of preaching competition, the deacons attempt to replace Pearson with the pompous Reverend Felton Cozy, whose preaching style is white. Cozy's style, however, fails to captivate most members of the congregation. Pearson is a great preacher in the folk tradition, moving his congregation to a frenzy with "barbaric thunder-poems." By contrast, Cozy, as one of the parishioners complains, does not give a sermon; he lectures. In an essay Hurston wrote on "The Sanctified Church," she explains this reaction: "The real, singing Negro derides the Negro who adopts the white man's religious ways. . . . They say of that type of preacher, 'Why he don't preach at all. He just lectures.'"

If Pearson triumphs over Cozy, he nevertheless ultimately falls. His sexual conduct destroys his marriage and leads to an unhappy remarriage with one of his mistresses, Hattie Tyson. He is finally forced to stop preaching at Zion Hope. Divorced from Hattie, he moves to another town, where he meets and marries Sally Lovelace, a woman much like Lucy. With her support, he returns to preaching. On a visit to a friend, however, he is tempted by a young prostitute and, to his dismay, succumbs. Although he has wanted to be faithful to his new wife, he will always be a pagan preacher, spirit *and* flesh. Fleeing back to Sally, he is killed when a train strikes his car.

In its presentation of folklore and its complex representation of cultural conflict, *Jonah's Gourd Vine* is a brilliant first novel, although Hurston does not always make her argument sufficiently clear. The novel lacks a consistent point of view. Though she endorses Pearson's African heritage and ridicules representatives of white cultural views, she also creates an admirable and very sympathetic character in Lucy Pearson, who is ruined by her husband's pagan behavior. Nor did Hurston seem to know how to resolve the cultural conflict she portrayed—hence, the deus ex machina ending.

Their Eyes Were Watching God

Type of work: Novel
First published: 1937

It was not until she wrote her next novel, *Their Eyes Were Watching God*, that Hurston learned to control point of view and presented a solution to the problem of white influences on black culture. *Their Eyes Were Watching God* is Hurston's most lauded work. It is the story of Janie Crawford Killicks Starks Woods, a thrice-married, twice-widowed woman who learns the hard way: through her own experience. Granddaughter of a slave and daughter of a runaway mother, Janie grows up not realizing her color until she sees a picture of herself among white children. Rather than worry about Janie in her adolescence, her grandmother marries her off to Logan Killicks, an old, narrow-minded, and abusive husband. Hoping for more to life than she has, Janie ends that marriage herself by walking off with Joe Starks, a passerby with a dream, who becomes the mayor of Eatonville, Florida, a new all-black town. Janie reigns as queen of the town, yet she is still unhappily under the control of a jealous, controlling husband.

The town is incensed when, after Starks's death, Janie runs off with Teacake Woods, a young, charming ne'er-do-well. Living with Teacake "on the muck"—picking and planting beans in the Everglades—Janie finds happiness. Teacake truly loves her and cherishes her company, and Janie and Teacake's home is the center of a community of lively, happy, hardworking folks. Janie ends up a widow again. In trying to save Janie from a rabid dog during a flood, Teacake is bitten. In his delirium, he threatens Janie's life, and she must shoot him.

Despite the tragedy in her life, Janie comes across as powerful and self-reliant. She moves from being controlled by men to being assertive and independent. She provides a positive image of the black woman who rises above her circumstances and learns to deal with life on her own terms. After Teacake's death and her trial, she returns to Eatonville with her head high. She is saddened but not defeated; she tells her friend Phoeby that she has "been a delegate to de big 'ssociation of life" and that she has learned that everybody "got tuh find out about livin' fuh they-selves."

Although Hurston's novel received some harsh criticism for being quaint and romantic and was out of print for years, it is now considered an important work for its understanding of the African American folkloric tradition, for its language, and for its female hero, a woman who struggles and successfully finds her own identity.

Moses, Man of the Mountain

Type of work: Novel
First published: 1939

With her third novel, *Moses, Man of the Mountain*, Hurston turned in a new direction, leaving the Eatonville milieu behind. The novel retells the biblical story of Moses via the folk idiom and traditions of southern rural blacks. Hurston leaves much of the plot of the biblical story intact—Moses does lead the Hebrews out of Egypt—but, for example, she shows Moses to be a great hoodoo doctor as well as a leader and lawgiver. In effect, Hurston simulated the creative processes of folk culture, transforming the story of Moses for modern African Americans just as slaves had adapted biblical stories in spirituals. Hurston may have reenacted an oral and communal process as a solitary writer, but she gave an imaginative rendering of the cultural process all the same.

Dust Tracks on a Road

Type of work: Autobiography
First published: 1942

Dust Tracks on a Road was written when Hurston was about fifty years old. The book poignantly describes what it was like to grow up poor, black, and female; it shows an energetic woman who overcomes odds to achieve a liberated, rewarding life. Hurston was born in Eatonville, Florida, America's first incorporated black community. Her father was a driving force in the community; her mother died when she was nine. The liberating force for Hurston was her love of knowledge. While at the black grammar school, she won a reading contest, receiving books that ignited her imagination. In turn, she learned about real life at Joe Clarke's store, the meeting place of the men in town.

After her mother's death, she was moved from place to place. It was her own initiative that released her from her circumstances. When she learned that an actress in a traveling Gilbert and Sullivan troupe was looking for a lady's maid, she approached the woman with "I come to work for you." When her service ended—a service that had been a marvelous education in humanity and the arts—she went back to night school, then to Howard University and Barnard College.

At Barnard, working under anthropologist Franz Boas, she studied the folklore of her people in Polk County, Florida. This began a lifelong interest in the roots of her people. Yet some of Hurston's greatest friends and confidants were the upper-class whites she met both in school and after. Author Fannie Hurst, singer Ethel Waters, and critic Carl Van Vechten were among the many who encouraged her and introduced her to other writers of her times. Hurston at times bemoans her own people and their plight. She sees their disillusionment and oftentimes ill-suited efforts to break out of a stereotype. She lovingly describes the black race as not a race chosen by God but "a collection of people who overslept our time and got caught in the draft."

Hurston's descriptions of her own dedication and hard work inspire the reader to see what a poor African American woman could achieve with forwardness and luck. Her sensitive pictures of her race show people who have the power to overcome obstacles and succeed. Her generous view of humanity and lack of prejudice against anyone because of background or color give the reader a hopeful vision for the future in which love, hope, and hard work make the American Dream possible for anyone.

Seraph on the Suwanee

Type of work: Novel
First published: 1948

Seraph on the Suwanee, Hurston's last novel, marks another dramatic shift in her writing. With this novel, however, she did not create a new context for the representation of folk culture. Rather, she turned away from the effort to present black folklore. *Seraph on the Suwanee* is set in the rural South, but its central characters are white. Hurston apparently wanted to prove that she could write about whites as well as blacks, a desire that surfaced, no doubt, in response to the criticism and disinterest her work increasingly faced in the 1940's. Yet, even when writing of upwardly mobile southern "crackers," Hurston could not entirely leave her previous mission behind. Her white characters, perhaps unintentionally, often use the black folk idiom.

Although Hurston's novels, with the exception of the last, create contexts or develop other strategies for the presentation of folklore, they are not simply showcases for folk traditions; black folk culture defines the novels' themes. The most interesting of these thematic renderings appear in Hurston's first two novels. Hurston knew that black folk culture was composed of brilliant adaptations of African culture to American life. She admired the ingenuity of these adaptations but worried about their preservation. Would a sterile, materialistic white world ultimately absorb blacks, destroying the folk culture they had developed? Her first two novels demonstrate the disturbing influence of white America on black folkways.

Suggested Readings

Boyd, Valerie. *Wrapped in Rainbows: The Life of Zora Neale Hurston*. New York: Scribner, 2003.

Cronin, Gloria L., ed. *Critical Essays on Zora Neale Hurston*. New York: G. K. Hall, 1998.

Hemenway, Robert E. *Zora Neale Hurston: A Literary Biography*. Urbana: University of Illinois Press, 1977.

Hill, Lynda Marion. *Social Rituals and the Verbal Art of Zora Neale Hurston*. Washington, D.C.: Howard University Press, 1996.

Howard, Lillie P. *Zora Neale Hurston*. Boston: Twayne, 1980.

Hurston, Lucy Anne. *Speak, So You Can Speak Again: The Life of Zora Neale Hurston*. New York: Doubleday, 2004.

Hurston, Zora Neale. *Zora Neale Hurston: A Life in Letters*. New York: Doubleday, 2002.

Lyons, Mary E. *Sorrow's Kitchen: The Life and Folklore of Zora Neale Hurston*. New York: Charles Scribner's Sons, 1990.

Plant, Deborah G. *Zora Neale Hurston: A Biography of the Spirit*. Westport, Conn.: Praeger, 2007.

West, Margaret Genevieve. *Zora Neale Hurston and American Literary Culture*. Gainesville: University Press of Florida, 2005.

Witcover, Paul. *Zora Neale Hurston*. New York: Chelsea House, 1991.

Yanuzzi, Della. *Zora Neale Hurston: Southern Storyteller*. Springfield, N.J.: Enslow, 1996.

Contributors: Janine Rider, Warren J. Carson, and Deborah Kaplan

David Henry Hwang

Born: Los Angeles, California; August 11, 1957

Chinese American

Hwang is the first playwright to depict the identity, culture, and history of Chinese Americans in mainstream American theater.

Principal works

DRAMA: *F.O.B.*, pr. 1978, pb. 1983; *The Dance and the Railroad*, pr. 1981, pb. 1983; *Family Devotions*, pr. 1981, pb. 1983; *Broken Promises: Four Plays*, pb. 1983 (includes *F.O.B.*, *Family Devotions*, *The Dance and the Railroad*, and *The House of Sleeping Beauties*); *Sound and Beauty*, pr. 1983 (2 one-acts; *The House of Sleeping Beauties*, pb. 1983, and *The Sound of a Voice*, pb. 1984); *As the Crow Flies*, pr. 1986; *Rich Relations*, pr. 1986, pb. 1990; *Broken Promises*, pr. 1987 (includes *The Dance and the Railroad* and *The House of Sleeping Beauties*); *M. Butterfly*, pr., pb. 1988; *One Thousand Airplanes on the Roof*, pr. 1988, pb. 1989 (libretto; music by Philip Glass); *F.O.B., and Other Plays*, pb. 1990; *Bondage*, pr. 1992, pb. 1996 (one act); *The Voyage*, pr. 1992, pb. 2000 (libretto; music by Glass); *Face Value*, pr. 1993; *Golden Child*, pr. 1996, pb. 1998; *Trying to Find Chinatown*, pr., pb. 1996; *The Silver River*, pr. 1997 (music by Bright Sheng); *Peer Gynt*, pr. 1998 (adaptation of Henrik Ibsen's play); *Aida*, pr. 2000 (with Linda Wolverton and Robert Falls; music by Elton John; lyrics by Tim Rice; adaptation of Giuseppe Verdi's opera); *Flower Drum Song*, pr. 2001, pb. 2003 (adaptation of Richard Rodgers and Oscar Hammerstein's musical)

SCREENPLAYS: *M. Butterfly*, 1993 (adaptation of his play); *Golden Gate*, 1994; *Possession*, 2001 (with Neil LaBute and Laura Jones; adaptation of A. S. Byatt's novel)

TELEPLAYS: *My American Son*, 1987; *The Lost Empire*, 2001

David Henry Hwang (wang) is a second-generation Chinese American. From his earliest plays, Hwang has been concerned with the Chinese American experience. Hwang has identified three developmental phases in his early work. His "assimilationist" phase was motivated by the overwhelming desire to be accepted by white American culture. Hwang's first play, *F.O.B.*, exemplifies this first period. Dave, a Chinese American, reacts negatively to a "fresh-off-the-boat" Chinese, Steve, because Steve exhibits all the stereotypic mannerisms that Dave has tried to suppress his entire life.

In college, Hwang lived in an all-Asian dormitory and was caught up in an "isolationist-nationalist" phase. During this phase, Hwang was primarily concerned with writing for a Chinese American audience. This resulted in *The Dance and the Railroad*, which recaptures the history of the Chinese American railroad strike of 1867, and *Family Devotions*, which encourages Chinese Americans to reject negative Western perceptions and remember their Chinese heritage.

After the isolationist phase, Hwang next became interested in the love story. He adapted two classic Japanese love stories and wrote a play without identified Asian characters. Although not successful, this last experiment led directly to Hwang's masterpiece, *M. Butterfly*, in which a French diplomat carries on an affair with a Chinese actress for years, only to discover that "she" is really a man. Identity is explored as Hwang shows how the Frenchman Gallimard falls in love with an Asian stereotype. Gallimard commits suicide at the loss of his lover, a role-reversal of Giacomo Puccini's *Madama Butterfly* (1904). Wanting to advocate a broader forum against sexism and racism in literature, Hwang created *Bondage*, an allegory of love that challenges a variety of prejudices. *Bondage* takes place in a fantasy bondage parlor where domination is subverted when stereotypes are rejected by masked participants.

The historical and cultural identity of Chinese Americans is at the heart of Hwang's plays, which present a significant exploration of the evolving identity of Asians in a pluralistic society.

The Dance and the Railroad

TYPE OF WORK: Drama
FIRST PRODUCED: 1981, pb. 1983

The Dance and the Railroad is a history play based on the Chinese railroad workers' strike of 1867. It reveals a significant event in the Chinese American past, rejecting the stereotype of submissive coolies and depicting assertive men who demanded their rights in spite of great personal risk. Originally intended as a contribution toward the reclaiming of the Chinese American past, it accomplished much broader artistic goals.

Ma, a young Chinese emigrant who has been in America only four weeks, comes to warn Lone, a performer, that the other Chinese do not like his superior attitude. Hired to build the railroad across the Sierras, they are now in the fourth day of a strike against the labor practices of the "white devils." The Chinese have demanded an eight-hour workday and a fourteen-dollar-a-week increase in pay. Lone is estranged from the other Chinese because he refuses to waste time drinking and gambling and instead practices the traditional Chinese opera. Captivated by Lone's beautiful dance, Ma decides to become a performer when he returns to China a wealthy man. Lone scoffs at Ma's naïve beliefs that America is a place with a mythical Gold Mountain, that his cheating Chinese coworkers are his friends, and that he will ever be able to portray the great Gwan Gung, god of fighters. Lone tells Ma that if he is to succeed he must face reality and willingly accept being shunned by the "already dead" Chinese men. Undaunted by this challenge, Ma begins to practice

Chinese opera. Ma is subsequently shocked, however, to learn that if he works hard, he might successfully portray the Second Clown. Lone reveals how he spent eight years in opera school training to play Gwan Gung, only to be "kidnapped" by his parents and sent to the Sierras to work. Ma is determined and practices by spending the night in the "locust" position, a metaphor for the emigrant awakening. Lone returns, reporting that the strike is over. The Chinese have achieved their eight-hour day but only an eight-dollar-a-week raise. Ma finally realizes that, although a few Chinese men in America might achieve their dreams, most become dead to China. Ma and Lone improvise a Chinese opera revealing their voyages to America and experiences on the Gold Mountain. When the mountain fights back, Lone is exhilarated but Ma falls, his spirit broken. Now a realist, Ma returns to work with the "already dead" men, while Lone continues practicing for the Chinese opera.

Hwang contrasts two portraits of emigrant Chinese becoming Americans. Ma loses his innocence, discards his traditions, and joins the "already dead" laborers. Lone adapts Chinese mythology and tradition to his American experience. The Asian community has lauded Hwang's work, praising its depiction of the lives of Chinese Americans.

David Henry Hwang

Family Devotions

Type of work: Drama
First produced: 1981, pb. 1983

Family Devotions was written when Hwang was primarily interested in writing for and about the identity of Asian Americans. The play is autobiographical in that Hwang was raised an evangelical Christian; *Family Devotions* advocates casting off the Western mythology imposed upon Asian cultures.

The play is set in an idealized house with an enclosed patio and tennis court, representing a shallow, materialistic American Dream. The extended families of Ama and Popo, first-generation Chinese Americans, are awaiting the arrival of Di-Gou, their brother whom they have not seen for thirty years and who is arriving from Communist China. As they anticipate Di-Gou's arrival, the women discuss the atrocities of the Communists, whose evil rule they are certain Di-Gou will be grateful to escape. The family descended from the great Chinese Christian evangelist See-goh-poo, and, as a boy, Di-Gou witnessed her miracles, so Ama and Popo anticipate hearing Di-Gou repeat his fervent testimony. When he arrives, however, Di-Gou quietly disavows ever being Christian. Di-Gou confides to Popo's grandson, Chester, that to establish a true American identity, he must believe the stories "written on his face," and these stories reflect many generations.

In act 2 the sisters organize a family devotional and invite Di-Gou to witness for Christ, but a family squabble erupts. Di-Gou is left with the women, who physically force him to submit before their neon cross. They implore him to remember See-goh-poo's miracles. Chester rushes in to rescue Di-Gou, and the scene transforms into a kind of Chinese opera. Di-Gou rises up speaking in tongues, the gas grill bursts into flames, and Chester interprets the revelation: Di-Gou witnessed See-goh-poo give birth out of wedlock, claiming evangelicalism to deceive her family. Di-Gou proclaims that because they now know the truth, their stories are meaningless. The old sisters collapse, dead, and Di-Gou realizes that "no one leaves America." The play ends with Chester standing where Di-Gou first stood, and the "shape of his face begins to change," a metaphor for the beginning acceptance of his Chinese heritage.

Family Devotions is an allegory depicting a cultural awakening of the individual. The world is reversed; "civilized" Christians behave as heathens, and the "heathen" Asian offers wisdom, solace, and love. Hwang calls for Asian Americans to embrace their Asian heritage.

M. Butterfly

Type of work: Drama
First produced: 1988, pb. 1988

M. Butterfly is Hwang's fictionalized account of a real French diplomat who carried on an affair with a Chinese opera singer for twenty years, only to discover she was actually a man. Hwang's compelling drama examines themes of sexual and racial stereotyping, Western imperialism, the role illusion plays in perceptions, and the ability of one person truly to know another.

M. Butterfly contrasts Rene Gallimard with Pinkerton in Giacomo Puccini's *Madama Butterfly* (produced, 1904; published, 1935). Gallimard sees himself as awkward, clumsy at love, but somehow blessed with the utter devotion of Song Liling, a beautiful Oriental woman. Hwang uses the word "Oriental" to convey an exotic, imperialistic view of the East. Gallimard becomes so absorbed with his sexist perception of Asian women that it distorts his thinking. He tests Liling's devotion by neglecting and humiliating her, ultimately forcing her to admit she is his "Butterfly," a character she has publicly denounced.

Unknown to Gallimard, Liling is a Communist agent, manipulating him to extract information about the Vietnam War. At the embassy Gallimard finds increased status because of his Oriental affair. When his analysis of East-West relations, based entirely on his self-delusions, prove wrong, Gallimard is demoted and returned to France. His usefulness spent, Liling is forced to endure hard labor, an official embarrassment because "there are no homosexuals in China." Eventually, the Communists send Liling to France to reestablish his affair with Gallimard. When Gallimard is caught and tried for espionage, it is publicly revealed that Liling is a man. Liling now changes to men's clothing, effecting a complete role-reversal between Liling and Gallimard. Liling becomes the dominant masculine figure while Gallimard becomes the submissive feminine figure. Preferring fantasy to reality, Gallimard becomes "Butterfly," donning Liling's wig and kimono, choosing an honorable death over a dishonorable life.

M. Butterfly demonstrates the dangers inherent in living a life satisfied with shallow stereotypes and misconceptions. Gallimard's singular desire for a submissive Oriental woman was fulfilled only in his mind. It blinded him to every truth about his mistress, refusing even to accept the truth about Liling until he stood naked before him. It first cost him his career, then his wife, then his dignity, then his lover, and finally his life. Even when he is confronted by the truth, Gallimard can only respond that he has "known, and been loved by, the perfect woman."

Bondage

Type of work: Drama
First produced: 1992, pb. 1996

Bondage, a one-act play set in a fantasy bondage parlor, is an exploration of racial, cultural, and sexual stereotypes. It is presented as an allegory depicting their overwhelming influence in society and offering one alternative for society's progressing beyond them. The play demonstrates Chinese American playwright Hwang's development beyond exclusively Asian American themes to encompass the destructiveness of all stereotyping, be it racial, cultural, or sexual.

Mark, identifiable only as a male, is the client of dominatrix Terri, identifiable only as a female, in a fantasy bondage parlor. Both characters' identities are fully disguised. They are merely a man and a woman who assume the characteristics required for whatever fantasy is suggested. During this encounter, however, both Mark and Terri refuse to accept the stereotypes associated with their fantasy roles.

Terri informs Mark that today he will be a Chinese man and she will be a blond woman. She immediately characterizes Mark as a horn-rimmed-glasses-wearing engineer afraid of her because she is popular with cowboys and jocks. Mark rejects her Asian stereotypes and, in turn, uses blond stereotypes to describe her. A personal confrontation ensues because Mark will not accept her ridicule.

This leads to male-female stereotyping, and on to progressive levels of racial stereotyping. As they are unable to resolve this confrontation, they move on to become a white man and a black woman, with underlying stereotyped images of the white liberal. Terri charges that he may try to "play" all races, but she has already "become" all races. Next they assume the roles of a Chinese American man and an Asian American woman, exploring intercultural stereotypes. Finally they explore Mark's need for penitence as a stereotypical businessman, which drives him to the bondage parlor to be dominated and humiliated in a fantasy world as he dominates and humiliates in the real one. The plight of both men and women, and the roles society forces upon them, dominate the final confrontation. Her resistance having been worn down by Mark's arguing, Terri begins to remove her disguise. She offers Mark his moment of victory, but instead he, too, removes his mask. When he confesses his real love for Terri, she reveals herself—they are as the original fantasy, an Asian man and a blond woman. Their confrontation has put the stereotypes of their disparate groups behind them. They see each other as individuals and are ready to move beyond their fantasies.

Hwang's optimism that society can move beyond oppressing societal stereotypes pervades *Bondage*. He presents a balanced attack on all stereotyping, showing that regardless of cultural, political, or sexual identity, society will only move forward when all stereotypes are destroyed and people are regarded as individuals.

Suggested Readings

Chen, Tina. "Betrayed into Motion: The Seduction of Narrative Desire in *M. Butterfly*." *Hitting Critical Mass: A Journal of Asian American Cultural Criticism* 1, no. 2 (Spring, 1994): 129-154.

Hwang, David Henry. "The Demon in David Henry Hwang." Interview by Misha Berson. *American Theatre* 15, no. 4 (April, 1998): 14-18.

_______. "*M. Butterfly*: An Interview with David Henry Hwang." Interview by John Lewis DiGaetani. *The Drama Review: A Journal of Performance Studies* 33, no. 3 (Fall, 1989): 141-153.

Kondo, Dorinne K. *About Face*. New York: Routledge, 1997.

Moy, James S. *Marginal Sights: Staging the Chinese in America*. Iowa City: University of Iowa Press, 1993.

Shin, Andrew. "Projected Bodies in David Henry Hwang's *M. Butterfly* and *Golden Child*." *MELUS* 27, no. 1 (Spring, 2002): 177-197.

Shinakawa, Karen. "Who's to Say? Or, Making Space for Gender and Ethnicity in *M. Butterfly*." *Theatre Journal* 45 (October, 1993): 349-362.

Skloot, Robert. "Breaking the Butterfly: The Politics of David Henry Hwang." *Modern Drama* 33, no. 1 (March, 1990): 59-66.

Street, Douglas. *David Henry Hwang*. Boise, Idaho: Boise State University Press, 1989.

Weinraub, Bernard. "Fleshing Out Chinatown Stereotypes." *New York Times*, October 14, 2000, section 2, pp. 7, 27.

Contributor: Gerald S. Argetsinger

Gish Jen

Born: Yonkers, New York; 1956

Chinese American

Drawing on the tension between the two cultural poles, Jen reflects on the lives of Asian Americans and "typical Americans."

Principal works

LONG FICTION: *Typical American*, 1991; *Mona in the Promised Land*, 1996; *The Love Wife*, 2004

SHORT FICTION: "In the American Society," 1987 (in *The New Generation: Fiction for Our Time from America's Writing Programs*; Alan Kaufman, editor); "The Water-Faucet Vision," 1988 (in *Best American Short Stories, 1988*); "The White Umbrella," 1990 (in *Home to Stay: Asian American Women's Fiction*; Sylvia Watanabe and Carol Bruchac, editors); *Who's Irish: Stories*, 1999

Gish Jen emerged as a promising new writer in the early 1990's, when her stories and articles began appearing in such prominent publications as *The New Yorker*, *The Atlantic Monthly*, *The New York Times*, and the *Boston Globe*. Jen is a second-generation Asian American who grew up in Scarsdale, New York, a privileged suburb of New York City. She was educated at Harvard University, Stanford's School of Business, and later the University of Iowa's prestigious Writers' Workshop. Since completing her education, she has worked in the publishing industry and has been the writer-in-residence at Yale University and Williams College.

Her first works, written while she was studying at Iowa, were published under her given name, Lillian. Friends recommended that she change her first name to "Gish," the nickname that she had gone by ever since her school classmates christened her after the famous silent film star, Lillian Gish. Jen has stated in interviews that she likes the double accented syllables of "Gish Jen," with its ambiguous gender identity. All of her later work has been published under that name.

Jen's concern over taxonomy is evident in her work, where verbal games and idiom play an important role. One of her distinguishing features as a writer is her acute ear for the way in which people speak. She has a gift for capturing the syntax of nonnative speakers of English in a way that illuminates not only their intended meaning but also the inadequacies of trying to pour the meaning of one language into another. A consistent theme running throughout the body of Jen's work is the way cultures interact and overlap. The tensions she chronicles are carried out at the mythic level, specifically in the way the expectations and legends about the

United States differ from those of Jen's Asian forebears.

Many critics have pointed out that Jen's perspective is inevitably that of an outsider: as a daughter of privilege, with an Ivy League education, looking at the East, and as an Asian American woman viewing American society with a cool distance denied a writer who is unalloyed with any other society. The magic of Jen's work is the ease with which she can move between the two cultures she inhabits. Jen joins a growing list of Asian American women writers, such as Maxine Hong Kingston and Amy Tan, who in the late twentieth century have found a voice. These writers have added the richness of their insights and poetry into a literary and cultural tradition where they had not previously been heard.

Gish Jen (J. D. Sloan)

Typical American

Type of work: Novel
First published: 1992

Jen's reputation was established with *Typical American*. The novel developed from her short story "In the American Society," in which the problems of the Chang family were first presented. In *Typical American* Jen returns to the Chang family to explicate the themes that the story introduced. Jen also interpolated the text of her story "The Water-Faucet Vision" into the book. The novel follows a young Chinese man, Ralph Chang, who comes to the United States to do graduate work in engineering. The novel dramatizes the cultural differences that Ralph Chang, his wife Helen, and his sister Theresa encounter. Ralph's expectations about America collide with the realities of academic politics, leaking roofs, and the superficiality of American culture. The family learns to navigate through this new and threatening society by distancing themselves from it. They use derogatory expressions, such as "typical American," to convey their sense of the shallowness and commerciality of American life. China is still very much part of the Changs' inner lives, a touchstone of comparison for all that they now find threatening. China for them represents all that is unsullied and the purity of the inner self. Much of the novel's satiric fire derives from this tension between the two cultural poles. By the end of the novel, Jen achieves a truly comic resolution, when her characters realize that they, too, have become "typical Americans." The reader is left with the sense that the Changs' inner Chinas are just as illusory as their initial impressions of America had been.

Questioned about her use of a male protagonist in *Typical American*, Jen says that she was trying to "figure out what reality was like for her parents." Jen's position as a second-generation American, aware of both her parents' culture and the one in which she grew up, allows her the comic scope for drawing a sharp satiric portrait. Ralph Chang's America proves not to be the one for which the young engineer hopes, but a more practical, drearier reality in which he manages a pancake restaurant.

Mona in the Promised Land

Type of work: Novel
First published: 1996

Mona in the Promised Land continues the story of the Changs, this time focusing on their teenage daughter Mona. The story takes place in the 1970's, and Mona has repudiated her Chinese identity by assimilating into the Jewish culture of the upscale New York suburb where the family has moved. After increasing incomprehension between the generations as the elder Changs try to understand what has happened to their daughter, Jen finishes with a comic paean to multiculturalism as Mona marries, is reconciled with her parents, and considers having her Jewish husband change his name to Changowitz.

Mona in the Promised Land has a jacket cover showing a bagel superimposed on a bowl of noodles in a familiar blue-and-white Chinese design. Peering through the hole in the bagel is a face, presumably representing Mona Chang, the young protagonist. The image perfectly captures the crossover of ethnic identities to be explored in this humorous novel. Faced with all the usual uncertainties of adolescents, Mona feels further singled out in the family's new upscale neighborhood of Scarshill in New York as the daughter of Chinese immigrant parents. Her parents have some traditionally strict notions of how a good Chinese girl should behave, with her older sister Callie already setting the pattern for stereotypical model minority success by getting into Harvard.

Yet Jen has set the novel in the 1960's, a time of adolescent behavior on a massive social scale, when pushing boundaries, testing limits, breaking patterns, in both extremely positive and negative ways, seem natural. So, at first, Mona gets along well with her mainly Jewish classmates as the only Asian student in her eighth-grade class. By tenth grade, Mona and her best friend Barbara Gugelstein have spent so much time at events for Jewish youth that Mona persuades a liberal rabbi to tutor her in Judaism, a religion she feels is right for her because its axiom is to "ask, ask, ask," not "obey, obey, obey." This is but one of a few other boundaries she pushes as she grows into adulthood.

The natural rebelliousness of many adolescents, the social idealism of the 1960's and 1970's, the questioning religion of a people known for centuries of displacement from their promised land—Jen weaves these different forces into a comic pattern seemingly effortlessly. At the core of all these movements lies a search for identity, for one's place in the world. The Chang family members encompass the options for ethnic identity: the immigrant parents will always be Chinese; the college-educated Callie learns to be Asian American; the free-spirited Mona chooses to join another ethnic group altogether.

Exhibiting the same creative use of language that she did in her first novel, *Typical American*, Jen sustains a lighthearted tone through the youthful romps while touching upon some profound and perplexing issues.

The Love Wife

Type of work: Novel
First published: 2004

Jen's third novel, *The Love Wife*, is narrated by a melange of voices which, together and separately, chronicle the story of the Wong family. As a graduate student in the Midwest, tender-hearted Carnegie Wong impulsively adopts Lizzy, an Asian foundling. Then he meets and marries Janie Bailey, whom his mother promptly renames Blondie (with all the negative connotations intact). Before the rehearsal dinner Mama Wong, who longs for a genuine Chinese daughter-in-law, offers each a million dollars not to marry. Predictable generational and ethnic conflicts ensue, but the redoubtable Mama Wong, who once swam from Mainland China to Taiwan with a basketball under each arm, never gives up, even after she develops Alzheimer's disease and is institutionalized.

Further complications arise. Fourteen years later, the Wongs have two adopted daughters, rebellious Lizzy and the younger, more empathetic Wendy, as well as their unexpected biological son Bailey, blond and blue-eyed like his mother. Mama Wong strikes from the grave when Lan, a distant relative from Communist China, is summoned to be the children's nanny. Blondie fears that Lan is the secondary "love wife" that Carnegie always should have had and begins to feel very much an outsider in this family.

Misinformation and misunderstandings abound. The difficulties inherent in an interracial marriage are viewed through both Blondie and Carnegie, two people still in love, while a great gulf emerges between Lan and her American family. Even as Lan feels she is being treated like a servant, Carnegie finds himself surprisingly attracted to her. Author Jen has the rare ability to intuit all sides of a highly emotional issue and render them sympathetically and with humor through the eyes of her characters.

Suggested Readings

"About Gish Jen." *Ploughshares* 26, no. 2/3 (2000): 217-222.

Gonzalez, Begona Simal. "The (Re)Birth of Mona Changowitz: Rituals and Ceremonies of Cultural Conversion and Self-Making in *Mona in the Promised Land*." *MELUS* 26, no. 2 (2001): 225-242.

Jen, Gish. "The Intimate Outsider." Interview by Marilyn B. Snell. *New Perspectives Quarterly* 8, no. 3 (1991): 56-60.

_______. "*MELUS* Interview: Gish Jen." Interview by Yoko Matsukawa. *MELUS* 18 (Winter, 1993): 111-120.

Samarth, Manini. "Affirmations: Speaking the Self into Being." *Parnassus* 17, no. 1 (1991): 88-102.

Storace, Patricia. "Seeing Double." *The New York Review of Books* 38 (August 15, 1991): 9-12.

Contributor: James Barbour

Ruth Prawer Jhabvala

Born: Cologne, Germany; May 7, 1927

Jewish

Throughout her work, Jhabvala addresses the problem of alienation and the conflicts of individuals who are geographically and spiritually adrift.

Principal works

LONG FICTION: *To Whom She Will*, 1955 (pb. in U.S. as *Amrita*, 1956); *The Nature of Passion*, 1956; *Esmond in India*, 1958; *The Householder*, 1960; *Get Ready for Battle*, 1962; *A Backward Place*, 1965; *A New Dominion*, 1972 (pb. in U.S. as *Travelers*, 1973); *Heat and Dust*, 1975; *In Search of Love and Beauty*, 1983; *Three Continents*, 1987; *Poet and Dancer*, 1993; *Shards of Memory*, 1995; *My Nine Lives: Chapters of a Possible Past*, 2004

SCREENPLAYS: *The Householder*, 1963; *Shakespeare Wallah*, 1965 (with James Ivory); *The Guru*, 1968; *Bombay Talkie*, 1970; *Autobiography of a Princess*, 1975 (with Ivory and John Swope); *Roseland*, 1977; *Hullabaloo over Georgie and Bonnie's Pictures*, 1978; *The Europeans*, 1979 (with Ivory); *Quartet*, 1981 (with Ivory); *The Courtesans of Bombay*, 1982; *Heat and Dust*, 1983 (based on her novel); *The Bostonians*, 1984 (with Ivory; based on Henry James's novel); *A Room with a View*, 1986 (based on E. M. Forster's novel); *Maurice*, 1987 (based on Forster's novel); *Madame Sousatzka*, 1988 (with John Schlesinger); *Mr. and Mrs. Bridge*, 1990 (based on Evan S. Connell, Jr.'s novels); *Howards End*, 1992 (based on Forster's novel); *The Remains of the Day*, 1993 (based on Kazuo Ishiguro's novel); *Jefferson in Paris*, 1995; *Surviving Picasso*, 1996; *A Soldier's Daughter Never Cries*, 1998 (based on Kaylie Jones's novel); *The Golden Bowl*, 2000 (based on James's novel); *Le Divorce*, 2003 (with Ivory; based on Diane Johnson's novel)

SHORT FICTION: *Like Birds, Like Fishes, and Other Stories*, 1963; *A Stronger Climate: Nine Stories*, 1968; *An Experience of India*, 1971; *How I Became a Holy Mother, and Other Stories*, 1976; *Out of India: Selected Stories*, 1986; *East into Upper East: Plain Tales from New York and New Delhi*, 1998

TELEPLAYS: *The Place of Peace*, 1975; *Jane Austen in Manhattan*, 1980; *The Wandering Company*, 1985

The novelist and screenwriter Ruth Prawer Jhabvala (jahb-VAH-lah) was the daughter of culturally assimilated German-Jewish parents who were forced to flee to England in 1939, when Ruth Prawer was twelve years old. She became a

British subject in 1948 and married C. S. H. Jhabvala, a Parsi architect, in 1951. The couple moved to Delhi, India, where they reared three daughters and Jhabvala became a full-time writer.

In "Myself in India," the introduction to *Out of India: Selected Stories*, Jhabvala declares that, despite having spent most of her adult life in India and having an Indian family, she remained European. Her early works, set in India, reflect the detached, ironic viewpoint of an alien. After Jhabvala's first novel, *To Whom She Will*, critics designated her the Jane Austen of middle-class Delhi urban society; categorized as comedy of manners, her work was praised for its wit and accuracy of observation. The five novels and three volumes of short stories she wrote during the next fifteen years maintained a similar tone, though it darkened considerably as the self-deceptions of her characters deepened. In the 1960's Jhabvala entered artistic partnership with the newly founded film production team of Ismael Merchant and James Ivory and started writing screenplays and adapting the works of others, among them Henry James's *The Bostonians* and E. M. Forster's *A Room with a View* and *Howards End*; this new genre, in turn, influenced the style and structure of her novels. Thus, when *A New Dominion* appeared in 1972, critics noticed resemblances not to the work of Austen but to that of Forster.

Heat and Dust, which followed three years later and is even more complex and experimental, juxtaposes two stories, that of a colonial wife who left her husband for an Indian prince in the 1920's and that of her step-granddaughter, who fifty years later, goes to India to solve an old riddle and herself becomes captivated by the land. Often designated Jhabvala's masterpiece, *Heat and Dust* won the prestigious Booker Prize.

In 1974 Jhabvala moved to New York City; from then on she returned to Delhi only for three months each year. In the novels written since her move to the United States, the international theme expanded. *In Search of Love and Beauty*, for example, examines the lives of a group of German-Jewish refugees to America over a forty-year period. *Three Continents*, based loosely on the exploits of an Asian serial killer, tracks relationships between an American family and visiting Indians and Eurasians; the setting shifts from the United States to England and finally to India. Jhabvala continued to collaborate with Merchant and Ivory on films that include *The Remains of the Day*, which was an overwhelming critical success, and the less successful *Jefferson in Paris*. Jhabvala has won numerous awards,

Ruth Prawer Jhabvala (© Jerry Bauer)

most of them for her screenwriting; *Room with a View* and *Howards End* both won Academy Awards for best screenplay adaptation.

Throughout her writings Jhabvala has remained preoccupied with the problem of alienation and the conflicts of individuals who are geographically and spiritually adrift. Even when the locale changes, the themes remain the same. In *To Whom She Will*, for example, two lovers are separated by the fact that one is an anglicized Hindu, the other a Punjabi Hindu. *Heat and Dust* features parallel stories of love and betrayal, each involving a Western woman and an Indian man; the young narrator, a British woman, feels more distant from her Western hippie lover than from the Indian man by whom she conceives a child. In the American novels the theme of alienation becomes even more complex. The members of the immigrant family in *In Search of Love and Beauty* are strangers in New York; the family members in *Three Continents*, on the other hand, are entrenched in Connecticut yet choose to become aliens in India because they hope to find a spiritual reality there. *Poet and Dancer* explores the dangerous closeness between two cousins, Angel and Lara. *Shards of Memory*, placed in Manhattan, traces the history of a family of mixed Indians, British, and Americans who follow a charismatic religious leader called only "The Master" over four generations.

Although her writing is rarely autobiographical, it is always generated by the powerful perceptions of a woman born in Germany, reared in England, matrimonially bound to India, and now artistically active in New York City. It is impossible to thrust Jhabvala into any national or ethnic literary category, and few novelists since Henry James have so powerfully explored the international theme.

Poet and Dancer

Type of work: Novel
First published: 1993

Poet and Dancer opens with a prefatory account of how Helena Manarr entices an unnamed professional writer into reconstructing the elusive story of her dead beloved daughter Angel. Angel is the poet of the title, though her collected works amount to a few scrawled pages of literary juvenilia. Lara is its dancer, though she is too capricious to make a career of anything but destruction. Jhabvala's novel imagines the collision of stasis with motion, of selflessness with self-absorption, of poet with dancer.

In her early twenties, Lara seduces Angel's feckless father Peter, a business executive who, like several other characters, learns "how difficult it was to deny Lara anything she momentarily desired." He installs her in an apartment and convinces Angel to keep her company. Abandoning Helena, Angel submerges her identity in her willful cousin's and serves the other's increasingly irrational whims. Lara's bizarre shopping sprees and sexual escapades convince her psychotherapist father that she needs professional help. Angel's own dementia is apparent in her belief that she can save Lara by obliterating herself.

"She wasn't mad," demurs Roland, one of many whom Lara attracts and discards. "Just bad. . . . There are good people trying to do all right, and there are bad ones that pull them down and win." *Poet and Dancer* is a morality play that tests the respective strengths of evil and love.

Lara is a femme fatale powerless to restrain her own ruinous power. When extrovert Lara links up with introvert Angel, it is a fundamental fusion of elemental forces, and the result is explosive. Years later, the novel's self-effacing narrator is still contending with the fallout.

Suggested Readings

Agarwal, Ramlal G. *Ruth Prawer Jhbavala: A Study of Her Fiction*. New York: Envoy Press, 1990.

Booker, Keith M. *Colonial Texts: India in the Modern British Novel*. Ann Arbor: University of Michigan Press, 1997.

Chakravarti, Aruna. *Ruth Prawer Jhabvala: A Study in Empathy and Exile*. Delhi: B. R. Publishing, 1998.

Crane, Ralph J. *Ruth Prawer Jhabvala*. Twayne's English Authors Series 494. New York: Twayne, 1992.

Gooneratne, Yasmine. *Silence, Exile, and Cunning: The Fiction of Ruth Prawer Jhabvala*. New Delhi: Orient Longman, 1983.

Sucher, Laurie. *The Fiction of Ruth Prawer Jhabvala: The Politics of Passion*. New York: St. Martin's Press, 1989.

Contributors: Rosemary M. Canfield Reisman and Allene Phy-Olsen

Ha Jin
(Xuefei Jin)

Born: Jinzhou, Liaoning, China; February 21, 1956

Chinese American

Ha Jin presents a complex view of the ambivalences and hypocrisies that flourish in China's intensely nationalistic culture.

Principal works

LONG FICTION: *In the Pond*, 1998; *Waiting*, 1999; *The Crazed*, 2002; *War Trash*, 2004; *A Free Life*, 2007

POETRY: *Between Silences: A Voice from China*, 1990; *Facing Shadows*, 1996; *Wreckage*, 2001

SHORT FICTION: *Ocean of Words: Army Stories*, 1996; *Under the Red Flag*, 1997; *The Bridegroom*, 2000; *Quiet Desperation*, 2000

Born in Jinzhou, Liaoning Province, in northeastern China in 1956, Ha Jin—a pen name that Xuefei Jin adopted for easier pronunciation—was the first Chinese-born American writer to win both the National Book Award and the PEN/Hemingway Award. However, Jin became an English-language writer almost by happenstance. His father was an army officer. Therefore, when facing the choices between going to work in the countryside and joining the People's Liberation Army at age fourteen, he choose the latter, patrolling the border between Northern China and the Soviet Union for six years. After leaving the army, he worked as a railroad telegrapher in Harbin, the capital of Helongjian Province from 1975 to 1977 and taught himself English by listening to the radio. In 1988, he went to Helongjiang University, also in Harbin, a city he loved so much that he used the first character of it, Ha, in his pen name. He graduated with a B.A. degree in English in 1982. Then he moved with his father, who had just retired from the army, to their home province of Shangdong.

Two years later, Jin received his M.A. in American literature from Shandong University; there he was taught by visiting American Fulbright scholars and was exposed for the first time to the National Book Award-winning novels of William Faulkner and Flannery O'Connor. While Jin enjoyed reading these works, he never imagined he would one day follow in their authors' footsteps. He wanted to be a scholar and a translator.

Shortly after his marriage to a young mathematician, Lisha Bian, Jin was given the opportunity to pursue a scholarship overseas. In 1985 he went to the United

States to begin doctoral work on modern American poetry at Brandeis University in Waltham, Massachusetts. His wife joined him in the United States in 1987. He had planned to return to China after four years, but because of the shootings during the political protests in Beijing's Tiananmen Square in 1989, he decided to stay in the United States. It was difficult for him to find a job in academia. By then he had published a book of poems in English, *Between Silences*, so he thought if he continued to publish some books in English he might find a job teaching creative writing.

Although Jin was determined to write, he had only completed several unpublished short stories back in China. To him, choosing to write in English meant much labor and some despair. When he applied to the creative writing program at Boston University in 1991, Leslie Epstein, the program director, could not accept him because his English was not quite fluent. Epstein was impressed, however, by Jin's determination to write and allowed him to audit the courses. As a result, all the short stories in *Ocean of Words* were written during that audit year. When Jin reapplied to the program a year later, he was accepted as a full-time student.

In 1992, Jin received his Ph.D. degree from Brandeis. One year later he was accepted by Emory University as an assistant professor of creative writing. In the following years, he published two collections of short fiction: *Ocean of Words*, which received the PEN/Hemingway Award, and *Under the Red Flag*, which won the Flannery O'Connor Award. Jin's novel *In the Pond* was selected as a best fiction book of 1998 by the *Chicago Tribune*, and *Waiting*, a finalist for the *Los Angeles Times* Book Award for fiction, won the National Book Award for fiction in 1999 as well as the PEN/Faulkner Award (2000). His short stories have been included in the anthologies *The Best American Short Stories* (1997 and 1999), three Pushcart Prize anthologies, and *The Norton Introduction to Fiction* and *The Norton Introduction to Literature*, among others. He also became the Young J. Allen Professor of English and Creative Writing at Emory.

While American literary circles praised his effort to transform the figures, statements, ideas, and plans found in history books about China into universally accessible images of struggle, thus presenting a complex view of the ambivalences and hypocrisies that flourish in an intensely nationalistic culture, Ha Jin's works have, to date, received little attention in China.

Under the Red Flag

Type of work: Short fiction
First published: 1997

The twelve short stories collected in *Under the Red Flag*, which won Jin the Flannery O'Connor Award for Short Fiction in 1997, provide the reader with extraordinary insight into the living conditions and mentality of the people of rural Northeast China. This is the area where Jin grew up during the brutal times of the Cultural Revolution, when the Communists tried to disrupt traditional society, often replacing ancient customs of repression with a savagery of their own.

Ha Jin (Kalman Zabarsky)

Jin's stories show people living without privacy. In addition to private jealousies and gossip, they are beset by Communists who often misuse their power to further private acts of vengeance or aggression. "In Broad Daylight" shows the public humiliation and near-lynching of a sexually frustrated woman turned occasional prostitute. Because she beat one of the juvenile Red Guards for failing to pay her, his comrades descend upon her under the mantle of party authority, leading her husband to kill himself out of shame.

While living conditions are often grim and many characters outrightly selfish, *Under the Red Flag* also shows the common people's will to endure and survive. The young boys of the stories have to cope with vicious neighborhood bullies or even their own jealous fathers, yet most of them survive with their spirits intact.

Jin also reveals the random nature of life under Communist repression. In "Again, the Spring Breeze Blew," the young widow Lanlan becomes a hero after the rapist she killed turns out to be an escaped criminal instead of the nephew of a party official.

Overall, *Under the Red Flag* is a thoroughly enjoyable and fascinating collection which takes the American reader on an insider's tour of a harsh place. When Jin left Communist China after the Tiananmen Square massacre in 1989, his craft as a skillful writer quickly earned him the 1997 PEN/Hemingway Award for fiction, and *Under the Red Flag* continues this fine tradition.

In the Pond

Type of work: Novel
First published: 1998

In the Pond, Jin's first novel, has the same appeal as his short stories: His work is crisp, unnerving, dramatic, and dominated by full characters. This is an episodic novel in which the central character, Shao Bin, suffers through humiliation after humiliation in his quest for what he sees as justice.

The novel opens with Shao Bin's name being left off the list of workers at the fertilizer plant who will be given a larger apartment. He feels he has been treated unfairly and that others have been rewarded for political reasons. He responds with his art: Despite his position as a fitter in the plant, he is an accomplished artist, and so he draws a cartoon that lampoons his two supervisors (and archenemies in the novel), secretary Liu and Director Ma.

Liu and Ma respond with a pay cut, and Bin creates another art piece that attacks their greed and their anti-revolutionary tendencies. Bin never backs down from the threats launched his way, and occasionally, with his wife's prodding, he continues to look for justice at the commune level, then with the county hierarchy, and finally in Beijing. Because his case becomes so famous, his supervisors are unable to have him beaten up or simply to fire him. He is finally given a promotion by Liu and Ma's boss, where he will write and draw propaganda pieces for the party. Meanwhile, his wife is still yearning for something larger than the single room she must share with her husband and their young girl.

This is not a novel in which characters are fighting—à la Tiananmen Square—for an end to Communist rule or greater liberalization. The power of the novel comes from the quixotic attempt of the common worker with the uncommon talent and faith in art to find a suitable outlet for his talents. Jin has succeeded admirably in creating a fast-moving, very readable account of one imperfect man's search for some version of domestic and artistic happiness.

Suggested Readings

Basney, Lionel. "Keeping Company." *The Georgia Review* 50 (Fall, 1996): 601-608.

Garner, Dwight. "Ha Jin's Cultural Revolution." *The New York Times Magazine*, February 6, 2000, pp. 38, 40-41.

Gilbert, Roger. Review of *Between Silences*, by Ha Jin. *Partisan Review* 61 (Winter, 1994): 180-186.

"Ha Jin." *Writer* 114, no. 1 (January, 2001): 66.

Twitchell-Waas, Jeffrey. Review of *Wreckage*, by Ha Jin. *World Literature Today: A Literary Quarterly of the University of Oklahoma* 76, no. 1 (Winter, 2002): 109-110.

Zhang, Hang. "Bilingual Creativity in Chinese English: Ha Jin's *In the Pond*." *World Englishes* 21, no. 2 (July, 2002): 305-315.

Contributor: Guoqing Li

Charles Johnson

Born: Evanston, Illinois; April 23, 1948

African American

Johnson's philosophical fiction continues an African American literary tradition.

Principal works

LONG FICTION: *Faith and the Good Thing*, 1974; *Oxherding Tale*, 1982; *Middle Passage*, 1990; *Dreamer*, 1998

SHORT FICTION: *The Sorcerer's Apprentice*, 1986; *Soulcatcher, and Other Stories: Twelve Powerful Tales About Slavery*, 2001; *Dr. King's Refrigerator, and Other Bedtime Stories*, 2005

TELEPLAYS: *Charlie Smith and the Fritter Tree*, 1978; *Booker*, 1984; *The Green Belt*, 1996

NONFICTION: *Black Humor*, 1970 (cartoons and drawings); *Half-Past Nation Time*, 1972 (cartoons and drawings); *Being and Race: Black Writing Since 1970*, 1988; *Africans in America: America's Journey Through Slavery*, 1998 (with Patricia Smith); *I Call Myself an Artist: Writings By and About Charles Johnson*, 1999 (Rudolph P. Byrd, editor); *King: The Photobiography of Martin Luther King, Jr.*, 2000 (photographs by Bob Adelman); *Turning the Wheel: Essays on Buddhism and Writing*, 2003; *Passing the Three Gates: Interviews with Charles Johnson*, 2004 (Jim McWilliams, editor)

EDITED TEXT: *Black Men Speaking*, 1997 (with John McCluskey, Jr.)

Reared in a tight-knit midwestern black community, Charles Johnson remembers his childhood environment as loving and secure. An only child, he often read to fill up his time. Johnson especially loved comic books and spent hours practicing drawing in hopes of becoming a professional cartoonist. To this end he took a two-year correspondence course and was publishing cartoons and illustrations by the time he completed high school.

At the last minute, Johnson decided to attend Southern Illinois University rather than art school. There he became passionately drawn to the study of philosophy and to writing. During his first summer vacation he began to pursue another lifelong interest, the martial arts. Before his undergraduate college days were over he had published a book of his own cartoons, *Black Humor* (1970), had hosted a television series on drawing, and had worked as a reporter for the *Chicago Tribune*. In 1970, he married Joan New, whom he had met two years earlier.

After graduation, Johnson began working as a reporter for the *Illinoisan*; how-

Charles Johnson (Courtesy, Canongate Books)

ever, he had already decided to become a novelist. Over the next two years, with John Gardner as his mentor, he wrote six "apprentice novels." Finally, in 1974, he published *Faith and the Good Thing*, which he had extensively researched while completing his master's degree in philosophy and writing a thesis on Marxism.

Johnson continued his studies in philosophy at the State University of New York at Stony Brook, this time concentrating on phenomenology. *Oxherding Tale* is a work he intended, he wrote, to be a reply to German novelist Hermann Hesse's *Siddartha* (1922; English translation, 1951). Johnson fashioned *Oxherding* into a "neo-slave narrative for the second half of the twentieth century." A melding of Eastern thought, the American slave experience, and a sharp, witty twentieth century consciousness, *Oxherding Tale* traces the misadventures of Andrew Hawkins, a privileged slave given the finest education because of his status as the child of the plantation's black butler and his white mistress. Eventually, Andrew leaves home and begins to experience a variety of identities and to test various philosophical stances toward life. His tale culminates with his marriage, his reconciliation with his past, and his final encounter with Soulcatcher, the fugitive slave hunter long on his trail.

By the time *Oxherding Tale* was published, Johnson had accepted an invitation to teach creative writing at the University of Washington. There, he continued to write; in addition to numerous essays, book reviews, and works for television, his credits include a collection of short stories, *The Sorcerer's Apprentice*, *Being and Race: Black Writing Since 1970*, and his most acclaimed success, *Middle Passage*, winner of the National Book Award. Another neo-slave narrative in the style of *Oxherding Tale*, *Middle Passage* continues Johnson's quest to produce entertaining yet seriously philosophical black literature. Johnson also continues his commitment to the martial arts and to Eastern philosophy, especially Buddhism.

Faith and the Good Thing

Type of work: Novel
First published: 1974

Written from the fall of 1972 to the early summer of 1973 under the tutelage of John Gardner, *Faith and the Good Thing* is the metaphysical journey of eighteen-year-old Faith Cross, who believes that she is following her mother's deathbed instructions and the werewitch Swamp Woman's advice by searching the external world for the "Good Thing." This quest for the key that will release her and everyone else from servitude leads from Hatten County, Georgia, to Chicago, Illinois, and home again. Despite limitations inherent in the narrative form itself, occasional lapses in viewpoint, and infrequent verbal artifice, Johnson has created a magical novel of legendary characters and metaphysical import.

The diverse characters who people Faith's life enrich her explorations on both ordinary and extraordinary levels of existence, yet none can lead her to her Good Thing. Asthmatic, stuttering, alcoholic Isaac Maxwell insists that the real power is in money. Dr. Leon Lynch, who treats her mother, believes that the purpose of human life is death and fulfills his self-prophecy by committing suicide on Christmas Eve. Nervous Arnold Tippis, a former dentist (who lost his license because of malpractice), theater usher, and male nurse, rapes her physically and spiritually. His adaptations, like Faith's initial search, are external. Richard M. Barrett, former Princeton University professor, husband, and father, is now a homeless robber who dies on a Soldiers' Field park bench. An existentialist, he believes enough in her search to will her his blank Doomsday Book and to haunt her after his death on Friday nights at midnight until her marriage. Each character shares his path to his Good Thing with Faith, thereby allowing her to choose pieces for her own.

Faith's mystical odyssey, remembered with relish by a third-person narrator addressing his listeners "children," commits every individual to his own search and, through reflection, to the potential alteration of individual consciousness. Despite identifiable elements of naturalism, romanticism, allegory, the bildungsroman, and black folktales, of far greater importance is that *Faith and the Good Thing* creates its own genre of philosophical fiction in which the metaphysical and the real are integrated into a healing totality of being.

Until her return to Swamp Woman, Faith's choices for survival thrust her upon a path of intensifying alienation from herself and from her world. Her feelings of estrangement and depersonalization escalate to an existential fragmentation during her rape and subsequent periods of prostitution, chemical abuse, and marriage. With her decision to forsake her quest for the Good Thing, to manipulate the eminently unsuitable Isaac Maxwell into marriage, and to settle for a loveless middle-class existence, Faith cripples her sense of metaphysical purpose and sees herself as one of the "dead living," an "IT," her soul severed, "still as stone."

The advent of Alpha Omega Holmes, her hometown first love, enables Faith to recover vitality, but her dependence upon others since childhood for self-definition has been consistently destructive to Faith, who has lived in the past or the future and denied her present being. Holmes continues the pattern by deserting her when she announces that she is five months pregnant with his child. Rejected by Holmes and Maxwell, Faith turns to Mrs. Beasley, her former madam, who cares for her, delivers her baby daughter, and leaves the burning candle that is responsible for the fire that kills Faith's child and critically maims Faith. Repeatedly, psychic abandonment and betrayal have been the consequences of a failure to respect her own and others' process of becoming.

Nevertheless, at the summons of Swamp Woman's white cat, Faith returns to the werewitch's holy ground. Now near death, she is finally prepared to devote her total being to the search. Accepting Swamp Woman's revelations that everyone has a path and a "truth," Faith understands that all humans are the sum of their experiences and that she, as well as they, has no beginning and no end. Thus, she has the power to exchange existence with the esoteric, iconoclastic, witty magician Swamp Woman or to become anyone she wishes, thereby personifying Barrett's premise that thinking directs being. The Good Thing is the dynamic, nonpossessive, fluid freedom of the search itself.

Oxherding Tale

Type of work: Novel
First published: 1982

After *Faith and the Good Thing*, Johnson began thinking differently about the storyteller voice. He sought a means by which he could more fully and naturally embody philosophical issues within his characters. In *Oxherding Tale*, he has realized that voice, an intriguing first-person fusion of slave narrative, picaresque, and parable. In the first of two authorial intrusions, chapters 8 and 11, Johnson explains the three existing types of slave narrative. In the second, the author defines his new voice as first-person "universal," not a "narrator who falteringly interprets the world, but a narrator who *is* that world."

Yet the eight years that Johnson worked on his second novel, a novel he believes he was born to create, were fraught with frustration as he wrote and discarded draft after draft until, in 1979, he considered never writing again. Nevertheless, his passion for writing conquered the obstructions. Following a period of extended meditation, Johnson experienced a profound catharsis and eliminated the problematic static quality of the earlier drafts by refashioning the narrator-protagonist from black to mulatto and his second master from male to female.

Oxherding Tale, inspired by Eastern artist Kakuan-Shien's "Ten Oxherding Pictures," describes Andrew Hawkins's rite of passage, an often-humorous, metaphysical search for self through encounters that culminate in his nondualistic understanding of himself and the world. The narrator, born to the master's wife and the master's butler as the fruit of a comic one-night adventure, sees himself as belonging to neither the fields nor the house. Although Andrew lives with his stepmother and his father (recently demoted to herder), George and Mattie Hawkins,

Master Polkinghorne arranges his classical education with an eccentric Eastern scholar. An excellent student, Andrew nevertheless expresses his recognition of the dualism when he protests that he can speak in Latin more effectively than in his own dialect. As Andrew opens his mind to the learning of the ages, George Hawkins becomes progressively more paranoid and nationalistic. This delicate counterbalance is sustained throughout the novel until, at the end, the assimilated Andrew learns from Soulcatcher that his father was shot to death as an escaped slave.

At twenty, Andrew wishes to marry the Cripplegate plantation seamstress, Minty. Instead, he is sold to Flo Hatfield, a lonely woman who considers her eleven former husbands subhuman and who has the reputation of sexually using each male slave until, discarding him to the mines or through his death, she replaces him with another. Believing that he is earning the funds for his own, his family's, and Minty's manumission, Andrew cooperates. He finds himself quickly satiated, however, with the orgiastic physical pleasures Flo demands to conceal her psychic lifelessness. Thus, neither his father's intensifying spiritual separatism nor his mistress's concupiscence is a path Andrew can accept.

Andrew proceeds to seek out Reb, the Allmuseri coffinmaker in whose Buddhist voice he finds comfort, friendship, and enlightenment. Flo's opposite, Reb (neither detached nor attached) operates not from pleasure but from duty, acting without ulterior motives simply because something needs to be done. Together, the two escape Flo's sentence to her mines as well as Bannon the Soulcatcher, a bounty hunter, with Andrew posing as William Harris, a white teacher, and Reb posing as his gentleman's gentleman. When Reb decides to leave Spartanburg for Chicago because of Bannon, Andrew, emotionally attached to the daughter of the town doctor, decides that Reb's path is not appropriate for him to follow. Instead, his dharma (Eastern soul-sustaining law of conduct) is to be a homemaker married to Peggy. During their wedding ceremony, Andrew surrenders himself to his timeless vision of all that humanity has the potential to become.

The final chapter, "Moksha," like the last of Kakuan-Shien's ten pictures, reveals the absolute integration between self and universe. "Moksha" is the Hindu concept of ultimate realization, perpetual liberation beyond dualities, of self with the Great Spirit. In an illegal slave auction, the mulatto Andrew discovers and buys his dying first love, Minty. He, Peggy, and Dr. Undercliff unite to ease her transition from this world. Thus, the three move beyond self to *arete*, "doing beautifully what needs to be done," and begin the process of healing their world.

In *Oxherding Tale*, Johnson once again offers the experience of affirmation and renewal. Through the first-person universal voice of Andrew Hawkins, he constructs a tightly interwoven, well-honed portrait of actualization. Minute details, vivid visual imagery, and delicate polarities within and among the characters achieve an exacting balance between portrayal of the process and the process itself. Once again, the search does not belong solely to Johnson's characters; the search belongs to everyone who chooses to be free of "self-inflicted segregation from the Whole."

The Sorcerer's Apprentice

Type of work: Short fiction
First published: 1986

Each of the stories in *The Sorcerer's Apprentice* has a specific philosophic concept at the core of the narrative. "The Education of Mingo," which opens the collection, is informed by the argument that humans are ultimately not responsible for their actions if there is an omniscient deity in control of the universe. The story is grounded in a very down-to-earth situation involving a white man, Moses Green, who has trained an African slave, Mingo, to echo all of his desires, attitudes, preferences, and predilections. As Mingo begins to act beyond the specific instructions of his master, anticipating Green's subconscious and instinctual urges, the servant/master relationship is presented as a reciprocal form of entrapment, in which neither is truly free or completely himself. The costs of this arrangement are Green's permanent connection to his slave and Mingo's restriction to his status as menial, no matter how skilled or accomplished he becomes. The story is both a commentary on three centuries of slavery and a vivid expression of the inner conflicts of an essentially good man, whose well-meaning attempt to educate someone he regards as completely ignorant must lead to a disastrous, violent conclusion due to his own massive ignorance of Mingo's mind. The interlocking destiny of Green and Mingo, the secret sharers of each other's lives, points the story toward an indeterminate future, in which the racial clash of American life remains to be resolved. As the writer Michael Ventura has observed, the stories in *The Sorcerer's Apprentice* often "reveal the underside of the last or next," so that Cooter and Loftis, brothers in the succeeding story, "Exchange Value," are also trapped in an interlocking relationship that wrecks their ability to think with moral clarity or with any sense of self-preservation.

Located at the center of the collection, "China" is the most energetically affirmative story in *The Sorcerer's Apprentice*, closer in mood to Johnson's celebrated novels, *Oxherding Tale* or *Middle Passage*, than to his short fiction. Rudolph Lee Jackson, the protagonist, is a middle-aged man whose entire life has been a catastrophe of caution and avoidance. His marriage is devoid of passion or communication, he is physically feeble, psychically terrified, and steadily deteriorating from even this diminished condition. The story is not an open allegory, but Jackson is presented as an emblem of the frightened, semibourgeois, not-quite-middle-class black man, nearly completely emasculated by a retreat from the daily assaults of a racist society and further discouraged by the constant critical sarcasm of his wife Evelyn, whose disappointment and fear are understandable in terms of Jackson's apparent acceptance of defeat.

Johnson has criticized novels in which "portraits of black men . . . are so limited and one-sided" that they seem immoral. The direction of "China" is an opening away from what Johnson calls "an extremely narrow range of human beings"—exemplified by Jackson, who has a "distant, pained expression that asked: "Is this all?"—toward a kind of self-actualization and fulfillment, which Jackson achieves through a difficult and painful but energizing course in the philosophy and practice of martial arts. In some of his most engaging, vivid writing, Johnson describes the revitalization and growth that lead to Jackson's symbolic rebirth as a man, as he becomes more and more involved in the life of the kwoon. Initially, Evelyn resists everything about Jackson's enthusiastic, disciplined transformation, but at the story's conclusion, she is, despite her reservations and fears, awakened to the possibility of a life without the artificial, self-imposed limits that African Americans have adopted as a kind of protection from the pain of a three-centuries-long legacy of racial oppression. The story "Kwoon" is a further exploration of the mental condition at the heart of true physical power that martial arts can provide, and it illuminates the genuine humility that the strongest people know when they have moved beyond the ego trap of resistance to enlightenment.

"Alēthia" is the most explicitly philosophical of Johnson's short stories. It is narrated by a book-ruled professor, whose ordered, intellectually contained life is fractured when a student pulls him into a forest of uncontrolled passion, the necessary complement to his mental fortress. The two sides of human existence are expressed in the contrast between the professor's measured discourse and the raw reality of the netherworld to which his guide takes him. The word *alēthia* is drawn from the philosopher Max Scheler's term concerning a process that "calls forth from concealedness," and it stands for the revelation of an inner essence that has been previously suppressed—the "ugly, lovely black life (so it was to me) I'd fled so long ago in my childhood." Johnson's presentation of the professor is a commentary on the retreat that a preoccupation with the purely mental may produce and a statement about the futility of repressing aspects of the true self.

Middle Passage

Type of work: Novel
First published: 1990

Middle Passage, for which Johnson won the 1990 National Book Award, is the story of Rutherford Calhoun's life-changing journey aboard the slaver *Republic* in 1830. Like Johnson's earlier *Oxherding Tale*, this book is narrated by a young black man born into slavery but with a superior education, whose story is rooted in nineteenth century history but whose savvy, humorous voice bespeaks a twentieth century intellectual consciousness.

Rutherford's adventures begin when he stows aboard a ship to escape a woman determined to bring him to the altar. The *Republic*, a slaver, ships out to Africa; there it picks up a special cargo—a hold full of men, women, and children of the mystical Allmuseri tribe. The *Republic*'s captain also secretly brings on board a crate containing the captured Allmuseri god.

Middle Passage blatantly evokes *Moby Dick: Or, The Whale* (1851), "Benito Cereno," and Homer's *Odyssey* (c. 725 B.C.E., English translation, 1616) among others. Johnson flaunts, mocks, and turns on end these similarities: His dwarfish

Captain Falcon is a caricature of the crazed Ahab; the ringleaders of the rebelling Allmuseri are Babo, Fernando, and Atufel; Isadora, Rutherford's intended, knits by day and unravels her work by night to forestall marriage to her new suitor. The *Republic*'s voyage is a darkly comic version of the *Pequod*'s, but one highlighting slavery's role in American history and economy. Whereas Herman Melville's Ishmael asks the philosophical question, "Who ain't a slave?" Johnson's Falcon educates Rutherford in the fundamentals of capitalism by pointing out, "Who ain't up for auction when it comes to it?"

Fittingly, then, Johnson's novel does not end when Falcon dies, the *Republic* sinks, and Rutherford is rescued. Rather, these events deliver Rutherford into the clutches of the *Republic*'s owners, come to check up on their investment. Also aboard the rescue ship is Isadora and her fiancé, wealthy black New Orleans mobster Papa Zeringue. Once Zeringue is exposed as a part owner of the *Republic*, Isadora is free to marry Rutherford, who joyfully embraces marriage as an emotional haven in a cannibalistic world.

Middle Passage charts Rutherford's growth from a self-serving opportunist to a responsible man who values the ties that link human beings. His passage from a worldview based on multiplicity, individualism, dualism, and linearity to acceptance of the Allmuseri concept of "unity of being" opens him up to love, compassion, and commitment. Rutherford's growth into this new identity also seems to comment on Johnson's identity as a sophisticated black writer navigating his way through African American, American, Western, and Eastern traditions. Johnson calls *Middle Passage* his attempt to fill a literary void by producing "philosophical black literature." An admirer of writers such as Thomas Mann, Jean-Paul Sartre, Hermann Hesse, Herman Melville, and Ralph Ellison, who "understood instinctively that fiction and philosophy were sister disciplines," Johnson weds, in this work, his own interests in philosophy, African American history, and fiction.

In *Middle Passage*, Johnson reminds readers that the received American epic (literary and historical) has an African American counterpart, and he adds a new dimension to the slave narrative tradition by creating an African American narrator who speaks in a formidably intellectual voice. Johnson also insists that Rutherford be taken seriously simply as a human being engaged in exploring fundamental underpinnings of the human condition.

Dreamer

Type of work: Novel
First published: 1998

Beginning in Chicago, in the fateful summer of 1966, the year Martin Luther King, Jr., took his nonviolent branch of the Civil Rights movement north, *Dreamer* is (to borrow the subtitle of Herman Melville's *Billy Budd*) "an inside narrative," and doubly so. A number of chapters, though told in the third person, deal intimately with the workings of King's troubled mind. Longer and more numerous are the chapters narrated by Matthew Bishop, a college dropout whose job includes "recording the Revolution, preserving its secrets for posterity—particularly what took place in the interstices." Bishop's narrative focuses on one interstitial event in particular, the arrival of Chaym Smith, the King look-alike who paradoxically is everything that King is not, "the kind of Negro the Movement had for years kept away from the world's cameras." Smith has the Midas touch in reverse; he is a man whose intelligence and talent have been thwarted and misshapen. Yearning to be of service, to be like King, he is also filled with resentment and constitutes as great a threat to the movement and to King as the virulent racism that manifests itself in Chicago. The story of Smith playing Cain to King's Abel serves as the foundation for Johnson's informative and often absorbing examination of dreams and civil wars of several kinds: within the country, the black community, the Civil Rights movement, and individuals. There is enough material here for a meganovel, but Johnson deliberately opts for the smallness that is in keeping with his dominant theme: that everyone has a part to play.

Suggested Readings

African American Review 30, no. 4 (Winter, 1996).

Byrd, Rudolph P. *Charles Johnson's Novels: Writing the American Palimpsest.* Bloomington: Indiana University Press, 2005.

_______, ed. *I Call Myself an Artist: Writings by and About Charles Johnson.* Bloomington: Indiana University Press, 1999.

Coleman, J. W. "Charles Johnson's Quest for Black Freedom in *Oxherding Tale*." *African American Review* 29, no. 4 (Winter, 1995): 631-644.

Connor, Marc C., and William R. Nash, eds. *Charles Johnson: The Novelist as Philosopher*. Jackson: University Press of Mississippi, 2007.

Johnson, Charles. "An Interview with Charles Johnson." Interview by Charles H. Rowell. *Callaloo* 20 (Summer, 1997): 531-547.

Little, Jonathan. *Charles Johnson's Spiritual Imagination*. Columbia: University of Missouri Press, 1997.

Rowell, Charles H. "An Interview with Charles Johnson." *Callaloo* 20 (Summer, 1997): 531-547.

Scott, D. M. "Interrogating Identity: Appropriation and Transformation in *Middle Passage*." *African American Review* 29, no. 4 (Winter, 1995): 645-655.

Travis, M. A. "*Beloved* and *Middle Passage*: Race, Narrative, and the Critics' Essentialism." *Narrative* 2, no. 3 (October, 1994): 179-200.

Contributors: Grace McEntee, Leon Lewis, Joanne McCarthy, and Kathleen Mills

James Weldon Johnson

Born: Jacksonville, Florida; June 17, 1871
Died: Wiscasset, Maine; June 26, 1938

African American

One of the first to celebrate African American art forms, Johnson was a major figure in the Harlem Renaissance.

Principal works

LONG FICTION: *The Autobiography of an Ex-Coloured Man*, 1912

POETRY: *Fifty Years, and Other Poems*, 1917; *God's Trombones: Seven Negro Sermons in Verse*, 1927; *Saint Peter Relates an Incident: Selected Poems*, 1935

TRANSLATION: *The English Libretto of "Goyescas,"* 1915

NONFICTION: *Black Manhattan*, 1930; *Along This Way*, 1933 (autobiography); *Negro Americans, What Now?*, 1934; *The Selected Writings of James Weldon Johnson*, 1995 (2 volumes; Sondra Kathryn Wilson, editor)

EDITED TEXTS: *The Book of American Negro Poetry*, 1922; *The Book of American Negro Spirituals*, 1925; *The Second Book of American Negro Spirituals*, 1926

James Weldon Johnson was born in Jacksonville, graduated from Atlanta University in 1894, and went on to become one of the most versatile artists of his time. In addition to expressing his artistic talents, he led a successful professional life and was an influential civil rights advocate. After his graduation in 1894, Johnson became principal of Stanton School and edited a newspaper, the *Daily American*. He advocated civil rights in his articles in a time that saw a dramatic rise in the number of lynchings. He thus assumed a public role in the African American community. Encouraged by his brother Rosamond, Johnson and his brother went to New York in 1899 to work on a musical career. Their most lasting achievement of that period is the song "Lift Every Voice and Sing," also known as the African American national anthem. After having been appointed consul in Venezuela and Nicaragua, Johnson, after publication of *The Autobiography of an Ex-Coloured Man*, decided to attempt to support himself through literary work. He returned to New York to begin writing an influential column for the *New York Age*, commenting on literary matters and encouraging black literary activity. He published *The Book of American Negro Poetry* three years before Alain Locke's anthology *The New Negro* (1925) officially ushered in the Harlem Renaissance.

Beginning in 1916, Johnson was field secretary for the National Association for the Advancement of Colored People (NAACP), organizing new branches and looking into matters of racial injustice nationwide. In 1920, he became the first African

American secretary of the NAACP, a post he would hold until 1930. Johnson saw his civil rights work and his artistic activity as complementary, believing that the production of great works of art would improve African Americans' position in society. Johnson contributed major work to that effort with the publication of *God's Trombones*, bringing the language of the African American church into the realm of literature. Weldon also collected two volumes of African American spirituals, which made clear that this expression of African American folk spirit belonged to the world of art. His death in a car accident in 1938 interrupted Johnson in his wide-ranging efforts.

The Autobiography of an Ex-Coloured Man

TYPE OF WORK: Novel
FIRST PUBLISHED: 1912

The Autobiography of an Ex-Coloured Man was first published anonymously in 1912, but it did not become a success until it was reissued in 1927, at the height of the Harlem Renaissance. The novel chronicles the coming-of-age of its unnamed protagonist, who switches back and forth between ethnic identities until he finally decides to pass as a European American. Its most striking feature might well be that it calls the notion of ethnic identity into question.

In order to explore ethnic identity, Johnson has his protagonist experience both sides of the "color line," to use the famous phrase by W. E. B. Du Bois. Growing up believing himself European American, as the white-looking child of a light-skinned African American mother and a European American father, the protagonist discovers in school that he is African American. Having harbored prejudice against African Americans, he now becomes an object of prejudice. Once over this initial shock, he resolves to become famous in the service of African Americans. In order to learn about his mother's heritage, he leaves for the South, where he often finds himself an outsider to African American society. He knows little of African American folk customs, so at first he reacts to African Americans ambiguously. In this way, Johnson shows that the culture of one's up-

James Weldon Johnson (Library of Congress)

bringing is a more important factor in determining one's outlook on other cultures than are ethnic bloodlines.

After losing his money in the South, the protagonist eventually embarks on a musical career, which takes him to New York. He discovers ragtime there and is fascinated by it, renewing his resolve to become famous and intending to do so through African American music. After a sojourn in Europe, he returns to the South in order to learn more about the roots of African American music, which he calls "a mine of material" when visiting a religious meeting at which spirituals are sung. The reader discovers that the protagonist's interest in African American culture is mainly commercial. He nevertheless often comments enthusiastically on African American contributions to American culture. The protagonist gives up his idea of becoming famous through African American music, however, after witnessing a lynching. He returns North, marries a European American woman, and becomes a white businessman. In the end, he wishes he had followed his musical inclinations, which are connected to his African American heritage, instead of achieving material success. Thus, the novel shows that a hostile social climate can bring people to forsake their heritage but also that ethnic identity is partly a matter of choice.

Along This Way

Type of work: Autobiography
First published: 1933

Johnson claimed that one of the reasons for publishing his autobiography, *Along This Way*, was to make clear that his novel *The Autobiography of an Ex-Coloured Man* was not a record of his life. A public figure as important as Johnson hardly needed, however, a justification for adding another book to the growing shelf of autobiographies of distinguished African Americans, such as Frederick Douglass, Booker T. Washington, and W. E. B. Du Bois. In a controlled and often ironic narrative tone, Johnson not only provides insights into his life and times but also focuses on African American accomplishments in the hostile social climate that he battled against all of his life.

Despite a middle-class upbringing, a university degree, and immediate success first as a school principal, in passing the Florida bar examination—the first African American to do so—and then as songwriter, writer, consul, and civil rights activist, Johnson always committed himself to the cause of African Americans. When on university vacation, he spent three months teaching African American farmers' children in rural Georgia, realizing "that they were me, and I was they; that a force stronger than blood made us one." Accordingly, all his artistic work was committed to improving the social situation of African Americans and to exploring African American art forms. When embarking on his composing and songwriting career, he "began to grope toward a realization of the American Negro's cultural background and his creative folk-art." In much of his poetry, too, Johnson built on African American folk traditions. He did so because he believed in the uniqueness of the African American heritage, based as it was on a deep spirituality. Thus, he implies that African Americans are a main resource for the United States in matters of artistry and spirituality and that, in turn, the United States will be measured by how it treats African Americans. He pithily summarizes this belief in saying "that in large measure the race question involves the saving of black America's body and white America's soul."

A considerable part of the book is devoted to Johnson's fight for racial justice and his time in the leadership of the National Association for the Advancement of Colored People. Johnson reveals explicitly that his program for improving the social status of African Americans, despite his own artistic, legal, and political efforts, is really a moral one: "The only kind of revolution that would have an immediately significant effect on the American Negro's status would be a moral revolution." As *Along This Way* makes clear, Johnson did his best on all fronts.

Saint Peter Relates an Incident

Type of work: Poetry
First published: 1935

Johnson's most famous poems appear in *Saint Peter Relates an Incident*, including the title poem, "O Black and Unknown Bards," and "Lift Every Voice and Sing."

"Saint Peter Relates an Incident of the Resurrection Day," originally published in 1930, was written in response to the visit by mothers of highly decorated World War I soldiers to their sons' graves in France. The State Department, which sponsored the visit, sent white mothers in one ship and African American mothers in another, second-class ship. The poem imagines Saint Peter telling the assembled angels of Heaven an incident occurring on Judgment Day. The dead are called from their graves, and white war veterans, among them members of the Ku Klux Klan, gather together in order to escort the Unknown Soldier to Heaven. Once they liberate him from his grave, they are shocked to find that he is black and debate whether they should bury him again. Until the white war veterans knew the Unknown Soldier's color, they intended to honor him; his color alone turns their admiration into hatred. The Unknown Soldier marches triumphantly into Heaven, while, it is implied, the war veterans dismayed by his skin color end up in Hell. Johnson points out the bitter irony and absurdity of drawing a color line even after death, particularly when death was incurred in the service of one's country.

"O Black and Unknown Bards" originally appeared in *Fifty Years, and Other Poems* (1917). The title refers to the unknown creators of the spirituals, a musical form that Johnson regarded as artistic work of the first rank, a point he makes by comparing it with the creations of classical composers. Incorporating titles of actual spirituals, such as "Steal Away to Jesus" and "Go Down, Moses," into the poem, Johnson pays homage to African American folk art, admiring its spiritual and artistic accomplishments, and bridges the gap between folk art forms and so-called high art.

"Lift Every Voice and Sing," perhaps the work which has done most to keep Johnson's name alive, was originally composed as a tribute to Abraham Lincoln's birthday and set to music. It is still known as the African American national anthem. Inspirational in nature, the poem makes no direct reference to ethnicity but refers metaphorically to hardships endured by African Americans while also celebrating liberties won in hard struggle. The third and last stanza reminds the listeners to remain faithful to God and ends on a patriotic note, which claims the United States as African Americans' "native land."

Suggested Readings

Ahlin, Lena. *The "New Negro" in the Old World: Culture and Performance in James Weldon Johnson, Jessie Fauset, and Nella Larsen*. Lund, Sweden: Almqvist & Wiksell, 2006.

Bruce, Dickson D., Jr. *Black American Writing from the Nadir: The Evolution of a Literary Tradition, 1877-1915*. Baton Rouge: Louisiana State University Press, 1989.

Fleming, Robert E. *James Weldon Johnson*. Boston: Twayne, 1987.

Levy, Eugene. *James Weldon Johnson: Black Leader, Black Voice*. Chicago: University of Chicago Press, 1973.

Price, Kenneth M., and Lawrence J. Oliver, eds. *Critical Essays on James Weldon Johnson*. New York: G. K. Hall, 1997.

Wilson, Sondra K., ed. *In Search of Democracy: The NAACP Writings of James Weldon Johnson, Walter White, and Roy Wilkins, 1920-1977*. New York: Oxford University Press, 1999.

Contributor: Martin Japtok

Gayl Jones

Born: Lexington, Kentucky; November 23, 1949

African American

Jones's conventional gothic novels and short stories are among the most intense psychological portrayals of black female characters in African American literature.

Principal works

DRAMA: *Chile Woman*, pr. 1973, pb. 1974

LONG FICTION: *Corregidora*, 1975; *Eva's Man*, 1976; *Die Vogelfängerin*, 1986 (in German); *The Healing*, 1998; *Mosquito*, 1999

POETRY: *Song for Anninho*, 1981; *The Hermit-Woman*, 1983; *Xarque, and Other Poems*, 1985

SHORT FICTION: *White Rat: Short Stories*, 1977

NONFICTION: *Liberating Voices: Oral Tradition in African American Literature*, 1991

Poet, novelist, essayist, short-story writer, and teacher, Gayl Jones is best known for the intensity and probing nature of her gothic tales, which mix the conventions of the gothic with radically unconventional worlds of madness, sexuality, and violence. Jones began writing seriously at age seven under the encouraging and guiding influence of her grandmother, her mother, and her high school Spanish teacher, Anna Dodd. Later, her mentors would be Michael Harper and William Meredith at Brown University, where she earned two degrees in creative writing. She published her first and best-known novel, *Corregidora*, while still at Brown.

No stranger to the art of writing and storytelling, Jones grew up in a household of female creative writers: Her grandmother wrote plays for church production. Jones's mother, Lucille, started writing in fifth grade and read stories she had written to Jones and her brother. It is therefore not surprising that stories, storytelling, and family history are the sources of most of the material for her fiction.

In addition to her distinction as teller of intense stories about insanity and the psychological effects of violence on black women, another characteristic of Jones's art is her consistent use of the first person for her protagonists. Claiming neither "political compulsions nor moral compulsions," Jones is first and foremost interested in the "psychology of characters" and therefore seeks to examine their "puzzles," as she states, by simply letting her characters "tell their stories." Her interest in the character as storyteller permits her to evoke oral history and engage the African American tradition of storytelling, which she accomplishes in her novels *Corregidora* and *Eva's Man*.

Corregidora, a historical novel, is what Jones calls a blues narrative. The novel examines the psychological effects of slavery and sexual abuse on three generations of women, particularly Ursa, a professional blues singer. *Eva's Man*, Jones's more provocative and controversial second novel, explores the psychological effects of violence. Eva Medina Canada, the protagonist-narrator, tells in confusing but gripping detail the story of her violent reaction to her victimization in a male-dominated society. Jones continues her thematic concerns with *White Rat*, a volume of twelve short stories, and *Song for Anninho*, a long narrative poem. In addition to her fiction and essay writing, Jones teaches full-time, writes poetry, and conducts research.

Eva's Man

Type of work: Novel
First published: 1976

Eva's Man, Jones's provocative second novel, is a psychological tale of repression, manipulation, and suffering. It is a gothic story of madness—Eva's madness—and the psychological effects of violence on black women. From her prison asylum room, where she has been incarcerated for five years for poisoning, then castrating, her lover, Eva Medina Canada, the psychotic title character, narrates the events that led up to her bizarre and violent act. Although she has maintained a steadfast and defiant silence in response to the grinding interrogation of the male judicial authorities—the police and psychiatrists—Eva readily tells her story to the reader. Through time and space intrusions, many flashbacks, and a combination of dreams, fantasies, memories, interrogation, and exchanges between herself and her cellmate, Elvira, Eva tells everything except her motive.

In the unsequential narrative, Eva's story delineates unequivocally men's malevolence and women's natural acceptance of a destiny inevitably circumscribed by this malevolence. Eva's appropriating of and identification with the story of Queen Bee, the femme fatale whose love, like a deadly sting, kills off every man with whom she falls in love, suggests that women resign themselves to a female destiny. This horrid fatalism blames and punishes women for their sexuality. Paradoxically, since the drone is always at the service of the queen bee, it is women who have power to affirm or deny manhood. Aligning herself with the queen bee, Eva kills Davis, the drone, rather than submit to his excessive domination.

For Eva the lessons in the violent consequences of womanhood and female sexuality began early. Prepubescent Freddy, a neighbor boy, initiates her sexually with a dirty Popsicle stick. Her mother's lover, Tyrone, makes her feel him. She sees her father punish her mother's infidelity with rape. Cousin Alphonse solicits sex from her, and a thumbless man harasses her sexually. Moses Tribbs propositions her, thereby provoking her attack on him with a pocket knife. Her fifty-five-year-old husband James, out of jealousy, disallows a telephone in the house. Finally, Davis, her lover, imprisons and uses her for five days. To each of these men, Eva (like other women characters in the novel, including her mother) exists merely as an object to satisfy insatiable male sexual needs. In response to this objectification and violence by men, Eva remains steadfastly silent, choosing neither to explain her extreme action nor to defend herself.

Apart from the bizarreness of Eva's brutal act, which delineates the level of her madness, it is perhaps the exclusive use of the first-person narrative voice and the lack of authorial intrusion or questioning of Eva's viewpoint that make *Eva's Man* controversial and successful.

Suggested Readings

Ashraf, H. A. "'Relate Sexual to Historical.'" *African American Review* 34, no. 2 (2000): 273-297.

Bell, Bernard. "The Liberating Literary and African American Vernacular Voices of Gayl Jones." *Comparative Literature Studies* 36, no. 3 (1999): 247-258.

Coser, Stelamaris. *Bridging the Americas: The Literature of Paule Marshall, Toni Morrison, and Gayl Jones*. Philadelphia: Temple University Press, 1995.

Robinson, Sally. *Engendering the Subject: Gender and Self-Representation in Contemporary Women's Fiction*. Albany: State University of New York Press, 1991.

Wilcox, Janelle. "Resistant Silence, Resistant Subject: (Re)Reading Gayl Jones's *Eva's Man*." *Genders* 23 (1996): 72-96.

Yukins, Elizabeth. "Bastard Daughters and the Possession of History in *Corregidora* and *Paradise*." *Signs* 28, no. 1 (2002): 221-247.

Contributor: Pamela J. Olubunmi Smith

June Jordan

Born: Harlem, New York; July 9, 1936
Died: Berkeley, California; June 14, 2002

African American

A self-avowed anarchist who considered all poems political, Jordan's ambition was an acknowledged "people's poet."

Principal works

CHILDREN'S LITERATURE: *Who Look at Me*, 1969; *Dry Victories*, 1972; *Fannie Lou Hamer*, 1972; *New Life: New Room*, 1975; *Kimako's Story*, 1981

DRAMA: *In the Spirit of Sojourner Truth*, pr. 1979; *For the Arrow That Flies by Day*, pr. 1981; *Bang Bang Über Alles*, pr. 1986 (libretto; music by Adrienne Bo Torf); *I Was Looking at the Ceiling and Then I Saw the Sky*, 1995 (libretto and lyrics; music by John Adams)

LONG FICTION: *His Own Where*, 1971

POETRY: *Some Changes*, 1971; *New Days: Poems of Exile and Return*, 1974; *Things That I Do in the Dark: Selected Poetry*, 1977; *Passion: New Poems, 1977-1980*, 1980; *Bobo Goetz a Gun*, 1985; *Living Room: New Poems*, 1985; *Lyrical Campaigns: Selected Poems*, 1989; *Naming Our Destiny: New and Selected Poems*, 1989; *Haruko/Love Poems: New and Selected Love Poems*, 1993 (pb. in U.S. as *Haruko: Love Poems*, 1994); *Kissing God Goodbye: Poems, 1991-1997*, 1997; *Directed by Desire: The Collected Poems*, 2005

NONFICTION: *Civil Wars*, 1981; *On Call: Political Essays*, 1985; *Moving Towards Home: Political Essays*, 1989; *Technical Difficulties: African-American Notes on the State of the Union*, 1992; *Affirmative Acts: Political Essays*, 1998; *Soldier: A Poet's Childhood*, 2000

The essence of June Jordan's life reveals itself in her poetry and in her autobiographical writings, in particular in *Civil Wars* and her memoir *Soldier: A Poet's Childhood*. She was born in Harlem, the daughter of her father Granville, a Panamanian immigrant, and Mildred, her Jamaican mother. When she was five years old, her parents moved to Brooklyn, and Jordan began her education by commuting to an all-white school. She later attended Northfield School for Girls, a preparatory school in Massachusetts.

Her introduction to poetry came through her father, who forced her to read, memorize, or recite the plays and sonnets of William Shakespeare, the Bible, the poetry of Paul Laurence Dunbar, and the poetry of Edgar Allan Poe, as well as the novels of Sinclair Lewis and Zane Grey. At the age of seven, she began to write poetry herself. Unfortunately, her father's pedagogical methods also included beatings for unsatisfactory performance, but Jordan never questioned his love for her, affirming that he had the greatest influence on her poetic and personal development, having given her the idea that "to protect yourself, you try to hurt whatever is out there." Jordan's mother, who committed suicide in 1966, did not oppose her father's harsh treatment of her, and Jordan found this passivity harder to forgive than her father's brutality.

Her interest in poetry was developed at Northfield but was limited mainly to white male poets "whose remoteness from my world . . . crippled my trust in my own sensibilities . . . and generally delayed my creative embracing of my own . . . life as the stuff of my art."

In 1953, at Barnard College, Jordan met Michael Meyer, a white student at Columbia University. They were married in 1955, and Jordan followed her husband to the University of Chicago. The strain of their interracial marriage, at a time when such marriages were frowned upon by the dominant society, began to take its toll, and after a prolonged separation the couple eventually divorced in 1965, leaving Jordan to raise her son Christopher, born in 1958, by herself. Supporting herself at first as a technical writer, journalist, and assistant to Frederick Wiseman (producer of *The Cool World*, a film about Harlem), she began her academic career at the City College of New York in 1967. In 1969, she published her first book, *Who Look at Me*, a series of poetic fragments dealing with the problem of black identity in America, in which she tries to imagine what a white person might see when looking at an African American and what effect such a look can have on the person observed.

In 1970 Jordan traveled to Italy with funding from the Prix de Rome in Environmental Design, which she had won with the support of R. Buckminster Fuller. Her reflections on this journey are contained in her collection *New Days: Poems of Exile and Return*. A breakthrough in her career as a poet came with the publication in 1977 of her best-known collection, *Things That I Do in the Dark*, edited by Toni Morrison. She also won the Prix de Rome in Environmental Design (1970-1971), and in 1971 her book *His Own Where* was nominated for a National Book Award. She won the Lila Wallace-Reader's Digest Writer's Award (1995), the National Association of Black Journalists Award (1984), and the PEN Center USA West Freedom to Write Award (1991).

Jordan published more than twenty books in a variety of genres, including books for children and young adults, political essays, long fiction, plays, and even an opera libretto. She taught at Connecticut College, Sarah Lawrence College, Yale University, the State University of New York at Stony Brook, eventually taking up a professorship in African studies at the University of California, Berkeley. There she became the head of the popular outreach program Poetry for the People. She was a regular contributor to the liberal periodical *The Progressive*, an outspoken critic of American foreign aid policy, and an aggressive proponent of affirmative action. Jordan died in June, 2002, after losing her decade-long fight against breast cancer.

Jordan was a self-avowed anarchist activist who considered all poems to be political. Her poetic ambition was to be a "people's poet" in the fashion of Pablo Neruda, particularly a black people's poet. Her poetic output was to a large degree a

June Jordan (Jill Posener)

running commentary on the social and political life in the United States, with allusions to current events such as the 1991 Clarence Thomas/Anita Hill hearings, Jesse Jackson's 1984 presidential campaign, the 1991 police beating of Rodney King and subsequent trial, and even the controversial events surrounding boxer Mike Tyson. Although her tone is frequently sarcastic, angry, and strident, in some sense all of her poems are love poems. Her militancy and unwillingness to be conciliatory appear to be guided by her love for the oppressed and marginalized; her denunciation of the oppressors is accompanied by the call to the victims not to capitulate, to gain and to preserve a sense of self-love and self-worth and then put it into action.

Some Changes

Type of work: Poetry
First published: 1971

Jordan's first substantial collection of poems is divided into four parts, each dedicated to a particular facet of her life that she felt needed revision and change. These poems were written in the years after the suicide of her mother and the dissolution of her own marriage; as such they are an assertion of her new independence as a woman, mother, poet, sexual person, and politically autonomous citizen; therefore she dedicates the volume to "new peoplelife."

This "new peoplelife" involves making peace with her mother and father in the opening poem. For the former, she has a list of promises; her father she would "regenerate." In "Poem for My Family: Hazel Griffin and Victor Hernando Cruz," Jordan expands the meaning of "family" beyond the traditional nuclear family to include all suffering people of her race.

In several other poems in the first half of the collection, Jordan's role as a single, working mother translates into concern for children in general and for her own son in particular. The tone of many of these early poems is dark. In "Not a Suicide Poem," she asserts that

> no one should feel peculiar living
> as they do
> . . . [in] terrific reeking epidermal
> damage
> marrow rot . . .

Other poems, such as "The Wedding" and "The Reception," assert a married woman's personal autonomy. Most notable of these is "Let Me Live with Marriage," a clever deconstruction of Shakespeare's sonnet beginning "Let me not to the Marriage of True Minds." Jordan's wish is to be allowed "to live with marriage/ as unruly as alive/ or else alone and longing/ not too long alone."

After declaring her independence from family and marriage in the first half and coming to terms with her losses ("I Live in Subtraction"), she indicates her growing sense of racial pride and political empowerment in the later poems of *Some Changes*. "What would I do white?" she asks in the opening poem of the third section, in which she declares herself in solidarity with all black people, whom she has incorporated into her extended family. In the final section she expands this family yet more to include all people living in poverty and oppression ("47,000 Windows") before returning to memories of her father and her family's former home on Hancock Street in Brooklyn, emphasizing the emptiness of the house and the forlorn wandering of her father after her mother's suicide ("Clock on Hancock Street").

In the final poem of the collection, pessimistically titled "Last Poem for a Little While," the speaker is saying grace at a Thanksgiving dinner of 1969, in which she thanks God "for the problems that are mine/ and evidently mine alone" and asks her fellow diners to "Pass the Ham./ And wipe your fingers on the flag."

In *Some Changes* Jordan found her independent poetic identity, acknowledging the influence of Shakespeare, T. S. Eliot, Emily Dickinson, and Walt Whitman but striking out confidently on her own path.

Naming Our Destiny

Type of work: Poetry
First published: 1989

Naming Our Destiny: New and Selected Poems updates *Things That I Do in the Dark* to include her poetry up to 1989. It therefore gives the reader a good sense of which poems from her previous collections Jordan considered most worthy of attention. The volume's first section presents selections from *Things That I Do in the Dark* (1958-1977); the second contains poems from *Passion* (1977-1980); the third is a selection from *Living Room* (1985); the fourth is composed of new poems written between 1984 and 1989.

Part 2 includes her most anthologized piece, "A Poem About My Rights." Jordan claimed that this poem was written in response to having been raped a few months before and that she intended to express her psychological reaction to this event. She emphatically states that victims of violence must resist the temptation to internalize the blame for the violent act and put it squarely on the shoulders of the perpetrators. She then characteristically extrapolates from her personal tragedy to the situation of violated people everywhere: "I am the history of rape/ I am the history of the rejection of who I am." As the poem indicates and as Jordan stated in interviews, the difference between her rape and the situation in apartheid South Africa was, for her, minimal. Her anger at this violation finds expression in the menacing final lines of the poem: "but I can tell you that from now on my resistance/ my simple and daily and nightly self-determination/ may very well cost you your life."

The new poems in *Naming Our Destiny* are collected in the fourth section under the title "North Star," a reference to the abolitionist newspaper founded by Frederick Douglass in 1847 and to the constellation that served as the navigational guide to Africans making their escape from slavery. Consequently, most of these poems are unabashedly political, taking to task most of Jordan's adversaries: the Israeli occupiers of Palestine; Bernard Goetz, the New York subway vigilante; the white supremacist rulers of South Africa; Ronald Reagan and the Nicaraguan Contras; the Marcos regime in the Philippines; and even Benjamin Franklin for declaring that there could be no lasting peace with Native Americans, "till we have well-drubbed them" ("Poem for Benjamin Franklin"). Other poems pay homage to friends and fellow activists, such as Angela Davis ("Solidarity").

Technical Difficulties

Type of work: Essays
First published: 1992

The centerpiece of Jordan's political ideology was an exalted view of human entitlements and of the capacity of the nation-state to guarantee them. This list of entitlements—found in the seventh of the twenty-four essays in this volume—includes items that would endear her to the staunchest European Social Democrat.

Citizens have a claim to state-supported education—"and perpetual reeducation"—including graduate study. Both parents must receive paid leaves in the months surrounding a child's birth and should be offered "universal, state-controlled child care programs." Youths have a claim on "appropriate, universal sex education in our public schools, and universal teenage access to contraceptive means, including abortion, if necessary." She asserts that the "nationalization of vital industries" is also an entitlement: "to protect citizen consumers and citizen workers, alike, from the greed-driven vagaries of a free-market."

Unfortunately, many essays contradict the socialist-humanist philosophy upon which this view of entitlements rests. Jordan's pronouncements on educational policy, the Western literary canon, Martin Luther King, Jr., Jesse Jackson, the Constitution, liberalism, and feminism often sound like those of a black nationalist or Afro-centralist. Yet her 1986 University of California commencement address, reprinted here, sounds a note of cultural conservatism, and the first essay is a masterpiece of American patriotism. Jordan's lack of an introduction strengthens the impression that she was trying to please very different audiences. Nonetheless, this compilation casts light on the variety of views and stands she expressed and is valuable for the high quality of her descriptive essays. The ones that treat Brooklyn, where she grew up, are particularly fine.

Kissing God Goodbye

Type of work: Poetry
First published: 1997

This slender collection of poems written between 1991 and 1997 restates many of the themes of Jordan's previous collections, but despite Jordan's battle with breast cancer, the tone of these poems is more optimistic and conciliatory, compared to the anger and stridency of her earlier work. The volume is dedicated to an anonymous lover and to the "Student Poet Revolutionaries" in her Poetry for the People project at Berkeley. Except for a harsh critique of the American air campaign against Iraq ("The Bombing of Baghdad") and the Israeli devastation of Lebanon, the poems are more personal, introspective, and accepting, particularly "First Poem after Serious Surgery" and "merry-go-round poetry."

The majority are intimate haikus and other poems to b.b.L., clearly a treasured lover, but even the lyricism of "Poem #7 for b.b.L.,"

> Baby
> when you reach out
> for me
> I forget everything
> except
> I do remember to breathe. . . .

is tempered in the last lines by a claim to breathing room.

In the title poem, "Kissing God Goodbye," which brings the collection to an end, the kinder and gentler June Jordan gives way once more to the strident activist, pouring sarcasm on what she considers the bigoted rhetoric of the antiabortion movement Operation Rescue:

> You mean to tell me on the 12th day or the 13th
> that the Lord . . .
> decided who could live and who would die? . . .
> You mean to tell me that the planet
> is the brainchild
> of a single
> male
> head of household?

In *Kissing God Goodbye*, then, Jordan reasserts her position as a fearless critic of American society and public policy, reconfirming her reputation as one of today's most gifted American poets. The Kosovo poem, "April 10, 1999," will surely strike a responsive chord in many readers:

> Nothing is more cruel
> than the soldiers who command
> the widow
> to be grateful
> that she's still alive.

Suggested Readings

Brogan, Jacqueline V. "From Warrior to Womanist: The Development of June Jordan's Poetry." In *Speaking the Other Self: American Women Writers*, edited by Jeanne Campbell Reesman. Athens: University of Georgia Press, 1997.

Brown, Kimberly N. "June Jordan." In *Contemporary African American Novelists: A Bio-bibliographical Critical Sourcebook*, edited by Emmanuel S. Nelson. Westport, Conn.: Greenwood Press, 1999.

Erickson, Peter. "The Love Poetry of June Jordan." *Callaloo* 9, no. 1 (Winter, 1986): 221-234.

Kinloch, Valerie. *June Jordan: Her Life and Letters*. Westport, Conn.: Praeger, 2006.

Kinloch, Valerie, and Margret Grebowicz, eds. *Still Seeing an Attitude: Critical Reflections on the Work of June Jordan*. Lanham, Md.: Lexington Books, 2004.

MacPhail, Scott. "June Jordan and the New Black Intellectuals." *African American Review* 33, no. 1 (1999): 57-71.

Contributor: Franz G. Blaha

Cynthia Kadohata

Born: Chicago, Illinois; July 2, 1956

Japanese American

Kadohata is best known for her portrayal of a Japanese American family in her first novel, The Floating World.

Principal works

CHILDREN'S/YOUNG ADULT LITERATURE: *Kira-Kira*, 2004; *Weedflower*, 2006; *Cracker! The Best Dog in Vietnam*, 2007

LONG FICTION: *The Floating World*, 1989; *In the Heart of the Valley of Love*, 1992; *The Glass Mountains*, 1995

Cynthia Lynn Kadohata (kah-doh-HA-tah) aspired to be a journalist after she graduated from college, believing that only nonfiction can express the truth. Her parents, as were other Japanese Americans, were uprooted during World War II and traveled extensively across the country in search of work. Kadohata's keen observation of landscape and people during these long drives prepared her for her later career.

Kadohata changed her plans for the future after she was seriously injured in an automobile accident. While recuperating, she read extensively and discovered the power of fiction, its ability to say what could not be said otherwise. She tried her hand at writing short stories, and, after several rejections, one of her stories was accepted by *The New Yorker*. She felt encouraged to devote her life to writing fiction.

Kadohata's two attempts at obtaining formal instruction in creative writing were of little use to her. She found her own observations and travels to be more useful than any theoretical discussions. In her first novel, *The Floating World*, Kadohata drew upon her own experiences of moving with her family from various cities on the Pacific coast to Arkansas. The protagonist and narrator, Olivia Osaka, is a third-generation Japanese American whose years of growing up are typical of all adolescents. The novel was well received and commended for its portrayal of a Japanese American migrant family. The success of the novel enabled her to win awards from the Whiting Foundation and the National Endowment for the Arts.

In the Heart of the Valley of Love, Kadohata's second novel, depicts Los Angeles in the 1950's. Her picture of grim and bleak life in the years to come is based on the implications of the changing demographics in California in the 1990's. Living in a period when a widening chasm between the classes breeds discontent and lawlessness, the protagonist, Francie, a young woman of Asian-African American ancestry, undergoes traumatic experiences. She loses her parents and then her surrogate parents but eventually finds love, hope, and the possibility of renewal. She expresses Kadohata's optimism about the survival of a multicultural society in the future.

Kadohata is clearly influenced by writers such as Maxine Hong Kingston and Amy Tan, who draw upon their Chinese heritage. She adds another dimension to the multicultural experience by adding the Japanese American perspective.

The Floating World

Type of work: Novel
First published: 1989

The Floating World deals with the theme of identity at two levels. The narrator, Olivia Osaka, a girl of twelve at the beginning of this episodic novel, is, like all adolescents, trying to understand the world around her. In her case, the problems normally associated with growing up are further complicated by the fact that her parents are of Japanese origin. Thus Olivia has to find her place not just as an adult but as an American of Japanese descent.

The experiences recounted by Olivia take place in the 1950's and 1960's. The internment camps for the Japanese Americans had been disbanded soon after World War II, but the effects of their dislocation were still discernible. The title of the novel comes from the Japanese word *ukiyo*—the floating world—the world of gas station attendants, restaurants, and temporary jobs encountered by the Osaka family. Charles Osaka is constantly on the move with his wife and four children—Olivia and three sons—to seek better opportunities.

Olivia discovers that Charlie is not her biological father and that her charming, graceful mother still mourns the loss of her first love. Olivia is baffled by her mother's unhappiness, for she cannot understand why the love of a decent man like Charlie is not enough for her mother. Like all children in families with marital tensions, Olivia wonders if she and her brothers are responsible for the unhappiness of their parents.

Obasan, Olivia's grandmother, lives with them for some years before her death. For Olivia, she becomes the link with her Japanese heritage. She is fascinated yet repelled by the seventy-three-year-old tyrant. Olivia enjoys her grandmother's fantastic tales of growing up in Japan, but she abhors her strict, Japanese ways of disciplining the children. She hates Obasan while she is alive, but Olivia realizes later that the memories of her grandmother's stories and the observations in her diaries are invaluable in helping her understand the lives of her parents and of the Japanese American community.

In Gibson, Arkansas, the family stays long enough for Olivia to finish high school. During this period, she experiences her first love and begins to appreciate the hardships endured by the Japanese Americans. By the time she leaves for Los Angeles, she has learned certain truths about herself and her relationship to her community. She recognizes the fears and uncertainties that govern her parents' lives but has confidence in her own ability to overcome these uncertainties.

Olivia's narrative comes to an end with her decision to go to college. She has turned twenty-one, and her years in Los Angeles have given her time to learn independence, to make her own mistakes, and to come to terms with the memories of Obasan and her biological father. With the acceptance of her past and her hyphenated identity, Olivia seems ready to take her place in American society.

In the Heart of the Valley of Love

Type of work: Novel
First published: 1992

In the Heart of the Valley of Love is a futuristic novel depicting life in Los Angeles in the 2050's. Narrated by Francie, who comes to stay with her aunt in Los Angeles after she loses her African American father and Japanese mother to cancer, the novel portrays the decline of the once-prosperous city.

The picture that Francie draws of Los Angeles in the 2050's is clearly based on the demographical changes in California and the widening chasm between the rich and the poor in the 1990's. Kadohata envisions a bleak city where the nonwhites and poor whites make up 64 percent of the population and where extreme pollution causes unusual and unheard-of diseases. Shortages of all essential commodities have led to rationing of water and gas; corruption and lawlessness among officials are widespread. The city is clearly divided into the areas of haves and have-nots, and rioting by unhappy citizens is commonplace.

Cynthia Lynn Kadohata (George Miyamoto)

It is no surprise, then, that this city of despair is inhabited by "expressionless people." Young people lead undisciplined lives in the absence of responsible adults in their lives. They tattoo their faces and their bodies—a way of "obliterating themselves," according to the narrator.

Francie, too, is affected by the times. Her adoptive family is disintegrated after Rohn, her aunt's boyfriend, disappears. It is suspected that he has been arrested by the authorities. As her aunt risks her life and devotes all her time to tracing him, Francie drifts, like her young peers. She joins a community college where there are several other men and women in their twenties and thirties keeping themselves occupied in aimless activities. Eventually, she overcomes her cynical approach to love and life in general, for amid the ruins she sees signs of renewal of the land.

Francie observes at the end of the novel: "I didn't know whether, a hundred years from now, this would be called The Dark Century or The Century of Light. Though others had already declared it the former, I hoped it would turn out to be the latter." Her comment does little to diminish the chilling picture of a possible future for Los Angeles.

Suggested Readings

Kadohata, Cynthia. "Cynthia Kadohata." Interview by Lisa See. *Publishers Weekly*, August 3, 1992, 48-49.

Kakutani, Michiko. "Growing Up Rootless in an Immigrant Family." Review of *The Floating World*, by Cynthia Kadohata. *The New York Times*, June 30, 1989, p. C27.

_______. "Past Imperfect, and Future Even Worse." Review of *In the Heart of the Valley of Love*, by Cynthia Kadohata. *The New York Times*, July 28, 1992, p. C15.

O'Hehir, Diana. "On the Road with Grandmother's Magic." Review of *The Floating World*, by Cynthia Kadohata. *The New York Times Book Review*, July 23, 1989, p. 16.

Pearlman, Mickey, ed. *Listen to Their Voices: Twenty Interviews with Women Who Write*. New York: Norton, 1993.

Smith, Wendy. "Future Imperfect: Los Angeles 2052." Review of *In the Heart of the Valley of Love*, by Cynthia Kadohata. *The Washington Post Book World*, August 16, 1992, 5.

Contributor: Leela Kapai

William Melvin Kelley

Born: Bronx, New York; November 1, 1937

African American

Kelley invites readers to consider the difference that race makes in America, as well as the complexity of the individual's dilemma in response.

Principal works

LONG FICTION: *A Different Drummer*, 1962; *A Drop of Patience*, 1965; *dem*, 1967; *Dunfords Travels Everywheres*, 1970

SHORT FICTION: *Dancers on the Shore*, 1964

William Melvin Kelley was the only child of William Melvin Kelley, Sr., and Narcissa Agatha (Garcia) Kelley. His father was a journalist and an editor, for a time, at the *Amsterdam News*. When William was young, the family lived in an Italian American neighborhood in the North Bronx, but later his parents sent him to the Fieldston School, a small, predominantly white preparatory school in New York, where he became captain of the track team and president of the student council. In 1957, the year of his mother's death, Kelley entered Harvard, intending to study law. By the following year, however, the year of his father's death, he was studying fiction writing with author John Hawkes, and later, Archibald MacLeish. For the rest of his career (which he left unfinished) at Harvard, no other academic subject was relevant to him. Consumed by writing, he said, "I hope only to write fiction until I die, exploring until there is no longer anything to explore [about] the plight of Negroes as individual human beings in America."

In 1962, after the publication of his first novel, Kelley married Karen Isabelle Gibson, a designer, and worked as a writer, photographer, and teacher in New York, France, and the West Indies. He is the father of two children, Jessica and Ciratikaiji. Though he continued to work on a book entitled *Days of Our Lives* and occasionally appeared in print and in public life, Kelley, in large part, would maintain a quiet life. A 1997 *New Yorker* story, "Carlyle Tries Polygamy: How Many Are Too Many?," reveals that, despite almost thirty years of nearly complete fiction-publication silence, Kelley maintained interest in creatively pursuing some of the personages and ideas that appeared earlier in his short and long fiction. Anthologized selections of his fiction mostly appeared in late 1960's and 1970's anthologies of African American writers. He has been a nonfiction and fiction contributor to periodicals such as *Accent*, *Canto*, *Esquire*, *Jazz and Pop*, *Mademoiselle*, *Negro Digest*, *The New Yorker*, *The New York Times Magazine*, *The Par-*

William Melvin Kelley (Library of Congress)

tisan Review, *Playboy*, *Quilt*, *River Styx*, *Urbanite*, and *Works in Progress*.

Critics often fix on the interrelatedness of Kelley's four novels (and his short stories), and, indeed, though each novel is different in style, setting, characters, and even language, the ideas that spawned them are related and grow from one another. Critic Jill Weyant sees Kelley's work as a saga, in that the "purpose of writing a serious saga . . . is to depict impressionistically a large, crowded portrait, each individual novel presenting enlarged details of the whole, each complete in itself, yet evoking a more universal picture than is possible in a single volume." Kelley admits to the possible influence of other great writers of sagas, telling Roy Newquist in an interview, "Perhaps I'm trying to follow the Faulknerian pattern—although I guess it's really Balzacian when you connect everything. I'd like to be eighty years old and look up at the shelf and see that all of my books are really one big book."

A Different Drummer

Type of work: Novel
First published: 1962

A Different Drummer is Kelley's first and finest work, an enduring classic of African American literature. Kelley took his literary inspiration from American writer Henry David Thoreau's resounding celebration of individuality: "If a man does not keep pace with his companions, perhaps it is because he hears a different drummer. Let him step to the music which he hears, however measured or far away." Kelley then adapted this idea to the plight of African Americans in a fictional narrative built on a foundation of mythic imagination, American history all the way back to the slave trade, and the racial strife of the 1960's. The black experience of being perceived as different, as a despised people with trenchantly stereotyped racial characteristics, has been anything but positive. It is here, on this ground, that Kelley develops his narrative from two basic questions rooted deeply in the history of

American race relations: What would whites do without the black people they so abuse and denigrate but to whom they are so tied? Also, who might white people be without the prison of their own prejudice?

The novel takes place in the small town of Sutton, in a nameless, imaginary southern state, in June, 1957, when, mysteriously for the white citizens, "all the state's Negro inhabitants departed." The exodus is unconsciously led by the child-sized Tucker Caliban, who, like Rosa Parks (a black woman who refused to relinquish her bus seat to a white man in 1955), simply decided one day that he could no longer comply with the way things had always been in the South. The course of history, or at least his own family history, had to be changed. For four generations the Calibans were defined and limited by their service to the Willsons, and Tucker knows that he cannot reach his full human potential living in the template of the southern racial past. Thus he salts his land, kills his farm animals, axes the grandfather clock that symbolizes all the years of his family's servitude, sets fire to his house, and walks off into the sunset with his pregnant wife and his child. This peaceful, though revolutionary, act of individual initiative and vision is a direct outgrowth of and complement to the rebellion and flight of the massive legendary African whose story begins the novel. This African prince, Tucker's great-grandfather, refused to be enslaved, and it is perhaps his spirit that propels Tucker's quiet self-reliance generations later. Ironically, it is old white Mr. Harper who keeps the memory of the African alive for the white men of Sutton, telling the story on the porch of Thomason's store as often as anyone will listen.

Kelley mixes his multiple points of view between first- and third-person narration, using flashbacks to take his readers inside the heads of the southern whites, not the blacks, who occupy the small southern town of Sutton. The whites that interest Kelley are of two classes. Harry Leland and his young son, Mister Leland, represent the poor-white southerners who wish to break with the past, who wish to know black people as individuals and not as a subjugated mass. The Willsons represent the southern aristocracy, bound by the past and the money they made from slavery, but who are also educated and morally conflicted.

Tucker's opposite, a Harvard-educated black religious leader who comes down from the North to investigate the inspiration behind the exodus, becomes the novel's sacrificial lamb. The ultimately self-seeking Reverend Bennett Bradshaw is superfluous in Sutton; the people have led themselves out of their legacy of bondage and have no need of he who is not one of their own. He becomes flotsam of the most violent of southern white rituals, ironically taking up the cross that the people have left behind.

A Different Drummer is, indeed, as critic David Bradley writes, an "elegant" little book, masterful in its balance of scenes of stunning moment, delivered in the language and points of view of the people most in need of understanding them. Within its covers there is much to understand about the nature of freedom as an individual conviction that must be realized; all social change begins with a human being's belief in his or her own equality, and no lasting social change can happen without it.

A Drop of Patience

Type of work: Novel
First published: 1965

With *A Drop of Patience*, Kelley returns to the South to uncover the life of a blind black boy, Ludlow Washington, who is deposited in an institution and left to exist among the faceless masses that society, and particularly a segregated society, builds institutions to hide. Ludlow cannot walk away from his circumstances, like Tucker Caliban, because he is a child, and blind, so he must transcend in another way. He finds his means of self-expression and his route to finding a place in southern black society in his musical instrument, which is never identified but is clearly some sort of horn with several keys. Extremely talented, Ludlow is released to a black bandleader, who takes him to the small southern city of New Marsails to play with his group in a local bar. Ludlow is better than the other members of the band, however, and he has to hold his creative compulsion for avant-garde improvisation in check until he is old enough to be free of his contract, which is essentially indenture. Eventually he leaves the South and migrates to the North, becoming a leading jazz musician with his own band and enjoying relative freedom.

Though this is the framework for "one of the finest novels ever written about a jazz musician," according to critic Stanley Crouch, *A Drop of Patience* is not so much a novel about a musician as it is a novel about a blind boy coming to sexual maturity, and a black man who literally cannot see color (and is therefore able to override its coded constraints to discover deeper qualities in people) but who must come to social maturity in a superficial and pervasively race-bound society. It is a society that can drive a sane person mad, and it does this to Ludlow, who must, at bottom, be able to trust his own senses. At novel's end Ludlow chooses a course that will allow him to be a musician and to be a man among people who can see him.

dem

Type of work: Novel
First published: 1967

If *A Drop of Patience* is an enlarged detail of the people who left the imaginary southern state in *A Different Drummer*, then *dem* is an enlarged detail of the people who are incapable of seeing Ludlow Washington as a human being beyond his racial categorization. *dem* is the black perspective on American society's "us" and "them" dichotomy, and it makes sense that this novel is both a satire and a comedy. Satire typically employs sarcasm and irony to expose human folly or vice, and not only does comedic writing provide an absurd vehicle (lighthearted treatment) to transport an absurd commodity (pervasive race prejudice); it also provides the opportunity to temporarily "solve" this immense social problem with justice and laughter. In short, it provides catharsis.

Mitchell Pierce and his wife, Tam, are upper-middle-class white New Yorkers who are frank stereotypes. They are shallow, insular, cold, like mannequins or robots—devoid of the redeeming, individual, distinguishing features that human beings possess. Murder cannot move them, and love, to them, is a plot gleaned from soap operas. Tam gets pregnant by both her husband and her maid's black boyfriend and gives birth to twins, one white and one black. The rest of the novel is about Mitchell's ludicrous hunt through Harlem for the father of the black twin, whom he does not recognize when he sees him. For Mitchell, black people are simply a faceless race meant to serve him, and it never occurs to him that the money in his pocket cannot buy them.

Dunfords Travels Everywheres

Type of work: Novel
First published: 1970

Often dismissed by critics as "experimental," there is no doubt that *Dunfords Travels Everywheres* is a difficult book to read, but its inspiration is, after all, James Joyce's *Finnegans Wake* (1939). Critic Michael Wood notes that, like Joyce, Kelley "as a black American and a writer, is caught in the language and culture of an enemy country," and Kelley's two protagonists in this novel, Chig Dunford and Carlyle Bedlow, might be understood to be acting this out. The hallucinatory dream sequences, which connect the separate adventures of these two characters, are their common ground, their realm of unconscious constructions of language with African retentions, characterized by black idiomatic expressions and dialect, phonetic sounds and spellings, puns and exuberant wordplays. The Harvard-educated Chig Dunford, hanging out in an imaginary country in Europe with what amounts to imaginary white friends, blurts out two words that are revelatory. He changes his course and finds himself making a surreal transatlantic journey to America, which is, perhaps, his own "Middle Passage" to a destination of self-realization. By journey's end, he has encountered the Harriet of Ludlow Washington's healing in *A Drop of Patience* as well as his Harlem counterpart, Carlyle Bedlow, who figures prominently in *dem* and in some of Kelley's short fiction. Further, it might be argued that Chig's voyage to Harlem, to a place where he can be known, is an updated version of Tucker Caliban's journey away from "dem people's" race-based expectations of him.

Suggested Readings

Babb, Valerie M. "William Melvin Kelley." In *Afro-American Fiction Writers After 1955*, edited by Thadious M. Davis. Vol. 33 in *Dictionary of Literary Biography*. Detroit: Gale Research, 1984.

Bradley, David. Foreword to *A Different Drummer*, by William Melvin Kelley. New York: Doubleday, 1989.

Early, Gerald. Introduction to *A Drop of Patience*, by William Melvin Kelley. Hopewell, N.J.: Ecco Press, 1996.

Karrer, Wolfgang. "Romance as Epistemological Design: William Melvin Kelley's *A Different Drummer*." In *The Afro-American Novel Since 1960*, edited by Peter Bruck and Wolfgang Karrer. Amsterdam: Gainer, 1982.

Ro, Sigmund. *Rage and Celebration: Essays on Contemporary Afro-American Writing*. Atlantic Highlands, N.J.: Humanities Press, 1984.

Thomas, H. Nigel. "The Bad Nigger Figure in Selected Works of Richard Wright, William Melvin Kelley, and Ernest Gaines." *CLA Journal* 39, no. 2 (December, 1995).

Weyant, Jill. "The Kelley Saga: Violence in America." *CLA Journal* 19, no. 2 (December, 1975): 210-220.

Contributor: Cynthia Packard Hill

Adrienne Kennedy

Born: Pittsburgh, Pennsylvania; September 13, 1931

African American

Kennedy's surrealist plays are leading examples of African American drama.

Principal works

DRAMA: *Funnyhouse of a Negro*, pr. 1962, pb. 1969; *The Owl Answers*, pr. 1963, pb. 1969; *A Rat's Mass*, pr. 1966, pb. 1968; *The Lennon Play: In His Own Write*, pr. 1967, pb. 1968 (with John Lennon and Victor Spinetti); *A Lesson in Dead Language*, pr., pb. 1968; *Sun: A Poem for Malcolm X Inspired by His Murder*, pr. 1968, pb. 1971; *A Beast's Story*, pr., pb. 1969; *Boats*, pr. 1969; *Cities in Bezique: Two One-Act Plays*, pb. 1969; *An Evening with Dead Essex*, pr. 1973; *A Movie Star Has to Star in Black and White*, pr. 1976, pb. 1984; *Black Children's Day*, pr. 1980; *A Lancashire Lad*, pr. 1980; *Orestes and Electra*, pr. 1980; *Adrienne Kennedy in One Act*, pb. 1988; *The Alexander Plays*, pb. 1992; *The Ohio State Murders*, pr., pb. 1992; *June and Jean in Concert*, pr. 1995; *Sleep Deprivation Chamber*, pr., pb. 1996 (with Adam Patrice Kennedy)

NONFICTION: *People Who Led to My Plays*, 1986

MISCELLANEOUS: *Deadly Triplets: A Theatre Mystery and Journal*, 1990 (novella and journal); *The Adrienne Kennedy Reader*, 2001

Adrienne Kennedy's plays baffle and entice theater critics. In Kennedy, critics recognize a singularly able writer whose surrealism equals that of Tom Stoppard and Amiri Baraka. Edward Albee's early recognition of Kennedy's ability encouraged the yet-unpublished playwright to persist in her writing and led to the production of her *Funnyhouse of a Negro*.

Raised in a multiethnic neighborhood in Cleveland, Ohio, where her father, Cornell Wallace Hawkins, was an executive secretary for the Young Men's Christian Association and her mother, Etta Haugabook Hawkins, was a teacher, Kennedy was secure in her identity. She grew up associating with her neighbors: blacks, Jews, Italians, eastern Europeans. Where she lived, these people existed harmoniously, so Adrienne was not exposed to a racially motivated identity crisis until she entered Ohio State University in Columbus in 1949. There Kennedy felt isolated and inferior. Columbus's restaurants were still segregated, and there was little interaction between blacks and whites. By the time she graduated in 1953, her anger and her detestation of prejudice had eaten away at her in ways that would shape her future writing career.

Kennedy married Joseph Kennedy shortly after graduation and followed him to New York City, where they both attended Columbia University. She studied creative writing there from 1954 until 1956. In 1958, she studied at the American Theatre Wing, then at the New School for Social Research, and finally at Edward Albee's Circle-in-the-Square School in 1962, where she was the only black student. Albee's encouragement led to Kennedy's continuing her writing career.

Her drama examines the inner struggles people encounter as they cope with their identities in relation to the outside forces that confront them. Kennedy's plays are essentially without plot. Her leading characters have multiple personalities, reflecting aspects of their identities. She relies heavily on the use of masks, each reflecting the different identities of her characters and suggesting elements of African art and culture as well.

Funnyhouse of a Negro

Type of work: Drama
First produced: 1962, pb. 1969

The struggle of the individual with internalized social and cultural forces is the focal point of most of Adrienne Kennedy's plays. In particular, she focuses on the internal conflict of the African American, whose existence is a result of the violent blending of European and African cultures. This conflict in *Funnyhouse of a Negro* is imaged in the Negro Sarah's idolatrous love of her fair-skinned mother and rejection of her black father. The mother's whiteness has driven her insane; the father's darkness has tied him to revolution and bloodshed. Sarah's eventual escape is suicide.

The play is set in Sarah's space. The characters in the play are views of herself, or they are inspired by the objects in her room. The space is filled with relics of European civilization: dusty books, pictures of castles and monarchs, the bust of Queen Victoria. Sarah's occupation is writing, the geometric placement of words on white paper. The space is also a coffin; the white material of the curtain looks as though it has been "gnawed by rats." Throughout the play the space becomes more confining as the walls drop down. Eventually it becomes the jungle, overgrown and wild. In the context of the play's imagery of death, the jungle represents the earth's reclamation of the body.

On another level, the play is set within a "funnyhouse," an "amusement park house of horrors." Raymond and the Landlady are representations of the two grinning minstrel faces outside the funnyhouse. They are white society mocking the Negro's confusion. The bald heads and dropping walls are cheap effects designed to create confusion and fear; the mirrors in Raymond's room conceal true reflections, as distorted funnyhouse mirrors do.

Kennedy is also a woman writer, and the play makes a statement about the roles of black women and white women in society. The mother was light-skinned and beautiful by European standards. There was no destiny for her in society except madness: To be a light-skinned woman is to invite the rape of black men. Sarah is dating a white man, and this seems to give her some power in the scene with Raymond when she is the Duchess of Hapsburg. It is Raymond, however, who is asking the questions and who has control over the environment. Even the white female characters in the play who represent powerful figures are victims of hair loss; they, too, are unable to escape the dark man who pursues them.

Adrienne Kennedy (Library of Congress)

In the playwright's view, the world is a disturbing place. The lure of power is held out to women, when in fact they are powerless. For the Negro, to be assimilated into white society is to go mad or self-destruct.

Funnyhouse of a Negro invites the viewer into the mind of a very confused young black woman. The characters of the play are identified as facets of herself. She sees herself as omnipotent (Jesus), powerful (Queen Victoria, the Duchess of Hapsburg), and revolutionary (Patrice Lumumba). According to the dream logic of the play, these diverse characters all suffer from the conflict between their father, a black man, and their mother, a light-complexioned black woman who was raped and driven to insanity. The characters evoke the era of European colonialism, the zealotry of Christian missionaries, and the subsequent search for liberation by the peoples of Africa.

The Owl Answers

Type of work: Drama
First produced: 1963, pb. 1969

The same eschewal of linear progression in *Funnyhouse of a Negro* occurs in *The Owl Answers*, the first of two one-act plays appearing with *A Beast's Story* in the collection titled *Cities in Bezique*. Clara Passmore, the protagonist in *The Owl Answers*, like Sarah in *Funnyhouse of a Negro*, is a sensitive, educated young woman torn between the two cultures of which she is a part. Riveted by her fascination for a culture that seems to want no part of her, Clara, a mulatto English teacher from Savannah, Georgia, learns from her mother that her father, "the richest white man in town," is of English ancestry. She comes to London to give him a fitting burial at Saint Paul's Cathedral, among the "lovely English." Once there, she has a breakdown and is imprisoned in the Tower of London by William Shakespeare, Geoffrey

Chaucer, and William the Conquerer, who taunt her by denying her English heritage. Clara, who is the daughter of both the deceased William Mattheson and the Reverend Mr. Passmore (who, with his wife, adopted Clara when she was a child), is as firm in her claim to English ancestry as she is in her plans to bury her father in London.

Like Sarah in *Funnyhouse of a Negro*, Clara's true prison exists in her mind. Ironically, Clara Passmore, whose name suggests racial passing, passes only from human into animal form. In a final, violent scene in which the third movement of Haydn's Concerto for Horn in D accentuates the mental anguish of Clara and her mother, Clara's mother stabs herself on an altar of owl feathers. Clara, in the meantime, fends off an attack from a man whom she calls "God," who has assumed that the love she seeks from him is merely sexual. Clara, who has grown increasingly more owl-like as the play has progressed, utters a final "Ow . . . oww." In this play, as in *Funnyhouse of a Negro*, Kennedy leaves the audience with questions about the nature of spiritual faith in a world in which one calls on God, yet in which the only answer heard comes from the owl.

A Rat's Mass

Type of work: Drama
First produced: 1966, pb. 1968

A Rat's Mass is a play about the negative aspects of the black experience, about prejudice and hatred and rejection, about being an outsider with no hope of ever belonging, and about the failure of traditional institutions to offer any solutions to the problem. Brother Rat and Sister Rat represent the black population, Rosemary the white society that subjugates and oppresses, and the Procession of holy figures the uncaring, impersonal church, which offers neither succor nor forgiveness.

For Brother and Sister Rat, the pain of living black in a white world is realized in their adoration of Rosemary, the white child who is all that they can never be—"a descendant of the Pope and Julius Caesar and the Virgin Mary." Rosemary is the source of their feelings of rejection ("Colored people are not Catholics, are they?"), the instigator of their sin ("Rosemary said if I loved her I would do what she said"), the reminder of their guilt ("I will never atone you"). Clad in her white Communion dress, Rosemary is both the unattainable ideal and the avenging angel.

Perhaps what is most theatrical—and sometimes most frustrating to audiences about *A Rat's Mass* is the surrealistic quality of the play. The set, composed as it is of two black chains, a red aisle runner, and candles, evokes images of a Black Mass and forbidden rituals, creating inevitable unease in the audience. The main characters, who are described as "two pale Negro children," are part rat, part human, and as their despair mounts and their hope dies, they sound more and more like rats, less and less human. Adrienne Kennedy's choice of rats as representative of a maligned and mistreated minority is especially apt: Rats—unlike mice—evoke no sympathy, elicit only disgust and the desire to exterminate them, and conjure up images of filth and degradation, which are violently juxtaposed to the Holy Family and their entourage and Rosemary in her white dress. Most startling of the visual images in the play is the finale, in which the Holy Procession—composed of the familiar biblical figures who grace every Nativity scene ever displayed—guns down the fleeing Brother Rat and Sister Rat. This nightmarish ending provides strong reinforcement for one of the play's more pervasive ideas: that the organized church is responsible in large part for racism and hatred and indeed can be directly implicated in some of the deaths of oppressed peoples. The biblical characters so long held to be symbols of salvation and redemption become in this play the agents of destruction for a pair of innocent children, whose only fault is their color and their desire to emulate and be accepted by the dominant race and culture.

Like most of Adrienne Kennedy's plays, *A Rat's Mass* is a curious blend of monologue and dream vision, informed by highly evocative symbolism and incantatory dialogue, laced with references to mythical and historical figures. Neither her most ambitious nor her most important work, the play nevertheless is a good example of the kind of work that has earned Kennedy the acclaim of theater critics, scholars, and audiences. Like her better-known plays, *A Rat's Mass* is concerned with the anguish of not belonging, with the pain of rejection.

A Movie Star Has to Star in Black and White

Type of work: Drama
First produced: 1976, pb. 1984

The animal motif employed in *The Owl Answers* and *A Rat's Mass* is less apparent in *A Movie Star Has to Star in Black and White*. Clara Passmore of *The Owl Answers* returns for a "bit role" in which she reads from several of Kennedy's plays. The English literary tradition highly esteemed by the protagonist in *Funnyhouse of a Negro* and *The Owl Answers* is replaced by the American film tradition. Reinforcing the theme of illusion versus reality begun in *Funnyhouse of a Negro*, *A Movie Star Has to Star in Black and White* is actually a series of plays-within-a-play in which scenes from the films *Now, Voyager* (1942), *Viva Zapata* (1952), and *A Place in the Sun* (1961) take place in a hospital lobby, Clara's brother's room, and Clara's old room, respectively. As the title of the play indicates—as well as a stage note directing that all the colors be shades of black and white—Kennedy continues her experimentation with black-and-white color contrasts onstage. As in other plays by Kennedy, linear progression is eschewed, and the illusion of cinema merges with the reality of the life of Clara, a writer and daughter to the Mother and Father, the wife of Eddie, the mother of Eddie, Jr., and the alter ego of the film actresses.

Through lines spoken in the first scene by Bette Davis to Paul Henreid, the audience learns of Clara's parents' dream of success in the North, which ends in disappointment when they learn that racial oppression is not confined to the South. The scene takes place simultaneously on an ocean liner from *Now, Voyager* and in a hospital lobby in which Clara and her mother have come to ascertain the condition of Wally, Clara's brother, who lies in a coma.

Scene 2 moves to Wally's room, while Jean Peters and Marlon Brando enact lines from *Viva Zapata*. History repeats itself when it is revealed that Clara, like her mother before her, is having marital problems with her husband, Eddie. In the meantime, Marlon Brando's character changes the bedsheets onto which Jean Peters's character has bled, reminding the audience of Clara's miscarriage while Eddie was away in the armed services.

In the following scene, Shelley Winters and Montgomery Clift appear onstage in a small rowboat from the film *A Place in the Sun*. In this scene, Clara reveals her frustration as a writer who is black and a woman. She says that her husband thinks that her life is "one of my black and white movies that I love so . . . with me playing a bit part." The play ends with the news that Wally will live, but with brain damage. In the interim, Shelley Winters's character drowns as Montgomery Clift's character looks on, suggesting a connection between Clara's fantasy life in motion pictures and the real world, from which she struggles to escape.

Suggested Readings

Benston, Kimberly W. "*Cities in Bezique:* Adrienne Kennedy's Expressionistic Vision." *CLA Journal* 20 (1976).

Blau, Herbert. "The American Dream in American Gothic: The Plays of Sam Shepard and Adrienne Kennedy." *Modern Drama* 27 (1984): 520-539.

Bryant-Jackson, Paul, and Lois More Overbeck, eds. *Intersecting Boundaries: The Theatre of Adrienne Kennedy*. Minneapolis: University of Minnesota Press, 1992.

Curb, Rosemary. "Fragmented Selves in Adrienne Kennedy's *Funnyhouse of a Negro* and *The Owl Answers*." *Theater Journal* 32 (1980): 180-195.

Kennedy, Adrienne. "A Growth of Images." *Tulane Drama Review* 21 (1977): 41-47.

Kolin, Philip C. *Understanding Adrienne Kennedy*. Columbia: University of South Carolina Press, 2005.

McDonough, Carla J. "God and the Owls: The Sacred and the Profane in Adrienne Kennedy's *The Owl Answers*." *Modern Drama* 40 (1997): 385-402.

Meigs, Susan. "No Place but the Funnyhouse: The Struggle for Identity in Three Adrienne Kennedy Plays." In *Modern Drama: The Female Canon*, edited by June Schlueter. Rutherford, N.J.: Fairleigh Dickinson University Press, 1990.

Sollors, Werner. "Owls and Rats in the American Funnyhouse: Adrienne Kennedy's Drama." *American Literature: A Journal of Literary History, Criticism, and Bibliography* 63 (1991): 507-532.

Zinman, Toby Silverman. "'In the Presence of Mine Enemies': Adrienne Kennedy's *An Evening with Dead Essex*." *Studies in American Drama, 1945-Present* 6 (1991): 3-13.

Contributors: R. Baird Shuman, Kathryn Ervin Williams, E. D. Huntley, Sheila McKenna, and P. Jane Splawn

Jamaica Kincaid
(Elaine Potter Richardson)

Born: Saint Johns, Antigua; May 25, 1949

African American, Caribbean

Kincaid's short stories and novels are admired for their lyricism and for their insights into feminist and racial issues.

Principal works

CHILDREN'S LITERATURE: *Annie, Gwen, Lilly, Pam, and Tulip*, 1986 (with illustrations by Eric Fischl)

LONG FICTION: *Annie John*, 1985; *Lucy*, 1990; *The Autobiography of My Mother*, 1996; *Mr. Potter*, 2002

SHORT FICTION: *At the Bottom of the River*, 1983

NONFICTION: *A Small Place*, 1988; *My Brother*, 1997; *My Garden (Book)*, 1999; *Talk Stories*, 2001; *Among Flowers: A Walk in the Himalaya*, 2005

EDITED TEXTS: *The Best American Essays 1995*, 1995; *My Favorite Plant: Writers and Gardeners on the Plants They Love*, 1998; *The Best American Travel Writing 2005*, 2005

Jamaica Kincaid (kihn-KAYD) was born Elaine Potter Richardson on the tiny Caribbean island of Antigua. The family was poor, but she recalls her early years as idyllic. As does the protagonist of *Annie John*, Kincaid felt secure as the focus of her mother's attention. With the births of three younger brothers, however, Kincaid became increasingly alienated from her mother, and with adolescence, her alienation turned to bitter resentment.

In addition to her antipathy toward her mother, there were other reasons for Kincaid to leave her Caribbean home as soon as she was old enough to do so. As she points out in *A Small Place*, on Antigua blacks were still relegated to the bottom tiers of the social structure, just as they had been in the colonial past. Black women were even more repressed than black men. In her short story "Girl," which appears in the collection *At the Bottom of the River*, the mother makes it clear to her daughter that a woman's sole purpose in life is to wait on a man and to keep him happy.

Determined to find her way in the world, in 1966, the seventeen-year-old young woman left Antigua for the United States. Her impressions of the different country are reflected in her second semiautobiographical novel, *Lucy*. In common with the title character, Kincaid first supported herself by working as a live-in babysitter in New York City. Although Kincaid took high school and college

Jamaica Kincaid (Sigrid Estrada)

courses, in the main she educated herself by reading. Eventually she found a job on a magazine, turned out articles, and tried her hand at short stories. She was finding a new identity as a writer; in 1973, she took the name Jamaica Kincaid, in a sense inventing herself as a person. In 1978, "Girl" was published in *The New Yorker*, the first of many stories to appear there. Shortly thereafter, Kincaid married and moved to Vermont.

After an absence of nearly two decades, Kincaid returned to Antigua. Having found herself, Kincaid was now free, and in the years that followed she often took her children to visit her early home. By leaving her native island, Kincaid learned not only to understand herself but also to empathize with women who, like the protagonist in *The Autobiography of My Mother* and like her own mother, were assigned their identities in a society that permitted them no options.

At the Bottom of the River

Type of work: Short fiction
First published: 1983

Some critics call *At the Bottom of the River* a novel; others call it a collection of stories. Certainly the stories' interconnections lend a sense of continuity to this thin volume. Much of *At the Bottom of the River* is a recollection of Jamaica Kincaid's childhood on the Caribbean island of Antigua. The author captures the identity of this region and its people with remarkable accuracy in her sketches. By telling her stories largely from a child's point of view, Kincaid gracefully intermixes the outside world with her protagonist's mental world of dreams, images, fantasy, and mysticism.

The book's ten stories dwell upon racial and mother-daughter relationships. The daughter is obsessed by her mother, an overpowering love object for her. Her attempts to break from her maternal dependence are central to many of the sketches. The sketch "My Mother" recounts with great poignancy a girl's emotional odyssey from early childhood to the point of needing to loose herself from a reliance upon the mother she dearly loves. The narrative is disarmingly simple and direct. The child's dreamworld intrudes constantly upon the outside world, with which she must necessarily merge. She cries a "pond of tears" at separating from her mother. The girl's exile, expressed in the words "she [the mother] shook me out and stood me under a tree," is connected to her memory of the childhood punishment of being banished, when she had misbehaved, from her house to take her dinner under the breadloaf trees. This story is about lost innocence and the attempt to recapture it.

The sketch "At Last" considers the essence of things. The child asks what becomes of the hen whose feathers are scattered, whose flesh is stripped away, whose bones disappear. Kincaid broaches similar universal questions in "Blackness," in which she deals with the mystery of the generations, with the child who grows up to become a mother to the succeeding generation. The questions posed in this story are questions that puzzled the ancient Greek philosophers and that still puzzle thinking people everywhere.

Annie John

Type of work: Novel
First published: 1985

Annie John, Kincaid's first novel, is a story of a girl's coming-of-age. On a conscious level the protagonist is contemplating death, friendship, sexual desire, and the developments in her body; she is also experiencing a deeper need to cut herself off from her mother, even if in the process she must hurt them both. The novel is set on the Caribbean island of Antigua. As a young child, Annie John clings to her beautiful and loving mother. She likes to caress her, smell her perfume, take baths with her, and wear dresses made of the same fabric as hers. At school, Annie shows that she has a mind of her own, but at home she takes note of everything her mother says or does.

Soon, however, Annie begins to realize that human relationships are fragile. They can be dissolved by death, by infidelity, or by changes in one's feelings. At a new school, Annie finds herself abandoning her best friend, Gwyneth Joseph, for a dirty, defiant red-haired girl. At home, Annie betrays her mother's trust and love. She lies to her about unimportant matters, such as whether or not she has any marbles, and she even insults her. To some degree Annie is acting out her feelings about her parents' lovemaking and about her own sexual development. Annie is also reacting to her mother's evident embarrassment when Annie assumes a woman's identity. On a deeper level, Annie's love for her mother is so strong that only by rejecting her can she establish a space for herself and a personality of her own.

At school, Annie gets into trouble by writing under the picture of Christopher Columbus the same words that her mother had said in mockery of her father, Pa Chess. Clearly, Annie senses that there is a similarity between the colonial system, which guaranteed that blacks would remain low in the economic system, and the patriarchal family, which ensured the subordination of females. By the time she is fifteen, Annie is thoroughly miserable, loathing her mother, herself, and her existence. She becomes ill, and for almost four months she is bedridden, nursed by her mother, her father, and finally by her grandmother, Ma Chess, who appears mysteriously and evidently effects a cure. At last, when she is seventeen, Annie is sent to England. As the ship prepares to sail, Annie and her mother weep, and Annie relents enough to wave good-bye. Now free to find her own identity, she is free to love her mother, if only at a distance.

Lucy

Type of work: Novel
First published: 1990

Lucy is a thematic sequel to *Annie John*. Lucy is seventeen when the novel begins, newly arrived in the United States from Antigua to work as an au pair, watching the four girls of Lewis and Mariah, an upper-middle-class New York couple. Although the novel is set entirely outside Antigua and Lucy's mother never appears in it, Lucy's attempt to separate herself from her mother constitutes the main theme of the novel.

Mariah is presented as a loving but thoroughly ethnocentric white woman. A recurring example of this is her attempt to make Lucy appreciate the Wordsworthian beauty of daffodils, unaware that it is precisely because Lucy had to study Wordsworth's poetry about a flower that does not grow in Antigua that this flower represents the world of the colonizer to her. In fact, Mariah's unselfconscious, patronizing goodwill is exactly what Lucy loves most and yet cannot tolerate about her employer, because it reminds her of her mother.

When Lucy learns that Lewis is having an affair with Mariah's best friend, Dinah, she understands that this idyllic marriage is falling apart. When a letter from home informs her that her father has died, she is unable to explain to Mariah that her anger toward her mother is based on mourning the perfect love she had once felt between them. At the same time, her own sexuality begins to emerge, and she develops interests in young men. Wanting more space, she moves in with her friend Peggy, a young woman who represents a more exciting world to Lucy, cutting short her one-year au pair agreement. The novel ends with Lucy writing her name, Lucy Josephine Potter, in a book and wishing that she could love someone enough to die for that love. This ending clearly signals an act of self-possession (much like the self-naming at the end of *Annie John*), but it also signifies the loneliness of breaking away from others, even to assert oneself. Though *Lucy* is a much angrier novel than *Annie John*, Lucy's anger is best understood in terms of the writer's earlier autobiographical surrogate in *Annie John*; the melancholy that debilitates Annie at the end of her novel is turned into anger by Lucy.

The Autobiography of My Mother

Type of work: Novel
First published: 1996

This narrative, in seven episodes, recapitulates and foretells, in starkly poetic language, the events in Xuela Richardson Bailey's life. The fragmentary photograph of a Caribbean woman that introduces each section is completed in the seventh section.

The central fact of the narrator's life is the death of her mother when Xuela was born, its recital a repeated incantation. Her maternal grandmother was abandoned at birth by an unknown woman. Xuela's father, of Scottish and African ancestry, gave his daughter—along with his dirty clothes—to be cared for by the woman who did his laundry.

From this unpromising beginning, the narrator creates a life for herself in a world from which she expects nothing. A highly sensual woman, she nevertheless withholds herself emotionally from those who might have loved her, refusing to compromise her fierce personal independence. Aborting the children she conceives, she rejects motherhood. Her power comes from herself: "I could sense from the beginning of my life that I would know things when I needed to know them."

Kincaid works against the tradition of black women writers who portray women bonding with one another against the racist, patriarchal oppressor. The women in this narrative distrust or hate one another. Kincaid is fascinated by the politics of power. In her reading of Caribbean history, there are the victors and the vanquished—all failed human beings. The strength of the black woman comes not from her Carib-African heritage or from those whom she loves. She lives in the existential present, creating herself, refusing to mourn her fate or regret her past.

Suggested Readings

Bloom, Harold, ed. *Jamaica Kincaid*. Philadelphia: Chelsea House, 1998.

Bouson, J. Brooks. *Jamaica Kincaid: Writing Memory, Writing Back to the Mother*. Albany: State University of New York Press, 2005.

Davies, Carole Boyce. *Black Women, Writing, and Identity: Migrations of the Subject*. New York: Routledge, 1994.

Emery, Mary Lou. "Refiguring the Postcolonial Imagination: Tropes of Visuality in Writing by Rhys, Kincaid, and Cliff." *Tulsa Studies in Women's Literature* 16 (Fall, 1997): 259-280.

Ferguson, Moira. *Jamaica Kincaid: Where the Land Meets the Body*. Charlottesville: University Press of Virginia, 1994.

Gilmore, Leigh. *The Limits of Autobiography: Trauma and Testimony*. Ithaca, N.Y.: Cornell University Press, 2001.

MacDonald-Smythe, Antonia. *Making Homes in the West Indies: Constructions of Subjectivity in the Writings of Michelle Cliff and Jamaica Kincaid.* New York: Garland, 2001.

Mistron, Deborah. *Understanding Jamaica Kincaid's "Annie John."* Westport, Conn.: Greenwood Press, 1999.

Paravisini-Gerbert, Lizabeth. *Jamaica Kincaid: A Critical Companion.* Westport, Conn.: Greenwood Press, 1999.

Simmons, Diane. *Jamaica Kincaid.* New York: Twayne, 1994.

Contributors: R. Baird Shuman, Rosemary M. Canfield Reisman, Thomas Cassidy, Ann Davison Garbett, and Barbara Wiedemann

Martin Luther King, Jr.

Born: Atlanta, Georgia; January 15, 1929
Died: Memphis, Tennessee; April 4, 1968

African American

King's speeches and essays united, motivated, and mobilized people of all colors during the civil rights struggles of the 1950's and 1960's.

Principal works

NONFICTION: *Stride Toward Freedom: The Montgomery Story*, 1958; *The Measure of a Man*, 1959; *Letter from Birmingham City Jail*, 1963; *Strength to Love*, 1963; *A Martin Luther King Treasury*, 1964; *Why We Can't Wait*, 1964; *The Trumpet of Conscience*, 1967; *Where Do We Go from Here: Chaos or Community?*, 1967; *The Words of Martin Luther King, Jr.*, 1983, 1987; *A Testament of Hope: The Essential Writings and Speeches of Martin Luther King, Jr.*, 1986, 1991; *The Papers of Martin Luther King, Jr.*, 1992-2000 (4 volumes; Clayborne Carson, editor); *The Autobiography of Martin Luther King*, 1998 (Carson, editor); *A Knock at Midnight: Inspiration from the Great Sermons of Reverend Martin Luther King, Jr.*, 1998 (Carson and Peter Halloran, editors); *A Call to Conscience: The Landmark Speeches of Dr. Martin Luther King, Jr.*, 2001 (Carson, editor)

Martin Luther King, Jr., was formally ordained at the age of nineteen, in the church over which his father presided, thus officially beginning his public-speaking career. Within ten years, he had secured a position as pastor of a Montgomery, Alabama, church and had established himself as a civil rights leader by leading a boycott against the Montgomery public transportation system. After the successful conclusion of the boycott, King founded the Southern Christian Leadership Conference (SCLC) in the hope of harnessing the momentum of the movement to further the cause of racial equality.

Supported by a network of churches and civil rights organizations, King became the most vocal opponent to segregation and thus became a lightning rod for criticism and accolades. On August 28, 1963, King led a march on Washington, D.C., at which he delivered his best-known speech, "I Have a Dream." The following year, he was awarded the Nobel Peace Prize. Also during 1963 and 1964, King was arrested four times on charges such as parading without a permit, trespassing, and contempt of court. One of King's most powerful works, *Letter from Birmingham City Jail*, was composed while he was incarcerated during this time, and several other pieces were occasioned by the arrests and subsequent confinements.

The focus of most of King's writings was upon the necessity for all citizens to effect necessary social changes by using a system of passive resistance and economic empowerment. The tenets of his strategy were outlined in such speeches as "The Power of Nonviolence" (1957) and "Love, Law, and Civil Disobedience" (1961). In addresses such as "A Time to Break Silence" (1967), he spoke of the need for Americans to examine their beliefs about race and culture, with respect not only to conflicts within the United States but also in international relations, such as those with Vietnam.

King's later works, such as *Where Do We Go from Here: Chaos or Community?*, show King's reluctant recognition that the struggle for racial equality would be a long-term battle. Although he believed that civil rights would eventually be equally afforded to all Americans, he warned of the dangers of complacency and backsliding. In his final address ("I've Been to the Mountaintop"), given on April 3, 1968, he urged supporters of civil rights to continue the struggle in his absence. The next day, he was shot to death.

Stride Toward Freedom

Type of work: Activist manual
First published: 1958

Published in 1958, King's first major publication grew out of a speech he had made in San Francisco in 1956 about the Rosa Parks incident and its aftermath, which included the bombing of King's home and frequent death threats directed at him and at members of his family. This book provides a blueprint for the ways in which a repressed populace can resist oppression nonviolently by creating a unified front against their oppressors. In the Montgomery case, this was accomplished through the boycott of public transportation and of white merchants who depended on Montgomery's black population for much of their income.

The tactics King outlines in this book are foolproof. Merchants cannot force people to patronize them, so when an oppressed group shuns them, they must eventually yield to the demands of those staging the boycott. The only rub is that a boycott like that in Montgomery places difficult demands upon those supporting it.

Many Montgomery blacks depended on public transportation to get to their jobs. Arrangements had to be made to get them to those jobs by other means. Not patronizing local stores meant obtaining food and other necessities elsewhere. Survival under such conditions demanded planning and coordination. King became an expert in creating the master plans necessary to implement his followers' actions.

Stride Toward Freedom had considerable influence among black leaders associated with such organizations as the SCLC. It outlined the effectiveness of nonviolence. It cast the oppressed as victims of an unjust society rather than as aggressors pitted against the dominant society. When Mahatma Gandhi challenged the British Empire, he and his followers were greatly outnumbered, but through employment of Gandhi's nonviolent tactics, they appealed to the morality of their oppressors and, in the long term, achieved their ends against odds that initially seemed insurmountable. King devoutly believed that American blacks could succeed by employing similar tactics.

Letter from Birmingham City Jail

Type of work: Letter and social criticism
First published: 1963

Probably the single most memorable piece of writing produced by Martin Luther King, Jr., was written during the few days that he languished in Birmingham's city jail. This book, published in 1963, includes the full text of King's letter and outlines in considerable detail how the elaborate plans for the Birmingham protests evolved. King, painfully aware of the injustices visited upon blacks in Birmingham, came to the city because of these injustices. He was publicly denounced as an interloper. Newspaper articles about his interference and an open letter by six local clergymen contended that, since King wasn't a citizen of Birmingham, he had no right to intervene in what they considered a local matter.

King took the high moral ground, asserting his need to seek out injustice where it existed and to regard people in towns in which he did not reside as brothers. He considered it a moral imperative to concern himself with their welfare, particularly when they were clearly the victims of an established policy of racial discrimination imposed upon them by the white society. The changes King demanded in Birmingham were reasonable. He wanted blacks to be served at the city's lunch counters and to be permitted to use drinking fountains then available to whites only. He sought to desegregate public restrooms and fitting rooms in stores.

The crux of this book is its detailed account of how the SCLC's training committee used simulations to replicate what protesters might expect to experience at the hands of bigoted police officers and enraged white citizens. Rather than fighting back, protesters were advised to be quiet and to let their bodies go limp. They were urged to resist without bitterness, to receive verbal abuse and not reply, and to be beaten without retaliating.

Martin Luther King, Jr. (© The Nobel Foundation)

Arrested for his participation in the Birmingham protest, King wrote *Letter from Birmingham City Jail* on paper smuggled to him and then smuggled out of the jail. Although he spent only a few days in confinement before being bailed out through Harry Belafonte's efforts, this incarceration shaped King's future in many ways.

Why We Can't Wait

Type of work: Social criticism
First published: 1964

The hundredth anniversary of Abraham Lincoln's signing of the Emancipation Proclamation occurred in 1963. To commemorate that anniversary, Martin Luther King, Jr., wrote *Why We Can't Wait*. The book, published the following year, discussed the irony of celebrating this anniversary while blacks in many parts of the United States were still segregated, discriminated against, and oppressed. In most southern states, interracial marriage was still banned by outmoded and clearly unconstitutional miscegenation laws. And, though Lincoln's pen theoretically freed America's slaves, their grandchildren and great-grandchildren were, in much of the United States, denied the right to vote, to attend the schools of their choice, to eat in restaurants of their choosing, and to stay in hotels that, throughout the South, were designated "White Only."

In 1939, world-acclaimed singer Marian Anderson was denied the right to sing in Constitution Hall in the nation's capital, and forbidden from staying in any of Washington's major hotels, simply because of the color of her skin. Blacks were similarly humiliated throughout the South and in much of the North. They were underemployed and underpaid for the work they did.

School segregation, although perhaps not specifically mandated as it was in the South, was a fact of life in most northern cities largely because blacks could not rent or buy homes in the parts of town with the best schools. Many secondary schools in the inner cities had black enrollments of 97 percent or more.

In *Why We Can't Wait*, King deplored segregation, discrimination, and gradualism. Many southern political leaders, realizing that racial integration would inevitably be thrust upon them, devised plans to integrate the schools so gradually that they would in effect remain segregated far into the future. Making his case with impeccable logic and considerable factual evidence, King developed an airtight argument for immediate and decisive action. Before the decade was out, substantial progress had been made, largely because of King's pioneering and persistent efforts.

A Testament of Hope

TYPE OF WORK: Essays, interviews, speeches, and sermons
FIRST PUBLISHED: 1986, 1991

A Testament of Hope: The Essential Writings and Speeches of Martin Luther King, Jr., is a compendium of King's writings and of transcripts of some of his better-known interviews, speeches, and sermons, all of which were compiled and published at the request of his widow, Coretta Scott King. The book is divided into subject-matter sections and an appendix. The first section, "Religious: Nonviolence," explores the theological underpinnings of King's passive resistance philosophy. Because he was connected at an early age with the church, it is not surprising that many of the works in this section focus on the role of Christian love in the struggle for equal rights.

Most of the selections in the second section, "Social: Integration," are oriented toward the more practical aspects of the Civil Rights movement. Topics include the necessity of passive resistance, the need for eloquent speakers, and the difficulties caused by internal conflicts within the movement.

The third section, "Political: Wedged Between Democracy and Black Nationalism," addresses the difficulties King encountered while campaigning for immediate change; it was difficult to do so and not to lose the support of moderate and conservative sympathizers. This theme echoes through much of the next section, "Famous Sermons and Public Addresses," as well. The fourth section contains King's best-known speeches, including the "I Have a Dream" speech of 1963 and the "I've Been to the Mountaintop" speech, which was delivered shortly before King's death in 1968.

The fifth section of *A Testament of Hope* contains some of King's best-known essays, including the "Letter from the Birmingham Jail" (1963). In this and the title essay, King impugns not only the staunch conservatives who resist social change but also the apathetic moderates who, King charges, perpetuate social injustice. The sixth section, "Interviews," contains transcripts of conversations King had with Kenneth B. Clark, *Playboy* magazine, *Meet the Press*, and *Face to Face*. The sixth and final section contains King's more formal written works, those that were written as, or developed into, books.

James M. Washington, editor of *A Testament of Hope*, admits that, as a public figure, King sometimes had help with the invention and composition of the works contained in this volume. This collection is valuable, he asserts, not only as a record of what King actually penned but also of the principles he espoused and the ideals for which he stood. Because each section is arranged chronologically, it is possible to chart aspects of King's philosophical development. He changed in response to the changing political and social climate of America. His focus, however—the necessity of nonviolent civil disobedience in order to accomplish the greater good of racial equality—remains evident throughout.

Suggested Readings

Baldwin, Lewis V., ed. *The Legacy of Martin Luther King, Jr.: The Boundaries of Law, Politics, and Religion*. South Bend, Ind.: University of Notre Dame Press, 2002.

Branch, Taylor. *Parting the Waters: America in the King Years, 1954-1963*. New York: Simon & Schuster, 1988.

_______. *Pillar of Fire: America in the King Years, 1963-65*. New York: Simon & Schuster, 1998.

Dyson, Michael Eric. *I May Not Get There with You: The True Martin Luther King, Jr.* New York: Free Press, 2000.

Fairclough, Adam. *Martin Luther King, Jr.* Athens: University of Georgia Press, 1995.

Frady, Marshall. *Martin Luther King, Jr.* New York: Viking, 2002.

Friedly, Michael, and David Gallen. *Martin Luther King, Jr.: The FBI File*. New York: Carroll & Graf, 1993.

Garrow, David J. *Bearing the Cross: Martin Luther King, Jr., and the Southern Christian Leadership Conference, a Personal Portrait*. New York: William Morrow, 1986.

King, Coretta Scott. *My Life with Martin Luther King, Jr.* Rev. ed. New York: Henry Holt, 1993.

Oates, Stephen B. *Let the Trumpet Sound: A Life of Martin Luther King, Jr.* Reprint. New York: HarperCollins, 1994.

Peake, Thomas R. *Keeping the Dream Alive: A History of the Southern Christian Leadership Conference from King to the Nineteen-Eighties*. New York: P. Lang, 1987.

Contributors: T. A. Fishman and R. Baird Shuman

Thomas King

Born: Sacramento, California; April 24, 1943

Native American

King's primary subject is cultural clash: Native Americans, with their traditional culture and communal values, are sneered at by the white invaders, but they triumph through wit, cleverness, and resourcefulness.

Principal works

CHILDREN'S/YOUNG ADULT LITERATURE: *A Coyote Columbus Story*, 1992; *Coyote Sings to the Moon*, 2001
LONG FICTION: *Medicine River*, 1990; *Green Grass, Running Water*, 1993; *Truth and Bright Water*, 1999
SHORT FICTION: *One Good Story, That One*, 1993
NONFICTION: *The Truth About Stories: A Native Narrative*, 2003
EDITED TEXT: *All My Relations: An Anthology of Contemporary Canadian Native Fiction*, 1990

Thomas King was born to Robert Elvin King, a Cherokee Indian from Oklahoma, and Katheryn Konsonlas King, a Greek American. His father left the family when Thomas was five, and he and his brother, Christopher, were raised by their mother in Roseville, California. Upon graduation from Roseville High School, King worked at odd jobs, including those of ambulance driver and gambling croupier. He attended Sacramento State College from 1961 to 1962 and Sierra Junior College from 1962 to 1964, after which he worked his way to Australia and New Zealand and was employed there as a photojournalist. He returned to the United States in 1967 and took a job as a draftsman at Boeing Aircraft in Seattle. The following year he enrolled at California State College, Chico, because his mother had gone there. He graduated in 1970, with a B.A. in English. That year he married Kristine Adams. They had a son, Christian, in 1971.

At that point, King embarked upon a series of academic jobs, beginning as a counselor for American Indian students at the University of Utah and soon moving up to director of the new Native Studies Department. While working at Utah, he obtained an M.A. in English from his undergraduate alma mater in Chico. In 1973 he moved on to Humboldt State University in Arcata, California, where he was an associate dean for student services.

In 1977 King returned to the University of Utah, to work as coordinator of the History of the Indians of the Americas project. In 1979 he moved to Canada to take a position as chair of the Native Studies Department and remained there for the next ten years. His marriage ended in 1981. In 1986 he received a doctorate in English and American studies from the University of Utah; his dissertation was titled "Inventing the Indian: White Images, Native Oral Traditions, and Contemporary Native Writers." Also in the 1980's he and his partner, Helen Hoy, had two children: Benjamin Hoy (born in 1985) and Elizabeth King (1988).

In 1987 King began publishing short stories in magazines and anthologies. In 1989 he returned to the United States, taking a position as associate professor of American and Native studies at the University of Minnesota, Twin Cities. In 1990 King published his first novel, *Medicine River*, set at a Blackfoot reservation in Alberta, Canada, and edited *All My Relations: An Anthology of Contemporary Canadian Native Fiction*. In 1992 King published his first children's book, *A Coyote Columbus Story*; it won the Canadian Governor-General's Award for that year.

In 1993-1994 he took a leave of absence for the academic year to work as a story editor for the Canadian Broadcasting Company, where he wrote the teleplay for the adaptation of his novel *Medicine River*. Also in 1993, King published his best-known novel, the satirical *Green Grass, Running Water*, and a short-story collection, *One Good Story, That One*. In 1995 he returned to Canada with his partner and children. He took an academic appointment at the University of Guelph in Ontario.

Thomas King is an important figure in American Indian literature. He once noted with some amusement that, because he lives and teaches in Canada, he is often called a Canadian Native writer, though he was born in the United States and those of his tribe, the Cherokee, are not native to Canada. In his work, his primary subject is cultural clash: The American Indians, with their traditional culture and communal values, are sneered at and ignored, if not simply conquered, by the white invaders, but they triumph through wit, cleverness, and resourcefulness (often represented in King's fiction by the figure of the trickster in American Indian lore, Coyote).

Green Grass, Running Water

Type of work: Novel
First published: 1993

In King's best-known work, *Green Grass, Running Water*, four old Indians have escaped from a mental hospital and are on their way to fix the world. They call themselves the Lone Ranger, Ishmael, Robinson Crusoe, and Hawkeye, and their companion is the trickster Coyote. There is some confusion over whether they are men or women. The director of the hospital, Dr. Hovaugh, believes that their disappearances occur with startling regularity relative to natural disasters such as the Yellowstone fire of 1988. He sets out with a coworker to catch them before another disaster occurs.

While the old Indians' revisionist retelling of how the world began makes up one strand of the plot, in the other main line of the story King explores the lives of five

Indians whose relationships intertwine through either blood or romantic ties. Alberta works as a university professor and enjoys her independence and the attentions of both Lionel and Charlie. Though she has no desire to marry either man, she wants to have a child. Charlie, an attorney whose father was an actor in Western films, works for the company whose dam is blocked by Eli, Lionel's uncle. Eli has moved into his mother's cabin, which sits in the path of the dam, and refuses to move. Lionel accidentally fell from grace as a university employee and now sells televisions and thinks he may someday return to his studies. Latisha, Lionel's sister, runs the Dead Dog Cafe, has three children, and has survived an abusive marriage.

As the Blackfoot community prepares to celebrate the annual Sun Dance, these several lives converge, and the old Indians attempt to fix the world in their unreliable way, bringing both salvation and disaster.

Suggested Readings

Atwood, Margaret. "A Double-Bladed Knife: Subversive Laughter in Two Stories by Thomas King." *Canadian Literature* 124/125 (Summer/Spring, 1990): 243-250.

Donaldson, Laura. "Noah Meets Old Coyote: Or, Singing in the Rain, Intertextuality in Thomas King's *Green Grass, Running Water*." *SAIL: Studies in American Indian Literature* 7 (Summer, 1995): 27-43.

Ruppert, James. "Thomas King." In *Native American Writers of the United States*. Vol. 175 in *Dictionary of Literary Biography*. Detroit: Gale Group, 1997.

The World & I 8 (June, 1993).

Contributor: Arthur D. Hlavaty

Barbara Kingsolver

Born: Annapolis, Maryland; April 8, 1955

Euro-American

Kingsolver's works grip the reader long after the details of the individual characters and plots have faded, because they, like Kingsolver's own life, are grounded in a real world of ecopolitical action.

Principal works

long fiction: *The Bean Trees*, 1988; *Animal Dreams*, 1990; *Pigs in Heaven*, 1993; *The Poisonwood Bible*, 1998; *Prodigal Summer*, 2000

poetry: *Another America/Otra America*, 1992

short fiction: *Homeland, and Other Stories*, 1989

nonfiction: *Holding the Line: Women in the Great Arizona Mine Strike of 1983*, 1989; *High Tide in Tucson: Essays from Now or Never*, 1995; *Last Stand: America's Virgin Lands*, 2002 (photographs by Annie Griffiths Belt); *Small Wonder*, 2002; *Animal, Vegetable, Miracle: A Year of Food Life*, 2007 (with Steven L. Hopp and Camille Kingsolver)

edited text: *The Best American Short Stories, 2001*, 2001

Although Barbara Kingsolver (KIHNG-sawl-vur) cannot be called "Native American," her physician-father prided himself in his one-sixty-fourth Cherokee heritage, and her works often concern themselves with marginalized groups, including Native Americans, Central Americans, and women. She grew up in Kentucky and lived there for much of her early life, with stints in the Congo (now Zaire) in 1963 and later in the Caribbean (1967). Kingsolver was therefore exposed to a variety of different cultures, developing an appreciation of diversity. Studying at DePauw University on a piano scholarship, she received a B.A. in 1977, earned an M.S. in 1981 from the University of Arizona, and eventually became a freelance journalist and science writer. After publishing her first novel in 1988, she turned seriously to writing, and her work began to garner numerous awards, crowned in 2000 by the National Humanities Medal. Leaving Arizona after a quarter century, she and her husband settled on a farm in Virginia.

This background subtly invigorates *Animal Dreams* and *Pigs in Heaven* as Kingsolver adeptly coordinates the intricacies of plot lines that move across ecological, ethnobiological, and regional backdrops. Kingsolver links the plots of *The Bean Trees* and *Pigs in Heaven* through the narrative of Taylor Greer and the Cherokee infant she initially befriends and later adopts, Turtle (named for her tenacious

Barbara Kingsolver (Seth Kantner)

grip on her newfound mother). In these two novels Kingsolver introduces the primary themes that resound through her fiction, nonfiction, and poetry: the importance of children, the necessity for and intricacies of finding respect for different ethnic worldviews, and the overwhelming joy that accompanies seizing a life full of challenge based on one's dreams. Kingsolver's characters invariably opt for the challenges of love created amid the tensions of intercultural relationships.

This tension of choosing a life amid differing cultural commitments is particularly evident in *Animal Dreams*. Codi Noline searches for a committed path of her own, even as she steadfastly denies doing so. Codi discovers this path in her ability to help the residents of her father's hometown, Grace, confront the consequences of industrial pollution. It is an easy association to see Kingsolver's own emerging human rights activism in Codi's process of deciding to help the city of Grace fight the threat of pollution. Kingsolver enables Codi to dream herself beyond the demons of her own outcast childhood by discovering in herself the will to fight this external enemy. From Loyd Peregrina, a Pueblo Native American, Codi learns the following in an answer to the question, "What do . . . animals dream about?":

> I think they dream about whatever they do when they're awake. . . . Your dreams, what you hope for and all that, it's not separate from your life. It grows right up out of it. . . . If you want sweet dreams, you've got to live a sweet life.

Holding the Line

Type of work: Social history
First published: 1989

Kingsolver's novels and poems continue to grip the reader long after the details of the individual characters and plots have faded, because they, like Kingsolver's own life, are grounded in a real world of ecopolitical action. *Holding the Line: Women in the Great Arizona Mine Strike of 1983*, *High Tide in Tucson: Essays from Now or Never*, and *Small Wonder* admirably present Kingsolver's real-world engagement. In *Holding the Line*, Kingsolver unabashedly offers a biased account of the strike against the Phelps Dodge Copper Corporation in Morenci and Clifton, Arizona, in 1983. At the time, Kingsolver was working as a freelance journalist, and while *Holding the Line* certainly presents an account of the actual events of a real strike, what comes through even more clearly is Kingsolver's desire to show the unexpected strength of the women who enabled the strike to continue long after the men of Clifton had lost their determination. In this respect Kingsolver calls into question traditional gender roles in the American Southwest and reinforces a tradition of "machisma" that clearly has echoes in her exclusive use of female leading characters in her fiction.

Homeland, and Other Stories

Type of work: Short fiction
First published: 1989

In her stories, Kingsolver addresses conventional relationships in contemporary situations: single mothers juggling the responsibilities of rearing children and working; married couples considering parenthood or growing old; estranged lovers or families trying to bridge the gaps that they do not understand. The characters in these stories are trying to find themselves; adrift and rootless, they are searching for commitment, either externally or internally. Lack of communication between two or more people apparently stems from an inability to find common ground and creates inarticulate resentment or incomprehension, In "Island on the Moon," for example, an estranged mother and daughter overcome years of bitterness and the strange circumstances of being pregnant at the same time to be reconciled and to draw strength from each other.

The title story describes the relationship between a grandmother and granddaughter. Written from the granddaughter's point of view as a young girl, the story relates a disappointing trip taken by the family to the grandmother's homeland, which the latter does not even recognize. Through the young girl, Kingsolver seems to say that it is not the place that holds the memories and has significance; it is the people and the history they retain in their memories. In other words, it is not necessary to go home in order to remember where one came from.

Other stories deal with various issues, such as homosexuality, strikes and unions, or ethnicity, where the main character is faced with a life-changing decision that she or he must inevitably make alone. In "Rose-Johnny," Georgeann, a young girl living in a small, rural town, slowly becomes aware of the ostracism against a lesbian named Rose-Johnny, whom she has befriended. The subtle victimization that Rose-Johnny undergoes is poignantly related through Georgeann, who steadfastly remains true to her friendship with the woman, despite town pressure.

The oral richness of the stories in this collection will often find the reader looking for a listening audience. Kingsolver displays an unusual gift for storytelling, a gift that she has developed in these stories beyond the considerable talent she demonstrated in *The Bean Trees*.

Animal Dreams

Type of work: Novel
First published: 1990

Animal Dreams is chiefly a novel about coming home. Returning to her small hometown of Grace, Arizona, after a ten-year absence, thirty-two-year-old Cosima (Codi) Noline must come to terms with her tangled personal and family past. Codi has finished medical school, but she has abandoned her career after panicking during a difficult childbirth procedure. She desperately misses Hallie, her beloved younger sister, who has just left their Tucson apartment to dedicate her agricultural expertise to the Sandinista revolution in Nicaragua. Thus Codi reluctantly returns to Grace to work for a year as a high school biology teacher and to care for her father, Doc Homer. A stern and stubbornly independent man, he is suffering from Alzheimer's disease, and Kingsolver includes several chapters that dramatize his confused perspective on his life and family.

Kingsolver presents most of the action, however, through Codi's first-person point of view; and despite Codi's sense of failure and alienation, she is an immensely appealing narrator. Codi's supple voice, both conversational and highly alert, provides many witty observations on herself, the numerous supporting characters, and the rich cultural mix of the Southwest. Chief among those characters who help Codi find herself are Emelina Domingos, her high school friend and the mother of a large family, and Loyd Peregrina, a railroad engineer who courts Codi and helps her to appreciate the beauty and wisdom of the Native American worldview.

In addition to providing an entertaining story of personal relations, Kingsolver's novel also deepens the reader's concern for social issues through the struggles faced by her characters. Hallie's letters and Codi's frequent thoughts of her develop a sympathetic image of the Sandinista revolution and a disturbing indictment of U.S. support for the Contras. Similarly, Kingsolver stirs the reader through the spirited campaign that the women of Grace organize to save the town's river and orchards from industrial poisoning by the Black Mountain Mining Company. In sum, *Animal Dreams* is a richly engrossing novel in which people overcome personal and community nightmares through the shared work and joy of everyday life.

Another America

Type of work: Poetry
First published: 1992

Another America reflects Kingsolver's central concerns: displaced or marginalized women and minorities. The book's five sections return over and over to themes of violence, war, incest, rape, and other forms of abuse, drawing sketches of lives poignantly reflecting the hazards of living on the edge in late twentieth century America.

Using repeated images of war and destruction, Kingsolver recalls childhood fears of a Russian invasion, threatened Titan missile launches, Nagasaki, Central American brutality. The book establishes an equation between a war's rape of a culture and assaults against women through rape, incest, verbal violence, and other forms of brutal domination. Kingsolver's vision also encompasses victims of political violence in Central America, in particular those traumatized in Nicaragua and Mexico and in this country after coming here hoping to find a safe haven in the Land of the Free. Such ironies are multiple in this collection of poems; for Kingsolver, the personal is the political, while the political destroys the personal.

Adding power to *Another America* are the Spanish translations accompanying each poem, by Chilean immigrant Rebeca Cartes. This collection of poems is gut-wrenchingly frank: The poems' combined voices emerge as a strong, unflinching female presence, a champion of the prisoners of the margins, whether by virtue of gender, race, or class.

Pigs in Heaven

Type of work: Novel
First published: 1993

Pigs in Heaven is an unusual and provocative sequel that calls into question the moral certainties of its predecessor. In *The Bean Trees*, as the plucky young protagonist Taylor Greer drives southwest from Kentucky, she has a baby girl thrust upon her during a car repair stop on Cherokee land in Oklahoma. In this earlier novel, Taylor's act of taking and raising the girl seems unquestionably heroic, since the girl's mother is dead, Taylor has no desire to become a mother, and particularly since it is revealed later in the novel that the girl had been sexually abused.

Pigs in Heaven, on the other hand, suggests that perhaps Turtle (as Taylor has named her) needs to be returned to her Oklahoma tribe. Annawake Fourkiller, a young Cherokee lawyer whose spirit matches Taylor's own, is on a crusade to test the legality of adoptions that have taken a third of all Indian children out of their tribes and into non-Indian homes.

Kingsolver's achievement in the novel is to develop the conflict between mother love and tribal community on a three-dimensional human level. The reader comes to understand many political and cultural issues as well as to know and sympathize with many individuals on both sides of the conflict. In addition, Kingsolver's sharp ear for dialogue, her eye for revealing cultural detail, and her keen sense of humor all enliven a novel that is abundantly populated with entertaining characters. These characters include Taylor's sardonic mother Alice; a young woman named Barbie, who tries to model her life on the popular children's doll; Taylor's unconventional boyfriend Jax, who plays in a rock band; and Alice's childhood friend Sugar, who introduces her to Cherokee life in the fictional town of Heaven, Oklahoma.

Though *Pigs in Heaven* is not as rich an achievement as *Animal Dreams*, it nonetheless offers a fully satisfying narrative that dramatizes the plights, the humanity, and the humor of individuals and groups who survive on the margins of American society.

High Tide in Tucson

Type of work: Essays
First published: 1995

High Tide in Tucson is a collection of essays, stories, and meditations from Kingsolver's life as she raised her daughter Camille alone. Many of these essays focus on the landscape and culture of the American desert, and most also reflect Kingsolver's extensive training as a biologist. In "Semper Fi," for example, Kingsolver addresses the question of fidelity—first to the relatively mundane world of television football but ultimately to the pursuit of truth itself in investigations into the pseudoscience conducted by Samuel Morton, who in the nineteenth century used brain volume as a measure of ethnic superiority, and by his intellectual heirs (according to Kingsolver) Robert Herrnstein and Charles Murray in *The Bell Curve* (1994).

In the title essay, Kingsolver suggests a maxim that easily links her fiction, poetry, and nonfiction:

> In the best of times, I hold in mind the need to care for things beyond the self: poetry, humanity, grace. In other times when it seems difficult merely to survive and be happy about it, the condition of my thought tastes as simple as this: let me be a good animal today.

The Poisonwood Bible

Type of work: Novel
First published: 1998

After Orleanna Price's opening sortie, which serves as a prologue, readers of *The Poisonwood Bible* find that the Price family comes from Bethlehem, Georgia, at the beginning of the next section. Combined with the tension inherent in the title, their place of origin signals why Kingsolver calls the book a political allegory. What follows is the story of the Price family's arrival at, sojourn in, and leave-taking from the Congo as they try to spread God's Word among the lost. The novel is told in five distinct voices, those of Orleanna Price and her daughters Leah, Ruth, Rachel, and Adah. Nathan Price has no lines in the novel, despite his position as head of the family—mostly as family despot, feared and unresponsive to the pleas and needs expressed by the women in his care.

What readers learn of their existence is filtered through the eyes of distinctly different sisters and their mother, but all of it comes freighted with the message that

Nathan Price will refuse every native custom and way of being in favor of his own. This attitude causes suffering and loss. His refusal to plant his garden in the protected raised hillocks, as is the native practice, results in all of their plants being flooded out. Ironically, his tin-ear pronunciation of bangala, which he shouts out every Sunday, tells the Congolese people over and over that Jesus will make them itch like the poisonwood tree, instead of what he wishes to say, that Jesus is precious.

Language and miscommunication are central to the novel, and one daughter, Adah, speaks only in palindromes to herself and no one else for years. Rachel's perpetual misuse of words and Leah's dedication to learning French and Kikongo mirror their involvement with the new culture that they face. Leah remains in the struggling world of the Congo after her family returns to the United States, coping and forming a life in the same way that she labored to learn the languages. Rachel relocates and keeps a hotel in Africa, but she keeps to the white minority culture and does not probe for understanding of herself or acceptance with Africans. She is not introspective or critical about American involvement in Africa. When Adah emerges from her voiceless state, she becomes a doctor but decides to devote her life to discovering the "life histories of viruses." Orleanna lives a solitary life, compromised in health by her Congo years, and the youngest daughter, Ruth, lies in a Congolese grave before the family leaves the country.

Nathan Price, deserted by his wife and daughters after Ruth's death, continues preaching and moves further and further away from a life even remotely related to his former existence. He becomes suspect as a spirit man who can turn himself into a crocodile. Following an accident in which children drown in a river after their boat is overturned by a crocodile, villagers chase and corner Nathan in an old coffee field watchtower and burn the tower, with him in it. The rift in the Price family's lives, the devastation of the Congo, America's complicity in that process, and the forward movement of all—the Prices, the United States, the Congo—weave a complex pattern of miscommunication, exploitation, and power. One cannot read this book without thinking about what it means to be human and the responsibility that each person has to contribute to the good of all others on the planet.

Suggested Readings

Aay, Henry. "Environmental Themes in Ecofiction: *In the Center of the Nation* and *Animal Dreams*." *Journal of Cultural Geography* 14 (Spring, 1994).

DeMarr, Mary Jean. *Barbara Kingsolver: A Critical Companion*. Westport, Conn.: Greenwood Press, 1999.

Draper, James P. "Barbara Kingsolver." In *Contemporary Literary Criticism: Yearbook 1993*. Vol. 81. Detroit: Gale Research, 1994.

Fleischner, Jennifer, ed. *A Reader's Guide to the Fiction of Barbara Kingsolver: "The Bean Trees," "Homeland, and Other Stories," "Animal Dreams," "Pigs in Heaven."* New York: HarperPerennial, 1994.

Kingsolver, Barbara. Interview by Lisa See. *Publishers Weekly* 237 (August 31, 1990): 46.

Pence, Amy. "Barbara Kingsolver." *Poets and Writers* 21, no. 4 (July/August, 1993): 14-21.

Perry, Donna. *Backtalk: Women Writers Speak Out*. New Brunswick, N.J.: Rutgers University Press, 1993.

Ross, Jean W. "CA Interview." In *Contemporary Authors*. Vol. 134, edited by Susan M. Trotsky. Detroit: Gale Research, 1992.

Ryan, Maureen. "Barbara Kingsolver's Lowfat Fiction." *Journal of American Culture* 18, no. 4 (Winter, 1995): 77-123.

Wagner-Martin, Linda. *Barbara Kingsolver's "The Poisonwood Bible": A Reader's Guide*. New York: Continuum, 2001.

Contributors: Peter D. Olson and Karen L. Arnold

Maxine Hong Kingston

(Maxine Ting Ting Hong)

BORN: Stockton, California; October 27, 1940

CHINESE AMERICAN

Kingston's autobiographical books and her novel, brilliantly interweaving imagination and fact, convey Chinese American immigrant experience to a wide readership.

PRINCIPAL WORKS

LONG FICTION: *Tripmaster Monkey: His Fake Book*, 1989

SHORT FICTION: *The Woman Warrior: Memoirs of a Girlhood Among Ghosts*, 1976; *China Men*, 1980

NONFICTION: *Hawai'i One Summer*, 1987; *Conversations with Maxine Hong Kingston*, 1998 (Paul Skenazy and Tera Martin, editors); *To Be the Poet*, 2002

MISCELLANEOUS: *The Fifth Book of Peace*, 2003 (fiction and nonfiction)

Born Maxine Ting Ting Hong, Kingston spoke Say Up, a Cantonese dialect, as her first language. Her immigrant parents made their living in California by running a laundry. They struggled to retain their Chinese identity and values in a new world peopled by ominous aliens: immigration officials, teachers, non-Chinese. Kingston's mother admonished and inspired her six children, particularly her daughters, with talks of the disasters that befell women who broke men's rules and of legendary heroines who dared battle for justice.

Silent and wordless among "white ghosts," Kingston was also threatened in childhood and adolescence by the specter of traditional Chinese prejudices against women. "Better to raise geese than girls" was a family motto. Kingston nevertheless became an A student and entered the University of California at Berkeley, where she drank in all the idealism of the Civil Rights and anti-Vietnam War movements of the 1960's.

Kingston married classmate and actor Earll Kingston, and for many years she pursued a career as a teacher, first in California and then in Hawaii. Meanwhile, finding her voice and experimenting with the linguistic means by which she could express the rich imagery and rhythms of Chinese American speech in her writing, she began working on two autobiographical books simultaneously. Enthusiastic critical acclaim accompanied the publication of the best-selling *The Woman Warrior* and *China Men*. Often called novels, these autobiographies combine imaginative flights and her memories of Chinese myths with the facts of Chinese immigrant history. In these works, Kingston claims full citizenship for Chinese Americans. "We Chinese belong here. This is our country, this is our history, we are a part of America. If it weren't for us, America would be a different place." Kingston says that, in telling the story of the Chinese in America, a major influence was William Carlos Williams's *In the American Grain* (1925).

Besides asserting the justice of the struggle against racism, Kingston also affirms the right of women of all races to full equality. Her writings make important contributions to feminist literature and women's studies. She stands as the most widely read and influential interpreter of the Chinese American experience.

The Woman Warrior

Type of work: Memoir
First published: 1976

The Woman Warrior: Memoirs of a Girlhood Among Ghosts is an autobiographical novel of Kingston's life, illuminated by references to the women whose histories influenced her. In the United States, the meager opportunities available to Chinese immigrants force her parents to earn a living by running a small laundry. Kingston's mother, Brave Orchid, a midwife in China, is a forceful character who admonishes her daughter with ever-changing renditions of Chinese legends and myths as well as tales about women who have been driven to madness or death by a culture that has traditionally viewed girls and women as subordinate to boys and men.

In "No Name Woman," Kingston recalls the haunting story of her aunt, who gave birth to a child years after her husband had gone to America. Driven to madness by the persecution of vengeful neighbors, a disgrace to her kin, she drowns herself and the baby in the family well. "Now that you have started to menstruate what happened to her could happen to you," Brave Orchid cautions. It is one of many frightening lessons for the young Kingston as she becomes increasingly aware of the different expectations placed upon women by the Chinese traditions that continue to dominate the attitudes of immigrants.

The book takes its title, however, from Fa Mu Lan, the legendary woman warrior who, disguised as a man, sword in hand, goes forth to fight for justice. Kingston takes inspiration from this story and imagines herself an avenger of the hurts she experiences as a woman and an Asian American. As she acquires a nontraditional consciousness, her listing of grievances transcends personal and family hurts to embrace broader struggles against racism and war. Kingston loses her job at a real estate firm when she refuses to type invitations to a banquet at a restaurant that discriminates against African Americans. She also struggles to evade the expectations that she sees American girls facing: wearing makeup, becoming cheerleaders, learning to be typists, marrying rich men.

In the final chapter, "A Song for a Barbarian Reed Pipe," Kingston testifies to her passage out of the confinements and prejudices that obsess her parents. She discovers that she can speak her mind. She alludes to the story of the Chinese princess,

Ts'ai Yen, who, carried off by barbarians, finds her voice and sings high and clear like a flute, a song that blends the sounds of China and of the world beyond.

The Woman Warrior is distinguished by its rich, poetic language. Chinese oral tradition and classical literature blend with the myriad impressions crowding into the mind of a Chinese American girl striving to make sense of the competing mores of California's diverse populations.

China Men

Type of work: Memoir
First published: 1980

In *China Men*, Kingston tells the stories of her male relatives who came to America. The opening chapter, "Our Fathers," signals her intention to embrace the community of Chinese immigrants. She challenges readers to reconsider the Eurocentric version of American history by bringing to their attention the contributions of Chinese to the building of America.

Kingston weaves her narrative from a poetic association of folklore, fantasy, and fact. In "On Discovery," she relates a Chinese legend: the arrival in North America of Tang Ao during the reign of the Empress Wu (694-705). Captured and forced to become a transvestite, feet bound, face powdered and rouged, ears studded with jade and gold, Tang Ao was forced to serve meals to the court. The bewildering experience of this precursor is a metaphor for the emasculation of Chinese men in America as racism disempowered them, forcing them to perform women's tasks: laundering and cooking.

Maxine Hong Kingston (© Franco Salmoiraghi)

In America, Kingston's forefathers find themselves off center as they are marginalized by U.S. laws. A chapter on laws, in the middle of *China Men*, documents the legislation and court decisions that, beginning in 1868, systematically excluded Chinese immigrants from normal treatment until 1958. Particularly dehumanizing was the law prohibiting the immigration of the wives and children of Chinese men working in America.

Through the portraits of her many forefathers, Kingston describes a multitude of immigration experiences. Great-grandfather Bak Goong sails to Hawaii in the hold of a ship and works for endless years under the whip on a sugar plantation. His dream of saving enough money to reach Gold Mountain is a mirage. The story of grandfather Ah Goong details the courage and skills of the Chinese who built the most difficult and dangerous section of the transcontinental railroad. They worked for lower wages and endured longer hours than white laborers but were denied the right to own property and become citizens. Nevertheless, Ah Goong prophesies: "We're marking the land now. The tracks are numbered."

Kingston's father, Baba, a man of scholarly accomplishment in China, enters America full of hope, only to be reduced to washing other people's clothes. Then, demonstrating the changing status of the Chinese in America after World War II, his son, drafted into the U.S. Navy to serve in the Vietnam War, receives the highest level of security clearance. "The government was certifying that the family was really American, not precariously American but super-American." Kingston's brother declines the invitation to attend language school, however, because he fears his improved Chinese will be used by intelligence to "gouge Viet Cong eyes, cattleprod their genitals."

Kingston thus ends her chronicle of Chinese American history on a questioning note. The Chinese American is now a full citizen but must share in all that is questionable in American culture.

Tripmaster Monkey

Type of work: Novel
First published: 1989

Kingston says that *Tripmaster Monkey: His Fake Book*, her first true novel, was written after she had exhausted all the stories she knew about China. Yet, its title belies that claim for it reflects the novel's debt to the classic Chinese epic Journey to the West, wherein the king of the monkeys takes a trip to India in search of sacred scrolls. Nonetheless, the cultural amalgam that Kingston relishes is confirmed by her statement that she was thinking of Henry Louis Gates, Jr.'s *The Signifying Monkey* (1988) when she wrote the book. A densely packed four hundred pages, it is the story of the pranks and high jinks of twenty-three-year-old Chinese American hippie playwright Wittman Ah Sing, who lives in San Francisco in 1963 under the reign of Governor "Ray Gun" (Reagan). The book covers two months, September and October. Wittman is as free-spirited, independent, and garrulous as Walt Whitman, the nineteenth century American poet who is his namesake, yet he is equally Chinese as Monkey, the mythical trickster-saint who brought Buddhist scripture to China from India. Like Whitman, Wittman sings America and its multifarious facets, and the legacy he celebrates is the hallucinogenic culture of Berkeley in the 1960's.

Wittman's picaresque bohemian life is part serendipity and part fantastic journey, and his goal is to stage his epic dramatic production based on Chinese novels and folktales. Told in nine chapters of roughly equal length, the novel moves in a seamlessly chronological and fantastical story line, using third-person limited omniscient point of view. The reader accompanies Wittman on his adventures and is privy to his thoughts through the commentary of a wise, indulgent, and engagingly intrusive seer-narrator.

When the novel opens, Wittman has been out of college for a while and is puzzling about his future. As he walks the streets of San Francisco, he contemplates suicide in such a slapdash way that the reader cannot take him seriously. His observant mind and quick wit are attuned to nuances in the behavior of strangers and microscopic features of inanimate objects. Aboard a city bus, he reads aloud passages from Rainer Maria Rilke's *Die Aufzeichnungen des Malte Laurids Brigge* (1910; *The Notebooks of Malte Laurids Brigge*, 1930), regaling (or at least not annoying) fellow passengers. He enjoys a cappuccino with Nanci Lee, a beautiful Asian acquaintance and aspiring actress to whom he is romantically attracted. When he brings her to his apartment and reads his poetry to her, however, she neither understands nor appreciates his work and walks out.

After working on a play all night long and sleeping for a few hours, Wittman goes to his job as toy clerk at a department store. He offends customers and is inept at assembling a bicycle display. He attends a management trainee conference at a fancy hotel (under false colors, as he has been demoted) and embarrasses the three other Chinese Americans present. Back at the job, Wittman maneuvers a toy organ grinder monkey and a Barbie bride doll into an obscene position in full view of shocked customers, an action that gets him fired.

For something to do, Wittman sees the film *West Side Story* (1961), but he is put off by the falsity of Hollywood. He boards a bus for Oakland and endures the self-interested chatter of the plain, aggressive Chinese American girl next to him. His destination—a party at the home of good friends, recently married—promises a new destiny, for Wittman becomes enchanted by Taña de Weese, a Caucasian with long blond hair and sandals, who recites poetry while looking directly into Wittman's eyes.

Wittman, Taña, and a few other guests stay up all night, then share a breakfast omelet. Wittman reads aloud a long excerpt from his play, and everyone discusses acting in it. Wittman and Taña visit her apartment, which Wittman finds enchanting, and where they declare their love for each other. The next day they do some sightseeing and encounter a hippie claiming to be an ordained minister, who spontaneously marries them.

Their next stop is Sacramento, to visit Wittman's parents. His mother is hosting a game of mah-jongg, so Wittman is able to introduce Taña to family relatives and friends. He searches the house for his grandmother, but his mother is elusive about her whereabouts. His father, playing poker at a friend's house, also will not give Wittman a straight answer, except to say that they had taken her to Reno and she had not returned with them. Taña and Wittman drive to Reno but fail to find the grandmother. Instead, they enjoy an expensive restaurant dinner that is partially marred by racist jokes they overhear at an adjacent table.

The next morning Taña goes to work, and Wittman goes through the seemingly interminable application process for unemployment compensation. Later, meandering through the lights of Chinatown, he unexpectedly meets his grandmother. Her abandonment by Wittman's parents in the Sierra Nevada has worked to her advantage; she was picked up by a wealthy Chinese man who married her. She presses money into Wittman's grateful hands before they depart.

Wittman uses a pay telephone to contact friends and relatives—everyone he knows in the area—to assemble an acting company and an audience for his play, scheduled to open Halloween night. The play turns out to be a complex and fast-paced blend of slapstick and magic, wit and rage, with the actors playing eccentrics, freaks, and mythical heroes. The famous joined twins Chang and Eng Bunker, Chinese-Siamese immigrants who got rich appearing as a Civil War sideshow spectacle, enable Wittman to bring to the stage an embodiment of mixed identity, notes Kingston. The cast and growing audience love it, and critics rave. So frenzied are the events that the audience finds it impossible to take it all in at once. Police are called because of the pandemonium. It becomes a climactic free-for-all, with everyone fighting everyone else, and it culminates in an explosion of fireworks. A book that began with reference to suicide ends in a roaringly good time.

After things settle down, Wittman takes center stage and "talks story" about the formative influences in his life and the larger dilemma of all Chinese living in the United States. As his name echoes Walt Whitman's, so this is his equivalent of Whitman's "Song of Myself." His extended monologue is touching, bitter, and humorous as he describes his personal experiences of racial prejudice. His narrative reveals the agony, pain, and bafflement of trying to synthesize past Chinese heritage with present American culture, yet his invectives and fevered eloquence end in optimistic determination for the future.

The Fifth Book of Peace

Type of work: Autobiography and fiction
First published: 2003

To some degree, most of Kingston's prose mixes fiction and nonfiction, but in *The Fifth Book of Peace*—instead of blending into each other in some postmodernist mix of novel and history—the two forms are separated. The book has five parts. In the opening section, Kingston tells the story of the horrific October, 1991, Oakland fire, when her house, and all her possessions, including the draft of her novel-in-progress, were consumed.

In the second, shorter section, she relates the history of the mythic Chinese "Three Lost Books of Peace." The third section is the reconstruction of her own, fourth book of peace, the novel that was destroyed in the fire, the story of Wittman Ah Sing (the hero of Kingston's earlier *Tripmaster Monkey*) and his wife and young son immigrating to Hawaii during the Vietnam War and getting caught up in the antiwar movement there. In the fourth section, Kingston describes her peace efforts in the early 1990's, when, after the fire, Vietnam veterans started sending her stories of their own losses and she organized workshops for the writer veterans. The epilogue brings those efforts up to date.

Kingston's book is thus an unfinished novel enclosed by personal stories of loss (the Oakland fire) and reclamation (the workshops where Vietnam veterans work out their involvement in the war). The different parts do not perfectly coalesce, but all are finally about peace. "Things that fiction can't solve must be worked out in life," Kingston writes here, and *The Fifth Book of Peace* is her most poignant attempt to do just that.

Suggested Readings

Cheung, King-Kok. *Articulate Silences: Hisaye Yamamoto, Maxine Hong Kingston, Joy Kogawa*. Ithaca: Cornell University Press, 1993.

Gao, Yan. *The Art of Parody: Maxine Hong Kingston's Use of Chinese Sources*. New York: Peter Lang, 1996.

Huntley, E. D. *Maxine Hong Kingston: A Critical Companion*. Westport, Conn.: Greenwood Press, 2001.

Kingston, Maxine Hong. *Conversations with Maxine Hong Kingston*, edited by Paul Skenazy and Tera Martin. Jackson: University Press of Mississippi, 1998.

Ludwig, Sami. *Concrete Language: Intercultural Communication in Maxine Hong Kingston's "The Woman Warrior" and Ishmael Reed's "Mumbo Jumbo."* Cross Cultural Communication 2. New York: Peter Lang, 1996.

Simmons, Diane. *Maxine Hong Kingston*. New York: Twayne, 1999.

Skandera-Trombley, Laura, ed. *Critical Essays on Maxine Hong Kingston*. New York: G. K. Hall, 1998.

Smith, Jeanne Rosier. *Writing Tricksters: Mythic Gambols in American Ethnic Literature*. Berkeley: University of California Press, 1997.

Wong, Sau-Ling Cynthia, ed. *Maxine Hong Kingston's "The Woman Warrior": A Casebook*. New York: Oxford University Press, 2002.

Contributors: Joseleyne Ashford Slade and Jill B. Gidmark

Etheridge Knight

Born: Corinth, Mississippi; April 19, 1931
Died: Indianapolis, Indiana; March 10, 1991

African American

Knight opened the eyes of a nation to the views and experiences of prisoners, unveiling a humanity that most Americans, black or white, never knew existed.

Principal works

POETRY: "For Malcolm, a Year After," 1967 (a contribution to *For Malcolm: Poems on the Life and Death of Malcolm X*, 1967); *Poems from Prison*, 1968; *Black Voices from Prison*, 1970 (with others); *A Poem for Brother/Man (After His Recovery from an O.D.)*, 1972; *Belly Song, and Other Poems*, 1973; *Born of a Woman: New and Selected Poems*, 1980; *The Essential Etheridge Knight*, 1986

Etheridge Knight, one of Bushie and Belzora (Cozart) Knight's seven children, came into the world on April 19, 1931, near Corinth, Mississippi. During this time the United States was gripped by one of history's most sensational racial battles, the Scottsboro Boys trial. Nine black males, ages twelve to nineteen, were taken off a train near Scottsboro, Alabama, and charged with the rape of two Huntsville, Alabama, white women, Ruby Bates, eighteen, and Victoria Price, twenty-one. The incident seeded a cloud of white fear and rage that shadowed black men throughout the South for more than thirty years.

Angered by the racial segregation and disgusted by the backbreaking work of sharecropping, Knight dropped out of school after the eighth grade and left home. He wandered for about five years, then enlisted in the Army in 1947.

Knight was a medic, stationed in Guam, Hawaii, and at the battlefront in the Korean War until 1951, when he was wounded by a piece of shrapnel. In 1957, the now drug-addicted soldier was discharged. Drugs dominated his life. In 1960, Knight was sentenced to prison for a robbery in Indianapolis, Indiana, motivated by his need to buy drugs. Doing time at Indiana State Prison in Michigan City, Indiana, led Knight to self-discovery and an increased desire to be more than an outcast in America. Those yearnings prompted him to write.

Poems from Prison, his first collection, was published by Broadside Press in 1968, with an introduction by Pulitzer Prize-winning poet Gwendolyn Brooks. She mentored Knight, who eventually gained support from members of the Black Arts movement, which gave artistic voice to African Americans' struggles for social rights and political freedom. One of those members, poet Dudley Randall, was

Etheridge Knight (Judy Ray)

the founder and editor of Broadside Press. Another poet, Sonia Sanchez, married Knight. By year's end, Knight had gained a career, a wife, and three stepchildren: Morani, Mungu, and Anita Sanchez.

His fame peaked between 1968 and 1975, when the movement waned. An anthology of prison writings, *Voce negre dal carcere* (1968), first published in Laterza, Italy, broadened the popularity of Knight's work. Two years later, Pathfinder Press released *Black Voices from Prison* in the United States. Doors opened. The poet was writer-in-residence at the University of Pittsburgh (1968-1969), the University of Hartford (1969-1970), and Lincoln University (1972) in Jefferson City, Missouri. He received a 1972 National Endowment for the Arts grant and a 1974 Guggenheim Fellowship.

Knight's career was going well, but his personal life was in a downward slide. Drugs kept him in and out of Veterans Administration hospitals. The marriage to Sanchez crumbled into a 1972 divorce. On June 11, 1973, Knight married Mary Ann McAnally. The couple had two children: Mary Tandiwe and Etheridge Bambata. That same year, Broadside published the first collection of his poems written outside prison, *Belly Song, and Other Poems*. In 1978, he married Charlene Blackburn. The relationship is celebrated in *Born of a Woman*, and with her he had a son, Issac Bushie Knight. Knight continued to write. *The Essential Etheridge Knight* was released in 1986, but Knight never regained prominence. He died of lung cancer in 1991 in Indianapolis, Indiana.

Like many of the writers and painters during the Black Arts movement which surfaced in major urban centers between 1965 and 1975, Knight believed that a black artist's main duty was to expose the lies of the white-dominated society. In *Contemporary Authors*, he is quoted as saying that the traditional idea of the aesthetic drawn from Western European history demands that the artist speak only of the beautiful: "His task is to edify the listener, to make him see beauty of the world." That aesthetic definition was a problem because African Americans were identified in the traditional European mind as not beautiful. In fact, the broader society saw everything in African American life as ugly. Black artists hoped to erase that mindset. They saw art as a force through which they could move people of all races toward understanding and respect. In *Contemporary Authors*, Knight is quoted as saying that the African American writer has to perceive and conceptualize the collective aspirations, the collective vision of black people, and through his art form give back to the people the truth that he has gotten from them. He must sing to them of their own deeds, and misdeeds.

"Hard Rock Returns to Prison from the Hospital for the Criminal Insane"

Type of work: Poetry
First published: 1968, in *Poems from Prison*

In "Hard Rock Returns to Prison from the Hospital for the Criminal Insane," Knight turns an uncontrollable prisoner into a new-day folk hero. Hard Rock is a Paul Bunyan without a pretty fate. The author understood that most African American lives, even mythic ones, do not have happy endings. The poem also shows that sometimes heroes are not what most people (meaning whites) see as nice or pretty. In the language of the incarcerated, Knight laid out the heroic stature:

> "Ol Hard Rock! Man, that's one crazy nigger."
> And then the jewel of a myth that Hard Rock once bit
> A screw on the thumb and poisoned him with syphilitic spit.

To many, those details are as alienating as the description:

> Hard Rock was "known not to take no shit
> From nobody," and he had the scars to prove it:
> Split purple lips, lumped ears, welts above
> His yellow eyes, and one long scar that cut
> Across his temple and plowed through a thick
> Canopy of kinky hair.

The prisoner, Knight recognized, is an archetype of all black Americans, only nominally "free" but really imprisoned. In prison, the prisoner stays in a hole, a tiny cell devoid of light. The guards' intimidation cannot break the man's spirit, so the prison doctors give him a lobotomy. They take his ability to think. Knight saw that scenario as identical to the experience of the descendants of Africans in America. In Mississippi and other places, he had seen black people who tried to stand tall against the onslaught of racial oppression either killed or, like the fictional Hard Rock, tamed:

> A screw who knew Hard Rock
> From before shook him down and barked in his face
> And Hard Rock did *nothing*. Just grinned and looked silly.
> His eyes empty like knot holes in a fence.

The poem captures the disappointment and defeat Knight saw in black men on both sides of the walls:

> We turned away our eyes to the ground. Crushed.
> He had been our Destroyer, the doer of things
> We dreamed of doing but could not bring ourselves to do.

"The Idea of Ancestry"

Type of work: Poetry
First published: 1968, in *Poems from Prison*

Knight reflects on those connections in both "A Poem for Myself (Or Blues for a Mississippi Black Boy)" and "The Idea of Ancestry," in his *Poems from Prison*. In the first part of "The Idea of Ancestry," he wrote:

> Taped to the wall of my cell are 47 pictures: 47 black
> faces: my father, mother, grandmothers (1 dead), grand fathers
> (both dead), brothers
> sisters, uncles, aunts, cousins (1st & 2nd), nieces, and nephews.
> They stare
> across the space at me sprawling on my bunk. I know
> their dark eyes, they know mine. I know their style
> they know mine. I am all of them, they are all of me;
> they are farmers, I am a thief, I am me, they are thee.

After exploring the variety of their individualism, he concludes that differences cannot break family ties:

> I have the same name as 1 grandfather, 3 cousins, 3 nephews
> and 1 uncle. The uncle disappeared when he was 15, just took
> off and caught a freight (they say). He's discussed each year
> when the family has a reunion, he causes uneasiness in
> the clan, he is an empty space. My father's mother, who is 93
> and who keeps the Family Bible with everybody's birth dates
> (and death dates) in it, always mentions him. There is
> no place in her Bible for "whereabouts unknown."

Works written after prison extended Knight's reflections on connections. When considered to its fullest extent, what binds people is love. Knight's reflection on ancestry in "The Idea of Ancestry" reveals an understanding of a family, the accidental space where one shares traits and foibles with loved ones. Accidental refers to things outside a person's control. In the 1980 essay "The Violent Space," Hill acknowledged that "the form of the poem as well as the idea of ancestry in the poem also represents the problem of ancestral lineage for the Black race as a whole." The power to direct family lines was stripped from African Americans for generations. The practice of selling slaves without regard for emotional ties also made it hard to keep track of the existing linkages.

Suggested Readings

Andrews, William L., Frances Smith Fuller, and Trudier Harris, eds. *The Oxford Companion to African American Literature*. New York: Oxford University Press, 1997.

Ford, Karen. "These Old Writing Paper Blues: The Blues Stanza and Literary Poetry." *College Literature* 24, no. 3 (October, 1997): 84-103.

Hill, Patricia Liggins. "The Violent Space: The Function of the New Black Aesthetic in Etheridge Knight's Prison Poetry." *Black American Literature Forum* 14, no. 3 (1980).

Randall, Dudley. *Broadside Memories: Poets I Have Known*. Detroit: Broadside Press, 1975.

Vendler, Helen Hennessy, ed. *Part of Nature, Part of Us: Modern American Poets*. Cambridge, Mass.: Harvard University Press, 1980.

Contributor: Vincent F. A. Golphin

Joy Kogawa
(Joy Nozomi Goichi)

Born: Vancouver, British Columbia, Canada; June 6, 1935

Japanese American

Kogawa's novel Obasan *brings literature of the World War II internment camp experience to a new level of psychological depth and lyrical brilliance.*

Principal works

CHILDREN'S LITERATURE: *Naomi's Road*, 1986

LONG FICTION: *Obasan*, 1981; *Itsuka*, 1991; *The Rain Ascends*, 1995

POETRY: *The Splintered Moon*, 1967; *A Choice of Dreams*, 1974; *Jericho Road*, 1977; *Woman in the Woods*, 1985; *A Song of Lilith*, 2000; *A Garden of Anchors*, 2003

Joy Kogawa (koh-GAH-wah) grew up in the relatively sheltered environment provided by her minister father in Vancouver. That security was shattered with World War II relocation policies, which sent Japanese Canadians to internment camps in the inhospitable interior lands of Canada. The atomic bombs dropped on Hiroshima and Nagasaki by the United States also profoundly affected her.

As a young woman Kogawa attended the University of Alberta, the Anglican Women's Training College, and the Conservatory of Music. She married David Kogawa on May 2, 1957; they had two children, Gordon and Deirdre. The years 1967 to 1968 seem to have been a transitional period in Kogawa's life, since her first book of poems (*The Splintered Moon*, 1967) was published, she divorced David Kogawa, and she returned to college, attending the University of Saskatchewan, in those two years.

The next ten years of Kogawa's life were increasingly productive. Her second collection of poems, *A Choice of Dreams*, was published in 1974. Kogawa worked in the Office of the Prime Minister in Ottawa, Ontario, as a staff writer from 1974 to 1976. A third collection of poetry, *Jericho Road*, was published in 1977. During this time Kogawa worked primarily as a freelance writer. Kogawa contributed poems to magazines and journals in Canada and the United States.

In 1981, *Obasan* was published. Widely acclaimed as one of the most psychologically complex and lyrically beautiful novels on the topic of Japanese Canadians' wartime experiences, *Obasan* continues to intrigue readers and critics alike with its powerful story of a silent, reserved woman, Megumi Naomi Nakane, learning of the fate of her family in Japan many years after the fact. Naomi's experience of dispossession, relocation, and internment, as well as the loss of her parents, has made her ethnicity, her self-image, and her relationships with others deeply problematic. Published in 1986, *Naomi's Road* retells the tale of *Obasan* in a manner intended for child readers.

Itsuka is Kogawa's sequel to *Obasan*. *Itsuka* follows Naomi's political awakening and the healing of her wounds from the past.

Joy Kogawa

Obasan

Type of work: Novel
First published: 1981

Kogawa's *Obasan* has forced critics to include Asian Canadians in their study of ethnic literature; it is such a fine work no critic can ignore it. Kogawa has defined political and cultural connections between the Japanese immigrants of Canada and America. Both groups were held in internment camps during World War II. Their property was seized, and their families were often separated. In Canada and the United States the men of the families fought for their new countries while their wives, children, and siblings remained interned. Arguably one of the finest literary renderings of this experience, *Obasan* investigates what happened as a result of these practices.

Naomi Nakane, the protagonist of *Obasan*, appears emotionally paralyzed at the beginning of the novel. Unable to move beyond her own past in the camps and unable to reconcile the loss of her parents, Naomi has retreated into silence and isolation. Canada has essentially told Japanese Canadians that they are untrustworthy, second-class citizens at best, so Naomi retreats from her ethnic identity as well. Her Aunt Emily, however, is articulate, learned, professional, and politically active. Aunt Emily encourages Naomi to learn about the terrible things done to Japanese Canadians and to act on her anger. Naomi gains the impetus for change.

Shortly before the family's relocation to the internment camps (when Naomi is a child), Mrs. Nakane leaves to visit family in Japan. She never returns, and the family carefully guards the secret of her fate. It is only as a thirty-six-year-old adult that Naomi is given the letters that reveal her mother's story of disfigurement and subsequent death as a result of the atomic bombing. The mother, herself, has imposed silence on the other family members. Naomi tries to engage her mother's presence, to heal the rift between them, although her mother is not physically there. In writing the novel Kogawa has constructed an elaborate attempt to embrace the absent voice, to contain the mother in some manner useful to Naomi's own construction of identity.

Poetic passages describe this imagined reunion. Dream sequences also punctuate the narrative, providing the touching lyricism that moves the novel beyond most of the literature written around the internment camp experience. Bound with the sociopolitical analysis provided by Aunt Emily and Naomi's personal history, the novel sets high standards for literature on ethnic identity.

Suggested Readings

Cheung, King-Kok. *Articulate Silences: Hisaya Yamamoto, Maxine Hong Kingston, Joy Kogawa*. Ithaca, N.Y.: Cornell University Press, 1993.

Davidson, Arnold E. *Writing Against the Silence: Joy Kogawa's "Obasan."* Toronto: ECW Press, 1993.

Goldman, Marlene. "A Dangerous Circuit: Loss and the Boundaries of Racialized Subjectivity in Joy Kogawa's *Obasan* and Kerri Sakamoto's *The Electric Field*." *Modern Fiction Studies* 48, no. 2 (2002): 362-388.

Kanefsky, Rachelle. "Debunking a Postmodern Conception of History: A Defense of Humanist Values in the Novels of Joy Kogawa." *Canadian Literature* 148 (1996): 11-36.

Kruk, Laurie. "Voices of Stone: The Power of Poetry in Joy Kogawa's *Obasan*." *Ariel* 30, no. 4 (1999): 75-94.

Petersen, Nancy. *Against Amnesia: Contemporary Women Writers and the Crises of Historical Memory*. Philadelphia: University of Pennsylvania Press, 2001.

Contributor: Julie Tharp

Yusef Komunyakaa

(James Willie Brown)

Born: Bogalusa, Louisiana; April 29, 1947

African American

Komunyakaa's poems use jazz and blues rhythms, and his focus on the Vietnam War places him among the finest writers who have explored this difficult terrain.

Principal works

audio recordings: *Love Notes from the Madhouse*, 1998 (with John Tchicai); *Thirteen Kinds of Desire*, 2000 (with Pamela Knowles)

poetry: *Dedications and Other Darkhorses*, 1977; *Lost in the Bonewheel Factory*, 1979; *Copacetic*, 1984; *I Apologize for the Eyes in My Head*, 1986; *Toys in the Field*, 1986; *Dien Cai Dau*, 1988; *February in Sydney*, 1989; *Magic City*, 1992; *Neon Vernacular: New and Selected Poems*, 1993; *Thieves of Paradise*, 1998; *Talking Dirty to the Gods*, 2000; *Pleasure Dome: New and Collected Poems*, 2001; *Taboo: The Wishbone Trilogy, Part One*, 2004; *Gilgamesh: A Verse Play*, 2006 (with Chad Gracia)

translation: *The Insomnia of Fire*, 1995 (with Martha Collins; of poetry by Nguyen Quang Thieu)

nonfiction: *Blue Notes: Essays, Interviews, and Commentaries*, 1999 (Radiclani Clytus, editor)

edited texts: *The Jazz Poetry Anthology*, 1991 (with Sascha Feinstein); *The Second Set: The Jazz Poetry Anthology, Volume 2*, 1996 (with Feinstein)

The oldest of five children, Yusef Komunyakaa (YEW-sehf koh-muhn-YAH-kah), born James Willie Brown, had a strained relationship with his father, which he vividly chronicled years later in a fourteen-sonnet sequence titled "Songs for My Father," which appears in *Neon Vernacular*. The Bogalusa of Komunyakaa's childhood was a rural community in southern Louisiana that held few opportunities economically or culturally, especially for a young black man. The main industry was the single paper mill, one that turned "workers into pulp," according to one poem. There was a racially charged atmosphere. The public library admitted only whites; the Ku Klux Klan was still active. In "Fog Galleon," Komunyakaa writes of these difficulties:

I press against the taxicab
Window. I'm black here, interfaced
With a dead phosphorescence;
The whole town smells
Like the world's oldest anger.

Daydreaming and reading were ways of escaping and coping with a slow life. Daydreaming, which Komunyakaa now sees as an important creative act of his youth, is evident in his early identification with his grandfather's West Indian heritage. He took the name Komunyakaa from his grandfather, who, according to family legend, came to America as a stowaway from Trinidad. In the poem "Mismatched Shoes," Komunyakaa writes of this identification:

The island swelled in his throat
& calypso leapt into the air
. . . .
I picked up those mismatched shoes
& slipped into his skin. Komunyakaa.
His blues, African fruit on my tongue.

The Bible and a set of supermarket encyclopedias were his first books. He has noted the influence of the Bible's "hypnotic cadence," sensitizing him to the importance of music and metaphor. James Baldwin's *Nobody Knows My Name* (1961), discovered in a church library when Komunyakaa was sixteen, inspired him to become a writer. Jazz and blues radio programs from New Orleans, heard on the family radio, formed a third important influence. Komunyakaa speaks fondly of those early days of listening to jazz and acknowledges its importance in his work.

After graduation from high school in 1965, Komunyakaa traveled briefly and in 1969 enlisted in the Army. He was sent to Vietnam. He served as a reporter on the front lines and later as editor of *The Southern Cross*, a military newspaper. The experience of being flown in by helicopter to observe and then report on the war effort laid the groundwork for the powerful fusion of passion and detached observation that is a hallmark of his war poems, written years later. He was awarded the Bronze Star for his service in Vietnam.

Upon being discharged, Komunyakaa enrolled at the University of Colorado, where he majored in English and sociology, earning a bachelor's degree in 1975. A creative writing course there inspired him to pursue a master's degree in creative writing at Colorado State University, which he earned in 1978. He received his master of fine arts degree from the University of California, Irvine, in 1980. During this period he published limited editions of his first two short books of poems, *Dedications and Other Darkhorses* and *Lost in the Bonewheel Factory*.

Komunyakaa taught poetry briefly in public school before joining the creative writing faculty at the University of New Orleans, where he met Mandy Sayer, whom he married in 1985. That year he became an associate professor at Indiana University at Bloomington, where in 1989 he was named Lilly Professor of Poetry.

He later became a professor in the Council of Humanities and Creative Writing Program at Princeton University.

Yusef Komunyakaa (AP/Wide World Photos)

Because Yusef Komunyakaa's poetry is so rich in imagery, allusion, metaphor, musical rhythms, and ironic twists, it possesses a freshness and a bittersweet bite whether the subject is the raw beauty of nature or the passions and follies of human nature. He has said that poetry does not work for him without "surprises." His poetry surprises both in its technique—the juxtaposition of disparate images and sudden shifts in perspective—and in its subjects. Generally his poems have a sensual quality even though the subject matter varies greatly: childhood memories, family feuds, race, war, sex, nature, jazz. Scholar Radiclani Clytus commented early in Komunyakaa's career that the poet's interpretation of popular mythology and legend gave readers "alternative access to cultural lore. Epic human imperfections, ancient psychological profiles, and the haunting resonance of the South are now explained by those who slow drag to Little Willie John and rendezvous at MOMA." Komunyakaa's comment that "a poem is both confrontation and celebration" aptly captures the essence of his own work.

Copacetic

Type of work: Poetry
First published: 1984

Copacetic focuses primarily on memories of childhood and the persuasive influence of music. The narrator speaks of "a heavy love for jazz," and in fact musical motifs run throughout Komunyakaa's poetry. He has compared poetry to jazz and blues in its emphasis on feeling and tone, its sense of surprise and discovery, and its diversity within a general structure. Poems such as "Copacetic Mingus," "Elegy for Thelonious," and "Untitled Blues" convey the power of this kind of music, in which "art & life bleed into each other." Depending on the poem, music can serve as escape, therapy, or analogy. Often it is combined with richly sensual images, as in "Woman, I Got the Blues."

Dien Cai Dau

TYPE OF WORK: Poetry
FIRST PUBLISHED: 1988

The past wounds and present scars of the Vietnam War are the subjects of *Dien Cai Dau*, whose title means "crazy" in Vietnamese. The powerful yet exquisitely sensitive—and sensual—way in which Komunyakaa conveys the pain, loss, and psychic confusion of his experience in Vietnam found a receptive audience. Most present a moment or a reflection in a richly nuanced but undogmatic way. In "We Never Know" he juxtaposes a delicate image of dancing with a woman with the reality of an enemy in the field, whom he kills and whose body he then approaches. The moral ambiguity of the moment is highlighted by the tenderness with which the soldier regards the body:

> When I got to him
> a blue halo
> of flies had already claimed him.
> I pulled the crumbled photograph
> from his fingers.
> There's no other way
> to say this: I fell in love.
> The morning cleared again
> except for a distant mortar
> & somewhere choppers taking off.
> I slid the wallet into his pocket
> & turned him over, so he wouldn't be
> kissing the ground.

Poems such as "Tu Du Street" and "Thanks" are even more complex in their multiple, often conflicting, images. The former presents the bizarre reality of racial prejudice even in Vietnam, "where only machine gun fire bring us together." The women with whom the soldiers seek solace provide one common denominator:

> There's more than a nation
> inside us, as black & white
> soldiers touch the same lovers
> minutes apart, tasting
> each other's breath
> without knowing these rooms
> run into each other like tunnels
> leading to the underworld.

In "Thanks" the narrator gives thanks to an unspecified being for the myriad coincidences that saved him one day in the jungle as he "played some deadly/ game for blind gods." The poet provides no resolution or closure, just a series of powerful, haunting images:

Again, thanks for the dud
hand grenade tossed at my feet
outside Chu Lai. I'm still
falling through its silence.

Neon Vernacular

Type of work: Poetry
First published: 1993

Neon Vernacular won considerable critical acclaim as well as the Pulitzer Prize. In addition to culling the best from earlier books, it adds gems of its own, including the unrhymed sonnet sequence "Songs for My Father," fourteen powerful poems that chronicle the poet's complicated relationship with his dad. In "At the Screen Door," in which a former soldier murders because he cannot separate the past from the present, Komunyakaa returns to the psychological aftermath of Vietnam.

Thieves of Paradise

Type of work: Poetry
First published: 1998

Thieves of Paradise is an example of Komunyakaa's ability to experiment with form and ease the reader into accepting poetry that is unfamiliar. Much of the subject matter is familiar—the grim reality of war and its psychological aftermath, the body's hungers and betrayals, the allure of memory and imagination—but the presentation is fresh and intriguing. "Palimpsest" is a seemingly random, kaleidoscopic series of four-quatrain poems that move from "slavecatchers" to tanks in Beijing's Tiananmen Square to the backwoods to jazz musician Count Basie. By confronting uncomfortable truths, the poet writes, "I am going to teach Mr. Pain/ to sway, to bop."

Several, such as "Nude Interrogation," "Phantasmagoria," and "Frontispiece," are prose poems that force one to rethink the nature of the form, while Komunyakaa's images work on the emotions. "The Glass Ark" is a five-page dialogue between two paleontologists.

This collection includes the libretto "Testimony," about Charlie Parker, written in twenty-eight fourteen-line stanzas. It captures the reckless allure of the man and the time:

Yardbird
could blow a woman's strut
across the room . . . pushed moans through brass. . . . High

heels clicking like a high hat.
Black-beaded flapper. Blue satin
Yardbird, he'd blow pain & glitter.

Talking Dirty to the Gods

Type of work: Poetry
First published: 2000

Talking Dirty to the Gods stands apart from earlier works in its adherence to a strict, traditional form. Each of its 132 poems consists of sixteen lines, in four unrhymed quatrains. Much of the appeal of this collection stems from the freedom and friction Komunyakaa creates by presenting his unusual images and bizarre juxtapositions in a tightly controlled format. The gods he discusses are taken from the ancient and the modern worlds, the exotic and the commonplace. Whether discussing the maggot ("Little/ Master of earth"), Bellerophon, or Joseph Stalin, he is able to humanize his subject enough to win at least some sympathy from the reader.

Pleasure Dome

Type of work: Poetry
First published: 2001

The publication of *Pleasure Dome* led to laudatory reviews not only for its poetic achievement but also for its high purpose: "Nearly every page of these collected poems will pull you from your expectations, tell you something you did not know, and leave you better off than you were," said the reviewer for *Library Journal*, while *Booklist* praised Komunyakaa's "fluent creative energy, and his passion for living the examined life." *Pleasure Dome* is an extraordinarily rich collection of more than 350 poems. All earlier collections except *Talking Dirty to the Gods* are represented. There is also a section titled "New Poems" and another, "Early Uncollected." Among the new poems is "Tenebrae," a moving meditation on Richard Johnson, the black Indiana University music professor who committed suicide. The lines "You try to beat loneliness/ out of a drum" are woven throughout the poem with a cumulative, haunting effect.

Suggested Readings

Aubert, Alvin. "Yusef Komunyakaa's Unified Vision: Canonization and Humanity." *African American Review* 27 (Spring, 1993).

Conley, Susan. "About Yusef Komunyakaa: A Profile." *Ploughshares* 23, no. 1 (Spring, 1997): 202-207.

Gordon, Fran. "Yusef Komunyakaa: Blue Note in a Lyrical Landscape." *Poets & Writers* 28, no. 6 (November/December, 2000): 26-33.

Gotera, Vincente F. "Depending on the Light: Yusef Komunyakaa's *Dien Cai Dau*." In *America Rediscovered: Critical Essays on Literature and Film of the Vietnam War*, edited by Owen W. Gilman, Jr., and Lorrie Smith. New York: Garland, 1990.

Jones, Kirkland C. "Folk Idiom in the Literary Expression of Two African American Authors: Rita Dove and Yusef Komunyakaa." In *Language and Literature in the African American Imagination*, edited by Carol Aisha Blackshire-Belay. Westport, Conn.: Greenwood Press, 1992.

Kelly, Robert. "Jazz and Poetry: A Conversation." *The Georgia Review* 46 (Winter, 1992).

Ringnalda, Don. *Fighting and Writing the Vietnam War*. Jackson: University Press of Mississippi, 1994.

Weber, Bruce. "A Poet's Values: It's the Words over the Man." *The New York Times Biographical Service* 25 (May, 1994): 666-667.

Contributor: Danny Robinson

Jerzy Kosinski

Born: Lodz, Poland; June 14, 1933
Died: Manhattan, New York; May 3, 1991

Jewish

Kosinski is best known for his depiction of the Holocaust in The Painted Bird *and for his creation of characters who grapple with the absurdity and cruelty of contemporary life.*

Principal works

LONG FICTION: *The Painted Bird*, 1965; *Steps*, 1968; *Being There*, 1971; *The Devil Tree*, 1973, revised 1981; *Cockpit*, 1975; *Blind Date*, 1977; *Passion Play*, 1979; *Pinball*, 1982; *The Hermit of 69th Street: The Working Papers of Norbert Kosky*, 1988

SCREENPLAY: *Being There*, 1979 (adaptation of his novel; with Robert C. Jones)

NONFICTION: *The Future Is Ours, Comrade*, 1960 (as Joseph Novak); *No Third Path*, 1962 (as Joseph Novak); *Notes of the Author on "The Painted Bird,"* 1965; *The Art of the Self: Essays à Propos "Steps,"* 1968; *Passing By: Selected Essays, 1962-1991*, 1992; *Conversations with Jerzy Kosinski*, 1993 (Tom Teicholz, editor)

EDITED TEXT: *Sociologia Amerykánska: Wybór Prae, 1950-1960*, 1962

Jerzy Nikodem Kosinski (JUR-zee koh-ZIHN-skee) was born in Lodz, Poland, on June 14, 1933. His life was as incredible as any of his novels, which are, to some degree, autobiographical. In 1939, when he was six, World War II began. He was Jewish, and his parents, believing he would be safer in the remote eastern provinces of Poland, paid a large sum of money to have him taken there. He reached eastern Poland, where he was immediately abandoned; his parents thought he was dead. Instead, at this very young age, he learned to live by his wits in an area where the peasants were hostile and the Nazis were in power. The extreme experiences of that time were given artistic expression in his first novel, *The Painted Bird*. Kosinski survived the ordeal, and his parents found him in an orphanage at the end of the war. The stress of his experience had rendered him mute, and his irregular, wandering life had left him unfit to live normally with other people. Finally, in the care of his family, Kosinski regained his speech, and, studying with his philologist father, he completed his entire basic formal education in a year and entered the University of Lodz, where he eventually earned advanced degrees in history and political science.

By that time, Poland was an Iron Curtain country with a collectivized society. Kosinski, after his youthful years of lone wandering, had developed a fierce independence and could not endure communal life in which the individual was under scrutiny at every step. He knew he could not remain without getting into serious trouble with the government, so he put together an elaborate scheme to escape. Making the cumbersome bureaucracy work in his favor, Kosinski invented a series of sponsors, all highly regarded scientists according to the documents he forged for them, to write him letters of recommendation, which eventually enabled him to get a passport to study in the United States. He arrived in New York on December 20, 1957, twenty-four years old, with $2.80 in his pocket and a good textbook knowledge of English, though little experience in speaking the language. He lived any way he could, stealing food when necessary and constantly studying English. By March, he was fluent in the language, and within three years he had published *The Future Is Ours, Comrade*, a study of Soviet life that sold extremely well. Suddenly he was moderately wealthy, but that was only the beginning. Mary Hayward Weir, the young widow of steel magnate Ernest Weir and one of the wealthiest women in the United States, read his book and wrote him a letter of praise. They met and were soon married. All at once he was wealthy beyond his own dreams, owning villas in several countries, a vast yacht, a private jet. "I had lived the American nightmare," he said, "now I was living the American dream."

Five years later, in 1968, Mary Weir died of a brain tumor. The wealth, held by her in trust, went back to the estate. Kosinski had, during his marriage, written his first two novels, *The Painted Bird* and *Steps*, and he was a well-known, celebrated author. Needing to earn a living, he taught at Yale, Princeton, and Wesleyan universities. He continued to write novels; they continued to sell well, so that he was able to leave teaching to write full-time. He was remarried, to Katherina von Frauenhofer, in 1987.

Kosinski's life then fell into an active but regular and disciplined pattern. In season, he traveled to Switzerland to ski or to the Caribbean to play polo, and he made extensive American tours, granting innumerable interviews and publicizing his books. He was also internationally active in civil rights cases and served for two terms (the maximum allowed) as president of the International Association of Poets, Playwrights, Editors, Essayists, and Novelists (PEN). The rest of the time he spent working in his small apartment in Manhattan. On May 3, 1991, Jerzy Kosinski, suffering from a serious heart disorder and discouraged by a growing inability to work, apparently chose to end his own life.

Kosinski often wrote that the world is an arena of violence and pure chance, which was certainly true of his own life. In addition to the numerous violent fluctuations of his early life, on a 1969 trip his baggage was misplaced, by chance, delaying his plane flight. His eventual destination was the home of his friends Roman Polanski and Sharon Tate; had it not been for the delay, he would have been there the fateful night the Charles Manson gang murdered everyone in that house.

Always a highly visible figure, Kosinski became in the early 1980's the subject of unwelcome publicity. In an article in *The Village Voice* (June 29, 1982), Geoffrey Stokes and Eliot Fremont-Smith charged that a number of Kosinski's novels had been written in part by various editorial assistants whose contributions he failed to acknowledge and indeed systematically concealed. Stokes and Fremont-Smith further charged that Kosinski's accounts to interviewers of his trau-

Jerzy Kosinski (National Archives)

matic childhood experiences, his escape from Poland, and his first years in America have been contradictory and in some cases verifiably untrue. Finally, they suggested that Kosinski's acclaimed first novel, *The Painted Bird*, was actually written in Polish and then rendered into English by an unacknowledged translator. Kosinski denied all the charges. In *The Hermit of 69th Street*, which its protagonist calls a "roman à tease," he responds indirectly to the controversy by reflecting on the writer's craft, which, he concludes, is largely a process of borrowing and recasting narrative material.

The Painted Bird

Type of work: Novel
First published: 1965

The Painted Bird is one of the most powerful novels about World War II and the Holocaust. Since it only obliquely deals with both events, the novel is a kind of allegory for the senseless cruelty and brutality of any war. Kosinski claimed, falsely, that the novel was based on his own experiences. He was not averse to creating fiction in more than one realm; he was candid about this practice. The point of Kosinski's claim, it may be argued, is that the book's unspeakable brutalities are realistic—indeed, they are much less than what happened.

Characterization is notably thin in *The Painted Bird*, and even the narrator is two-dimensional. The scenes that he narrates are, however, often overwhelming, and the power of the novel comes in large part from its simple language and imagery.

At one level, this short, episodic novel is an allegory. Kosinski has written that the novel is a fairy tale experienced by a child rather than told to him, and this is an apt description. Each incident in *The Painted Bird* can be considered as a stepping-stone in an allegorical bildungsroman, or novel of education. In each encounter, the boy learns another lesson, only to discard it for a new lesson in the following chapter or incident—religion from the priest, politics from Gavrila, vengeance from Mitka and the Silent One, and so on. The final answer with which Kosinski leaves readers is ambiguous. At the end, the boy is losing the muteness into which the horror of the world forced him. There is evil in the world, surely, and, as the boy has seen, neither the religious nor the political solution cancels it—in fact, they often exacerbate it. The only thing that is certain is the individual.

At another level the novel is about not merely an individual boy but also the Holocaust of World War II. *The Painted Bird* can be read as one of the most powerful indictments of the madness and terror of the Holocaust in literature. Although the horrors depicted in *The Painted Bird* are much less brutal than the actuality—no death camps or gas ovens are in the novel—they are horrible for their starkness and immediacy; they are the concrete and individual horrors of one alien child in a world gone mad.

The major thematic question the novel raises is the one at the center of the Book of Job and other classic pieces of literature: What is one to make of the evil of the world? Kosinski has no clear answer—except that the novel, with all its horror, is its own answer. The boy begins to speak again; the novel is testimony to what he has witnessed—the powerful communication is that *The Painted Bird* exists.

For all of its realistic detail, the novel also has a symbolic meaning. There are a number of incidents that have this symbolic quality—the story to which the title makes reference, for example. The painted bird is an apt symbol for the boy himself. Lekh captures a bird, paints it, and releases it. The bird's own flock, not recognizing it, pecks the bird to death. This bird also represents all those who are marked as aliens and who thus are destroyed—including the millions in the death camps of World War II. Kosinski's novel, in language and theme, forces readers to confront the potential horror of human behavior, without recourse to easy answers.

Steps

Type of work: Novel
First published: 1968

Winner of the National Book Award in 1969, *Steps* is experimental fiction belonging to the "new wave" school led by the French author Alain Robbe-Grillet. Events dominate, and readers must participate in the action if they are to find meaning. Its unusual, brilliant tone and technique set the work apart from other fiction of its time.

In 1967, Kosinski received a Guggenheim Fellowship to write the novel. His purpose, as he explained it, was to discover the self through incidents that were symbolic of the world. He said that the book's characters and their relationships existed in a fissure of time between past and present.

The significance of the title is elusive. Steps should go somewhere, but these steps seem only to travel between experiences. Some readers see the steps as a moral descent into hell, but it is certain that the author hoped that the steps would be his narrator's progression toward self-discovery.

Place-names are not given. Poland may be the setting for some of the incidents, America that for others. The author lived in both places. There is no unifying plot, no order to time. Characters are like stick figures, stripped to their bare bones. They have no personality and are nameless. Only women are allowed admirable traits.

The narrator is a man trying to discover who he is in a world he considers hostile.

Having come from a Communist country where human beings are externally controlled, he is surprised to find that there are collective forces in the new country that prevent the self from being free. Both society and religion exert control over people.

Much of Kosinski's writing is autobiographical. He spews the horrors he encountered in Poland out onto his pages in graphic form, colored dramatically by his vivid imagination. The jobs held by his narrator are jobs that Kosinski, too, held at various times.

An outgrowth of his first novel, *The Painted Bird* (1965), in which he was a child, *Steps* shows the author as a young man. The incidents seem disconnected, like a mirror that has been broken and the fragments scattered. If the protagonist could only find the pieces and put them together again, perhaps he could look into the reflective surface and see himself clearly. His self is shattered like the narrative, and the chaotic society in which he lives seems shattered as well. A former photographer, Kosinski records each event in visual detail as a camera would see it. He uses sight to achieve neutrality. The book is almost totally without emotion.

The theme of the book may be that brutality and violence are so destructive that they make life meaningless. Dispassionate acceptance of crude, degrading acts in an uncaring world gives tremendous power to the narrative. Distinguished by a commanding structure, poetic prose, and, despite its portrayal of depravity, an underlying morality, the work has been called existential. Its epigraph from the *Bhagavad Gita* (c. fifth century B.C.E.) indicates that the author hoped for peace and happiness to be restored to human life. That cannot occur if manipulative sex and brutal violence are the sum total of an individual's experience. The stark reality of this powerful novel is an admonition to modern society that bizarre relationships and fragmented experiences are capable of destroying the self.

Suggested Readings

Bruss, Paul. *Victims: Textual Strategies in Recent American Fiction*. Lewisburg, Pa.: Bucknell University Press, 1981.

Everman, Welch D. *Jerzy Kosinski: The Literature of Violation*. San Bernardino, Calif.: Borgo Press, 1991.

Fein, Richard J. "Jerzy Kosinski." In *Contemporary Novelists*, edited by James Vinson. London: St. James Press, 1976.

Lavers, Norman. *Jerzy Kosinski*. Boston: Twayne, 1982.

Lilly, Paul R., Jr. *Words in Search of Victims: The Achievement of Jerzy Kosinski*. Kent, Ohio: Kent State University Press, 1988.

Lupack, Barbara Tepa. *Plays of Passion, Games of Chance: Jerzy Kosinski and His Fiction*. Bristol, Ind.: Wyndham Hall Press, 1988.

Sloan, James Park. *Jerzy Kosinski: A Biography*. New York: Dutton, 1996.

Tepa Lupack, Barbara, ed. *Critical Essays on Jerzy Kosinski*. New York: G. K. Hall, 1998.

Contributors: Norman Lavers, Charles L. P. Silet, David Peck, and Josephine Raburn

Stanley Kunitz

Born: Worcester, Massachusetts; July 29, 1905
Died: New York, New York; May 14, 2006

Jewish

Kunitz achieves a complexity and coherence unique in lyric poetry.

Principal works

POETRY: *Intellectual Things*, 1930; *Passport to the War: A Selection of Poems*, 1944; *Selected Poems, 1928-1958*, 1958; *The Testing-Tree: Poems*, 1971; *The Coat Without a Seam: Sixty Poems, 1930-1972*, 1974; *The Terrible Threshold: Selected Poems, 1940-1970*, 1974; *The Lincoln Relics*, 1978; *The Poems of Stanley Kunitz, 1928-1978*, 1979; *The Wellfleet Whale and Companion Poems*, 1983; *Passing Through: The Later Poems, New and Selected*, 1995; *The Collected Poems*, 2000

TRANSLATIONS: *Antiworlds and the Fifth Ace*, 1967 (with others; of Andrei Voznesensky's poetry); *Stolen Apples*, 1971 (with others; of Yevgeny Yevtushenko's poetry); *Poems of Akhmatova*, 1973 (of Anna Akhmatova; with Max Hayward); *Story Under Full Sail*, 1974 (of Voznesensky's poetry); *Orchard Lamps*, 1978 (of Ivan Drach's poetry)

NONFICTION: *A Kind of Order, a Kind of Folly: Essays and Conversations*, 1975; *Interviews and Encounters with Stanley Kunitz*, 1993 (Stanley Moss, editor)

EDITED TEXTS: *Living Authors: A Book of Biographies*, 1931; *Authors Today and Yesterday: A Companion Volume to "Living Authors,"* 1933 (with Howard Haycraft and Wilbur C. Hadden); *The Junior Book of Authors*, 1934, 2d edition 1951 (with Haycraft); *British Authors of the Nineteenth Century*, 1936 (with Haycraft); *American Authors, 1600-1900: A Biographical Dictionary of American Literature*, 1938 (with Haycraft); *Twentieth Century Authors: A Biographical Dictionary of Modern Literature*, 1942, 7th edition 1973 (with Haycraft); *British Authors Before 1800: A Biographical Dictionary*, 1952 (with Haycraft); *Twentieth Century Authors: A Biographical Dictionary of Modern Literature, First Supplement*, 1955, 7th edition 1990 (with Vineta Colby); *European Authors, 1000-1900: A Biographical Dictionary of European Literature*, 1967 (with Colby); *Contemporary Poetry in America*, 1973; *The Essential Blake*, 1987; *The Wild Card: Selected Poems, Early and Late*, 1998 (with David Ignatow); *The Wild Braid: A Poet Reflects on a Century in the Garden*, 2005 (with Genine Lentine)

MISCELLANEOUS: *Next-to-Last Things: New Poems and Essays*, 1985

The son of immigrants, Stanley Jasspon Kunitz (KEW-nihtz) was born July 29, 1905, in Worcester, Massachusetts. Kunitz's father, Solomon, descended from Russian Sephardic Jews, committed suicide shortly before Stanley was born—an event that was to haunt the poet and that stands behind some of his most important and best-known poems. His mother, Yetta Helen, of Lithuanian descent, opened a dry goods store to support herself, her son, and two older daughters and to repay accumulated debts. Reared principally by his sisters and a succession of nurses, Kunitz grew up with his father's book collection, into which, as he put it, he would "passionately burrow." Though his mother shortly remarried, his stepfather, of whom he was fond, died before Kunitz reached his teens.

Educated in Worcester public schools, Kunitz edited the high school magazine, played tennis, and was graduated valedictorian of his class. Winning a scholarship to Harvard, Kunitz majored in English and began to write poetry, subsequently winning the Lloyd McKim Garrison Medal for poetry in 1926. He was graduated summa cum laude in the same year, and he took his M.A. degree from Harvard the following year. He worked briefly as a Sunday feature writer for the Worcester *Telegram*, where he had worked summers during college. He also completed a novel, which he later "heroically destroyed."

In 1927, Kunitz joined the H. W. Wilson Company as an editor. With Wilson's encouragement, he became editor of the *Wilson Bulletin*, a library publication (later known as the *Wilson Library Bulletin*). While at Wilson, he edited a series of reference books, including *Authors Today and Yesterday: A Companion Volume to "Living Authors"* (1933; with Howard Haycraft and Wilbur C. Hadden), *British Authors of the Nineteenth Century* (1936; with Haycraft), *American Authors, 1600-1900: A Biographical Dictionary of American Literature* (1938), and *Twentieth Century Authors: A Biographical Dictionary of Modern Literature* (1942; with Haycraft).

In 1930, Kunitz married Helen Pearse (they were divorced in 1937) and published his first collection of poems, *Intellectual Things*. The book was enthusiastically received by reviewers. Writing in *Saturday Review of Literature*, William Rose Benét observed, "Mr. Kunitz has gained the front rank of contemporary verse in a single stride." In 1939, Kunitz married a former actress, Eleanor Evans (from whom he was divorced in 1958), a union that produced his only child, Gretchen.

Kunitz's tenure with the H. W. Wilson Company was interrupted by World War II, during which he served as a noncommissioned officer in charge of information and education in the Air Transport Command. His second collection, *Passport to the War: A Selection of Poems*, appeared in 1944. A reviewer of that volume for *The New York Times Book Review* noted, "Kunitz has now (it seems) every instrument necessary to the poetic analysis of modern experience." Kunitz was awarded a Guggenheim Fellowship in 1945 and began a second career as an itinerant teacher, first at Bennington College, at the behest of his friend, the poet Theodore Roethke, then at a succession of colleges and universities, including the State University of New York at Potsdam, the New School for Social Research, Queens College, Brandeis University, the University of Washington, Yale University, Princeton University, and Rutgers University's Camden Campus.

In 1958, Kunitz married the artist Elise Asher, published *Selected Poems, 1928-1958*, which was awarded the Pulitzer Prize for Poetry in 1959, and received grants from the National Institute of Arts and Letters and the Ford Foundation. During the 1960's, though based in New York City and Provincetown, Massachusetts, Kunitz was a Danforth Visiting Lecturer at colleges and universities throughout the United States. He also lectured in the Soviet Union, Poland, Senegal, and Ghana. In 1964, he edited a volume of the poems of John Keats and two years later translated selections from Russian poet Andrei Voznesensky's *Antiworlds and the Fifth Ace*. He continued to edit for the Wilson Company (with Vineta Colby, *European Authors: 1000-1900: A Biographical Dictionary of European Literature*, 1967) and coedited a memorial volume of essays on the poet Randall Jarrell. In 1968, along with artist Robert Motherwell and novelist Norman Mailer, he helped found the Fine Arts Work Center in Provincetown, a resident community of young artists and writers, and in 1969 he assumed the general editorship of the Yale Series of Younger Poets.

Stanley Kunitz (Library of Congress)

The Testing-Tree, a volume of poems and translations, appeared in 1971, prompting Robert Lowell to assert in *The New York Times Book Review*, "once again, Kunitz tops the crowd, the old iron brought to the white heat of simplicity." In 1974, Kunitz was awarded one of the nation's top official literary honors when he was appointed consultant in poetry to the Library of Congress. In addition to *The Testing-Tree* and the collection *The Poems of Stanley Kunitz, 1928-1978*, a book of essays and conversations titled *A Kind of Order, a Kind of Folly*, as well as three volumes of translations, appeared during the 1970's.

Kunitz published a thematic volume of old and new poems, *The Wellfleet Whale and Companion Poems*, in a limited edition in 1983, with the new poems later incorporated in *Next-to-Last Things: New Poems and Essays*, published in 1985. In recognition of his lifetime achievement, Kunitz was chosen as the first New York State poet, for the term 1987-1989.

In 1996, President Bill Clinton presented Kunitz with a National Medal of Arts. Kunitz's next volume of poems, *Passing Through: The Later Poems, New and Selected*, received the National Book Award for Poetry in 1995. In 1998, he received the Frost Medal from the Poetry Society of America. Two years later, in 2000, Congress named Kunitz the poet laureate of the United States, a post that carries a one-year term and provides its incumbent with an office in the Library of Congress and a stipend of $35,000 for the year. His wife died in 2004, and Kunitz followed her two years later, dying at his Manhattan home.

"Father and Son"

Type of work: Poetry
First published: 1944, in *Passport to War: A Selection of Poems*

"Father and Son" is about the desire for a source of psychological and spiritual certitude. It is also about the acute frustration in the individual prematurely deprived of one who could have provided it. Yet the poem is not for the fatherless or orphaned alone. In the ordinary course of life, everyone loses his or her parents. Later, one may yearn, consciously or not, for a bygone security that they represent. Such feeling does not require that security to have existed in fact. It is fueled by loss and by the alienation and dissolution that often follow from it. Moreover, the one lost may or may not have possessed the love requisite to this need.

The two-line stanza that concludes the poem reveals the fruit of the son's entreaties—a vision of the father's skull. Nothing remains to be conveyed. The brevity of this climax and denouement is arresting. The son's yearning and his belief in his father's love make "the white ignorant hollow of his face" an unexpected and shocking final image. Does the concluding couplet, then, cynically denigrate this yearning? Probably not, because this desire and its gratification are imagined as in a dream, suggesting their unconscious nature. The voice of the poem is not engaged in a realistic social exchange. What the son finally realizes is not the sort of rebuff one gets from an impatient realist. It is more like the half-conscious, desultory insight that follows a dream embodying some personal unhappiness. Such an insight could be as salutary in the long run as it is disquieting for the moment.

Maturity finally requires one to acknowledge that a dead source of surety cannot be otherwise. In addition, an absolute and dead guarantor of one's well-being, by its magical, unconscious empowerment, enslaves one. (The dead father's "indomitable love" has kept the son in "chains.") One may esteem that love, real or not, but one wishes the person who seeks it free of bondage as well. Thus, the terrible experience of the "white ignorant hollow" is ultimately liberating. Learning to live independently of perfect guidance is often a painful experience, but it vitalizes one's autonomy and self-reliance. The son is finally free to be a real moral agent, to act through his own judgment, even ignorance, there being no morally omniscient guide anyway, as the innocently "ignorant . . . face" makes clear.

"Three Floors"

Type of work: Poetry
First published: 1971, in *The Testing-Tree*

"Three Floors" is a short formal poem; divided into four rhyming stanzas, it resembles a ballad or hymn. The title suggests the interior of a house and raises the question of what is happening on each floor. The reader is thus led to expect some contrast or tension.

"Three Floors" is one of several poems in which Kunitz mentions his father—or rather the felt absence of his father. In the final stanza, the poem itself becomes a vehicle for the imagination, creating a father for the son. The child adds the possessive pronoun and the lowercase ("my father"—he cannot call him "Father") as he wills him into being. The father is "flying," though. Even as he is apprehended, he seems to be leaving. In a frenzy, the child perceives an elemental loss where the external world reflects his own amorphous grief.

Loss is at the heart of this poem. The mother is hardly real as she hovers on the other side of the door. The sister is soon to be lost, and the child is all too aware of her impending marriage. The father has never been there at all; he becomes a mystery to be solved. The child picks at the metaphorical lock of the family, hoping to discover his own identity. In the trunk, he finds only a hat that suggests a secret adult male society and a walking stick, with its implications of freedom and mobility. These powerful absences add up to a very real (if imagined) presence.

The sister has a fiancé—a "doughboy," or soldier—who has recently asked her to marry him. The boy listens as she plays the piano, one sound over and over, *Warum*. The word means "why" in German. The sister plays the song, almost absentmindedly, thinking of her soldier and the war. Behind loss is the question "Why?" The question, along with its rhythm, pervades the poem, establishing a fatal sense that some things have no reason. The father's death, the mother's anger, the child's internalized conflict—nothing makes sense. Without an answer, the child is fated to ask this question throughout his life. The imaginative act, then, is seen as a way of discovering meaning—of making a divided house, however briefly, whole.

In sixteen lines, "Three Floors" has peopled the house with ghosts: The mother is sensed but not seen, the sister is remembered as a scrap of song, and the few vestiges of the father are locked in a trunk. The small boy is literally caught in the middle between the past (his father's loss) and the future (his sister's marriage, his own manhood). The poet re-creates the various claims on his affections as he presents the immediate moment of the poem—the darkness and the visionary sight of his father flying. His private thoughts are depicted as turbulent, guilty, and psychologically necessary. The reader is drawn into the poem's emotional complex in such a way that childhood itself, with all of its confusions, is awakened in memory.

Suggested Readings

Barber, David. "A Visionary Poet at Ninety." *The Atlantic Monthly* 277, no. 6 (June, 1996): 113-120.

Braham, Jeanne, ed. *The Light Within the Light: Portraits of Donald Hall, Richard Wilbur, Maxine Kumin, and Stanley Kunitz*. Engravings by Barry Moser. Boston: David R. Godine, 2007.

Campbell, Robert. "God, Man, and Whale: Stanley Kunitz's Collected Poems Show His Work Is All of a Piece." *The New York Times Book Review* 150 (October 1, 2000): 16.

Henault, Marie. *Stanley Kunitz*. Boston: Twayne, 1980.

Kunitz, Stanley. *Interviews and Encounters with Stanley Kunitz*. Edited by Stanley Moss. Riverdale-on-Hudson, N.Y.: Sheep Meadow Press, 1993.

_______. "Translating Anna Akhmatova: A Conversation with Stanley Kunitz." Interview by Daniel Weissbort. In *Translating Poetry: The Double Labyrinth*, edited by Weissbort. Iowa City: University of Iowa Press, 1989.

Orr, Gregory. *Stanley Kunitz: An Introduction to the Poetry*. New York: Columbia University Press, 1985.

Plummer, William. "New Beginnings: At Ninety-five, Fledgling Poet Laureate Stanley Kunitz Finds Fresh Wood." *People Weekly* 54 (October 30, 2000): 159-160.

Vinson, James, ed. *Contemporary Poets*. 3d ed. New York: Macmillan, 1980.

Weisberg, Robert. "Stanley Kunitz: The Stubborn Middle Way." *Modern Poetry Studies* 6 (Spring, 1975): 49-57.

Contributors: David Rigsbee, David M. Heaton, and Judith Kitchen

Tony Kushner

Born: New York, New York; July 16, 1956

Jewish

Kushner's work brings together issues of national politics, sexuality, and community.

Principal works

CHILDREN'S LITERATURE: *Brundibar*, 2002 (illustrated by Maurice Sendak)

DRAMA: *A Bright Room Called Day*, pr. 1985, pb. 1991; *Yes Yes No No*, pr. 1985, pb. 1987 (children's play); *Hydriotaphia: Or, The Death of Dr. Browne*, pr. 1987, pb. 2000; *Stella*, pr. 1987 (adaptation of Johann Wolfgang von Goethe's play); *The Illusion*, pr. 1988, pb. 1992 (adaptation of Pierre Corneille's play *L'Illusion comique*); *Angels in America: A Gay Fantasia on National Themes (Part One: Millenium Approaches)*, pr. 1991, pb. 1992; *Widows*, pr. 1991 (with Ariel Dorfman; adaptation of Dorfman's novel); *Angels in America: A Gay Fantasia on National Themes (Part Two: Perestroika)*, pr. 1992, pb. 1993, revised pb. 1996; *Slavs! (Thinking About the Longstanding Problems of Virtue and Happiness)*, pr. 1994, pb. 1995; *The Good Person of Setzuan*, pr. 1994 (adaptation of Bertolt Brecht's play); *A Dybbuk: Or, Between Two Worlds*, pr. 1997, pb. 1998 (adaptation of S. Ansky's play *The Dybbuk*); *Terminating: Or, Lass Meine schmerzen nicht verloren sein, Or, Ambivalence*, pr., pb. 1998 (adaptation of William Shakespeare's sonnet 75); *Death and Taxes: Hydriotaphia, and Other Plays*, pb. 2000 (includes *Reverse Transcription*, *Hydriotaphia*, *G. David Schine in Hell*, *Notes on Akiba*, *Terminating*, and *East Code Ode to Howard Jarvis*); *Homebody/Kabul*, pr. 2001, pb. 2002, revised pb. 2004; *Caroline, or Change*, pr. 2003, pb. 2004 (book and lyrics by Kushner; music by Jeanine Tesori)

NONFICTION: *Tony Kushner in Conversation*, 1998 (Robert Vorlicky, editor); *The Art of Maurice Sendak, 1980 to the Present*, 2003

EDITED TEXTS: *Wrestling with Zion: Progressive Jewish-American Responses to the Israeli-Palestinian Conflict*, 2003 (with Alisa Solomon)

MISCELLANEOUS: *Thinking About the Longstanding Problems of Virtue and Happiness: Essays, a Play, Two Poems, and a Prayer*, 1995

Tony Kushner (KOOSH-nur) grew up in Lake Charles, Louisiana. His parents, musicians, immersed him in culture, leftist politics, and the arts. He returned to New York City, his birthplace, to attend Columbia University, where he studied medieval history, developed an interest in Marxist thought, and began to come to terms

Tony Kushner (Columbia University/Courtesy, Jay Thompson)

with his homosexuality. He underwent psychoanalysis during his early years in New York, attempting to "cure" himself of being gay. After graduating from Columbia in 1978, Kushner earned a Master in Fine Arts degree in directing from New York University in 1984.

Kushner is best known for *Angels in America: A Gay Fantasia on National Themes*, a play about life in Ronald Reagan's America and the pandemic of acquired immunodeficiency syndrome (AIDS). Much of *Angels in America*—and of Kushner's other work—focuses on political thought, especially the connections between world history and contemporary politics. Kushner's first major play, *A Bright Room Called Day*, uses an artistic character to draw explicit links between the rise of Nazism in Germany in the 1930's and what Kushner saw as the smothering conservatism of the 1980's. *Slavs!*, Kushner's sequel to *Angels in America*, opens with a character from *Perestroika*, Aleksii Antedilluvianovich Perlapsarianov, the world's oldest Bolshevik. The play focuses on a postsocialist world in which leftist politics has lost out to its more conservative counterparts. Kushner sees the loss of the Left to be a loss of hope and a foreboding of a dangerous, heartless future. These themes are also developed in *Angels in America*, but in *Slavs!* Kushner does not use sexuality as a major symbol, although two main characters of *Slavs!* are a lesbian couple.

Kushner writes what he has referred to as Theater of the Fabulous. His plots examine the close relationship between the public, political world and the private lives of people. An activist who has been arrested more than once at demonstrations against government inaction in the face of the AIDS crisis, Kushner sees himself as an inheritor of Bertolt Brecht's explicitly political theater. In order for theater to be socially relevant, moving, and artistically successful, Kushner believes that theater must be confrontational, that it must not leave its audience comfortable or satisfied with the status quo. Theater, for Kushner, is an art of engagement, with politics, with issues, and with audiences—and theater is always political.

Angels in America

Type of work: Drama
First produced: *Millenium Approaches*, 1991, pb. 1992 (part 1); *Perestroika*, 1992, pb. 1993 (part 2)

A two-part, seven-hour play, *Angels in America: A Gay Fantasia on National Themes* is an epic of life in America in the mid-1980's. In the play, self-interest has overtaken love and compassion, acquired immunodeficiency syndrome (AIDS) is decimating the gay male population, and victory in the ideological battle between liberals and conservatives seems to be going to the conservatives. Kushner's leftist politics are unmistakably present in his play, but *Angels in America* is not a polemic. Instead, it is a fantastic journey through the lives of two couples. One couple is Louis, a Jewish word processor, and Prior Walter, a former drag queen who has AIDS. The other is Joe Pitt, a Mormon republican and lawyer, and his wife, Harper. Another key player is the ethically questionable lawyer Roy Cohn, a dramatized version of the real person. (Cohn was counsel to Senator Joseph McCarthy during the "Communist witch-hunts" of the 1950's.) Cohn is dying of AIDS and is in the process of being disbarred.

Angels in America uses AIDS as a metaphor for an investigation of life in the 1980's. Kushner views the greed of that era as having frightening implications for personal relations. Louis spouts grand ideas in bombastic speeches but flees when faced with a lover who has AIDS. Louis is unable to face the responsibilities associated with caring for a person with AIDS. Joe, who becomes Louis's lover, abandons his wife, deciding that he can no longer repress his homosexuality. Cohn tries to enlist Joe's help in stopping the disbarment process by getting Joe a job in the Reagan administration, but Joe refuses.

Prior, the protagonist, is the character who suffers most. As AIDS-related complications jeopardize his health, he becomes more panicked. He also becomes a prophet after being visited by an angel at the end of part 1, *Millenium Approaches*. With the help of Hannah Pitt, Joe's mother, he learns how to resist the Angel and how to make the Angel bless him. In spite of his failing health, Prior tells the Angel: "We live past hope. If I can find hope anywhere, that's it, that's the best I can do. It's so much not enough, so inadequate. . . . Bless me anyway. I want more life."

This message of hope, near the end of part 2, *Perestroika*, affirms the movement of the play toward the interconnectedness of people across boundaries of race, religion, sexuality, or ideology. Julius Rosenberg and Ethel Rosenberg say kaddish over the dead body of Cohn. Hannah, a devout Mormon, nurses Prior, a stranger to her. Belize, a black, gay nurse, advises Cohn on his medical treatment. Louis and Prior get back together, as the epilogue reveals.

Suggested Readings

Brask, Per, ed. *Essays on Kushner's Angels*. Winnipeg, Man.: Blizzard, 1995.

Felman, Jyl Lynn. "Lost Jewish (Male) Souls: A Midrash on *Angels in America*." *Tikkun* 10, no. 3 (May, 1995): 27-30.

Fisher, James. *The Theater of Tony Kushner*. New York: Routledge, 2002.

_______, ed. *Tony Kushner: New Essays on the Art and Politics of the Plays*. Jefferson, N.C.: McFarland, 2006.

Geis, Deborah R., and Stephen F. Kruger. *Approaching the Millennium: Essays on "Angels in America."* Ann Arbor: University of Michigan Press, 1997.

Kushner, Tony. Interview by David Savran. In *Speaking on Stage: Interviews with Contemporary American Playwrights*, edited by Philip C. Kolin and Colby H. Kullman. Tuscaloosa: University of Alabama Press, 1995.

Osborn, M. Elizabeth, Terrence McNally, and Lanford Wilson. *The Way We Live Now: American Plays and the AIDS Crisis*. New York: Theatre Communications Group, 1990.

Vorlicky, Robert, ed. *Tony Kushner in Conversation (Triangulations)*. Ann Arbor: University of Michigan Press, 1997.

Contributor: Chris Freeman

Jhumpa Lahiri

Born: London, England; July 11, 1967

South Asian American

The child of Bengali immigrants, Lahiri writes with a luminous, graceful style that presents the mythic significance of food, ethnic customs, and other details of daily life.

Principal works

LONG FICTION: *The Namesake*, 2003
SHORT FICTION: *Interpreter of Maladies*, 1999; *Unaccustomed Earth*, 2008
NONFICTION: *Accursed Palace: The Italian Palazzo on the Jacobean Stage, 1603-1625*, 1997

Jhumpa Lahiri (JEWM-pah lah-HIH-ree) was born in London on July 11, 1967, to Bengali parents originally from Calcutta. Her mother, a teacher, and her father, a librarian, immigrated to the United States when she was a child, and Lahiri grew up in South Kingstown, Rhode Island. She was a shy child, uncomfortable in groups, who started writing ten-page "novels" during recess with friends, quiet girls like her who enjoyed stories. In one interview, Lahiri said she always hoped for rainy days so she could stay inside and write instead of having to run around the playground.

In high school, Lahiri stopped writing fiction, for she had no confidence in her ability in the form, and instead wrote articles for the high school newspaper. In college, she took some creative writing classes but still felt she might never succeed in writing fiction and thus decided to be an academic. After being turned down by a number of graduate schools, she got a job as a research assistant at a nonprofit organization, discovered the ease of writing with a computer, and began writing fiction again.

A second-generation immigrant, Lahiri found it difficult having parents who, even after living abroad for thirty years, still considered India home. She said she inherited a sense of exile from her parents, even though she felt more American than they. Lahiri, realizing that loneliness and a sense of alienation are hard for immigrant parents, thought that the problem for their children was that they feel neither one thing nor the other. Having visited India often, Lahiri said she never felt any more at home there than she did in the United States.

Much of Lahiri's time spent in Calcutta as a child was with her grandmother, which she said made it possible for her to experience solitude and which also encouraged her to see things from different points of view. Being a second-generation

American did not make her want to be a writer so much as it made her want to write, to seek solace by recording her observations in a place where she answered only to herself. The act of writing made it possible, she said, to withdraw into herself.

Because Lahiri went to Calcutta neither as a tourist nor as a former resident, she learned to observe things as an outsider, even though she felt she belonged there in some fundamental way. She said her first stories were set in Calcutta as a result of this combination of distance and intimacy. However, she claimed never to have thought consciously of trying to deal with questions of cultural identify in her writing as much as simply beginning with a conflict in a character's life.

Lahiri received her B.A. from Barnard College in New York City in 1989 and subsequently enrolled in Boston University's creative writing program, from which she received her M.A. in 1993. Lahiri also received an M.A. in English and an M.A. in comparative literature and the arts from Boston University. She earned her doctorate in Renaissance studies from Boston University in 1997 but decided she wanted to write fiction. She said that she worked for the Ph.D. out of a sense of duty and practicality, but pursuing it was never something she loved. She wrote stories on the side while doing the research for her dissertation. Lahiri worked in the summer of 1997 at *Boston* magazine as an intern, doing routine tasks and writing news stories. She received a fellowship at the Fine Arts Work Center in Provincetown, where she studied in 1997 and 1998. The experience at Provincetown changed everything: In seven months' time she got an agent, had a story published in *The New Yorker*, and got a book contract.

The title story of Lahiri's collection of stories *Interpreter of Maladies* was included in both *Best American Short Stories* and *Prize Stories: The O. Henry Awards*. *The New Yorker* named her one of the twenty best writers under the age of forty. She won the Transatlantic Review award from the Henfield Foundation, the Louisiana Review Award for Short Fiction, a fiction prize from *The Louisville Review*, the PEN/Hemingway Award, and ultimately the Pulitzer Prize for *Interpreter of Maladies* in 2000.

The Namesake

Type of work: Novel
First published: 2003

The Namesake, Lahiri's first novel, fulfilled the promise of her short stories. *The Namesake* portrays both the immigrant experience in America and the complexity of family loyalties that underlies all human experience. Ashoke and Ashima Ganguli, after an arranged marriage in India, immigrate to America where Ashoke achieves his dream of an engineering degree and a tenured position in a New England college. Their son Gogol, named for the Russian writer, rejects both his unique name and his Bengali heritage.

In a scene central to the novel's theme, Ashoke gives his son a volume of Nikolai Gogol's short stories for his fourteenth birthday, hoping to explain the book's significance in his own life. Gogol, a thoroughly Americanized teenager, is indifferent, preoccupied with his favorite Beatles recording. Such quietly revealing moments give the narrative its emotional power. The loneliness of lives lived in exile is most poignantly revealed in the late-night family telephone calls from India, always an announcement of illness or death. Gogol earns his degree in architecture, but happiness in love eludes him. An intense love affair with Maxine draws him into a wealthy American family, revealing the extreme contrasts between American and Indian family values. Gogol's marriage to Moushumi, who shares his Indian heritage, ends in divorce.

Lahiri's conclusion achieves a fine balance. Ashima, now a widow, sells the family home and will divide her time between America and Calcutta. Gogol, at thirty-two, discovers in his father's gift of Gogol's short stories a temporary reconciliation with his name and the heritage he has rejected.

Suggested Readings

Bellafante, Ginia. "Windows into Life." *Time* 154 (August 2, 1999): 91.

Crain, Caleb. "Subcontinental Drift." *The New York Times Book Review*, July 11, 1999, 11-12.

Curtis, Sarah. "Strangers and Neighbours." *The Times Literary Supplement*, October 22, 1999, 25.

Flynn, Sean. "Jhumpa Lahiri." *Esquire* 134 (October, 2000): 172.

"Jhumpa Lahiri." *People* 54 (December 25, 2000): 138.

Kakutani, Michiko. "Liking America, but Longing for India." *The New York Times*, August 6, 1999, p. E48.

Keesey, Anna. "Four New Collections Show the Elastic Quality of Short Fiction." *The Chicago Tribune*, August 8, 1999, p. 4.

O'Grady, Megan. Review of *Interpreter of Maladies*, by Jhumpa Lahiri. *The Village Voice* 104 (April 19, 1999): 59-60.

Todd, Tamsin. "At the Corner Delhi." *The Washington Post*, October 7, 1999, p. C8.

Contributor: Charles E. May

Nella Larsen

Born: Chicago, Illinois; April 13, 1891
Died: New York, New York; March 30, 1964

African American

Larsen's novels are among the first to portray realistically the dilemma of identity for biracial women.

Principal works

LONG FICTION: *Quicksand*, 1928; *Passing*, 1929
SHORT FICTION: "Sanctuary," 1930
MISCELLANEOUS: *An Intimation of Things Distant: The Collected Fiction of Nella Larsen*, 1992 (also as *The Complete Fiction of Nella Larsen*, 2001)

In common with her protagonists—Helga Crane in *Quicksand* and Clare Kendry in *Passing*—Nella Larsen, throughout her life, never thoroughly resolved the crisis of her identity. Larsen often invented details about her life to suit her audience and the effect she wanted to have on it; it may be said that she learned this habit of invention from her parents. Mystery surrounds her identity because she wanted it that way.

Even in such matters as her birth certificate, school records, and early childhood whereabouts, it is possible that no absolutely definitive history will arise. Thadious M. Davis, in the biography *Nella Larsen, Novelist of the Harlem Renaissance: A Woman's Life Unveiled*, makes a thorough summary of the information available on the basics of Larsen's identity. Nella Larsen was born Nellie Walker, child of a Danish woman and a cook designated as "colored." The baby was designated, therefore, as "colored." When the girl entered school, she did so under the name Nellie Larson. It is possible that her supposed stepfather, Peter Larson, was in fact the same person as her "colored" father, Peter Walker, and that Peter Walker had begun to pass for white. Nellie Larson also attended school as Nelleye Larson. In 1907, she began to use the surname Larsen. The 1910 census of her household does not include her (her officially white sister, Anna, is mentioned), perhaps because her birth certificate, with the word "colored," was being disassociated from the family. Later, she adopted the first name Nella; with marriage, she became Nella Larsen Imes. Larsen thus had considerable experience in her life with such issues as passing and identity.

After completing a nursing degree at Lincoln Hospital, Larsen worked as a nurse at Tuskegee Institute in Alabama. As does her character Helga, Larsen quickly tired of the uplifting philosophy at Tuskegee and headed north. Larsen worked for the New York City Department of Health and married Elmer S. Imes.

Between 1921 and 1926, Larsen worked for the New York City Public Library in Harlem. There, Larsen became involved with Harlem Renaissance writers, capturing her own following with the publication of several critically acclaimed short stories. Shortly afterward, Larsen wrote *Quicksand*, a novel for which she was awarded a Harmon Award in literature. Following the success of this book and her next novel, *Passing*, Larsen became the first African American woman to receive the prestigious Guggenheim Fellowship.

Nella Larsen (Department of State)

Her popularity ended, however, with the public embarrassment of being accused in 1930 of plagiarizing one of her short stories, "Sanctuary," and a messy divorce from her husband, whose unfaithfulness was the talk of the town. Larsen's readership abandoned her, and she retreated to nursing at New York City's Gouverneur Hospital, transferring to Metropolitan Hospital in 1961. In 1963, she endured a period of depression that may have been because her white sister (or perhaps half sister) had shunned Larsen for the last of many times. In 1964, her absence from work being noted, Larsen was found dead in her apartment.

Larsen enjoyed literary success only briefly during her lifetime. Her literary talents and achievements went largely unrecognized until reappraisal of women's literature elevated her works as contributing a distinctive voice to American literature.

Quicksand

Type of work: Novel
First published: 1928

Quicksand, Larsen's masterpiece, is the story of Helga Crane's quest, through a series of excursions in black and white society, for racial identity and acceptance. Her rejection by her black father and by her white stepfather and her mother's early death leave Helga an orphan subject to the charity of white relatives, who pay for her education.

Helga's search begins with her brief tenure at Naxos, a Southern black college, where she fails to assimilate the racial attitudes of middle-class educated blacks there who expound the philosophy of racial uplift. She escapes to Chicago and then New York. Despite associations with middle-class blacks there, she still feels detached from the culture. A monetary gift from her uncle and his advice to visit her mother's sister in Denmark take Helga abroad. In Denmark, Helga rejects becoming her relatives' social showpiece of primitivism and a marriage proposal from an artist who sees in Helga "the warm, impulsive nature of the women of Africa" and "the soul of a prostitute."

Hearing a Negro spiritual at a symphony concert, Helga can no longer resist returning to America. When she returns, she finds that Robert Anderson, her only love interest, has married her mentor. Anderson underscores Helga's alienation when, despite his clandestine sexual advances, he rejects her. Devastated, Helga finds herself at a storefront revival, where she experiences a spiritual conversion. The intensity of emotion and her weak health occasion her meeting the Reverend Mr. Pleasant Green, a scurrilous "jack-leg" preacher who takes advantage of this opportunity to gain a wife and sexual partner. Transplanted to the South and drowning in the domestic hell of babies and marriage, Helga bids an angry and bitter farewell to her dreams and resigns herself to "the quagmire in which she had engulfed herself." She resolves to get out of her predicament, but she understands "that this wasn't new. . . . [S]omething like it she had experienced before." Life offers no healing balm for Helga, as her journey ends in the squalor of a filthy house, the revulsion she feels for her slovenly, lecherous husband, and her ultimate failure to find any redeeming purpose or value for her life.

Larsen's character is more than the archetypal tragic mulatto. Helga's restlessness and predictable flights from her cultural surroundings portray a woman uncomfortable with and deeply confused about her identity. Larsen was among the first to render depth and dimension to the emotional and physical motivations for her mixed-race characters' actions.

Passing

Type of work: Novel
First published: 1929

Like *Quicksand*, *Passing* centers on the marginalization of African American women. Some literary critics have maintained that Larsen's choice of title—and, indeed, the book's main theme—only strengthens the effect of the characters' isolation. However, most scholars consider the novel to be the finest treatment of the concept of hidden racial identity in modern American literature.

The novel's protagonist, Clare Kendry, escaped from cruel, racist aunts by "passing"—that is, by using her light skin color to join the white community and to adopt a white identity. Her childhood friend, Irene Redfield, lives her life in fear and carefully avoids any hint of danger. Seeking a safe lifestyle, she has married, but her marriage hangs by a thread. She does, however, take an active role in Harlem's middle-class black society, and it is through her friendship with Redfield that Kendry begins to rediscover her identity as an African American. The women are able to maintain their friendship despite Kendry's absorption into white society, and Redfield does not chastise her friend for her decision. In fact, the women are first reunited at a party at which Irene herself has "passed" as white in order to seek refuge from the tumult of Chicago's rough neighborhoods.

Larsen is careful to point out that Kendry's life as a white woman is far from idyllic. In some ways, any advantage Kendry might have had as a white person is replaced in her mind by the disadvantages created by her lack of money (compared to her relatively prosperous white acquaintances). She seeks comfort in Redfield's Harlem, but her period of self-exploration comes to an abrupt halt when her husband, John Bellew, discovers Kendry's real identity and rejects her entirely. Much hinges on the novel's climax, in which Kendry attends a Christmas party with Redfield and her husband Brian. Redfield has become increasingly jealous of the affection between her husband and her friend and begins to feel that Kendry may be trying to dissolve her marriage. As the party continues, Kendry falls from a sixth-floor window and is killed. Several critics, though, have argued that she was pushed by Redfield.

In many ways, the success of this scene (and the novel as a whole) rests on Larsen's depiction of the relationship between the two women. When Kendry's husband storms into the party, calling his wife a "damned nigger," Redfield rushes to her friend's side in a gesture that seems, on its surface, to be a loving act of defense. However, Larsen reveals Redfield's thoughts: "One thought possessed her. She couldn't have Clare Kendry cast aside by Bellew. She couldn't have her free." Redfield's well-being is dependent on her friend's entrapment; Redfield is unable to draw any kind of distinction between her desire for and her desire to be Kendry, nor is she able to reconcile these desires. The complex web that Larsen constructs around and between these four characters (but most especially between the two women) is further tangled by the novel's lack of resolution. It never becomes clear whether Kendry was killed or whether she killed herself. The reader is left unsatisfied, unless he or she can be satisfied with ambiguity, as Larsen had to be in her own life.

Suggested Readings

Bontemps, Arna, ed. *The Harlem Renaissance Remembered*. New York: Dodd Mead, 1984.

Davis, Thadious M. *Nella Larsen, Novelist of the Harlem Renaissance: A Woman's Life Unveiled*. Baton Rouge: Louisiana State University Press, 1994.

Defalco, Amelia. "Jungle Creatures and Dancing Apes: Modern Primitivism and Nella Larsen's *Quicksand*." *Mosaic: A Journal for the Interdisciplinary Study of Literature* 38, no. 2 (June, 2005): 19-25.

Huggins, Nathan. *Harlem Renaissance*. New York: Oxford University Press, 1971.

Knadler, Stephen. "Domestic Violence in the Harlem Renaissance: Remaking the Record in Nella Larsen's *Passing* and Toni Morrison's *Jazz*." *African American Review* 38, no. 1 (Spring, 2004): 99-118.

Larson, Charles R. *Invisible Darkness: Jean Toomer and Nella Larsen*. Iowa City: University of Iowa Press, 1993.

McLendon, Jacquelyn Y. *The Politics of Color in the Fiction of Jessie Fauset and Nella Larsen*. Charlottesville: University of Virginia Press, 1995.

Miller, Erika M. *The Other Reconstruction*. New York: Garland, 2000.

Singh, Amritjit. *The Novels of the Harlem Renaissance: Twelve Black Writers, 1923-1933*. State College: Pennsylvania State University Press, 1976.

Wall, Cheryl A. *Women of the Harlem Renaissance*. Bloomington: University of Indiana Press, 1995.

Contributors: Betty L. Hart and Anna A. Moore

Evelyn Lau

Born: Vancouver, Canada; July 2, 1971

Chinese American

Lau's writing features young women, often entangled in prostitution, drug abuse, and bizarre sexual subcultures, who are in search of love and acceptance.

Principal works

LONG FICTION: *Other Women*, 1995

POETRY: *You Are Not Who You Claim*, 1990; *Oedipal Dreams*, 1992; *In the House of Slaves*, 1994

SHORT FICTION: *Fresh Girls, and Other Stories*, 1993; *Choose Me: Stories*, 1999

NONFICTION: *Runaway: Diary of a Street Kid*, 1989; *Inside Out: Reflections on a Life So Far*, 2001

Evelyn Lau started to write when she was six years old in 1977; at fourteen, her self-described obsession with writing led her to run away from her Chinese Canadian family, who did not permit her to pursue this passion. Keeping journals and penning poetry kept Lau's spirit alive while she descended into a nightmare world of juvenile prostitution, rampant drug abuse, and homelessness.

Lau left the streets at sixteen, and wrote *Runaway: Diary of a Street Kid* (1989) about her experience. She also published her first collection of poetry, *You Are Not Who You Claim*, in which her harrowing ordeals find artistic expression. The persona of Lau's poetry is often a woman who resembles Lau, and her voice hauntingly evokes the mostly futile search for human warmth and genuine affection in a nightmare adult world.

In Lau's poetry and fiction, lovemaking can end sadly. Thus, "Two Smokers" ends on a note of complete alienation: While the sleeping lover of the persona "gropes at the wall" and "finds flesh in his dreams," the woman "watches the trail of smoke" from her cigarette "drift towards the ceiling,/ hesitate, fall apart."

The haunting lucidity, freshness of imagination, and stunning power of Lau's writings have earned for her important literary prizes. Her first poetry collection won the Milton Acorn People's Poetry award, and her second collection, *Oedipal Dreams*, which contains many interrelated poems reflecting on a young woman's relationship with her married psychiatrist and lover, was nominated for the Governor-General's Award, Canada's highest literary honor. Perhaps most important, Lau's youth has given her writing a sharp awareness of the startling coexistence of mainstream and alternative lifestyles. Her poems and stories feature many a professional man who shows pictures of his children to the teenage sex worker whom he has hired to be his dominatrix. Similarly, the persona of *In the House of Slaves* watches a squirrel as a customer drips hot wax on her body. As has the author, the main character of *In the House of Slaves* has lived simultaneously in the world of pop culture adolescence and in hell.

Runaway

Type of work: Autobiography
First published: 1989

Based on the journals that Lau kept, *Runaway: Diary of a Street Kid* chronicles her two-year experience as a young Chinese Canadian woman who left home because she could no longer stand her parents' oppression of her desires to write poetry. She sought to be anything but an obsessively studious, meekly obedient model pupil. *Runaway* became Lau's start in a successful career as a young writer.

After telling of her terrible life at home in a prologue, Lau's autobiography opens on the first day after she ran away from home: March 22, 1988. Staying with friends at first, she attempts suicide on the day she is turned in to the authorities. Recovering at a mental hospital, Lau falls into Canada's well-developed social safety net designed to rescue troubled teenagers.

For months, Lau tries to put distance between her old and new selves as she self-destructively experiments with drugs and sex. Twice she goes to the United States only to turn herself in to be shipped back home to Vancouver. She frustrates social workers and her two psychiatrists, who are unable to prevent her descent into teenage prostitution and drug abuse.

Throughout the chronicle of Lau's ordeal, the reader becomes aware of her extremely low self-esteem and her self-loathing, which her parents' perfectionistic behavior has instilled in her. The reader almost cries out in despair at Lau's inability to value herself, even as her budding career as a writer begins with awards and letters of acceptance for her poetry.

Despite her ability to keep up with her writing and her occasionally seeing her position with lucidity, Lau refuses to stop hurting herself. She becomes attached to unsuitable men such as Larry, a drug addict on a government-sponsored recovery program, which he abuses with cunning. To keep Lau, Larry provides her the potent pharmaceuticals without which she could not abide his presence.

In the end, Lau frees herself of Larry, lives on her own in a state-provided apartment, and readies herself for college. Her writing has sustained her through dark hours, and, at sixteen, she is only a short time away from turning the journals into a manuscript. *Runaway* does not have a real closure. The reader leaves Lau as she seems to have overcome the worst of her self-abusive behavior, yet her life is still a puzzle waiting to be sorted out completely. In the epilogue added in a 1995 edition, Lau provides a firm sense that she has found a way out of the crisis of her adolescent life.

Fresh Girls, and Other Stories

Type of work: Short fiction
First published: 1993

Fresh Girls, and Other Stories, Lau's collection of short stories, centers on young women who seek love and human affection in a netherworld of prostitution and bizarre, alternative sexual lifestyles. Many of the stories' protagonists live on two or more levels. They often wear a mask during the sex work they perform but have retained a different identity in which they long for a more conventional life and for loving acceptance.

Lau's stories are told from the perspective of the young women, who chase after a dream that continues to elude them. The reader is made to share, for example, the sadness of the drug-addicted teenage narrator of the title story. Looking around the massage parlor where she works, she suddenly recognizes that, although many of her friends still look nice in regular clothes and outside their work, they have lost that special youthful freshness after which their clients lust with such depravity.

The astonishing ease with which men and women cross from an arcane subculture of sadomasochism to a mainstream life that is officially unaware and innocent of the other world is described with brilliant sharpness in "The Session" and "Fetish Night." Alternate identities are taken on quickly, and discarded just as easily, as young women agree to perform strange sexual acts on men who want to live out their secret fantasies and change from a position of power into that of helpless submission.

A core of stories explores the unhappy relationships of young women in love with older, married men who refuse to commit to their new lovers. In these stories, a man's wedding band takes on the identity of a weapon "branding" the narrator's skin. Fiercely subjective in her view, the protagonist of "Mercy" feels that "we are victims of each other," as she sexually tortures her lover on his wife's birthday.

The pain of the experience sometimes proves too much for the young women to bear. Out of a feeling of self-hatred and despair, "Glass" implies, a dejected girl cuts her wrists while she smashes her window, ready to follow the falling glass onto the street below. What gives artistic shape to Lau's collection is her unflinching, sympathetic look at a world that is alien to most readers. Her young, often nameless narrators are allowed to speak for themselves and scrutinize their tortured identities. In Lau's stories, the literary perspective is not that of a prurient voyeur who looks in but that of young souls who look out. Lau's stories challenge readers to examine the abyss of their own lives.

Suggested Readings

Dieckmann, Katherina. Review of *In the House of Slaves*, by Evelyn Lau. *Village Voice Literary Supplement*, April, 1994, 32.

Halim, Nadia. Review of *In the House of Slaves*, by Evelyn Lau. *The Canadian Forum* 73 (October, 1994): 41.

James, Darlene. Review of *Runaway: Diary of a Street Kid*, by Evelyn Lau. *Maclean's*, November 13, 1989, 81.

Contributor: R. C. Lutz

Wendy Law-Yone

Born: Mandalay, Burma (now Myanmar); April 1, 1947

Asian American

Law-Yone's novels describe the alienation caused by harsh upbringings, political turmoil, and immigration.

Principal works

LONG FICTION: *The Coffin Tree*, 1983; *Irrawaddy Tango*, 1993

SHORT FICTION: "Ankle," 1988 (in *Grand Street 7.3*); "Drought," 1993 (in *Slow Hand: Women Writing Erotica*; Michelle Slung, editor)

NONFICTION: *Company Information: A Model Investigation*, 1980.

The novels of Wendy Law-Yone (law YOH-neh) reflect the events in her turbulent life. In 1962, while a teenager in Burma, she watched her country become a military dictatorship and imprison her father, a newspaper publisher and political activist. In 1967, attempting to leave the country, she was captured and held for two weeks before being released. After living in Southeast Asia, she immigrated to America in 1973. She graduated from college two years later and worked as a writer, publishing in the *Washington Post Magazine* and researching and writing *Company Information: A Model Investigation* (1980).

Her first novel, *The Coffin Tree*, portrays an Asian American immigrant in a different situation than that of many other novels. In many books, protagonists need to choose between, or reconcile, their native culture and American culture. Law-Yone's heroine, however, lacks connections to both cultures. Growing up with no mother and a distant father, she develops no attachment to Burma and is never nostalgic. When she and her brother immigrate, however, she remains detached from and unenthusiastic about America. Unable to express or follow her own desires, she obeys her tyrannical father and grandmother in Burma and her deranged brother in America. When brother and father die, twisted logic leads her to attempt suicide to fulfill her newly "uncovered . . . identity." Although she survives, institutional treatment engenders only a mild affirmation of life: "Living things prefer to go on living."

Irrawaddy Tango also describes a woman living more for others than herself: In a fictionalized Burma, a friend inspires her to love dancing. She marries an officer who becomes the country's dictator; when kidnapped by rebels, she agrees to be their spokeswoman. After her rescue, she helps other refugees before drifting into homelessness in America; she then returns to publicly reconcile with the dictator. Despite her political activities, she evidences no commitment to any cause and also can express herself only by violence, finally murdering her husband.

Law-Yone does not fully account for her heroines' alienation and lack of self-esteem, though possible factors include unhappy childhoods—with cold fathers and absent mothers. Politics is also corrosive in Law-Yone's fiction, leading parents and spouses to neglect personal relationships. Finally, fate forces some to lead unrewarding lives. The absence of easy answers in her fiction demonstrates her maturity as a writer.

The Coffin Tree

TYPE OF WORK: Novel
FIRST PUBLISHED: 1983

The Coffin Tree explores a young woman's growth into adulthood from the perspective of two cultures: Burma and the United States. Against the backdrop of large-scale political instability and threat of war in Burma, Law-Yone depicts a subtle kind of brutality at work beneath the veneer of prosperity and efficiency in the United States. The narrator's matter-of-fact description of the rebuffs and humiliation that she experiences in her attempt to adapt to a foreign culture is a powerful indictment of the United States' insensitivity to its immigrant population. The narrator and her half brother Shan are educated and speak English, but this does not prevent them from being misunderstood and maligned by Americans who show no understanding that people from other cultures operate according to different codes of behavior. *The Coffin Tree* suggests that cruelty caused by a failure to empathize with one's fellow human beings can take many guises. For example, the narrator's employer in New York does not give her a chance to explain her absence from work because his thinking is controlled by negative stereotypes. He thoughtlessly fires her just when she has spent her last money on a doctor's house call to the mentally ill Shan, who has malaria.

Ultimately, however, the main focus of the novel is not on the narrator's eventual cultural assimilation, which is glossed over in a few paragraphs, but on her inner emotional state. Her dreams are as important to her as waking reality. While not always as overtly symbolic as in her dream of the threatening half-man, half-horse whose energy, impatience, and violence are suggestive of her father, most of the dreams nevertheless disclose her anxieties and her longings. Yet, though the narrator's explanation of her feelings and motives constitutes the novel's reason for being, she never indulges in self-pity or self-justification. As she records events, memories, and emotions, the rapid pace and alternating settings drive the narrative forward without sentimentality. Incorporated stories and legends add a touch of the mythic to the realism of the novel. Law-Yone portrays a broad range of human experience in *The Coffin Tree* without straying from her central focus on the narrator's search for meaning.

The process of a young person's developing individuality and the formation of gender roles are pervasive concerns in contemporary American society. Law-Yone shows that the narrator has the same basic psychological needs as young American women, even though Burmese culture dictates different practices and standards regarding communication, social interaction, and family ties. Law-Yone also reveals through her depiction of patients in a mental hospital that psychological disorders are not restricted to any one social or ethnic group but tend to be rooted in personal history and family relationships.

Irrawaddy Tango

Type of work: Novel
First published: 1993

Irrawaddy Tango is a worthwhile successor to *The Coffin Tree*. Although *Irrawaddy Tango* is set mainly in fictitious "Daya," the country is recognizably Myanmar, replete with repressive military dictatorship and rebel guerrillas.

The novel details the picaresque career of its protagonist-narrator, Irrawaddy Tango, who seems to develop through four phases of popular archetypes of female identity: first, an Evita-like phase during which the small-town girl Tango becomes a dance champion and a dictator's wife; second, a Patty Hearst phase during which First Lady Tango, now a wealthy socialite, is kidnapped by guerrillas and brainwashed into bonding with, bedding with, and speaking for her abductors; third, a joyless-luckless Asian American woman phase (à la Amy Tan) where she marries her American rescuer and immigrates to America only to discover anomie and alienation; and fourth, a spider woman phase in which Tango returns to Daya, empowers herself sexually, mates with the dictator (her former husband), and destroys him.

Through these phases, Tango's character develops, like the dance itself, with exhilarating dips and lifts of fortune, dizzying reversals of plot, and in movements charged with sinister power and unassuaged sensuality. *Irrawaddy Tango* is a tale told with brilliant flashes of detail, psychological penetration, and erotic candor. It is not flawless, however, having its longueurs of plot and a self-centered protagonist with whom it is difficult to empathize. Nevertheless, it does perform the signal service of shedding light and focusing attention upon the political plight of an often ignored area of darkness in the heart of Southeast Asia.

Suggested Readings

Bow, Nancy. "Interview with Wendy Law-Yone." *MELUS* 27, no. 4 (2002).

Forbes, Nancy. "Burmese Days." *The Nation*, April 30, 1983.

Law-Yone, Wendy. "Life in the Hills." *The Atlantic Monthly*, December, 1989, 24-36.

Ling, Amy. "Wendy Law-Yone." In *The Oxford Companion to Women's Writing in the United States*, edited by Cathy N. Davidson and Linda Wagner-Martin. New York: Oxford University Press, 1995.

Milton, Edith. "Newcomers to New York." *The New York Times Book Review*, May 15, 1983.

Tharoor, Shashi. "The Most Dangerous Dance." Review of *Irrawaddy Tango*, by Wendy Law-Yone. *The Washington Post Book World*, January, 1994.

Tsukiyama, Gail. "Long Journey of a Tango Queen." Review of *Irrawaddy Tango*, by Wendy Law-Yone. *The San Francisco Chronicle*, March 20, 1994.

Contributors: Gary Westfahl and Patricia L. Watson

Gus Lee

Born: San Francisco, California; August 8, 1946

Chinese American

Lee's novels capture the dilemma of an Asian American youth who tries to please the demands of two opposing cultures.

Principal works

LONG FICTION: *China Boy*, 1991; *Honor and Duty*, 1994; *Tiger's Tail*, 1996; *No Physical Evidence*, 1998

NONFICTION: *Chasing Hepburn: A Memoir of Shanghai, Hollywood and a Chinese Family's Fight for Freedom*, 2002

Gus Lee came to writing late in life, at age forty-five, after careers in the military and as a lawyer. In 1989, his daughter asked him a question about his mother, and that simple question led to his first book, *China Boy*, in 1991. Born in San Francisco in a tough black neighborhood, the Panhandle, Lee found his childhood full of danger on the streets. At home he felt divided. His father and mother had come from mainland China in the early 1940's and were wealthy and educated. His father had a military background and had fought for the Nationalist army. His mother had been educated by Christian missionaries. Lee's mother died when he was five years old, and his new stepmother had new ideas about the traditional Chinese ways. Lee had to fight in the streets, with the help of boxing courses he took at the Young Men's Christian Association (YMCA). He also had to battle at home with his stepmother, who wanted him to become more American.

His first novel, *China Boy*, uses many autobiographical events to tell the story of a young boy, Kai Ting, who is growing up in San Francisco. Skinny, weak, and timid, Kai Ting finds a friend at the neighborhood YMCA, learns self-defense, and returns to the streets with more confidence.

Lee describes the early days as being very stifled by rules at home. Lee rebelled against his controlling stepmother, reading his homework but refusing to concentrate. He got good grades but was not involved. Lee's father also attempted to direct him, objecting to the Christianity that the stepmother taught her stepson and projecting an atheistic approach that Lee felt was not right. Lee kept his mind focused on one goal: He wanted to become a West Point cadet. When he was appointed, he felt great relief, even though his life away from home as a plebe would be hellish. Lee actually found the harassment as a plebe at West Point to be easier than living at home.

His second novel, *Honor and Duty*, also uses Kai Ting as his fictional hero and

Gus Lee (Asian Week)

takes this character through many tough days at West Point. Kai Ting must obey the older cadets, he must study mathematics, and he must obey the West Point honor code. Coming upon a group of cadets who are cheating, Kai Ting agonizes about reporting them to the authorities, knowing that they will be removed from West Point if he informs on them.

In Lee's life, after a long tenure as an Army Command Judge Advocate and later as senior Deputy District Attorney in Sacramento, Lee found himself unfulfilled. Then his daughter's question provoked Lee to write about an Asian American adjusting to life in the United States.

China Boy

Type of work: Novel
First published: 1991

China Boy is the story of Kai Ting, the American-born son of a Shanghai refugee family. Ending an odyssey across both friendly and unfriendly terrain, the Ting family finally settles in San Francisco.

China Boy is a bildungsroman, or rite-of-passage story. Although the novel covers only approximately one and a half years of Kai's life, it depicts a pivotal point in his growth, a time of great change and uncertainty out of which he will gather strength and survive or to which he will succumb. With the death of his mother, the physical and emotional distance of his father, the cruelty of his stepmother, and the everyday violence that he faces on his neighborhood streets, Kai is plunged into a seemingly inescapable dungeon. To escape, Kai has to draw on the very last dregs of a personal integrity—the somehow unquenchable resilience of a seven-year-old—in order to salvage a childhood gone awry. Facing violence both within and without his home, Kai nevertheless soldiers along and, despite incredible odds, neutralizes a neighborhood bully in the defining battle of his short life. This culminating act signals a breakthrough for Kai, and the novel leaves the reader with the hope that with one battle won, Kai is set to win others and, ultimately, to win the long war of his childhood.

The novel is also about displacement, about the suspension between two clearly defined, seemingly irreconcilable cultures. The culture represented by Kai's mother (Mah-mee) and Uncle Shim seems, with Mah-mee's death, to slip away with each day. Kai, speaking a five-year-old's broken "Songhai," is the flotsam from that culture. The reality of a relentlessly alien culture is all around him, but without its language, without recognizable points of reference to help him in his transition, Kai is in danger of becoming both a refugee from one culture and an unwanted stranger in another.

Ultimately, though, the novel is about the possibility of reconciliations: between past and present, between ethnicity and nationality, between passivity and action. There is time for Kai to recollect the lost pieces of his past in order to give direction and purpose to his present. Confronted by racism both at home and on the streets, Kai is befriended and aided by individuals who recognize the inherent stranger in themselves and who see in Kai only the human quality of need. Physically and emotionally brutalized by both his stepmother and the neighborhood boys, Kai is unable to retaliate. His understanding of *yuing chi*, or karma, seems to feed his childish fatalism. With the bodybuilding and mind-building at the YMCA, however, Kai seems finally to be able both to assert himself and to preserve his integrity. In the novel's epilogue, Kai confronts his stepmother at their doorway. He has just survived his fight with the bully, and his clothes are drenched with blood. Edna is concerned only that he has rung the doorbell too early and that she will once again have to bleach the blood—the Asiatic blood—out of his clothes. As a recognition of his past and present, of his ethnicity, of his action, of his new self, Kai tells her, "You are not my Mah-mee! . . . I ain't fo' yo' pickin-on, no mo'!"

Suggested Readings

Shen, Yichin. "The Site of Domestic Violence and the Altar of Phallic Sacrifice in Gus Lee's *China Boy*." *College Literature* 29, no. 2 (2002): 99-114.

Simpson, Janice C., and Iyer Pico. "Fresh Voices Above the Noisy Din." *Time* 137 (June 3, 1991): 66-67.

So, Christine. "Delivering the Punch Line: Racial Combat as Comedy in Gus Lee's *China Boy*." *MELUS* 21, no. 4 (1996): 141-155.

Stone, Judy. "Gus Lee: A China Boy's Rites of Passage." *Publishers Weekly* 243, no. 12 (March 18, 1996): 47-49.

Contributors: Larry Rochelle and Pat M. Wong

Li-Young Lee

Born: Jakarta, Indonesia; 1957

Chinese American

Lee's writing is inspired by his relation to his father and his family.

Principal works

POETRY: *Rose*, 1986; *The City in Which I Love You*, 1990; *Book of My Nights: Poems*, 2001

NONFICTION: *The Winged Seed: A Remembrance*, 1995

When Li-Young Lee's first collection of poetry, *Rose*, was published, its Chinese American author had lived in America for twenty-two of his twenty-nine years. The poet's immigrant experience, his strong sense of family life, and his recollections of a boyhood spent in Asia have provided a background to his writing.

Lee was born in Jakarta; his Chinese parents were exiles from Communist China. They traveled until their arrival in Pittsburgh in 1964. The sense of being an alien, not a native to the place where one lives, strongly permeates Lee's poetry and gives an edge to his carefully crafted lines. There is also a touch of sadness to his poetry: The abyss lurks everywhere, and his personae have to be circumspect in their words and actions, since they, unlike a native, can take nothing for granted in their host culture. Looking at his sister, the speaker in "My Sleeping Loved Ones" warns "And don't mistake my stillness/ for awe./ It's just that I don't want to waken her."

Faced with a new language after his arrival in America, Lee became fascinated with the sound of words, an experience related in "Persimmons." Here, a teacher slaps the boy "for not knowing the difference/ between persimmon and precision." After college work at three American universities, Lee focused on his writing. Before the publication of his second collection, *The City in Which I Love You*, he received numerous awards.

Lee has always insisted that his writing searches for universal themes, and the close connection of his work to his life cannot be discounted. His father, for example, appears in many poems. Lee offers, in *The Winged Seed*, a factual yet poetic account of his young life. Lee's poetry and his prose reveal a writer who appreciates his close family and strives to put into words the grief and the joy of a life always lived in an alien place.

The Winged Seed

Type of work: Memoir
First published: 1995

To a large extent, *The Winged Seed: A Remembrance* is a lyrical and sometimes surrealistic memorializing of Lee's father and the author's relationship with him. This memoir is also, as its title indicates, the saga of the Lee family's participation in the twentieth century diaspora of Asians fleeing from the political upheavals of Asia and seeking to take root in the promise of America. Thus the book is a complex fabric made up, on one hand, of a highly subjective psychological history about the formation of dominant themes and images in a poetic imagination that is woven, on the other hand, with factual history of world events.

By the time Lee was born, his father, Kuo Yuan, had already left China, which had been taken over by the Communist regime. He had migrated to Jakarta, Indonesia, and become a vice president at Gamaliel University in the late 1950's, a time when President Sukarno was blaming his country's economic woes on its Chinese inhabitants. Swept into the undertow of ethnic cleansing, Kuo Yuan was imprisoned in 1959. Physically abused, he bribed his way into less harsh incarceration in an insane asylum. There Kuo Yuan preached the gospel powerfully, first to inmates and then to their jailers.

By bribery and luck, the Lee family escaped to Hong Kong, where Kuo Yuan preached to throngs numbering in the thousands. Thence they immigrated in 1964 to the United States, where, at the age of forty, he attended theological school. A changed and subdued man, he was appointed a minister in a Pennsylvania town whose congregation called him their "heathen minister." Kuo Yuan emerges as an intelligent, gifted, tenacious survivor with traits of integrity and spiritual power that did not flourish on American soil.

Li-Young Lee

Although Lee's father is the dominant presence in the book, Lee also provides fascinating glimpses of his mother, Jiaying. There are brilliantly recollected vignettes of her life growing up in the privileged class of China. Jiaying was living in the French quarter of Tientsin when Lee's father joined her destiny with his. In Lee's memoir, Jiaying emerges as a capable mother and fiercely loyal wife.

One gathers that Lee's early childhood experiences in Indonesia played a formative role in shaping his imagination, even though there are few overt references to those experiences in his poetry. In Indonesia, Lee was largely cared for by his Javanese nanny, Lammi. Through her, he became aware of family conflicts and love affairs; more important, Lammi took Lee to her village home, where he watched performances of *wayang* (Indonesian folk theater) and imbibed the mythological tales they dramatized. Through Lammi and her friends, Lee was exposed to stories of spellbinding *bomohs*, medicine men and women whose power was confirmed by the Lee family's experience of hailstorms bombarding their house until their mother agreed to sell it. Lee's early childhood exposure to the folk art and shamanistic tradition of Southeast Asia may have contributed to the qualities of mythic resonance and paraordinary sensation that mark some of his writing.

The Winged Seed is a finely wrought memoir affording fascinating insights into the formation of a literary imagination and the origins of the most powerful images and themes that stir it. The book also provides revealing glimpses of some decisive political moments in twentieth century China and Indonesia.

Suggested Readings

Hesford, Walter A. "*The City in Which I Love You:* Li-Young Lee's Excellent Song." *Christianity and Literature* 46, no. 1 (Autumn, 1996): 37-60.

Lee, Li-Young. "Li-Young Lee." Interview by James Kyung-Jin Lee. In *Words Matter: Conversations with Asian American Writers*, edited by King-Kok Cheung. Honolulu: University of Hawaii Press, 2000.

_______. "Li-Young Lee." Interview by Bill Moyers. In *The Language of Life*. New York: Doubleday, 1995.

_______. "Poems from God: A Conversation with Li-Young Lee." Interview by Amy Pence. *Poets and Writers* 29 (November/December, 2001): 22-27.

_______. "To Witness the Invisible: A Talk with Li-Young Lee." Interview by Tod Marshall. *The Kenyon Review*, Winter, 2000, 129-147.

Lee, Li-Young, and Shawn Wong. *Li-Young Lee*. Los Angeles: Lannan Literary Videos, 1995.

Slowick, Mary. "Beyond Lot's Wife: The Immigration Poems of Marilyn Chin, Garrett Hongo, Li-Young Lee, and David Mura." *MELUS* 25, no. 3 (Fall/Winter, 2000): 221-242.

Zhou, Xiaojing. "Inheritance and Invention in Li-Young Lee's Poetry." *MELUS*, Spring, 1996, 113-132.

Contributors: R. C. Lutz and C. L. Chua

Gerda Lerner
(Gerda Hedwig Kronstein)

Born: Vienna, Austria; April 30, 1920

Jewish

Lerner's goal is to bring women's history back into the light so that women may be educated, encouraged, and emboldened by the struggles and achievements of their predecessors.

Principal works

LONG FICTION: *No Farewell*, 1955

NONFICTION: *The Grimké Sisters from South Carolina: Rebels Against Slavery*, 1967 (biography); *The Woman in American History*, 1971; *Women Are History: A Bibliography in the History of American Women*, 1975; *A Death of One's Own*, 1978; *The Majority Finds Its Past: Placing Women in History*, 1979; *Women and History, Volume 1: The Creation of Patriarchy*, 1986; *Women and History, Volume 2: The Creation of a Feminist Consciousness, from the Middle Ages to 1870*, 1993; *Why History Matters: Life and Thought*, 1997; *Fireweed: A Political Autobiography*, 2002

EDITED TEXT: *Black Women in White America: A Documentary History*, 1972; *The Female Experience: An American Documentary*, 1976

Born Gerda Hedwig Kronstein, Gerda Lerner is a seminal figure in women's history. She grew up in a bourgeois household in Vienna in the 1920's and 1930's. Lerner's father, Robert Kronstein, owned a pharmacy, and her mother, Ilona Kronstein, was an amateur painter who occupied herself with cultural pursuits.

Lerner became interested in politics at an early age. In her autobiography, *Fireweed*, she states that her childhood taught her about resistance to authority and the necessity of questioning the values of those in power. Born a Jew, she became an agnostic at the age of fourteen and refused to go through with her bat mitzvah. In 1934, she witnessed the first of what were to be many political upheavals that affected her, a workers' strike that was violently repressed by the Viennese government. As a student, she embraced various progressive political causes, sometimes secretly, and excelled in her studies.

In 1938, after the Nazi occupation of Austria, her father immigrated to Lichtenstein, where he had established a satellite business. Like many Jews, Robert Kronstein was concerned that Austria was becoming increasingly anti-Semitic under the Nazis during this period prior to World War II, and, like others, he made plans for his family to emigrate. Partly in preparation for such a departure, Lerner became engaged to a young medical student named Bobby Jerusalem, who was in the process of immigrating to the United States. Lerner and her mother were arrested and imprisoned shortly thereafter in an attempt by the government to pressure her father to return. They spent just over a month in prison, during which time Lerner turned eighteen, and they were released, with orders to leave the country. Ironically, although they were under deportation orders, they were at first unable to obtain emigration permits.

On September 9, 1938, Lerner, her younger sister Nora, and their mother left Austria to join their father in Lichtenstein. In April of 1939, having secured a visa from the U.S. consul in Switzerland after being sponsored by her fiancé and his family, Gerda Lerner arrived in New York City, while her mother remained in France, her father in Lichtenstein, and her sister in Switzerland. She married Jerusalem, who had changed his name to Jensen, within a week of her arrival in the United States. She and Jensen continued to be involved in progressive political activities, as they had while living in Vienna. The marriage was short-lived, lasting just a year and a half.

Shortly after the breakup of her first marriage, she met her second husband, Carl Lerner, in the world of the New York theater business. Carl was a Communist and a director and producer of small theatrical events at the time. He had recently been left by his wife. Gerda and Carl moved to Reno, Nevada, temporarily in order to obtain divorces from their respective spouses, and from there they went to Hollywood, where they both obtained menial employment. They were married on October 6, 1941. Lerner began writing and publishing short stories at this time, and her husband obtained a job as an apprentice film editor at Columbia Pictures. They had two children, Stephanie and Dan.

In 1946, Lerner formally joined the Communist Party and continued to engage in progressive political action, supporting such causes as the Civil Rights movement and the antinuclear movement. Her husband, already a Communist, was blacklisted in the Hollywood film industry, and the family moved back to New York in 1949. Lerner's novel, *No Farewell*, which she finished in 1951 after working on it for twelve years, was rejected by numerous American publishers but accepted by an Austrian firm. The novel was translated into German and was well received in Austria. Lerner also wrote and published shorter pieces during this period, including performance works and pamphlets for the Civil Rights Congress. In 1954 she, along with five other people, started a short-lived cooperative publishing house. The English version of *No Farewell* was one of the books that the cooperative published.

In 1958 she resumed her formal education as a student at New York's New School for Social Research. Planning to write a historical novel on the Grimké sisters, Lerner became involved in historical research. This experience made her realize that the work she really wanted to do was to promote the history of women. She refocused her initial idea of a historical novel and instead wrote a biography of the Grimké sisters, which served as her doctoral dissertation and was published in 1967. She was awarded a Ph.D. from Columbia University in 1966.

Lerner has taught at many universities, notably at Sarah Lawrence College, where she founded the first graduate program in women's history, and at the University of Wisconsin, Madison, where she established a Ph.D. program in women's history in 1984. Her most influential works are *The Creation of Patriarchy* and its sequel, *The Creation of a Feminist Consciousness*. In these books, Lerner argues for the existence of a prehistoric matriarchal culture. She asserts that the subjugation of women was the first form of institutionalized dominance and that other forms of oppression, such as classism and racism, grew out of men's control over women. In *The Creation of a Feminist Consciousness*, Lerner discusses the rise of feminist responses to patriarchal oppression among women from the Middle Ages to 1870. She argues that women have been deprived of their history and that this deprivation has had a significant negative impact on the status of women in general. Her goal in producing these books is to bring that history back into the light so that women may be educated, encouraged, and emboldened by the struggles and achievements of their predecessors.

Among the many distinctions that Lerner has received are election as president of the Organization of American Historians. *The Creation of Patriarchy* won the Joan Kelly Memorial Prize. Lerner has received fellowships from the National Endowment for the Humanities, the Ford Foundation, the Eli Lilly and Company Foundation, and the Guggenheim Foundation. She was also the 2002 recipient of the Bruce Catton Prize for lifetime achievement in historical writing and is a founding member of the National Organization for Women.

The Creation of a Feminist Consciousness

Type of work: History
First published: 1993

In her two-volume *Women and History*, Lerner ranges over the whole of Western history from prehistory to the late nineteenth century, examining the origins of patriarchy (in *Volume 1: The Creation of Patriarchy*) and the long process by which women began to "think their way out" of their systematic subordination (in *Volume 2: The Creation of a Feminist Consciousness*).

In this second volume, Lerner rigorously plumbs her disparate sources to help answer her question of how feminist consciousness developed. Such a consciousness could only emerge once autonomous women'sorganizations and a knowledge of women's history were established. These were preconditions for a progressive development. Earlier, a perceptive woman might discover important arguments to combat women's supposed inferiority—and yet she could not have known or used the work of predecessors a generation or even several hundred years before. Lerner's great insight is that women's subordination could not be changed as long as their history remained largely inaccessible to each succeeding generation. Lerner analyzes women's struggle for education; the importance of mysticism, biblical criticism, and religious thought for women's autonomous development; how the concept of motherhood gave women authority; the uses of female creativity; the beginnings of female spaces and networks; and the development of women's history.

Far-reaching and well written, *The Creation of a Feminist Consciousness* will function as an excellent general text for the nonspecialist in women's history, but there is plenty of new detail and insight for the professional historian as well. The bibliography is very helpful, arranged topically, chronologically, and by individual.

Suggested Readings

"Gerda Lerner." In *Feminist Writers*, edited by Pamela Kester-Shelton. Detroit: St. James Press, 1996.

Lerner, Gerda. "Resistance and Triumph." Interview by Joan Fischer. *Wisconsin Academy Review* 48, no. 2 (Spring, 2000).

Rutland, Robert Allen, ed. *Clio's Favorites: Leading Historians of the United States, 1945-2000*. Columbia: University of Missouri Press, 2000.

Contributor: Michele Leavitt

Audre Lorde

Born: Harlem, New York; February 18, 1934
Died: Christiansted, St. Croix, U.S. Virgin Islands; November 17, 1992

African American

Lorde's poetry, essays, and autobiographical fiction are among the best American black lesbian feminist writings.

Principal works

POETRY: *The First Cities*, 1968; *Cables to Rage*, 1970; *From a Land Where Other People Live*, 1973; *New York Head Shop and Museum*, 1974; *Between Our Selves*, 1976; *Coal*, 1976; *The Black Unicorn*, 1978; *Chosen Poems, Old and New*, 1982 (revised as *Undersong: Chosen Poems, Old and New*, 1992); *A Comrade Is as Precious as a Rice Seedling*, 1984; *Our Dead Behind Us*, 1986; *Need: A Chorale for Black Woman Voices*, 1990; *The Marvelous Arithmetics of Distance: Poems, 1987-1992*, 1993; *The Collected Poems of Audre Lorde*, 1997

NONFICTION: *Uses of the Erotic: The Erotic as Power*, 1978; *The Cancer Journals*, 1980; *Zami: A New Spelling of My Name, a Biomythography*, 1982; *Sister Outsider: Essays and Speeches*, 1984; *I Am Your Sister: Black Women Organizing Across Sexualities*, 1985; *Apartheid U.S.A.*, 1986; *A Burst of Light: Essays*, 1988; *The Audre Lorde Compendium: Essays, Speeches, and Journals*, 1996; *Conversations with Audre Lorde*, 2004 (Joan Wylie Hall, editor)

The parents of Audre Lorde (AW-dree lohrd) emigrated from Grenada to New York City in 1924. Lorde, the youngest of three girls, was born in 1934. She recounted many of her childhood memories in *Zami*, identifying particular incidents that had an influence or effect on her developing sexuality and her later work as a poet. She attended the University of Mexico (1954-1955) and received a B.A. from Hunter College (1959) and an M.L.S. from Columbia University (1961). In 1962, she was married to Edwin Rollins, with whom she had two children before they were divorced in 1970.

Prior to 1968, when she gained public recognition for her poetry, Lorde supported herself through a variety of jobs, including low-paying factory work. She also served as a librarian in several institutions. After her first publication, *The First Cities*, Lorde worked primarily within American colleges and free presses. She was an instructor at City College of New York (1968-1970), an instructor and then lecturer at Lehman College (1969-1971), and a professor of English at John Jay College of Criminal Justice (1972-1981). From 1981 to 1987, she was a professor of English at Hunter College at CUNY, and she became a Thomas Hunter

Audre Lorde (Ingmar Schullz/Courtesy, W. W. Norton)

Professor for one year there (1987-1988). She also served as poetry editor of the magazine *Chrysalis* and was a contributing editor of the journal *Black Scholar*.

In the early 1980's, she helped start Kitchen Table: Women of Color Press, a multicultural effort publishing Asian American and Latina as well as African American women writers. In the late 1980's, Lorde became increasingly concerned over the plight of black women in South Africa under apartheid, creating Sisterhood in Support of Sisters in South Africa and remaining an active voice on behalf of these women throughout the remainder of her life. She also served on the board of the National Coalition of Black Lesbians and Gays. With the companion of her last years, the writer and black feminist scholar Gloria I. Joseph, she made a home on St. Croix in the U.S. Virgin Islands. Shortly before her death in 1992 she completed her tenth book of poems, *The Marvelous Arithmetics of Distance*.

The First Cities *and* Cables to Rage

Type of work: Poetry
First published: 1968, 1970

In her early collections of poetry, *The First Cities* and *Cables to Rage*, Lorde expressed a keen political disillusionment, noting the failure of American ideals of equality and justice for all. When Lorde used the pronoun "we" in her poetry, she spoke for all who have been dispossessed. In "Anniversary," for example, she wrote, "Our tears/ water an alien grass," expressing the separation between those who belong and those who do not. In poems such as "Sowing," the poet revealed the land's betrayal of its inhabitants by showing images of destruction juxtaposed to personal rage: "I have been to this place before/ where blood seething commanded/ my fingers fresh from the earth."

She also demonstrated a concern for the children of this earth in "Blood-birth": Casting about to understand what it is in her that is raging to be born, she wondered how an opening will come "to show the true face of me/ lying exposed and together/ my children your children their children/ bent on our conjugating business." The image of the warrior, the one who must be prepared to go about the business of existing in an unjust world, signifies the need to take care of those not yet aware of unfulfilled promises.

If the rage in her early poems appears "unladylike," Lorde was setting out to explode sexual typecasting. Certainly, there was nothing dainty about her sharp images and powerful assessments of social conditions. As she confronted harsh realities, the portrayals were necessarily clamorous. Yet the poet's rage did not lead to a blind rampage. In "Conversation in Crisis," the poet hoped to speak to her friend "for a clear meeting/ of self upon self/ in sight of our hearth/ but without fire." The poet must speak honestly and not out of false assumptions and pretenses so that real communication can occur. The reader and listener must heed the words as well as the tone in order to receive the meaning of the words. Communication, then, is a kind of contractual relationship between people.

From a Land Where Other People Live *and* Between Our Selves

TYPE OF WORK: Poetry
FIRST PUBLISHED: 1973, 1976

In the collections *From a Land Where Other People Live* and *Between Our Selves*, Lorde used a compassionate tone to tell people about the devastation of white racism upon African Americans. She mixes historical fact with political reality, emphasizing the disjunction that sometimes occurs between the two. In "Equinox," Lorde observed her daughter's birth by remembering a series of events that also occurred that year: She had "marched into Washington/ to a death knell of dreaming/ which 250,000 others mistook for a hope," for few at that time understood the victimization of children that was occurring not only in the American South but also in the Vietnam War. After she heard that Malcolm X had been shot, she reread all of his writings: "the dark mangled children/ came streaming out of the atlas/ Hanoi Angola Guinea-Bissau . . ./ merged into Bedford-Stuyvesant and Hazelhurst Mississippi."

From the multiplicity of world horrors, the poet returned to her hometown in New York, exhausted but profoundly moved by the confrontation of history and the facts of her own existence. In "The Day They Eulogized Mahalia," another event is present in the background as the great singer Mahalia Jackson is memorialized: Six black children died in a fire at a day care center on the South Side; "firemen found their bodies/ like huddled lumps of charcoal/ with silent mouths and eyes wide open." Even as she mourned the dead in her poems, the poet seems aware of both the power and the powerlessness of words to effect real changes. In the poem, "Power," Lorde writes,

The difference between poetry and rhetoric
is being ready to kill
yourself
instead of your children.

Once the event has occurred, one can write about it or one can try to prevent a similar event from occurring; in either case, it is not possible to undo the first event. Therefore, as a society, people must learn from their errors and their failures to care for other people. Lorde even warned herself that she must discern and employ this crucial difference between poetry and rhetoric; if she did not, "my power too will run corrupt as poisonous mold/ or lie limp and useless as an unconnected wire."

Coal

Type of work: Poetry
First published: 1976

Coal explores Audre Lorde's identities as a black woman, mother, wife, and lover of women. Several of her life issues are examined and refracted in the poems. Lorde's lifelong journey toward claiming her West Indian, African American heritage is given voice in "Coal"; her motherhood is the subject of "Now That I Am Forever with Child"; and her women-centered existence is described in "On a Night of the Full Moon."

As a black woman of West Indian heritage, Audre Lorde knew the struggles of black Americans to claim their place and voice in American society. Raised in Harlem during the 1930's and 1940's, Lorde became aware of racism at an early age. The poem "Coal" claims a positive, strong voice for Lorde—a voice deeply embedded in her black heritage.

In "Coal," Lorde effectively transforms black speech into poetry: "I/ is the total black, being spoken/ from the earth's inside." Lorde defines poetic speech as a force that embraces blackness; then, she goes on to question how much a black woman can speak, and in what tone. Yet "Coal" defines Lorde as a black female poet who breaks the boundaries of silence and proclaims the sturdiness of power of her own words: "I am Black because I come from the earth's inside/ now take my word for jewel in the open light."

Fire imagery suffuses the book. The fire that marks the edges of many poems defines the anger and hostility engendered by a patriarchal and racist society. Lorde learns to empower herself by using the fire of anger and despair to create her own vision of spiritual and sexual identity. Embarked on her own journey toward truth, Lorde proclaims in the poem "Summer Oracle" that fire—which she equates with a warming agent in a country "barren of symbols of love"—can also be a cleansing agent. Fire burns away falsehoods and lets truth arise.

Lorde was widely praised by her contemporaries for her determination to see truth in everyday life. *Coal* could be called an uneven book, but her portraits of city life, love, anger, and sorrow make *Coal* a book of poetic transition from which Lorde would emerge into a life of more radical feminism and richer fulfillment.

The Cancer Journals

Type of work: Memoir
First published: 1980

The Cancer Journals, Lorde's documentation and critique of her experience with breast cancer, is a painstaking examination of the journey Lorde takes to integrate this crisis into her identity. The book chronicles Lorde's anger, pain, and fear about cancer and is as frank in its themes of "the travesty of prosthesis, the pain of amputation, and the function of cancer in a profit society," as it is unflinching in its treatment of Lorde's confrontation with mortality.

Lorde speaks on her identity as a black, lesbian, feminist mother and poet with breast cancer. She illuminates the implications the disease has for her, recording the process of waking up in the recovery room after the biopsy that confirms her cancer, colder than she has ever been in her life. The following days, she prepares for the radical mastectomy through consultation with women friends, family, her lover, and her children. In the days that follow, Lorde attributes part of her healing process to "a ring of women like warm bubbles keeping me afloat" as she recovers from her mastectomy. She realizes that after facing death and having lived, she must accept the reality of dying as "a life process"; this hard-won realization baptizes Lorde into a new life.

The journal entries for 1979 and 1980, written while Lorde recovered from the radical mastectomy she chose to forestall spread of the disease, show Lorde's integration of this emergency into her life. She realizes that she must give the process a voice; she wants to be more than one of the "socially sanctioned prosthesis" women with breast cancer, who remain quiet and isolated. Instead, Lorde vows to teach, speak, and fight.

At the journal's end, Lorde chooses to turn down the prosthesis offered her, which she equates with an empty way to forestall a woman's acceptance of her new body and, thus, her new identity. If, Lorde realizes, a woman claims her full identity as a cancer survivor and then opts to use a prosthesis, she has made the journey toward claiming her altered body, and life. Postmastectomy women, however, have to find their own internal sense of power. *The Cancer Journals* demonstrates a black, feminist, lesbian poet's integration of cancer into her identity.

Zami

Type of work: Novel
First published: 1982

Zami: A New Spelling of My Name, Lorde's prose masterpiece, examines a young black woman's coming to terms with her lesbian sexual orientation. An autobiographical novel, *Zami* has earned a reputation as much for its compelling writing as for its presentation of a coming-of-age story of a black lesbian feminist intent on claiming her identity.

At the age of nineteen, Zami flees New York City, where she was raised by her West Indian parents, for Mexico. There, she falls in love with an older expatriate woman named Eudora, who opens up her sensual life to the younger woman. Through her relationship with Eudora, Zami realizes the paralyzing consequences of the "racist, patriarchal and anti-erotic society" that Eudora fled when she left the United States. Zami returns to live in the "gay girl" milieu of Greenwich Village in the 1950's. She commits herself to a long-term relationship with Muriel, a white woman with whom she builds a home. Muriel completes the sexual awakening that Eudora began. Muriel is threatened, however, when Zami enters therapy and enrolls in college. As Zami forges an identity that integrates her sensual, intellectual, and artistic sides, Muriel moves out of the Greenwich Village apartment. Zami moves forward, even in grief, toward her newfound life.

Erotic language and scenes pepper the story. Zami learns to accept her own erotic impulses toward women, and her acceptance leads her into a larger life where love for women is central. Her eroticism is about the acceptance of the stages of a woman's physical life. Eros is also language that she uses to infuse her poems with life. As Zami goes to college, begins to send out her own poetry, and opens to life while Muriel declines, she meets a female erotic figure of mythic proportions: Afrekete.

Years earlier, Zami met a black gay woman whom she named Kitty: a woman of pretty clothes and dainty style. The two women meet again at the novel's end. Kitty has become a fully erotic woman, who has assumed the mythic name Afrekete. After her liaison with Afrekete, Zami finds that her own life has become a bendable, pliable entity that challenges myths and, in the end, makes a new myth of its own.

Undersong

Type of work: Poetry
First published: 1992

Three decades of production and the work from Lorde's first five published collections form her 1992 collection titled *Undersong: Chosen Poems, Old and New*, a reworking of her 1982 work, *Chosen Poems, Old and New*. This volume is not a "selected poems" collection in the usual meaning of the term, because it contains no work from her centrally important *The Black Unicorn*, which she considered too complex and too much of a unit to be dismembered by excerpting; *Undersong* also holds little of *Our Dead Behind Us*. Thus, a large chunk of Lorde's strongest work is missing—including most of the poems in which she conjured and confronted "the worlds of Africa."

As Lorde states in an introduction, her revisions of *Chosen Poems, Old and New* were undertaken to clarify but not to recast the work—necessitating that she "propel [herself] back into the original poem-creating process and the poet who wrote it." Lorde returned to her work of *Chosen Poems, Old and New* after Hurricane Hugo wrecked her home in the Virgin Islands and she found "a waterlogged but readable copy of [the book], one of the few salvageable books from [her] library." The drama of the incident seemed to take an allegorical cast and inspired her to treat the anchoring of her poems in truth with the same fierce honesty she had devoted to confronting her childhood, her blackness, and her sexual identity. She thus seemed determined to keep her poetry under spiritual review with the same intensity that she devoted to the infinite difficulties of being an African American woman and lesbian in late twentieth century America. The changes she made in this collection seem limited to the excising of a handful of early poems, substituting others previously unpublished, and reworking line breaks and punctuation to give more space and deliberate stress to each stanza and image.

The themes of the book largely circulate on two central axes: The notion of changeable selves—the broken journey toward self—is a recurrent motif, as is her consuming involvement with issues of survival. In examining changeable selves, she juxtaposes the longing for completion with the awareness of change as a paradoxical condition of identity. In "October," Lorde appeals to the goddess Seboulisa, elsewhere described as the "Mother of us all":

> Carry my heart to some shore
> my feet will not shatter
> do not let me pass away
> before I have a name
> for this tree
> under which I am lying
> Do not let me die still
> needing to be stranger.

As the final couplet hints, the counterpoint to the search for self is the search for connection, and to that end, dialogue is used as a structuring device, creating a sense of companionship won in the face of a proudly borne singularity.

Poems with images of destruction also abound: the dead friend Genevieve; the father who "died in silence"; the "lovers processed/ through the corridors of Bellevue Mattewan/ Brooklyn State the Women's House of D./ St. Vincent's and the Tombs"; "a black boy (Emmett Till) hacked into a murderous lesson"; the lost sisters and daughters of Africa and its diaspora, whose "bones whiten/ in secret." Lorde's dual themes of the unending search for identity and a struggle for survival heighten the impact of the word "nightmare," which cycles endlessly throughout Lorde's work. The word represents her expression for history as glimpsed in surreal previsions and "Afterimages" (the title of a poem linking her memories of Emmett Till's lynching to television pictures of a Mississippi flood). One looks in vain for a "positive" counterweight, before realizing that the nightmare, for Lorde, is not a token of negativity but rather symbolizes the denied and feared aspects of experience that must be recalled and accepted for change to occur.

The Marvelous Arithmetics of Distance

Type of work: Poetry
First published: 1993

In her final collection of poems, *The Marvelous Arithmetics of Distance* (published posthumously), Lorde displays a personal, moving, bare, and striking set of work that strives for poignant reckonings with her family. "Legacy—Hers" is about her mother, "bred for endurance/ for battle." "Inheritance—His" is about her father. She also has farewells to her sister, whom she forgives ("both you and I/ are free to go"), and to her son, whom she challenges ("In what do you believe?"). She has many bouquets for Gloria, her partner.

She also visits her characteristic theme of politics in this collection. For example, she writes cinematically about the destruction wrought by U.S. foreign policy in a ferocious "Peace on Earth: Christmas, 1989":

> the rockets red glare where
> all these brown children
> running scrambling around the globe
> flames through the rubble
> bombs bursting in air
> Panama Nablus Gaza
> tear gas clouding the Natal sun.
> THIS IS A GIFT FROM THE PEOPLE OF THE UNITED
> STATES OF AMERICA
> quick cut
> the crackling Yule log
> in an iron grate.

In "Jesse Helms," which begins "I am a Black woman/ writing my way to the future," she takes on the bigotry of the senator from North Carolina with intentional crudeness:

> Your turn now jessehelms
> come on its time
> to lick the handwriting
> off the walls.

In this sparse and commanding book, perhaps the most arresting lines are those in which she wrestles with the nearness of her own death. In "Today is not the day," she writes:

> I am dying
> but I do not want to do it
> looking the other way.
> Audre Lorde never looked the other way.

Suggested Readings

Avi-Ram, Amitai F. "*Apo Koinou* in Lorde and the Moderns: Defining the Differences." *Callaloo* 9 (Winter, 1986): 193-208.

Bloom, Harold, ed. *Black American Women Poets and Dramatists*. New York: Chelsea House, 1996.

De Veaux, Alexis. *Warrior Poet: A Biography of Audre Lorde*. New York: W. W. Norton, 2004.

Hull, Gloria T. "Living on the Line: Audre Lorde and *Our Dead Behind Us*." In *Changing Our Own Words: Essays on Criticism, Theory, and Writing by Black Women*, edited by Cheryl A. Wall. New Brunswick, N.J.: Rutgers University Press, 1989.

Lorde, Audre. "Sadomasochism: Not About Condemnation." Interview by Susan Leigh Star. In *A Burst of Light: Essays*, by Lorde. Ithaca, N.Y.: Firebrand Books, 1988.

Olson, Lester C. "Liabilities of Language: Audre Lorde Reclaiming Difference." *Quarterly Journal of Speech* 84, no. 4 (November, 1998): 448-470.

Opitz, May, Katharine Oguntoye, and Dagmar Schultz, eds. *Showing Our Colors: Afro-German Women Speak Out*. Translated by Anne V. Adams. Amherst: University of Massachusetts Press, 1992.

Perreault, Jeanne. *Writing Selves: Contemporary Feminist Autography*. Minneapolis: University of Minnesota Press, 1995.

Contributors: Cynthia Wong and Sarah Hilbert

Eduardo Machado

Born: Havana, Cuba; June 11, 1953

Cuban American

Machado's plays explore the conflicts between capitalism and communism, heterosexuality and homosexuality, and Cuban identity and Cuban American identity.

Principal works

DRAMA: *1979*, pr. 1991; *Worms*, pr. 1981; *Rosario and the Gypsies*, pr. 1982 (one-act musical; book and lyrics by Machado, music by Rick Vartoreila); *The Modern Ladies of Guanabacoa*, pr., pb. 1983; *There's Still Time to Dance in the Streets of Rio*, pr. 1983; *Broken Eggs*, pr., pb. 1984; *Fabiola*, pr. 1985, pb. 1991; *When It's Over*, pr. 1987 (with Geraldine Sherman); *Why to Refuse*, pr. 1987 (one act); *Across a Crowded Room*, pr. 1988; *A Burning Beach*, pr. 1988; *Don Juan in New York City*, pr. 1988 (two-act musical); *Once Removed*, pr., pb. 1988, revised pr. 1994; *Wishing You Well*, pr. 1988 (one-act musical); *Cabaret Bambu*, pr. 1989 (one-act musical); *Related Retreats*, pr. 1990; *Stevie Wants to Play the Blues*, pr. 1990, revised pr. 1998 (two-act musical); *The Floating Island Plays*, pb. 1991, pr. 1994 (as *Floating Islands*; cycle of four plays; includes *The Modern Ladies of Guanabacoa*, *Fabiola*, *In the Eye of the Hurricane*, and *Broken Eggs*); *In the Eye of the Hurricane*, pr., pb. 1991; *Breathing It In*, pr. 1993; *Three Ways to Go Blind*, pr. 1994; *Between the Sheets*, pr. 1996 (music by Mike Nolan and Scott Williams); *Cuba and the Night*, pr. 1997; *Crocodile Eyes*, pr. 1999; *Havana Is Waiting*, pr., pb. 2001 (originally pr. 2001 as *When the Sea Drowns in Sand*)

SCREENPLAY: *Exiles in New York*, 1999

TRANSLATION: *The Day You'll Love Me*, pr. 1989 (of José Ignacio Cabrujas's play *El día que me quieras*)

Eduardo Machado (eh-DWAHR-doh mah-CHAH-doh) arrived from Cuba in 1961, at age eight, with his brother Jesús, five years younger, as a "Peter Pan" child. The Peter Pan Project, a collaboration between a United States-based Roman Catholic bishop and the United States Central Intelligence Agency, brought fourteen thousand Cuban children to the United States without their parents, ostensibly to "save" them from communism and from the governmental policies under Fidel Castro. Arriving with no knowledge of English and undergoing major culture shock, the brothers were sent to an aunt and uncle in Hialeah, Florida, who had their own children as well as other immigrant relatives living with them. Machado's first memory of the United States is celebrating Halloween by trick-or-treating, believing that they had been sent out truly begging, as the children had moved from an economically privileged childhood in Cuba to poverty in the United States. His parents came a year later.

The house in which Machado had lived in Cuba was taken by the government and transformed into a school. His father, a self-professed "professional rich man's son," initially could not find work in United States. Machado finished growing up in Canoga Park, a suburb of Los Angeles. By the time Machado was sixteen, his father had succeeded economically as an accountant. Machado's parents later divorced, reportedly due to his father's infidelity, which has been an item in his dramatic work.

Machado began his acting career in 1978 at the Padua Hills Playwrights Festival, where he met Maria Irene Fornes, a Cuban immigrant playwright who would become a major influence on his work. He became her assistant on her *Fefu and Her Friends* (1977) at the Ensemble Studio Theater. Machado began writing plays at the suggestion of a therapist, who recommended writing an imaginary letter forgiving his mother for sending him away.

By 2002, Machado had written twenty-seven plays, all but seven dealing with his family or Cuba in some way. In New York City, as part of INTAR (International Arts Relations) Hispanic American Arts Center, he wrote *The Floating Island Plays* (*The Modern Ladies of Guanabacoa*, *Fabiola*, *Broken Eggs*, *In the Eye of the Hurricane*) between 1983 and 1991. He has been commissioned to write plays for The Public Theater, the Roundabout Theatre Company, and Wind Dancer Productions. He took his first trip back to Cuba in December, 1999, followed in rapid succession by two more visits to his homeland. Machado says he has always been at the mercy of politics. Critics say his works show his conflicts: capitalism versus communism, heterosexuality versus homosexuality, Cuban identity versus Cuban American identity.

Machado has taught at Sarah Lawrence College, New York University, the Mark Taper Forum, The Public Theater, and the Playwrights Center in Minneapolis. He has headed Columbia University's graduate playwriting program in the School of Arts since 1997 and has been an artistic associate of the Cherry Lane Alternative, the Off-Broadway Cherry Lane Theatre's nonprofit wing.

Machado received a 1995 National Theater Artist Residency to be playwright-in-residence at Los Angeles's Mark Taper Forum. He has been awarded grants from the National Endowment for the Humanities, the Rockefeller Foundation, and the City of Los Angeles for his works. He received a National Endowment for the Arts grant for a one-act play at Ensemble Studio Theatre. He first debuted *When the Sea Drowns in Sand* at the twenty-fifth annual Humana Festival of New American Plays. It has since been rewritten and performed as the autobiographical *Havana Is Waiting*.

Gender-Bending Plays

Although Machado's early works often examine issues of immigrant identity, he leaves his immigrant theme behind with such major works as *Stevie Wants to Play the Blues*, a musical about a female singer who transforms herself into a man, and *Don Juan in New York City*, which is chiefly about sexual ambivalence in the age of AIDS. The latter play, a work that is operatic in scope and amplitude, centers on D. J. (Don Juan), an experimental filmmaker, as a retrospective of his work is planned and executed. Apparently bisexual, D. J. is torn between a female singer-celebrity, Flora, and his trashy male lover, Steve. His conflict is enacted against the backdrop of the AIDS epidemic: D. J.'s good friend, Paul, a female impersonator, has taken refuge in the guise of Carole Channing and is preparing first for a concert of Channing's songs and subsequently for a successful suicide, as he eludes the depredations of AIDS. The baroque action is further complicated by actual film clips from D. J.'s creations and by passionate songs performed by two mysterious figures, Abuelo and Mujer, representatives of the world of traditional heterosexual love for which the classic Don Juan was known.

Machado has called *Stevie Wants to Play the Blues* a "gender-bender," a genre in which he examines premises about sexuality and takes the characters through surprising and unconventional revelations about their gender identifications. Other plays in which he toys with the notion of sexual identity are *Related Retreats*, about the lives of writers at an arts colony under the tutelage of a female guru, and *Breathing It In*, about a motley band of lost souls who congregate around a male/female guru couple who espouse the individual's embracing the woman-nature within. It at once satirizes groups such as Werner Erhard's individual, social transformation technique (EST) and the women's movement of the 1970's and 1980's and concocts a string of variations on sexual transformation among its characters.

Suggested Readings

Armengol Acierno, María. *The Children of Peter Pan*. Needham, Mass.: Silver Burdett Ginn, 1996.

Brand, Ulrika. "A Master Playwright Teaches His Discipline: An Interview with Eduardo Machado." *Columbia News*, June 28, 2001.

Brantley, Ben. "Eduardo Machado." *New York Times Magazine*, October 23, 1994, 38-41.

Conde, Yvonne. *Operation Peter Pan: The Untold Exodus of Fourteen Thousand Cuban Children*. New York: Routledge, 1999.

Muñoz, Elias Miguel. "Of Small Conquests and Big Victories: Gender Constructs in *The Modern Ladies of Guanabacoa*." In *The Americas Review* 20, no. 2 (Summer, 1992): 105-111.

Ortiz, Ricardo L. "Culpa and Capital: Nostalgic Addictions of Cuban Exile." *Yale Journal of Criticism* 10, no. 1 (Spring, 1997): 63-84.
Sterling, Kristin. "The Return to Cuba Helps Eduardo Machado Find Home and Inspiration." *Columbia News*, October 29, 2001.
Triay, Victor Andrés. *Fleeing Castro: Operation Peter Pan and the Cuban Children's Program*. Gainesville: University Press of Florida, 1998.

Contributors: Debra D. Andrist and David Willinger

Claude McKay

Born: Sunny Ville, Jamaica; September 15, 1889
Died: Chicago, Illinois; May 22, 1948

African American, Caribbean

McKay's writings capture the dialect of his native Jamaica, ushered in the Harlem Renaissance, and added a black voice to the early years of Soviet Communism.

Principal works

LONG FICTION: *Home to Harlem*, 1928; *Banjo: A Story Without a Plot*, 1929; *Banana Bottom*, 1933

POETRY: *Constab Ballads*, 1912; *Songs of Jamaica*, 1912; *Spring in New Hampshire, and Other Poems*, 1920; *Harlem Shadows*, 1922; *Selected Poems of Claude McKay*, 1953

SHORT FICTION: *Gingertown*, 1932

NONFICTION: *A Long Way from Home*, 1937 (autobiography); *Harlem: Negro Metropolis*, 1940

MISCELLANEOUS: *The Passion of Claude McKay: Selected Poetry and Prose, 1912-1948*, 1973 (Wayne F. Cooper, editor; contains social and literary criticism, letters, prose, fiction, and poetry)

Claude McKay was the youngest of eleven children in a rural Jamaican family. His parents instilled pride in an African heritage in their children. McKay's brother Uriah Theophilus and the English folklorist and linguist Walter Jekyll introduced McKay to philosophy and literature, notably to English poetry.

When he was nineteen McKay moved to Kingston and worked as a constable for almost a year. Encouraged by Jekyll, McKay published two volumes of poetry in Jamaican dialect in 1912, *Songs of Jamaica* and *Constab Ballads*. The first collection echoes McKay's love for the natural beauty of Jamaica while the second reflects his disenchantment with urban life in Kingston.

In 1912 McKay left Jamaica for the United States and studied at Tuskegee Institute in Alabama and at Kansas State College before moving to Harlem in 1914. His most famous poem, "If We Must Die," was published in 1919 and proved to be a harbinger of the Harlem Renaissance. The poem depicts violence as a dignified response to racial oppression.

Soon thereafter McKay published two other volumes of poetry, *Spring in New Hampshire, and Other Poems* and *Harlem Shadows*, which portray the homesickness and racism that troubled McKay in the United States. Some of McKay's poems were anthologized in Alain Locke's *The New Negro* (1925), the bible of the Harlem Renaissance.

McKay also spent time in Europe and North Africa. In the Soviet Union in 1922 and 1923, he was lauded as a champion of the Communist movement and published a poem in *Pravda*. While in France in the 1920's, McKay preferred Marseilles over the white expatriate community in Paris.

McKay wrote three sociological novels about the attempts of black people to assimilate as outsiders in various places around the world: *Home to Harlem* is set in Harlem, *Banjo* in Marseilles, and *Banana Bottom* in Britain and Jamaica. The seamy realism of black urban life depicted in the first novel did not appeal to African American thinkers such as W. E. B. Du Bois, who preferred more uplifting and optimistic black art.

McKay continued to examine the place of black people in Western culture in his autobiography, *A Long Way from Home*, and in some of his posthumously published *Selected Poems of Claude McKay*. His conversion to Catholicism in his final years was the last step in his search for aesthetic, racial, and spiritual identity.

Home to Harlem

Type of work: Novel
First published: 1928

This novel is an account of life in Harlem as seen through the experiences of Jake, who has come to regard Harlem as his hometown and is constantly comparing it with other places in his experience. Though the brief sojourn of Jake gives a linear development to the plot, *Home to Harlem* is actually a cyclical novel, for it is apparent that Jake has opened and closed one episode of his life in Petersburg, Virginia, another in Europe (with the Army), and a third in Harlem, before entering on yet another in Chicago with Felice.

Home to Harlem is essentially a story without a plot. Felice is lost for a time and then found by chance. Everything else in the novel is introduced to let the reader know what life is like in Harlem. Life in the Black Belt is depicted as serendipitous, often unfair, and dangerous. The participation of the Haitian immigrant Ray in the life of Jake is short-lived and fundamentally ineffective. In this way, McKay seems to suggest that there is no possibility of amelioration from the outside and from would-be saviors who are transient and not from within the social structure.

On the other hand, Jake, who is part of Harlem and who has become accustomed to its harshness and brutality, can see the possibility of finding love, affection, and even self-satisfaction and self-improvement by leaving it all behind. Prostitution, he seems to suggest, is nothing to hold against a woman if society has forced her into it for survival.

McKay, a longtime resident of Harlem after migrating from Jamaica, thought of Harlem as dehumanizing in the extreme. His attitude is reflected in Ray's comment that if he married Agatha he soon "would become one of the contented hogs in the pigpen of Harlem, getting ready to litter little black piggies." It is this image that McKay presents throughout the novel: Where people are overcrowded and treated like animals, they become animals.

It is the pervasive contrast between Jake and Ray that gives *Home to Harlem* its principal thematic development. Jake is forthright, versatile, optimistic, and persevering; he comes in contact with Ray, who is deliberate, cynical, pessimistic, and unpredictable. Jake is impressed by the intellect and interests of Ray, yet he discerns that a person made "impotent by thought" is irrelevant to the lives of Harlem's masses. Jake is principled: He will be unemployed rather than be a strikebreaker; he will live with a woman, but he will not be a kept man; he sees that the white world is one of materialism and opportunism, but he does not want to participate in it; he sees that the lives of the black folk are difficult, but he does not succumb to the blandishments of purported prophets and saviors. Nevertheless, he feels that he can survive and perhaps even succeed in life. The dialectic permeates the novel.

Only occasionally does McKay allow his own political and social views to intrude explicitly. The black-white issue that absorbed him in his journalism is never directly introduced, though it can be discerned by implication. The authorial voice is to be seen in Jake and Ray, for they represent the two sides of McKay himself: the body and the mind.

Banjo

TYPE OF WORK: Novel
FIRST PUBLISHED: 1929

Banjo: A Story Without a Plot is an episodic narrative involving a small group of relatively permanent residents of the Vieux Port section of Marseilles, France, and a larger cast of incidental characters who are encountered briefly in the varied but fundamentally routine activities of unemployed black seamen trying to maintain a sense of camaraderie and well-being. It is, therefore, basically a picaresque fiction that offers a measure of social criticism.

The novel reiterates McKay's constant themes: that the folk rather than the black intelligentsia represent the best in the race; that blacks should have a high regard for their heritage and hence a racial self-esteem; that the ideal life is one of vagabondage, of natural gusto and emotional response, allowing one to "laugh and love and jazz and fight." The breakup of the beachboys at the end of parts 2 and 3 suggests that cohesiveness is less powerful among McKay's favorite people than individualism—the very characteristic of the materialistic, commercial class that Ray inveighs against in his numerous diatribes and asides. Ironically, this assertion of individuality plays into the arms of those classes and attitudes that Ray sees as inimical to racial betterment.

Ray is the mouthpiece for an unrelenting indictment of white civilization. In his eyes, its chief shortcomings are crass commercialism; an unwarranted sense of racial superiority; hypocrisy (white Europeans assert that they make the best pornographic films, yet they condemn the uninhibited—even justifiable—sexuality of the blacks); nauseating patriotism, rather than internationalism; standardization; and Calvinist attitudes toward sex, alcohol, music, and entertainment.

Yet the behavior of Banjo and the others is far from admirable—if one excepts Ray, who is moderate, literate, and emotional. When he arrives in port, Banjo has 12,525 francs—a considerable sum—but quickly spends it on a girl who leaves him as soon as he is broke. He is wholly improvident and far from admirable. Accordingly, it is difficult to maintain any sympathy for him and to feel that he is anything more than a wastrel, a womanizer, a loafer, and an impractical dreamer.

If McKay means *Banjo* to be a paean to the free life, the life of the spirit and the emotions untrammeled by responsibilities, he seems to be suggesting that his motley sybarites are enviable models. They most certainly are not: They are irresponsible and without any admirable ambition. Their parallels are the Europeans who attend the "blue" cinema, who are rootless, affected, and suffering from ennui. (Their Satanism and sexual aberrations have cut them off from their cultural bearings.) It is hard to believe that the beachboys—and Banjo in particular—are to be admired for their instinctive, spontaneous, sensual behavior. Moreover, at the end most of them express their dissatisfaction with pointless drifting, with unemployment, with poverty, and with temporary liaisons dependent on money alone. It is little wonder, then, that *Banjo* has been criticized for not having a clearly defined and defensible theme. Similarly, one can see a weakness in Banjo's saying that his instrument is his "buddy," that it is more than a "gal, moh than a pal; it's mahself." The Jazz Age had not ended, but the banjo was a symbol of a past era, and its owner, who places a thing above persons, seems to be disoriented. Banjo has become an anachronism.

Banana Bottom

Type of work: Novel
First published: 1933

Banana Bottom is the story of a young Jamaican woman's discovery of her country, her people, and herself. The novel begins with the return to Jamaica of twenty-two-year-old Tabitha "Bita" Plant, who has been abroad for seven years. After a flashback in which he explains the reasons for her absence, McKay tells the story of Bita's life from her homecoming to her marriage, concluding with a brief epilogue that shows her as a contented wife and mother.

Banana Bottom is based on a less simplistic view of the black experience than some critics have assumed. A close look at the novel shows how far McKay's underlying meaning is from the easy dichotomy between a white society of repression, which is evil, and a black culture of expression, which is good, with all the characters lined up on one side or the other.

One of McKay's major themes has little to do with that kind of dichotomy. His Jamaica is almost entirely black, and the social hierarchy that he finds so stultifying is maintained by blacks, not by whites. The reason that the highly educated, intelligent, charming Bita can aspire no higher than her seminarian is that, in the view of her own society, no one so dark in skin color can marry a professional man or a government official. Granted, the Jamaican system is based on the old white colonial belief in black inferiority; however, it is not whites who enforce this social stratification. By showing how this system traps people of unquestionable ability at an arbitrary level in society, McKay is arguing for a change of mind within the black community itself.

An even more important theme of *Banana Bottom* is the issue of what lifestyle is most fulfilling for a black person, specifically for an intelligent, well-educated individual such as Bita. Again, it has been easy for critics to see the prudish and repressed Priscilla Craig as the representative of white society and Herald Newton Day as an example of a black man destroyed when he attempts, like his white sponsor, to repress his black sexual vitality. McKay, however, does not make arbitrary classifications of either his whites or his blacks. In Malcolm Craig's dedication to black freedom and autonomy and in Squire Gensir's passion for black culture, McKay shows that some whites are capable not only of kindness but also of selflessness.

Similarly, he uses two of Bita's suitors to show that black people are not necessarily noble. Certainly both Hopping Dick Delgado and Tack Tally are unworthy of McKay's heroine. Unlike both Herald and Tack, the man whom Bita chooses is a truly free one who finds the meaning of life not in the supernatural but in nature itself, in his wife, in his family, in his own sexual vitality, and in the land to which he is devoting his life. Instead of denying Bita the expression of her own identity, Jubban encourages her even in those interests that are not his own. The life that Bita and Jubban build together, then, is not a rejection of one culture or another but a fusion of the best of two worlds.

Poetry

McKay has been posthumously proclaimed Jamaica's national poet, and he has been the subject of an international conference of literary scholars. Paul Laurence Dunbar, Countée Cullen, and Langston Hughes also helped in the development of modern African American poetry, but only Hughes could legitimately be proposed as a better and more important poet than McKay.

Although there are some true gems of both concept and expression in McKay's initial two volumes of poetry, it is unlikely that any except Jamaicans and scholars will take any real pleasure in reading them. Even in 1912, McKay's mentor Walter Jekyll thought it necessary to add extensive footnotes to *Songs of Jamaica* to explain the poems' contractions, allusions, and pronunciations, and both a glossary and footnotes were added to *Constab Ballads*. There is no doubt that McKay's use of dialect in his poems was an advance on the use of dialect by such predecessors as Dunbar, who used it largely for either comic or role-establishing purposes;

Claude McKay (Library of Congress)

McKay used dialect for social verisimilitude, to attempt to capture the Jamaican inflections and idiom, to differentiate the speech of the folk from that of the colonial classes. Upon quitting Jamaica for the United States, however, McKay discontinued his use of dialect, even when, in some of his American "protest" poems that make use of African American diction, dialect would be appropriate and even effective.

Spring in New Hampshire, and Other Poems, McKay's first volume of poetry in Standard English, which was published in London, and *Harlem Shadows*, which appeared two years later in New York, established him as a major poet in the black community and as a potentially important one in English literature. *Harlem Shadows*, with its brilliant evocation of life in the black ghetto of New York City, more than any other book heralded the beginning of the Harlem Renaissance, from which developed the great florescence of African American culture in subsequent years.

In his post-Jamaican poetry, McKay became attached almost exclusively to the sonnet form, eschewed dialect, and he showed no strong inclination to experiment with rhyme, rhythm, and the other components of the sonnet. Further, he displayed the influence of his early reading of the English Romantics, and in the words of Wayne Cooper, McKay's biographer, "his forthright expression of the black man's anger, alienation, and rebellion against white racism introduced into modern American Negro poetry an articulate militancy of theme and tone which grew increasingly important with time."

The sense of being a black man in a white man's world pervades McKay's poetry, as does the sense of being a visionary in the land of the sightless—if not also the sense of being an alien (an islander) in the heart of the metropolis. As John Dewey noted, "I feel it decidedly out of place to refer to him as the voice of the Negro people; he is that, but he is so much more than that." McKay is the voice of the dispossessed, the oppressed, the discriminated against; he is one of the major poetic voices of the Harlem Renaissance; he is one of a select group of poets who have represented the colonized peoples of the world; and he is one of the voices for universal self-respect and brotherhood.

Suggested Readings

Cooper, Wayne F. *Claude McKay: Rebel Sojourner in the Harlem Renaissance*. Baton Rouge: Louisiana State University Press, 1987.

Gayle, Addison, Jr. *Claude McKay: The Black Poet at War*. Detroit: Broadside Press, 1972.

Giles, James R. *Claude McKay*. Boston: Twayne, 1976.

Hathaway, Heather. *Caribbean Waves: Relocating Claude McKay and Paule Marshall*. Bloomington: Indiana University Press, 1999.

Holcomb, Gary E. "Diaspora Cruises: Queer Black Proletarianism in Claude McKay's *A Long Way from Home*." *Modern Fiction Studies* 49, no. 4 (Winter, 2003): 714-746.

James, Winston. "Becoming the People's Poet: Claude McKay's Jamaican Years, 1889-1912." *Small Axe: A Caribbean Journal of Criticism*, no. 13 (March, 2003): 17-46.

_______. *A Fierce Hatred of Injustice: Claude McKay's Jamaica and His Poetry of Rebellion*. New York: Verso, 2001.

LeSeur, Geta. "Claude McKay's Marxism." In *The Harlem Renaissance: Revaluations*, edited by Amritjit Singh, William S. Shiver, and Stanley Brodwin. New York: Garland, 1989.

Rosenberg, Leah. "Caribbean Models for Modernism in the Work of Claude McKay and Jean Rhys." *Modernism/Modernity* 11, no. 2 (April, 2004): 219-239.

Schwarz, A. B. Christa. *Gay Voices of the Harlem Renaissance*. Bloomington: Indiana University Press, 2003.

Tillery, Tyrone. *Claude McKay: A Black Poet's Struggle for Identity*. Amherst: University of Massachusetts Press, 1992.

Contributors: Douglas Edward LaPrade, Rosemary M. Canfield Reisman, A. L. McLeod, and Richard A. Eichwald

Reginald McKnight

Born: Fürstenfeldbruck, Germany; February 26, 1956

African American

Although McKnight refrains from political statement in his fiction and refuses to accept or to promote any singular concept of black identity, he believes art should "get under your skin."

Principal works

LONG FICTION: *I Get on the Bus*, 1990; *He Sleeps*, 2001

SHORT FICTION: *Moustapha's Eclipse*, 1988; *The Kind of Light That Shines on Texas*, 1992; *White Boys*, 1998

EDITED TEXTS: *African American Wisdom*, 1994; *Wisdom of the African World*, 1996

Reginald McKnight was born in Fürstenfeldbruck, Germany, to military parents in 1956. His father Frank was a U.S. Air Force noncommissioned officer, and his mother Pearl was a dietitian. Because of his military background, McKnight has lived all over the world, moving a total of forty-three times. After a brief stint in the U.S. Marine Corps, McKnight earned an associate degree in anthropology (1978) from Pikes Peak Community College and a B.A. in African literature (1981) from Colorado College. He received the Thomas J. Watson Fellowship to study folklore and literature in West Africa, so he spent a year teaching and writing in Senegal. In 1987, he earned an M.A. in English with an emphasis in creative writing from the University of Denver. McKnight has taught at Arapahoe Community College, the University of Denver, and the University of Maryland at College Park. He married Michele Davis in 1985 and has two daughters. He is the recipient of a National Endowment for the Arts Fellowship, an O. Henry Award, the Kenyon Review Award for excellence (which he received twice), a PEN/Hemingway Special Citation, a Pushcart Prize, the Drue Heinz Literature Prize, the Watson Foundation Fellowship, the Whiting Writers' Award, and the Bernice M. Slote Award.

McKnight's work is a refreshing change from much of the black protest literature of the 1970's and 1980's. While white people are often presented as unpleasant, annoying, and mean-spirited, they are seldom presented as outrightly diabolical. McKnight deliberately refrains from political statement in his fiction, believing that art has the higher purpose of bringing a sense of joy to the reader, the type of joy that makes one think that "life is deep, limitless, and meaningful." Yet he does not believe that art should be harmless. "It should get under your skin," he says. McKnight refuses to accept or to promote any singular concept of black identity; instead, he respects the diversity of black experience found in the United States and elsewhere.

Like many writers, McKnight draws heavily on personal experience to find subject matter for his stories. For example, several stories found in his collections are set in West Africa with an anthropologist as the narrator. Other stories include the painful experience of being one of a handful of black children in a school. His experience in the military is also woven into several stories. His stories, however, are no mere transcription of personal experience. He is equally successful in portraying the experiences of black working-class males.

Many of McKnight's stories are boldly experimental in point of view, tone, style, and concept. His stories set in West Africa are particularly notable for their non-Western philosophical views and the incorporation of the fantastic. For example, in "The Homunculus: A Novel in One Chapter" (found in *The Kind of Light That Shines on Texas*), the protagonist is a young writer in a fairy-tale-like place who becomes so consumed with his writing that it becomes a flesh-and-blood likeness of himself. McKnight's work is characterized by his successful, convincing use of multiple voices.

"Uncle Moustapha's Eclipse"

Type of work: Short fiction
First published: 1988, in *Moustapha's Eclipse*

"Uncle Moustapha's Eclipse," the title story of McKnight's first collection, is narrated in the broken English of a Senegalese interpreter working for an American anthropologist living in Africa. This story has the feel of a folktale; that is, it is clearly meant to teach a lesson. Uncle Moustapha is a successful peanut farmer, who lives in a small African village with his three wives and seven children. His only problem is that he constantly thinks of death; he would not have this problem if he had not adopted the white man's tradition of celebrating his birthday.

On the eve of his sixtieth birthday (or at least what he has designated as his birthday), he goes to bed anticipating an eclipse of the sun, which has been predicted for the next day. On the following morning, a white scientist arrives to set up his viewing equipment on Uncle Moustapha's land. The scientist warns Moustapha not to view the eclipse directly with naked eyes. At first, Moustapha complies and views the eclipse properly through the scientific equipment. However, he quickly becomes overjoyed with the eclipse, believing that it was sent to him as a gift from Allah and his ancestors. Moustapha runs to fetch his favorite wife, Fatima. They rush together to the baobab tree, which is believed to house the spirits of their ancestors. After a brief prayer, Moustapha experiences a rush of heightened sensory perceptions. He turns to stare at the eclipse with his eyes wide open, so that he can see "it all in supreme detail." As he returns home, the world seems more beautiful to him than ever before, except for a black shape that begins to flicker on and off in his left eye.

The ending of the story is ambiguous. It is not clear whether he goes blind or it is death that is finally coming to Uncle Moustapha. However, he has no regrets because he has seen "what no other living soul has seen today." Clearly, he does not believe that going blind or even dying is too great a price to pay for such a magnificent experience.

The Kind of Light That Shines on Texas

Type of work: Short fiction
First published: 1992

At first glance, the seven stories collected in *The Kind of Light That Shines on Texas* appear discrete and unrelated, so varied are they in style and form. Yet inherent within this collection is an overriding concern with the black American self—more specifically, with the black American male self: with its formation, its definition, its ruination.

Stylistically, McKnight's stories move from the fablelike opening story, "The Homunculus: A Novel in One Chapter," through a series of more realistic narratives, to the futuristic concluding tale, "Soul Food." McKnight frequently places the storytelling responsibility upon a first-person voice, and just as frequently these voices tell their stories in a language that is sharp and colloquial and distinctive.

McKnight's vision in his short fiction focuses upon the nature of the black American male and upon the forces that define black American male selfhood. Most of the central figures in these stories are young black American men—artists, drug dealers, military personnel—whose behavior in the present is inextricably linked to elements of their individual and their racial past: violence, subjugation, maternal dominance. They are men who challenge the stereotypes; they are paradoxical characters who smoke crack and read BRAVE NEW WORLD ("Roscoe in Hell"), who write story-length letters to friends they haven't seen in years ("Quitting Smoking"), who join the Marines and express their very human fears in the action of very personal wars ("Peacetime"). Two of the most successful stories in this collection (the title story, and "Into Night"), though, deal with the childhood experiences, experiences which McKnight suggests are especially significant in the formation of the black adult character. What finally emerges from these stories is a difficult, troubling notion of what it means to be black and male in an increasingly multicultural America.

In the O. Henry Award-winning title story of *The Kind of Light That Shines on Texas*, McKnight explores the ambivalence of friendship, not just between blacks and whites but also between blacks and blacks. Clinton Oates, the narrator, is one of three black children in his sixth-grade class in Waco, Texas. Oates, who is eager to prove himself inoffensive to whites, feels embarrassed by the presence of Marvin Pruitt, a black boy who fulfills most negative black stereotypes. Pruitt "smelled bad, was at least two grades behind, was hostile, dark skinned, homely, close-mouthed." Pruitt sleeps away most of the schoolday; the other black child is a large, passive girl who refuses to speak.

This class is full of older children, including a sixteen-year-old white bully, Kevin Oakley, who is just looking for a reason to fight with Oates. One day, their coach (who probably wants to see Oates get hurt) singles out the two boys for a game of "murder ball," using two hard-pumped volleyballs instead of the usual red rubber balls. Completely in fair play, Oates hits Oakley square in the face, causing a nosebleed and the boy's humiliation. Shortly afterward, in the locker room, Oakley threatens to attack Oates after school. Oates sees Pruitt, an innocent bystander, and asks, "How come you after me and not him?" Oates escapes from Oakley that afternoon by getting on the bus early, but he cannot escape the implications of what he had said in the locker room. Clearly, Oates meant that Pruitt deserved to be picked on or beaten up because he so neatly fit all the negative stereotypes of blacks.

The next morning, Oakley predictably picks a fight with Oates. Surprisingly, Pruitt intervenes on Oates's behalf, with a disdainful "git out of my way, boy." This action shows that Pruitt is, without a doubt, morally superior to Oates, the nice young black who is only too eager to do his "tom-thing." The reader is left to believe that Pruitt knows exactly what Oates had meant in the locker room, but he still rises above this black-on-black racial insult. While never exactly friends, the black boys' relationship proves that blood is, indeed, thicker than water.

"Quitting Smoking"

Type of work: Short fiction
First published: 1992, in *The Kind of Light That Shines on Texas*

This story, also found in *The Kind of Light That Shines on Texas*, is narrated by a working-class black man, Scott Winters, who lives with his white lover, Anna. Their relationship does not work, partly because Scott cannot stop smoking, partly because race becomes a barrier, and partly because Scott cannot bring himself to share his deepest secret with her. Scott began smoking in his late teens to hide the smell of reefer from his parents. He discovers that he likes the buzz from cigarettes better than any other "high." When he meets Anna—a vegetarian, health nut, and feminist—he naturally and easily loses his desire to smoke and to eat meat. One night, Anna confides to him an incident of acquaintance rape. This confidence immediately reminds him of a time in his teens that he and three other males witnessed the abduction of a woman into a car. The woman struggled and screamed for help, but none of the young men intervened on her behalf. Nagged by this memory, Scott goes out and buys a pack of cigarettes.

What follows is a story of cigarette addiction that anyone who has ever smoked will find familiar. He continues to sneak out for smokes in the middle of the night. He begins to keep an arsenal of cover-up supplies in his truck—gum, toothpaste, mouthwash, deodorant, and air freshener. Cigarettes become his secret infidelity.

When Anna confronts him with a cigarette she has found, Scott vows to quit but does not. Scott's deeper problem is that he cannot bring himself to confess to Anna what he had allowed to happen to the woman who had been abducted and perhaps raped or killed.

One night, he makes elaborate preparations for this confession; he cleans the house, makes dinner, and buys wine and flowers. Scott tentatively approaches the subject by saying, "I wouldn't be surprised if you hated men." Anna, who has grown distant for other reasons, counters, "I'm surprised I don't hate black men. The guy who raped me was black." Scott, who feels this racial insult as an almost physical injury, immediately packs his bags and walks out the door. Both partners are guilty of erecting barriers that destroy the relationship, but only Anna chose to use race as a weapon.

"The White Boys"

Type of work: Short fiction
First published: 1998, in *White Boys*

This story opens with yet another move for a black military family. The Oates are, in many ways, a typical black middle-class family. Both parents are strict, even to the point of violence. Two particularly nasty beatings of the young protagonist Derrick are recounted in this narrative. His two siblings Dean and Alva are spared similar beatings, mostly because they are less conspicuous or odd than Derrick. Both parents greatly fear that one of their children will bring shame or trouble to their home. They know, only too well, that white people will conjure up the worst possible racial stereotypes at the slightest provocation.

The day after they move in, Derrick provides this type of provocation by innocently scooping snow off of his neighbor's car. The neighbor, Sergeant Hooker, vehemently hates blacks, following his childhood experience of growing up in a predominantly black neighborhood in Baltimore. His mother, with whom he no longer communicates, even married a black man. Ironically, Hooker's best friend from childhood was also black. Furious over the Oates's moving next door, Hooker sets out to instill racial hatred equal to his own in his three sons. The youngest son Garrett is determined to hate Derrick, but a friendship begins to grow between the two boys. When Hooker discovers this friendship, he devises a diabolical scheme to scare Derrick away permanently. He plans to take Derrick and his three sons on a fishing trip, during which time the four whites will stage a mock lynching of Derrick. Garrett, unable to confront his father or to warn Derrick, comes up with his own scheme to save his friend. On the Friday before this fateful weekend, he calls Derrick a nigger, not just once but repeatedly. His act destroys their friendship (exactly what his father wanted) but saves Derrick from a far more horrific experience.

In an interview, McKnight has said that the stories in *White Boys* should produce this response: "It's too bad that blacks and whites don't get along very well today."

This response is exactly what this story produces. There is every reason except race that the Hookers and Oateses should have been good friends and neighbors.

Suggested Readings

McKnight, Reginald. "An Interview with Reginald McKnight." Interview by Renée Olander. *The Writer's Chronicle* 3 (February, 2000): 5-14.

_______. "We Are, in Fact, a Civilization." Interview by William Walsh. *Kenyon Review* 16, no. 2 (Spring, 1994): 27-42.

Megan, Carolyn. "New Perceptions on Rhythm in Reginald McKnight's Fiction." *Kenyon Review* 16, no. 2 (Spring, 1994): 56-62.

Peterson, V. R. "Picks and Pans—*The Kind of Light That Shines on Texas*." *People* 37, no. 15 (April 20, 1992): 39-40.

Contributor: Nancy Sherrod

Terry McMillan

Born: Port Huron, Michigan; October 18, 1951

African American

McMillan's novels and short stories explore the complex relationships among urban black women of the late twentieth century, their families, and the men in their lives.

Principal works

LONG FICTION: *Mama*, 1987; *Disappearing Acts*, 1989; *Waiting to Exhale*, 1992; *How Stella Got Her Groove Back*, 1996; *A Day Late and a Dollar Short*, 2001; *The Interruption of Everything*, 2005

SCREENPLAYS: *Waiting to Exhale*, 1995 (adaptation of her novel; with Ronald Bass); *How Stella Got Her Groove Back*, 1998 (adaptation of her novel; with Bass)

NONFICTION: *The Writer as Publicist*, 1993 (with Marcia Biederman and Gary Aspenberg)

EDITED TEXT: *Breaking Ice: An Anthology of Contemporary African-American Fiction*, 1990

Terry McMillan was reared near Detroit by working-class parents and later moved to Los Angeles, where she attended community college and read widely in the canon of African American literature. In 1979, at the age of twenty-eight, she received her bachelor of science degree from the University of California, Berkeley. In 1987, she began a three-year instructorship at the University of Wyoming, Laramie, and in 1988 received a coveted fellowship from the National Endowment for the Arts. After teaching in Tucson at the University of Arizona from 1990 to 1992, McMillan pursued writing as her full-time career.

The environment in which McMillan's views were formed prepared her for early marriage and a family, not the life of an intellectual and an artist. Her failure as an adult to meet the expectations of her culture and family created pressures that her work has consistently sought to address. Not surprisingly, her own struggle to adapt to cultural expectations resulted in an emphasis in her work on the tension in relationships between professional and blue-collar blacks, between women and men, and between members of the nuclear family. *Mama* depicts an acceptance by an intellectual daughter of her flawed mother. *Disappearing Acts* follows a love affair between a professional, responsible woman and an uneducated tradesman. *Waiting to Exhale* builds an ambitious collage of images from all three types of relationships.

McMillan's fiction addresses the archetypal dilemma of the disadvantaged—

Terry McMillan (© Marion Ettlinger)

escaping the limitations imposed by one's culture and family while trying to preserve the advantages they inevitably offer. This dilemma leads her characters into conflicts of ideology; their struggle is the struggle for truth, their quest the search for meaning.

While some reviewers have attacked McMillan for her use of vulgar language, others have defended its realism and immediacy. The same is true of the explicit sexual references throughout her work, and indeed for her character portrayals themselves. Critics observe that MacMillan's characters all seem at times to have been exaggerated to achieve a calculated effect. McMillan's popularity, however, suggests that she understands her craft and that her audience approves her purpose.

Mama

Type of work: Novel
First published: 1987

Mama is set in a town called Point Haven, Michigan, not far from Detroit. The book is dedicated to McMillan's mother. Like her, the book's protagonist, Mildred Peacock, is a poor, uneducated black woman who has remained with her abusive husband in the hope that he will help support their five children. As the novel begins, however, Crook Peacock has beaten Mildred one time too many. She kicks him out and divorces him. As the title suggests, Mildred sees motherhood as her primary role in life. McMillan shows her dealing with unscrupulous employers, scheming to outwit rent collectors and welfare workers, and even prostituting herself in order to feed her family.

Mildred's efforts to be a good mother are stymied by her addiction to alcohol and her inability to resist attractive men. Ironically, she gets married a second time to a man she does not love, or even like, simply because she needs his income. Her third marriage is no better. That husband, who is a much younger man, walks out on Mildred when he finds family responsibilities too burdensome.

Though education gives most of McMillan's other heroines many more options than Mildred has, their experiences with men are not very different from hers. Like her, they come to depend not on men but on other women, either family members or close friends. In Mildred's case, it is her eldest daughter, Freda, who both inspires her to keep going and, on occasion, offers the wise counsel that Mildred desperately needs.

Disappearing Acts

Type of work: Novel
First published: 1989

McMillan's second novel is a romantic comedy set in New York. The main characters in *Disappearing Acts* are Zora Banks, a musician and teacher, and Franklin Swift, a construction worker. One of their problems is that Franklin does not seem motivated to better himself. Another is that Zora and Franklin are not honest with each other. When he loses his job, he does not tell Zora; when she terminates a pregnancy, she does not even consult him. The next time she becomes pregnant, she decides to have the baby. Franklin gets furious and Zora puts him out. Franklin takes refuge in alcohol and cocaine. However, he finally returns to her with his addictions conquered and some solid plans for the future.

McMillan undoubtedly drew the inspiration for *Disappearing Acts* from her life in New York, but, like any other artist, she invented her characters and changed details. Nevertheless, in 1990, McMillan's former boyfriend, Leonard Welch, sued McMillan and her publishers, alleging that the character of Swift presented an unflattering portrait of Welch. Ironically, critics agree that Swift is presented as a basically good person. At any rate, the case was decided in McMillan's favor.

McMillan's artistic integrity is also illustrated by her insistence on using alternating monologues in *Disappearing Acts*, telling the story first through Zora's eyes and then from Franklin's perspective. When her publisher insisted that she rewrite the book, making Franklin the sole narrator, McMillan changed publishers.

Waiting to Exhale

Type of work: Novel
First published: 1992

Waiting to Exhale, McMillan's third novel, was an instant popular success when it was first published in 1992. The book found wide acceptance, both critical and public, largely because of the honesty of its character portrayals and the timeliness of its themes. All four main characters in *Waiting to Exhale* are seeking the acceptance of culture and family but are also determined to escape their limiting influences. The conflicts that arise in the lives of the characters reflect the concerns of black feminist writers in general, and critics generally regard McMillan as having a finger on the pulse of 1990's educated black women. The novel's popularity is a reflection of the growing number of middle-class African Americans who wish to participate in black cultural life and preserve its heritage.

The title of *Waiting to Exhale* is a metaphor for the tension in each of the novel's four protagonists' lives. All are waiting to find the right man, and each is figuratively holding her breath until he comes along. Each protagonist's story delineates a different type of coping strategy for the alienation and anxiety each suffers. In the face of criticism from their families, their culture, and themselves, the four women develop a friendship that enables them to stand fast against the many temptations to "settle" for an unhealthy relationship. The novel's setting, Phoenix, implies the possibility of glorious rebirth, but the symbolic implications are muted and ultimately unfulfilled; still, the characters achieve integration and a new sense of identity through their relationships with one another.

Savannah takes a cut in pay to move to Phoenix, where her old roommate from college, Bernadine, is living the perfect life. By the time Savannah completes the move, Bernadine's marriage is in shambles, her husband and the father of their two children having deserted her with his young blond bookkeeper. Robin, a mutual friend, is frustrated, self-conscious, and anxious, looking for self-esteem through the eyes of the men she meets. Gloria, their hairdresser, is the single mother of a sixteen-year-old son, whose emerging sexuality creates fear in her and hostility in him. Savannah moves, Bernadine spends, Robin casts horoscopes, and Gloria eats; ultimately all their defense mechanisms crumble under one anothers' affectionate but witheringly, relentlessly honest scrutiny.

How Stella Got Her Groove Back

Type of work: Novel
First published: 1996

Like *Disappearing Acts*, *How Stella Got Her Groove Back*, is a love story. However, this time her novel is unabashedly autobiographical. McMillan's alter ego, Stella Payne, is a successful forty-two-year-old woman with a wonderful son much like McMillan's own, Solomon Welch. In a breathless, first-person narrative, Stella explains how she happened to choose Jamaica for a vacation and describes her chance encounter with Winston Shakespeare, a handsome young man half her age. What begins as attraction turns out to be true love. Nevertheless, Stella cannot forget the difference in their ages, though it seems not to trouble Winston.

Back in California, Stella discovers that she has lost her job. However, she has invested so wisely over the years that money is not a real problem. She even sees this development as an opportunity to take her life in a new direction. This uncharacteristic optimism, she realizes, is the result of her involvement with Winston. Stella does not waste any time. She makes a second trip to Jamaica, this time taking her son and her niece with her. They get along famously with Winston. As the book ends, Winston is in California with Stella, and they are planning to marry. McMillan dedicated the novel to Jonathan Plummer, her own Jamaican husband.

Reviewers felt that *How Stella Got Her Groove Back* lacked both the craftsmanship and the realism of McMillan's other novels. With its happily-ever-after ending, it was generally dismissed as a romance.

A Day Late and a Dollar Short

Type of work: Novel
First published: 2001

Of the six major characters in *A Day Late and a Dollar Short*, Viola Price is the most important. Viola is a matriarch much like McMillan's own mother. She still feels responsible for her children, her grandchildren, and even her former husband Cecil. Viola knows that her hardworking, well-to-do oldest daughter, Paris, is addicted to pills; that her second daughter, Charlotte, is possessed by her jealous hatred of Paris; and that her youngest child, Janelle, is too afraid of her second husband to admit that he has raped her daughter. Viola's son, Lewis, is an alcoholic whose hot temper keeps landing him in jail. Viola also has one grandson who is gay and another who was headed for college until his girlfriend got pregnant. Even Cecil is a worry; he has a young girlfriend who Viola believes takes advantage of him.

A Day Late and a Dollar Short begins with Viola lying in a hospital bed worrying about her family. It ends with her reaching out to them from beyond the grave in a final attempt to set them straight and to bring the family closer together. Although the use of six narrative voices sometimes leads to confusion, *A Day Late and a Dollar Short* is considered one of McMillan's most appealing novels.

The Interruption of Everything

Type of work: Novel
First published: 2005

McMillan began by writing about young, ambitious women like herself. As she has grown older, however, so have her characters. *The Interruption of Everything* is about middle age. Marilyn Grimes, the heroine of the novel, is a forty-four-year-old woman whose children have gone off to college, leaving her with a live-in mother-in-law, a mother showing signs of Alzheimer's disease, a sister too addicted to drugs to care for her own children, and a husband who seems to be having his own midlife crisis. Fortunately, Marilyn has two girlfriends to provide the support she desperately needs.

One reason for McMillan's broad appeal is that, though she never pretends that life is easy, she assures women that they have the inherent strength to handle whatever comes their way. In *The Interruption of Everything*, McMillan holds the attention of her readers with one plot complication after another. Marilyn becomes pregnant; her husband goes to Costa Rica to find himself; her son brings a peculiar crew home from college; and her former husband reappears, looking better than she remembered. The dialogue is as irreverent and as sparkling as McMillan's readers expect, and *The Interruption of Everything* ends on an optimistic note.

Suggested Readings

Dandridge, Rita B. "Debunking the Motherhood Myth in Terry McMillan's *Mama*." *CLA Journal* 41, no. 4 (1998): 405-416.

Ellerby, Janet Mason. "Deposing the Man of the House: Terry McMillan Rewrites the Family." *MELUS* 22, no. 2 (1997): 105-117.

Harris, Tina M., and Patricia S. Hill. "'Waiting to Exhale' or 'Breath(ing) Again': A Search for Identity, Empowerment, and Love in the 1990's." *Women and Language* 21, no. 2 (1998): 9-20.

Henderson, Mae Gwendolyn. "Speaking in Tongues: Dialogics, Dialectics, and the Black Woman Writer's Literary Tradition." In *Reading Black, Reading Feminist: A Critical Anthology*, edited by Henry Louis Gates, Jr. New York: Meridian, 1990.

Hernton, Calvin C. *The Sexual Mountain and Black Women Writers*. New York: Doubleday, 1987.

Patrick, Diane. *Terry McMillan: An Unauthorized Biography*. New York: St. Martin's Press, 1999.

Richards, Paulette. *Terry McMillan: A Critical Companion*. Westport, Conn.: Greenwood Press, 1999.

Contributors: Andrew B. Preslar and Rosemary M. Canfield Reisman

D'Arcy McNickle

Born: St. Ignatius, Montana; January 18, 1904
Died: Albuquerque, New Mexico; October 18, 1977

Native American

In novels, short stories, children's books, and scholarly works, McNickle focuses on communication problems between Native Americans and the dominant culture.

Principal works

LONG FICTION: *The Surrounded*, 1936; *Runner in the Sun: A Story of Indian Maize*, 1954; *Wind from an Enemy Sky*, 1978

SHORT FICTION: *The Hawk Is Hungry, and Other Stories*, 1993

NONFICTION: *They Came Here First: The Epic of the American Indian*, 1949; *Indians and Other Americans: Two Ways of Life Meet*, 1959 (with Harold Fey); *The Indian Tribes of the United States: Ethnic and Cultural Survival*, 1962 (revised as *Native American Tribalism: Indian Survivals and Renewals*, 1973); *Indian Man: A Biography of Oliver La Farge*, 1971

Born to a Scotch-Irish father and a French Canadian mother of Cree heritage, D'Arcy McNickle (DAHR-see muhk-NIHK-ehl) knew from an early age the problems of mixed identity that many Native Americans experience. Reared on a northwestern Montana ranch, McNickle, along with his family, was adopted into the Salish-Kootanai Indian tribe. Attending Oxford University and the University of Grenoble in France after completing his undergraduate education at the University of Montana, McNickle was as firmly grounded in Native American culture as he was in the white world.

Completing his formal education when the United States was gripped by the Depression, McNickle was among the writers who joined the Federal Writers' Project, with which he was associated from 1935 to 1936. His first novel, *The Surrounded*, was an outgrowth of this association. This book focuses on how an Indian tribe disintegrates as the United States government encroaches upon and ultimately grabs tribal lands and then sets out to educate the Native American children in such a way as to denigrate their culture and integrate them into the dominant society. Like McNickle, the protagonist of this novel, Archilde, has a mixed identity, being the offspring of a Spanish father and a Native American mother.

In his children's book, *Runner in the Sun*, McNickle deals with similar questions of identity centering on the inevitable conflicts between whites and Native Americans. The Native Americans strive in vain to preserve their culture and retain their grazing lands.

Such also is the focus of McNickle's posthumous novel, *Wind from an Enemy Sky*, in which tribal lands are condemned for the building of a dam, and the sacred medicine bundle is given to a museum for display. McNickle also produced several works of nonfiction that grew out of his tenure with the Bureau of Indian Affairs and his directorship of the bureau's division of American Indian development.

The Surrounded

Type of work: Novel
First published: 1936

The Surrounded has strong autobiographical overtones. The novel focuses on Archilde, through whom the readers see the identity conflicts that trouble the racially mixed hero. Archilde is caught between the white and the Indian cultures, neither of which is unambiguously good or bad, making his position even more difficult.

One of the ways that the novel emphasizes this cultural conflict is by describing many characters and events as opposing pairs. Catharine LaLoup Leon and Max Leon, for example, each present to Archilde some of the positive aspects of Indian and white culture, respectively. The Indian dancing on the Fourth of July, full of ancient meaning and beauty, is contrasted with the white people's meaningless dance in a dark, bare hall.

The novel expresses particular concern for the decline of Native American culture. McNickle describes in great detail the transformation of Mike and Narcisse as the older women prepare them for the dance, emphasizing the beauty of traditional culture. McNickle applies his expertise as an anthropologist to the detailed explanation of all the old dances, stressing each dance's particular meaning. This is contrasted with the scene at the Fourth of July dance, where white people come to laugh disrespectfully at the old men as they move slowly through the only dances that they are still allowed to do.

In addition, *The Surrounded* presents an interesting view of nature. Archilde goes into the wilderness to be alone, and nature is generally seen as an ally to the Indians, who can live in mountain caves and hunt for their food if they so choose. The scene in which Archilde sees the cloud-cross in the sky, and ignores it because the bird ignores it, stresses the preeminence of nature. Archilde remembers this experience and teaches this same lesson to Mike and Narcisse: If the birds are not frightened by signs and demons, they should not be, either. Nature is seen as a better source of encouragement and truth than are the priests.

An interesting aspect of the novel is the presence of two especially strong female characters. Elise is reckless and determined to get what she wants. She can ride and hunt as well as any man. She takes the initiative, not only in her relationship with Archilde but also in their escape into the mountains. She, like Catharine, is not afraid to kill when Archilde is threatened. Catharine is held in high regard, not only among the Indians but also among the whites (which is one reason that Max married her in the first place). Even in her advanced age, she hunts for herself. Her death is described as a triumphant moment. She dies unafraid, surrounded by her Indian family and friends.

The plot structure of *The Surrounded* demonstrates a certain circularity and reflects the work's thematic concern for Archilde's identity. Archilde left the reservation, trying to put some distance between himself and his people. When he returns, it is only for a short and final visit. Yet he continues to stay as he becomes increasingly entangled in events on the reservation. The apparent inaction—staying—is actually the action that helps him determine his identity as an Indian. He does not succeed in going to Portland to be a fiddler or even in running his father's farm. Archilde succeeds in finding his identity at those times when he feels most connected to his tribal heritage: at the dance and at his mother's death. His identity comes not from breaking away and succeeding in isolation but from living in his proper context, with his people and his land.

Wind from an Enemy Sky

Type of work: Novel
First published: 1978

In *Wind from an Enemy Sky*, McNickle writes of the difficult period in American history during which the United States government attempted to subdue Native Americans peacefully. McNickle, a government employee for most of his life, presents a balanced view of what occurred during this period in one small Native American enclave in the Flathead Lake-St. Ignatius area of Montana.

On the surface, McNickle presents the story of a Native American extended family that includes Pock Face, who, carrying his grandfather's rifle, steals furtively into a canyon where white developers have built a dam on tribal land. The Little Elk Indians equate the damming of their river with its murder. The dam has an immediate negative impact upon fishing and farming on their tribal lands. As Pock Face and Theobald, his cousin, approach the dam, they spy a white man walking across its surface. Pock Face fires one shot. Jim Cooke, ironically on his last day of work before going east to marry, dies instantly.

The remainder of the story revolves around the government's efforts to mete out justice to the murderer. This surface story, however, provides the justification for a compelling subtext that illustrates the difficulties involved when one well-established culture attempts to impose itself upon another. *Wind from an Enemy Sky*, maintaining throughout an objective view of two disparate cultures, proffers a poignant political and social statement about culture and values in multiethnic settings.

Wind from an Enemy Sky is concerned largely with the inability of the Native American and dominant societies in the United States to communicate productively with each other. As McNickle presents it, Native American society is deeply suspicious of the dominant society that has, through the years, oppressed it. Promises made have seldom been promises kept. The suspicions that keep Indians from interacting productively with government agencies are spawned not by paranoia but rather by extensive bitter experience.

The dam the government built has diverted a river on which the Indians depend. The waters that the dam captures will nourish the fields of white homesteaders, to whom the government has sold Indian lands at $1.25 an acre. The Native Americans look upon these land sales as forms of robbery. Added to this justifiable charge is the charge that white officials have kidnapped Indian children and sent them to distant government schools against their will.

McNickle suggests the inevitability of tragedy in dealings between Native Americans and representatives of the dominant society. He also demonstrates how some Native Americans—Henry Jim and The Boy, for example—move into the white world or attempt to straddle the two worlds, placing them in impossible positions. For Henry Jim, it is impossible to shake the Native American heritage, which the dying man finally embraces again.

Suggested Readings

McNickle, D'Arcy. *D'Arcy McNickle's "The Hungry Generations": The Evolution of a Novel.* Edited by Birgit Hans. Albuquerque: University of New Mexico Press, 2007.

Parker, Dorothy R. *Singing an Indian Song: A Biography of D'Arcy McNickle.* Lincoln: University of Nebraska Press, 1992.

Purdy, John Lloyd, ed. *The Legacy of D'Arcy McNickle: Writer, Historian, Activist.* Norman: University of Oklahoma Press, 1996.

_______. *Word Ways: The Novels of D'Arcy McNickle.* Tucson: University of Arizona Press, 1990.

Ruppert, James. *D'Arcy McNickle.* 1962. Reprint. Boise, Idaho: Boise State University Press, 1988.

Contributors: R. Baird Shuman and Kelly C. Walter

James Alan McPherson

Born: Savannah, Georgia; September 16, 1943

African American

McPherson's stories are preoccupied not only with what it means to be a black person in modern America but also with how the individual responds to a culture plagued by racial discrimination.

Principal works

SHORT FICTION: *Hue and Cry*, 1969; *Elbow Room*, 1977

NONFICTION: *Why I Like Country Music*, 1982; *Crabcakes*, 1998; *A Region Not Home: Reflections from Exile*, 2000; *Hallowed Ground: A Walk at Gettysburg*, 2003

EDITED TEXTS: *Railroad: Trains and Train People in American Culture*, 1976 (with Miller Williams); *Fathering Daughters: Reflections by Men*, 1998 (with DeWitt Henry)

James Alan McPherson earned degrees from Morris Brown College (B.A., 1965), Harvard Law School (LL.B., 1968), and the Iowa Writers' Workshop (M.F.A., 1971). He has taught at the University of Iowa, the University of California, Harvard University, Morgan State University, and the University of Virginia. Besides being a contributing editor of *The Atlantic Monthly*, he held jobs ranging from stock clerk to newspaper reporter. In the early 1980's, McPherson began teaching fiction writing in the Writers' Workshop at the University of Iowa in Iowa City. After writing *Elbow Room* (which won the 1978 Pulitzer Prize in fiction and was nominated for the National Book Award), McPherson primarily focused on nonfiction essays that center on the need for African Americans to help define the cultural realities of contemporary American life. His first book in twenty years, *Crabcakes*, focuses on his ultimate understanding of what makes people human.

McPherson is one of the writers of fiction who form the second major phase of modern writing about the African American experience. Indebted, like all of his generation, to the groundbreaking and theme-setting work of Richard Wright, Ellison, and Baldwin, McPherson shies away from doctrinaire argumentation about racial issues. Rather, he uses these issues to give his work a firmly American aura, which includes a preoccupation not only with what it means to be a black person in modern America but also with how the individual responds to a culture that often is plagued by subtle and not-so-subtle racial discriminations. Hence, there are times when blackness becomes for McPherson a metaphor for the alienation experienced by the individual in contemporary society.

This comprehensive concern with American culture informs all of McPherson's work, including those pieces that are included in the prose and poetry collection compiled by McPherson and Miller Williams, titled *Railroad: Trains and Train People in American Culture*. A celebration, a lament, and a plea, this volume deals with the passing of the great era of passenger railcar service in the United States. To McPherson, the liberating motion integral to the railroad is important, but so is the sense of place and time that builds for his characters much of their sense of self. McPherson's characters are often confined by the conventions of locale, yet McPherson is not a regional writer in the usual sense of the word; he can bring to life stories set in Tennessee, Virginia, Boston, Chicago, or London.

Because of the tension in this body of work between the individual and the community, McPherson's people often feel alienated, lonely, and unable fully to reach or to maintain contact with acquaintances, friends, families, or lovers. Yet such isolation may lead to a character's growth to near-tragic stature. The integrity of the individual is thus asserted even while a narrator may worry over the deep inability of any person to penetrate into the heart and mind of another. Such recognitions contribute to the sympathetic portrayal even of unpromising characters. It should be noted that the reader is not given solutions in McPherson's fiction, only access to degrees of awareness of the mysteries of race, sexuality, identity, and love. Reading McPherson, a reader may be reminded of Baldwin's presentation of agonizingly complex racial and sexual problems, of Saul Bellow's portrayal of characters battling absurdity and despair, and of the struggle of characters, both in Baldwin and in Bellow, toward the ameliorating but no less mysterious experience of love.

"Gold Coast"

Type of work: Short fiction
First published: 1969, in *Hue and Cry*

McPherson's first volume of short fiction, *Hue and Cry*, is an often-grim affair, containing stories of loneliness, destitution, defeat, sexual alienation, and racial tension. A prime example of this early work is "Gold Coast," winner of *The Atlantic Monthly*'s 1968 fiction prize. The narrator of this story is an "apprentice janitor" in a hotel near Harvard Square in Boston, a hotel that has seen better days and is now populated with aging singles or couples who are almost as disengaged from the mainstream of Boston life as is the superintendent of the building, James Sullivan. Listening to Sullivan and observing the people in the apartments, the narrator, Robert, seeks to gather information for the stories and books he hopes to write. For Robert, being a janitor is in some ways a whim; in addition to gleaning experiential details from rubbish bins, he is constructing his life along romantic lines. Hence, Robert notes that, almost nightly,

> I drifted off to sleep lulled by sweet anticipation of that time when my potential would suddenly be realized and there would be capsule biographies of my life on dust jackets of many books, all proclaiming: "He knew life on many levels. From shoeshine boy, free-lance waiter, 3rd cook, janitor, he rose to. . . ."

Naïve but witty, the narrator humors Sullivan, putting up patiently with the Irishman's redundant reminiscing and opinionated ramblings on society and politics. Sullivan, however, comes to rely on Robert's company; he turns from the horrors of life in the filthy apartment he shares with his obscene, insane wife to interminable conversations with Robert.

Robert's sympathetic tolerance of Sullivan emanates from his sense of the pathetic isolation of Sullivan from human contact and from Robert's recognition for the first time of the terrors of aging. Robert is the archetypal youth coming to awareness of old age as a time of foreshortened expectations and straitened lifestyles, of possible despair and near dehumanization. The apprentice janitor can tolerate Sullivan and his new knowledge while his relationship with the rich, lovely Jean goes well, but Jean and he are soon torn apart by social forces. In fact, they play a game called "Social Forces," in which they try to determine which of them will break first under social disapproval of their interracial relationship. When the game defeats them, Robert first is comforted by and then pulls back from his friendship with the dejected Sullivan, who is especially upset over the loss of his dog.

When Robert finally leaves his briefly held janitorial position, he does so with both relief and guilt over his abandonment of Sullivan. He knows, however, that he is "still young" and not yet doomed to the utter loneliness of the old man. McPherson suggests that the young, nevertheless, will inevitably come to such bleak isolation and that even the temporary freedom of youth is sometimes maintained at the expense of sympathy and kindness. There are dangers in being free, not the least of which are the burden of knowledge, the hardening of the self, and the aching realization of basic, but often unmet, human needs. This theme of loss is picked up in the volume's title story, "Hue and Cry," which includes this interchange between two characters:

> "Between my eyes I see three people and they are all unhappy. Why?"
>
> "Perhaps it is because they are alive. Perhaps it is because they once were. Perhaps it is because they have to be. I do not know."

These voices cannot make sense of the losses to which life dooms McPherson's characters, nor does Robert. He simply moves away from the hotel to enjoy, while he can, youth and his sense of potential.

"A Solo Song: For Doc"

Type of work: Short fiction
First published: 1969, in *Hue and Cry*

The theme of old age and its defeats is further developed in McPherson's well-received "A Solo Song: For Doc," a story that displays well the author's rhythmic and precise control of narration conceived of as speech. McPherson resolves to initiate readers of all races into a facet of their culture that is quickly passing out of sight. The narrator, an aging waiter on a railroad line, tells a young listener about the good old days in the service and about their embodiment, a waiter called Doc Craft. "So do you want to know this business, youngblood?" begins the teller of the tale, and he goes on, "So you want to be a Waiter's Waiter? The Commissary gives you a book with all the rules and tells you to learn them. And you do, and think that is all there is to it." This "Waiter's Waiter" then proceeds to disillusion the "youngblood" by describing the difficult waiter's craft—the finesse, grace, care, and creativity required to make the job into an art and to make that art pay. The grace and dedication displayed by men of Doc Craft's generation is shown to be losing ground to the contemporary world of business in which men such as "Jerry Ewald, the Unexpected Inspector," lie in wait to trap heroes like Doc Craft and to remove them from the service that keeps them alive. The narrator specifies what kept Doc on the road: having power over his car and his customers, hustling tips, enjoying women without being married to them, getting drunk without having to worry about getting home. The shift from passenger to freight service on the railroad, however, begins the company's attempt to fire Doc and also initiates Doc's rise to heroic stature. Older ways of work and life yield to new technology, and, like the oldtime railroad, Doc Craft is doomed; Ewald catches Doc on a technicality about iced-tea service, and the waiter is fired.

Clearly, McPherson's thematic preoccupations and love of the railroad have coalesced in this story. He captures the complexity, richness, and hardships of the lives of African American traveling men, as well as the initiative and kinship developed by black workers. Movement, adventure, freedom, self-expression, craftsmanship, commitment, exuberance, and endurance—these qualities mark both Doc Craft and the railroad as valuable American entities. Yet the passing of Doc carries McPherson's sense of the epic loss suffered by an America that has allowed the railroad, the metaphoric counterpart of imaginative integration of all kinds, to decay.

"Why I Like Country Music"

Type of work: Short fiction
First published: 1977, in *Elbow Room*

Even while remaining faithful to McPherson's characteristic themes, *Elbow Room*, his second volume, includes stories that reach a kind of comic perfection. One example is “Why I Like Country Music.” The narrator, a southern-born black, addresses to his northern-born wife an explanation of his love of square-dance music. His wife will not believe or accept this preference, but the narrator quietly insists on it. In one sense, this insistence and the narration that justifies it may be viewed as evidence of the eternal and invincible isolation of the human heart from sympathetic understanding even by loved ones. The forces of memory and of individual development work to isolate human beings from one another. Further, the narrator’s insistence that the South Carolina traditions of his youth have given to him preferences and ideas alien to those of the New York-born tends to strengthen this theme of the coherence but separateness of the self.

Such thematic reverberations, however, do not form the main concern of this story. Rather, the narrator tells us of a comic case of childhood puppy love; he explains that he loves country music because it is permanently associated in his mind with a girl in his fourth-grade class whose name was Gweneth Larson. Born in Brooklyn and redolent of lemons, Gweneth is for the narrator an object of first love. The moments when he square-danced with her in a school May Day celebration were etched in his mind as moments of surpassing joy and love. Far from exploring alienation, the story celebrates the endurance of such affection.

McPherson’s comedy is never heavy-handed, always a matter of a light tone or a moment of incongruity. An example occurs when the narrator describes the calling of the Maypole teams to the playground for their performance:

> “Maypole teams *up*!” called Mr. Henry Lucas, our principal, from his platform by the swings. Beside him stood the white Superintendent of Schools (who said later of the square dance, it was reported to all the classes, “Lord, y’all square dance so *good* it makes me plumb *ashamed* us white folks ain’t takin’ better care of our art stuff”).

“A Loaf of Bread”

Type of work: Short fiction
First published: 1977, in *Elbow Room*

A more somber story in *Elbow Room*, “A Loaf of Bread,” addresses important issues associated with racism and assimilation by depicting the isolation of the African American middle class. As in many of his other stories, McPherson expresses hope for the evolution of a model of American identity toward which all Americans can proudly gravitate. In “A Loaf of Bread,” he explores the difference between exploitation and participation of African Americans in American society.

Store owner Harold Green charges higher prices for goods in his store in an African American neighborhood than in the stores he owns in white neighborhoods. Consequently, as an act of restitution for exploiting the black community, Green decides that the best solution is to open his store and give away his merchandise free of charge to members of the exploited black community. The ensuing frenzy leaves Green’s store in complete disarray, totally depleted of merchandise.

Nelson Reed, the leader of the community protest against Green, returns to the store later in the day to pay Green one dollar for the loaf of bread that his wife had taken from the store that morning. Reed is evidently seeking the status of a participating consumer versus an exploited one. Characteristic of McPherson's writing, characters in difficult situations struggle for some measure of success. However, Reed's attempt to receive equitable treatment as an American citizen is nullified by Green's response.

Similar to other fiction written by McPherson, the overall plot of "A Loaf of Bread" appears to argue for an American citizenship that eradicates racial boundaries and produces a coherent, color-blind American society. However, McPherson believes that racial exclusion continues to exist like an undeviated line from decades past and that acts of racial prejudice continue to demonstrate the pervasiveness of racial chauvinism. Furthermore, pointing fingers and using the "we/they" phrase in reference to other races only proliferate prejudice and isolation.

In "A Loaf of Bread," the hope for the black community to achieve unified American citizenship seems to be superseded by the lure of participating as a consumer in the marketplace. McPherson suggests that the African American middle class has abandoned the process of discarding some of the traditions of their fathers and embracing a sense of commonality with the white world. Consequently, the African American middle class becomes further isolated from the mainstream of American society. It is notable that in both his comedy "Why I Like Country Music" and his very somber "A Loaf of Bread," McPherson remains firmly focused on the human personality, which is for him the incentive for narration and the core of his art.

Suggested Readings

Beavers, Herman. *Wrestling Angels into Song: The Fictions of Ernest J. Gaines and James Alan McPherson*. Philadelphia: University of Pennsylvania Press, 1995.

Cox, Joseph T. "James Alan McPherson." In *Contemporary Fiction Writers of the South*, edited by Joseph M. Flora and Robert Bain. Westport, Conn.: Greenwood Press, 1993.

Laughlin, Rosemary M. "Attention, American Folklore: Doc Craft Comes Marching In." *Studies in American Fiction* 1 (1973): 221-227.

McPherson, James Alan. "Interview with James Alan McPherson." Interview by Bob Shacochis. *Iowa Journal of Literary Studies* 4 (1983): 6-33.

Reid, Calvin. "James Alan McPherson: A Theater of Memory." *Publishers Weekly* 244 (December 15, 1997): 36-37.

Wallace, Jon. *The Politics of Style: Language as Theme in the Fiction of Berger, McGuane, and McPherson*. Durango, Colo.: Hollowbrook, 1992.

_______. "The Story Behind the Story in James Alan McPherson's *Elbow Room*." *Studies in Short Fiction* 25 (Fall, 1988): 447-452.

Contributors: Alvin K. Benson, Cheryl Herr, and Edward Huffstetler

Haki R. Madhubuti
(Don L. Lee)

Born: Little Rock, Arkansas; February 23, 1942

African American

Madhubuti exhibits a total dedication to black pride, unity, power, and, as he puts it, "identity, purpose and direction" focused on black "nationbuilding."

Principal works

POETRY: *Think Black*, 1967 (revised 1968 and 1969); *Black Pride*, 1968; *Don't Cry, Scream*, 1969; *We Walk the Way of the New World*, 1970; *Directionscore: Selected and New Poems*, 1971; *Book of Life*, 1973; *Killing Memory, Seeking Ancestors*, 1987; *GroundWork: New and Selected Poems of Don L. Lee/Haki R. Madhubuti from 1966-1996*, 1996; *Heartlove: Wedding and Love Poems*, 1998; *Run Toward Fear: New Poems and a Poet's Handbook*, 2002

NONFICTION: *Dynamite Voices: Black Poets of the 1960's*, 1971; *From Plan to Planet, Life Studies: The Need for Afrikan Minds and Institutions*, 1973; *Enemies: The Clash of Races*, 1978; *Black Men: Obsolete, Single, Dangerous?*, 1990; *Claiming Earth: Race, Rage, Rape, Redemption—Blacks Seeking a Culture of Enlightened Empowerment*, 1994; *Tough Notes: A Healing Call for Creating Exceptional Black Men—Affirmations, Meditations, Readings, and Strategies*, 2002

EDITED TEXTS: *To Gwen with Love: An Anthology Dedicated to Gwendolyn Brooks*, 1971 (with Francis Ward and Patricia L. Brown); *Say That the River Turns: The Impact of Gwendolyn Brooks*, 1987; *Confusion by Any Other Name: Essays Exploring the Negative Impact of "The Blackman's Guide to Understanding the Blackwoman,"* 1990; *Why L.A. Happened: Implications of the '92 Los Angeles Rebellion*, 1993; *Black Books Bulletin: The Challenge of the Twenty-first Century*, 1995; *Million Man March, Day of Absence: A Commemorative Anthology—Speeches, Commentary, Photography, Poetry, Illustrations, Documents*, 1996 (with Maulana Karenga); *Releasing the Spirit: A Collection of Literary Works from "Gallery Thirty-Seven,"* 1998 (with Gwendolyn Mitchell); *Describe the Moment: A Collection of Literary Works from "Gallery Thirty-Seven,"* 2000 (with Mitchell)

MISCELLANEOUS: *Earthquakes and Sunrise Missions: Poetry and Essays of Black Renewal, 1973-1983*, 1984

Haki R. Madhubuti (HAH-kee mah-dew-BEW-tee)—who changed his name from Don Luther Lee to his Swahili name in 1973—was born in Little Rock, Arkansas, and moved to Chicago with his parents Jimmy and Maxine Lee midway through his childhood. After graduating from high school, Madhubuti continued his education at Wilson Junior College, Roosevelt University, and the University of Illinois at Chicago Circle. His formal education was tempered, however, by a wide range of jobs that increased his rapport with varied classes and individuals within the black community. After serving in the United States Army from 1960 to 1963, Madhubuti returned to Chicago to begin an apprenticeship as curator of the DuSable Museum of African History, which he continued until 1967. Meanwhile, he worked as a stock department clerk for Montgomery Ward (1963-1964), a post office clerk (1964-1965), and a junior executive for Spiegel's (1965-1966).

By the end of 1967, Madhubuti's reputation as a poet and as a spokesman for the new black poetry of the 1960's had grown sufficiently to enable him to support himself through publishing and teaching alone. He was writer-in-residence at Cornell University from 1968 to 1969. Similar positions followed at Northeastern Illinois State College (1969-1970) and the University of Illinois at Chicago Circle (1969-1971), where he combined poet-in-residencies with teaching black literature. From 1970 to 1975, Madhubuti taught at Howard University, except for a year at Morgan State College where he was writer-in-residence from 1972 to 1973.

The extensive popular reception of his poetry and the increasing frequency of his social essays made him a favorite (if controversial) reader and lecturer with black college students across the country. His influence and popularity also enabled him to found, in Chicago, the Institute of Positive Education in 1971, which became the publisher of *Black Books Bulletin*, edited by Madhubuti, and for which he served as director from 1971 to 1991. He also became the publisher and editor of Third World Press, one of the largest and most successful independent African American book publishers. In conjunction with his publishing roles, Madhubuti also served as a professor of English and director of the Gwendolyn Brooks Center for Black Literature and Creative Writing at Chicago State University, and he assumed important executive positions with a number of Pan-African organizations such as the Congress of African People.

Think Black

Type of work: Poetry
First published: 1967

Several poems in Madhubuti's first book, *Think Black*, are testimonial as well as vengeful; it is clear in these poems that Madhubuti had been "liberating" himself for several years and only then was testifying to that personal struggle through accommodation. He was to say later, in "Black Sketches" (*Don't Cry, Scream*), that he "became black" in 1963 and "everyone thought it unusual;/ even me."

Both the accommodationist period and the reactive phase are seen in *Think*

Black, but the point of view is nearly always that of a reaction against accommodation. In "Understanding But Not Forgetting," Madhubuti speaks of his family life and his "early escape/ period, trying to be white." Among his images are those of an intellectual accommodationist who "still ain't hip," an uneducated grandmother "with wisdom that most philosophers would/ envy," misery-filled weekends with "no family/ but money," a twenty-two-year-old sister with "five children," a mother involved in prostitution but "providing for her family," and a cheating white newspaper distributor who kept "telling/ me what a good boy I was." Reexamining his childhood and adolescence in this poem, Madhubuti concludes: "About positive images as a child—NONE," and further that "About negative images as a child—all black." In his attempt to understand his social conditioning and view it in the larger context of American culture, he is forced to conclude that education, democracy, religion, and even the "BLACK MIDDLE CLASS" (to which he has aspired) have failed him because of "the American System." It is, in fact, those very outcasts of the black community itself—the grandmother and the prostitute-mother, who "read Richard Wright and Chester Himes/ . . ./ [bad books," that offer examples of survival against overwhelming oppression.

Black Pride

Type of work: Poetry
First published: 1968

Madhubuti had not, however, accomplished much more at that time than rejection of the value system that had created his anger and despair: The awareness of *how* to "think black" is vague. The last poem in the book, "Awareness," is a chant of only three words: "BLACK PEOPLE THINK." In the variations of syntactical arrangement of these words, however, one is left with the unmistakable impression that he will struggle to learn from those outcasts of mainstream society just what it means to "THINK BLACK." These lessons are the heart of his second book, *Black Pride*, which is still reactive but nevertheless substantial in its discovery of identity. While many of these poems remain confessional, there is an increase in the clarity of Madhubuti's sociopolitical development. In the brief lead poem, "The New Integrationist," he announces his intention to join "negroes/ with/ black/ people." The one-word lines of the poem force the reader to contemplate not only the irony in his use of "integration" but also the implications inherent in the labels "negro" and "black." It is an appropriate keynote for the fulfillment of that vague awareness with which his first book ended.

Perhaps the growth in self-identity that characterizes *Black Pride* begins, paradoxically, most clearly in "The Self-Hatred of Don L. Lee." The confessional stance of the poet first acknowledges a love of "my color" because it allowed him to move upward in the accommodationist period; it "opened sMALL/ doors of/ tokenism." After "struggling" through a reading list of the forerunners of cultural nationalism, Madhubuti then describes a breakthrough from "my blindness" to "pitchblack// awareness." His "all/ black// inner/ self" is now his strength, the basis for his self-identity, and he rejects with "vehement/ hatred" his "light/ brown/ outer" self, that appearance which he had previously exploited by accepting the benefits of tokenism. While Madhubuti had escaped accommodation by this time, he had not yet ceased to react to it; instead of having skin too dark, he had skin too light. He was, as black oral tradition puts it, "color-struck." He had, however, moved much deeper into the problem of establishing an identity based on dignity rather than denigration.

The growth of identity and black pride still remains, then, a function of what is not blackness instead of what is, or will become, Madhubuti's new Black Nation. In several poems such as "The Primitive," Madhubuti describes the loss of black values under American slavery and the subsequent efforts of blacks to imitate their oppressors who "raped our minds" with mainstream images from "T.V. . . ./ Reader's Digest// tarzan & jungle jim," who offered "used cars & used homes/ reefers & napalm/ european history & promises" and who fostered "alien concepts/ of whi-teness." His message here is blunt: "this weapon called/ civilization// [acts] to drive us mad/ (like them)." For all of his vindictive bitterness, however, Madhubuti addresses himself to the black community more than he does to white America—self-reliance for self-preservation emerges as the crucial issue. As he suggests in the final poem "No More Marching Now," nonviolent protest and civil rights legislation have been undermined by white values; thus, "public/ housing" has become a euphemism for "concentration camps." His charge is typically blunt: "you better wake up// before it's too late."

Haki R. Madhubuti (Courtesy, St. Norbert College)

Although the first two volumes of Madhubuti's poems exist in the tension between accommodation and reaction, they do show growth in the use of language as well as in identity and pride. His work, at times, suffers from clichéd rhetoric and easy catchphrases common to exhortation, but it also possesses a genuine delight in the playfulness of language even while it struggles forward in the midst of serious sociopolitical polemic. In his division of "white," for example, where the one-syllable word is frequently cut into the two-syllable "whi-te" or the second syllable is dropped completely to the next line, Madhubuti demonstrates more than typographical scoring for the sound of his poem, for he displays the fragmentation between ideals and the implementation of those ideals in American culture. In contrast, "Black man" appears frequently as one word, "blackman," sometimes capitalized and sometimes not—to emphasize the gradual dissolution of the individual's ego, to suggest the necessity for unity in the community for which he strives. Capitalization, in a similar way, sometimes connotes pride in his use of "BLACK." At other times, he uses derogatory puns, such as when "U.S." becomes "u ass." His models are street language, urban speech patterns, jazz improvisation, the narrative form of the toast, and the general inventiveness of an oral tradition that belongs wholly to black culture.

Don't Cry, Scream

TYPE OF WORK: Poetry
FIRST PUBLISHED: 1969

These early poems continue to develop both thematically and technically in Madhubuti's next two books, *Don't Cry, Scream* and *We Walk the Way of the New World*, in which he began to outline his revolutionary program. Critic Marlene Mosher suggests that these works are consciously much less antiwhite and much more problack in their sociopolitical commitment. Madhubuti's artistic commitment fused completely with his politics; as he says in the preface to *Don't Cry, Scream*, "there is *no* neutral blackart." Black poetry is seen as "culture building" rather than as a tool to criticize either white society or blacks who seek assimilation. In this programmatic work, the hate, bitterness, and invective of the earlier two books give way to music, humor, and a gentler insistence on change. The poems are more consciously crafted than previously, but they do not compromise their essentially urgent political fervor.

In perhaps the most widely anthologized poem by Madhubuti, "But He Was Cool, or: he even stopped for green lights," he humorously undermines the stance of black radicals who are far more concerned with the appearance of being a revolutionary than with a real commitment to working for change in the black community. His satire here is more implicit than explicit, for the reader views the "supercool/ ultrablack" radical in "a double-natural" hairstyle and "dashikis [that] were tailor made." His imported beads are "triple-hip," and he introduces himself "in swahili" while saying "good-by in yoruba." Madhubuti then becomes more explicit in his satire by dividing and modifying "intelligent" to read "ill tel li gent," but he quickly moves back to implication by a rapidly delivered "bop" hyperbole that describes the radical as "cool cool ultracool . . ./ cool so cool cold cool/ . . . him was air conditioned cool" and concludes that he was "so cool him nick-named refrigerator." The dissonance of the last word with the "ice box cool" earlier in the delivery clashes not only in sound but also in economic and political connotation. This radical is so busy acting the role of a revolutionary that he has been seduced by the very goals of Western culture that Madhubuti is rejecting: money, power, and sex. By his superficial use of gestures, the "radical" has taken himself even further away from an awareness of the real needs in the black community. In the aftermath of riots in "detroit, newark, [and] chicago," the would-be revolutionary must still be informed that "to be black/ is/ to be/ very-hot." Despite the humor, music, and wordplay in one of Madhubuti's most consciously and carefully "aesthetic" poems, the message is still primarily political. Although the poem does react to the shallowness of the radical, it is worth noting that the poem is no longer essentially reactive in its tone; by the very act of informing the radical of his ignorance in the closure of the poem, the implication is established that even this caricature has the possibility of redemption in Madhubuti's version of Black Nationalism.

Throughout *Don't Cry, Scream*, Madhubuti begins to embrace a wider range of sensibilities in the black community while continuing to denounce those who would betray the needs of black people. In "Black Sketches," he describes Republican Senator Ed Brooke from Massachusetts (then a self-proclaimed liberal advocate of civil rights) as "slashing/ his wrist/ because somebody/ called him/ black," and portrays the conservative (relative to Madhubuti) Roy Wilkins as the token figure on the television show, "the mod squad." He is relentless in his attack on black leaders who work within mainstream politics. In another poem, however, "Blackrunners/ blackmen or run into blackness," Madhubuti celebrates the Olympic medal winners Tommie Smith and John Carlos for their Black Power salutes in 1968 during the awards ceremony. One could hardly describe their gesture as revolutionary, but Madhubuti accepts and praises their symbolic act as a sign of solidarity with his own sense of revolutionary change. In other poems, he is equally open to the role of black women, intellectuals, and Vietnam veterans. By the final poem of the volume, he is even willing to concede that the "negroes" whom he has denounced in earlier work may also be receptive to his political message. In "A Message All Blackpeople Can Dig (& a few negroes too)," Madhubuti announces that "the realpeople" must "move together/ hands on weapons & families" in order to bring new meanings "to// the blackness,/ to US." While not exactly greeting antagonists with open arms (the parenthetical shift to the lower case in the title is quite intentional), his emphasis has changed from the coarse invective found in *Think Black* to a moral, political force that proceeds in "a righteous direction." Not even whites are specifically attacked here; the enemy is now perceived as "the whi-timind," attitudes and actions from "unpeople" who perpetuate racism and oppression. The message, in short, is now much closer to black humanism than it ever has been before: "blackpeople/ are moving, moving to return this earth into the hands of/ human beings."

We Walk the Way of the New World

Type of work: Poetry
First published: 1970

The seeds for a revolutionary humanism planted at the close of *Don't Cry, Scream* blossom in *We Walk the Way of the New World*. The flowers are armed to be sure, but in signaling this change, the author's introduction, "Louder but Softer," proclaims that the "cultural nihilism" of the 1960's must give way to the "New World of black consciousness" in which education and self-definition (in the context of the community) will create not noisy, pseudorevolutionaries but self-confident leaders who pursue "real" skills—"doctors, lawyers, teachers, historians, writers"—for ensuring the survival and development of African American culture. Madhubuti's scope and purpose in this book are no less committed than they had been before, but they are far more embracing, compassionate, and visionary. His concern is the establishment of "an ongoing process aimed at an ultimate definition of our being." The tone of urgency ("We're talking about our children, a survival of a people") remains constant and clear, but its directions have moved completely "from negative to positive." While the ideas are not new in *We Walk the Way of the New World*, they do form Madhubuti's most consciously articulated and poetically designed program: Of the three sections that shape the book, "Black Woman Poems," "African Poems," and "New World Poems," he says, "Each part is a part of the other: Blackwoman is African and Africa is Blackwoman and they both represent the *New World*." What is new in the fourth volume, then, is the degree of structural unity and, to a certain extent, a greater clarity in describing the specific meaning of *Nguzo Saba*, a black value system: "design yr own neighborhoods/ . . . teach yr own children/ . . . but/ build yr own loop// feed yr own people// [and] protect yr own communities."

The unifying metaphor for the book is the pilgrimage into the New World. Arming the heroic, everyman figure "blackman" (unnamed because he is potentially any black man in the service of community rather than in pursuit of individual, egotistical goals) with a knowledge of the contrasts between black women who are positive role models (with their love tied inextricably to black consciousness) and black women who aspire to imitate white middle-class, suburban women, Madhubuti then distinguishes the values of precolonial Africa from those that have become "contaminated" by Western industrialization. Here his emphasis is on rural communalism, loving family life, and conserving natural resources. By the final section, "blackman" has ceased to function as a depersonalized hero and is embodied in the individuality (having derived such from the community) of real black men, women, and children. This section largely recapitulates the themes and messages of earlier work, but it does so in an affirmative tone of self-asserted action within *kawaida*, African reason and tradition. In the long apocalyptic poem "For Black People," Madhubuti dramatically represents a movement of the entire race from a capitalistic state of self-defeating inactivity to a socialistic economy where mutual love and respect result in an ecologically sound, peacefully shared world of all races (although the "few whi-te communities/ . . . were closely watched"). The movement of the poem, symphonic in its structure, is, in fact, the culmination of Madhubuti's sociopolitical growth and artistic vision to this point.

Book of Life

Type of work: Poetry
First published: 1973

With *Book of Life*, Madhubuti introduces little new thought, but his ideas are expressed in a much more reserved political tone and poetic structure. His role is that of the visionary prophet, the wise sage offering advice to the young children who must inevitably carry on the struggle to build the New World which he has described. Indeed, the book's cover shows a photograph of his own son in the center of a star, and the volume is dedicated to him "and his sons, and their sons." Throughout the book, photographs of Madhubuti sitting or fishing with his son testify to his affirmation of the future. His introduction still affirms "black world unity" and looks to *kawaida* as the source of this new African frame of reference, but only six new poems speak explicitly to the political dimensions of his vision. The second section, captioned after the title of the book, is composed of ninety-two meditations that echo Laozi's *Dao De Jing* (c. third century B.C.E.). The language is simple but profound; the tone is quiet but urgent; the intended audience seems to be his son, but the community overhears him; the poetics are nearly devoid of device from any cultural context, but the force of the didacticism is sincere and genuine. Madhubuti, thinking of black poets who talk "about going to the Bahamas to write the next book," denounces those "poets [who] have become the traitors." It may well be that his sense of betrayal by black artists whom he had expected to assist him in his struggle for the New World and his own growing quietism combined to bring an end to his poetry—at least since the 1973 publication of this work. He seems to have followed his own proverb in *Book of Life*: "best teachers/ seldom teach/ they be and do."

Madhubuti demonstrated an astonishingly rapid growth in his poetry and thought—in only six years. With that sort of energy and commitment, it is not surprising that he should do what he has asked of others, shunning the success of the "traitors": to be and do whatever is necessary for the building of the New World. For Madhubuti, that necessity has meant a turning away from publishing poetry and a turning toward the education of the future generation. One might quite easily dismiss Madhubuti as a dreamer or a madman, but then one would need to recall such visionaries as William Blake, who was dismissed too much and too soon.

Earthquakes and Sunrise Missions *and* Killing Memory, Seeking Ancestors

Type of work: Poetry
First published: 1984, 1987

In the 1980's, the growth in Madhubuti's poetry was clearly evident. A sizable portion of his later poems teach through the impact of artful language, rather than sounding merely teacherly. Madhubuti's two poetry collections of the 1980's, *Earthquakes and Sunrise Missions* (which also includes prose essays) and *Killing Memory, Seeking Ancestors*, represent some of his strongest writing as he trusts that his keen observation will yield a bold enough political statement.

For example, in "The Shape of Things to Come," written about the earthquake in Naples, Italy, he observes: "quicker than one can pronounce free enterprise/ like well-oiled rumors or elastic lawyers smelling money/ plastic coffins appear and are sold/ at dusk behind the vatican on the white market./ in Italy in the christian month of eighty/ in the bottom of unimaginable catastrophe/ the profit motive endures as children replenish the earth/ in wretched abundance."

Poems from these volumes, such as "Abortion," "Winterman," "The Changing Seasons of Life," "White on Black Crime," and "Killing Memory" all reflect his increased technical control and subtle political commentary. Poems collected here also show that, ideologically, Madhubuti no longer continues to fight all the old battles. Christianity gets a break now, as do some white individuals. He has not, however, wavered in his fundamental commitment to black liberation and in his belief that cultural awareness can ignite and help sustain progressive political struggle. The love in him and for his mission has not diminished. If anything it has grown.

Heartlove

Type of work: Poetry
First published: 1998

Ten years after the publication of his previous volume of poetry, Madhubuti produced *Heartlove: Wedding and Love Poems*, an elegant collection drawn solely from Madhubuti's poetry and prose and designed to capture and celebrate the essence of love in marriage, family meditations, caring, commitment, and friendships. Acting as a poetic script for the cast of a wedding—minister, bride and groom, the maid of honor, and the best man—Madhubuti counsels, "rise with the wisdom of grandmothers, rise understanding that creation is on-going, immensely appealing and acceptable to fools and geniuses, and those of us in between."

Each poem offers words of encouragement and advice to new couples or words of tribute to the lives that have influenced Madhubuti's. From "Wedding Poems" to "Quality of Love" to "Extended Families," *Heartlove* addresses crucial questions about building partnerships and the struggle to preserve community.

Suggested Readings

Hooper, Lita. *Art of Work: The Art and Life of Haki R. Madhubuti*. Chicago: Third World Press, 2007.

Jennings, Regina. *Malcolm X and the Poetics of Haki Madhubuti*. Jefferson, N.C.: McFarland, 2006.

Madhubuti, Haki R. "Hard Words and Clear Songs: The Writing of Black Poetry." In *Tapping Potential: English Language Arts for the Black Learner*, edited by Charlotte K. Brooks et al. Urbana, Ill.: Black Caucus of the National Council of Teachers of English, 1985.

_______. "Interview with Haki Madhubuti." In *Heroism in the New Black Poetry: Introductions and Interviews*, edited by D. H. Melhem. Lexington: University Press of Kentucky, 1990.

Mosher, Marlene. *New Directions from Don L. Lee*. Hicksville, N.Y.: Exposition Press, 1975.

Palmer, R. Roderick. "The Poetry of Three Revolutionists: Don L. Lee, Sonia Sanchez, and Nikki Giovanni." In *Modern Black Poets: A Collection of Critical Essays*, edited by Donald B. Gibson. Englewood Cliffs, N.J.: Prentice-Hall, 1973.

Randall, Dudley. "Broadside Press: A Personal Chronicle." In *The Black Seventies*, edited by Floyd B. Barbour. Boston: Porter Sargent, 1970.

Thompson, Julius E. "The Public Response to Haki R. Madhubuti, 1968-1988." *The Literary Griot: International Journal of Black Expressive Cultural Studies* 4, nos. 1/2 (Spring/Summer, 1992): 16-37.

Contributors: Sarah Hilbert and Michael Loudon

Clarence Major

BORN: Atlanta, Georgia; December 31, 1936

AFRICAN AMERICAN

The author of novels, short fiction, poetry, and critical studies, Major writes in a range of styles, from the conventional to the experimental. All his work exhibits lyricism and a fascination with language.

PRINCIPAL WORKS

LONG FICTION: *All-Night Visitors*, 1969; *NO*, 1973; *Reflex and Bone Structure*, 1975; *Emergency Exit*, 1979; *My Amputations*, 1986; *Such Was the Season*, 1987; *Painted Turtle: Woman with Guitar*, 1988; *Dirty Bird Blues*, 1996; *One Flesh*, 2003

POETRY: *The Fires That Burn in Heaven*, 1954; *Love Poems of a Black Man*, 1965; *Human Juices*, 1966; *Swallow the Lake*, 1970; *Private Line*, 1971; *Symptoms and Madness*, 1971; *The Cotton Club*, 1972; *The Syncopated Cakewalk*, 1974; *Inside Diameter: The France Poems*, 1985; *Surfaces and Masks: A Poem*, 1988; *Some Observations of a Stranger at Zuni in the Latter Part of the Century*, 1989; *Parking Lots: A Poem*, 1992; *Configurations: New and Selected Poems, 1958-1998*, 1998; *Waiting for Sweet Betty*, 2002

SHORT FICTION: *Fun and Games*, 1990

NONFICTION: *Dictionary of Afro-American Slang*, 1970 (also known as *Juba to Jive: A Dictionary of African-American Slang*, 1994); *The Dark and Feeling: Black American Writers and Their Work*, 1974; *Necessary Distance: Essays and Criticism*, 2001; *Come by Here: My Mother's Life*, 2002; *Conversations with Clarence Major*, 2002 (Nancy Bunge, editor)

EDITED TEXTS: *Writers Workshop Anthology*, 1967; *Man Is Like a Child*, 1968; *The New Black Poetry*, 1969; *Calling the Wind: Twentieth-Century African-American Short Stories*, 1993; *The Garden Thrives: Twentieth-Century African-American Poetry*, 1996

Clarence Major was born in Atlanta, Georgia, grew up on the South Side of Chicago, and served in the U.S. Air Force from 1955 to 1957. He studied at the Chicago Art Institute, graduated from the State University of New York at Albany, and earned a Ph.D. from the Union of Experimenting Colleges and Universities. Major taught at a number of universities, both in the United States and abroad, and after 1989 at the University of California at Davis. In addition to his fiction and poetry, Major has exhibited and published paintings and photographs. He has also been an editor and columnist and has lectured widely. He has been married twice and has lived in various parts of the United States and for extended periods in France and Italy.

Critic Jerome Klinkowitz has written that the central achievement of Major's career

> has been to show just how concretely we live within the imagination—how our lives are shaped by language and how by a simple act of self-awareness we can seize control of the world and reshape it to our liking and benefit.

"An Area in the Cerebral Hemisphere"

Type of work: Short fiction
First published: 1975, in *Statements*

This story, which first appeared in the literary magazine *Statements*, is the best example of Major's postmodernist style, fragmentary and barely coherent but with a powerful edge to it. The story centers on a young African American woman, a visit by a friend, and the young woman's thoughts about her father and her own life. These events are parceled out in a style that dispels meaning: "The friend lit a cigarette and sat on the sounds of her own voice. Motion. And made a blowing sound," Major writes early in this story, and, a little later on, "And mother's couch was eaten by what might easily have been taxicabs with hooks on them. Anything can happen. (In any case, swift traffic was known to move through her living room.)" This metaphor of motion runs through the story, but it hardly ties together the various fragmented incidents and scraps of dialogue. What readers are left with is Major's brilliant and poetic use of language.

Fun and Games

Type of work: Short fiction
First published: 1990

Clarence Major's short-story collection *Fun and Games* was nominated for the *Los Angeles Times* Book Critics Award in 1990. While the volume represents Major's short fiction through the 1980's, it is a good barometer of his continuing fictional interests and forms. The sixteen stories in the volume are divided into five parts: Section 1 contains three stories (including the realistic "My Mother and Mitch" and "Ten Pecan Pies"), section 2 also has three shorter and more surreal stories, section 3 contains six stories, section 4 has three, and section 5 comprises "Mobile Axis: A Triptych," three interconnected short fictions. While Major is capable of one form of social realism (as in "Letters"), he more regularly leans toward a staccato, fragmentary prose fiction in which the links are missing among characters and incidents ("The Horror" and the title story).

"The Exchange," for example, is a fairly realistic and even comic story about a faculty exchange gone horribly wrong. When the narrator and his wife arrive on the opposite coast to begin the yearlong exchange, they find a dilapidated house. Worse, when they return to their own home at the end of the year, their exchangees have turned the house into a replica of their own—down to the moldy contents of the refrigerator. Likewise, the collection's title story is a first-person narration about a man's three or four girlfriends, who keep leaving him and returning. The story is comic and at the same an oblique commentary on transience and commitment in contemporary society.

More common in *Fun and Games*, however, are the themes found in "Mother Visiting," a short, three-page story that violates most of the conventions of fictional verisimilitude. While the story touches upon a number of contemporary issues (notably sex and violence), its postmodernist style emphasizes the play of language over sense. Likewise in the short story "Virginia," the dazzling use of language and image has replaced the demands of plot.

"My Mother and Mitch"

Type of work: Short fiction
First published: 1990, in *Fun and Games*

This story won the Pushcart Prize for fiction in 1989 and leads off the *Fun and Games* collection. In some ways it does not resemble Major's other short fiction, being a leaner and less experimental coming-of-age story. "My Mother and Mitch" centers on the date that Tommy Anderson's mother had with Mitch Kibbs when Tommy was a teenager in Chicago in 1951. Mitch had dialed a wrong number and then kept calling to talk with Tommy's mother, even after he discovered that she was black. The climax of the story comes when Mitch asks her to meet him in a restaurant, and Tommy watches the white man and his mother talking at the counter of a predominantly black eatery. The story is barely about interracial dating, for the couple never meet again after that night. What is more important is what the young Tommy discovers about his single mother: "I learned for the first time that she did not always know what she was doing. It struck me that she was as helpless as I sometimes felt." That knowledge makes the adolescent Tommy feel closer to his mother: "there she was, just finding her way, step by step, like me. It was something wonderful anyway." The story may remind readers of Sherwood Anderson's "Death in the Woods," for Tommy is retelling the tale many years later and still trying to get it right and discover its meaning through the retelling. In its lean re-creation of the spare events here, the story may also remind readers of Raymond Carver and other minimalist short-story writers of the late twentieth century, who forsake long exposition and elaborate descriptions for the psychological revelations of a single voice.

"Ten Pecan Pies"

Type of work: Short fiction
First published: 1990, in *Fun and Games*

"Ten Pecan Pies" uses still another fictional style, here a third-person, more traditional narration. The story was first published in *Seattle Review*, is reprinted in the first section of *Fun and Games*, and may remind readers of William Faulkner or Truman Capote in its rural southern setting and voices. "Ten Pecan Pies" concerns one Christmas in the Flower household, when the patriarch Grady Flower has kept two bags of pecans to himself and will not let his wife make her annual Christmas pies. The other preparations for Christmas—finding and decorating a tree, for example—go on, but Grady hoards the pecans in his room until Christmas Eve, when Thursday finally shames her husband and then, when he gives in, "suddenly kisse[s] the side of his face. The first time in years." The story has other tensions—the drunken son Slick John killing the rabbits in front of his niece, Gal, for example—but the overwhelming feeling of the story is lyrical and nostalgic. Thursday douses the fire in the stove, the story concludes, "Yet the warmth stayed."

"Scat"

Type of work: Short fiction
First published: 1993, in *Calling the Wind*

"Scat" was the only story of his own that Clarence Major selected for *Calling the Wind*, the collection of twentieth century African American fiction he published in 1993, so readers can assume he thinks the story is important, but it is also representative of a certain comic-surreal style Major mastered. The story covers a nightmare cab ride the narrator and his white girlfriend take into New York City with a cabdriver who subjects them to a monologue about the dangers of Manhattan, where the couple want to go, and the relative safety of Brooklyn, where the cabdriver lives. In his frustration at the cabdriver's tales of the "superstitious practices" and "voodoo rites" in Manhattan, the narrator counters with his own stories of body snatching in Brooklyn. Readers conclude the story still not knowing who is crazier: the cabdriver, who talks knowingly of the "evil art of capnomancy," or the narrator, who speaks of "the Plot, I mean the Sacrifice" and seems equally deranged. Perhaps, if one pursues the definition of the tale's title, the story is the fictional equivalent of jazz singing with nonsense syllables, each voice trying to outdo the other.

Suggested Readings

Bell, Bernard W. "Introduction: Clarence Major's Double Consciousness as a Black Postmodernist Artist." *African American Review* 28 (Spring, 1994): 5-10.

_______, ed. *Clarence Major and His Art: Portraits of an African American Postmodernist*. Chapel Hill: University of North Carolina Press, 2001.

Bolling, Doug. "A Reading of Clarence Major's Short Fiction." *Black American Literature Forum* 13 (1979): 51-56.

Klinkowitz, Jerome. "Clarence Major's Innovative Fiction." *African American Review* 28 (Spring, 1994): 57-63.

O'Brien, John. "Clarence Major." In *Interviews with Black Writers*. New York: Liveright, 1973.

Selzer, Linda Furgerson. "Reading the Painterly Text: Clarence Major's 'The Slave Trade: View from the Middle Passage.'" *African American Review* 33 (Summer, 1999): 209-229.

Weixlmann, Joe. "Clarence Major: A Checklist of Criticism." *Obsidian* 4, no. 2 (1978): 101-113.

Contributor: David Peck

Bernard Malamud

Born: Brooklyn, New York; April 26, 1914
Died: New York, New York; March 18, 1986

Jewish

Malamud's works present the outsider, usually a Jew, who epitomizes the individual who must make moral choices.

Principal works

LONG FICTION: *The Natural*, 1952; *The Assistant*, 1957; *A New Life*, 1961; *The Fixer*, 1966; *The Tenants*, 1971; *Dubin's Lives*, 1979; *God's Grace*, 1982; *The People*, 1989

SHORT FICTION: *The Magic Barrel*, 1958; *Idiots First*, 1963; *Pictures of Fidelman: An Exhibition*, 1969; *Rembrandt's Hat*, 1973; *The Stories of Bernard Malamud*, 1983; *The People, and Uncollected Stories*, 1989; *The Complete Stories*, 1997 (Robert Giroux, editor)

NONFICTION: *Talking Horse: Bernard Malamud on Life and Work*, 1996 (Alan Cheuse and Nicholas Delbanco, editors)

Bernard Malamud (MAL-uh-mewd) spent his youth in a setting much like that in *The Assistant*. His father was the owner of a small, struggling grocery store. His mother died when he was an adolescent. As a youth he had the freedom to wander around Brooklyn becoming intimately acquainted with the neighborhood. It was not a Jewish neighborhood, but Malamud came to understand the Jewish experience through his hardworking parents, immigrants from Russia.

Malamud began writing stories in high school, and his writing career reflects the discipline and determination of many of his characters. After graduating from Erasmus Hall High School, he earned a bachelor's degree from City College of New York. He then attended Columbia University and earned the master's degree that enabled him to teach. He taught immigrants in evening school in Brooklyn, then in Harlem, for eight years, while writing short stories, before getting a job at Oregon State College in Cascadia, Oregon. There he wrote four novels and a collection of short stories. Malamud received the National Book Award for the short-story collection, *The Magic Barrel*, in 1959. He also received the Pulitzer Prize in fiction and the National Book Award for *The Fixer* in 1967. He accepted a position at Bennington College in Vermont in 1961, where he spent the rest of his teaching career, except for two years as a visiting lecturer at Harvard.

Malamud's work has an allegorical quality like that of Nathaniel Hawthorne. His stories also reflect the Eastern European storytelling tradition. In this he is like such Yiddish writers as Sholom Aleichem and Isaac Leib Peretz. When Malamud describes, for example, a luckless character (called, in Jewish culture, a *schlemiel*) living in Brooklyn in the twentieth century, that person seems quite like someone living in the Jewish section of a Polish village. Malamud also captures in his works the sense of irony that pervades the folk stories of a people who recognize themselves as the chosen people and as the outcasts of society.

Bernard Malamud (© Jerry Bauer)

Malamud saw this paradoxical position as being the plight of all humanity, and he found in the Jew the ideal metaphor for the struggling human being. Acceptance of Jewish identity becomes, for his characters, acceptance of the human condition. Fusing this theme with a style that utilizes irony and parable, realism and symbolism, he presents the flourishing of the human spirit in an everyday reality of pressure and pain.

The Natural

TYPE OF WORK: Novel
FIRST PUBLISHED: 1952

The Natural is a modern retelling of the story of Percival, the Grail knight, and his quest to restore plenty to his desolate land. It chronicles the efforts of Roy Hobbs to lead the New York Knights baseball team to the pennant. At the beginning, Roy, nineteen, is on his way to Chicago for a tryout with the Cubs when he meets the mysterious Harriet Bird. When he can explain his purpose in life only in terms of self-interest, Harriet shoots him.

Fifteen years later, Roy attempts a comeback with the Knights and quickly establishes himself as the greatest slugger in baseball history—with the help of his magical bat, Wonderboy, suggestive of the tree of fertility, Percival's lance, and Excalibur, King Arthur's sword. When he gives in to the temptations of the corrupt Memo Paris, however, Roy goes into a slump. He recovers through the influence of Iris Lemon, representative of fertility, life, and responsibility, but he ultimately rejects her and sells out to Memo's gambler friends. He has one more chance to redeem himself.

The wasteland-Holy Grail legend is combined with baseball history and lore, including the 1949 shooting of Eddie Waitkus, the 1919 Black Sox scandal and the consequent disgrace of Shoeless Joe Jackson, Babe Ruth's career, and "Casey at the Bat," to depict the moral complexities of contemporary American life, the opportunities for heroism offered by America, and moral obligations placed on the hero. The sufferings of the Christlike protagonists in Malamud's novels are the ultimate tests of their humanity. Roy Hobbs fails as a hero because he does not recognize Iris's goodness or his own selfishness. He fails to grow up morally, a growth necessary to revitalize a decadent society. He fails as a baseball hero, yet his suffering can make him succeed as a man.

The Assistant

Type of work: Novel
First published: 1957

In *The Assistant*, Malamud carefully structures his realistic second novel so that the story of the intertwined fates of Frank Alpine and the Bobers grows to symbolize self-discipline and suffering. The hero, Frank Alpine, unlike the hero of Malamud's *The Natural* (1952), achieves self-integration and the subsequent identification with a group.

Frank enters the life of the Bobers when he comes with Ward Minoque, who represents his worst self, to the struggling neighborhood store of Morris Bober to steal. Unlike Ward, Frank immediately recognizes Morris as a suffering human being. Indeed, Morris is the suffering Jew, an Everyman. Now old, he has achieved none of his dreams and must deprive his daughter, Helen, of her dream of attending college.

To expiate his crime and to change his life, Frank returns to the store and, promising to work for nothing, persuades Morris to use him as an assistant. Unaware that Frank is the one who stole from him, Morris helps the hungry and homeless Frank with room and board and a small salary. Morris then becomes the moral guide Frank never had.

Frank begins to change, but his progress is fitful, and he steals small sums from the register. His moral growth is accelerated by his falling in love with Helen, an idealistic young woman who will give Frank her love if he earns it. Motivated by this hope and a memory of the beauty of the selfless life of Saint Francis of Assisi, Frank tries to discipline himself. When Frank has nearly won the love of Helen, his hopes slip away when Morris, who suspects that Frank has been stealing, catches him with his hand in the register. Sent away from the store on the day he expects Helen to proclaim her love, Frank gives in to despair and frustration. First saving her from rape by Ward, he then forces himself on her against her will.

Alienated from the Bobers, Frank's redemption comes when he moves beyond himself. The opportunity arises when Morris is hospitalized and then dies. Frank takes over the store when Helen and her mother are too overwhelmed by their misfortunes to protest. To support them all, he works two jobs. Though he sometimes questions the dreary life to which he has submitted himself, he patiently endures, replacing Morris, whose example he has internalized. After a year, Frank even sends Helen to college. He then reflects his new attitudes by having himself circumcised, a symbolic act of his transformation.

The Fixer

Type of work: Novel
First published: 1966

Based on the story of a Russian Jew, Mendel Beiless, who was tried and acquitted in czarist Russia for the ritual murder of a Christian child, *The Fixer* artistically re-creates that history. It also represents, in its theme, persecution in general. Malamud creates in this novel a story like a parable, similar in theme and style to his other works, that recounts the protagonist's spiritual growth and affirms personal dignity and moral integrity even in a world that seems incomprehensible. Yakov Bok, the hero, a Jew, comes to define himself, value suffering, and feel most free when most confined.

Yakov, a fixer or handyman, has had bad luck. With little work in his Jewish village and a wife first disappointing him in being childless then deserting him, he feels himself a prisoner of his circumstances. He sets off for Kiev, a city known for its anti-Semitism, in hopes of changing his life. In Kiev, Yakov, finding no work in the Jewish sector, begins looking outside the ghetto, which is illegal. Coming upon a drunken man who is lying unconscious in the street, Yakov helps the drunk, although Yakov recognizes him as an anti-Semite. To reward Yakov, the man offers him a job, which Yakov accepts with misgivings because it is outside the ghetto. One day Yakov reads in the paper of the ritual murder of a Christian child. The next day he is accused of the murder and put in prison. He is held for thirty months before being brought to trial.

The next three-quarters of the novel describes Yakov's physical agonies and spiritual growth while imprisoned. This growth is presented in his actions, dreams, hallucinations, perceptions, and memories during the daily suffering he undergoes—from deprivation of basic necessities and the torture of poisoning and chaining to the humiliation of the daily physical searches. During this time, he learns.

He discovers the strength of hate, political power, and historical events and sees that an individual is, by force, a political being. Secretly reading the Old then the New Testament, he feels connected with his people yet fully appreciates the story of Christ. He develops compassion for the suffering of others. He acknowledges the suffering of the guard, who tells his story. Yakov forgives his wife and acknowledges his own part in their failed relationship. He accepts fatherhood, symbol of adulthood and personal identity, by declaring paternity to her illegitimate child, enabling her to return to life in her village without shame. At the same time, he refuses to sign any documents that will free him by blaming other Jews. He also refuses to admit guilt. He finds, in identifying with his group and in willingly suffering for them that, despite what may happen to him, he is free.

Suggested Readings

Abramson, Edward A. *Bernard Malamud Revisited*. New York: Twayne, 1993.

Avery, Evelyn, ed. *The Magic Worlds of Bernard Malamud*. Albany: State University of New York Press, 2001.

Bloom, Harold, ed. *Bernard Malamud*. New York: Chelsea House, 2000.

Davis, Philip. *Experimental Essays on the Novels of Bernard Malamud: Malamud's People*. Lewiston, N.Y.: Edwin Mellen Press, 1995.

Malamud, Bernard. Introduction to *The Stories of Bernard Malamud*. New York: Farrar, Straus, Giroux, 1983.

Ochshorn, Kathleen. *The Heart's Essential Landscape: Bernard Malamud's Hero*. New York: Peter Lang, 1990.

Richman, Sidney. *Bernard Malamud*. Boston: Twayne, 1966.

Sío-Castiñeira, Begoña. *The Short Stories of Bernard Malamud: In Search of Jewish Post-immigrant Identity*. New York: Peter Lang, 1998.

Smith, Janna Malamud. *My Father Is a Book: A Memoir of Bernard Malamud*. Boston: Houghton Mifflin, 2006.

Watts, Eileen H. "Jewish Self-Hatred in Malamud's 'The Jewbird.'" *MELUS* 21 (Summer, 1996): 157-163.

Contributor: Bernadette Flynn Low

Malcolm X

(Malcolm Little)

Born: Omaha, Nebraska; May 19, 1925
Died: New York, New York; February 21, 1965

African American

Malcolm X went from being a street hustler to being a black leader and a symbol of fearless resistance against oppression.

Principal works

NONFICTION: *The Autobiography of Malcolm X*, 1965 (with Alex Haley); *Malcolm X Speaks*, 1965; *The Speeches of Malcolm X at Harvard*, 1968; *By Any Means Necessary*, 1970; *The End of White World Supremacy*, 1971

Malcolm X's (born Malcolm Little) early years were marked by unsettling events: His family, threatened by the Ku Klux Klan in Omaha, moved to Lansing, Michigan, only to have their house burned down by a white hate group. Malcolm's father died in 1931 under mysterious circumstances, leaving his mother with the task of raising eight children. Malcolm eventually moved to Boston in 1941 and to New York in 1943, where he first experienced the street life of the African American urban poor. After becoming a burglar, he received a six-year prison term for armed robbery. In prison, he converted to the Nation of Islam and read voraciously on philosophy, theology, and history. The Nation of Islam helped him to acquire self-respect and gave him a new worldview, one that celebrated African American history and culture and in which whites were seen as forces of evil. Two years after his release, Malcolm—who by then had changed his last name to "X" in order to shed any links to a past in which white slave masters gave African American slaves their last names—became minister of the New York Temple Number Seven and the national spokesperson for the Nation of Islam. He brought unprecedented attention to the Nation: At a time when much of the United States was still segregated, Malcolm X voiced fearlessly what others only thought and denounced white racist practices.

Advocating strong moral codes and behaviors, Malcolm X became disenchanted with the Nation, suspecting the covert immorality of some leaders. After leaving the Nation of Islam, Malcolm X went on a pilgrimage to Mecca, where his warm reception by white Muslims (and his earlier contact in America with white students and journalists) led him to reject his earlier declarations that all whites were evil, and he accepted Orthodox Islam as his faith. He adopted the name el-Hajj

Malik el-Shabazz. Malcolm X traveled to Africa, meeting African leaders and recognizing the links between imperialist oppression of Africa and the situation of African Americans. Malcolm X was assassinated in New York after beginning to build Organization of Afro-American Unity, which featured cross-racial alliances and an international outlook.

The Autobiography of Malcolm X

Type of work: Autobiography
First published: 1965

The Autobiography of Malcolm X was hailed as a literary classic shortly after it appeared. Its description of Malcolm X's discovery of an African American identity continues to inspire its readers. The two most memorable phases of Malcolm X's life described in his autobiography, and quite possibly the two phases most formative of his identity, are his self-education and religious conversion while in prison and his last year of life, in which he set out to organize a multiracial coalition to end racism. The first of these phases followed a difficult childhood and life as a criminal. In prison, Malcolm X felt inspired by fellow inmates to improve his knowledge. He started on a rigorous program of reading books on history and philosophy. He also worked on his penmanship and vocabulary by copying an entire dictionary. His readings revealed to him that school had taught him nothing about African and African American history. School had also been silent on the crimes that Europeans and European Americans had committed against people of color. In prison, members of the Nation of Islam urged Malcolm X to reject the negative self-image he had unconsciously adopted and to replace it with black pride.

Malcolm X (Library of Congress)

Malcolm X taught the Nation's doctrine of black self-reliance after his release from prison, and he married Betty Shabazz, eventually becoming the father of six children. Disappointed by the divergence between the practices of some of the leaders of the Nation of Islam and the rules of self-discipline and honor that the Nation taught, he left the Nation and, after traveling to Mecca, became an orthodox Muslim. Islam and his experiences in the Middle

East and Africa also changed his outlook on racial relations. Before, he had seen an unbridgeable gulf between African Americans and European Americans. His positive experiences with white Muslims, white students, and white reporters caused him to reevaluate that position. Deciding that cooperation between whites and blacks was possible, he remained devoted to the liberation of people of African descent to the end of his life.

The Autobiography of Malcolm X is important as an account of the life of a charismatic American intellectual. The book is also an important literary work in the African American tradition of the autobiographies of Frederick Douglass and W. E. B. Du Bois and in the American tradition of Benjamin Franklin. Like Douglass and Franklin, Malcolm X can be described as a self-made man.

Suggested Readings

Breitman, George. *The Assassination of Malcolm X*. 3d ed. New York: Pathfinder, 1991.

Carson, Clayborne. *Malcolm X: The FBI File*. New York: Carroll & Graf, 1991.

Clarke, John. *Malcolm X: The Man and His Times*. 1969. Reprint. Trenton, N.J.: African World Press, 1990.

DeCaro, Louis A. *On the Side of My People: A Religious Life of Malcolm X*. New York: New York University Press, 1996.

Dyson, Michael Eric. *Making Malcolm: The Myth and Meaning of Malcolm X*. New York: Oxford University Press, 1995.

Gallen, David. *Malcolm X as They Knew Him*. New York: Carroll & Graf, 1992.

Goldman, Peter. *Death and Life of Malcolm X*. 2d ed. Urbana: University of Illinois Press, 1979.

Jenkins, Robert L., and Mfanya Donald Tryman, eds. *The Malcolm X Encyclopedia*. Westport, Conn.: Greenwood Press, 2002.

Perry, Bruce. *Malcolm: The Life of a Man Who Changed Black America*. Barrytown, N.Y.: Station Hill Press, 1991.

Sales, William W., Jr. *From Civil Rights to Black Liberation: Malcolm X and the Organization of Afro-American Unity*. Boston: South End Press, 1994.

Contributor: Martin Japtok

Paule Marshall

Born: Brooklyn, New York; April 9, 1929

African American, Caribbean

Marshall's major contribution to literature is her deep understanding of the human psyche, especially that of black women. Her women characters are complex, with deep reservoirs of strength that can be called upon when needed.

Principal works

LONG FICTION: *Brown Girl, Brownstones*, 1959; *The Chosen Place, the Timeless People*, 1969; *Praisesong for the Widow*, 1983; *Daughters*, 1991; *The Fisher King*, 2000

SHORT FICTION: *Soul Clap Hands and Sing*, 1961; *Reena, and Other Stories*, 1983; *Merle: A Novella and Other Stories*, 1985

Paule Marshall (PAH-lee MAHR-shahl) was born in Brooklyn, New York, to Samuel Burke and Ada Clement Burke, who immigrated to New York from Barbados shortly after World War I and joined the growing community of West Indian immigrants in Brooklyn. She was born to parents who had brought with them to America a strong sense of pride and tradition that was an integral part of West Indian culture, and she was nourished by a community of people who revered their West Indian heritage, even as they embraced the advantages that America afforded them. Her parents continually returned to their homeland of Barbados, taking their small daughter with them.

Being of both African American and Caribbean ancestry helped to shape Paule Marshall as a woman and as a writer. She first traveled to Barbados as a nine-year-old child. When she visited the island as a young woman just starting out on a writing career, she began to develop a deeper appreciation for the West Indian culture—its rituals, its customs, its people and language—and a greater sense of pride in her West Indian heritage. She was most impressed with the strength and character she observed in West Indian women, qualities she saw reflected in the women of the Brooklyn community where she had grown up. The lives of these women, whom she calls her "literary foremothers," were to become the major focus of her novels. Their use of language and their storytelling skills influenced Marshall's style, and their strength and deep sense of pride are the essential qualities of the female characters she creates.

Marshall wrote poetry as a child and listened to the talk of women, both preparing her for her career as a powerful and poetic writer. In the opening of *Reena, and*

Other Stories, she describes the influence of her mother, woman relatives, and other female friends on her experience in an essay called "From the Poets in the Kitchen":

> They taught me my first lesson in the narrative art. They trained my ear. They set a standard of excellence. This is why the best of my work must be attributed to them; it stands as testimony to the rich legacy of language and culture they so freely passed on to me in the workshop of the kitchen.

Marshall attended Brooklyn College, where she received a bachelor's degree in 1953, graduating magna cum laude and Phi Beta Kappa. After leaving Brooklyn College, Marshall went to work as a researcher and later as a feature writer for *Our World* magazine. In 1955, she enrolled as a graduate student at Hunter College (City University of New York) but continued to write for *Our World*, where her assignments carried her to Brazil and the West Indies. In 1957, she married Kenneth Marshall, with whom she had one son, Evan Keith. Her trips to the Caribbean islands were rewarding in that they provided her an opportunity to return to the land of her ancestors. While there, she immersed herself in the culture, absorbing the nuances of language, customs, and traditions that were to figure so prominently in her novels.

In 1960, Marshall received a Guggenheim Fellowship, which allowed her to complete her second work, a collection of novellas, *Soul Clap Hands and Sing*. Eight years passed, however, before the publication of her second novel. In that interim, she worked for *New World*, a Caribbean magazine, produced several short stories, and continued work on her novel. So committed was she to her craft that she would often obtain a baby-sitter, over her husband's objections, and go every day to the home of a friend in order to continue her writing. She divorced Kenneth Marshall in 1963.

In 1970, Marshall was married for the second time, to Nourry Menard, a Haitian businessman—a man with whom she said she had an "open and innovative marriage," one that gave her the time and freedom to pursue her work. In the fall of 1970 she took the position of lecturer on creative writing at Yale University. She also lectured on black literature at several colleges and universities, including the University of Oxford, Columbia University, Michigan State University, Lake Forest College, and Cornell University. Marshall combined her writing career with teaching and became a professor at Virginia Commonwealth University in Richmond, Virginia.

Brown Girl, Brownstones

Type of work: Novel
First published: 1959

In *Brown Girl, Brownstones*, Marshall begins to develop the self-identity theme through the character of Selina Boyce, a girl moving from childhood into adolescence in Brooklyn and caught between two cultures, the American culture in which she lives and the Barbadian culture of her ancestors, the customs of which are carefully observed in her household.

The novel treats the problems she encounters in trying to reconcile these two disparate parts of herself. She is a "divided self," feeling little connection with either the "bajan" community or the larger white community. She rejects her Barbadian heritage and its "differentness" and yearns to be a part of the white community, which rejects her. The sense of isolation that she feels is the source of all her problems.

At the climax of the novel, the "divided self" is integrated as Selina finally accepts her heritage and discovers that with acceptance comes wholeness. She resolves her conflict with her mother, she makes peace with the Barbadian Association, and she leaves Brooklyn to begin her travels. As she passes through her old neighborhood, she feels psychically connected to all the people who helped create her integrated self. As a final symbolic act, she tosses behind one of her two Barbadian bangle bracelets and retains the other as a reminder of her link with the past. Selina has finally learned that true selfhood begins with the acceptance of one's own history.

Soul Clap Hands and Sing

Type of work: Short fiction
First published: 1961

Marshall's first collection of shorter works, *Soul Clap Hands and Sing*, contains four longer short stories, almost novellas. They are given the titles of the settings: "Barbados," "Brooklyn," "British Guiana," and "Brazil." In each, the main character is an older man, and the stories explore how that man has failed to live his life fully, for whatever reasons. This failure is indicated by the title of the collection, taken from the William Butler Yeats poem "Sailing to Byzantium," which includes the lines "An aged man is but a paltry thing/ A tattered coat upon a stick, unless/ Soul clap its hands and sing." In each case, the failure of the man to allow his soul to "clap hands" has led to the emptiness or aridity of his life. Thus, he is forced to realize his failure to live truly through the intervention of a woman who, in some way, exposes his inadequacies.

In "Barbados," Mr. Watford, who has returned to his native island after having worked single-mindedly throughout his adult life in the United States just so he can return for this purpose, lives like a white colonizer. He has built a house, bought plantation land, and planted coconut trees, which he tends faithfully, despite years of accumulated fatigue. He has never completely finished his house, however, and he lives in total isolation, proud of the fact that he needs no one and no one needs him. It takes a young native woman, foisted on him as a servant, to reveal the paucity of his life, the emptiness of his days. He recognizes that he has not been able to bear the responsibility for the meaninglessness of his life, but when he goes to confront the young woman with the hope of some renewal, he is capable only of attacking her verbally, to which she responds, "you ain't people, Mr. Watford, you ain't people." It is this that destroys him: He has not been able to be a part of the people who bore him and has not found sustenance living the same way as those who oppressed him.

In "Brooklyn," an aging Jewish professor, who has been banned from teaching by the Red-baiters of the McCarthy era, attempts to coerce a young black woman who is taking his class to spend some time at his summer home. She refuses but in the end returns to his class for the final and takes him up on his invitation, only to express her outrage as well as the freedom that she now feels. She has also felt an outcast from her own people, while unable to trust whites. Now she has the courage to live not as her parents have taught her but as she chooses. Professor Max Berman, on the other hand, is forced to recognize that it is his failure to believe in or stand up for anything that has resulted in his loneliness and misery. Interestingly, in "Barbados" the female protagonist is not given a name, while here she is named only in dialogue as Miss Williams.

"British Guiana" explores the present of Gerald Motley, a man who is indeed a motley collection of races; he could have been taken for white, because of the British army officer who was one of his ancestors, or black, for the slave woman that officer had been intimate with, or East Indian, from some Hindu who also had a part in his creation. He has achieved a certain amount of success as the head of a radio station, but he knows that he has failed to live his life fully. Although as a young man

Paule Marshall (AP/Wide World Photos)

he had shown a great ability and had rejected his middle-class background to organize a strike, he had been bought off by a job in radio, which forces him to copy the whites who have colonized his country. When he attempts to penetrate the jungle, to prove his worth to himself, he is prevented by another motley person, Sybil, an African Chinese woman with whom he is involved. He is forever conscious of his betrayal of himself and also of Sybil's part in this, which results in a life of cynicism and taking the easy way. At the end of the story, when Sybil, whom he might have married, returns to visit, his last act is to bargain with her for a protégé who despises him but deserves a chance. In the conclusion, he realizes that he is going to die a failure by his own doing.

The final story in the book, "Brazil," reminds the reader of Carson McCullers's *The Ballad of the Sad Café* (1951) in that it is the story of what appears to be a strange love affair between a white woman of epic proportions and a black dwarf. In this story, the dwarf is a performer who goes by the name of O Grande Caliban and has teamed up with a blond of Germanic appearance to perform a comic and athletic act. He has decided that it is time to retire, but his mistress does not wish to do so. One of the interesting things about the story is the breaking of the traditional white reader's expectations; it is the undersized black man who is trying to end a relationship with the Aryan-looking female. He has become so famous as Caliban, however, that no one, not even his wife, knows him as he had been. He has been living a lie so long that he cannot convince people of the truth anymore, and so he destroys everything.

The Chosen Place, the Timeless People

Type of work: Novel
First published: 1969

The Chosen Place, the Timeless People is set in the West Indies, specifically Bournehills, a remote part of one of the Caribbean islands. Here, Marshall expands the identity theme, focusing not on the individual self but rather on the collective self of a community of people in search of a common bond. While Merle Kimbona is the protagonist of the novel and a strong female character—a mulatto who has returned to Bournehills to become mistress of a large estate left to her by her white father after spending many adventuresome years in Europe—she is really not the central figure of the novel. At the center of the novel are the people of Bournehills, who, having been oppressed first by slavery, then by their own people, search for some common thread of unity. They discover this in Carnival, an annual ritual in which the people reenact the story of Cuffee Ned, who led a slave revolt against the slaveholder Percy Byram.

The plot turns with a visit by a team from an American philanthropic organization sent to Bournehills to provide aid to this underdeveloped country. The team consists of a Jewish American social scientist, Saul Amron; his wife, Harriet; and two returning natives of Bournehills, Allen Fuso and Vere. During their stay on the island, the outsiders interact with the natives, observing their rituals and customs and contrasting them with their American experience. As guests at the estate of Merle Kimbona, now a political activist, they also become involved in the political affairs of Bournehills.

The contrasts between the two cultures are apparent throughout the novel. The high-tech white society, represented by the machine—in this case the machines in the sugarcane factory—enslave the people of Bournehills in much the same way they had been enslaved by Percy Byram. Also it is the machine—the American automobile—that takes the life of the Bournehills native Vere.

Marshall brings together characters from many backgrounds and classes—black and white; upper, middle, and lower classes; natives and outsiders—in this "chosen place." The ritual reenactment of their history at Carnival is the common thread that binds all classes of people in Bournehills, and it also connects them to their African ancestry and Western culture.

Praisesong for the Widow

Type of work: Novel
First published: 1983

In *Praisesong for the Widow*, Marshall continues the theme of self-discovery through her protagonist, Avey Johnson, a middle-aged, middle-class black woman on a Caribbean cruise with two of her women friends. Avey is haunted by a recurring dream about a story told to her by her great-aunt, with whom she had spent summers in Tatem, South Carolina, of how the African slaves who landed at Tatem had immediately turned back toward the sea, walking across the water back to their home in Africa.

Deciding to leave the ship before the cruise is over and return home, Avey misses her flight to New York and is stranded in Grenada just at the time of the annual excursion to the island of Carriocou. Here, again, Marshall uses ritual to reveal to Avey the importance of connecting to her African ancestry. In a scene that is almost surreal she is transported to Carriocou, where this annual ritual is to take place. Reluctant to participate at first, Avey eventually joins in the ritual and discovers the meaning of her recurring dream. The landing of the Ibos in South Carolina and their return to Africa by the mythic walk on water symbolize the link between Africa and all black people of the diaspora. In participating in this ritual, Avey becomes aware that she can achieve wholeness only if she becomes reconnected to her African roots.

Reena, and Other Stories

Type of work: Short fiction
First published: 1983

Reena, and Other Stories is a collection of previously printed works gathered together for the first time in 1983 by Feminist Press. It begins with Marshall's autobiographical essay, "From the Poets in the Kitchen," which had originally been published in *The New York Times Book Review*'s series called "The Making of a Writer." This essay celebrates the women in Marshall's life who helped form her thought and shape her voice. The collection includes two of the stories discussed above, "Brooklyn" and "Barbados," previously published in *Soul Clap Hands and Sing*. Also included is a novella, *Merle*, which has been excerpted from her 1969 novel *The Chosen Place, the Timeless People* but was extensively reshaped and rewritten. Marshall wrote autobiographical headnotes to each story, which help to place them in the context of her experience and development as a writer.

The first story in the collection, "The Valley Between," was, as Marshall explained, "my very first published story, written when I could barely crawl, never mind stand up and walk as a writer." In it, the characters are white, a deliberate decision as Marshall herself was at the time married to Kenneth E. Marshall, a marriage she describes as "an early, unwise first marriage," and she wished to disguise the autobiographical elements in it. It is the story of a marriage falling apart because the wife (and mother of a small child) continues to grow, while the husband wishes her to remain the same, to be nothing more than a wife and mother. Published in August, 1954, it is a story well before its time in its depiction of the stifling expectations placed upon a woman of talent and energy.

The title story, "Reena," is unusual in that it was commissioned by *Harper's Magazine* for a special supplement on "The American Female," published in October of 1962. Intended by the editors to be an article on the African American woman, the story instead became a thinly disguised fiction concerning the women whom Marshall knew best: "those from an urban, working-class and lower middle-class, West Indian American background who, like [Marshall herself], had attended the free New York City colleges during the late forties and fifties."

A first-person narrator named Paulie recounts her meeting again after twenty years with a friend from her childhood, Reena, formally named Doreen, who—being a child who shapes her own life as best she can in a world that discriminates against women, African Americans, and particularly African Americans from the West Indies—had transformed herself into Reena, "with two ees!"

The meeting place is at the funeral of Aunt Vi, Reena's aunt, a woman who represents the strong, nurturing, enduring women "from the poets in the kitchen" and who will reappear in Marshall's fiction. Having been out of touch for so long, Reena and Paulie have much to discuss, and much of the story is Reena's recounting of what has been happening in her life: the struggle for meaningful work; her relationship with her family, particularly her mother; relationships with white men (usually unsuccessful) and with black men, who have to learn how to relate to and accept a strong, educated, ambitious black woman; childbearing; radical politics; and loneliness. In almost essayistic form, this story provides an intimate glimpse into the struggle, suffering, and successes of this group of African American women.

"To Da-duh, in Memoriam" is based on a visit that Marshall made to her maternal grandmother in Barbados when she was nine. Da-duh is another of the ancestor figures who populate Marshall's fiction, like Aunt Vi in the previous story and Merle in the story of that same name; as Marshall says, "Da-duh turns up everywhere."

Merle

Type of work: Short fiction
First published: 1985

Another example of ancestor figures appears in the novella *Merle*, Marshall's heroine, Merle, is "part saint, part revolutionary, part obeah woman," a woman who, wherever she goes, exhorts people to resist oppression, while on a personal level she is "still trying to come to terms with her life and history as a black woman, still seeking to reconcile all the conflicting elements to form a viable self." Merle is the same woman whom Paule Marshall creates in other guises, calling into being a new character for twentieth century American literature. Merle epitomizes Marshall's compelling portrayals of women, brining to life for her readers a vision of the direction in which the world should be going by showing readers the people whom the world desperately needs to listen to and emulate.

Daughters

Type of work: Novel
First published: 1991

Like the protagonists of most of Marshall's other novels, the protagonist of *Daughters*, Ursa MacKensie, is a woman caught between two cultures: the African American culture of her mother, Estelle, and the Caribbean culture of her father, Primus. The action of the novel is divided almost equally between New York City, where Ursa lives, and Triunion, the West Indian island where her parents reside, her father being a leading politician, known from his boyhood as the PM (prime minister). Although firmly rooted in the urban culture of New York, where she is pursuing a career as a young black professional, Ursa keeps one foot planted in the small Caribbean island through her relationship with her doting father, a relationship strengthened by frequent letters and periodic visits.

In this novel, Marshall again explores the themes of identity and the attempt to bridge the gap between two cultures. The novel addresses the integration of the two cultures on several levels, the first being the marriage of Ursa's parents—her African American mother to her West Indian father. The second is the birth of their daughter, Ursa-Mae, who physically integrates the two cultures. Then, the African American and West Indian cultures are geographically and spiritually linked as Ursa's mother moves to Triunion with her husband and becomes integrated into that community.

As in *The Chosen Place, the Timeless People*, much of the novel is devoted to the workings of Triunion politics and their effect upon the Triunion people, the marriage of Primus and Estelle, and Ursa. Its setting and wide array of characters provide Marshall the opportunity to explore the theme of self-discovery from a number of perspectives.

Suggested Readings

Alexander, Simone A. James. *Mother Imagery in the Novels of Afro-Caribbean Women*. Columbia: University of Missouri Press, 2001.

Collier, Eugenia. "The Closing of the Circle: Movement from Division to Wholeness in Paule Marshall's Fiction." In *Black Women Writers, 1950-1980*, edited by Mari Evans. Garden City, N.Y.: Anchor Press/Doubleday, 1984.

Coser, Stelamaris. *Bridging the Americas: The Literature of Paule Marshall, Toni Morrison, and Gayl Jones*. Philadelphia: Temple University Press, 1995.

DeLamotte, Eugenia C. *Places of Silence, Journeys of Freedom: The Fiction of Paule Marshall*. Philadelphia: University of Pennsylvania Press, 1998.

Denniston, Dorothy Hamer. *The Fiction of Paule Marshall*. Knoxville: University of Tennessee Press, 1995.

Hathaway, Heather. *Caribbean Waves: Relocating Claude McKay and Paule Marshall*. Bloomington: Indiana University Press, 1999.

McClusky, John, Jr. "And Called Every Generation Blessed: Theme, Setting, and Ritual in the Works of Paule Marshall." In *Black Women Writers, 1950-1980*, edited by Mari Evans. Garden City, N.Y.: Anchor Press/Doubleday, 1984.

Macpherson, Heidi Slettedahl. "Perception of Place: Geopolitical and Cultural Positioning in Paule Marshall's Novels." In *Caribbean Women Writers*, edited by Mary Condé and Thorunn Lonsdale. New York: St. Martin's Press, 1999.

Waxman, Barbara Frey. "Dancing out of Form, Dancing into Self: Genre and Metaphor in Marshall, Shange, and Walker." *MELUS* 19 (Fall, 1994): 91-106.

Contributors: Mary LeDonne Cassidy, Theodore C. Humphrey, and Gladys J. Washington

Ved Mehta

Born: Lahore, British India (now Pakistan); March 21, 1934

South Asian American

Mehta vividly describes the cultures in which he has lived and the experience of exile and blindness.

Principal works

NONFICTION: *Face to Face*, 1957 (autobiogaphy); *The Fly and the Fly Bottle: Encounters with British Intellectuals*, 1963 (essays); *The New Theologian*, 1966 (essays); *Portrait of India*, 1970; *Daddyji*, 1972 (autobiography; part of the Continents of Exile series); *Mahatma Gandhi and His Apostles*, 1977 (biography); *The New India*, 1978; *Mamaji*, 1979 (autobiography; part of the Continents of Exile series); *Vedi*, 1982 (autobiography; part of the Continents of Exile series); *The Ledge Between the Streams*, 1984 (autobiography; part of the Continents of Exile series); *Sound-Shadows of the New World*, 1985 (autobiography; part of the Continents of Exile series); *The Stolen Light*, 1989 (autobiography; part of the Continents of Exile series); *Up at Oxford*, 1993 (autobiography; part of the Continents of Exile series); *Rajiv Gandhi and Rama's Kingdom*, 1994; *Remembering Mr. Shawn's "New Yorker": The Invisible Art of Editing*, 1998 (autobiography; part of the Continents of Exile series); *A Ved Mehta Reader: The Craft of the Essay*, 1998; *All for Love*, 2001 (autobiography; part of the Continents of Exile series); *Dark Harbor: Building House and Home on an Enchanted Island*, 2003 (autobiography; part of the Continents of Exile series); *The Red Letters: My Father's Enchanted Period*, 2004 (autobiography; part of the Continents of Exile series)

Ved Mehta (vehd MEH-tah) has been telling the story of his own life for most of his career. This story includes the cultures in which he has lived. Mehta was born into a well-educated Hindu family in Lahore in 1934. At the age of three he lost his eyesight as a result of meningitis. Mehta's education took him away from his close-knit family and sent him to places that must have seemed like different worlds: Arkansas in the era of segregation, a college campus in suburban Southern California, and Oxford University. As a staff writer for *The New Yorker* and in his many books, Mehta makes those different worlds, including the world of blindness, come alive to the reader.

Mehta published his first book, *Face to Face*, when he was twenty-two. It is a highly readable account of his childhood, of his family's sufferings during the partition of India (they had to flee their native city when it became part of the new Muslim nation of Pakistan), and of his experiences as a student in America. The central subject, however, is Mehta's blindness and the ways in which he learns to be independent and successful despite his disability.

For many years after the appearance of *Face to Face*, Mehta allowed no hint of his disability to appear in his work, which he filled with visual descriptions. He published a novel and became a master of nonfiction. He wrote books introducing Indian culture and politics to Western readers; Mehta has also written a series of books on the excitement of intellectual life. In books on history and philosophy, theology, and linguistics, Mehta makes clashes of ideas vivid by describing intellectuals not only as thinkers but as people.

When Mehta returned to autobiography, beginning with *Daddyji*, he stopped suppressing the fact of his blindness. Instead, he tried to make the things that had formed his identity—his family, his disability, his experiences at schools for the blind, and the colleges and universities where he studied—as vivid as his other subjects. Beginning with biographies of his mother and father and working ahead through five more books to his graduation from Oxford, Mehta presents the story of his life, always as an exile seeking his place in the world, with eloquence and frankness.

Continents of Exile

Type of work: Autobiography

First published: *Daddyji*, 1972; *Mamaji*, 1979; *Vedi*, 1982; *The Ledge Between the Streams*, 1984; *Sound-Shadows of the New World*, 1985; *The Stolen Light*, 1989; *Up at Oxford*, 1993; *Remembering Mr. Shawn's "New Yorker": The Invisible Art of Editing*, 1998; *All for Love*, 2001; *Dark Harbor: Building House and Home on an Enchanted Island*, 2003; *The Red Letters: My Father's Enchanted Period*, 2004

In the Continents of Exile series, Mehta set himself the task of remembering and interpreting his life. In these volumes, he examines his development from childhood through his career as a writer to his efforts to build a home and family. Mehta's quest for self-understanding is also an introduction to the several different cultures through which Mehta has passed. From childhood Mehta has been an outsider seeking to understand worlds of which he is not fully a part. The loss of his eyesight at age three made him an exile in the world of the sighted, and his almost heroic struggle to secure an education sent him into exile—to Bombay from his native Punjab, to the United States, and to England. In describing his experiences, Mehta also gives the reader the flavor of different worlds, including India before and after its partition into India and Pakistan in 1947, Arkansas during segregation, suburban California in the tranquil 1950's, Oxford before the upheavals of the 1960's, and the world of blindness.

Continents of Exile is in some ways a sequel to Mehta's first book, *Face to Face* (1957). That book, written while Mehta was still an undergraduate, tells the story of his life up to almost the point reached in the seven later volumes. It lacks, however, the breadth, frankness, and detachment of the later volumes. In Continents of Exile, Mehta explores the power of memory. He has discovered that, with the aid of some research, memory yields much more than one might think. He also can analyze his experience with more detachment than his younger self could.

The series begins with biographies of Mehta's father and mother, *Daddyji* and *Mamaji*. Mehta's father's family embraced Western influences, the English language, and an "unsuperstitious" form of Hinduism. Mehta's mother's family was more resistant to Western influences, and Mehta's mother often sought cures through charms and native treatments. In telling the stories of his very different parents and their nevertheless successful marriage, Mehta recalls the world of a close-knit family. He left the family to seek an education. *Vedi* and *The Ledge Between the Streams* describe Mehta's childhood, including his first experience of exile at a boarding school for the blind in Bombay and his family's flight from their home during the chaos following partition.

The next three volumes chronicle Mehta's education in America and England. In *Sound-Shadows of the New World* (1985) Mehta recounts his years at the Arkansas School for the Blind. *The Stolen Light* takes Mehta to Pomona College in Claremont, California, where he is both a great success and an outsider. *Up at Oxford* describes Mehta's years at Balliol College and sketches portraits of some promising minds he met there.

The period covered in *The Stolen Light* was particularly important for Mehta. Most of the book concerns Mehta's experiences at Pomona College, though there are excursions elsewhere; letters and journal extracts from those years are interspersed in the narrative as well. Occasionally Mehta shifts forward to the 1980's, tracing the subsequent fates of some of the people whom he knew in college and in a few instances describing recent meetings with them. It was during this time that he wrote—or rather dictated—his first book, a fledgling autobiography; his account of the process of composing that book, and the special part played in it by the young woman who served as his amanuensis, is fascinating. He recounts the romantic dreams that mingled with his intellectual ambitions, and the unromantic reality of his first sexual experience. While much of the interest of the book lies in Mehta's personal history, *The Stolen Light* is also absorbing as an account of a particular place and time and as a gallery of memorable portraits. Mehta's father, profiled earlier in *Daddyji*, the first book in the sequence, figures prominently here, as does Ethel Clyde, an eccentric millionaire who became Mehta's patron—a character of truly Dickensian proportions.

In *Remembering Mr. Shawn's "New Yorker,"* Mehta explains his estrangement as a young man from his native India, but most of his memoir concerns the consequences of his decision to forsake pursuing a Ph.D. in history at Harvard in 1960 to become a contributor to *The New Yorker*. Mehta offers a vivid picture of the New York literary world of the 1960's and depicts the eccentric behavior of many of his fellow writers for the sophisticated weekly magazine. Mehta describes the famously seedy 43rd Street offices of *The New Yorker* and the day-to-day operations of the magazine with regular contributors like himself going through a painstaking process of writing, rewriting, and waiting before their pieces appeared in print. An attitude of the magazine before anything else was imbued by William Shawn, who joined *The New Yorker* in 1933 and became its editor in 1952, succeeding the legendary Harold Ross. Shawn lived for his work and expected nothing less of his staff. Mehta offers a loving, perhaps idealized, portrait of the editor he saw as his mentor and father figure. The young writer and his editor became entwined in numerous ways from Mehta's becoming an honorary member of the Shawn family to Shawn's writing the jacket copy for Mehta's books.

The next book in the series, *All for Love*, focuses on Mehta's struggle to find love by recounting four love affairs he had while a writer for *The New Yorker* in the 1960's and 1970's. His emotions and those of his lovers are presented through their letters, which recount the intimate and at times banal details of their relationships while revealing the wide range of emotions underlying such intimacies. The book's final section, presenting Mehta's psychoanalysis, recounts his exchanges with his therapist and was found by some critics to be both disappointingly narcissistic and unnecessary. However, looming over the narrative is Mehta's blindness—which, though never mentioned during his relationships, to a large degree prompted his psychotherapy. The book is therefore a chronicle of Mehta's journey toward complete self-acceptance, a necessary precursor to love. *All for Love* is thus the first volume in the series to address Mehta's relationship with his blindness. He has refused to accept this part of his identity as a disability—a denial in large part at the root of his success but which does not serve him well in his quest to find a wife.

The penultimate book of the series, *Dark Harbor* is the aptly named story of Mehta's drive to build a safe haven, a home, in an unlikely place: on a Maine vacation island that would generally be considered inaccessible to a modestly paid writer and a blind man. The psychological and logistical difficulties Mehta must surmount—becoming accustomed to the island's wild environment, navigating his way there by plane, overcoming the panic he briefly feels when first left alone on the airstrip—are paralleled by the evolution of his marriage and the process of building a house in this unlikely setting.

The final volume, *The Red Letters* (referring to love letters), was prompted by Mehta's father, who wanted his son to work with him on a novel about a love affair. Mehta soon surmised that the narrative was about his parents—not their own relationship, but its compromise when Mehta's father went outside the marriage. The book is as much the story of the effect of this news on the son as it is a figurative revision of the original biographies of Mehta's parents, *Daddyji* and *Mamaji*. Mehta realizes that his child's-eye view of both parents must be rewritten, and he himself must undergo a "belated growing up." Like the other novels in the Continents of Exile series, *The Red Letters* weaves this personal story into the framework of history and the contrasting cultures of British India and modern America.

Suggested Readings

Embree, Ainslie. Review of *The Ledge Between the Streams*, by Ved Mehta. *The New York Times Book Review*, May 6, 1984.

Malcolm, Janet. "School of the Blind." *The New York Times Book Review*, March 9, 1986.

Mehta, Ved. Interview by Stella Dong. *Publishers Weekly*, January 3, 1986.

Slatin, John M. "Blindness and Self-Perception: The Autobiographies of Ved Mehta." *Mosaic* 19, no. 4 (Fall, 1986): 173-193.

Sontag, Frederick. "The Self-Centered Author." *New Quest* 79 (July/August, 1989): 229-233.

Contributors: Brian Abel Ragen and Christina J. Moose

Louise Meriwether

Born: Haverstraw, New York; May 8, 1923

African American

Meriwether often uses the first-person point of view and draws on her own experience to make compelling fiction about the black experience.

Principal works

children's literature: *The Freedom Ship of Robert Smalls*, 1971; *The Heart Man: Dr. Daniel Hale Williams*, 1972; *Don't Ride the Bus on Monday: The Rosa Parks Story*, 1973

long fiction: *Daddy Was a Number Runner*, 1970; *Fragments of the Ark*, 1994; *Shadow Dancing*, 2000

short fiction: "Daddy Was a Number Runner," 1967; "A Happening in Barbados," 1968; "The Thick End Is for Whipping," 1968; "That Girl from Creektown," 1972; "Fragments of the Ark," 1984; "I Loves You Rain," 1988

nonfiction: "James Baldwin: The Fiery Voice of the Negro Revolt," 1963; "No Race Pride," 1964; "The Negro: Half a Man in a White World," 1965; "The New Face of Negro History," 1965; "The Black Family in Crisis," 1984

Louise Jenkins Meriwether was the third of five children and the only daughter. Her parents, Marion Lloyd Jenkins and Julia Jenkins, had migrated from South Carolina to New York in search of work. Meriwether spent her youth in Harlem. She graduated from Central Commercial High School in Manhattan and received a B.A. in English from New York University. She received an M.A. in journalism from the University of California, Los Angeles, after moving there with her first husband, Angelo Meriwether. That marriage ended in divorce, as did her second marriage to Earl Howe.

In California Meriwether worked as a legal secretary and real estate salesperson, wrote for both the *Los Angeles Sentinel* and *The Los Angeles Times*, and became the first African American story analyst for Universal Studios. She also became a staff member of the Watts Writers' Workshop, and in 1967 she published her first short story, "Daddy Was a Number Runner," in the Watts Writers' Workshop issue of the *Antioch Review*. A second story, "A Happening in Barbados," also appeared in the *Antioch Review*; here she probes the dynamics of interracial relationships between black men and white women, as well as the relationships between African American and white women. The story aroused the attention of a Prentice-Hall editor who asked to see chapters from Meriwether's novel in progress, *Daddy Was a Number Runner*.

Meriwether's first two novels are concerned with the fact that African Americans are missing from the pages of American history. *Daddy Was a Number Runner* chronicles one year in the life of a twelve-year-old girl in Depression-era Harlem. Although not strictly autobiographical, the novel shows a number of correlations between Meriwether's life and that of the main character, Francie Coffin. Both spent their adolescence in Harlem, and both have mothers who are domestic workers and fathers who turn to running numbers—a type of illegal street lottery game—because they cannot find work and must support a family. The novel is an insider's view of an economic racism that ends in the destruction of one family.

On her return to New York in 1970 Meriwether began to write biographies of African Americans for elementary school and juvenile readers in an attempt to counteract the absence of African American role models available to children. In 1971 she published *The Freedom Ship of Robert Smalls*, a biography of a man born a slave who won his freedom by commandeering a Confederate ship; he eventually returned to South Carolina, where he was elected to Congress for five terms. In *The Heart Man: Dr. Daniel Hale Williams* Meriwether traces the life, struggles, and eventual triumph of the first African American heart surgeon. Although he was the first doctor of any race to perform a successful heart operation, he was excluded from white professional societies. Nevertheless, he opened Provident Hospital in Chicago in 1891, the first hospital in the United States to admit both white and black patients. In *Don't Ride the Bus on Monday: The Rosa Parks Story* Meriwether documents the story of the woman often called the Mother of the Civil Rights Struggle, a modest yet courageous African American woman who in refusing to give up her seat on a bus launched one of the most significant eras in American history.

Meriwether was always involved politically. Her work with the Congress of Racial Equality (CORE) in Bogalusa, Louisiana, led to her short story "That Girl from Creektown," in which she explores racism and sexism. Along with John Henrik Clarke she wrote and distributed the pamphlet *Black Americans Stay out of South Africa*, which grew out of her activities in support of the Organization of African Unity and other groups that encouraged African American entertainers' boycotting South Africa.

Meriwether taught fiction workshops in New York and writing courses at Sarah Lawrence College. She received a grant from the Mellon Foundation for research for her second novel, *Fragments of the Ark*, which incorporates the earlier story "I Loves You Rain." The slave Peter Mango, the protagonist of the novel, resembles Robert Smalls (like Smalls, Mango hijacks a Confederate ship and turns it over to Union forces), and Meriwether intersperses other actual people and events in the book. As with other works, a narrative in the first person and the use of actuality and her own autobiography lend immediacy, a hallmark of Louise Meriwether's writing. In *Shadow Dancing*, Meriwether returned to a contemporary setting, tracing the ups and downs of a marriage between two artistically driven African Americans, a writer and a theater director.

Fragments of the Ark

Type of work: Novel
First published: 1994

Fragments of the Ark is an exciting historical novel that describes the adventures of a group of runaway slaves who not only find freedom but also help to liberate the South as heroes in the Civil War. The central figure is Peter Mango, who steals the Confederate gunboat *Swanee* and delivers it to the Union naval blockade at Charleston, South Carolina. A talented sea captain, Peter pilots various Union ships along the Sea Island coast of South Carolina for the duration of the war. Yet all is not smooth sailing: Several of his Gullah friends who have also sought freedom are killed in various battles, and Peter's marriage to the troubled Rain is not without its persistent tensions. In the end, however, Peter and his family are living free in Beaufort, where he has been elected as a delegate to the Freedman's Convention in Charleston.

The novel is full of history, as Peter and other characters interact with the historical figures—General William Tecumseh Sherman, Harriet Tubman—of the 1860's; Peter even gets to meet Abraham Lincoln not long before his assassination. Much of the historical information, however, is awkwardly forced into the narrative through newspaper accounts and letters. In fact, *Fragments of the Ark* would probably work best as a novel for adolescent readers, who would be captured by the romantic plot and educated by all the historical information, especially by the important role that African Americans played in their own liberation. Adult readers, however, may find the contemporary slang and the authorial editorializing a little too unrealistic for their taste.

Suggested Readings

Dandridge, Rita B. "From Economic Insecurity to Disintegration: A Study of Character in Louise Meriwether's *Daddy Was a Number Runner*." *Negro American Literature Forum* 9 (Fall, 1975): 82-85.

Duboin, Corinne. "Race, Gender, and Space: Louise Meriwether's Harlem in *Daddy Was a Number Runner*." *CLA Journal* 45, no. 1 (September, 2001): 26-40.

McKay, Nellie. Afterword to *Daddy Was a Number Runner*, by Louise Meriwether. New York: Feminist Press, 1986.

Wade-Gayles, Gloria Jean. *No Crystal Stair: Visions of Race and Gender in Black Women's Fiction*. Rev. ed. Cleveland: Pilgrim Press, 1997.

Walker, Melissa. "Harbingers of Change: Harlem." In *Down from the Mountaintop: Black Women's Novels in the Wake of the Civil Rights Movement, 1966-1989*. New Haven, Conn.: Yale University Press, 1991.

Contributor: Muriel W. Brailey

Arthur Miller

Born: New York, New York; October 17, 1915
Died: Roxbury, Connecticut; February 10, 2005

Jewish

Miller's plays are widely regarded to be among the best plays ever written by an American.

Principal works

DRAMA: *Honors at Dawn*, pr. 1936; *No Villain*, pr. 1937; *The Man Who Had All the Luck*, pr. 1944, pb. 1989; *All My Sons*, pr., pb. 1947; *Death of a Salesman*, pr., pb. 1949; *An Enemy of the People*, pr. 1950, pb. 1951 (adaptation of Henrik Ibsen's play); *The Crucible*, pr., pb. 1953; *A Memory of Two Mondays*, pr., pb. 1955; *A View from the Bridge*, pr., pb. 1955 (one-act version); *A View from the Bridge*, pr. 1956, pb. 1957 (two-act version); *Collected Plays*, pb. 1957 (includes *All My Sons*, *Death of a Salesman*, *The Crucible*, *A Memory of Two Mondays*, and *A View from the Bridge*); *After the Fall*, pr., pb. 1964; *Incident at Vichy*, pr. 1964, pb. 1965; *The Price*, pr., pb. 1968; *The Creation of the World and Other Business*, pr. 1972, pb. 1973; *The Archbishop's Ceiling*, pr. 1977, pb. 1984; *The American Clock*, pr. 1980, pb. 1982; *Arthur Miller's Collected Plays, Volume II*, pb. 1981 (includes *The Misfits*, *After the Fall*, *Incident at Vichy*, *The Price*, *The Creation of the World and Other Business*, and *Playing for Time*); *Two-Way Mirror*, pb. 1984; *Danger: Memory!*, pb. 1986, pr. 1987; *Plays*, pb. 1988-1995 (5 volumes); *The Last Yankee*, pb. 1991, pr. 1993; *The Ride Down Mt. Morgan*, pr., pb. 1991; *Broken Glass*, pr., pb. 1994; *Mr. Peter's Connections*, pr. 1998, pb. 1999; *Resurrection Blues*, pr. 2002; *Finishing the Picture*, pr. 2004

LONG FICTION: *Focus*, 1945; *The Misfits*, 1961

SCREENPLAYS: *The Misfits*, 1961; *Everybody Wins*, 1990; *The Crucible*, 1996 (adaptation of his play)

SHORT FICTION: *I Don't Need You Any More*, 1967; *Homely Girl, a Life: And Other Stories*, 1995; *Presence*, 2007

TELEPLAY: *Playing for Time*, 1980

NONFICTION: *Situation Normal*, 1944; *In Russia*, 1969 (photo essay; with Inge Morath); *In the Country*, 1977 (photo essay; with Morath); *The Theater Essays of Arthur Miller*, 1978 (revised and expanded, 1996; Robert A. Martin, editor); *Chinese Encounters*, 1979 (photo essay; with Morath); *"Salesman" in Beijing*, 1984; *Conversations with Arthur Miller*, 1987 (Matthew C. Roudané, editor); *Spain*, 1987; *Timebends: A Life*, 1987; *Arthur Miller and Company*, 1990

(Christopher Bigsby, editor); *The Crucible in History, and Other Essays*, 2000; *Echoes Down the Corridor: Collected Essays, 1947-2000*, 2000; *On Politics and the Art of Acting*, 2001

MISCELLANEOUS: *The Portable Arthur Miller*, 1995 (Christopher Bigsby, editor)

Arthur Miller first achieved success as a dramatist with *All My Sons*. *Death of a Salesman*, widely regarded as Miller's most important play, contains many of the themes of identity that give distinction to Miller's plays: the tension between father and son, the dangerous material lure of the American Dream, the influence of memory on the formation of personality, and the common man in a tragic situation.

Partly in response to the anticommunist hysteria that was led by Senator Joseph McCarthy and the House Committee on Un-American Activities that swept the nation in the early 1950's, Miller wrote *The Crucible*. In 1955, Miller was denied a passport by the State Department, and in June, 1956, he was accused of left-wing activities and called before the committee. Unlike the girls in *The Crucible*, Miller refused to name others, and he was convicted of contempt of Congress in 1956, only to be fully exonerated by the United States Court of Appeals in 1958. During the turbulent summer of 1956 Miller also divorced his college sweetheart Mary Slattery and quickly married the famous actress Marilyn Monroe. Reflections of those two events recur throughout Miller's works and give shape to the identity of many of his major characters.

After completing the screenplay for *The Misfits*, which starred Monroe, Miller divorced the actress and married Inge Morath, events that may be reflected in *After the Fall*. Miller's later years saw the publication of his influential *The Theater Essays of Arthur Miller*, numerous revivals of his major plays, and his illuminating autobiography *Timebends: A Life*.

Arthur Miller (Inge Morath/Magnum)

Miller lectured at the University of Michigan in the mid-1970's, thereafter retiring to an estate in Roxbury, Connecticut. There he continued to write and pursue his love of carpentry and gardening. In 1997, he petitioned the Czech government to halt arrests of dissident writers. During the 1980's, he directed *Death of a Salesman* in Beijing, China. Throughout the 1990's, Miller received numerous honors for his achievements. In early 2002, his wife died, and three years later, in early 2005, Miller died at his home in Connecticut.

Death of a Salesman

Type of work: Drama
First produced: 1949, pb. 1949

Death of a Salesman, widely regarded as Miller's best and most important play, chronicles the downfall and suicide of Willy Loman, a ceaselessly struggling New England salesman driven by dreams of success far greater than he can achieve. Almost a classical tragedy in its form, *Death of a Salesman* has provoked much controversy due to the unheroic nature of its protagonist. Although the play, like its Greek forebears, conveys a sense of the inevitability of fate, Willy himself possesses no greatness in either achievement or status. Willy's sheer commonness, rather, gives the play its power. In *Death of a Salesman*, Miller shows that tragedy comes not only to the great but also to the small.

On its most fundamental level, *Death of a Salesman* depicts the disintegration of Willy's personality as he desperately searches for the moment in his memory when his world began to unravel. The play's action is driven primarily by Willy's volcanic relationship with grown son Biff, who is every inch the failure that his father is. Willy's grandiose dreams of happiness and material success conflict with the reality of his failures as a salesman, as a husband to his wife Linda, and as a father to his two boys, Biff and Happy. The alternation between present action and presentations of Willy's delusional "memories" forms the play's thematic center. Willy's memory is populated by figures who idealize success, most notably his brother Ben, who became rich; Dave Singleman, a fabulously successful and well-liked salesman; and the woman in Boston with whom Willy has had an affair. Countering those empty fantasies are the realities of Howard, Willy's unsympathetic boss; Charley, Willy's best friend and neighbor (who gives Willy the money he needs to pay his bills); Charley's successful son Bernard; and of course Biff, who refuses to accept Willy's delusions. "We never told the truth for ten minutes in this house!" Biff says at one point. Willy cannot accept the piercing truth of Biff's description: "You were never anything but a hard-working drummer who landed in the ash can like all the rest of them!" Rather, Willy commits suicide by crashing his car. The play's final tragic irony comes out in the play's last scene: Although Willy strove all his life to be well-liked and remembered, his funeral is attended only by his close family and friends. Neither he nor they are finally free, but only alone.

Suggested Readings

Bigsby, Christopher, ed. *Arthur Miller and Company*. London: Methuen, 1990.
_______. *The Cambridge Companion to Arthur Miller*. Cambridge, England: Cambridge University Press, 1997.
Bloom, Harold, ed. *Arthur Miller*. New York: Chelsea House, 1987.
_______. *Arthur Miller's "Death of a Salesman."* New York: Chelsea House, 1988.

Brater, Encoh. *Arthur Miller: A Playwright's Life and Works*. New York: Thames & Hudson, 2005.

_______, ed. *Arthur Miller's America: Theater and Culture in a Time of Change*. Ann Arbor: University of Michigan Press, 2005.

Gottfried, Martin. *Arthur Miller: His Life and Work*. Cambridge, Mass.: Da Capo Press, 2003.

Koorey, Stefani. *Arthur Miller's Life and Literature*. Metuchen, N.J.: Scarecrow Press, 2000.

Martine, James. *Crucible: Politics, Property, and Pretense*. New York: Twayne, 1993.

Murphy, Brenda. *Miller: Death of a Salesman*. New York: Cambridge University Press, 1995.

Schleuter, June, and James K. Flanagan. *Arthur Miller*. New York: Frederick Ungar, 1987.

Contributor: Gregory W. Lanier

Henry Miller

Born: New York, New York; December 26, 1891
Died: Pacific Palisades, California; June 7, 1980

Jewish

Creator of a first-person style that deftly mixes fact, philosophy, and fantasy, and known for his sexual frankness, Miller correctly predicted that the full value of his work would not be appreciated during his lifetime.

Principal works

DRAMA: *Just Wild About Harry: A Melo-Melo in Seven Scenes*, pb. 1963

LONG FICTION: *Tropic of Cancer*, 1934; *Black Spring*, 1936; *Tropic of Capricorn*, 1939; *The Rosy Crucifixion*, 1949-1960, 1963 (includes *Sexus*, 1949, 2 volumes; *Plexus*, 1953, 2 volumes; *Nexus*, 1960); *Quiet Days in Clichy*, 1956

NONFICTION: *Aller Retour New York*, 1935; *What Are You Going to Do About Alf?*, 1935; *Max and the White Phagocytes*, 1938; *Money and How It Gets That Way*, 1938; *The Cosmological Eye*, 1939; *Hamlet*, 1939, 1941 (2 volumes; with Michael Fraenkel); *The World of Sex*, 1940, 1957; *The Colossus of Maroussi: Or, The Spirit of Greece*, 1941; *The Wisdom of the Heart*, 1941; *The Angel Is My Watermark*, 1944 (originally pb. in *Black Spring*); *Murder the Murderer*, 1944; *The Plight of the Creative Artist in the United States of America*, 1944; *Semblance of a Devoted Past*, 1944; *The Air-Conditioned Nightmare*, 1945; *The Amazing and Invariable Beauford Delaney*, 1945; *Echolalis: Reproductions of Water Colors by Henry Miller*, 1945; *Henry Miller Miscellanea*, 1945; *Maurizius Forever*, 1945; *Obscenity and the Law of Reflection*, 1945; *Why Abstract?*, 1945 (with Hilaire Hiler and William Saroyan); *Patchen: Man of Anger and Light, with a Letter to God by Kenneth Patchen*, 1946; *Of, by, and About Henry Miller: A Collection of Pieces by Miller, Herbert Read, and Others*, 1947; *Portrait of General Grant*, 1947; *Remember to Remember*, 1947; *Varda: The Master Builder*, 1947; *The Smile at the Foot of the Ladder*, 1948; *The Waters Reglitterized*, 1950; *The Books in My Life*, 1952; *Nights of Love and Laughter*, 1955 (Kenneth Rexroth, editor); *Argument About Astrology*, 1956; *A Devil in Paradise: The Story of Conrad Mourand, Born Paris, 7 or 7:15 P.M., January 17, 1887, Died Paris, 10:30 P.M., August 31, 1954*, 1956; *The Time of the Assassins: A Story of Rimbaud*, 1956; *Big Sur and the Oranges of Hieronymus Bosch*, 1957; *The Red Notebook*, 1958; *The Henry Miller Reader*, 1959 (Lawrence Durrell, editor); *The Intimate Henry Miller*, 1959 (Lawrence Clark Powell, editor); *Reunion in Barcelona: A Letter to Alfred Perlès*, 1959; *To Paint Is to Love Again*, 1960; *The*

Michael Fraenkel-Henry Miller Correspondence, Called Hamlet, 1962 (2 volumes); *Stand Still Like the Hummingbird*, 1962; *Watercolors, Drawings, and His Essay "The Angel Is My Watermark,"* 1962; *Books Tangent to Circle: Reviews*, 1963; *Lawrence Durrell and Henry Miller: A Private Correspondence*, 1963 (George Wickes, editor); *Greece*, 1964; *Henry Miller on Writing*, 1964 (Thomas H. Moore, editor); *Letters to Anaïs Nin*, 1965; *Selected Prose*, 1965 (2 volumes); *Order and Chaos chez Hans Reichel*, 1966; *Collector's Quest: The Correspondence of Henry Miller and J. Rivers Childs, 1947-1965*, 1968; *Writer and Critic: A Correspondence*, 1968 (with W. A. Gordon); *Insomnia: Or, The Devil at Large*, 1970; *My Life and Times*, 1971 (Bradley Smith, editor); *Henry Miller in Conversation with Georges Belmont*, 1972; *Journey to an Unknown Land*, 1972; *On Turning Eighty*, 1972; *Reflections on the Death of Mishima*, 1972; *First Impressions of Greece*, 1973; *Reflections on the Maurizius Case*, 1974; *Letters of Henry Miller and Wallace Fowlie, 1943-1972*, 1975; *The Nightmare Notebook*, 1975; *Books of Friends: A Tribute to Friends of Long Ago*, 1976; *Four Visions of America*, 1977 (with others); *Gliding into the Everglades, and Other Essays*, 1977; *Sextet*, 1977; *Henry Miller: Years of Trial and Triumph*, 1978; *My Bike and Other Friends*, 1978; *An Open Letter to Stroker!*, 1978 (Irving Stetner, editor); *Some Friends*, 1978; *Joey: A Loving Portrait of Alfred Perlès Together with Some Bizarre Episodes Relating to the Other Sex*, 1979; *Notes on "Aaron's Rod" and Other Notes on Lawrence from the Paris Notebooks of Henry Miller*, 1980 (Seamus Cooney, editor); *The World of Lawrence: A Passionate Appreciation*, 1980 (Evelyn J. Hinz and John J. Teumissen, editors); *Reflections*, 1981; *The Paintings of Henry Miller*, 1982; *From Your Capricorn Friend: Henry Miller and the "Stroker," 1978-1980*, 1984; *Dear, Dear Brenda*, 1986; *Letters from Henry Miller to Hoki Tokuda Miller*, 1986 (Joyce Howard, editor); *A Literate Passion: Letters of Anaïs Nin and Henry Miller*, 1987; *The Durrell-Miller Letters, 1935-1980*, 1988; *Henry Miller's Hamlet Letters*, 1988; *Henry Miller and James Laughlin: Selected Letters*, 1996 (George Wickes, editor)

Henry Valentine Miller was born in the Yorkville section of Manhattan. His father, Heinrich, drank heavily; his mother, Louise, was stern and domineering; his only sibling, Lauretta, was mentally retarded. Miller spent most of his youth in Brooklyn, living in Williamsburg from 1892 to 1900 and Bushwick from 1901 to 1907. An earnest reader, he enjoyed close friendships with neighborhood boys but felt inhibited among his female peers. In 1909 he entered the City College of New York but soon left. After beginning work as a cement company clerk, he embarked on a rigorous physical regimen that included pacing cyclists on their weekend races. In the years that followed Miller moved from job to job, meeting many people, including the anarchist Emma Goldman during a trip west. Upon his return to New York, he worked in his father's tailor shop. In 1917 Miller married the pianist Beatrice Sylvas Wickens; their child Barbara was born two years later. In 1920 he began a four-year stint as the employment manager of Western Union.

Frustrated in an unhappy marriage, Miller became infatuated with June Edith

Smith, whom he met in a dance hall in 1923; the following year he left Western Union, divorced Beatrice, married June, and tried to develop his literary skills. During the emotionally turbulent years that followed, he and June eked out a bohemian existence, earning money through a variety of schemes. In an outburst of creativity in 1927 Miller sketched the notes that formed the basis of *Tropic of Capricorn* and the trilogy *The Rosy Crucifixion*. In 1930 Miller left June in the United States and embarked on his second visit to Europe, eventually arriving in Paris; he and June were divorced by proxy in 1934. That same year he received world attention as a result of the publication of *Tropic of Cancer*. Besides garnering much praise for him, the work gained worldwide notoriety for itself and Miller because of its sexual frankness (*Tropic of Cancer*, *Tropic of Capricorn*, *The Rosy Crucifixion*, and other works by Miller were banned in the United States and Great Britain until the 1960's). During this period Miller wrote the epistolary *Aller Retour New York*, a scathing account of a visit to Manhattan, and the wide-ranging correspondence with Michael Fraenkel that comprised the *Hamlet* books. He also began his close relationship with Anaïs Nin, who provided him with financial and emotional support and sparked his interest in D. H. Lawrence.

Henry Miller (Larry Colwell)

Tropic of Capricorn, Miller's most stylistically complex work, appeared in 1939. Many readers in the United States who did not first encounter Miller's writing via smuggled editions of his books did so through the collection *The Cosmological Eye*, which included his short story "Max" as well as an essay on director Luis Buñuel's film *L'Âge d'or* (1930). Leaving France in 1939, Miller traveled to Greece, where he visited Lawrence Durrell and met raconteur George Katsimbalis, a kindred spirit whom he dubbed "the Colossus of Maroussi." His book by the same title is often cited as his greatest work. In 1944 Miller moved to Big Sur, California, and married Janina M. Lepska, with whom he had two children before their divorce in 1952. Miller then married Eve McClure in 1953; the two were divorced in 1962.

In 1957 Miller was elected to the National Institute of Arts and Sciences; in 1960 he served as a judge at the Cannes International Film Festival. Grove Press first published *Tropic of Cancer* for distribution in the United States in 1961; subsequent legal action established the company's right to bring Miller's banned writings to a receptive public. In 1962, Miller established a home in Pacific Palisades, California, where he lived until his death in 1980. There he reaped the pleasures and difficulties of his fame, lending his support to artists, small presses, and literary magazines while pursuing his interests in nonfiction writing and watercolor painting. His unhappy fifth and last marriage, to Hiroki "Hoki" Tokuda, lasted from 1967 to 1978. Miller appeared in Warren Beatty's film *Reds* (1981) and served as the focus of several documentaries and recordings.

Miller believed that the full value of his work would not be appreciated during his lifetime, since the restricted distribution of many of his writings focused attention on the scandalous aspects of his genius rather than its overall substance. The misleading attribution by Grove Press of the pornographic *Opus Pistorum* (1983; also known as *Under the Roofs of Paris*) to Miller, who penned only a small portion of the work, exemplifies the difficulties engendered by his notoriety. In a literary era populated with portraits of paralyzed and pessimistic intellectuals, Miller employed his expressive first-person narrative voice, developed over a lifetime of compulsive letter writing, to celebrate spiritual growth and creativity.

Tropic of Cancer

Type of work: Novel
First published: 1934

Even in the twenty-first century, *Tropic of Cancer* still has the power to startle and overwhelm a reader. Its wild, violent language, its immense force, its radiant paeans to the historic beauty of Paris, and its unsettling descriptions of a society in an advanced state of decomposition reflect a bottom dog's sense of the world that is still relevant and disturbing.

Even the fairly explicit sexual passages retain the power to shock and disturb, not because of their pornographic content but because they show the psychotic self-absorption of people ruined by social stratification and personal egocentricity. Miller wrote the book as a declaration of his own survival after a wrenching psychic experience, and his exuberant embrace of nearly every aspect of existence is a reflection of his discovery that he had found a voice and a form appropriate to the ideas and ambitions he had been harboring for his entire adult life. Before the book was published, Nin read the manuscript and accurately described the protagonist as "the mould-breaker . . . the revolutionist," and the revolution Miller was proclaiming was part of the modernist enterprise of challenging conventional but no longer viable authority.

One aspect of this challenge was the form of the book itself. It was begun originally as a kind of journal called "Paris and Me," and Miller eventually divided the book into fifteen sections. It has little character development, however, beyond the narrator's personal journey, a discontinuous sense of chronology, no plot in any familiar sense, no real dramatic events, and no conclusion. Instead, the narrative drifts and drives from "the fall of my second year in Paris" (in 1929) and continues in rhythmic lurches to the spring of 1931, but time is elastic. Days and months have no particular meaning, as the narrator has no regular job or any other specific schedule. This enables him to roam freely, at random primarily, so that he is able to avoid all the traps that have led his companions to spiritual destruction.

Certain motifs recur throughout the book. There are many scenes of male bonding, including men eating, drinking, arguing, complaining, and womanizing together. One of the most striking among these is section 8, in which Miller describes Van Norden, a nonspiritual man, as a mechanical monster who is something of a double for the protagonist. These sections are often bracketed with descriptions of women from the perspective of male lust. In passages such as the one in section 3, where the protagonist celebrates the qualities of Germaine, a whore he finds admirable, Miller is criticizing the narrowness and self-centered posturing of the men in the book. These passages are often also apostrophes to the mythic beauty and mysterious power of Woman, what Norman Mailer calls Miller's "utter adoration," reflecting "man's sense of awe."

A third motif includes an introduction of the comic into almost everything so that mundane difficulties become a source of humor rather than a cause for concern. This capacity for appreciating the comic aspect of a generally frustrating and discouraging pattern of searching for food, love, friendship, and so on is what separates the protagonist from nearly everyone else, and this gives Miller, as his fourth motif, a pure vision of ecstasy generated by the almost delirious contemplation of beauty in many forms, particularly in the city itself.

Section 13 offers Miller's powerful tribute to artist Henri Matisse, constructed in terms of the artist's use of light—a continuing fascination for Miller, who sets it against the darkness and sterility of the cancerous world. The fact that the protagonist can emerge from a realm of human decomposition with his sense of wonder at the phenomena of the universe intact is what makes the book exhilarating in spite of all the failure it examines. As the book moves toward a conclusion, or at least an ending or stopping, Miller becomes more and more rhapsodic, exclaiming "I love everything that flows," in a tribute to writer James Joyce.

On the last pages of the book, after a bizarre interlude spent teaching at a boys' school in Dijon (a job Nin helped Miller obtain), the protagonist steps out of a doomed culture and into a landscape of serenity. For a moment, as he regards the River Seine, he is able to imagine himself merging with the great flow of cosmic energy that animates the universe, his own manic energy temporarily spent and his psychic demons relegated to the realm he has left. The culmination of the artist's development at the end of *Tropic of Cancer* is, as Jay Martin says, proof that he is now the man who can write the book.

Tropic of Capricorn

Type of work: Novel
First published: 1939

If Miller's first novel, *Tropic of Cancer*, can be seen as a modern version of Dante's *Inferno*, then *Tropic of Capricorn* is clearly Miller's version of Dante's *Purgatorio*.

The earlier book describes a world of sex and surreal violence without love. This novel opens in a similarly hellish environment, but the central character (a fictional version of the author) recognizes its nature, passes through a series of purgatorial punishments, and emerges possessed of an angelic or paradisiac vision.

The book opens with Miller living in New York and working as personnel manager of the Cosmodemonic Telegraph Company. He describes himself as a clown living in an insane world, dominated by his deadly business life, violence at home in a loveless marriage, and crazy random sex. With the lesson of his father's broken spirit before him, he dreams of the imaginative freedom he finds in books but sinks into a torpor of despair at the life around him. The only force that keeps him from giving in to his despair is the sensuous power he finds in sex. The middle portion of the book is a catalog of sexual encounters, present and remembered, all explicitly described in Miller's uniquely explosive language. This sexual landscape is purgatorial, filled with suffering and betrayal and loss but ultimately liberating.

The book is dedicated to "Her," a woman like Dante's Beatrice who opens to him a vision of life beyond the wheel of destiny. He achieves resurrection from the tomb of the telegraph company in a vision of life as love. He calls himself Gottlieb Leberecht Muller, a God-loved and loving, right-living man who has baptized himself anew. In his new angelic identity as a man who has walked out on himself, a happy rock in the divine stream of life, he meets Mona (Her) and begins a new life as an artist with both death and birth behind him.

Suggested Readings

Brown, J. D. *Henry Miller*. New York: Frederick Ungar, 1986.

Dearborn, Mary V. *The Happiest Man Alive: A Biography of Henry Miller*. New York: Simon & Schuster, 1991.

Ferguson, Robert. *Henry Miller: A Life*. New York: Norton, 1991.

Gottesman, Ronald, ed. *Critical Essays on Henry Miller*. New York: G. K. Hall, 1992.

Jahshan, Paul. *Henry Miller and the Surrealist Discourse of Excess: A Poststructuralist Reading*. New York: P. Lang, 2001.

Lewis, Leon. *Henry Miller: The Major Writings*. New York: Schocken Books/Random House, 1986.

Mathieu, Bertrand. *Orpheus in Brooklyn: Orphism, Rimbaud, and Henry Miller*. Paris: Mouton, 1976.

Mitchel, Edward, ed. *Henry Miller: Three Decades of Criticism*. New York: New York University Press, 1971.

Widmer, Kingsley. *Henry Miller*. Rev. ed. Boston: Twayne, 1990.

Contributors: David Marc Fischer and Leon Lewis

Anchee Min

Born: Shanghai, China; 1957

Chinese American

Min's powerful story of the Cultural Revolution is about rebellion against political and sexual repression.

Principal works

long fiction: *Katherine*, 1995; *Becoming Madame Mao*, 2000; *Wild Ginger*, 2002; *Empress Orchid*, 2004; *The Last Empress*, 2007

nonfiction: *Red Azalea*, 1994 (personal narrative)

Born in Shanghai, Anchee Min (ahn-chee mihn) experienced political turmoil from an early age. During her childhood, Min's family was forced to move into a series of shabby apartments while her parents were demoted from their teaching positions to become factory workers. Min joined the Red Guards in elementary school and underwent a wrenching introduction to political survival when she was forced to denounce her favorite teacher as a Western spy.

Min's major experience with the clash between personal and political needs came at seventeen when she was assigned to an enormous collective farm. Forced to become a peasant in order to become a "true" revolutionary, Min witnessed the destruction of a friend whose relationship with a man led to her madness and his death. Min therefore knew the danger she faced when she fell in love with the leader of her workforce, the charismatic Yan. The two eventually began a sexual relationship that violated the strictures against premarital sex and committed the "counterrevolutionary crime" of lesbianism.

Fighting to maintain her relationship with Yan and to survive the brutal life on the farm, Min received an unexpected respite when she was chosen to audition for the lead in a propaganda film, by Jiang Qing, wife of Mao Zedong, the Communist dictator of China. Min's return to Shanghai thrust her into an even more ruthless environment than the collective farm—the Shanghai film industry. Min was rescued finally through her relationship with the enigmatic "Supervisor," the film's producer, who became Min's lover and protector. Min's deliverance, however, was short-lived. Qing's fall from power in 1976 brought about the political destruction of those associated with her. The Supervisor was able to save Min from return to the collective farm, but he was unable to keep her from being demoted to a menial position within the film studio.

Faced with an uncertain future and continued repression, Min accepted an offer from the actress Joan Chen, a fellow film student in Shanghai, to immigrate to the

United States, arriving in 1984. While learning English, she worked at a variety of jobs and received a Master of Fine Arts degree from the Art Institute of Chicago in 1990.

The great strength of Min's autobiography, *Red Azalea*, is its combination of frank narrative and lyrical description. Linking the personal and the political, Min uses sexuality as a metaphor for the individual's hunger for connection; sexual freedom thus indicates political freedom, and sexual expression becomes a revolutionary act.

Red Azalea

Type of work: Autobiography
First published: 1994

In strikingly effective prose, Min reveals her determination to retain her individuality against the force of Mao's Cultural Revolution and its determination to submerge her into the role chosen by China's Communist Party.

Red Azalea is a coming-of-age story. Min writes of her struggles with issues of identity and sexuality within the repressive environment of Mao Zedong's Cultural Revolution (1966-1976). With this focus she differs from other Chinese men and women writing about their lives in the same period in two ways: in the intensely personal journey she relates and in the simple but powerful prose she writes.

Min is proud to be identified with the nation as a young Red Guard. Still, in her home life she is a Chinese daughter, until her name is blacked out in her family's official residence papers as she leaves for Red Fire Farm. At the farm, she and her comrades work in rows, sleep in crowded, sex-segregated dorms, and study and recite Mao's teachings. This new life is difficult, but in her commander, Yan Sheng Yan, Min finds a role model of heroic response to the Party and its decrees. At the same time Min is newly conscious of sexual yearnings, which she is supposed to repress until the Party allows them. Min and Yan listen to each other's stories and experience the intimacy of a close friendship. Their joy becomes dangerous when the two women move to sexual intimacy.

This great love falters when Min is selected to go to Shanghai and compete for the starring role in Madame Mao's film/opera *Red Azalea*. In Shanghai, Min struggles between her need for Yan and her ambition to be a star. Despite her efforts, she loses the competition and is shunted to the lowly job of set-clerk. Finally, when Yan takes a male lover, Min feels as if she does not exist anymore.

Min attracts the attention of the powerful Supervisor. He is a mysterious man, womanish in his demeanor and dress, a Party loyalist but attracted to Min's individuality. She is excited by his attention, not because of any sexual attraction but because he is the key to fulfilling her heretofore thwarted ambitions to be a star. They become lovers, risking their lives by doing so. He arranges for a screen test, ousts Min's competitor, and gives Min a new chance for the starring role. She cannot say the words as he wants, and in a powerful scene he convinces Min not to play the role of Red Azalea, the ultimate Chinese heroine, but to *be* Red Azalea.

At this point, however, China changes: Mao dies, and Madam Mao and her cohorts, including the Supervisor, fall out of favor. Min is once again told to return to Red Fire Farm, but in a final act of generous love the Supervisor arranges for her to be reassigned to her post as set-clerk—probably for the rest of her life. Thus Min's story ends. She seems a Party-controlled menial laborer, luckily escaping punishment for her antirevolutionary actions.

In the epilogue, Min states that after six years, in 1984, she left China for America. In *Red Azalea* she tells her story, her personal story of love affairs, of romance, the story that in the years of the Cultural Revolution was not to be told, not to be lived. She is Red Azalea, a Chinese heroine, because she narrates in her own voice the intimately human story she lived in China's recent history. The true revolutionary, one concludes, was Min.

Empress Orchid

Type of work: Novel
First published: 2004

Empress Orchid is a brilliant re-creation of another tumultuous period in Chinese history, the late 1800's, when the empire was threatened from without by European imperialists and from within by its own decadence and corruption. Its heroine was a real person, Tsu Hsi, called "Orchid" because of her beauty. An impoverished girl whose impeccable Manchu lineage took her to court as one of the many wives of the young Emperor Hsien Feng, Orchid eventually became an empress and one of the most powerful people in China.

On her arrival in the Forbidden City, Orchid finds herself a virtual slave, her very life threatened both by a spiteful chief eunuch and by her female rivals. However, Orchid makes her way into the emperor's bed, pleases him as a sexual partner, and then so impresses him with her grasp of public affairs that she remains with him as an unofficial adviser. After Orchid bears him an heir, her power seems assured; however, Hsien Feng gives authority over the child to the unworldly Empress Nuharoo, who turns him into a little tyrant.

The ailing Hsien Feng dies when the boy is five. Now Orchid has to get control of her son away from Nuharoo, protect him and herself while she gets rid of her sinister enemy Su Shun, and establish a new regime in which she will be the power behind the throne. *Empress Orchid* ends with the heroine embarking on her ascent to power.

Suggested Readings

Huntley, Kristine. Review of *Becoming Madame Mao*, by Anchee Min. *Booklist*, March 15, 2000, 1293.

Jolly, Margaretta. "Coming out of the Coming out Story: Writing Queer Lives." *Sexualities* 4, no. 4 (November, 2000): 474-496.

Min, Anchee. "Anchee Min: After the Revolution." Interview by Roxane Farmanfarmaian. *Publishers Weekly* 247, 23 (June 5, 2000): 66-67.

Quan, Shirley. Review of *Becoming Madame Mao*, by Anchee Min. *Library Journal*, March 15, 2000, 128.

Scott, A. O. "The Re-education of Anchee Min." *The New York Times Magazine*, June 18, 2000, 44.

Seaman, Donna. Review of *Katherine*, by Anchee Min. *Booklist*, April 1, 1995, 1378.

Smith, Sarah A. Review of *Katherine*, by Anchee Min. *New Statesman and Society*, August 25, 1995, 33.

Xu, Wenying. "Agency via Guilt in Anchee Min's *Red Azalea*." *MELUS* 25, nos. 3/4 (Fall/Winter, 2000): 203-219.

Contributors: Margaret W. Batschelet and Francine Dempsey

Nicholasa Mohr

Born: New York, New York; November 1, 1935

Puerto Rican

Mohr writes of Puerto Ricans in New York, and her work features feminist characters.

Principal works

long fiction: *Nilda*, 1973 (juvenile); *Felita*, 1979 (juvenile); *Going Home*, 1986 (sequel to *Felita*)

short fiction: *El Bronx Remembered: A Novella and Stories*, 1975; *In Nueva York*, 1977; *Rituals of Survival: A Woman's Portfolio*, 1985; *The Song of El Coquí, and Other Tales of Puerto Rico*, 1995; *A Matter of Pride, and Other Stories*, 1997

The daughter of Puerto Rican immigrants, Nicholasa Mohr (NIH-koh-LAH-sah mohr) documents life in New York City's barrios. Mohr examines the Puerto Rican experience from the perspective of girls and young women. Her female characters face multiple social problems associated with the restrictions imposed upon women by Latino culture. The struggle for sexual equality makes Mohr's literature central to Latina feminism.

Mohr's characters are an integral part of her realistic portrayal of life in a barrio. The parallels between her characters and her experience are evident. Nilda Ramírez, for example, is a nine-year-old Puerto Rican girl who comes of age during World War II. She also becomes an orphan and is separated from her immediate family. There are close parallels between these events and those of Mohr's life. In other stories as well girls must face, alone, social adversity, racism, and chauvinistic attitudes. Gays also frequently appear in her work. Gays and girls or young women (especially those who have little or no family) have often been subjected to mistreatment in the male-dominated Puerto Rican culture.

Mohr, a graphic artist and painter, studied at the Brooklyn Museum Art School from 1955 to 1959. Her advocacy to the social underclass is visible in her visual art, which includes elements of graffiti. Her use of graffiti in her art attracted the attention of a publisher who had acquired several of her paintings. Believing that Mohr had a story to tell, the publisher convinced her to write a short autobiographical piece on growing up Puerto Rican in New York. Many changes later, that piece became *Nilda*, her first novel, which has earned several prizes. Mohr has also drawn pictures for some of her literary work.

New York City is as important to Mohr's writing as her Puerto Rican characters.

The city, with its many barrios, provides a lively background to her stories. Her short-story collections *El Bronx Remembered* and *In Nueva York* stress the characters' relationship to New York. Mohr's work can be described as cross-cultural, being a careful and artistic portrait of Puerto Rican culture in New York City.

El Bronx Remembered

Type of work: Short fiction
First published: 1975

Mohr's *El Bronx Remembered* is a collection of short stories depicting life in a Puerto Rican barrio in New York City during the 1960's and 1970's. Well known for her treatment of child, adolescent, and young adult characters, Mohr concentrates on subjects of particular importance to those age groups. Mohr's narratives do not offer a denunciation of the troubled lives of these immigrants and children of immigrants. Instead, her stories bring forward voices that were often, in literature, considered unimportant. Female characters of several age groups and social backgrounds stand out for analysis.

Mohr writes from autobiographical memories; she grew up in a barrio much like the one in her stories. In her hands, the barrio is a strong presence that affects the lives of her characters in myriad ways. City life and traditional Puerto Rican family values are set against one another, producing the so-called Nuyorican culture, or Puerto-Rican-in-New-York culture. The clashes within that hybrid culture are the thematic center of Mohr's short stories.

The introduction to the collection sets a strong historical context for the stories. The 1940's saw an increase in Puerto Rican migration to New York. The arrival of thousands of immigrants changed the ethnic constitution of the city, especially of Manhattan's Lower East Side and the South Bronx. El Bronx, as it is called by the Puerto Ricans, became home to new generations of Puerto Rican immigrants. The center of Nuyorican culture, El Bronx challenges the Nuyorican characters in their struggle to survive in a world of rapid economic and technological changes.

The short stories in *El Bronx Remembered* speak openly about the struggles of the first immigrants with linguistic and other cultural barriers and with racist attitudes within institutions. Mohr's stories, however, attempt to go beyond social criticism. Puerto Rican characters challenge such obstacles. Some succeed in their attempts. Others are overwhelmed by city life, facing the barrio's multiple problems, including drug abuse and gang-related troubles. The message, however, is not pessimistic. Although some characters succumb to tragedy because they are ill prepared to face adversity, others around them survive by learning from the plight of the weak.

Mohr's contribution to ethnic American literature is significant. She has made an important contribution to Latino literature by describing Puerto Rican life in New York City. Her writing has a twofold significance. One, it links the Puerto Rican experience to that of other groups, emphasizing women's issues and those of other marginal characters, such as gays, within the Puerto Rican community. Two, Mohr's work provides a link between the literature written in English about Puerto Rican life in the United States and the literature in Spanish on Puerto Rican issues.

Suggested Readings

Benson, Sonia G., Rob Nagel, and Sharon Rose, eds. *UXL Hispanic American Biography*. Detroit, Mich.: UXL, 2003.

Laezman, Rick. *One Hundred Hispanic-Americans Who Shaped American History*. San Mateo, Calif.: Bluewood Books, 2002.

Mohr, Nicholasa. "An Interview with Author Nicholasa Mohr." Interview by Nyra Zarnowski. *The Reading Teacher* 45, no. 2 (October, 1991): 106.

Quintana, Alvina E., ed. *Reading U.S. Latina Writers: Remapping American Literature*. New York: Palgrave Macmillan, 2003.

Contributor: Rafael Ocasio

N. Scott Momaday

Born: Lawton, Oklahoma; February 27, 1934

Native American

Momaday's works are poetically brilliant accounts of the landscape, the sacredness of language, and self-knowledge.

Principal works

CHILDREN'S LITERATURE: *Circle of Wonder: A Native American Christmas Story*, 1994

DRAMA: *The Indolent Boys*, pr. 1994

LONG FICTION: *House Made of Dawn*, 1968; *The Ancient Child*, 1989

POETRY: *Angle of Geese, and Other Poems*, 1974; *The Gourd Dancer*, 1976

NONFICTION: "The Morality of Indian Hating," 1964; *The Journey of Tai-me*, 1967 (memoir; revised as *The Way to Rainy Mountain*, 1969); "The Man Made of Words," 1970; *Colorado: Summer, Fall, Winter, Spring*, 1973 (with David Muench); *The Names: A Memoir*, 1976; *Ancestral Voice: Conversations with N. Scott Momaday*, 1989 (with Charles L. Woodard)

EDITED TEXT: *The Complete Poems of Frederick Goddard Tuckerman*, 1965

MISCELLANEOUS: *In the Presence of the Sun: Stories and Poems, 1961-1991*, 1992; *The Man Made of Words: Essays, Stories, and Passages*, 1998; *In the Bear's House*, 1999

Among the most widely read and studied Native American authors, N. Scott Momaday (MAWM-ah-day) manifests, in his writings, a keen awareness of the importance of self-definition in literature and life. From 1936 onward, his family moved from place to place in the Southwest, eventually settling in Albuquerque, where Momaday attended high school. He entered the University of New Mexico in 1954 and later studied poetry at Stanford University. In 1963, he received his doctorate in English and since then has held teaching jobs at various Southwestern universities.

In a semiautobiographical work, *The Way to Rainy Mountain*, Momaday writes that identity is "the history of an idea, man's idea of himself, and it has old and essential being in language." Momaday defines his characters in terms of their use or abuse of language; usually his characters find themselves relearning how to speak while they learn about themselves. Even the title of one of Momaday's essays, "The Man Made of Words," indicates his contention that identity is shaped by language. "Only when he is embodied in an idea," Momaday writes, "and the idea is realized in language, can man take possession of himself."

The forces that shape language—culture and landscape—are also crucial in Momaday's works. To Russell Martin, Western writing is concerned with the harsh realities of the frontier that "could carve lives that were as lean and straight as whittled sticks." This harsh landscape is present in Momaday's work also, but he has a heartfelt attachment to it. Having a spiritual investment in a place, in Momaday's writing, helps a person gain self-knowledge. To an extent, issues of identity were important to Momaday as well. Son of a Kiowa father and a Cherokee mother, Momaday belonged fully to neither culture. Furthermore, much of his early childhood was spent on a Navajo reservation, where his father worked, and he grew up consciously alienated from the surrounding culture.

To combat rootlessness, the imagination and its expression in language are essential. "What sustains" the artist, he writes in *The Ancient Child* "is the satisfaction . . . of having created a few incomparable things—landscapes, waters, birds, and beasts." Writing about the efforts of various people to maintain traditional culture in the face of the modern world, Momaday occupies a central place in the American literary landscape.

House Made of Dawn

Type of work: Novel
First published: 1968

House Made of Dawn, Momaday's first novel, is the story of an outcast who learns that his being is bound up in his culture. The novel, which relates the experiences of a mixed-race World War II veteran, was a signal achievement, winning the Pulitzer Prize in fiction for Momaday in 1969 and paving a way for other Native American novelists.

It begins with Abel's return to his ancestral village. Although he is so drunk that he does not recognize his grandfather, Abel's troubles run much deeper. He feels cut off from the Tanoan tribe yet unwilling to live in white America. Even more disturbing to Abel is his inability to "say the things he wanted" to anyone. His inability to express himself hampers his achieving a true identity. Wrapped up in his own problems, Abel is jealous and violent toward those who do participate in Tanoan culture. While at Walatowa, Abel loses a competition to an albino Indian and murders him.

After his release from prison, Abel tries to build a new life in California, where he comes in contact with a small community of Indians, who are also alienated from their cultures. The leader of this exile community is John Tosamah, a self-proclaimed priest of the sun, who sermonizes on the failure of white society to recognize the sacredness of the American landscape and of language. Tosamah victimizes Abel, however. Eventually, Abel is cast out of this group and is savagely beaten by a sadistic police officer, Martinez.

After the beating, Abel is physically what he was once only psychologically: an invalid. He returns to Walatowa, where his grandfather is dying. Aware that he

N. Scott Momaday (© Thomas Victor)

must embrace his Tanoan heritage, if only to perform the burial rites for his grandfather, Abel begins to heal psychologically. At the novel's end, Abel participates in another ceremony, this time a race between the young men of the tribe, which his grandfather had won years before. Abel finds "a sort of peace of mind" through participation but is certainly not healed by it. Unable to keep pace with the others, Abel keeps stumbling and falls behind. Abel's position in the tribe likewise remains unsettled. On the threshold between the world of his grandfather and that of modern America, on the threshold between spiritual values and lack of faith, Abel can do little but keep running, which becomes a gesture of hope and healing.

The Ancient Child

Type of work: Novel
First published: 1989

A complex and richly evocative work, Momaday's *The Ancient Child* is the story of two Native Americans—a middle-aged painter and a young woman—who come to a fuller understanding of themselves. Native American folklore and mythology are woven into their story, lending cultural and psychological depth to the two's quests for, essentially, rebirth.

Locke Setman, called "Set" throughout the novel, is in many ways a representative Momaday protagonist because he is cut off from his past and therefore lives an unexamined life. Brought up in an orphanage by an embittered academic, Set's connection to the Kiowa culture of his ancestors is tenuous. Because Set does not know his past, "it was in Set's nature to wonder, until the wonder became pain, who he was." His quest to achieve a more profound sense of self begins when he receives a telegram begging him to attend the funeral of one Kope' mah. Mystified by a past he has never known, Set goes to the funeral and meets Grey, who is training to become a medicine woman because she "never had . . . to quest after visions."

Like Set, Grey has not achieved her true identity, largely because she rejects the modern world. After being raped by a white farmer, she goes to live in an abandoned sod house in a ghost town. She literally dwells in the past. She speaks

Kiowan fluently, so she is befriended by Kope' mah, and becomes the link between Set's past and his future. When the two meet, Grey gives Set a medicine bag containing "the spirit of the bear." The bear, Set's unacknowledged totem animal, is as much a curse as a blessing, however, since the life that Set has lived must be stripped away before his true identity can be recognized. Set suffers a mental breakdown, and his nightmares are dominated by "a dark, impending shape" that draws him into itself, into "the hot contamination of the beast."

Eventually, when he is completely stripped of illusions, Set is drawn back to Kiowan tribal lands, and back to Grey. Set is healed and the two forge a relationship, one tied to an awareness of themselves and their culture. Grey teaches Set to speak the language of her people, and by the novel's end Set is profoundly aware of his place in their culture: "he knew . . . its definition in his mind's eye, its awful silence in the current of his blood." He belongs.

The Man Made of Words

Type of work: Essays
First published: 1998

Readers may consider *The Man Made of Words* a collection of random prose, as Momaday notes in his preface, but he sees both unity in the collection and evidence of his development as a writer. Part 1 consists of essays on Native American subjects, part 2 of travel accounts to Europe and Native American sites, and part 3 of anecdotes and observations on Native American and other subjects. How these pieces are unified is indicated by Momaday in the first essay, "The Arrowmaker," which recounts a Kiowa legend that Momaday interprets as an allegory of existence. In the legend, a Kiowa arrowmaker draws on his sense of identity and shrewd language to dispose of a lurking enemy. The arrowmaker becomes "the man made of words" and Momaday's prototype.

The Man Made of Words is thus the record of an existential act: how Momaday has used writing to define and hold on to his Native American identity. The cultural abyss that Momaday has bridged is suggested by numerous autobiographical glimpses in the collection. He grew up on a Kiowa homestead near Rainy Mountain Creek in Oklahoma and on the Navajo reservation in New Mexico. He now travels the world, has numerous friends in artistic and intellectual circles, likes fine food and wine, and has learned to fly.

The collection also records Momaday's views on such topics as language, the oral tradition, and the land. He believes that the Native American oral tradition gives words their true, sacred value, while the print culture brought by European settlers debases language. Similarly, the land and places revered by Native Americans are threatened. A recurrent theme throughout the collection is the decline and loss of the sacred.

Suggested Readings

Charles, Jim. *Reading, Learning, Teaching N. Scott Momaday*. New York: Peter Lang, 2007.

Isernhagen, Hartwig. *Momaday, Vizenor, Armstrong: Conversations on American Indian Writing*. Norman: University of Oklahoma Press, 1999.

Mason, Kenneth C. *Ancestral Voice: Conversations with N. Scott Momaday*. Interviews by Charles L. Woodard. Lincoln: University of Nebraska Press, 1989.

_______. "Beautyway: The Poetry of N. Scott Momaday." *South Dakota Review* 18, no. 2 (1980): 61-83.

Momaday, N. Scott. *Conversations with N. Scott Momaday*. Edited by Matthias N. Schubnell. Jackson: University Press of Mississippi, 1997.

Roemer, Kenneth J. *Approaches to Teaching "The Way to Rainy Mountain."* New York: Modern Language Association, 1990.

Scarberry-Garcia, Susan. *Landmarks of Healing: A Study of "House Made of Dawn*." Albuquerque: University of New Mexico Press, 1990.

Schubnell, Matthias. *N. Scott Momaday: The Cultural and Literary Background*. Norman: University of Oklahoma Press, 1985.

Schweninger, Lee. *N. Scott Momaday*. Detroit: Gale Group, 2001.

Trimble, Martha Scott. *N. Scott Momaday*. Boise, Idaho: Boise State College, 1973.

Velie, Alan R. *Four American Indian Literary Masters*. Norman: University of Oklahoma Press, 1982.

Contributor: Michael R. Meyers

Alejandro Morales

Born: Montebello, California; October 14, 1944

Mexican American

In Morales's work, a gritty depiction of the racism, oppression, and violence that afflict the poor and minority cultures of America coexists with fantastic or "magically real" interventions such as ghosts and the mythic powers of culture.

Principal works

LONG FICTION: *Caras viejas y vino nuevo*, 1975 (Old Faces and New Wine, 1981; also known as *Barrio on the Edge*, 1998); *La verdad sin voz*, 1979 (*Death of an Anglo*, 1988); *Reto en el paraíso*, 1983; *The Brick People*, 1988; *The Rag Doll Plagues*, 1992

Alejandro Morales (ah-lay-HAHN-droh moh-RAL-ehs) is a leading Chicano writer and professor at the University of California, Irvine (UCI). Born in Montebello, California (locally considered "East L.A."), Morales grew up in a secure and loving working-class home, though in the midst of a more turbulent barrio. Witnessing the gang fights, drug deals, homelessness, and chaos on the streets of his neighborhood while still in high school, Morales decided to become a writer who would chronicle his community. He recorded his neighborhood experiences in his journals and then set out for college, first to earn a B.A. from California State University, Los Angeles, and then an M.A. (1971) and Ph.D. (1975) in Spanish from Rutgers University. Morales became a professor in the Department of Spanish and Portuguese, with an appointment in film studies at UCI, teaching courses on Latin American literature. He married Rohde Teaze on December 16, 1967, and they had two children, Alessandra Pilar and Gregory Stewart.

After finishing his Ph.D., Morales pursued publication of his first novel, *Old Faces and New Wine*, which was based on his youthful journal writings. Offers from American publishing companies proved elusive because of his challenging, experimental prose style and because the journals were initially written in Spanish. His early fiction reflects Morales's anger at the exploitation of his parents, who worked in manufacturing, his despair over the conditions of the barrio, and his struggles against the racism, subtle and overt, he experienced in the academic world early in his teaching career. The result is an arresting prose style; readers of Morales's early fiction have to work to make connections between events and their meanings and must also learn to comprehend the peculiar dialect he constructs to describe his subject. Often criticized by reviewers, especially for the way he bends both Spanish and English, Morales has written substantial literature that, because it is not easily accessible, has received less attention than other Mexican American literature of his generation.

Morales wrote two more novels in Spanish, but then, seeking a wider audience in the United States, he wrote *The Brick People* and *The Rag Doll Plagues* in English. The critical success of these two works has positioned Morales as a leading Chicano novelist. Since the late 1980's, he has become a noted spokesman for Chicano writers—and Chicano culture—writing reviews and essays on Mexican American literature and Latino films and conducting interviews with other Chicano writers and poets.

Besides his stylistic innovations, Morales's early publications demonstrate his interest in local history and biography. For example, his most popular novel, *The Brick People*, is based on the lives of his parents, who immigrated to California from Mexico and lived and worked at the Simmons Brick Plant in Pasadena, California. *The Brick People* chronicles the immigration to California of an entire generation of Mexican Americans at the turn of the twentieth century and describes how their labor helped build the growing metropolis of Los Angeles in the early 1930's. It narrates the Mexican laborers' exploitation by the paternalistic brick manufacturer. In interviews, public conversations, and symposia, Morales is fond of describing the Simmons brick, which graces the landscaping of his Southern California home, remarking that, like the brick, the lives and labors of Mexican Americans are embedded in the history and geography of California.

Morales's later works, such as *The Rag Doll Plagues*, evince a strong interest in science, medicine, and technology. In these works, plots revolve around technological change and the effects of science on social evolution. This turn toward science and its social implications reflects Morales's interest in how history is shaped and recorded and how it thus guides the present and future. Furthermore, writing about science and technology gives Morales a metaphorical language for describing the ongoing evolution of Mexican American culture, as Mexican Americans, or Chicanos, increasingly integrate with Anglos, Asian Americans, and African Americans, especially in California. In Morales's allegorical fiction is a mixture of two compelling literary styles that reflect both his realism and his optimism. A gritty depiction of the racism, oppression, and violence that afflict the poor and minority cultures of America sits side by side on the page with fantastic or "magically real" interventions such as ghosts and the mythic powers of culture. Morales's continuing experimentation reflects his often stated devotion to developing his mastery of the craft of writing.

The Rag Doll Plagues

Type of work: Novel
First published: 1992

The Rag Doll Plagues is a collection of stories that offer an absorbing panoramic view of the continuing encounter of European and Native American and of English and Spanish-speaking cultures in the Americas. It is divided into three books. In book 1, Gregorio Revueltas, sent by his king to improve health conditions in seventeenth century Mexico, encounters a plague that threatens to depopulate the colony and weaken Spain's empire. Revolted by the primitive savagery and amorality of the colonials, Revueltas nevertheless grows to care for them and eventually sees himself as a Mexican. Important to this transformation is his vision of two men who often appear to guide his efforts.

In book 2 a young California doctor, Gregory Revueltas, falls in love with Sandra Spear, a hemophiliac actress. As a result of a transfusion, she develops AIDS during the first years after its identification. Seeking help, he returns with her to Old Mexico, where he and Sandra rediscover the ancient Mexican/Indian spiritual traditions that help her to think of death as a positive transformation, traditions that seem verified in Gregory's guiding visions of his ancestor, Gregorio.

Book 3 takes place at the end of the twenty-first century in Lamex, an extrapolated administrative region that comprises most of western Mexico and the southwestern United States. Gregory Revueltas, state doctor, deals with frequent plagues that erupt from centers of organic pollution that have become living entities. He discovers that Mexicans from the highly polluted Mexico City area have developed a genetic mutation that makes their blood, given in transfusion, a cure for most lung ailments. He, too, is led by the visionary presence of his ancestor, Gregorio. At the end of this book, Revueltas, as narrator, reflects upon the multiple ironies of Mexicans' new place in American civilization.

Suggested Readings

Gurpegui, José Antonio, ed. *Alejandro Morales: Fiction Past, Present, Future Perfect*. Tempe, Ariz.: Bilingual Review/Press, 1996.

Gutiérrez-Jones, Carl. "Rancho Mexicana: USA Under Siege." In *Rethinking the Borderlands: Between Chicano Culture and Legal Discourse*. Berkeley: University of California Press, 1995.

Libretti, Tim. "Forgetting Identity, Recovering Politics: Rethinking Chicano/a Nationalism, Identity Politics, and Resistance to Racism in Alejandro Morales's *Death of an Anglo*." *Post Identity* 1, no. 1 (Fall, 1997): 66-93.

Contributors: Dean Franco, Adrienne Pilon, and Terry Heller

Toni Morrison
(Chloe Anthony Wofford)

Born: Lorain, Ohio; February 18, 1931

African American

Morrison is the first African American woman to receive the Nobel Prize in Literature.

Principal works

CHILDREN'S LITERATURE: *The Big Box*, 1999 (with Slade Morrison and Giselle Potter); *The Book of Mean People*, 2002 (with Morrison); *The Ant or the Grasshopper?*, 2003 (with Morrison); *The Lion or the Mouse?*, 2003 (with Morrison); *Remember: The Journey to School Integration*, 2004

DRAMA: *Dreaming Emmett*, pr. 1986

LONG FICTION: *The Bluest Eye*, 1970; *Sula*, 1973; *Song of Solomon*, 1977; *Tar Baby*, 1981; *Beloved*, 1987; *Jazz*, 1992; *Paradise*, 1998; *Love*, 2003

NONFICTION: *Playing in the Dark: Whiteness and the Literary Imagination*, 1992; *Conversations with Toni Morrison*, 1994 (Danille Taylor-Guthrie, editor); *Birth of a Nation'hood: Gaze, Script, and Spectacle in the O.J. Simpson Case*, 1997; *Remember: The Journey to School Integration*, 2004

EDITED TEXTS: *To Die for the People: The Writings of Huey P. Newton*, 1972; *The Black Book: Three Hundred Years of African American Life*, 1974; *Race-ing Justice, En-gendering Power: Essays on Anita Hill, Clarence Thomas, and the Construction of Social Reality*, 1992; *Deep Sightings and Rescue Missions: Fiction, Essays, and Conversations*, 1996 (of Toni Cade Bambara)

Toni Morrison was born Chloe Anthony Wofford; her family was blue-collar midwestern. Her parents had migrated from the South in search of a better life. From her parents and grandparents, Morrison acquired a background in African American folklore; magic and the supernatural appear with frequency in her work.

At Howard University, where she earned a bachelor's degree, she changed her name to Toni. After receiving a master's degree in English from Cornell University, she taught at Texas Southern University and then at Howard, where she met Jamaican architect Harold Morrison. Their marriage ended after seven years. A single mother, Toni Morrison supported herself and two sons as a senior editor at Random House, where she encouraged the publication of African American literature. She has continued to teach at various universities, including Harvard, Yale, and Princeton.

Originally, Morrison did not intend to be a writer. She has said she began to write because she could not find herself, a black woman, represented in American fiction. In a conversation with novelist Gloria Naylor, published in *Southern Review*, Morrison speaks of reclaiming herself as a woman and validating her life through the writing of her first book, *The Bluest Eye*, in which a young black girl prays for the blue eyes that will bring her acceptance.

Morrison celebrates the culture of strong black women that she remembers from her childhood, especially in *Sula*, *Song of Solomon*, and *Beloved*. She believes that being able to recognize the contribution and legacy of one's ancestors is essential to self-knowledge. Her characters are forced to confront their personal and social histories and are often drawn back to their African heritage.

Some black male critics have challenged Morrison on the grounds that her male characters are too negative, but the literary world has honored her. In 1988, *Beloved* was awarded the Pulitzer Prize for fiction. In 1989 she was named Robert F. Goheen Chair in the Humanities at Princeton University, a title she held until her retirement in 2006. In 1993, Morrison became the second American woman and the first African American woman to receive the Nobel Prize in Literature. In 2005, Oxford University honored her with a doctorate of letters.

The Bluest Eye

Type of work: Novel
First published: 1970

In *The Bluest Eye*, Morrison shows how society inflicts on its members an inappropriate standard of beauty and worth, a standard that mandates that to be loved one must meet the absolute "white" standard of blond hair and blue eyes. Morrison's narrator says that two of the most destructive ideas in history are the idea of romantic love (canceling both lust and caring) and the idea of an absolute, univocal standard of beauty.

In the novel, the most extreme victim of these destructive ideas is Pecola, who finds refuge in madness after she has been thoroughly convinced of her own ugliness (confirmed when she is raped by her own father, Cholly). Mrs. Breedlove, Pecola's mother, is another victim who gets her idea of an unvarying standard of beauty from romantic motion pictures that glorify white film stars. When she realizes the impassible gap between that ideal and her physical self (she has a deformed foot and two missing teeth), she also gives up any hope of maintaining a relationship with Cholly, her husband, except one of complete antagonism and opposition. Mrs. Breedlove even comes to prefer the little white girl she takes care of at work to her own daughter, Pecola, whom she has always perceived as ugly.

The ideal of unattainable physical beauty is reinforced by the sugary, unattainable world of the family depicted in the school readers—of Mother and Father and Dick and Jane and their middle-class, suburban existence. The contrast between that false standard of life and the reality lived by the children makes them ashamed of their reality, of the physical intimacy of families in which the children have seen their fathers naked.

Although Pecola is thoroughly victimized, Freida and Claudia MacTeer, schoolmates of Pecola, do survive with some integrity and richness. Freida seems to accept Shirley Temple as the ideal of cuteness, but her sister Claudia, a center of consciousness in the novel, responds with anger and defiance, dismembering the hard, cold, smirking baby dolls she receives at Christmas. What Claudia really desires at Christmas is simply an experience of family closeness in the kitchen, an experience of flowers, fruit, and music, of security.

Claudia's anger at the white baby dolls springs from a conviction of her own reality and her own worth. In defense of her own individuality, Claudia rejects Shirley Temple and "Meringue Pie," the high yellow princess, Maureen Peal. It is that defense of her own reality that makes Claudia sympathize with Pecola and try to defend her, even to the point of sacrificing Freida's money and her own.

Claudia is especially puzzled and regretful that nobody says "poor baby" to the raped Pecola, that nobody wants to welcome her unborn baby into the world. It would be only natural, "human nature," it seems, for people to sympathize with a victim and rejoice at the creation of a human life. Instead, the springs of human sympathy have been dammed up by social disapproval. Suffering from the self-hatred they have absorbed from the society around them, the black community maintains inflexible social standards and achieves respectability by looking down on Pecola. The two MacTeer sisters appeal to nature to help Pecola and her unborn baby, but nature fails them just as prayer did: No marigolds sprout and grow that year. The earth is unyielding. The baby is stillborn. Eventually, even the two girls become distanced from Pecola, whose only friend is an imaginary one, a part of herself who can see the blue eyes she was promised. Pecola functions as a scapegoat for the society around her, and Claudia's sympathy later grows into an understanding of how the community used Pecola to protect itself from scorn and insult. What finally flowers in Claudia is insight and a more conscious respect for her own reality.

Sula

Type of work: Novel
First published: 1973

Sula also explores the oppressive nature of white society, evident in the very name of the "Bottom," a hillside community which had its origin in the duplicitous white treatment of an emancipated black slave who was promised fertile "bottom land" along with his freedom. In a bitterly ironic twist, the whites take over the hillside again when they want suburban houses that will catch the breeze. In taking back the Bottom, they destroy a place, a community with its own identity. In turn, the black community, corrupted by white society, rejects Sula for her experimenting with her life, for trying to live free like a man instead of accepting the restrictions of the traditional female role.

Sula provokes the reader to question socially accepted concepts of good and evil. As Sula is dying, she asks her girlhood friend Nel, "How do you know that you were the good one?" Although considered morally loose and a witch by the townspeople, the unconventional Sula cannot believe herself to be an inferior individual. Contrasting the traditional role of mother and church woman that Nel has embraced, Sula's individuality is refreshing and intriguing. Despite her death, Sula maintains an independence that ultimately stands in proud opposition to the established network of relationships that exist within conventional society.

The novel shows that the Bottom society encompasses both good and evil. The people are accustomed to suffering and enduring evil. In varying degrees, they accept Eva's murder of her drug-addict son, Plum, and Hannah's seduction of their husbands, one after another. The community, nevertheless, cannot encompass Sula, a woman who thinks for herself without conforming to their sensibilities. They have to turn her into a witch, so that they can mobilize themselves against her "evil" and cherish their goodness. Without the witch, their goodness grows faint again. Like Pecola, Sula is made a scapegoat.

Growing up in the Bottom, Sula creates an identity for herself, first from the reality of physical experience. When she sees her mother Hannah burning up in front of her eyes, she feels curiosity. Her curiosity is as honest as Hannah's admission that she loves her daughter Sula the way any mother would but that she does not like her. Hearing her mother reject her individuality, Sula concludes that there is no one to count on except herself.

In forging a self, Sula also draws on sexual experience as a means of joy, as a means of feeling sadness, and as a means of feeling her own power. Sula does not substitute a romantic dream for the reality of that physical experience. She does finally desire a widening of that sexual experience into a continuing relationship with Ajax, but the role of nurturing and possession is fatal to her. Ajax leaves, and Sula sickens and dies.

A closeness to the elemental processes of nature gives a depth to the lives of the Bottom-dwellers, although nature does not act with benevolence or even with consistency. Plum and Hannah, two of Eva's children, die by fire, one sacrificed by Eva and one ignited by capricious accident. Chicken Little and several of those who follow Shadrack on National Suicide Day drown because acts of play go wrong and inexplicably lead to their destruction. Sula's supposed identity as a witch is connected to the plague of robins that coincides with her return to the Bottom. The people of the Bottom live within Nature and try to make some sense of it, even though their constructions are strained and self-serving.

On one level, Sula refuses any connection with history and family continuity. Her grandmother Eva says that Sula should get a man and make babies, but Sula says that she would rather make herself. On the other hand, Sula is a descendant of the independent women Eva and Hannah, both of whom did what they had to do. It is at least rumored that Eva let her leg be cut off by a train so that she could get insurance money to take care of her three children when BoyBoy, her husband, abandoned her. When her husband died, Hannah needed "manlove," and she got it from her neighbors' husbands, despite community disapproval. In their mold, Sula is independent enough to threaten Eva with fire and to assert her own right to live, even if her grandmother does not like Sula's way of living.

To flourish, Morrison suggests, conventional society needs an opposite pole. A richness comes from the opposition and the balance—from the difference—and an acceptance of that difference would make scapegoats unnecessary. The world of the Bottom is poorer with Sula dead and out of it.

Song of Solomon

Type of work: Novel
First published: 1977

Song of Solomon, Morrison's third novel, received the 1978 National Book Critics Circle Award for fiction. In her first work to feature a male protagonist, she established the rich narrative voice for which she has become famous. Macon "Milkman" Dead, grandson of a slave, evolves from a self-centered youth to a man of compassion and understanding. He completes this transition as he searches for his family origins, thus exemplifying Morrison's belief in the importance of ancestors.

Originally, Milkman desires to know as little as possible about his family. Torn by the ongoing conflict between his parents, he sets out to find his inheritance, which he believes to be gold in the possession of his father's sister, Pilate. Instead, Milkman's quest leads him out of the Midwest to discover his true heritage, his ancestors. He gains pride in his family when he encounters old men who remember his father and grandfather. Before long he is more interested in locating his people than in the gold.

At the town of Shalimar, in Virginia, after the symbolic initiation of a night hunt, Milkman recognizes his own selfishness. He learns that a child's game, the town itself, and many of the people bear some version of his great-grandfather Solomon's name. The figure of Solomon is based upon a legend of the Flying African, who escaped slavery by leaping into the air and flying home to Africa. Milkman realizes that his great-grandfather has become a folk hero.

Heritage is symbolized by the importance of names. The powerful and eccentric Pilate wears her name, laboriously copied from the Bible by her father, in her mother's snuffbox, which has been made into an earring. She always carries her parents with her. Pilate, an imposing woman who has no navel, struggled with her identity in her teens, when she determined to live by her own rules. One of Morrison's strong, independent women, she cuts her hair short like a man's and becomes a bootlegger for practical reasons. She is also a mythic figure, birthing herself after the death of her mother. Pilate communicates comfortably with her father's ghost, a friendly presence that appears and tells her what she needs to know. She carries his bones around with her in a tarp. He is her guide to maturity; in turn, she becomes Milkman's. Through her, Milkman learns what she already accepts: "When you know your name, you should hang on to it."

Tar Baby

Type of work: Novel
First published: 1981

Toni Morrison (Alfred A. Knopf)

Tar Baby explores three kinds of relationships: the relationship between blacks and whites; the relationships within families, especially between parents and children; and the relationship between the American black man and black woman. In the epigraph to the novel, Saint Paul reproaches the Corinthians for allowing contentions to exist among their ranks; the quote serves to foreshadow the discord that abounds in the novel's relationships.

In *Tar Baby*, Morrison depicts not a self-contained black society but an onstage interaction between blacks and whites. The novel juxtaposes two families, a white family of masters and a black family of servants. The white family includes a retired candy-maker, Valerian Street, and his wife Margaret, once the "Principal Beauty of Maine," who is now in her fifties. The couple's only son Michael lives abroad; his arrival for Christmas is expected and denied by various characters.

The black family consists of the husband, Sydney Childs, who is Valerian's valet and butler, and the wife, Ondine, who serves as cook and housekeeper. They are childless, but their orphan niece Jadine plays the role of their daughter. (Valerian has acted as Jadine's patron, paying for her education at the Sorbonne.)

The pivotal character, however, who enters and changes the balance of power and the habitual responses of the families, is a black man who rises out of the sea. His true name is Son, although he has gone by other aliases. The veneer of politeness and familiarity between the characters is shaken by Son's abrupt appearance. Uncomfortable racial and personal assumptions are put into words and cannot be retracted. The Principal Beauty is convinced that Son has come to rape her: What else would a black man want? (Jadine is convinced that if Son wants to rape anyone, it is she, not Margaret.) Sydney finds Son a threat to his respectability as a Philadelphia black because when Son appears, the white people lump all blacks together. Ondine seems less threatened, but most of her energy goes into her running battle with the Principal Beauty. Jadine is apprehensive at Son's wild appearance, and later she is affronted by his direct sexual approach. Only Valerian welcomes Son. He sees him as a vision of his absent son Michael, and he invites him to sit down at the dining table and be a guest.

Son's coming is the catalyst that causes time-worn relationships to explode when Michael does not come for Christmas. His failure to appear leads to the revelation that the Principal Beauty abused her son as a child, pricking him with pins and burning him with cigarettes. Ondine, the black woman, finally hurls this accusation at Margaret, the white woman, and makes explicit what the two women have known mutually since the beginning. Valerian, who has been haunted by the memory of Michael as a lonely child who would hide under the sink and sing to himself, is hit with a reality much harsher than he has known or admitted.

Structured as it is in terms of families, the whole novel revolves around family responsibilities, especially between parents and children. Michael Street does not come home for Christmas, but the abuse he suffered as a child seems to justify his absence. Thus, the undutiful mother Margaret has thrown the whole family off balance. In the black family, later in the novel, attention is drawn to the undutiful daughter Jadine, although it seems implied that she has learned this undutifulness, partly at least, from whites, wanting her individual success to be separate from family ties and responsibilities.

This undutifulness also springs from a question of identity. In Paris, even before she comes to Valerian's island, Jadine feels affronted by a beautiful, proud, contemptuous African woman in yellow, who buys three eggs and carries them on her head. She is herself and embodies her tradition consummately, exhibiting balance and physical grace that symbolize spiritual poise. Jadine feels diminished and threatened by the African woman, who spits at her. The scorn sends Jadine back to her family, Sydney and Ondine.

Jadine is similarly disturbed by her dream of the women with breasts, the mothers, who reproach her for not joining that chain of mothers and daughters who become mothers with daughters. Although Jadine herself is an orphan, reared by Ondine and Sydney and owing much to their care, she refuses to take the self-sacrificing role of the woman who cares for her family. Jadine wants money and the power it brings in the white world. After a little more modeling, she wants to run her own business, perhaps a boutique. Also, she may choose a white husband, like the man who bought her a seductive sealskin coat.

Jadine is the Tar Baby of the novel, and Son is Brer Rabbit from the Uncle Remus stories. As the Tar Baby, Jadine acts as a possible trap for Son set by his enemies, white society. Jadine, who has absorbed many white values, wants money and success. Son wants something purer, something associated with nature (he is associated with the sea and the beauty of the savannas) and with family tradition. Nature, direct physical experience, and family traditions that are integral to personal identity are all important values in Son's existence. Son has a home—the completely black town of Eloe—and there he abides by the ideas of respectability held by his father and his Aunt Rosa. (He asks Jadine to sleep at Aunt Rosa's, apart from him, and he comes to her secretly only when she threatens to leave if he does not.) To amuse herself in the traditional town, in which she is uncomfortable, Jadine takes photographs of the people and steals their souls, stealing their individual beauty and grace. In the photographs, they seem graceless, poor, and stupid, even to Son, who usually sees them with loving eyes.

Individually, Son and Jadine love each other, but they seem unable to find a world in which they can both thrive. Yet Son is an undaunted lover, unwilling to let Jadine go, even when she flees from him. Son tries to return to Isle de Chevaliers, Valerian's island, to get news of Jadine, but the only way he can get there seems to be through the help of Thérèse, the half-blind, fifty-year-old black woman who says that her breasts still give milk. Thérèse takes him by boat to the island of the horsemen. Son has said that he cannot give up Jadine, but Thérèse tells him to join the fabled black horsemen who see with the mind. At the end of the novel, Son is running toward his destiny, whether that be Jadine and some way to make her part of his world or the black horsemen who ride free through the hills. Readers do not know what Son's fate is to be; they only know that Son is running toward it, just as Brer Rabbit ran from his enemy Brer Fox and from the Tar Baby. Like Milkman Dead at the end of *Song of Solomon*, Son leaps into mythic possibility; like Brer Rabbit, Son, the black man, is a figure with the power to survive.

Beloved

Type of work: Novel
First published: 1987

Beloved's dedication, "Sixty Million and More," commemorates the number of slaves who died in the middle passage—from Africa to the New World. Morrison's protagonist, Sethe, is modeled upon the historical figure of a fugitive Kentucky slave, who in 1851 murdered her baby rather than return it to slavery.

A pregnant Sethe flees on foot to Cincinnati, Ohio, sending her children ahead by way of the Underground Railroad. Her overwhelming concern is to join her baby daughter, who needs her milk. On the bank of the Ohio River she goes into labor, her delivery aided by a white girl who is herself fleeing mistreatment. The new baby is named Denver. Although Sethe reaches her destination, slave-catchers soon follow to return her to Kentucky. Frantic, she tries to kill her children rather than submit them to slavery, but she succeeds only with the older baby. "Beloved" is carved on the child's tombstone.

Sethe accepts her identity of black woman, escaped slave, wife, mother. Her antagonist is life, which has taken so much from her. She and Paul D, the man who becomes her lover, are the last survivors of Sweet Home, the Kentucky farm that was neither sweet nor home to them. Their charge is to endure memory and accept the unforgivable past.

A vengeful spirit, that of the dead baby, invades Sethe's house. After Paul D drives it away, a strange young woman appears in the yard, and they take her in. Her name is Beloved. She is the ghost of Sethe's dead child. She is also, less clearly, a ghost from the slave ships and an African river spirit. She alters relationships in the household, exerting control over the two adults and Denver. Denver hovers over Beloved; Beloved dotes on Sethe. Once Sethe recognizes Beloved as her daughter, she struggles to make amends while Beloved grows plump and cruel.

Denver develops a new identity. At eighteen, she is self-centered, jealous, and lonely. Beloved becomes her dear companion. Gradually, Denver grows aware that Beloved's presence is destroying Sethe, who loses her job along with her meager income and begins to waste away. Denver, who has rarely ventured past her own yard because of the neighbors' hostility, realizes that only she can save her mother. Terrified, she walks down the road to seek work from strangers and, by accepting this responsibility, becomes a woman.

Morrison expected this painful, fiercely beautiful novel to be controversial. Instead, it was widely praised, receiving the Pulitzer Prize for fiction in 1988.

Jazz

Type of work: Novel
First published: 1992

Toni Morrison's Pulitzer Prize-winning best seller *Beloved* was a hard act to follow, but her new novel, *Jazz*, is an adventurous, richly imagined work that extends her range into Afro-American city life.

Jazz begins with a terse, anecdotal story that seems closely akin to such blues ballads as "Frankie and Johnny." Joe Trace, a door-to-door salesman in his fifties, has a "deepdown, spooky love" for eighteen-year-old Dorcas, but he shoots her when their three-month-old affair goes awry. Joe's wife Alice then takes a strange revenge by bursting in on Dorcas's funeral and trying to slash the dead girl's face.

Playing off this sensational opening story, Morrison's quirky narrative voice ranges in many directions, much as a jazz musician might improvise on the opening statement of a melody. In a vividly sensuous style, the author brings to life both the excitement of Jazz Age Harlem, to which many African Americans migrated after World War I, and the racism, violence, and unresolved mysteries of the places they left behind. She compels the reader to care for Joe, Alice, Corcas, and many other characters by vividly dramatizing both their individual passions and their discoveries of their own unique identities. Ultimately, it is the power of Morrison's narrator and characters to renew and reinvent themselves—much as a jazz musician plays upon an old melody.

Paradise

Type of work: Novel
First published: 1998

Paradise, Morrison's first novel since she was awarded the 1993 Nobel Prize in Literature, rises easily to the level of her best work. It takes place in Ruby, Oklahoma, the second incarnation of an all-black town originally founded by a group of former slaves. Ruby remains largely isolated from the rest of the world, and its inhabitants prefer it that way. The town leaders are men who have inherited a passion for freedom, religion, and respect, but their passion has gradually become distorted into a fanaticism that will brook no contradiction. They resist any challenge to tradition.

Ruby's patriarchy is ignored by the five independent women who come one by one to live in an old mansion known as the Convent, some seventeen miles from town. The women are Consolata, a former servant at the Convent; Mavis, a battered wife; Gigi, the free-spirited activist; Seneca, who slices her skin with razors; and Pallas, a lonely little rich girl. In the course of the novel they find peace through Consolata, who becomes the consoler her name suggests as she intuitively instructs them in the rites of a very old religion. They exemplify a separation from the rigid, authoritarian ways of Ruby.

The novel begins at its climax, with an attack by the town vigilantes against the Convent, then winds through past events to return to that same attack. Morrison offers a delightful blend of complex characters and magical language. The novel is elliptical, told in Morrison's rich, storyteller voice, creating an effect of increasing illumination, introducing people and events as gradually as dawning light clarifies the interior of a room.

Suggested Readings

Bloom, Harold, ed. *Toni Morrison*. New York: Chelsea House, 1990.

Conner, Marc C., ed. *The Aesthetics of Toni Morrison: Speaking the Unspeakable*. Jackson: University Press of Mississippi, 2000.

Fultz, Lucille P. *Toni Morrison: Playing with Difference*. Urbana: University of Illinois Press, 2003.

Furman, Jan. *Toni Morrison's Fiction*. Columbia: University of South Carolina Press, 1996.

_______, ed. *Toni Morrison's "Song of Solomon."* New York: Oxford University Press, 2003.

Harris, Trudier. *Fiction and Folklore: The Novels of Toni Morrison*. Knoxville: University of Tennessee Press, 1991.

Kubitschek, Missy Dehn. *Toni Morrison: A Critical Companion*. Westport, Conn.: Greenwood Press, 1998.

McKay, Nellie Y., ed. *Critical Essays on Toni Morrison*. Boston: G. K. Hall, 1988.

Otten, Terry. *The Crime of Innocence in the Fiction of Toni Morrison*. Columbia: University of Missouri Press, 1989.

Peach, Linden, ed. *Toni Morrison*. New York: St. Martin's Press, 1998.

Samuels, Wilfred D., and Clenora Hudson-Weems. *Toni Morrison*. Boston: Twayne, 1990.

Contributors: Joanne McCarthy, Kate Begnal, and Nika Hoffman

Walter Mosley

Born: Los Angeles, California; January 12, 1952

African American

Mosley brought a new perspective to the hard-boiled detective genre with an African American detective and settings in Watts and South Central Los Angeles.

Principal works

CHILDREN'S LITERATURE: *Forty-Seven*, 2005

LONG FICTION: *RL's Dream*, 1995; *Always Outnumbered, Always Outgunned*, 1997; *Blue Light*, 1998; *Walkin' the Dog*, 1999; *The Man in My Basement*, 2004; *Fortunate Son*, 2006; *The Wave*, 2006; *Killing Johnny Fry*, 2007; *Diablerie*, 2008

LONG FICTION (EASY RAWLINS SERIES): *Devil in a Blue Dress*, 1990; *A Red Death*, 1991; *White Butterfly*, 1992; *Black Betty*, 1994; *Gone Fishin'*, 1996; *A Little Yellow Dog*, 1996; *Bad Boy Brawly Brown*, 2002; *Little Scarlet*, 2004; *Cinnamon Kiss*, 2005; *Blonde Faith*, 2007

LONG FICTION (FEARLESS JONES SERIES): *Fearless Jones*, 2001; *Fear Itself*, 2003; *Fear of the Dark*, 2006

SHORT FICTION: *Futureland: Nine Stories of an Imminent World*, 2001; *Six Easy Pieces: Easy Rawlins Stories*, 2003

NONFICTION: *Workin' on the Chain Gang: Shaking Off the Dead Hand of History*, 2000; *What Next: A Memoir Toward World Peace*, 2003; *Life Out of Context: Which Includes a Proposal for the Non-Violent Takeover of the House of Representatives*, 2006; *This Year You Write Your Novel*, 2007

EDITED TEXTS: *Black Genius: African American Solutions to African American Problems*, 1999 (with others); *The Best American Short Stories, 2003*, 2003 (with Katrina Kenison)

With the publication of his first detective novel, *Devil in a Blue Dress*, Walter Mosley (MOHZ-lee) accomplished the difficult feat of bringing a fresh perspective to that genre, the hard-boiled detective story, in which few writers have equaled—and none has improved—upon the style as it was as originally fashioned by Raymond Chandler and Dashiell Hammett. The terse prose, sarcastic wit, and tough-guy action that mark their books have served as the yardstick against which all newcomers are measured and most are found wanting. Mosley, however, succeeded in carving out a place for himself within the genre. Although his books are, like Chandler's, set in Los Angeles, Mosley's detective is African American and his world is the world of Watts and South Central. That setting may be geographically close to Chandler's "mean streets," but it is light-years away from them in every other regard. Mosley's detective, Ezekiel "Easy" Rawlins, moves within the setting of his creator's own childhood, and his community is the one in which Mosley was raised.

Born in the Watts district of Los Angeles, Mosley is the son of an African American father, who worked as a school custodian, and a white, Jewish mother, who was employed as a clerk by the Board of Education. Mosley grew up listening to stories of his father's youth in the South and of his mother's Russian Jewish family. After graduating from high school, he enrolled first in Goddard College in Vermont and later graduated from Johnson State College. A brief period in graduate school at the University of Minnesota ended when he moved to Boston to continue his relationship with the dancer/choreographer Joy Kellerman, whom he married in 1987.

While living in Boston, Mosley worked as a caterer and a potter. Following his move to New York with Kellerman in 1982, he switched to computer programming. He had always been an avid reader, but it was only after reading Alice Walker's novel *The Color Purple* (1982) that he realized for the first time that there was a place in literature for his own experience. He was inspired to try his hand at writing and completed a novella entitled *Gone Fishin'* while attending creative writing classes at New York's City College. In that work, which remained unpublished until 1996, he first used the character who later became the focus of his detective novels, Ezekiel "Easy" Rawlins.

Based in part on his father's experiences as a black man from the South who had immigrated to Los Angeles after World War II, the saga of Easy Rawlins is also the history of that city's African American community. Although the novels' structure is that of the traditional detective novel, Mosley's ultimate intent is to chronicle the community in which he was raised and the changes it had undergone since the late 1940's. Like the author, Rawlins is a veteran who finds that his military service overseas does not bring him more respect or better treatment back home.

The first book in the Easy Rawlins series, *Devil in a Blue Dress*, opens with Easy's being laid off from his defense plant job and undertaking some investigative work in an effort to meet his mortgage payments. The plot is set at a time when Los Angeles's African American community was in its heyday: Stores and jazz clubs lined Central Avenue, and black Americans expected that their contributions to the war effort would bring them a share of the postwar prosperity. Easy's investigation into a woman's disappearance, however, reveals just how wide the economic and social gap between the races had remained. *Devil in a Blue Dress* brought Mosley an Edgar nomination from the Mystery Writers of America and firmly established his reputation as a writer.

In his second book, *A Red Death*, Mosley draws on his dual heritage as both an African American and a Jew in his portrayal of the relationship—increasingly frayed in more recent years—between the African American and Jewish communities. The novel is set during the McCarthy era and finds Easy forced to cooperate with the Federal Bureau of Investigation (FBI) in their investigation of a Jewish union organizer, an Eastern European who reawakens Easy's dark memories

Walter Mosley (Courtesy, Allen & Unwin)

of the liberation of the concentration camps. Mosley is often identified solely in terms of his African American heritage, but in *A Red Death* he acknowledges his mother's legacy.

Mosley's books often focus on racial discrimination and the frustration and rage it can engender. Easy's dealings with the police are sometimes marked by gross injustice and brutality, which instill in him an anger that he only rarely dares to express. *White Butterfly*, Mosley's third novel in the series, deals with discrimination against the entire African American community as the murders of several black women are ignored until a white woman also falls victim to the killer. The next book, *Black Betty*, also explores the tremendous disparity in the way people of different races are treated; here the title character is a once-vibrant and seductive woman who works as a maid in the home of a wealthy and powerful white family.

Mosley's love of blues music led him to venture outside the detective genre for his fifth novel, *RL's Dream*, a well-received portrait of a dying blues musician and the culture that shaped his life. With *A Little Yellow Dog*, Mosley returned to Easy Rawlins, by this time a school janitor in 1963. His efforts to get off the street seem about to come to naught when he becomes involved in a double murder revolving around an attractive white teacher at the school. *Always Outnumbered, Always Outgunned* again leaves Easy for another character, Socrates Fortlow, a former convict trying to come to terms with life in Watts in a series of fourteen interconnected short stories. Fortlow reappears in *Walkin' the Dog*. *Blue Light* marked Mosley's foray into science fiction. The novel concerns mysterious blue lights that flicker in the Northern California skies, causing those they strike to develop a higher understanding of human purpose. *Walkin' the Dog* returns to the character of Socrates Fortlow, still facing moral dilemmas in the Los Angeles ghetto. *Fearless Jones* introduced yet another eponymous protagonist, working the private detective gig in 1950's Los Angeles. *Bad Boy Brawly Brown* returns to Easy Rawlins, this time struggling through the racial tensions simmering in Los Angeles in 1964 and the rise of black militancy.

For all of Mosley's forays into other genres and other characters, it is his Easy Rawlins novels that receive the greatest attention, for in them Mosley illuminates a part of Los Angeles history that had been long ignored. In the detective series he created books that are both familiar and startlingly original, taking his readers down a much-traveled road to a new destination.

A Little Yellow Dog

Type of work: Novel
First published: 1996

An early morning when Easy Rawlins is seduced by a beautiful young teacher and a dead body is found on the school grounds sets in motion a wild and complex plot involving larceny, drug dealing, and multiple deaths. Easy had arranged for a new job in an attempt to avoid danger and to provide a steady living for his foster children, but Idabell Turner and her problems (the corpse is that of her brother-in-law) trap him in more murder and mayhem.

With the support of his friend and a backup muscle, Mouse Alexander, Easy tries to get himself off the hook despite the dark suspicions of Sergeant Sanchez, a homicide detective who is convinced that Easy is a murderer and that he is also responsible for a rash of burglaries of school equipment. Easy makes a variety of deals with menacing criminals to deflect suspicion from himself, to rescue friends from dire situations, and incidentally to try to find who killed Idabell's brother-in-law, her husband, and Idabell herself. He also has time to fall in love with a beautiful stewardess named Bonnie Shay.

A final deal backfires. Mouse is fatally wounded as he and Easy try to deliver a shipment of drugs in exchange for a cessation of violence against Easy's friends. Easy survives but in the end discovers that Bonnie Shay had killed Idabell's husband. Turner had tried to force Bonnie into drug running and had raped her. The possibility of further romance between Easy and Bonnie is one of the few bright spots in the grim ending of this gritty and tough novel.

Suggested Readings

Coale, Samuel. *The Mystery of Mysteries: Cultural Differences and Designs.* Bowling Green, Ohio: Bowling Green State University Popular Press, 1999.

Lock, Helen. "Invisible Detection: The Case of Walter Mosley." *MELUS* 26 (Spring, 2001): 77-89.

Smith, David L. "Walter Mosley's *Blue Light*: (Double Consciousness)^2." *Extrapolation* 42 (Spring, 2001): 7-26.

Wesley, Marilyn C. "Knowledge and Power in Walter Mosley's *Devil in a Blue Dress*." *African American Review* 35 (Spring, 2001): 103-116.

Young, Mary. "Walter Mosley, Detective Fiction, and Black Culture." *Journal of Popular Culture* 32 (Summer, 1998): 141-150.

Contributor: Janet E. Lorenz

Thylias Moss

Born: Cleveland, Ohio; February 27, 1954

African American

In addition to writing about the African American experience, Moss deconstructs the idea of God, liberating it from the controlling religious paradigm.

Principal works

CHILDREN'S/YOUNG ADULT LITERATURE: *I Want to Be*, 1993
DRAMA: *The Dolls in the Basement*, pr. 1984; *Talking to Myself*, pr. 1984
POETRY: *Hosiery Seams on a Bowlegged Woman*, 1983; *Pyramid of Bone*, 1989; *At Redbones*, 1990; *Rainbow Remnants in Rock Bottom Ghetto Sky*, 1991; *Small Congregations: New and Selected Poems*, 1993; *Last Chance for the Tarzan Holler*, 1998; *Slave Moth: A Narrative in Verse*, 2004; *Tokyo Butter: A Search for Forms of Deirdre*, 2006
NONFICTION: *Tale of a Sky-Blue Dress*, 1998 (memoir)

Awards earned by Thylias Moss (THIH-lee-ahs mahs) who became an English professor at the University of Michigan in 1992, include a Guggenheim, a National Endowment for the Arts Award, and a prestigious MacArthur Fellowship in 1996. Born Thylias Rebecca Brasier, Moss was the daughter of Calvin Brasier, a tire recapper, and Florida Brasier, a housekeeper. With their adored only child, the Brasiers lived in an attic apartment owned by the Feldmans, a Jewish couple who treated Thylias as though she were their own grandchild.

After the Feldmans sold the house, the thirteen-year-old daughter of the new owners, Lytta, baby-sat for the young Thylias and treated her with extreme cruelty, a fact the youngster never told her parents. Lytta victimized her physically, verbally, and sexually, forcing darkness into an otherwise idyllic childhood. It is this relationship that forms the focus of Moss's memoir, *Tale of a Sky-Blue Dress*.

Moss started school at Louis Pasteur Elementary School, a friendly, racially mixed school where her intelligence and gifted violin playing were encouraged. She sometimes led the class, contributed to discussions, wrote plays and poems, and eagerly played the violin. When she was nine, her family moved to a primarily white neighborhood. At the Benjamin Franklin School in her new neighborhood, she was treated indifferently and denied a school-issued violin as well as attendance in the accelerated classes she had been in previously. She grew resentful, withdrawn, and sullen but found solace in writing.

Moss attributes her remarkable ear for poetry to regular church attendance, where she first became aware of the power of the spoken word. Apparently what she learned stayed with her; her poetry readings, which encourage audience participation and use many voices, are popular and widely known. (In 1991 she won the annual Dewar's Profiles Performance Artist Award in poetry.)

It was also in church that she met her husband, John Moss, who was in military service and later became a University of Michigan administrator. They married when she was nineteen and eventually had two sons, Dennis and Ansted. After marrying, she spent two unhappy years at Syracuse University and then worked for several years in a Cleveland business, where she ultimately became a junior executive. She enrolled at Oberlin College and graduated in 1981 with the top academic record in her class. Later, she earned her M.F.A. in creative writing from the University of New Hampshire, where the well-known poet Charles Simic inspired her and recognized her talent. She taught at Phillips Academy in Andover, Massachusetts, and won an artist's fellowship from the Massachusetts Arts Council in 1987 that enabled her to work on her second book of poetry, *Pyramid of Bone*.

Pyramid of Bone

Type of work: Poetry
First published: 1989

This collection was short-listed for the National Book Critics Circle Award. Moss's poetry is both earnest and comic, embracing both extremes of this apparent dichotomy. In one poem she will move between a polemic tone and an irony that recognizes few boundaries. She is comfortable taking on even the most sacred cows. In "A Form of Deicide," God plays the part of her father, walking Moss down the aisle to turn her over to her husband: ". . . He will/ always be my Father, but another man will be/ my husband and I will look at him in ways God/ does not want to be seen. . . . Ever the strong, silent type. . . ."

Moss deconstructs the idea of God, liberating it from the controlling religious paradigm. Religion is a common theme in Moss's work, which often reimagines the Christian tradition with its various symbols, including angels, devils, and God. These terms are redefined in new and different ways, rendering them fresher and certainly more personal. Just as Moss is adventurous in her language, she is equally adventurous in her use of form. She juxtaposes instructions and dialogue, uses tercets to frame a poem written in quatrains, inserts italicized refrains as ironic comments on stanzas, and writes remarkable prose poems. Among the latter are "The Warmth of Hot Chocolate," spoken in the voice of an angel, "Renegade Angels," and "Dear Charles," an epistolary poem.

"Dear Charles" illustrates another of Moss's themes: the overwhelming influences that shape people of color. A woman writes to a black man of a tornado, which becomes a metaphor of her experience of him: "Not Charles, though, who, male and all, gives birth to tornadoes; little pieces of him drop off and spin madly. . . . Forgive me, but the way I feel, I can deal with you only in the third person, which is the same as dealing with the Third World." Charles replies in the voice of a black "everyman," who was turned into a storm by the weight of black history.

Many of Moss's poems deal with the African American experience, bearing titles like "Lunchcounter Freedom," "The Lynching," and "*Nigger* for the First Time." Still, she is reluctant to be classified as a "black woman poet." "I am a person," she has said, "whose ancestors were brought to this country from Africa. But it has not very much of anything to do with how I view the world." With a distinctive voice and a worldview that overlap the boundaries of race, this work brought her wide recognition as a groundbreaking poet.

Tale of a Sky-Blue Dress

Type of work: Memoir
First published: 1998

In this memoir, Moss probes her silent submission to several years of physical and sexual abuse by her teenage babysitter, who was supposed to care for her after school. This abuse so destroyed young Thylias's self-esteem that as a teenager she was sexually exploited by two older men and underwent a traumatic late-term abortion. Even as an adult, she cannot satisfactorily explain why she did not report her torment to her parents, except to believe that they could not have comprehended the nature of such evil.

Moss's salvation, in childhood and now as a wife, mother, and English professor at the University of Michigan, was—and is—her gift for language. Her tortured childhood is, she says, reflected in her poetry, leaving her "with a need to make sense of humanity's defects and psychologies." Her love of beauty, expressed in an explosion of images, is elicited by the world of nature, science, and the people she observes with such keen insight. In her journey toward redemption, she describes the cruelty of the public schools, slow to recognize giftedness in a black child, and the anti-intellectualism of the fundamentalist church that suppressed her aspirations. With this work, and through the love of the compassionate man she married, Moss reclaimed her self-identity.

Suggested Readings

Hammer, Langdon. "Invisible Things." *The American Scholar* 74, no. 2 (Spring, 2005): 49ff.

Kitchen, Judith. "Poetry Reviews." *Georgia Review*, Winter, 1998, 763-765.

Winston, Jay. "The Trickster Metaphysics of Thylias Moss." In *Trickster Lives: Culture and Myth in American Fiction*, edited by Jeanne Campbell Reesman. Athens: University of Georgia Press, 2001.

Contributor: Sheila Golburgh Johnson

Bharati Mukherjee

Born: Calcutta, India; July 27, 1940

South Asian American

Mukherjee is perhaps the foremost fiction writer describing the experience of Third World immigrants to North America.

Principal works

long fiction: *The Tiger's Daughter*, 1972; *Wife*, 1975; *Jasmine*, 1989; *The Holder of the World*, 1993; *Leave It to Me*, 1997; *Desirable Daughters*, 2002; *The Tree Bride*, 2004

short fiction: *Darkness*, 1985; *The Middleman, and Other Stories*, 1988

nonfiction: *Kautilya's Concept of Diplomacy*, 1976; *Days and Nights in Calcutta*, 1977 (with Clark Blaise); *The Sorrow and the Terror: The Haunting Legacy of the Air India Tragedy*, 1987 (with Blaise); *Political Culture and Leadership in India: A Study of West Bengal*, 1991; *Regionalism in Indian Perspective*, 1992

Bharati Mukherjee (bah-RAH-tee MEWK-ehr-jee) was born to an upper-caste Bengali family and received an English education. The most important event of her life occurred in her early twenties, when she received a scholarship to attend the University of Iowa's Writers' Workshop. Her fiction reflects the experimental techniques fostered at such influential creative writing schools.

At the University of Iowa, Mukherjee met Clark Blaise, a Canadian citizen and fellow student. When they moved to Canada she became painfully aware of her status as a nonwhite immigrant in a nation less tolerant of newcomers than the United States. The repeated humiliations she endured made her hypersensitive to the plight of immigrants from the Third World. She realized that immigrants may lose their old identities but not be able to find new identities as often unwelcome strangers.

Mukherjee, relying on her experience growing up, sought her salvation in education. She obtained a Ph.D. in English and Comparative Literature and moved up the career ladder at various colleges and universities in the East and Midwest until she became a professor at Berkeley in 1989. Her first novel, *The Tiger's Daughter*, was published in 1972. Like all her fiction, it deals with the feelings of exile and identity confusion that are experienced by immigrants. Being female as well as an immigrant, Mukherjee noted that opportunities for women were so different in America that she was exhilarated and bewildered. Many of her best stories, dealing with women experiencing gender crises, have a strong autobiographical element.

Darkness, her first collection of stories, was well reviewed, but not until the publication of *The Middleman, and Other Stories* did she become internationally prominent. She is dealing with perhaps the most important contemporary phenomenon, the population explosion and flood of immigrants from have-not nations. Mukherjee makes these newcomers understandable to themselves and to native citizens, while shedding light on the identity problems of all the anonymous, inarticulate immigrants of America's past. Her protagonists are not the "huddled masses" of yesteryear; they are talented, multilingual, enterprising, often affluent men and women who are transforming American culture. Mukherjee's compassion for these newcomers has made her one of the most important writers of her time.

The Middleman, and Other Stories

Type of work: Short fiction
First published: 1988

The Middleman, and Other Stories deals with the clash between Western and Third World cultures as technology and overpopulation join diverse peoples in tragicomic relationships. "A Wife's Story" is a good example of Mukherjee's storytelling technique. It is told in the present tense, begins abruptly, and has an interest, characteristic of literary minimalism, in brand names and consumerism. The narrator sees her Indian husband through American eyes when he visits her in New York City, where she is attending college. He is captivated by the meretricious glamour and abundance of consumer goods. The narrator realizes how Americanized she has become and how comically provincial her husband appears.

Alfred Judah in "The Middleman" is a man without a country, a Jew living in Central America and hoping to make his way to the United States. Some think he is an Arab and others think he is an Indian; he is despised by everyone. In "Orbiting," an American woman is living with an Afghan lover who is another man without a country, unable to obtain legal entry into any of the developed countries being flooded with immigrants.

In "Buried Lives," an Indian who is prospering in Sri Lanka abandons his responsibilities for a new life in America. After leading a terrifying underground existence, he finds himself engaged to be married in Germany. "Danny's Girls" is about immigrants who come to the United States for a better life and who become prostitutes. "Jasmine" has a similar theme.

"The Management of Grief"

Type of work: Short fiction
First published: 1988, in *The Middleman, and Other Stories*

Based on an actual event—the Sikh terrorist bombing of an Air India plane on June 23, 1985, which killed all 329 passengers and crew—"The Management of

Grief" is Mukherjee's "tribute to all who forget enough of their roots to start over enthusiastically in a new land, but who also remember enough of their roots to survive fate's knockout punches." Mukherjee's story focuses on Shaila Bhave in the hours, days, and months following the deaths of her husband and two young sons. The story focuses on her forms of grief and guilt, which are specific to her culture. As an Indian wife, she never spoke her husband's name or told him she loved him—simple acts that Westerners take for granted. Her grief reveals who Shaila is, was, and will be. As do many of the characters in Mukherjee's stories and novels, she finds herself caught between cultures, countries, and existences. "At thirty-six," she considers, "I am too old to start over and too young to give up. Like my husband's spirit, I flutter between two worlds."

One of the worlds is Indian, including the highly supportive Hindu community in Toronto, from which she feels strangely detached. The Hindu community in Toronto is itself part of a larger Indian immigrant community that includes Muslims, Parsis, atheists, and even the Sikhs, tied by religion if not necessarily by politics to those responsible for the bombing, which is part of a struggle for autonomy being waged by Sikh extremists in India. Even within Toronto's Hindu community there are divided allegiances as parents "lose" their children to Western culture no less than to terrorist bombs. The other world, the "West," or more specifically Canada, is equally problematic, especially for Indian immigrants such as Mrs. Bhave, who are made to feel at best marginalized, at worst excluded altogether. She experiences the insensitivity of police investigators, the inadequacy of news coverage (the implicit message is that the victims and their families are not really Canadian), and finally the well-intentioned but ineffectual efforts of a government social worker's textbook approach to "grief management." The social worker enlists Mrs. Bhave's help in assisting those who have not been "coping so well."

Bharati Mukherjee (Tom Victor)

The story's complex identity theme is reflected in its spatial diversity. It follows Mrs. Bhave from Toronto to Ireland (to identify remains) and then to India, where she believes she hears her husband's voice telling her: "You must finish alone what we started together." This seemingly irrational link to tradition, including her thinking that her husband and sons "surround her like creatures in epics," gives her the strength to leave India and return to Canada. Although she does not assume, as some of the older relatives do, that God will provide, she is provided for and in a way that precludes the reader's seeing her as entirely representative. Thanks to her husband's savings and the sale of their house, she is financially secure and so can afford to heed her dead husband's final admonition: "Go, be brave." Her future, including her future identity, may be uncertain, but in that uncertainty Shaila Bhave finds her freedom, one inextricably rooted in loss.

The Holder of the World

Type of work: Novel
First published: 1993

The Holder of the World is a complex narrative tour de force. On one level, it is the story of an extraordinary, and extraordinarily (even implausibly) modern young woman from seventeenth century Massachusetts, Hannah Easton, who becomes a Hindu king's lover in India. On another level, it is an attempt by the narrator—present-day thirtysomething "asset-hunter" Beigh Masters—to reconstruct Hannah's life. On yet a third level, the book is the author's—Mukherjee's—attempt to prove that "everything in history . . . is as tightly woven as a Kashmiri shawl," that "there are no accidents." That this attempt is only partly successful is only to be expected; such conceits are a large and honorable part of any novelist's motivation.

Like any very good, complex work of narrative, *The Holder of the World* is "about" several things at once. It is a feminist and very contemporary rewriting of the story of early British imperialism. It is an audacious rewriting of Nathaniel Hawthorne's classic American novel *The Scarlet Letter*. It is an essay on the great literary topic of the present day: the meeting and mixing of peoples. "Of all the qualities I admire in Hannah Easton that make her entirely our contemporary in mood and sensibility, none is more touching to me than the sheer pleasure she took in the world's variety," comments Beigh, the narrator. *The Holder of the World* is an important, engrossing novel that will stimulate much lively discussion.

Suggested Readings

Alam, Fakrul. *Bharati Mukherjee*. New York: Twayne, 1996.

Bowen, Deborah. "Spaces of Translation: Bharati Mukherjee's 'The Management of Grief.'" *Ariel* 28 (July, 1997): 47-60.

Chua, C. L. "Passages from India: Migrating to America in the Fiction of V. S. Naipaul and Bharati Mukherjee." In *Reworlding: The Literature of the Indian Diaspora*, edited by Emmanuel S. Nelson. Westport, Conn.: Greenwood Press, 1992.

Drake, Jennifer. "Looting American Culture: Bharati Mukherjee's Immigrant Narratives." *Contemporary Literature* 40 (Spring, 1999): 60-84.

Fakrul, Alam. *Bharati Mukherjee*. New York: Twayne, 1996.

Mukherjee, Bharati. "Interview." In *Speaking of the Short Story: Interviews with Contemporary Writers*, edited by Farhat Iftekharuddin, Mary Rohrberger, and Maurice Lee. Jackson: University Press of Mississippi, 1997.

Nazareth, Peter. "Total Vision." *Canadian Literature: A Quarterly of Criticism and Review* 110 (1986): 184-191.

Nelson, Emmanuel S., ed. *Bharati Mukherjee: Critical Perspectives*. New York: Garland, 1993.

Scheer-Schäzler, Brigitte. "'The Soul at Risk': Identity and Morality in the Multicultural World of Bharati Mukherjee." In *Nationalism vs. Internationalism: (Inter)National Dimensions of Literature in English*, edited by Wolfgang Zach and Ken L. Goodwin. Tübingen: Stauffenburg, 1996.

Schlosser, Donna. "Autobiography, Identity, and Self-Agency: Narrative Voice in Bharati Mukherjee's *Jasmine*." *English Language Notes* 38 (December, 2000): 75-92.

Contributors: Bill Delaney and Robert A. Morace

Albert Murray

Born: Nokomis, Alabama; May 12, 1916

African American

"The mainstream is not white but mulatto," Murray wrote in The Omni-Americans. *His novels, poetry, and essays ponder the implications of this statement, exploring the richness of African American culture and its immersion in American cultural life.*

Principal works

LONG FICTION: *Train Whistle Guitar*, 1974; *The Spyglass Tree*, 1991; *The Seven League Boots*, 1996; *The Magic Keys*, 2005

POETRY: *Conjugations and Reiterations*, 2001

NONFICTION: *The Omni-Americans: New Perspectives on Black Experience and American Culture*, 1970; *South to a Very Old Place*, 1971; *The Hero and the Blues*, 1973; *Stomping the Blues*, 1976; *Good Morning Blues: The Autobiography of Count Basie*, 1985 (as told to Albert Murray); *The Blue Devils of Nada: A Contemporary American Approach to Aesthetic Statement*, 1996; *Conversations with Albert Murray*, 1997 (Roberta S. Maguire, editor); *Trading Twelves: The Selected Letters of Ralph Ellison and Albert Murray*, 2000 (Albert Murray and John F. Calhoun, editors); *From the Briarpatch File: On Context, Procedure, and American Identity*, 2001

After receiving his B.A. from Tuskegee Institute and his M.A. from New York University, Murray taught literature at Tuskegee; for a while he also directed the College Little Theatre. Beginning in 1943 Murray served in the U.S. Air Force, from which he retired in 1962 as major. He lectured at several universities, including Columbia University's Graduate School of Journalism, Colgate University, University of Massachusetts, University of Missouri, and Barnard College; he was also writer-in-residence at Emory University and professor of creative writing at Barnard College and Dupont Visiting Scholar at Washington and Lee universities.

Like his friend and fellow Tuskegee alumnus Ralph Ellison, Murray derived much of the content and style of his work from music. In his first book-length work, *The Omni-Americans*, he explores the complicated relationships among cultures in the United States, asserting that "any fool can see that the white people are not really white, and that black people are not black. They are all interrelated one way or another." Far from being an Africanist, Murray nevertheless argues for recognition of the particular aesthetic that is "a central element in the dynamics of U.S. Negro life-style." This aesthetic depends on improvisation and stylization, where improvisation is experimenting with the possibilities and stylization is developing these possibilities into a unique personal statement. The interaction of these largely African solutions within an American context has created an African American expressive culture encompassing music, dance, language, religion, sports, fashions, physical deportment, and food. Yet Murray insists that the "omni-Americans" of his title are also all American people, perhaps even all humanity, who have created the mulatto culture and identity he describes.

South to a Very Old Place converts his description of African American identity into an intellectual autobiography composed as a set of improvisational essays. Begun at the request of Willie Morris for a *Harper's* magazine series called "Going Home in America," the book explores not only the geographical South of Murray's youth but also the South of cultural and intellectual historians, journalists, novelists, storytellers, and musicians of all ethnicities and locations, whom Murray engages in actual or imagined conversation throughout the book.

In 1972 Murray gave three public lectures at the University of Missouri. In *The Hero and the Blues*, the published version of those lectures, Murray continues his meditation on the role of the artist and the function of literature in society. Murray eloquently describes a blues aesthetic in literature from Thomas Mann to Ernest Hemingway and reflects on heroic action and the quest for selfhood in terms of the blues dynamic, which he defines as antagonistic cooperation. Heroes become heroic by overcoming obstacles. The sinister circumstances that inspire heroism also demand that the hero continue to grow in response to their challenge. Murray discusses stylization and improvisation as the means of experimenting within a tradition and developing unique solutions to ongoing problems. Thus in opposition to protest fiction, which fails to offer solutions, hope, or heroes, Murray praises heroic art—the blues—as the victory of art and metaphor over the human situation.

In 1973 Murray published the first of two loosely autobiographical novels, *Train Whistle Guitar*. Through the eyes and ears of the narrator, Scooter, and his best friend Little Buddy Marshall, Murray reveals a concrete and multishaded blues culture, from summer baseball's blue skies to the steel-blue freight trains whistling through Gasoline Point, Alabama. Scooter begins his narrative sorting through stories about the mysterious bluesman Luzana Cholly and ends by solving a riddle he is late even in coming to recognize, the riddle of his own past. In verbal riffs celebrating the specificity of real life picnics, schoolrooms, barbershops, and music of the twelve-string guitar and the honky-tonk piano, Murray fixes in words the history and texture of Southern rural African American community and vernacular culture.

Stomping the Blues is, as the title indicates, an exploration of African American rhythm- and body-centered music in its many guises: religious expression, song, dance, swing, be-bop, and "equipment for living." Essentially a cultural history, *Stomping the Blues* combines Murray's inimitable literary style with the perceptions of a trained musician and the point of view of a cultural analyst. Murray regards blues music as heroic, not sorrowful, and stomping the blues as a cultural purification ritual.

The Spyglass Tree briefly recapitulates the events of Murray's earlier novel before launching into Scooter's experiences during four years on an Alabama college campus. *The Seven League Boots* continues Scooter's story; after graduating from college, he becomes a bass player with a Duke Ellington-esque pianist and composer at the height of the Swing era.

From the Briarpatch File is a collection of Murray's essays that offers a good introductory overview of his work and his major themes. In *Conjugations and Reiterations*, Murray let his fascination with the blues and other musical forms take hold of his words and create poetry. Wordplay and rhythm make his poems as much oral lyrics as they are words printed on a page.

The Spyglass Tree

Type of work: Novel
First published: 1991

The first section of *The Spyglass Tree* concerns Scooter's polymath college roommate, nicknamed "Snake" because his prodigious intellectual accomplishments remind Scooter of a snake doctor. At the same time he is studying literature, drama, poetry, botany, chemistry, geography, electronics, and military history, Snake mentors Scooter in constructing miniature stage sets, greenhouses, and model airplanes, and Scooter reflects on how these things are connected. Friendships, community, family, baseball, and the combination of childhood educators and fairy godmothers that steered him toward a college education weave through his thoughts on the present shape and future trajectory of his life. In the book's second half Scooter, later in college, negotiates trickier territory. For keeping cool in a crisis that had threatened to turn into a rural race war, Scooter lands a summer job from a local businessman and scores a bass fiddle from the blues singer. This instrument becomes his talisman for the larger world he is about to enter. Central to this novel are Snake's and Scooter's efforts to integrate intellectual inquiry with everyday living, a task to which Murray dedicated himself throughout his career.

The Blue Devils of Nada

Type of work: Essays
First published: 1996

The phrase "the blues aesthetic" suggests origins deep in African American culture, but, as the subtitle of *The Blue Devils of Nada: A Contemporary American Approach to Aesthetic Statement* suggests, Murray is concerned to define the place of the blues idiom, which for him means what others call "jazz," in American culture at large. For Murray, who has been making this point incisively for a quarter of a century, there is no "white" American culture; he describes and praises American mainstream culture as mulatto. Nor is there any "black" American culture, if by that is meant a culture of African Americans that does not reflect their interaction with Americans of every ethnic heritage. The blues idiom is itself not "African" but arises out of the confrontation of American and European musical elements in the transforming context of America.

Much of this book is devoted to the work and personalities of three giants of the blues idiom: Louis Armstrong, Count Basie, and Duke Ellington. Murray does not offer technical analysis of the music; he is rather concerned to define its meanings for his vision of American culture. He then, more boldly, extends the blues aesthetic to the African American painter Romare Bearden, and finally, and more boldly still, to the white American writer Ernest Hemingway.

One need not agree with every point that Murray makes (few readers will) to realize that Murray's approach to culture is provocative and often illuminating in itself and a challenge to all versions of separatism and to many versions of multiculturalism. The liveliness of his mind and the range of his interests make Albert Murray an always engaging and stimulating companion to the reader. Not for the first time in his career, he has produced a book for which readers should be grateful.

The Seven League Boots

Type of work: Novel
First published: 1996

The Seven League Boots, third in the Scooter series after *Train Whistle Guitar* and *The Spyglass Tree*, Scooter, now more often called "Schoolboy" (having finished a stint at Tuskegee), embarks on an exploration of the great world. Divided into three parts, titled "The Apprentice," "The Journeyman," and "The Craftsman," the novel follows Schoolboy across the country as he tours with the great jazz band led by the Bossman, clearly modeled on Duke Ellington. Upon leaving the band, Schoolboy flourishes in Hollywood and enjoys a rewarding sojourn in Europe. When readers last see him, he is on his way home on a visit.

Murray's theme is the possibility embodied in a young man like Scooter/Schoolboy, a possibility that cannot be realized through reductive definition by race, ethnicity, or nationality. Scooter absorbs all the influences, black and white, American and European, to which he is exposed, integrates them within himself, and brings them all back home. Not merely a protagonist, he is a hero, an "adequate man," to use a formulation Murray has employed elsewhere. As part of an ongoing meditation on Murray's chief themes, *The Seven League Boots* is unfailingly interesting. As a novel, it is rather more problematic. The hero's will encounters too little resistance from the world to generate the tensions that inform a fully realized work of fiction. Nevertheless, Murray's many admirers will regard this book as a must. Readers curious to make Murray's acquaintance might do best to begin with one of his nonfiction works, such as *The Omni-Americans*, *Stomping the Blues*, or *South to a Very Old Place*.

Suggested Readings

Carson, Warren. "Albert Murray: Literary Reconstruction of the Vernacular Community." *African-American Review* 27, no. 2 (Summer, 1993): 287-296.

Fairbanks, Carol, and Eugene A. Engeldinger. *Black American Fiction: A Bibliography*. Metuchen, N.J.: Scarecrow Press, 1978.

Karrer, Wolfgang. "The Novel as Blues: Albert Murray's *Train Whistle Guitar*." In *The Afro-American Novel Since 1960: A Collection of Critical Essays*, edited by Peter Bruck and Wolfgang Karrer. Amsterdam: B. R. Grüner, 1982.

Wideman, John. "*Stomping the Blues*: Ritual in Black Music and Speech." *American Poetry Review* 7, no. 4 (1978): 42-45.

Contributor: Gena Dagel Caponi

Walter Dean Myers

Born: Martinsburg, West Virginia; August 12, 1937

African American

Myers writes realistic stories about young African Americans coping with complex social and ethical issues and finding values to live by.

Principal works

children's/young adult literature: *Where Does the Day Go?*, 1969; *The Dancers*, 1972; *The Dragon Takes a Wife*, 1972; *Fly, Jimmy, Fly!*, 1974; *Fast Sam, Cool Clyde, and Stuff*, 1975; *The World of Work: A Guide to Choosing a Career*, 1975; *Social Welfare*, 1976; *Brainstorm*, 1977; *Mojo and the Russians*, 1977; *Victory for Jamie*, 1977; *It Ain't All for Nothin'*, 1978; *The Young Landlords*, 1979; *The Black Pearl and the Ghost: Or, One Mystery After Another*, 1980; *The Golden Serpent*, 1980; *Hoops*, 1981; *The Legend of Tarik*, 1981; *Won't Know Till I Get There*, 1982; *The Nicholas Factor*, 1983; *Tales of a Dead King*, 1983; *Motown and Didi: A Love Story*, 1984; *Mr. Monkey and the Gotcha Bird*, 1984; *The Outside Shot*, 1984; *Crystal*, 1987; *Sweet Illusions*, 1987; *Fallen Angels*, 1988; *Me, Mop, and the Moondance Kid*, 1988; *Scorpions*, 1988; *The Mouse Rap*, 1990; *Now Is Your Time! The African-American Struggle for Freedom*, 1991; *Mop, Moondance, and the Nagasaki Knights*, 1992; *The Righteous Revenge of Artemis Bonner*, 1992; *Somewhere in the Darkness*, 1992; *Brown Angels: An Album of Pictures and Verse*, 1993 (poetry); *Malcolm X: By Any Means Necessary*, 1993; *A Place Called Heartbreak: A Story of Vietnam*, 1993; *Young Martin's Promise*, 1993; *Darnell Rock Reporting*, 1994; *The Glory Field*, 1994; *Glorious Angels: A Celebration of Children*, 1995 (poetry); *One More River to Cross: An African-American Photograph Album*, 1995; *Shadow of the Red Moon*, 1995; *The Story of the Three Kingdoms*, 1995; *How Mr. Monkey Saw the Whole World*, 1996; *Slam!*, 1996; *Smiffy Blue, Ace Crime Detective: The Case of the Missing Ruby, and Other Stories*, 1996; *Toussaint L'Ouverture: The Fight for Haiti's Freedom*, 1996; *Harlem*, 1997; *Amistad: A Long Road of Freedom*, 1998; *Angel to Angel: A Mother's Gift of Love*, 1998; *At Her Majesty's Request: An African Princess in Victorian England*, 1999; *Monster*, 1999; *The Journal of Joshua Loper, a Black Cowboy*, 1999; *The Journal of Scott Pendleton Collins, a WWII Soldier*, 1999; *The Blues of Flat Brown*, 2000; *145th Street*, 2000 (short stories); *Bad Boy: A Memoir*, 2001; *The Greatest: Muhammad Ali*, 2001; *The Journal of Biddy Owens: The Negro Leagues*, 2001; *Three Swords for Granada*, 2002; *The Beast*, 2003; *Blues Journey*, 2003 (Christopher Myers, illustrator); *The Dream Bearer*, 2003; *Antarctica: Journeys to the South Pole*, 2004; *Here in Harlem: Poems in Many Voices*, 2004; *I've Seen the Promised Land*, 2004 (Leonard Jenkins, illustrator); *Shooter*, 2004; *USS Constellation: Pride of the American Navy*, 2004; *Autobiography of My Dead Brother*, 2005 (Myers, illustrator)

Walter Dean Myers was born in West Virginia into a large family. When he was three years old, his mother died. Burdened by poverty, his father sent Myers to live with foster parents in New York City. The foster parents, Herbert and Florence Dean, raised the boy in Harlem, which Myers remembers as teeming with life and excitement. Myers changed his original middle name, Milton, to Dean in honor of his foster parents.

Myers's foster mother read to him every day until he could read for himself. Myers was a good student in the sense that he was literate, but he became known as a discipline problem in school. He had a speech impediment that prevented people from understanding what he was saying. His classmates teased him, and Myers responded with anger. He spent many days in the principal's office or on suspension.

He received some guidance from his fifth-grade teacher, who thought that writing words down would help him with his speech problem. He filled notebooks with poems and stories but did not consider writing as a career. When not in school, Myers hung out with the street gangs and played basketball until it was too dark to see. Later in his life, the game of basketball would be a prominent feature in several of his books.

Walter Dean Myers (Courtesy, HarperCollins)

At age sixteen, Myers dropped out of school and joined the Army the next year. After his tour of duty, he returned to Harlem and worked in a series of low-paying jobs. At the same time, he began to write for magazines.

In 1968, Myers entered a writing contest sponsored by the Council on Interracial Books for Children and won first place in the picture-book category for *Where Does the Day Go?* Myers wrote a few more books for preschoolers before directing his efforts toward teenagers. *Fast Sam, Cool Clyde, and Stuff* was his first young adult novel. He would go on to win several American Library Association (ALA) Notable Book Awards and Best Books for Young Adults Citations, Newbery Honors, Parents' Choice Awards, and Coretta Scott King Awards. He was the first recipient of the Michael L. Printz Award for excellence in young adult literature in 2000 for his powerful book *Monster*.

For twenty years, Myers worked as an editor during the day and wrote fiction at night. When he was laid off by the company for which he worked, he became a full-time writer. As a result, Myers has been prolific, publishing more than sixty books for young people. A father of three children, he and his family made their home in New Jersey.

Hoops

TYPE OF WORK: Children's/young adult literature
FIRST PUBLISHED: 1981

In *Hoops*, Myers makes the game of basketball symbolize the game of life. Basketball was one of Myers's loves; it was an escape from the frustrations of school, a time to bond with other kids his age, and just plain fun. He depicts the basketball scenes in his books with astounding clarity and from an insider's perspective. *Hoops* seems at first to be an action-packed sports novel, but it is revealed as a moral tale about choices and integrity.

The main character in *Hoops* is seventeen-year-old Lonnie Jackson, who clings to a dream that he will become a professional basketball player. He is a senior in high school and is feeling tense about what his next steps in life will be. Basketball could be a way out of Harlem, a way to accrue status in the world, and a way to gain some self-esteem. Lonnie is one of the best players in Harlem. He believes a real chance exists that his dream could come true.

Lonnie rarely stays at home with his mother. He has an arrangement with the manager of a hotel called The Grant where he does some cleaning in exchange for a place to sleep. One of the first incidents in the book is a robbery at a liquor store across the street from the hotel. While the criminals are herding staff and customers into the back, Lonnie grabs a case of Scotch to sell. This incident paints a picture of Lonnie's environment and of his own cunning adaptation to it.

Myers often uses the first-person viewpoint to engage his young adult readers. Lonnie's thoughts and feelings are skillfully articulated, exposing conflicts and concerns about love, sex, money, family, and honor. Specifically, Lonnie's conflicts in *Hoops* revolve around basketball, his mother, his girlfriend, and Cal. Cal, a former pro player who was ousted from the league for gambling, coaches Lonnie's team. He is now a semi-homeless alcoholic but still possesses enough caring to warn Lonnie about the ugly side of the game. Lonnie starts to look up to Cal, whom he at first considered a useless wino. As Lonnie grows closer to Cal, however, he sees a broken man with a broken past who still manages to instill trust in the team members.

The story builds to its climax with the team playing in a tournament, with big gambling money riding on the outcome. Cal is ordered by mob leaders to keep Lonnie out of the game, which would result in the team's loss. Cal tells Lonnie that basketball is like life: "Everybody plays the game with what they got." At first, Cal does sit Lonnie down, but as the tournament game progresses, he suddenly calls for Lonnie, and the team wins the game. However, this spells doom for Cal, who is viciously stabbed in the team locker room.

Hoops takes place in a terrifying world where gangs roam the streets in malicious packs and Lonnie's girlfriend is injected with heroin because she learns about a mobster's involvement in the tournament fix. The reader follows Lonnie's growth from a tough, self-centered kid who cares about nothing except basketball to a more mature young man who sees that even a person as fallen as Cal can overcome his weakness and become a moral force in the midst of corruption.

Fallen Angels

Type of work: Children's/young adult literature
First published: 1988

Myers dedicated *Fallen Angels* to his brother who was killed in the Vietnam War. Myers himself joined the Army at age seventeen because it seemed to him that he had few other options. The protagonist of *Fallen Angels*, Richie Perry, is also seventeen when he enlists in the Army. The young man believes at first that he will not see any combat because he has injured his knee stateside. However, he soon discovers that the wheels of paperwork processing grind slowly in the Army, and he finds himself in the muggy jungles of Vietnam.

The story is one of courage, conflict, and deep numbing confusion about a soldier's role in the Vietnam War. Myers tells the story from Richie's point of view and spares the reader no detail of the young man's terror, the firefights and bombings, the killings, and the deaths of his companions, who are the fallen angels to which the book's title refers. Realistic language and settings play an important role in helping contemporary readers relate to the environment of brutal fighting in a Southeast Asian jungle.

There is racial tension in the novel, but it is overshadowed by the intense fear and confusion generated by the war. The language can be vulgar, yet it fits the raw, rugged life that the characters experience out in the jungle. The environment is overwhelming: Death and injury surround Richie and his comrades, dwarfing the concerns of ordinary life (otherwise known as the World).

Initially, Richie yearns to get back to the World, back to his stateside, civilian life. Gradually, he begins to shed his childlike dream of being a hero to his younger brother and focuses on the crucially important issue: staying alive. He realizes that he does not know how to pray and starts to form a spiritual outlook. He begins to love the men that fight alongside him, to think not only of himself but also of his comrades in arms. Myers makes it clear that the war has changed Richie forever and that the World has become the foreign land.

Monster

Type of work: Children's/young adult literature
First published: 1999

Monster is presented in an unusual format: a screenplay interspersed with facsimiles of a handwritten journal. The book is illustrated with photographs, court sketches, even fingerprints. It won for Myers the first Michael L. Printz Award for excellence in young adult literature.

The fictional author of this screenplay/journal is sixteen-year-old Steve Harmon. He has been accused of acting as a lookout during a homicide. If he is convicted, he could spend the rest of his life in prison. The book describes his weeks of incarceration, his trial, and its outcome. Steve writes in the screenplay format because he wants to become a filmmaker and because it is a way to distance or disassociate himself from the unfolding nightmare of his life. He can see himself and others as simply actors in a motion picture.

As the book opens, Steve has already learned that the best time to cry in jail is at night. When other prisoners are screaming and yelling, a little sniffle cannot be heard. He realizes that he must not show weakness in jail, just as he could not show weakness on the street. When he looks in the small scratched mirror over the steel sink in his cell, he does not recognize himself. He starts to wonder if he is becoming some kind of evil changeling. Within the first page of the book, Myers characteristically creates a clear picture of Steve and his predicament. Myers grabs the reader's attention immediately by using the first-person viewpoint to express the character's emotions and by describing a harsh, disturbing setting in sharp physical detail.

The prosecutor calls Steve a monster during opening arguments. Steve begins to wonder obsessively if he is a good person or a monster after all. What constitutes a good person? In Steve's milieu, drug use, petty crimes, and running the streets are just a part of life. His alleged presence during the robbery/homicide raises questions about his choices. Just as his survival in prison depends on displaying a hardened exterior, so his survival on the streets depended on doing little jobs for gang leaders.

Steve insists in his journal that "he didn't do nothing." However, his defense lawyer, Ms. O'Brien, has some concerns. She is afraid that the jury will not "see a difference between [him] and all the bad guys taking the stand," that Steve might be tarred with the same brush as his fellow defendants. Steve intuits that Ms. O'Brien thinks he is guilty and is merely doing her job in the courtroom. Myers does not state the facts of the crime in the book, so the reader is left wondering if Steve was or was not a lookout at the crime scene. This question is literally illustrated by two captioned photographs in the book. They both appear to be stills from a store's videotape, showing Steve in the store. The captions read: "What was I doing?" and "What was I thinking?" It is not clear if the photographs are anxious figments of Steve's imagination or telltale hints that he was actually in that store.

Finally, Steve is found not guilty. He spontaneously reaches out to hug Ms. O'Brien, who turns away stiffly, indicating that there is something bad about Steve despite his acquittal. *Monster* is thoroughly ambiguous about Steve's role in the crime. It is ambiguous about Steve's basic nature, his goodness or badness. The book leaves the reader to ponder about whether guilt equals badness and whether acquittal equals innocence.

Suggested Readings

Bishop, Rudine Sims. *Presenting Walter Dean Myers*. Boston: Twayne, 1991.

Jordan, Denise M. *Walter Dean Myers: Writer for Real Teens*. Berkeley Heights, N.J.: Enslow, 1999.

Snodgrass, Mary Ellen. *Walter Dean Myers: A Literary Companion*. Jefferson, N.C.: McFarland, 2006.

Contributor: Janet M. Ball

Gloria Naylor

Born: New York, New York; January 25, 1950

African American

Naylor's exploration of black communities stresses the relationship between identity and place.

Principal works

LONG FICTION: *The Women of Brewster Place: A Novel in Seven Stories*, 1982; *Linden Hills*, 1985; *Mama Day*, 1988; *Bailey's Café*, 1992; *The Men of Brewster Place*, 1998; *1996*, 2004

NONFICTION: *Conversations with Gloria Naylor*, 2004 (Maxine Lavon Montgomery, editor)

EDITED TEXT: *Children of the Night: The Best Short Stories by Black Writers, 1967 to the Present*, 1995

When she gave her introverted daughter a journal from Woolworth's, Gloria Naylor's mother opened the door to her child's writing career. In high school, two experiences shaped Naylor's emerging identity: Nineteenth century English literature taught her that language can be a powerful tool, and Martin Luther King, Jr.'s 1968 assassination turned her to missionary work. Instead of going to college, for the next seven years she traveled as a Jehovah's Witness, abandoning the work in 1975, when she began to feel constrained by the lifestyle.

At Brooklyn College, her introduction to black history and the discovery of such literary foremothers as Zora Neale Hurston and Toni Morrison gave her the inspiration to try writing herself. Completing her first novel, the best seller *The Women of Brewster Place*, signified, she has indicated, her taking hold of herself and attempting to take her destiny into her own hands. After winning a scholarship to Yale University, Naylor discovered that, for her, graduate training was incompatible with writing fiction. She nevertheless completed a master's degree in 1983, when the Afro-American Studies department allowed her second novel, *Linden Hills*, to fulfill the thesis requirement. *Linden Hills* illustrates the effects of materialism on an elite all-black community that lacks a spiritual center.

During the 1980's, demand for Naylor as a lecturer and writer-in-residence grew, and she garnered top-notch honors, receiving a fellowship from the National Endowment for the Arts (1985), the Candace Award of the National Coalition of 100 Black Women in 1986, and a Guggenheim Fellowship in 1988. She was a scholar-in-residence at the University of Pennsylvania in 1986, a visiting lecturer at Princeton University in 1986-1987, a visiting professor at New York University in

1986 and Boston University in 1987, a Fannie Hurst Visiting Professor at Brandeis University in 1988, and a senior fellow at Cornell University's Society for the Humanities in 1988. Her novel *Mama Day* won the National Book Award.

The central feature of all of Naylor's novels is an enclosed black community where characters learn to embrace their identities in the context of place. Naylor's powerful settings combine elements of the ordinary with the otherworldly, allowing for magical events and mythic resolutions. For example, *Mama Day* takes place on the imaginary island of Willow Springs and weaves the history of the Day family from the point of view of the powerful matriarch Mama Day, a conjure woman. Naylor's own family history provides her with a rich sense of community, but she paradoxically treasures solitude. Married briefly, she refuses to remarry or have children and teaches writing to keep from being too much of a recluse. Naylor's strength is portraying convincing multigenerational characters in specific settings.

The Women of Brewster Place

Type of work: Novel
First published: 1982

Naylor's first novel, *The Women of Brewster Place*, won the American Book Award for First Fiction in 1983 and was made into a film. Actually a novel in seven stories, it presents a series of interconnected tales about seven women who struggle to make peace with their pasts. The allegorical setting is Brewster Place, a dead-end ghetto street whose distinctive feature is the brick wall that bottles economic and racial frustration inside. Two interdependent themes bind the stories together: The violence that men enact on women is counteracted by the healing power of community. The novel's innovative structure is key to Naylor's purpose. Exploring the lives of different women on Brewster Place, Naylor attempts to create a microcosm of the black female experience in America.

The microcosm consists of seven African American women representing a range of ages, backgrounds, and sexualities. The first character introduced is Mattie Michael, whose fierce love for her son twice costs her the security and pride of a happy home. Her hard-won strength becomes the force that helps other women, such as Mattie's oldest friend, Etta Mae Johnson, and Lucielia Louise Turner (Ciel), whom Mattie helped raise. One of the most powerful scenes of the novel is the one in which Mattie saves Ciel, who loses her desire to live after the tragic deaths of her two children. Kiswana Browne is a would-be revolutionary who attempts to reclaim her African heritage and to improve Brewster Place by renouncing her parents' elite Linden Hills lifestyle. Cora Lee, her opposite, is a single mother of seven who wants babies but not children. Last are Lorraine and Theresa, the couple whom Brewster Place cruelly rejects when they seek a haven that will tolerate their love for each other. Women's dual identity as mother and daughter is a highlighted conflict throughout.

The symbolism of Brewster Place's brick wall contributes to the horrific climax when Lorraine is gang-raped in the alley formed by the wall, her blood spattering the bricks. Her effort to fight back, delayed by the trauma, causes her to attack Ben, the janitor who treats her like a daughter. She murders him with a brick. The novel appears to end triumphantly when the women tear down the wall, brick by brick, at a block party that celebrates the power of community. This is a deceptive resolution, however, because the block party has happened only in Mattie's dream. The ambiguity of the ending gives the story a mythic quality by stressing the continual possibility of dreams and the results of their deferral.

Gloria Naylor (AP/Wide World Photos)

Linden Hills

Type of work: Novel
First published: 1985

The community feelings of Brewster Place, from which the women gain a positive sense of identity, somehow make the ghetto's problems seem less awesome, paradoxically, than those of Linden Hills, an affluent suburb. If Brewster Place is a ghetto, Linden Hills is a hell. Naylor underlines this metaphor by deliberately modeling her novel *Linden Hills* after Dante's *Inferno*. Linden Hills is not a group of hills, but only a V-shaped area on a hillside intersected by eight streets. As one travels down the hill, the residents become richer but lower on the moral scale. Lester and Willie, two young unemployed poets who perform odd jobs for Christmas money (they are the modern counterparts of Vergil and Dante), take the reader on a guided tour.

Lester's sister Roxanne deems black Africans in Zimbabwe unready for independence; one young executive, Maxwell Smyth, encourages another, Xavier Donnell, no longer to consider Roxanne as a prospective corporate bride; and Dr. Daniel Braithwaite has written the authorized twelve-volume history of Linden Hills without making a single moral judgment. Other sellouts are more personal: The young lawyer Winston Alcott leaves his homosexual lover to marry respectably, and Chester Parker is eager to bury his dead wife in order to remarry.

Significantly, Linden Hills is ruled by men. The archfiend is Luther Nedeed, the local undertaker and real estate tycoon who occupies the lowest point in Linden Hills. Speaking against a low-income housing project planned for an adjacent poor black neighborhood, Nedeed urges outraged Linden Hills property owners to make common cause with the racist Wayne County Citizens Alliance. Most damning of all, however, is that Nedeed disowns his own wife and child and imprisons them in an old basement morgue; the child starves, but the wife climbs up to confront the archfiend on Christmas Eve.

Mama Day

Type of work: Novel
First published: 1988

If *Linden Hills* strains credulity, then the main setting of *Mama Day* is even more unbelievable, if not downright mythical: Willow Springs, a southern coastal island relatively unwashed by the tides of racism. The island is populated by the descendants of white slaveholder Bascombe Wade and his black wife Sapphira and of other slaves that he freed and deeded land to back in 1823. Since that time, the island has been plagued mainly by malaria, Union soldiers, sandy soil, two big depressions, and hurricanes. The fictitious barrier island lies off the coast of South Carolina and Georgia but is owned by no state. Willow Springs is a backwater of history where the people have been mostly left to themselves, and they have developed a black American culture strongly connected to the land, to their historical beginnings, and even to their African roots.

Willow Springs is a daring concept—an effort to imagine what black life might have been like in America if left free to develop on its own. Naylor acknowledges the concept's utopian aspects by drawing parallels between Willow Springs and the magical island in William Shakespeare's *The Tempest* (1611). Yet the conjuring that goes on in Willow Springs recalls the conjuring in *Sundiata: An Epic of Old Mali* (a translation of the thirteenth century African epic published in 1965) and the good magic and bad magic still practiced in parts of Africa. Also very real are the closeness to the land, the recognized status of individuals within the community, the slow pace of life, and the presence of the past—things that rural southerners, black and white, miss when they move to northern cities.

In the novel, such a person is Ophelia "Cocoa" Day, who was born on Willow Springs and raised by her grandmother Abigail and great-aunt Miranda "Mama" Day (descendants of Bascombe and Sapphira Wade). Cocoa left Willow Springs to work in New York City, but she is drawn back to the island for regular August visits. In New York, the novel's other setting, Cocoa meets George Andrews, a black engineer who was raised in an orphanage, and they eventually get married. The contrasts between the two—George gentle and straightforward, Cocoa spoiled and insecure—suggest the novel's underlying cultural clash, but this split does not become critical until George visits Willow Springs with Cocoa.

While George appreciates black life on Willow Springs, it is way beyond his urbanized, rationalistic range, particularly when a hurricane hits and when he becomes involved in a conjuring match between Mama Day and her nemesis, Ruby.

Mama Day has a wealth of knowledge about herbs and various natural phenomena that she uses for the purposes of healing and aiding new life. The reader senses that much has been passed down to her from others who no longer live but whose spirits nourish the rich fabric of Willow Springs. In contrast, the evil-spirited Ruby uses the same knowledge, mixed with hoodoo, to kill anyone whom she perceives might take away her man, Junior Lee. Several women have already met terrible fates because they had contact with the philandering Junior Lee.

Unfortunately, at a party given in honor of Cocoa and George, Junior Lee follows Cocoa out to the porch and attempts to rape her, and Ruby catches him. The next day, Ruby sees Cocoa walking down the road and asks her to stop; Ruby apologizes for Junior Lee's behavior and offers to massage and braid Cocoa's hair the way she did when Cocoa was little. Right before the party, Mama Day had felt a big hurricane coming and death in the air. During the hurricane Cocoa becomes disoriented, and huge welts cover her head and face. Mama Day realizes that Ruby has poisoned Cocoa by rubbing nightshade into her head. Mama Day cuts off Cocoa's hair and works a counteracting salve into her scalp, but Cocoa is already badly poisoned.

Meanwhile, the hurricane has wreaked terrible havoc and taken out the wooden bridge between Willow Springs and the mainland. With all the boats destroyed and no telephones, George exhausts himself working to restore the bridge and get Cocoa off the island to a doctor. His efforts do not succeed, however, and in desperation he is forced to try Mama Day's solution. She sends him to "the other place," the island's original homeplace, to get whatever he finds behind an old brooding hen. Doubting George finds nothing, is attacked by the old hen, and dies of a weak heart.

George's doubts and weak heart represent the limits of his rationalistic outlook, his inability to participate fully in the island's culture and to comprehend Mama Day's powers. There is no doubt that those powers are real. Before George undertakes his fatal mission, Mama Day deals with Ruby by calling out three warnings, whacking each side of Ruby's house with a stick, and sprinkling a circle of silvery dust around the house. The results are two lightning strikes on Ruby's house, the second one exploding it with Ruby inside.

Bailey's Café

Type of work: Novel
First published: 1992

Set in 1948, *Bailey's Café*, Naylor's fourth novel, is her self-described "sexual novel." Similar to *The Women of Brewster Place*, it tells the tragic histories of female characters who suffer simply because they are sexual. The underlying structure of blues music recasts these feminist rewritings of biblical stories. The characters' own blues-influenced narrations provide the equivalent of melody, and the male narrator supplies the connecting texts linking one story to another.

The proprietor of Bailey's Café, who is the narrator, sets the pattern by telling how he was saved by Bailey's Café, a magical place. It is a café that does not serve customers, and its magic is not the redemptive kind. The café provides "some space, some place, to take a breather for a while" by suspending time. Not fixed in any one city, it is "real real mobile," so that anyone can get there. It features a back door that opens onto a void where patrons re-create scenes to help them sustain life or, alternatively, to end it. The street on which Bailey's Café may be found contains three refuges that form a "relay for broken dreams": Bailey's Café, Gabe's Pawnshop, and Eve's Boardinghouse and Garden.

Eve transforms her suffering into a haven. She aids only those women who know what it means to "walk a thousand years." Her boarders include Esther, who hates men because of the sexual abuse she suffered as a child bride; Peaches, a woman so beautiful she disfigures herself; Jesse, a spunky heroin addict; and Mariam, a fourteen-year-old Ethiopian Jew who is pregnant but still a virgin. The community also includes men. The unforgettable Miss Maple is a man who forges a strong identity despite the racism that threatens his manhood. The novel explores positive models of masculinity and steadily subverts the idea that sexual women are whores. Such a characterization oppresses all women, who must transcend the personal consequences of this destructive label.

The arrival of the outcast and pregnant Mariam threatens to disrupt the characters' safety because the birth could destroy their world: "For all we knew, when that baby gave its first cry, this whole street could have just faded away." The women on the street fear they will find themselves back in "those same hopeless crossroads in our lives." Instead, the baby is born in Mariam's homeland, magically re-created in the void. All the characters gather to celebrate its arrival. Their participation in the Jewish birth ceremony brings hope for the future and shows the healing power of a diverse community.

The Men of Brewster Place

Type of work: Novel
First published: 1998

Naylor's return to Brewster Place gave her readers the opportunity to revisit the male characters introduced in the first book (generally portrayed negatively) and see them in a different light. No longer assuming background roles, they are up front, giving an account of their actions in the first book. In *The Women of Brewster Place*, Mattie's son Basil skipped town while awaiting sentencing, causing his mother to lose the property she had put up for his bail. Here Basil does return, check in hand, to repay his mother for her loss; however, she is dead, and his unfulfilled desire to make amends leads him into a detrimental relationship and a prison sentence. Eugene, absent from his daughter's funeral in the first book, is in fact on site. His grief compels him to undergo a harsh punishment, one that has much to do with the fact that he could never tell Ciel that he is gay. C. C. Baker, responsible for the vicious gang rape of Lorraine, executes another heinous crime in this book but gives the reader insight into his tragic character. When he squeezes the trigger to kill his brother, he does so with eyes closed, thanking God "for giving him the courage to do it. The courage to be a man."

In *The Men of Brewster Place*, Naylor seems to be acknowledging that there is, after all, more than one side to a story and that she is ready to let the whole story be known. Passages from the first book provide continuity between the two works, as does the resurrected voice of Ben, the janitor killed by Lorraine. Reminiscent of the character Bailey in *Bailey's Café*, Ben is both character and narrator.

However, Naylor brings some new voices to Brewster Place when she introduces Brother Jerome and Greasy. These characters link together the lives of the men living in Brewster Place. Brother Jerome is a retarded child with an ability to play the piano that speaks of genius. The blues that pour from his fingers speak to the lives of each man, rendering their conditions tangible. Greasy makes his brief but memorable appearance in the story called "The Barbershop," leaving the men to carry the burden of his self-inflicted demise. Naylor's portrayals of these two characters are perhaps the most moving of the book. These characterizations, along with the complexity of all the male characters, point to a Naylor who is taking a broader view. She had prefaced *The Women of Brewster Place* with a poem by Langston Hughes that asked the question, "What happens to a dream deferred?" In *The Men of Brewster Place*, she seems ready to acknowledge that deferred dreams are not only the province of women.

Suggested Readings

Gates, Henry Louis, Jr., and K. A. Appiah, eds. *Gloria Naylor: Critical Perspectives Past and Present*. New York: Amistad, 1993.

Kelley, Margot Anne, ed. *Gloria Naylor's Early Novels*. Gainesville: University Press of Florida, 1999.

Montgomery, Maxine Lavon. "Authority, Multivocality, and the New World Order in Gloria Naylor's *Bailey's Café*." *African American Review* 29, no. 1 (Spring, 1995): 27.

Naylor, Gloria. "An Interview with Gloria Naylor." Interview by Charles H. Rowell. *Callaloo* 20, no. 1 (Winter, 1997): 179-192.

Naylor, Gloria, and Toni Morrison. "A Conversation." *The Southern Review* 21 (Summer, 1985): 567-593.

Puhr, Kathleen M. "Healers in Gloria Naylor's Fiction." *Twentieth Century Literature* 40, no. 4 (Winter, 1994): 518.

Rowell, Charles H. "An Interview with Gloria Naylor." *Callaloo* 20, no. 1 (Winter, 1997): 179-192.

Stave, Shirley A., ed. *Gloria Naylor: Strategy and Technique, Magic and Myth*. Newark: Delaware University Press, 2001.

Whitt, Margaret Earley. *Understanding Gloria Naylor*. Columbia: University of South Carolina Press, 1998.

Contributors: Christine H. King, Jacquelyn Benton, and Harold Branam

Fae Myenne Ng

Born: San Francisco, California; 1956

Chinese American

Ng brings the perspective of an Asian American to the American experience of immigration and assimilation.

Principal works

LONG FICTION: *Bone*, 1993
SHORT FICTION: "A Red Sweater," 1986; "Backdaire," 1989
NONFICTION: "False Gold: My Father's American Journey," 1993

The writing of Fae Myenne Ng (fay myehn ehng) depicts a cultural divide between her assimilated generation and that of her Chinese parents. Reared in San Francisco's Chinatown by working-class parents who emigrated from China, Ng acquired an excellent education, receiving degrees from the University of California at Berkeley and an M.F.A. from Columbia University. *Bone*, her first novel, took her ten years to write, during which time she supported herself as a waitress and temporary worker, as well as by a grant from the National Foundation for the Arts. Like Leila, the narrator of the novel, Ng is an educated woman who understood her parents' working-class world. In the novel, the Chinese mother is a poorly paid, overworked garment worker. The father holds down a series of dead-end jobs that include janitor, dishwasher, houseboy, and laundry worker. The couple have worked their fingers to the bone to provide for their daughters. *Bone* is a tribute to the family's father, who represents a generation of Chinese men who sacrificed their personal happiness for the sake of their families. Ng's inspiration was the old Chinese men living alone and impoverished in single-room occupancy hotels in Chinatown. Chinese America's bachelor society came to America to work the gold mines, to build the railroads, and to develop California agriculturally. These immigrants became men without roots.

The novel also depicts the conflicts of the family's three daughters with their old-fashioned parents. There is the middle daughter Ona, whose suicide suggests she could not adjust to American society and maintain her identity as a dutiful Chinese daughter. Nina, the youngest daughter, affirms a modern identity and escapes to New York City. Leila, the eldest daughter, is a complicated combination of the old Chinese ways and new American cultural patterns. As does Nina, the rebellious daughter, Ng moved to New York City. Leila, with her ability to assimilate the new while keeping faith with the past, is the daughter who most mirrors Ng's identity as an Asian American. Ng's work adds to the tradition of the immigrant novel.

Bone

Type of work: Novel
First published: 1993

Ng's *Bone* continues in a tradition of Asian American novels by women that mediate between the demands of addressing issues of gender and ethnicity. As a woman writing from a strongly patriarchal cultural heritage, Ng has had to create new strategies in order to express the paradox of resistance to and affirmation of her cultural heritage.

Bone relates the story of the Leong family, which has recently suffered the death by suicide of the Middle Girl, Ona. Ona committed suicide by jumping from one of Chinatown's housing projects. She left no note, and although the police reported she was "on downers," or depressants, there was no apparent cause for the suicide. The novel is narrated by the First Girl, Leila Fu Louie, Ona's half sister and the eldest daughter in the Leong family. Leila's attempts to come to terms with her sister's death, and thereby her own life, lead her to muse about incidents from their childhood and the everyday circumstances of the present. The novel unfolds in a series of stories that move from the present into the past.

The children of immigrants have often been called upon to translate for their parents. Their ability to switch from the language of their parents to the English of their birthplace makes them the bridge between the customs of the Old World and the expectations and demands of the New. This enormous responsibility can become an overwhelming burden. Although Leila must continually face the chasm between her parents' expectations and her own reality, her ability to build a bridge of translation is grounded in her strong need and appreciation for the family.

Her youngest sister, Nina, the End Girl, refuses to shoulder this burden of translation. Her rebellion has caused her to move to New York, far away from her parents in San Francisco's Chinatown. She declares her independence by refusing to lie about her life in order to appease her parents. It is the self-imposed silence of Ona, however, that is at the center of the novel. Ona, the middle child, is caught in the middle; she learned too well how to keep secrets.

Ng does not seek to solve the mystery of Ona's death in this novel. It is a mystery that is unsolvable; rather, through the narrative voice of Leila, Ng explores the languages and silences of love, grief, assimilation, avoidance, anger, guilt, and, finally, acceptance. Ng, who grew up in San Francisco, is the daughter of Chinese immigrants and in an interview explained the title of her novel: "Bone is what lasts. And I wanted to honor the quality of endurance in the immigrant spirit."

Bone is a journey into a territory that is the common heritage of all second-generation immigrant Americans and the particular traditions of Chinese immigrants. The path to assimilation into American society is fraught with contradictions and ambivalence. Ng provides few answers; she simply reveals one family's experience.

Suggested Readings

Eder, Richard. "A Gritty Story of Assimilation." *Los Angeles Times*, January 14, 1993, p. E5.

Jones, Louis B. "Dying to Be an American." *The New York Times Book Review*, February 7, 1993, 7, 9.

Kakutani, Michiko. "Building on the Pain of a Past in China." *The New York Times*, January 29, 1993, p. C26.

Stetson, Nancy. "Honoring Her Forebears." *Chicago Tribune*, April 4, 1993, p. C12.

Wong, Sau-Ling Cynthia. *Reading Asian-American Voices: From Necessity to Extravagance*. Princeton, N.J.: Princeton University Press, 1993.

Contributors: Margaret Boe Birns and Jane Anderson Jones

John Okada

Born: Seattle, Washington; September, 1923
Died: Seattle, Washington; February, 1971

Japanese American

Okada introduced Japanese American literature to the United States.

Principal work

LONG FICTION: *No-No Boy*, 1957

John Okada was a Nisei, or second-generation Japanese American. He grew up in the Pacific Northwest and witnessed the internment of 120,000 Japanese Americans during World War II. Unlike the character Ichiro in *No-No Boy*, however, Okada was not a no-no boy (a person who answered no to two critical questions on the loyalty questionnaire—refusing to serve in the American armed forces and refusing to forswear allegiance to Japan and pledge loyalty to the United States). He volunteered for military service and was sent to Japanese-held islands to exhort Japanese soldiers to surrender. The experience helped him shape his perspective on the war.

After he was discharged from the military in 1946, Okada went to the University of Washington and Columbia University. He earned two B.A. degrees and an M.A. degree studying, in his own words, "narrative and dramatic writing, history, sociology." He started working on *No-No Boy* while he was an assistant in the Business Reference Department of the Seattle Public Library and at the Detroit Public Library. After a stint as a technical writer for Chrysler Missile Operations of Sterling Township, Michigan, he and his wife Dorothy moved back to Seattle. *No-No Boy* was completed in 1957. Okada had a hard time trying to find publishers who were interested in his work. *No-No Boy* was first published by Charles Tuttle of Tokyo. After Okada died, his wife offered all of his manuscripts, including the one of his second novel, to the Japanese American Research Project at the University of California at Los Angeles. They were rejected. Dorothy burned them shortly after, when she was preparing to move.

Okada was proud to be a Japanese American. He examined the double consciousness of the Japanese American community. *No-No Boy* portrays the psychological confusion and distress experienced by many Japanese Americans, especially second-generation Japanese Americans (U.S. citizens by birth, culturally Japanese) during and after World War II. *No-No Boy* portrays the struggle of those who are caught between two worlds at war.

No-No Boy

Type of work: Novel
First published: 1957

No-No Boy depicts a second-generation Japanese American's struggle to balance his loyalty to the Japanese culture, to his parents, and to his country, the United States. Ichiro Yamada is interned during World War II. He is put in jail for answering no to the two critical questions on the allegiance questionnaire. His two negative answers are his refusal to serve in the American armed forces and his refusal to forswear allegiance to Japan and pledge loyalty to the United States. After he is released from prison, Ichiro moves back to Seattle and is caught between two seemingly irreconcilable worlds. On one side, there are his parents, who are very proud of being Japanese. On the other side, there is the United States, a country to which he still feels he belongs.

During his search for his identity, Ichiro meets several people who help shape his perspective on himself and on his relationship with America. One of his close friends, Kenji, joins the military during the war. He loses a leg and has only two years to live. What Kenji physically goes through, Ichiro experiences emotionally. Being a no-no boy, Ichiro is looked down upon by his brother and other Japanese Americans who believe he has betrayed the country. During one of their conversations, Kenji and Ichiro jokingly discuss whether they want to trade places. The fact that both of them are willing to do it comments on the kind of social environment they have to deal with and on the choices they have made.

Kenji also introduces Ichiro to Emi, a person who can empathize with Ichiro's experience. Emi's husband has left her because he is ashamed of his brother Mike and of Emi's father, who elect to be repatriated back to Japan. Mike is a World War I veteran. He is incensed by how Japanese Americans are treated by their own government during World War II and eventually decides to go back to a country he does not know or love. Emi saves Ichiro from plunging into an emotional abyss. They find a friend and companion in each other. After witnessing the death of his friend, Freddie, who is also a no-no boy, Ichiro starts to think about his own future. In "the darkness of the alley of the community" that is "a tiny bit of America," he starts to chase that faint and elusive insinuation of promise as it continues "to take shape in mind and in heart."

Suggested Readings

Inada, Lawson Fusao. "The Vision of America in John Okada's *No-No Boy*." In *Ethnic Literatures Since 1776: The Many Voices of America*, edited by Wolodymyr T. Zyla et al. Lubbock: Interdepartmental Committee on Comparative Literature, Texas Tech University, 1978.

Ling, Jinqi. "Race, Power, and Cultural Politics in John Okada's *No-No Boy*." *American Literature* 67, no. 2 (1995).

Sato, Gaile K. Fujita. "Momotaro's Exile: John Okada's *No-No Boy*." In *Reading the Literatures of Asian America*, edited by Shirley Geok-lin Lim and Amy Ling. Philadelphia: Temple University Press, 1992.

Sumida, Stephen H. "Japanese American Moral Dilemmas in John Okada's *No-No Boy* and Milton Murayama's *All I Asking for Is My Body*." In *Frontiers of Asian American Studies: Writing, Research, and Commentary*, edited by Gail M. Nomura et al. Pullman: Washington State University Press, 1989.

Contributor: Qun Wang

Simon J. Ortiz

Born: Acoma Pueblo, New Mexico; May 27, 1941

Native American

Ortiz's poetry and other works express both the grief and loss associated with past abuse and the suffering of veterans. His work as a whole, however, expresses optimism and hope.

Principal works

CHILDREN'S LITERATURE: *The People Shall Continue*, 1977; *Blue and Red*, 1982; *The Good Rainbow Road*, 2004

POETRY: *Naked in the Wind*, 1971; *Going for the Rain*, 1976; *A Good Journey*, 1977; *Fight Back: For the Sake of the People, for the Sake of the Land*, 1980 (poetry and prose); *From Sand Creek: Rising in This Heart Which Is Our America*, 1981; *A Poem Is a Journey*, 1981; *Woven Stone*, 1992; *After and Before the Lightning*, 1994; *Telling and Showing Her: The Earth, the Land*, 1995; *Out There Somewhere*, 2002

SHORT FICTION: *Howbah Indians*, 1978; *Fightin': New and Collected Stories*, 1983; *Men on the Moon: Collected Short Stories*, 1999

NONFICTION: *Traditional and Hard-to-Find Information Required by Members of American Indian Communities: What to Collect, How to Collect It, and Appropriate Format and Use*, 1978 (with Roxanne Dunbar Ortiz); *The Importance of Childhood*, 1982

EDITED TEXTS: *A Ceremony of Brotherhood, 1680-1980*, 1981 (with others); *Earth Power Coming: Short Fiction in Native American Literature*, 1983; *Speaking for the Generations: Native Writers on Writing*, 1998

MISCELLANEOUS: *Song, Poetry, and Language: Expression and Perception*, 1977

Simon Joseph Ortiz (ohr-TEES) is a native of the Acoma Pueblo. He grew up in Deetseyaamah, a rural village of the Acoma Pueblo community, a place also called McCartys, New Mexico. His parents, Joe L. and Mamie Toribio, along with other members of his clan and residents of his birthplace, shaped his values and provided him with an emotional and cultural home that has grounded him in his life and work.

His father, a woodcarver and elder of the tribe, worked for the Santa Fe Railroad. He imbued his son with a respect for his culture and a sense of connection with all living things. His mother, a potter and storyteller, passed along legends and myths engendering reverence for everyday activities and stories, ancient and new, that form personal and cultural identity.

Ortiz's first significant contact with the American, or the "Mericano," culture came when he and his family relocated to Skull Valley, Arizona, a residential site for railroad workers. There Ortiz first contrasted his life in the minimal housing provided by the railroad company with the lives of suburban Americans as presented in the "Dick and Jane" stories in the elementary school readers. Soon he would leave his family in order to attend the Bureau of Indian Affairs School, St. Catherine's, in Gallup, New Mexico. Efforts to Americanize native students by punishing them for speaking their own language left the homesick child feeling lonely and estranged. Later he attended high school in Grants, New Mexico, and became in many ways a typical high school student while excelling in academics and leading his peers.

His parents prized education and learning and encouraged Ortiz to continue his education. After high school, he began work at Kerr-McGee, a uranium mine in Grants, thinking the job might lead to a career in science. Instead it took him from typing in an office to laboring in the open pits, an experience he would recall in *Fight Back*. In 1962, he began to study chemistry at Fort Lewis College. He left to enlist in the United States Army, serving from 1963 to 1966. This experience reinforced for him the differences between the Mericano and Indian cultures and the lack of respect for American Indians that prevailed.

After military service he enrolled in the University of New Mexico, where he began studying literature and creative writing. He was accepted into the writing program at the University of Iowa, where he earned an M.F.A. in 1969. Soon afterward his poems were being accepted for publication in journals and magazines. In 1976, his first major collection of poems, *Going for the Rain*, was published to critical acclaim and introduced him as a major American Indian voice.

Ortiz became an established poet, teaching writing, lecturing, and gaining an audience. He has taught at San Diego State University; the Institute of American Artists in Santa Fe, New Mexico; Navajo Community College; College of Marin in Kentfield, California; the University of New Mexico; Sinte Gleska College in Rosebud, South Dakota; and Lewis and Clark College, in Portland, Oregon. He has been honored by the National Endowment for the Arts, the Lila Wallace-Reader's Digest Fund, and the Lannan Foundation. He has received the "Returning the Gift" Lifetime Achievement Award, the WESTAF Lifetime Achievement Award, and the New Mexico Governor's Award for Excellence in Art. He received the Pushcart Prize for Poetry for *From Sand Creek* and was honored poet in the White House Salute to Poetry and American Poets, 1980.

As his career moved forward, Ortiz published other collections of poems, stories, essays, and children's books and edited anthologies. Both his artistic work and his interviews have been anthologized. He has been the subject of analytical and critical articles. He had three children: Raho Nez, Rainy Dawn, and Sara Marie. Sara Marie was born after he married Marlene Foster in 1981. That marriage ended in divorce in 1984.

Despite the positive reception of his work and the satisfactions derived from family and children, Ortiz has suffered the disorientation and alienation that many native people have experienced in assimilating into the Mericano culture. In addition to feelings of anger, rejection, and dislocation, he has suffered bouts of alcoholism. His career has been punctuated with periods of struggle to overcome alcohol abuse.

Many poems and collections, such as *From Sand Creek*, express both the grief and loss associated with past abuse and the suffering of veterans. However, Ortiz's work as a whole expresses optimism and hope. He reiterates his belief in the healing, sustaining value of story. He looks to Coyote of native lore and sees in this clever, scrappy transformer a symbol of native people able to survive and embrace their cultural values. He adopts the voice of Coyote, describing himself as a survivor who can pull himself back together and restore himself through a symbolic fragment that recalls his origins.

Reflecting the high value he places on his people and their land, Ortiz took the office of lieutenant governor for the Acoma Pueblo in 1989. Later he moved to Toronto, Canada, where he continued to practice his art.

Woven Stone

Type of work: Poetry
First published: 1992

Woven Stone gathers three books previously published, collections primarily of poetry but also including stories, essays, and narratives interspersed amid the poems. Like many contemporary Native American writers, Ortiz is concerned with connecting the heritage of Indian thought and practice ranging over more than one thousand years with the difficulties of life in America for Indians today.

The first section, "Going for the Rain," is divided into four parts: "The Preparation," which covers Ortiz's earliest memories and his education with his family, as well as his first acquaintance with the myth and lore of his people; "Leaving," which follows his initiation into the world of strangers beyond his community; "Returning," which details his confusion as he tries to integrate his experiences in the "Mericano" world with his background and beliefs; and "The Rain Falls," which presents a fuller understanding of the meaning of the myths he has heard. The second section, "A Good Journey," traces his experience in American society as he searches for a sense of direction and a sense of self. The final one, "Fight Back: For the Sake of the People, For the Sake of the Land," is a forceful, eloquent expression of Ortiz's political convictions. Here he discusses ways in which Native Americans have been exploited from the arrival of Spanish colonialists to the present, alternating poem/song with a very direct narrative description of the uranium mines on his homeground and their effect on the landscape.

Utilizing the language and rhythms of his community's oral tradition and the open forms of contemporary American poets such as Gary Snyder, Ortiz expresses the philosophical perspective—especially the reciprocal relationship between land and people—of a modern man with ties to "an ancient age." His work is accessible, and this volume offers an excellent way to begin learning about Native American culture as well as the clarity and power of an accomplished American poet.

Suggested Readings

Capulti, Jane. "The Heart of Knowledge: Nuclear Themes in Native American Thought and Literature." *American Indian Culture and Research Journal* 16, no. 4 (1992): 1-27.

Coltelli, Laura, ed. *Winged Words: American Indian Writers Speak.* Lincoln: University of Nebraska Press, 1990.

Litz, A. Walton. "Simon J. Ortiz." In *The American Writers*, supp. 4, part 2. New York: Charles Scribner's Sons, 1996.

Rader, Dean. "Luci Tapahonso and Simon Ortiz: Allegory, Symbol, Language, Poetry." *Southwest Review* 82, no. 2 (Spring, 1997): 75-92.

Smith, Patricia Clark. "Coyote Ortiz: *Canis latrans latrans* in the Poetry of Simon Ortiz." In *Studies in American Indian Literature*, edited by Paula Gunn Allen. New York: Modern Language Association of America, 1983.

Wiget, Andrew. *Simon Ortiz.* Boise, Idaho: Boise State University Press, 1986.

Contributor: Bernadette Flynn Low

Judith Ortiz Cofer

Born: Hormigueros, Puerto Rico; February 24, 1952

Puerto Rican

Ortiz Cofer's fiction, poems, and essays describe the strengths and conflicts of Puerto Ricans, especially women, on the island and on the mainland.

Principal works

CHILDREN'S LITERATURE: *Call Me Maria*, 2004

DRAMA: *Latin Women Pray*, pr. 1984

LONG FICTION: *The Line of the Sun*, 1989; *The Meaning of Consuelo*, 2003

POETRY: *Peregrina*, 1986; *Reaching for the Mainland*, 1987; *Terms of Survival*, 1987; *Reaching for the Mainland, and Selected New Poems*, 1995

SHORT FICTION: *Latin Women Pray*, 1980; *Among the Ancestors*, 1981; *The Native Dancer*, 1981; *An Island Like You: Stories of the Barrio*, 1995

NONFICTION: *Silent Dancing: A Partial Remembrance of a Puerto Rican Childhood*, 1990; *Woman in Front of the Sun: On Becoming a Writer*, 2000

EDITED TEXTS: *Letters from a Caribbean Island*, 1989; *Sleeping with One Eye Open: Women Writers and the Art of Survival*, 1999 (with Marilyn Kallet); *Riding Low on the Streets of Gold: Latino Literature for Young Adults*, 2003

MISCELLANEOUS: *The Latin Deli: Prose and Poetry*, 1993; *The Year of Our Revolution: New and Selected Stories and Poems*, 1998

Judith Ortiz Cofer (ohr-TEES KAH-fur) did not begin writing for publication until after she had been in the United States for more than twenty years. During those years, however, she frequently returned to Puerto Rico to visit her extended family. Her writing is informed by her bicultural experiences: one in the urban apartment buildings in English-speaking New Jersey, where her father stressed the importance of learning American language and customs to succeed, and the other in the traditional island community where her mother and other Spanish-speaking relatives taught her not to forget her heritage.

Ortiz Cofer is bilingual, but she writes primarily but not exclusively in English. For example, her grandmother's home, filled with the community of women who nurtured the writer as a child, is warmly referred to as *la casa de Mamá*, or simply her *casa*. Neither solely Puerto Rican nor simply American, Ortiz Cofer straddles both cultures and intermingles them in her writing. Although most of her life has been spent in New Jersey—where her father was stationed in the Navy—and later Florida and Georgia, she considers herself a Puerto Rican woman. She identifies this connection to the island not merely through geographical association but also by invoking and reclaiming her family, their stories, and her memories through her writing.

Judith Ortiz Cofer (John Cofer)

As a Puerto Rican woman, Ortiz Cofer was expected to marry, bear children, and define herself through these relationships. She dreamed, however, of becoming a teacher and later a writer. Although she was married to Charles John Cofer in 1971 and later gave birth to a daughter, she did not follow the traditional Puerto Rican path of the married woman. After completing a bachelor's degree in 1974 from Augusta College, she earned a master's degree in English from Florida Atlantic University and received a fellowship to do graduate work at Oxford University in 1977. She taught English and creative writing at various schools in Florida before settling at the University of Georgia in 1984. In addition to her academic career, she also became a widely anthologized and acclaimed writer. Ortiz Cofer's writing pays homage to the strictly defined and highly ritualized lives of Puerto Rican women, but her life and her act of writing break that mold; she redefines what it means to be a Puerto Rican woman.

Silent Dancing

Type of work: Autobiographical essays and poetry
First published: 1990

Silent Dancing: A Partial Remembrance of a Puerto Rican Childhood is Ortiz Cofer's collection of fourteen essays and accompanying poems looking back on her childhood and adolescence in Hormigueros, Puerto Rico, and Paterson, New Jersey. Her father joined the Navy before she was born, and two years later he moved them to Paterson, where he was stationed. When he went to sea for months at a time, he sent his wife and children back to Puerto Rico until he returned to New Jersey.

While her father urged the family to assimilate into the American melting pot and even moved them outside the Puerto Rican neighborhoods in New Jersey, her mother remained loyal to her own mother's home on the island. Her mother's quiet sadness emerges throughout the book, such as the voice of the poem "*El Olvido*" that warns that to forget one's heritage is to "die/ of loneliness and exposure."

The memoir chronicles significant moments, beginning with her birth ("They Say"). "*Quinceañera*" tells of the custom of a girl's coming-of-age party (at age fifteen). Her grandmother prepares her for Puerto Rican womanhood. The adult narrator also explores her and her mother's memories of the yearly trips to Puerto Rico in "Marina" and "The Last Word."

The central theme in the book is the traditional Puerto Rican "script of our lives," which circumscribes "everyone in their places." The narrator struggles with her family's expectations for her to become a traditional Puerto Rican woman: domestic, married, and fertile. This script allows little room for individual identity, so the maturing narrator focuses on those characters who rewrite the script and extemporize their own lives ("Some of the Characters").

The embodiment of Puerto Rican tradition is Mamá, the grandmother who ironically gives Ortiz Cofer the tools that enable her to redefine her own role. In "More Room," for instance, Ortiz Cofer tells the story about Mamá expelling her husband from her bedroom to avoid giving birth to even more children, thus liberating herself to enjoy her children, her grandchildren, and her own life. Similarly, "Tales Told Under the Mango Tree" portrays Mamá's queenly role as the matriarchal storyteller surrounded by the young women and girls of the family as she passes on *cuentos* (stories) about being a Puerto Rican woman, such as the legend of the wise and courageous María Sabida who is not controlled by love and is "never a victim."

Silent Dancing is ultimately a *Künstlerroman*, the story of an artist's apprenticeship. Ortiz Cofer has revised the script for her life as a Puerto Rican woman by inheriting Mamá's role as storyteller; she redefines what it means to be a Puerto Rican woman and tells her stories to a wider audience.

The Meaning of Consuelo

Type of work: Novel
First published: 2003

The novel's narrator is Consuelo (which means "one who consoles"), the elder daughter in a family that is making its way into the middle class in the suburbs of San Juan, Puerto Rico's largest city. While her father works in a hotel and admires anything modern or American, her mother stays bonded to the old island ways and to her "familia," primarily the females who are the guardians both of tradition and morals. Milagra, or Mili, is the younger daughter—beautiful, flighty, and increasingly strange.

In her early teens and burdened with watching over her little sister, Consuelo develops a sensitive awareness of her parents' troubled marriage, her cousin Patricio's imaginative but odd behavior (he is homosexual), and her own need for a selfhood not bound by the family's sense of "tragedia," a kind of island doom that she is determined to elude. Ortiz Cofer employs Spanish words in her text, but always in an appropriate and understandable fashion. Language and culture are an inimitable part of the story. Consuelo develops a crush on an attractive boy, initiates sex with him, gets shunned by her high school peers when he spreads stories ("cuentos") about her, panics when she realizes she is an outcast, the "la fulana" of her own life, but does not succumb.

Ortiz Cofer has written a tale about a young woman who rises above her fate while her poor sister drowns in her own. If this tale is a little too predictable for some, perhaps too heavy-handed in the telling, it may be the kind of young adult story that impressionable females need to read.

Suggested Readings

Acosta-Belén, Edna. "A *MELUS* Interview: Judith Ortiz Cofer." *MELUS* 18, no. 3 (Fall, 1993): 83-97.

Bost, Suzanne. "Transgressing Borders: Puerto Rican and Latina Mestizaje." *MELUS* 25, no. 2 (Summer, 2000): 187-211.

Faymonville, Carment. "New Transnational Identities in Judith Ortiz Cofer's Autobiographical Fiction." *MELUS* 26, no. 2 (Summer, 2001): 129-158.

Jago, Carol. *Judith Ortiz Cofer in the Classroom: A Woman in Front of the Sun*. Urbana, Ill.: National Council of Teachers of English, 2006.

Ortiz Cofer, Judith. "Puerto Rican Literature in Georgia? An Interview with Judith Ortiz Cofer." Interview by Rafael Ocasio. *The Kenyon Review* 14, no. 4 (Fall, 1992): 43-50.

Contributor: Nancy L. Chick

Louis Owens

Born: Lompoc, California; July 18, 1948
Died: Albuquerque, New Mexico; July 26, 2002

Native American

Owens's scholarship, autobiographical nonfiction, and novels deal with themes of mixed-blood identity, place, social class, family, human relationship to the natural world, and disillusionment.

Principal works

LONG FICTION: *Wolfsong*, 1991; *The Sharpest Sight*, 1992; *Bone Game*, 1994; *Nightland*, 1996; *Dark River*, 1999

NONFICTION: *American Indian Novelists: An Annotated Bibliography*, 1985 (with Tom Colonnese); *John Steinbeck's Re-Vision of America*, 1985; *The Grapes of Wrath: Trouble in the Promised Land*, 1989; *Other Destinies: Understanding the American Indian Novel*, 1992; *Mixedblood Messages: Literature, Film, Family, Place*, 1998; *I Hear the Train: Reflections, Inventions, Refractions*, 2001

The works of Louis Dean Owens, a novelist and cultural critic of mixed Choctaw, Cherokee, Irish, and French ancestry, express observations from his mixed-blood perspective about contemporary American culture, with a particular focus on ethnicity and class. He was the son of Hoey Louis and Ida Brown Louis, who had nine children. Hoey Louis worked at various jobs, including farm labor, managing a chicken ranch, dowsing for a well-driller, working in a laundry, and driving a truck. Ida Louis sometimes worked as a waitress. The family moved back and forth between Mississippi, where they lived in a two-room cabin on the Yazoo River, and California, where they lived in the Santa Lucia mountains, the Salinas Valley, San Leandro, and, finally, Atascadero. Owens wrote autobiographically of his working-class childhood and his family history in *Mixedblood Messages* and *I Hear the Train*. He worked at various places from the age of nine, including in fields, a chicken ranch, a mushroom farm, and a can factory.

Gene Owens, Louis's older brother, was the first member of the extended family to graduate from high school, and Louis Owens became the second. He attended community college for two years, then was admitted to the University of California, Santa Barbara (UCSB), under an equal opportunity program. He worked summers fighting fires for the United States Forest Service. While at UCSB he met Kiowa novelist and professor N. Scott Momaday, who influenced Owens to pursue his study of American Indian literature. Owens received his B.A. in 1971 and an M.A. in English in 1974. In 1975, he married his wife, Polly, whom he had met while a student at UCSB; they would have two daughters, Elizabeth and Alexandra.

Owens began and then dropped out of a graduate program at Arizona State University. He then worked as a forest ranger. Eventually he entered graduate school at the University of California, Davis, and received a Ph.D. in 1981. He spent a year at the University of Pisa, Italy, on a Fulbright scholarship in 1980-1981, then became an assistant professor of English at California State University, Northridge, in 1982. In 1984 he moved to the University of New Mexico. A brief stint as professor of literature at the University of California, Santa Cruz (1989-1994), served as the inspiration for the novel *Bone Game*. He returned to the University of New Mexico in 1994. In 2001 he moved to a professorship at the University of California, Davis. He held a New Mexico Humanities Grant (1987), was a National Endowment for the Humanities Fellow (1987), and won a National Endowment for the Arts Fellowship (1989).

As a scholar, Owens addressed the failure of the American Dream in the works of John Steinbeck (*Steinbeck's Re-Vision of America*) and carried out a project of recovery of American Indian writers, both in a coauthored (with Tom Colonnese) reference work, *American Indian Novelists: An Annotated Critical Bibliography*, and in his work of criticism of American Indian fiction, *Other Destinies*. His scholarship, autobiographical nonfiction, and novels are intertwined in that they deal with themes of mixed-blood identity, place, humans' relationship to the natural world, social class, familial relationships, and disillusionment. His first novel, *Wolfsong*, focuses on the natural world and the question of American Indian identity. A young American Indian man who has left his home in Washington State to go to college returns for his uncle's funeral, takes a job as a logger, and discovers a plan to strip-mine in a wilderness area. *The Sharpest Sight* focuses on family and mixed-blood identity. Owens borrowed many details from his own family for this work, including the names of his father and grandfather and the story of his older brother, a Vietnam War veteran.

Bone Game makes a connection between a historical murder in Spanish colonial times and a series of murders of students taking place on a university campus (suggested by, but not based on, serial killings that took place in Santa Cruz in the 1970's). *Nightland* continues Owens's themes of environmentalism, the destructiveness of money and capitalism, family relations, the questionable value of higher education, and mixed-blood identity in a plot set in motion by the discovery of a sack full of (drug) money. It is in *Dark River*, however, that all of Owens's themes and his literary theories are brought together, combining humor and tragedy in a postmodern narrative. On July 26, 2002, Owens died of a self-inflicted gunshot wound.

The Sharpest Sight

Type of work: Novel
First published: 1992

The setting of *The Sharpest Sight* shifts between rural Northern California and the dark swamps of Mississippi. Attis McCurtain, a mixed-blood Choctaw and emotionally scarred Vietnam veteran, has been murdered and his body is being carried toward the sea by a muddy, rain-swollen river. Attis's best friend, mixed-blood Hispanic policeman Mundo Morales, sets out to discover the person responsible for the murder. At the same time, the dead man's brother, Cole, embarks upon his own primordial search: the search for his brother's bones.

At first glance this book shares some aspects of the mystery thriller, but closer examination proves that it is much more than that. The novel's best writing derives from its informed focus on cultural collisions and its almost mythical quality. Ghosts and shadows speak aloud: in dreams and in fact. Cole McCurtain is magically summoned—by his full-blood Uncle Luther and the wonderfully drawn Onatima ("Old Lady Blue Wood")—to the ancestral Choctaw homeland in the swamps of Mississippi. It is in the dark swamp that the frightened and restless spirit of Attis McCurtain awaits the discovery and picking of his bones—the picking of the bones of the dead being a powerful and essential rite in early Choctaw cosmology.

In *The Sharpest Sight*, Owens provides an insider's look at the search for traditional cultural values in a world gone slightly screwy and for a mainstream America that is largely ignorant and unappreciative of its native cultures. In *The Sharpest Sight*, a book full of signs and wonders, those who attend can discover truths that are quite wonderful to encounter.

Bone Game

Type of work: Novel
First published: 1994

In *Bone Game*, Owens succeeds in blending Native American folklore with the traditional mystery genre to create a unique novel of intrigue, suspense, and wonder. Cole McCurtain is a recently divorced, mixed-blood professor of American Indian studies at the University of Santa Cruz. Trying to build a new life and attempting to come to terms with his mixed heritage, Cole's turmoil is reflected in a dreamlike encounter with an Indian who is painted half white and half black and who carries small bones resembling dice. Cole is not sure if the Indian is human, the ghost of a long-dead medicine man, or the incarnation of the gambler of American Indian mythology. Not only does this strange apparition foreshadow Cole's identity crisis as he struggles with his Indian heritage but also seems to be mysteriously connected to a series of vicious murders in Santa Cruz.

When he meets Alex, a full-blood Navaho colleague and a cross-dressing trickster, Cole begins to reconnect with his Indian background. Although the murders continue, Cole is not really concerned until his daughter Abby becomes a potential target. Finally, Cole's father Hoey, his great-uncle Luther, and his aunt Onatima, all powerful Choctaw shamans, travel from Mississippi to help Cole and Abby, because as Luther says, "This story's so big, Cole sees only a little bit of it."

Magical Realism is at work in *Bone Game*. By combining the enigmatic character of the spiritual world with mundane and often violent human existence, Owens expands the limits of the mystery genre. The result is a thoroughly enjoyable, intriguing, and haunting reading experience.

Suggested Readings

Daniel, G. Reginald. Review of *Mixedblood Messages: Literature, Film, Family, Place*, by Louis Owens. *Biography* 23, no. 3 (Summer, 2000): 572-578.

Helstern, Linda Lizut. *Louis Owens*. Boise, Idaho: Boise State University Press, 2005.

Kilpatrick, Jacquelyn, ed. *Louis Owens: Literary Reflections on His Life and Work*. Norman: University of Oklahoma Press, 2004.

Lalonde, Chris. *Grave Concerns, Trickster Turns: The Novels of Louis Owens*. Norman: University of Oklahoma Press, 2002.

Studies in American Indian Literatures 10, no. 2 (1998).

Contributor: Renny Christopher

Cynthia Ozick

Born: New York, New York; April 17, 1928

Jewish

Ozick's fiction describes the difficulty of observing Jewish traditions in America's secular, assimilationist society.

Principal works

DRAMA: *Blue Light*, pr. 1994 (adaptation of her short story "The Shawl")

LONG FICTION: *Trust*, 1966; *The Cannibal Galaxy*, 1983; *The Messiah of Stockholm*, 1987; *Heir to the Glimmering World*, 2004 (also known as *The Bear Boy*)

POETRY: *Epodes: First Poems*, 1992

SHORT FICTION: *The Pagan Rabbi, and Other Stories*, 1971; *Bloodshed and Three Novellas*, 1976; *Levitation: Five Fictions*, 1982; *The Shawl*, 1989; *The Puttermesser Papers*, 1997

NONFICTION: *Art and Ardor*, 1983; *Metaphor and Memory: Essays*, 1989; *What Henry James Knew, and Other Essays on Writers*, 1993; *Fame and Folly: Essays*, 1996; *Portrait of the Artist as a Bad Character, and Other Essays on Writing*, 1996; *Quarrel and Quandry: Essays*, 2000; *The Din in the Head*, 2006

EDITED TEXT: *The Best American Essays, 1998*, 1998

MISCELLANEOUS: *A Cynthia Ozick Reader*, 1996

Cynthia Ozick (OH-zihk) recalls her grandmother telling her stories, invariably conveying a lesson, about girlhood in a Russian Jewish village. From her drugstore-owning parents, she overhead "small but stirring adventures" confided by their Bronx neighbors. "Reading-lust" led her to fairy tales, to bachelor's and master's degrees in literature, and to a self-taught education in Judaism's textual tradition. From these various influences, Ozick creates fiction noted for its range and inventiveness. Her reputation is based largely on her short fiction. Ozick has more than once won the O. Henry Award.

Ozick's first book, however, was a novel, *Trust*. It concerns a young woman's search for identity. A predominant theme in Ozick's work has been the difficulty of sustaining one's Jewish identity in America's secular, assimilationist society. Assimilated, rootless Jews are frequently objects of satire in her fiction. What Ozick proposes, in terms of language, is a New Yiddish, understandable to English speakers yet preserving the tone and inflections of Yiddish, a language that is facing extinction as a result of the Holocaust and assimilation.

For Ozick, the Orthodox Jewish moral code remains the standard against which life and art are measured. America's materialistic culture, she maintains, is essentially pagan and therefore hostile to Judaism. This conflict is clearly evident in "The Pagan Rabbi," a story in which attraction to nature drives the title character to suicide. The idea that the artist competes with God as creator also concerns Ozick. Particularly in "Usurpation (Other People's Stories)," Ozick intimates that writers are congenital plagiarizers and, more seriously, usurpers of God. The hubris of a person attempting godlike creation is approached humorously in "Puttermesser and Xanthippe," in which the female protagonist fashions a female golem, first to help with the housework, then to reform New York City. So convinced is Ozick of the pervasiveness of idolatrous ambition that her heroines display an arrogant singlemindedness that is more often associated with men. In the story "The Shawl" and its sequel, the novella *Rosa*, Ozick, herself a mother, imagines a woman who idolizes the memory of a daughter murdered by the Nazis.

Ozick's vigilance against idolatry extends to her narrative style. Postmodernist, self-referential techniques—asides, interruptions, and explanations—alert readers to the illusions of fiction. Ironic in effect, they also deflate authorial claims to being like God.

The Pagan Rabbi, and Other Stories

Type of work: Short fiction
First published: 1971

The Pagan Rabbi, and Other Stories, Ozick's first collection of short stories, was nominated for the National Book Award. Short fiction would subsequently form the basis of Ozick's literary reputation. The collection's seven stories—originally published in various periodicals—explore interrelated themes that mark Ozick's work: Jewish identity, the lure of secularism, and the vocation of the artist. In Ozick's view, Western civilization, rooted in Greek paganism, extols nature and physical existence and is therefore hostile to Judaism. The Western artistic tradition, moreover, dares usurp God's role as creator.

A prominent symbol in the title story, "The Pagan Rabbi," is the tree on which the protagonist eventually hangs himself with his prayer shawl. The tree's dryad and the heretical rabbi have coupled. In "The Dock-Witch," the protagonist's immersion in nature also leads to sexual union with a pagan goddess, yet because he is a Gentile, lacking Judaism's horror of idolatry, his seduction is guilt-free.

Lust for the world's beauty undoes these characters; lust for the world's acclaim corrupts others. In "Virility," an immigrant Jewish poet, who anglicizes his name to Edmond Gates, becomes a literary sensation, until he confesses that an elderly aunt wrote his verses. When poems are published under her name after her poverty-induced death, the same gift that when considered his was declared "seminal and hard" is dismissed as "a spinster's one-dimensional vision." Along with satirizing associations between sexuality and artistry, Ozick condemns Gates for rejecting kin and heritage. He lives out the rest of his life in penitential drag and dies a suicide.

Cynthia Ozick (Julius Ozick)

The aging Yiddish poet Herschel Edelshtein of "Envy: Or, Yiddish in America" is in futile pursuit of a translator who would free him from the obscurity of writing in a dying language; meanwhile, he rails against popular American Jewish novelists, for whom history is a "vacuum." In "The Suitcase," a notable German architect and his son's Jewish mistress engage in a paradigmic struggle, as Jew cannot allow Gentile to forget history, particularly its production of an Adolf Hitler.

Some critics have questioned the accessibility of Ozick's work, with its self-consciously Jewish style and content. Others find that its imaginative reach transcends its specifics of cultural origin.

"The Shawl"

Type of work: Short fiction
First published: 1989, in *The Shawl*

Ozick's most anthologized work, "The Shawl," condenses within seven pages the horrors of the infamous Nazi concentration camps. This prize-winning story reverberates with images and themes common in Ozick's work: the Holocaust, World War II refugees, and secret enmity. Chilling imagery leaves the reader's senses buzzing like the electrified fence against which Rosa's fifteen-month-old child, Magda, is thrown. Through Ozick's powerful, yet uncharacteristically simple language, the reader shares the spiritually elevating love that Rosa, a young mother, has for her infant daughter as well as her forbidden despair over Magda's barbaric murder.

Initially, the shawl provides warmth and protection as it hides the secret child. When Rosa can no longer suckle, the shawl magically nourishes Magda with the "milk of linen." In its third life-giving role, the shawl provides companionship, as Magda silently laughs with it as if it were the sister she never had. Without the shawl, Magda, separated from her source of life, is completely vulnerable. Her secret existence is instantly discovered, and her brief life brutally extinguished.

The central metaphor, the shawl, wraps baby Magda and the story in many layers of interpretation. Ozick has crafted her three characters in the fashion of a fifteenth century morality play. In a morality play, each character represents moral qualities or abstractions. Similarly, Ozick's characters represent three states of existence. Magda, wound in the magical shawl, is Life, full of warmth and imagination. Rosa, who no longer experiences hunger, "a floating angel," is Spirit. Stella, always so cold that it has seeped into her hardened heart, is Death.

Metaphorically, when Spirit looks away, Death, jealous of the warmth of Life, takes the life-source away, thus killing Life. The secret hatred that Stella harbors toward Magda is only surpassed by the disturbing images Rosa has of starving Stella cannibalizing the delicious-looking infant.

A powerful story, whether read literally or interpreted metaphorically, "The Shawl" offers a private insight into the chillingly painful world created by World War II Germany. Rosa's loss is humankind's loss, and the gut-wrenching pain she experiences as she sucks out what little taste of Magda's life remains in the shawl is the pain of the modern world, gagged and left speechless by inhumanity.

Suggested Readings

Alkana, Joseph. "'Do We Not Know the Meaning of Aesthetic Gratification?' Cynthia Ozick's *The Shawl*, the Akedah, and the Ethics of Holocaust Literary Aesthetics." *Modern Fiction Studies* 43 (Winter, 1997): 963-990.

Bloom, Harold, ed. *Cynthia Ozick: Modern Critical Views*. New York: Chelsea House, 1986.

Burstein, Janet Handler. "Cynthia Ozick and the Transgressions of Art." *American Literature: A Journal of Literary History, Criticism, and Bibliography* 59 (March, 1987): 85-101.

Cohen, Sarah Blacher. *Cynthia Ozick's Comic Art: From Levity to Liturgy*. Bloomington: Indiana University Press, 1994.

Fargione, Daniela. *Cynthia Ozick: Orthodoxy and Irreverence—A Critical Study*. Rome: Aracne, 2005.

Fisch, Harold. "Introducing Cynthia Ozick." *Response* 22 (1974): 27-34.

Friedman, Lawrence S. *Understanding Cynthia Ozick*. Columbia: University of South Carolina Press, 1991.

Kauvar, Elaine M. *Cynthia Ozick's Fiction: Tradition and Invention*. Bloomington: Indiana University Press, 1993.

Lowin, Joseph. *Cynthia Ozick*. New York: Twayne, 1988.

Ozick, Cynthia. "An Interview with Cynthia Ozick." *Contemporary Literature* 34 (Fall, 1993): 359-394.

Pinsker, Sanford. *The Uncompromising Fiction of Cynthia Ozick*. Columbia: University of Missouri Press, 1987.

Strandberg, Victor. *Greek Mind, Jewish Soul: The Conflicted Art of Cynthia Ozick*. Madison: University of Wisconsin Press, 1994.

Contributors: Amy Allison and Leslie Pearl

Grace Paley

Born: New York, New York; December 11, 1922
Died: Thetford Hill, Vermont; August 22, 2007

Jewish

Paley's short stories and poems are among the finest contemporary Jewish American and feminist fiction.

Principal works

POETRY: *Leaning Forward*, 1985; *New and Collected Poems*, 1992; *Begin Again: Collected Poems*, 2000

SHORT FICTION: *The Little Disturbances of Man: Stories of Men and Women in Love*, 1959; *Enormous Changes at the Last Minute*, 1974; *Later the Same Day*, 1985; *The Collected Stories*, 1994; *Here and Somewhere Else*, 2007 (with Robert Nichols)

NONFICTION: *Conversations with Grace Paley*, 1997 (Gerhard Bach and Blaine H. Hall, editors); *Just as I Thought*, 1998

MISCELLANEOUS: *Long Walks and Intimate Talks: Stories and Poems*, 1991 (with paintings by Vera Williams)

Grace Paley (PAY-lee) began writing short stories in the mid-1950's, in her thirties, after having two children. She was born to Russian Jewish immigrants and was educated at Hunter College and New York University. She studied poetry with the famous British poet W. H. Auden. In 1942, she married Jess Paley, a veteran, freelance photographer, and cameraman.

After the war, the couple moved to lower Manhattan. Her early interest in poetry and her ability as a storyteller and listener led her to write about her family experiences. Growing up as the Depression waned, Paley was optimistic, and her choice to marry and have children was made with the same liveliness and independence as was her decision to write. One of her first stories, "Goodbye and Good Luck," shows boldness in protagonist Rosie Lieber's decision to live with a lover and marry late in life, despite the disapproval of her family.

In the fifteen years after the publication of *The Little Disturbances of Man*, there was little separation between her identity as writer and her identities as mother, teacher at Sarah Lawrence College, and peace activist. Paley's writings typically have a distinctive personal voice. Published in *Enormous Changes at the Last Minute*, the stories that flowed from her experiences as a mother, family member, New Yorker, activist, and teacher include "A Subject of Childhood" and "Faith in a Tree," which focus on the attachment between mother and child and on the lives of women trying to end war and protect the future through peaceful protests.

Influenced by the sounds of New York neighborhoods, the identities of her characters also include many cultures and dialects—Yiddish, black, and Puerto Rican, for example. The themes of listening, voice, and telling one's story occur throughout much of her work. Stories such as "A Conversation with My Father," "The Story Hearer," and "Zagrowsky Tells" echo the conversations of her Jewish parents, and feature one or more characters—most often women or Jewish Americans—who must shape narratives as a way of shaping their history and the world.

In 1972, Paley and her husband were divorced. Paley married her friend and co-activist Robert Nichols, and the couple settled in Greenwich Village. In 1973, she was a delegate to the World Peace Conference in Moscow. Throughout the 1970's and 1980's, she continued her writing and teaching and always her activism. She condemned Soviet repression of human rights, demonstrated in Washington, D.C., against nuclear weapons, campaigned against U.S. government policy in Central America, and visited Nicaragua and El Salvador. Her stories appeared in *The Atlantic*, *Esquire*, and other well-known magazines.

In the 1990's Paley continued to teach in the New York City area, particularly at Sarah Lawrence College, but by the end of the decade she had retired, dividing her

Grace Paley (Dorothy Marder)

time between her Vermont home and her Greenwich Village apartment. She died in Vermont from breast cancer on August 22, 2007.

Enormous Changes at the Last Minute

Type of work: Short fiction
First published: 1974

With the publication of *Enormous Changes at the Last Minute*, Paley's reputation as a writer burgeoned. Her unique blend of poetic concision and concern for women's contributions to the future made her an important feminist voice in contemporary literature. In this collection, identity is a personal and a social issue in the struggle for a peaceful world. Most of the characters are middle-aged women, such as Faith Darwin, who resembles, but is not intended to be, Paley's alter ego; others are simply those about whom stories are told—the children who have died or suffered from neglect, poverty, drug abuse, and the Vietnam War.

The main characters in these stories act with defiance and hope. In "Enormous Changes at the Last Minute," Alexandra is a middle-aged social worker who accidentally becomes pregnant through a liaison with Dennis, a cabdriver, poet, and commune member. Instead of joining the commune, Alexandra invites several of her pregnant clients to come live with her, a "precedent in social work which would not be followed or even mentioned in state journals for about five years." In the story "Wants," the woman narrator meets with her ex-husband, who criticizes her, telling her that she'll "always want nothing." In answer to herself and the reader, she recites the things she has wanted in her life, including ending the war before her children grew up. In "The Long-Distance Runner," Faith Darwin takes a long run through her old neighborhood and ends up living with the black family who now occupies her childhood apartment. All three of these women examine themselves midway, finding, as Faith does, that a "woman inside the steamy energy of middle age" may learn "as though she was still a child what in the world is coming next."

The collection's most acclaimed story, "A Conversation with My Father," features Faith, who, in dialogue with her father (modeled after Paley's father, I. Goodside, M.D.), invents the story of a middle-aged woman who becomes a junkie trying to identify with her son's generation. Faith's father laments the "end of a person" but is more upset when Faith adds her characteristic openness: In the "after-story life," the junkie becomes a "receptionist in a storefront community clinic." On one hand, Faith's response is emblematic of the way in which Paley's characters will not, as Faith's father exclaims, look tragedy "in the face." On the other hand, other stories in the collection—namely, "The Little Girl," "Gloomy Tune," and "Samuel"—do precisely that. These stories study the identities of the victimized—the teenage girl who is raped and strangled by a drug addict, the neglected boy branded in violence and delinquency, the black boy dying in a freak subway accident. "Never again will a boy exactly like Samuel be known," states the narrator.

Later the Same Day

Type of work: Short fiction
First published: 1985

Paley's *Later the Same Day* contains the stories of people speaking in the varied dialects of New York City. In these stories, identity is formed through people's acts and through their unique stories. As in Paley's earlier collection, *Enormous Changes at the Last Minute*, Faith Darwin is a recurring character, but here she is the mature woman, looking back at her life. In "The Story Hearer," for instance, Faith is asked to tell her lover, Jack, the story of her day. Despite her effort to "curb [her] cultivated individualism," she ends up sidetracking, watering her "brains with time spent in order to grow smart private thoughts." Jokingly, Faith comments on men's love of beginnings and thus suggests that women move through stories and time quite differently, tempted by the private rather than the "public accounting" of life. Similarly, in "Zagrowsky Tells," "Lavinia: An Old Story," and "In This Country, but in Another Language, My Aunt Refuses to Marry the Men Everyone Wants Her To," identity is a matter of individual stories told in first-person narratives and ethnic dialects.

In "The Story Hearer," Faith wants to rise above her time and name but finds herself "always slipping and falling down into them, speaking their narrow language." In "The Expensive Moment," Faith's friends and families respond to the aftereffects of China's Cultural Revolution, relating their experiences to America's "revolutions" of the 1960's. A visiting Chinese woman quickly identifies herself as still a Communist, but later in the story, another Chinese woman asks about children and "how to raise them." Like Faith and other mothers in Paley's fiction, these women "don't know the best way." In a world and country divided by different voices, different genders, and different politics, there is still possibility for community and for common identities. "Friends" pays tribute to Faith's dying friend Selena and the circle of women who go to visit her. Dying sets her apart from the others, but Selena is a mother, as are they, of a child in a generation "murdered by cars, lost to war, to drugs, to madness."

Later the Same Day was highly acclaimed by critics for its sensitivity to human and ethnic identity and for its experiments with storytelling. It continues to be significant in light of feminist concern with world peace, relationships among women, theories of women's language, and the importance of finding one's own voice.

Suggested Readings

Aarons, Victoria. "Talking Lives: Storytelling and Renewal in Grace Paley's Short Fiction." *Studies in American Jewish Literature* 9 (1990): 20-35.

Arcana, Judith. *Grace Paley's Life Stories: A Literary Biography*. Urbana: University of Illinois Press, 1993.

Bach, Gerhard, and Blaine Hall, eds. *Conversations with Grace Paley*. Jackson: University Press of Mississippi, 1997.

DeKoven, Marianne. “Mrs. Hegel-Shtein’s Tears.” *Partisan Review* 48, no. 2 (1981): 217-223.

Isaacs, Neil D. *Grace Paley: A Study of the Short Fiction*. Boston: Twayne, 1990.

Marchant, Peter, and Earl Ingersoll, eds. “A Conversation with Grace Paley.” *The Massachusetts Review* 26 (Winter, 1985): 606-614.

Meyer, Adam. “Faith and the ‘Black Thing’: Political Action and Self-Questioning in Grace Paley’s Short Fiction.” *Studies in Short Fiction* 31 (Winter, 1994): 79-89.

Paley, Grace. *Conversations with Grace Paley*. Edited by Blaine H. Hall. Jackson: University of Mississippi Press, 1997.

Schleifer, Ronald. “Grace Paley: Chaste Compactness.” In *Contemporary American Women Writers: Narrative Strategies*, edited by Catherine Rainwater and William J. Scheick. Lexington: University Press of Kentucky, 1985.

Taylor, Jacqueline. *Grace Paley: Illuminating the Dark Lives*. Austin: University of Texas, 1990.

Contributor: Andrea J. Ivanov